PSALTER
HYMNAL

PSALTER HYMNAL

Including the psalms, Bible songs,
hymns, ecumenical creeds,
doctrinal standards, and
liturgical forms of the
Christian Reformed Church in
North America

Grand Rapids, Michigan

Scripture taken from the HOLY BIBLE, NEW
INTERNATIONAL VERSION. Copyright © 1973, 1978,
1984, International Bible Society. Used by permission of
Zondervan Bible Publishers.

Library of Congress Cataloging-in-Publication Data
Psalter Hymnal
        Principally English words; some words in Dutch,
French, and Spanish.
        "Fourth edition of the official book of praise produced
by the Christian Reformed Church"—Pref.
        Includes indexes.
        1. Christian Reformed Church—Hymns.   2. Hymns,
English.   3. Christian Reformed Church—Liturgy.
I. Christian Reformed Church.
M2124.C55P7   1987   87-751144
ISBN 0-930265-35-1

Design: Dean Heetderks
Music typography: Cliff Lehman
Copyright administration: Laura Van Tol

CONTENTS

PREFACE

The 1987 *Psalter Hymnal* is the fourth edition of the official book of praise produced by the Christian Reformed Church. In 1977 synod appointed a committee to revise and improve the psalm and hymn sections of the 1959 edition of the hymnal. The 1987 edition is the fruit of their work—a book of worship to help God's people move into the twenty-first century.

The Revision Committee greatly expanded the contents of earlier editions of the *Psalter Hymnal*. Part of that growth was fueled by the tremendous worldwide outpouring of new songs for Christian worship that began in the 1960s and continues to this day. The other part of the expansion occurred as a result of a careful look back; the committee added some of the great hymns of past centuries that had not been included in previous editions. The cultural and musical variety of the new songs for worship in this hymnal coincides with the growing cultural and ethnic diversity in the Christian Reformed Church.

The Revision Committee began its work by studying the musical heritage of the Christian Reformed Church. Before 1934 only psalms were sung in public worship. And until 1914—when the 1912 United Presbyterian *Psalter* was adopted as the denomination's first English-language psalter—these psalms were sung in Dutch to the melodies of the sixteenth-century Genevan Psalter. Our *Psalter* edition also contained translations of doctrinal standards and liturgical forms. The first edition of the *Psalter Hymnal* (1934) retained the 150 psalms found in the United Presbyterian *Psalter*, restored several Genevan tunes, and, for the first time, added hymns. The second edition, published in 1959, two years after the denomination's centennial, retained the same structure and included several new hymns. A third edition in 1976 left the psalms and hymns unchanged; the only changes in this edition occurred in the confessional and liturgical sections. However, a *Psalter Hymnal Supplement,* published two years earlier, introduced the church to new hymns, paving the way for the 1987 edition.

The music in the 1987 edition is divided into three sections. The first section contains all 150 psalms, returning to the long-standing Reformed tradition of presenting one complete versification of each psalm set to a single melody; the psalms follow the numerical order in which they appear in the Bible. The second section, new to the *Psalter Hymnal,* includes 86 Bible songs based on passages of Scripture from Genesis to Revelation. These are followed by the third and largest section, the 405 hymns.

In addition to music, the worship edition of the 1987 *Psalter Hymnal* contains the liturgical forms used by the Christian Reformed Church, doctrinal standards that are shared with many other churches in the Reformed tradition, and ecumenical creeds that bind us to Christians everywhere. Because the number of liturgical forms has grown over the years, not all synodically approved forms could be included in this edition. Synod 1984 approved a list for inclusion, replacing some of the older forms with their newer counterparts.

The psalms, Bible songs, and hymns in this book are no less confessional than the creeds and doctrinal confessions. The songs together contain the prayer and praise of God's people of every age and, increasingly, from every place. In these songs we pray with the psalmist who looked forward to the coming of Christ's kingdom, even as we look forward to its completion. In our songs we take up the prayers of the saints who have rested from their labors, who await with us the return of Christ. And in this edition we present several new songs as our particular gift to the church. We see Christ's kingdom growing across the earth, and we join our voices in praise to God with those far away in place as well as in time.

For all these gifts of prayer, praise, and confession, we give thanks to God. May this book of worship help enrich our worship as we unite heart, mind, and voice in praise to God.

The Revision Committee:

Emily R. Brink, *Editor*	Anthony Hoekema	Verlyn Schultz
Shirley Boomsma	Bert Polman	Calvin Seerveld
Dale Grotenhuis	Marie Post	Dale Topp
John Hamersma	Jack Reiffer	Jack Van Laar

Acknowledgments

Work on the 1987 edition of the *Psalter Hymnal* began with a synodically appointed committee of twelve in 1977. Those twelve people, named above, worked regularly on this project for nine years. The editor remained a member of the committee until 1983, when she joined the staff at CRC Publications.

The church owes a great debt to those faithful eleven who volunteered their time and energies with unflagging devotion and commitment to their task. As work progressed, more and more people were drawn into the project—CRC Publications' board members and synodical delegates who faithfully reviewed every text and tune, singing through many of them during their long meetings; consultants who reviewed new texts, added guitar chords to the music, or who prepared and reviewed drafts of indexes; production assistants who conscientiously attended to the minute details of preparing final manuscripts for publication. In addition, many churches participated in the sampler program and offered suggestions and encouragement.

For all these people, and many more who contributed from time to time, CRC Publications offers thanks and gratitude on behalf of the church. Our lives were enriched as we grew in knowledge and appreciation of the many different dimensions, gifts, and talents combined in this project. The *Psalter Hymnal* is truly produced by, as well as for, the church.

INTRODUCTION TO THE PSALMS, BIBLE SONGS, AND HYMNS

I n developing the contents of the new book of worship, the Revision Committee was guided by the following statement of principle (revised from the 1959 edition), adopted by Synod 1979.

Statement of Principle

The music of the church should be appropriate for worship—that is, it should be liturgical and have aesthetic integrity. The music of worship should serve the dialogue between God and his people. It must be true to the full message of the Scriptures and reflective of biblical Christian experience. Along with the biblical motif, the music of worship should give expression to the other motifs of liturgy: the catholic, the confessional, and the pastoral. The music of worship should satisfy the aesthetic laws that are conditions of good art,

such as imaginative craftsmanship and seriousness of expression. It should reflect the church at worship today and throughout the ages in ways that are relevant, enduring, festive, and dignified.

The four liturgical motifs listed in the Statement of Principle—the biblical, the catholic, the confessional, and the pastoral—are present in all worship and ought to complement one another. They may not be equally obvious in each worship service, but they should all be appropriately represented in the flow of worship services throughout the year.

The music of the church should be biblical. Texts and tunes must serve worship in ways true to biblical patterns for liturgy and must be faithful to the full range of the revelation of God and of his works in creation. Bible songs and psalms must be faithful to the original meaning and context of the Scripture passage. Hymn texts are to be true to Scripture and to the testimony of the Holy Spirit.

In working out this principle, the Revision Committee first debated whether to retain all 150 psalms. Since hymns were introduced in 1934, psalm singing has steadily declined in Christian Reformed worship. However, three considerations convinced the committee not only to retain all the psalms but also to attempt to prepare a psalter that could revitalize psalm singing. One consideration was tradition; the Christian Reformed Church is one of the few Reformed denominations that has retained the entire psalter. The second consideration was the increased interest in psalm singing in other Christian communions. Renewed interest in Bible study, increased use of the lectionary, and the publication of several new translations of the Bible have all contributed to more regular use of psalms in worship and have stimulated many new musical compositions based on the psalms. The third and most fundamental consideration was that the Book of Psalms is God's gift of song to the church. Although most of today's poets probably would write fewer laments and more songs of praise than the psalmists did, every psalm has meaning for Christians in some time or place. For the sake of those suffering persecution and calling out for justice, we have kept even the difficult imprecatory psalms—praying even as we sing them that we may be spared the conditions that caused such anguished prayer.

The Bible-song section expands the singing of Scripture. In it, well-known canticles have been supplemented by settings of other passages from the Old and New Testaments, including many new songs set in simple folk styles. Several

additional familiar and beloved psalm settings from earlier editions of the *Psalter Hymnal* have been included in this section.

The hymns range from songs based very closely on passages of Scripture to texts by poets throughout the ages. Each text was examined for its consonance with scriptural truths.

The music of the church should be catholic. Our music should express not only the unity of a single denomination or congregation but also the unity of the church throughout the world and from all ages. We celebrate the communion of the saints when we sing ancient prayers and songs from a variety of the Christian communities, cultures, and traditions that make up the body of Christ. In addition, because we worship together as families, the music of the church ought to include songs that our little ones can sing and understand. To meet these many different needs, this edition contains a great variety of styles.

A few songs are printed in both English and another language: Spanish (9), French (2), and Dutch (2). The Spanish texts are included to celebrate the growing cultural and ethnic diversity in the church. The French texts serve as a tribute both to the original language of the Genevan Psalter and to the continuing use of French in Reformed congregations in French-speaking Canada. The Dutch texts remind us of the cultural heritage of the Christian Reformed Church.

Although most of the tunes in this hymnal are of Western European origin and style, several melodies from other sources were included: Afro-American (23), Hispanic (9), Israeli (5), and Asian (3).

Certain songs that appeared in earlier editions—especially songs from the heavily represented nineteenth century—

have been deleted from the 1987 edition. However, the best of that great hymn-writing era was retained and balanced with hymns both older and more contemporary. The emphasis in this edition of the *Psalter Hymnal* has shifted consciously from a more subjective and pietistic approach to our faith, characteristic of the nineteenth century, to a broader concern with our calling as Christians to live in full awareness of our societal relationships and kingdom tasks.

The music of the church should be confessional. While part of the worldwide body of Christ, we stand in a particular tradition—that part of God's people named Reformed. Since our music must reflect our confessional and doctrinal understanding of Scripture, the emphasis is on the communal rather than on the individualistic, and our songs deal with topics like infant baptism and God's sovereignty. That doesn't mean that every aspect of a given teaching must be present in every song on that topic. A text is not to be judged by what it fails to say, unless in its failure a false impression is conveyed.

The music of the church should be pastoral. Each part of the body of Christ worships in a particular time and place and has a unique set of needs. Each worshiping congregation needs both to identify with an already-familiar body of songs and to find new songs for worship that enrich its understanding of its particular place in God's kingdom. The 1987 *Psalter Hymnal* retains many familiar songs from previous editions and adds much of what has become familiar in recent years. New songs from many different sources and styles were included to reflect the increasing diversity in the church.

In all these ways—biblical, catholic, confessional, and pastoral—the music of the church serves the dialogue between God and his people, containing God's word to us and our response to him. The church's music also provides a way for us to address others. Since God's people serve as his ambassadors to the whole world, the church's songs must witness to God's wondrous acts of saving love and must call all people and nations to honor and obey the King of kings and Lord of lords. Psalm 100 exemplifies all three aspects of address:

> All people that on earth do dwell,
> sing to the LORD with cheerful voice.
> Serve him with joy, his praises tell,
> come now before him and rejoice!

At one and the same time, God addresses us in his Word, we sing praise and thanksgiving to God, and we address each other together with all of creation in witness of God's goodness, faithfulness, and mercy.

The Texts

The words that we speak to God and for God must excel in craftsmanship and clarity. The Revision Committee applied the Reformation principle of worshiping in the vernacular: the committee updated many older texts, removing archaic language while at the same time trying to remain sensitive to the original poetry. Because the older pronoun and verb forms (e.g., thee, thou, wast, wert) are rapidly disappearing in worship, both in prayer and in Scripture versions, they were frequently changed in the song texts as well. Texts also were revised to avoid gender-specific terms by using more inclusive language. In keeping with current translations of Scripture, pronouns for God remain anthropomorphically masculine.

Most of the psalm texts in previous editions date from the 1912 *Psalter*, which frequently included more than one complete or partial setting for a given psalm. The decision to return to one complete versification for each of the psalms according to their numerical order in the Bible is an attempt to respect the integrity of each psalm as a poetic unit. That decision, coupled with the decision to add a section of Bible songs, resulted in the commissioning of many new versifications for this edition. Most texts are based on the Revised Standard Version (RSV) and the New International Version (NIV) of the Bible. Like those Bible versions, our Psalm and Old Testament song texts distinguish between the two most common Hebrew names for God: the name *YHWH* is rendered in capital letters as "LORD," and *Adonai* is written "Lord," with small letters. The word "Jehovah" is no longer used.

Paragraph units within the psalms were honored as much as possible within the limits of the metrical forms. The committee also worked to retain original images, memorable phrases, and important names from biblical history. Since the versifier's primary considerations were faithfulness to Scripture and clarity, a few unrhymed versions were included.

Each psalm versification was reviewed for faithfulness to the Hebrew original by John Stek, professor of Old Testament at Calvin Seminary and author of the notes on the Psalms in *The NIV Study Bible*. The texts, with Stek's comments, were then reviewed by Henrietta Ten Harmsel, professor emeritus of English at Calvin College and author of several translations of Dutch poetry that are similar to the psalm versifications in their meter, rhyme, and accent.

The number of hymn texts has more than doubled from previous editions. The Revision Committee searched through more than one hundred English-language hymnals and compiled a list of over one

thousand texts for consideration. The selection process for choosing the hymns from that list was based on several factors, including balance and variety. The songs were chosen from every period of hymn writing and include several that are published here for the first time anywhere.

Although the hymns are organized much as they were in previous editions, in this edition categories are identified both in the table of contents and on each page. "The Church at Worship" category is structured according to the order of worship as discussed in the 1968 Liturgical Report and includes songs intended for particular liturgical actions. Because of the greater number of hymns overall, most sections in this category have more than doubled in size from the 1959 edition. Some sections—Word of God, Dedication and Offering, and Lord's Supper—have more than tripled. The increase reflects a growing liturgical consciousness and the practice of celebrating the Lord's Supper more frequently than in the past.

The second category, "The Church Year," includes an Epiphany section, which is new to the *Psalter Hymnal*. The section celebrates the wise men's coming to worship the newborn King as the epiphany (manifestation) of Christ the Savior to the Gentiles and includes songs on the continuing revelation and ministry of Christ. "The Church Year" category also includes an entire section devoted to celebrating Christ as the ascended and victorious King of creation, thus emphasizing the ascension and reign of Christ as one of the most significant events in salvation history.

The third category of hymns, "The Church in the World," follows the structure of *Our World Belongs to God: A Contemporary Testimony*. The category begins with creation and follows the course of salvation history, including the redemptive work of Christ and the work of the Holy Spirit in leading the church. After several hymns dealing with the Christian life, the category culminates in an entire section devoted to the new creation, when Christ will return to establish his kingdom on the new earth. The hymns on the new creation are closely linked to the Advent section: even as we remember the first coming of Christ during Advent, we look forward to his second coming at the end of this age. The hymn section concludes with responses and doxologies.

The Music

A hymn functions in worship only when the gathered congregation joins voices in singing the text. The tune exists to empower the text and so to strengthen the communal prayer and praise of God's people.

In every section of this hymnal the committee sought to balance familiar songs with new songs, old songs with recently written songs, songs challenging in structure with songs of childlike simplicity.

The tunes vary greatly in length and style. Although the traditional metric structure predominates, styles range from short choruses to antiphonal songs to chantlike songs. Forty melodies from the

Genevan Psalter are included, almost all restored to their original rhythms.

Tunes were chosen for their singability and according to their suitability for a given text. Most tunes were set in four-part harmony, although several are intended for unison singing. The pitch for many tunes was lowered in order to make them more accessible for unison singing.

Several songs have alternative accompaniments and descants. Many, particularly those with relatively simple harmonies, include guitar chords. When a brief introduction to a song is sufficient, introduction marks ⌐ ⌐ are provided as an aid to the organist. However, when a song is unfamiliar to a congregation, the organist should play through the entire tune.

The songs contained in this edition of the *Psalter Hymnal* are offered with the hope and prayer that they move from the printed page into the hearts, minds, and voices of God's people, who then use these songs to lift gloriously exuberant sounds of praise to God. May the joyful noises of worshiping congregations everywhere delight our Creator God and so impress our unbelieving neighbors that they too may be drawn to join their voices with ours in singing praise to our God and Savior. To God alone be all the glory.

Abbreviations (used in credits for text and tune sources)

alt.	altered		LM	long meter (88 88)
adapt.	adapted (by)		LMD	long meter double
arr.	arranged by		PM	peculiar meter
attr.	attributed to		para.	paraphrased by
b.	born		rev.	revised by
c.	circa (around)		SM	short meter (66 86)
cent.	century		SMD	short meter double
CM	common meter (86 86)		st.	stanza(s)
CMD	common meter double		tr.	translated by
desc.	descant by		vers.	versified by
harm.	harmonized by			

PSALMS

How Blest Are They Who, Fearing God

1 How blest are they who, fear - ing God, from
2 How blest are they who make God's law their
3 Their lives are nour - ished like a tree set
4 The wick - ed, like the driv - en chaff, are
5 The LORD will guard the right - eous well, their

sin re - strain their feet, who will not with the
trea - sure and de - light, and med - i - tate up-
by the riv - er's side— its leaf is green, its
blown a - cross the land; they shall not gath - er
way to him is known; the way of sin - ners,

wick - ed stand, who shun the scorn - er's seat.
on that word with glad - ness day and night.
fruit is sure: so all their works a - bide.
with the just, nor in the judg - ment stand.
far from God, shall sure - ly be o'er - thrown.

Text: Psalm 1; vers. Psalter, 1912, alt.
Tune: Charles Wesley (the younger), 1757–1834

CM
EPWORTH

Wherefore Do the Nations Rage

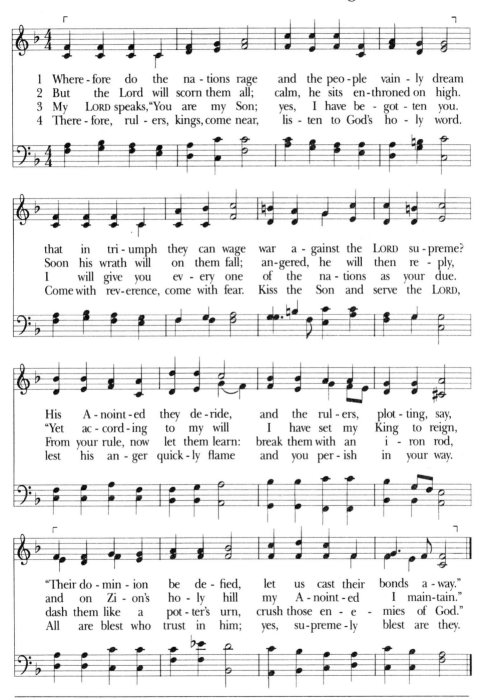

1 Where-fore do the na-tions rage and the peo-ple vain-ly dream
2 But the Lord will scorn them all; calm, he sits en-throned on high.
3 My LORD speaks,"You are my Son; yes, I have be-got-ten you.
4 There-fore, rul-ers, kings,come near, lis-ten to God's ho-ly word.

that in tri-umph they can wage war a-gainst the LORD su-preme?
Soon his wrath will on them fall; an-gered, he will then re-ply,
I will give you ev-ery one of the na-tions as your due.
Come with rev-erence, come with fear. Kiss the Son and serve the LORD,

His A-noint-ed they de-ride, and the rul-ers, plot-ting, say,
"Yet ac-cord-ing to my will I have set my King to reign,
From your rule, now let them learn: break them with an i-ron rod,
lest his an-ger quick-ly flame and you per-ish in your way.

"Their do-min-ion be de-fied, let us cast their bonds a-way."
and on Zi-on's ho-ly hill my A-noint-ed I main-tain."
dash them like a pot-ter's urn, crush those en-e-mies of God."
All are blest who trust in him; yes, su-preme-ly blest are they.

Text: Psalm 2; vers. Psalter, 1912, alt.
Tune: Dick L. Van Halsema, 1952; harm. Psalter Hymnal, 1987.
Harmonization © 1987, CRC Publications

77 77 D
MONSEY CHAPEL

3

O Lord, My Enemies

1 O Lord, my en-e-mies rise up to con-quer me;
2 When I cry out to pray, God hears each word I say;
3 A - rise, O God, a - rise! I know you hear my cries,

they show-er me with taunt - ing. From ev - ery side they say
he an-swers from his moun - tain. I rest and go to sleep
for all my foes are fly - ing. De - liv - er me, O Lord;

that God has gone a - way while trou-bles still are mount - ing.
and rise, for God will keep his own in his pro - tec - tion.
give them their sure re - ward for all their fierce de - fy - ing.

Text: Psalm 3; vers. Paul Shuart, 1982
Tune: Louis Bourgeois, 1551; harm. Howard Slenk, 1985
Text and harmonization © 1987, CRC Publications

667 667 D
GENEVAN 3

But God is still my shield: he helps me on the field;
Why should I ev - er fear the thou-sands who ap - pear
You strike those on the cheek who war a - gainst the meek,

God gives me back my glo - ry. All through the long dark night
with e - vil to sur-round me? Why should I be a - fraid
with hate and hurt op-press - ing. The god - less are de-stroyed;

my God takes up the fight, holds back my foes be - fore me.
when God is still my aid to con-quer those a - round me?
your help a - lone has stood. O grant us, LORD, your bless - ing.

Lord, Hear Me When I Call to You

1 Lord, hear me when I call to you;
re - lieve my ag - o - ny. You are a true and
right - eous God: be mer - ci - ful to me.

2 You peo - ple, why per - sist in lies,
in tram-pling on God's name? How long will you seek
worth - less gods that bring de - spair and shame?

3 Know that the Lord has set a - part
the god - ly as his heirs; I know that when I
call on him, the Lord will hear my prayers.

4 In an - ger do not sin, but think
on all that God has done. Pre - sent to God a
right - eous heart and trust the Ho - ly One.

5 Though many others ask in doubt,
   "Who shows us any good?"
we pray with fervor, "Let your face
   shine over us, O Lord."

6 You fill my heart with greater joy
   than others get from wine.
Their harvest may be plentiful,
   but happiness is mine!

7 I will lie down and sleep in peace;
   my rest is calm and sure.
I know that you alone, O Lord,
   can make my life secure.

Text: Psalm 4; vers. Bert Witvoet, 1984. © 1987, CRC Publications
Tune: Dale Grotenhuis, 1985, ©

CM
PHILIP

Hear, O LORD, My Urgent Prayer

1 Hear, O LORD, my ur - gent prayer as I
2 You do not de - light in sin or in
3 By your mer - cy and your grace I will
4 Save me from de - ceit - ful ways; li - ar's
5 Let those trust - ing you sing praise; grant them

come to seek your care. With each morn - ing
tales that li - ars spin. Haugh - ty ones you
➤ come be - fore your face. Fear - ing foes, I
throats are o - pen graves. Make them bear their
joy to fill their days. Those who al - ways

light I raise voice and heart in prayer and praise.
will de - feat with all those who love de - ceit.
➤ bow to pray: lead me, LORD, make straight my way.
guilt, O LORD, for by choice they spurn your word.
seek the right are pro - tect - ed by your might.

Text: Psalm 5; vers. Marie J. Post, 1983
Tune: Timothy Hoekman, 1979
Text and music © 1987, CRC Publications
This music in a higher key: 289

77 77
TEBBEN

6

LORD, Chasten Not in Anger

1 LORD, chas-ten not in an - ger, nor in your wrath re-buke me.
2 Turn to me now, up - hold me; for your love's sake re-store me.
3 Pain and dis-tress o'er - whelm me, I cry all night for mer - cy,
4 All who love e - vil, leave me, for God has heard my weep-ing:

Give me your heal-ing word. My soul and bod - y lan - guish;
O save me by your grace. For death ends all re - mem - brance;
my bed is wet with tears. My eyes can weep no lon - ger;
my foes are put to shame. Turned back, no more to grieve me,

I wait for you in an - guish. How long, how long, O LORD?
it wraps the tongue in si - lence. How can the dead sing praise?
my en - e - mies seem stron - ger, my aw - ful foes and fears.
they sud - den - ly shall leave me. All glo - ry to his name!

Text: Psalm 6; vers. Clarence P. Walhout, 1982
Tune: Genevan Psalter, 1542; harm. Howard Slenk, 1985
Text and harmonization © 1987, CRC Publications

776 D
GENEVAN 6

Psalm 6: Alternative harmonization with melody in the tenor

1 LORD, chas-ten not in an - ger, nor in your wrath re-buke me.
2 Turn to me now, up - hold me; for your love's sake re-store me.
3 Pain and dis-tress o'er-whelm me, I cry all night for mer - cy,
4 All who love e - vil, leave me, for God has heard my weep - ing:

Give me your heal-ing word. My soul and bod - y lan - guish;
O save me by your grace. For death ends all re - mem - brance;
my bed is wet with tears. My eyes can weep no lon - ger;
my foes are put to shame. Turned back, no more to grieve me,

I wait for you in an - guish. How long, how long, O LORD?
it wraps the tongue in si - lence. How can the dead sing praise?
my en - e - mies seem stron - ger, my aw - ful foes and fears.
they sud-den - ly shall leave me. All glo - ry to his name!

Text: Psalm 6; vers. Clarence P. Walhout, 1982. © 1987, CRC Publications
Tune: Genevan Psalter, 1542; harm. Claude Goudimel, 1564

776 D
GENEVAN 6

7   O LORD My God, from You Alone Comes Aid

1 O LORD my God, from you a - lone comes aid.
2 If I have been un - fair to friends or foes,
3 A - gainst my fu - rious foes in an - ger rise,
4 The LORD, my judge, will sure - ly come to save,
5 Be - cause the LORD in ev - ery time and place

Save me from those who make me sore a - fraid,
if on my hands the soil of mal - ice shows,
▸ and show your - self as judge be - fore all eyes.
while stub - born hearts will know his right - eous wrath.
brings his sal - va - tion, jus - tice, mer - cy, grace,

who, like a li - on, stalk and drag me off,
if there are wrongs that still must be un - done,
▸ O right - eous God, who search - es minds and hearts,
His sharp - ened sword is quick; his ar - rows flame
I will in ev - ery thought and deed and word

Text: Psalm 7; vers. Marie J. Post, 1981. © 1987, CRC Publications
Tune: Geist und Lehr-reiches Kirchen und Haus Buch, Dresden, 1694; harm. Johann S. Bach, 1685–1750

10 10 10 10 84
SO GIEBST DU

while   no   one comes to   save   me   or   to   help.
then   let   those foes   who   stalk   my   steps   come near
▸ try   me   ac - cord - ing   to   my   right - eous - ness.
and   threat - en those   con -   ceiv -   ing, spawn - ing   sin,
give   thanks and praise to   God,   the   right - eous LORD.

What   have   I   done, O   LORD,   I   cry, that   I   should   die?
to   tram - ple   me   un -   til   I   lie   in   dust   to   die.
▸ De - fend, LORD, my   in -   teg - ri - ty   with your   de - cree.
who   in   the   traps   they   have pre-pared them-selves   are   snared.
No   oth - er   gift   can   sat - is - fy   the   LORD   Most   High.

8 LORD, Our Lord, Your Glorious Name

Descant

5 With do-min-ion crowned, we stand o'er the crea-tures

1 LORD, our Lord, your glo-rious name all your won-drous
2 In-fant voic-es chant your praise, tell-ing of your
3 Moon and stars in shin-ing height night-ly tell their
4 Who are we that we should share in your love and
5 With do-min-ion crowned, we stand o'er the crea-tures

of your hand; all to us sub-jec-tion yield,

works pro-claim; in the heavens with ra-diant signs
glo-rious ways; weak-est means work out your will,
► Mak-er's might; when I view the heavens a-far,
ten-der care— raised to an ex-alt-ed height,
of your hand; all to us sub-jec-tion yield,

in the sea and air and field. How great your name!

ev-er-more your glo-ry shines.
might-y en-e-mies to still.
► then I know how small we are. How great your name!
crowned with hon-or in your sight!
in the sea and air and field.

Text: *Psalm 8; vers. Psalter, 1912, alt.*
Tune: *William F. Sherwin, 1877; desc. Emily R. Brink, 1987. Descant © 1987, CRC Publications*

77 77 4 *with refrain*
EVENING PRAISE

LORD, in all the earth, how great your name! Yours the name of

G Refrain | **D7** G C

LORD, our Lord, in all the earth, how great your name! Yours the name of

match - less worth, ex - cel - lent in all the earth. How great your name!

G | D7 | G | G/D D7 G

match - less worth, ex - cel - lent in all the earth. How great your name!

9 Wholehearted Thanksgiving to You I Will Bring

1 Whole-heart-ed thanks-giv-ing to you I will bring;
2 My foes were turned back-ward in ut-ter de-spair;
3 You chid-ed the na-tions, the wick-ed de-stroyed;
4 The LORD will e-ter-nal-ly sit on his throne,

in praise of your mar-vel-ous works I will sing.
they stum-bled and per-ished be-cause you were there.
their names you e-rased and for-ev-er made void.
es-tab-lish-ing it for his judg-ment a-lone.

For joy I will shout and ex-ult-ing-ly cry
For you have de-fend-ed my right and my cause;
The foe is con-sumed and com-plete-ly dis-graced,
He right-eous-ly judg-es the world with his might;

in praise of your name, LORD my God, O Most High.
you sat in just judg-ment, up-hold-ing your laws.
their cit-ies up-root-ed, their mem-ory e-rased.
all peo-ples will know that his judg-ment is right.

Text: Psalm 9; vers. The Book of Psalms for Singing, 1975, alt.
Tune: C. Ferdinand Walther, 1811–1887

11 11 11 11
WALTHER

5 The LORD is a stronghold, a bulwark, a tower,
for all the oppressed in their dark troubled hour.
Those knowing your name, LORD, trust you for your grace;
you have not forsaken those seeking your face.

6 Sing praise to the LORD, who in Zion does dwell;
among all the peoples his mighty deeds tell.
The cry of the poor never fades from his ear;
their blood he avenges; he always will hear.

7 LORD, see what I suffer from malice and hate.
Have mercy! O lift me away from death's gate,
that I with the Daughter of Zion may voice
your praises, and in your salvation rejoice.

8 The nations are sunk in the pit they prepared;
their feet in the net which they hid are ensnared.
The LORD by his judgment has made himself known,
and by their own works are the wicked o'erthrown.

9 The wicked shall perish in death's dark abode,
with all of the lands who are heedless of God.
No longer forget the just cause of the weak,
nor banish forever the hope of the meek.

10 Arise, LORD, let sinners not think themselves strong;
let peoples be judged in your presence for wrong.
Strike terror within them, O LORD; make them see
that nations, though pompous, must still bend the knee.

Why Do You Stand So Far Away, O Lord?

Unison

1 Why do you stand so far a - way, O Lord?
2 The wick - ed boast a - bout their hearts' de - sires;
3 They pros - per and in pride ig - nore your law;
4 Their mouths are filled with oaths and lies and threats;

Why do you hide your - self in trou - bled times?
the cov - et - ous re - nounce and spurn the Lord.
at all their foes they on - ly puff in scorn.
be - neath their tongues are e - vil thoughts and deeds.

In ar - ro - gance the wick - ed trap the poor;
In pride they see no need to seek for aid;
With - in their hearts they think, "I am se - cure;
They lie in am - bush near the vil - lage street;

they catch the weak in schemes they have de - vised.
in all their thoughts they say, "There is no God."
through-out my life my hap - pi - ness is sure."
the in - no - cent they mur - der and de - feat.

Text: Psalm 10; vers. The Book of Psalms for Singing, 1975, alt.
Tune: Carl F. Schalk, 1979, ©

10 10 10 10
FLENTGE

5 The helpless one is crushed and trampled down;
   another victim falls beneath their might.
   At heart they think, "God has forgotten this;
   he hides his face, so he will never see."

6 Arise, O Lᴏʀᴅ, lift up your hand, O God!
   Do not forget the helpless and the poor.
   Why do the wicked proudly scoff at God
   and say, "He will not call me to account"?

7 O God, you note injustice and distress
   that you may take it all into your hands.
   The helpless ones commit themselves to you,
   for you give help to orphans and the poor.

8 O break the wicked evildoers' arm!
   Seek out the secret sin they try to hide.
   The Lᴏʀᴅ is King through all eternity;
   all sinful ones will perish from his land.

9 Lᴏʀᴅ, you will hear the longing of the meek;
   strengthen their hearts, incline your ear to them.
   You will defend the orphan and the poor
   that evil ones may terrify no more.

11   The LORD Is My Strength and My Refuge

1 The LORD is my strength and my ref - uge.
2 "When mor - al foun - da - tions are shak - en,
3 The LORD weighs the good and the e - vil.
4 But God loves the just and the up - right;

My coun - sel - ors vain - ly ad - vise:
then what can the right - eous ones do?"
The vi - o - lent stir up his rage;
he holds them with - in his em - brace.

"O flee like a bird to your moun - tain,
The LORD from his throne sees all peo - ple
his soul burns in ha - tred a - gainst them;
The LORD turns in love toward the right - eous;

for en - e - mies plot your de - mise.
and tests if their ac - tions are true.
his an - ger they get as their wage.
the up - right shall look on his face.

Text: Psalm 11; vers. Clarence P. Walhout, 1983
Tune: Roy Hopp, 1984
Text and music © 1987, CRC Publications

98 98
HILLCREST

Help, LORD, for Those Who Love Your Truth   12

1 Help, LORD, for those who love your truth have van - ished.
2 Do not deal gent - ly with such ly - ing peo - ple.
3 God knows the poor have been op - pressed and ru - ined.
4 The prom - is - es of God are pure as sil - ver—

Are there trust - wor - thy per - sons far or near?
De - stroy all those who boast and have no shame,
God knows the need - y groan and gives them care:
as pure as sil - ver sev - en times re - fined.

It seems that all speak lies and flat - ter neigh - bors.
whose brag - ging lips re - flect a heart of e - vil.
"Now I will grant the safe - ty that they long for."
Though all the wick - ed flour - ish and be hon - ored,

No one these days is hon - est or sin - cere.
"No one can stop our speech," these li - ars claim.
Our God will hear and an - swer ev - ery prayer.
God will pro - tect his own; the LORD is kind.

Text: Psalm 12; vers. Marie J. Post, 1983
Tune: Louis Bourgeois, 1551; harm. Howard Slenk, 1985
Text and harmonization © 1987, CRC Publications

11 10 11 10
GENEVAN 12

13 How Long Will You Forget Me, LORD

1 How long will you for - get me, LORD, and hide your face from me? How long must I with heav - y heart en - dure anx - i - e - ty? How long, how long will en - e - mies boast tri - umph o - ver me?

2 Come close to me and an - swer, LORD, bring light to my sad eyes, or I will sleep the sleep of death, re - viled by en - e - mies. Then they will say, "What can you do? We tri - umphed o - ver you!"

3 But I have trust - ed in your love and in your sav - ing grace. And I will sing to God the LORD my thank - ful hymns of praise, for ev - ery hour and day I see the LORD is good to me.

Text: Psalm 13; vers. Marie J. Post, 1982
Tune: traditional; harm. Dale Grotenhuis, 1986
Text and harmonization © 1987, CRC Publications

86 86 86
THE CHURCH'S DESOLATION

The Foolish in Their Hearts Deny

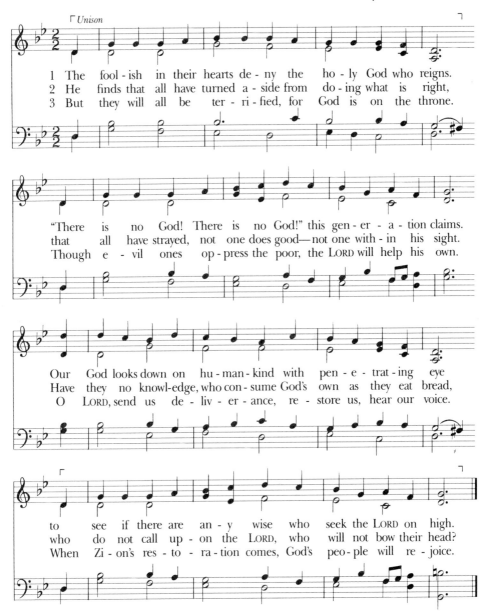

Unison

1 The fool-ish in their hearts de-ny the ho-ly God who reigns.
2 He finds that all have turned a-side from do-ing what is right,
3 But they will all be ter-ri-fied, for God is on the throne.

"There is no God! There is no God!" this gen-er-a-tion claims.
that all have strayed, not one does good—not one with-in his sight.
Though e-vil ones op-press the poor, the LORD will help his own.

Our God looks down on hu-man-kind with pen-e-trat-ing eye
Have they no knowl-edge, who con-sume God's own as they eat bread,
O LORD, send us de-liv-er-ance, re-store us, hear our voice.

to see if there are an-y wise who seek the LORD on high.
who do not call up-on the LORD, who will not bow their head?
When Zi-on's res-to-ra-tion comes, God's peo-ple will re-joice.

Text: Psalm 14; vers. Marie J. Post, 1983
Tune: Richard L. Van Oss, 1984
Text and music © 1987, CRC Publications

CMD
MAPLE AVENUE

LORD, Who Are They That May Dwell

1 LORD, who are they that may dwell
2 They lead an in - cor - rupt life
3 They do no wrong to their friends
4 They stand by what they have vowed,
5 Now these are they who may dwell

with - in the courts of your house? And by what
and do the thing that is right. They speak the
► and will not slan - der their name. They scorn the
al - though it be to their hurt. They do not
with - in the courts of the LORD. Their lives shall

lives do they show they dwell on your ho - ly hill?
truth from their heart and use not their tongue for harm.
► one who is false but love those who fear the LORD.
sin with their wealth and will not be swayed with bribes.
nev - er be moved; they stand in their God, se - cure.

Text: Psalm 15; vers. James E. Seddon, 1971, alt.
Tune: Norman L. Warren, 1971
Text and music © 1973, Hope Publishing Co. All rights reserved. Used by permission.

77 77
STELLA CARMEL

Protect Me, God: I Trust in You

1 Pro - tect me, God: I trust in you. I tell you now,
2 Your peo - ple are a cho - sen race, and I de - light
3 LORD God, you are my food and drink; my work for you
4 Thank you, my LORD, for warn - ing me; by night and day

"You are my Lord; on you my hap - pi - ness de - pends."
in faith - ful friends, but pa - gan ways I will not share.
is joy in - deed; glad is the her - i - tage that's mine.
you guide my thoughts. With you be - fore me, I stand firm.

Refrain

Pro - tect me, God: I trust in you.

5 So now I'm glad in heart and soul,
   for I have found security—
   among the dead I shall not rot. *Refrain*

6 Not death, but life, shall be my path;
   abundant joy your presence grants,
   an honored place, and happiness. *Refrain*

Text: Psalm 16; vers. Michael Saward, 1970
Tune: M. Christian T. Strover, 1973
Text and music © 1973, Hope Publishing Co. All rights reserved. Used by permission.

888 with refrain
MEPHIBOSHETH

17

LORD, Listen to My Righteous Plea

1 LORD, lis - ten to my right - eous plea; you will not
2 I know that you will hear my prayer and show the
3 Be - neath the shad - ow of your wings pro - tect me
4 Their hearts are hard, they speak with pride, they track me
5 For your own peo - ple you pro - vide; with gifts their

find de - ceit in me as my prayers rise.
mar - vel of your care to those who trust.
from all e - vil things sur - round - ing me.
down from ev - ery side like li - on's prey.
chil - dren you sup - ply from your great store.

Ex - am - ine me and probe my heart to see that
LORD, as the ap - ple of your eye may I be
Pro - tect me from my en - e - mies who plot with
By your great power and maj - es - ty rise up, O
At dawn I will be sat - is - fied, when I in

I have kept a - part from ways of sin.
kept in safe - ty by your might - y hand.
cal - cu - lat - ing ease to take my life.
LORD, and res - cue me from such as these.
right - eous - ness a - bide be - fore your face.

Text: Psalm 17; vers. Helen Otte, 1982
Tune: Jack Grotenhuis, 1983
Text and music © 1987, CRC Publications

884 D
BERNARD

Psalm 18: Alternative arrangement with the melody in canon

Tune: Joseph Parry, 1879; arr. Donald Busarow in All Praise to You, Eternal God, *1980.*
Arrangement © 1980, Augsburg Publishing House. Reprinted by permission.

77 77 D
ABERYSTWYTH

How I Love You, Lord, My God

1 How I love you, Lord, my God, you, my rock and
2 All cre - a - tion reeled and rocked, moun - tains quaked when
3 From on high the Lord reached down, seized me with his
4 With the faith - ful you are true, to the pure you

for - tress strong; con - stant ref - uge, might - y shield—
God came down, soar - ing on the wings of wind,
power - ful arm; when the floods en - gulfed my soul,
show your grace, but to crook - ed hu - man - kind

I will praise you in my song. Snares of death en -
fire and hail - stones all a - round. Then his nos - trils,
he de - liv - ered me from harm. God the Lord, my
you re - veal an an - gry face. You, Lord, bring the

tan - gled me, hell - ish tor - rents fright - ened me; but you
with a blast, split the sea that bil - lowed there; when the
strong sup - port, brought me to a spa - cious place, for it
haugh - ty low, save the hum - ble from their plight, and you

Text: Psalm 18; vers. Ada Roeper-Boulogne, 1985. © 1987, CRC Publications
Tune: Joseph Parry, 1879
This music in a higher key: 578

77 77 D
ABERYSTWYTH

heard my des - perate cry, and your hand has set me free.
LORD un - leashed his wrath, earth's foun - da - tions were laid bare.
is his great de - light to re - ward my right-eous ways.
keep my lamp a - glow, turn my dark - ness in - to light.

5 All God's promises are sure.
  Who is God besides the LORD?
  He is perfect in his ways.
  Who the Rock except our God?
  It is God who gives me strength;
  he enables me to stand
  high above the battlefield,
  held up by his powerful hand.

6 God prepares me well for war,
  makes my feet as swift as deer,
  arms me with salvation's shield,
  makes my pathway broad and sure.
  I pursued my enemies
  till they fell beneath my feet,
  beat them fine like blowing dust,
  low like dirt that lines the street.

7 God has rescued me from strife
  with the nations all around.
  He has made me head of all;
  foreign leaders now bow down.
  Yes, the LORD exalted me
  over all my enemies;
  they obey all my commands,
  cringing low on trembling knees.

8 God the LORD, my Savior, lives!
  To my Rock be all the praise!
  He has overcome my foes,
  shown me his unfailing grace.
  LORD, I will extol your name
  and make all your blessings known.
  You give victory to your king,
  give his heirs a royal throne.

The Spacious Heavens Tell

1 The spa-cious heav - ens tell the glo - ry of the LORD;
2 God's per - fect law is good, for it re - vives the soul
3 Who can dis - cern their wrongs? For - give my hid - den faults.

the skies his work pro - claim. Each day and night is heard
and makes the sim - ple wise. The pre-cepts of the LORD
Keep me from will - ful sins. May they not rule my life;

their voice in all the earth; they glo - ri - fy God's name.
give joy un - to the heart and light un - to the eyes.
then I will blame - less be, not guilt - y of great sin.

Text: Psalm 19; vers. Helen Otte, 1987
Tune: Genevan Psalter, 1542; harm. Dale Grotenhuis, 1985
Text and harmonization © 1987, CRC Publications
Another setting of Psalm 19: 429

666 D 667 D
GENEVAN 19

Each day the might-y sun re - joic - es in its run,
All God's com-mands are sure— the fear of God is pure,
All of these words and thoughts, re - flec - tions of my heart,

a - ris - ing in the morn - ing— a bride-groom com - ing forth,
for - ev - er-more en - dur - ing— more pre - cious than pure gold
in praise to you I of - fer. May this, my sac - ri - fice,

a run - ner on the course— bright shin - ing in its glo - ry.
or hon - ey from the comb; to keep them is re - ward - ing.
be pleas-ing in your sight, my Rock and my Re-deem - er.

In the Day of Need

1 In the day of need may your answer be the LORD;
2 May the LORD God grant you success in all your plans;
3 Now I know that God will encourage those he loves;
4 There are some who boast of the weapons of the world,

may the God of Jacob strengthen you.
may he give you all your heart's desire.
he will hear and answer from on high.
but the power of God is all our pride.

May he send you
May we sing for
Not a word shall
Those who arm for

help from his high and holy place, and sup-
joy when we see the battle won, when the
fail of the promise he has made, nor the
war shall one day collapse and fall, but God's

port you for the glory of his name.
LORD has heard and answered every prayer.
works of his victorious right hand.
people stand and in their King prevail.

Text: Psalm 20; vers. Christopher M. Idle, 1969
Tune: Norman L. Warren, 1972
Text and music © 1973, Hope Publishing Co. All rights reserved. Used by permission.

12 9 12 11
SAMSON

The King Rejoices in Your Strength

1 The king rejoices in your strength, O LORD, and
in your care. You granted all his heart's desire, and
you have heard his prayer. You welcomed him with every
kind of grace you could unfold. Rich blessings you have
given him; you crowned his head with gold.

2 He asked for life from you, O LORD: you gave it
endlessly. His glory shines because you gave him
strength and majesty. You blessed him, LORD, by being
near; his trust is firm and sure. Because of your unfailing love our king will stand secure.

3 Your hand, O king, will sieze your foes; they cringe before your name. When you appear, God will destroy them
all with dreadful flame. They plot and scheme but flee a-
way before your arrow's flight. All praise to you, O
LORD, our God; we glory in your might.

Text: Psalm 21; vers. Marie J. Post, 1985. © 1987, CRC Publications
Tune: Supplement to the New Version, 1708

CMD
ST. MATTHEW

22

My God! O My God!

1 My God! O my God! Have you left me a - lone?
2 Yet you are the Ho - ly One, Is - ra - el's King,
3 Yet I am a worm who is laughed at and mocked,
4 Since I was a ba - by, de - pen - dent and weak,

Why have you for - sak - en me, deaf to my groan?
to whom all our fa - thers and moth - ers did sing.
de - spised by the god - less who saun - ter a - bout.
I nes - tled in safe - ty, LORD, close to your cheek.

I cry to you dai - ly and plead late at night,
They count - ed on you to come through when they prayed;
"His help is the LORD! Fool - ish fel - low," they sneer,
Please don't go a - way, for deep trou - ble is near!

but you do not an - swer or pit - y my plight.
when - ev - er they trust - ed, then you al - ways saved.
"let God set him free since he counts him so dear."
Who else can se - cure me and keep a - way fear?

Text: Psalm 22; vers. Calvin Seerveld, 1985, ©
Tune: Welsh, 17th cent.
Other settings of Psalm 22: 160, 239, 240, 542

11 11 11 11
MALDWYN

5 Surrounding brute beasts make me shudder with fright,
and jaws of fierce lions are ready to bite.
My bones seem disjointed, I can't catch my breath—
my heart melts like wax, and I face cruel death.

6 Like dogs they surround me, I cringe and I groan;
they pierce through my hands and my feet to the bone.
They measure me out for the kill, as they gloat.
They scatter their dice for my garments and coat.

7 My God! O my God! Do not leave me exposed.
Voracious, these dogs only deepen my woes.
These beasts, mad with violence, want me to die:
O stop them, Almighty, and answer my cry!

8 I shout out your praise to your saints who endure.
Praise God, all you faithful: his comfort is sure.
The LORD has not left me or hidden his face;
I cried out for help, and God saved me in grace.

9 Those hungry for fullness will feast with the LORD.
All peoples will worship the God they ignored.
Yes, even the proud will be humbled in dust
to honor God's power—the LORD whom we trust!

10 I thank you, my LORD, I may sing with your folk
to seal here in worship the vows which I spoke,
so new generations shall pass on in faith
that you, O my God, keep your children all safe!

The LORD, My Shepherd, Rules My Life

Descant
5 Your good - ness and your gra - cious love pur-

1 The LORD, my shep - herd, rules my life and
2 The LORD re - vives my fail - ing strength, he
3 Though in a val - ley dark as death, no
4 While all my en - e - mies look on, you
5 Your good - ness and your gra - cious love pur-

sue me all my days; your house, O LORD, shall

gives me all I need; he leads me by re -
makes my joy com - plete; and in right paths, for
e - vil makes me fear; your shep - herd's staff pro -
spread a roy - al feast; you fill my cup, a -
sue me all my days; your house, O LORD, shall

be my home— your name, my end - less praise.

fresh - ing streams; in pas - tures green I feed.
his name's sake, he guides my fal - tering feet.
tects my way, for you are with me there.
noint my head, and treat me as your guest.
be my home— your name, my end - less praise.

Text: Psalm 23; vers. Christopher M. Idle, 1977. © 1982, Hope Publishing Co. All rights reserved. Used by permission.
Tune: Jessie Seymour Irvine, 1872; harm. David Grant, 1872; desc. W. Baird Ross, 1871–1950
Other settings of Psalm 23: 161, 162, 550

CM
CRIMOND

The Earth and the Riches

1 The earth and the rich-es with which it is stored,
2 Then who may as-cend to the hill of the LORD,
3 Who then are the cho-sen our LORD God will bless?
4 O gates, lift your heads high, O doors, o-pen wide;
5 O gates, lift your heads high, O doors, o-pen wide;

the world and its peo-ple be-long to the LORD.
who stand in his pres-ence while hear-ing his word?
► On whom will our Sav-ior pour out right-eous-ness?
the King of all glo-ry will then come in-side.
the King of all glo-ry will then come in-side.

Se-cure-ly he an-chored the world and, with ease,
Those show-ing clean hands, who are hon-est and true;
► On these, God's own peo-ple, his cov-e-nant race,
Who is he, the King of all glo-ry we sing?
Who is he, the King of all glo-ry we sing?

es-tab-lished its per-ma-nent place on the seas.
those who are trust-wor-thy in all that they do.
► for they are the ones who are seek-ing his face.
The LORD strong and might-y, our con-quer-ing King!
Al-might-y and glo-rious, the LORD is the King!

Text: Psalm 24; vers. Marie J. Post, 1982. © 1987, CRC Publications
Tune: Charles H. Gabriel, 1856–1932
Another setting of Psalm 24: 163

11 11 11 11
LANSING

25

LORD, to You My Soul Is Lifted

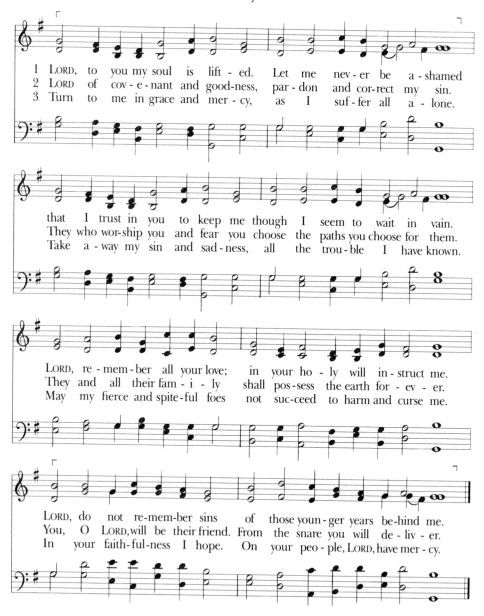

1 LORD, to you my soul is lift - ed. Let me nev - er be a - shamed
2 LORD of cov - e - nant and good-ness, par - don and cor-rect my sin.
3 Turn to me in grace and mer - cy, as I suf - fer all a - lone.

that I trust in you to keep me though I seem to wait in vain.
They who wor-ship you and fear you choose the paths you choose for them.
Take a - way my sin and sad - ness, all the trou - ble I have known.

LORD, re - mem - ber all your love; in your ho - ly will in - struct me.
They and all their fam - i - ly shall pos-sess the earth for - ev - er.
May my fierce and spite-ful foes not suc-ceed to harm and curse me.

LORD, do not re-mem-ber sins of those youn - ger years be-hind me.
You, O LORD, will be their friend. From the snare you will de - liv - er.
In your faith-ful-ness I hope. On your peo - ple, LORD, have mer - cy.

Text: Psalm 25; vers. Stanley Wiersma, 1980
Tune: Louis Bourgeois, 1551; harm. Howard Slenk, 1985
Text and harmonization © 1987, CRC Publications

87 87 78 78
GENEVAN 25

Lord, Speak for Me, for I Am Yours

1 Lord, speak for me, for I am yours; and test my mind and heart. I walk with stead-y trust in you, nor from your ways de - part.

2 Try me, O Lord, if I be true and walk in right-eous-ness. Your love for-ev-er leads my way; I trust your faith-ful-ness.

3 I do not sit with those who cheat— the false who love pre-tense. I do not fol-low where they go, nor count them as my friends.

4 I wash my hands in in-no-cence and seek your al-tar, Lord, and, sing-ing there with thank-ful voice, your might-y works re-cord.

5 I love your house, O might-y Lord, I love the ho-ly place where you in your great glo-ry dwell; you vis-it us in grace.

6 O do not sweep me down to death
with those who thirst for blood.
Their right hands overflow with bribes;
they turn away from good.

7 I walk in my integrity;
redeem me, Lord, in grace.
Securely now I stand, O Lord;
in worship I bring praise.

Text: Psalm 26; vers. Marie J. Post, 1983. © 1987, CRC Publications
Tune: Leo Sowerby, 1962. © 1964, Abingdon Press. Used by permission.

CM
PERRY

27 The LORD God Is My Light and My Salvation

1 The LORD God is my light and my sal - va - tion—
2 One thing I ask my lov - ing LORD to grant me:
3 Hear me, O LORD, when I in des - per - a - tion
4 Do not de - sert me, LORD of my sal - va - tion,

whom shall I fear? He is my shel - tering wall.
that I may dwell for - ev - er in his house,
cry out for help; be mer - ci - ful to me.
al - though my moth - er and my fa - ther do.

When en - e - mies a - rise and turn a - gainst me,
to gaze up - on the beau - ty of the LORD God,
LORD, hear my cry and heed my sup - pli - ca - tion;
Teach me your way of truth, O LORD, and lead me

they stum - ble on their slip - pery paths and fall.
to seek him in his ho - ly dwell - ing place.
O an - swer, gra - cious LORD, this ur - gent plea.
to walk the lev - el paths I long to know.

Text: Psalm 27; vers. Marie J. Post, 1980
Tune: Louis Bourgeois, 1551; harm. Dale Grotenhuis, 1986
Text and harmonization © 1987, CRC Publications
Another setting of Psalm 27: 164

11 10 11 10 10 10 10 10
GENEVAN 27

I will not fear though en - e - mies as - sault;
For in the day of trou - ble and of strife,
The LORD to me has spo - ken, "Seek my face."
False wit - ness - es a - rise to block my ways,

my con - fi - dence in God e - ras - es doubt.
God in his shel - ter will pre - serve my life.
My heart says, "Yes, LORD, I will seek your face."
but I am con - fi - dent and trust your grace,

Though bat - tles rage, the LORD will keep me near;
High on a rock I'll lift my voice and sing;
Re - mem - ber me, your ser - vant; do not hide.
that I will see the good - ness of the LORD.

I trust in him and I shall nev - er fear.
with shouts of joy my prais - es I will bring.
Do not be an - gry, LORD; stay at my side.
Hope in the LORD! Be strong and trust his word.

O Lord My Rock, in Desperation

1 O Lord my Rock, in des-per-a-tion I plead for
2 I cry, O Lord, for help and mer-cy; I lift my
3 They act so friend-ly to their neigh-bors but har-bor
4 Be-cause they dis-re-gard God's do-ings, and all his

you to hear my cry. For if you should re-main in
plead-ing hands in prayer. Lord, do not drag me off with
mal-ice in their heart. Lord, pun-ish them for spite and
jus-tice they de-spise, our Lord will cast them down in

si-lence, I know that I would sure-ly die.
sin-ners while wick-ed peo-ple stand and stare.
out-rage, and set their e-vil lives a-part.
an-ger and he will nev-er let them rise.

5 O praise our God, the Lord eternal;
   he heard my cry and turned to me.
   He is my strength, my shield and helper;
   in him my joy will always be.

6 God is the strength of his anointed,
   a fortress to the ones he chose.
   As shepherd, save and bless your people;
   keep them secure from all their foes.

Text: Psalm 28; vers. Marie J. Post, 1982. © 1987, CRC Publications
Tune: Mary J. Hammond, 1920

98 98
SPIRITUS VITAE

Psalm 28: Alternative harmonization with melody in the tenor

1 O LORD my Rock, in des - per - a - tion I plead for
2 I cry, O LORD, for help and mer - cy; I lift my
3 They act so friend - ly to their neigh - bors but har - bor
4 Be - cause they dis - re - gard God's do - ings, and all his

you to hear my cry. For if you should re - main in
plead-ing hands in prayer. LORD, do not drag me off with
mal - ice in their heart. LORD, pun - ish them for spite and
jus - tice they de - spise, our LORD will cast them down in

si - lence, I know that I would sure - ly die.
sin - ners while wick - ed peo - ple stand and stare.
out - rage, and set their e - vil lives a - part.
an - ger and he will nev - er let them rise.

Text: Psalm 28; vers. Marie J. Post, 1982
Tune: Mary J. Hammond, 1920; harm. Emily R. Brink, 1987
Text and harmonization © 1987, CRC Publications

98 98
SPIRITUS VITAE

29 Give Glory to God, All You Heavenly Creatures

1 Give glo-ry to God, all you heav-en-ly crea-tures;
2 The voice of the LORD rolls out o-ver the wa-ters;
3 The voice of the LORD now is break-ing the ce-dars;
4 The voice of the LORD whips out light-ning-like flash-es.
5 The crea-tures now wor-ship the God of all pow-er;

all glo-ry and pow-er be-long to the LORD!
it thun-ders and ech-oes his glo-ry a-broad.
he shat-ters the trees while Mount Leb-a-non quakes.
The voice of the LORD makes the des-ert to reel.
all crea-tures re-spond, "May God's glo-ry in-crease."

So drop to your knees and re-spect what is ho-ly,
The voice of the LORD is ma-jes-tic and might-y;
God speaks: all the hills jump like an-te-lopes star-tled—
The voice of the LORD sets the oak tree a-whirl-ing.
The LORD gives his peo-ple their strength and all bless-ing;

be qui-et and lis-ten: the voice of the LORD!
its pow-er re-sounds, and his crea-tures are awed.
the voice of the LORD makes us crea-tures to shake.
God strips for-ests bare by the force of his gale.
the LORD shall en-cir-cle his peo-ple with peace.

Text: Psalm 29; vers. Calvin Seerveld, 1983, ©
Tune: Charles H. Gabriel, 1856–1932

12 11 12 11
ARLES

I Worship You, O LORD

1. I worship you, O LORD, for you have raised me up; I cried to you for help, and you restored my life. You brought me back from death and saved me from the grave.

2. Sing praises to the LORD, all those who know his name; for while his wrath is brief, his favor knows no end. Though tears flow for a night, the morning brings new joy.

3. I said, "I am so strong, I never shall be moved"; but you, LORD, shook my life—my heart was in distress. I cried out for your help and pleaded for your grace:

4. "What good am I when dead, while lying in the grave? Can dust recount your love, the grave proclaim your praise?" O hear me, gracious LORD, in mercy be my aid!"

5. My mourning you have turned to dancing and to joy; my sadness you dispelled as gladness filled my soul. And so I'll sing your praise, my God, through all my days.

Text: Psalm 30; st. 1–3, 5 vers. James Seddon, 1973, alt.; st. 4 vers. Calvin Seerveld, 1982
Tune: Norman L. Warren, 1969
Text and music © 1973, Hope Publishing Co. All rights reserved. Used by permission.

66 66 66
BISHOP TUCKER

31 I Seek My Refuge in You, LORD

1 I seek my ref-uge in you, LORD; then let me not be
2 You are my rock and for-tress, LORD: lead me in all my
3 I hate all those who trust false gods; I ev-er trust in
4 Be mer-ci-ful to me, O LORD; my strength has failed, con-

put to shame. LORD, lis-ten to my anx-ious cries
trou-bled ways. A - lert me, LORD, to hid-den traps;
God a-lone. You knew the an-guish of my soul
sumed with grief. I am for-got-ten, bro-ken, lost;

for help that nev-er seems to come. Be my strong rock to
safe-guard-ed I shall spend my days. My spir-it, LORD, I
and heard each trou-bled, pain-ful groan. You an-swered me in
LORD, come and bring my soul re-lief. I am a hor-ror

shel-ter me, a ref - uge to which I can flee.
now com-mend in - to your gra-cious, sav-ing hand.
love and grace and set me in a spa-cious place.
to each friend, and e - vil schem-ers plot my end.

Text: Psalm 31; vers. Marie J. Post, 1985. © 1987, CRC Publications
Tune: La Scala Santa, Ireland, 1681; arr. Erik Routley, 1985. Arrangement © 1985, Hope Publishing Co.
All rights reserved. Used by permission.

88 88 88
COLERAINE

5 I trust in you: you are my God.
My times are in your gracious hand.
LORD, shine your face on me in love;
keep me from shame. By your command
put wicked liars all to shame,
who slander those that bear your name.

6 How great your goodness kept in store
for those who cling to you for aid.
You hide them in a secret place
and keep them safe and unafraid.
They are secure from stabbing lies
and plots that enemies devise.

7 The mercy of the LORD is sure—
to me he showed his saving care.
When I felt cut off from your sight,
you did not leave me in despair.
You saints, you faithful, trust his word.
Be strong, take heart, hope in the LORD.

How Blest Are They Whose Trespass

1 How blest are they whose tres-pass has free-ly been for-given,
2 While I kept guilt-y si-lence, my strength was spent with grief:
3 So let the god-ly seek you in times when you are near;
4 "I gra-cious-ly will teach you the way that you should go,
5 The sor-rows of the wick-ed in-crease from year to year,

whose sins are whol-ly cov-ered be-fore the sight of heaven.
your hand was heav-y on me; my soul found no re-lief.
▸ no whelm-ing floods shall reach them or cause their hearts to fear.
and, with my eye up-on you, help you my coun-sel know.
but those who trust the LORD God know love in-stead of fear.

Blest they to whom the LORD God does not im-pute their sin,
But when I owned my tres-pass and did not hide my sin,
▸ O LORD, you are my ref-uge, you are my hid-ing place,
Then do not be un-rul-y or slow to un-der-stand;
Then in the LORD be joy-ful, in song lift up your voice;

who have a guile-less spir-it, whose heart is true with-in.
then you for-gave my guilt, LORD, re-stored my life with-in.
▸ and you sur-round me al-ways with songs of sav-ing grace.
be not per-verse, but will-ing to heed my wise com-mand."
be glad in God, you right-eous: re-joice, O saints, re-joice!

Text: Psalm 32; vers. Psalter, 1912, alt.
Tune: Chrétien Urhan, 1834; arr. Edward F. Rimbault, 1867

76 76 D
RUTHERFORD

Psalm 33: Alternative harmonization with melody in the tenor

Tune: *Genevan Psalter, 1551; harm. Claude Goudimel, 1564*

Rejoice! Sing Praise to Your Creator

1 Re - joice! Sing praise to your Cre - a - tor, for it is
2 God spoke his word to make the heav - ens; his spir - it
3 The LORD up - sets the plans of na - tions; he frus - trates
4 The LORD on high looks down from heav - en; he sees all
5 Our souls wait for the LORD, our keep - er; he is our

good to praise the LORD. Make mu - sic with gui - tar and
gave the stars their birth. He gath - ers all the o - ceans'
▶ all that they de - vise. But God's own plans stand firm for -
peo - ple he has made. No king is saved by might or
help, he is our shield. Shout loud - ly, praise the LORD, and

trum - pet; blend skill - ful - ly each note and word.
wa - ters in store - hous - es a - round the earth.
▶ ev - er, and all his pur - pos - es are wise.
ar - my; a war - rior's horse will not give aid.
trust him who has our life and fu - ture sealed.

Text: Psalm 33; vers. Marie J. Post, 1980. © 1987, CRC Publications
Tune: Genevan Psalter, 1551; harm. Claude Goudimel, 1564, alt.
Another setting of Psalm 33: 449

PM
GENEVAN 33

All God's words are truth - ful. All his works are faith - ful.
Who should not a - dore him, stand in awe be - fore him?
► Bless - ed is that na - tion, ev - ery gen - er - a - tion
Our LORD sees with fa - vor those who love their Sav - ior—
God, our lov - ing Sav - ior, keeps us safe for - ev - er.

He loves right - eous - ness. To the earth and heav - ens
What he spoke was done: place and life were giv - en
► for whom God is LORD. Bound to him for - ev - er,
keeps his eye on them. Death's bonds he will sev - er,
Ho - ly is his name! God the LORD is lov - ing,

con - stant care is giv - en with un - fail - ing love.
to seas, earth, and heav - en. Let all fear the LORD!
► noth - ing now can sev - er God from those he chose.
save their lives for - ev - er— God will save from death.
al - ways, all ways prov - ing hope is in the LORD.

LORD, I Bring My Songs to You

1 LORD; I bring my songs to you, ev - ery day de - clar - ing praise. All the meek shall hear my words al - ways tell - ing of your ways. Join with me your heart and voice, praise the LORD, in him re - joice.

2 I sought God, he an - swered me; he de - liv - ered me from fear. Look to him; your face will shine, free from shame and from de - spair. Lo, the an - gel of our God camps near those who fear the LORD.

3 Taste and see that God is good, shel - tering all who love his name. Fear the LORD and heed his word; those who fear him know no shame. Li - ons young from hun - ger cry; God his own will sat - is - fy.

4 Come, my chil - dren, hear me speak. This is how to fear the LORD: If good days you would en - joy, keep your tongue from ly - ing words. Turn from e - vil, do the good, seek the peace that comes from God.

Text: Psalm 34; vers. Marie J. Post, 1985. © 1987, CRC Publications
Tune: Freylinghausen's Geistreiches Gesangbuch, 1704; rev. Werner's Choralbuch, 1815

77 77 77
RATISBON

5 God the LORD sees all our needs;
   he will answer us in grace.
   But against all evil ones
   God will surely turn his face.
   When the contrite cry, he hears,
   saving them and ending fears.

6 Though our troubles multiply,
   God the LORD will save his own.
   He will turn the wrong aside,
   keep unbroken every bone.
   Wicked ones the LORD condemns,
   but his servants he defends.

35

O Lord, Arise, Come Help Me Now

1 O Lord, a - rise, come help me now.
2 Let them be turned back in dis - may
3 Then in the Lord will I re - joice
4 Un - right - eous wit - ness - es a - rise

Con - tend with those who seek my life. Con - front my
who plot my ru - in and dis - grace. Then may the
and in his sav - ing work de - light. Then my whole
a - gainst me, caus - ing me dis - tress. I treat - ed

en - e - mies, O Lord; pro - tect me with your
an - gel of the Lord drive them like chaff be -
be - ing will ex - claim, "Who can com - pare with
them with love and care; when they were ill, I

Text: Psalm 35; vers. Helen Otte, 1985. © 1987, CRC Publications
Tune: J. G. Wagner's Sammlung alter und neuer, 1742; harm. Johann S. Bach, 1685–1750, alt.

88 88 88
GOTTLOB

might - y	shield.	Come speak	your	re - as - sur - ing
fore	the	wind.	O LORD, may	their	de - ceit	and
you,	O	LORD?	You res - cue	those	who	are	op -
prayed	and	wept.	As though they	were	my	own,	I

word	that	my	sal - va - tion	is	the	LORD.
lies	trap them and	take	them	by	sur - prise.
pressed;	the	poor and	need - y	call	you	blest."
mourned,	but	still they	treat - ed	me	with	scorn.

5 How long will you look on, O LORD?
  Save me from their contempt and rage.
  Then I will thank and praise your name
  amid the crowds of worshipers.
  Let not my enemies rejoice
  who plot deceit with mocking voice.

6 Do not be far from me, O Lord;
  arise and vindicate my cause.
  Let those who hope for my release
  be glad and shout, "The LORD is great!"
  Then I will speak with thankful voice and
  in your righteousness rejoice.

36   My Heart Speaks Out on Those Who Sin

1 My heart speaks out on those who sin, who day and
2 Your love, O LORD, ex - tends to heaven; your faith - ful -
3 How pre - cious is your con - stant love! O LORD, you
4 From you a liv - ing foun - tain flows, and in your
5 But may the proud not tram - ple me or drive me

night give birth to lies. There is no fear of
ness tran - scends the sky. Your jus - tice e - quals
▸ keep man - kind and beast. All crea - tures find their
light we see the light. Main - tain your love to
out of your do - main. See how the wick - ed

God in them; they are no lon - ger good or wise.
o - cean depths; your right - eous - ness is moun - tain high.
▸ rest in you; with joy a - bun - dant they shall feast.
faith - ful folk, your truth to those who love the right.
can - not stand; thrown down, they will not rise a - gain!

Text: Psalm 36; vers. Bert Witvoet, 1981. © 1987, CRC Publications
Tune: J. Frederick Wolle, 1923

LM
PALMARUM

Psalm 36: Alternative accompaniment and descant

2 Your love ex - tends to heaven; your faith - ful -
4 From you a foun - tain flows, and in your

ness tran - scends the sky. Your jus - tice e - quals
light we see the light. Main - tain your love to

o - cean depths; your right - eous - ness is moun - tain high.
faith - ful folk, your truth to those who love the right.

Text: Psalm 36; vers. Bert Witvoet, 1981
Tune: J. Frederick Wolle, 1923; arr. Roy Hopp, 1987
Text and arrangement © 1987, CRC Publications

LM
PALMARUM

When Evil People Sin

1 When e - vil peo - ple sin and wrong sup-press - es right,
2 Be still be - fore the LORD, wait pa - tient - ly for him,
3 The wick - ed fight the poor, but God will scorn their stealth.
4 The god - less bor - row much and then do not pay back.

re - mem - ber, they will fade a - way and with - er o - ver - night.
and do not fret when wick-ed - ness suc - ceeds to make life grim.
The lit - tle that the right-eous hold is bet - ter than sin's wealth.
The right-eous give and give a - gain—their chil-dren have no lack.

Com - mit your way to God; trust him to bless the right.
Re - frain from an - gry ways and wor - ries that de - stroy.
The LORD up - holds his own; their bless - ings will in - crease.
My steps are from the LORD, who helps my feet to stand.

He gives you all your heart's de - sire when he is your de - light.
All those who look to God their LORD his king-dom shall en - joy.
But all the wick-ed come to naught—their power will sure - ly cease.
I stum-ble but I do not fall: God holds me with his hand.

Text: Psalm 37; vers. Bert Polman, 1985; based on a text by Christopher Idle. © 1987, CRC Publications
Tune: Joseph Parry, 1841–1903

SMD
DINBYCH

5   Shun evil and do good;
      then you will live in peace.
   The LORD protects his suffering saints,
      but wicked lives will cease.
     The righteous speak the truth,
      their tongues with wisdom flow;
  the law of God is in their heart.
      He saves them from the foe.

6   The LORD will bless your land
      if you but keep his way.
  Though wicked people grow like trees,
      they soon will pass away.
     Salvation comes from God
      who saves us from the wrong,
and those who seek his shelter find
      a refuge safe and strong.

38

Rebuke Me Not in Anger, LORD

1 Re - buke me not in an - ger, LORD; your ar - rows
2 My sin - ful fol - ly brought me low; bowed down, I
3 You know my sighs and weak - ness, Lord, my blind - ed
4 My mouth is mute, I can - not speak; my ear is

wound and bring de - spair. My guilt is like a
groan in an - guished grief. I have no strength, for
eyes and throb - bing heart. Friends and com - pan - ions
deaf, I can - not hear. I wait for you to

heav - y load that is too much for me to bear.
I am crushed and spend my days with no re - lief.
stand far off while oth - ers plot to seek my hurt.
an - swer, LORD, to si - lence those who boast and jeer.

5 My pain is ever with me, LORD,
   for I have sinned against your laws.
   My foes are mighty—those who hate
   and slander me without a cause.

6 Do not forsake me, O my LORD;
   do not go far from me, my God.
   Come quickly, help me now, I pray,
   O Lord, my Savior and my God.

Text: Psalm 38; vers. Helen Otte, 1985. © 1987, CRC Publications
Tune: Hesperian Harp, 1848; harm. Louise McAllister, 1958

LM
BOURBON

Once I Said, "I Must Keep Quiet"

1 Once I said, "I must keep qui - et; else I sin in
2 "LORD, are you re - veal - ing lim - its, how my days look
3 "Why, O Lord, must I be wait - ing when my hope is
4 "But, my LORD, your heav - y bur - den wears me out and
5 "Can you see, LORD, I am cry - ing? Do not spurn my

harsh dis - pute. Just to see the wick - ed near me an - gers
in your sight? Just a breath and fleet - ing shad - ow slip - ping
▸ still in you? Keep me, LORD, from sin and trou - ble, from the
weighs me down. All your dis - ci - pline for sin - ning hurts and
sore un - rest. I pass by like those be - fore me, yet I

me, but I stay mute." Yet I could not hold my fu - ry,
by in use - less flight? Yes, I know our lives are frag - ile,
▸ wrong I would pur - sue. Save me from the fool's loud laugh-ter—
bows me to the ground. Must you eat a - way my trea - sures
claim to be your guest! No more sad - ness— give me glad - ness,

burned to vent my sharp cri - tique; then, at last, I had to speak:
that we seem to work in vain— all we have is oth - ers' gain.
▸ I was si - lent, I for - got: you con - trol my trou - bled lot.
like a moth? I'm but a breath. Are you fac - ing me with death?
be my hope be - fore I cease. LORD, dear LORD, I beg for peace."

Text: Psalm 39; vers. Calvin Seerveld, 1983, ©
Tune: Evan Morgan, 1846–1920

87 87 87 7
TYDDYN LLWYN

40

I Waited Patiently for God

1 I wait-ed pa-tient-ly for God; he turned to me and
2 You do not want a sac-ri-fice; in-stead, you claim my
3 Do not with-hold your mer-cy, LORD; pro-tect me with your
4 May all who seek to take my life be put to shame and

heard my cry. He pulled me from de-struc-tion's pit and set my
life, my all. I come to you o-be-dient-ly; to do your
love and truth. For trou-bles now sur-round my life, my sins have
suf-fer scorn. But all who seek you will re-joice and say, "The

feet on sol-id ground. He put a new song in my
will is my de-light. Be-fore your peo-ple I pro-
o-ver-tak-en me. They o-ver-whelm my fail-ing
LORD be mag-ni-fied!" Yet I am poor and need-y,

Text: Psalm 40; vers. Bert Polman, 1980. © *1987, CRC Publications*
Tune: Joseph Parry, 1870

LMD
MERTHYR TYDFIL

mouth. How blest are those who trust the LORD. My God, your deeds and
claim the gos-pel of your right-eous-ness. I do not hide your
heart; I can-not see, my way is dark. Be pleased, O LORD, to
LORD; please turn to me and hear my cry. You are my help, my

plans are great; they num-ber more than I can count.
love and truth, but speak of your great faith-ful-ness.
res - cue me; come quick-ly and re - store my life.
Sav - ior God! Do not de - lay, re - mem-ber me.

41

How Blest Are Those Who Thoughtfully

1 How blest are those who thought-ful-ly   the poor and weak be-friend:
2 I said, "Have mer-cy, heal me, LORD, and all my sin for-give."
3 O LORD, be mer-ci - ful to me; let jus-tice now pre-vail.

The LORD de-liv-ers them from harm; his bless-ings have no   end.
My en - e - mies have said in scorn, "We hope you will not live!"
I   know that you are pleased with me, for all my foes do fail.

The LORD will not sur - ren-der them when en · e-mies op - press;
My friend, whom I have trust-ed much, who of-ten shared my bread,
In my in-teg-ri - ty, O LORD, you hold me in your hand

in sick-ness he sus-tains their life and heals those in dis-tress.
has turned a-gainst me like my foes: they all would see me dead.
to live with you for - ev-er-more. O praise the LORD! A - men!

Text: Psalm 41; vers. Bert Polman, 1985
Tune: Roy Hopp, 1984
Text and music © 1987, CRC Publications

CMD
GREELEY

Psalm 42: Alternative harmonization with instrumental descants for stanza 3

Tune: Louis Bourgeois, 1551; bass and desc. Johann Crüger, 1658

87 87 77 88
GENEVAN 42

As a Deer in Want of Water

1 As a deer in want of water, so I
2 Bit - ter tears of lam - en - ta - tion are my
3 O my soul, why are you griev - ing, why dis -
4 From the land be - yond the Jor - dan, in my
5 I will say to God, my for - tress, "Why have

long for you, O LORD. All my heart and be - ing
food by night and day. In my deep hu - mil i -
qui - et - ed in me? Put your hope in God, be -
grief I think of you; from the foot - hills of Mount
you for - got - ten me? Why must I pro - ceed in

fal - ter, thirst - ing for your liv - ing word.
a - tion "Where is now your God?" they say.
liev - ing he will still your ref - uge be.
Her - mon I will still re - mem - ber you.
sad - ness, hound - ed by the en - e - my?"

When shall I be - hold your face? When shall I
When my sor - rows weigh on me, then I bring
I a - gain shall praise his grace for the com -
As the wa - ters plunge and leap, storm - y trou -
Their re - bukes and scoff - ing words pierce my bones

Text: Psalm 42–43; vers. Psalter Hymnal, 1987. © 1987, CRC Publications
Tune: Louis Bourgeois, 1551; harm. Johann Crüger, 1658

87 87 77 88
GENEVAN 42

re - ceive your grace? When shall I, your prais - es
to mem - o - ry how with throngs I would as -
▶ fort of his face; he will show his help and
bles o'er me sweep. Day and night God's song is
like point - ed swords, as they say with proud de -

voic - ing, come be - fore you with re - joic - ing?
sem - ble, shout - ing prais - es in your tem - ple.
▶ fa - vor, for he is my God and Sav - ior.
with me as a prayer to him who loves me.
fi - ance, "Where is God, your firm re - li - ance?" *Repeat st. 3*

Psalm 43

6 Vindicate me, God, my Father,
    come and plead my urgent cause,
for my enemies forever
    threaten me and flout your laws.
    I am safe with you alone;
    why do you reject your own?
LORD, I need your help and blessing;
keep me safe from this oppressing.

7 Send your light and truth to lead me:
    send them forth to be my guide.
To your mountain let them bring me,
    to the place where you reside.
    Then, O God, I will come near
    and before your throne appear,
to my Savior praises bringing
with the harp and joyful singing. *Repeat st. 3*

43 Defend Me, LORD, from Those Who Charge Me

1 De - fend me LORD, from those who charge me with shame - ful
2 Send out your light and truth to lead me, to bring me
3 My soul, why are you weak and down - cast, why do you

in - sults, lies, and slurs. Come, save your ser - vant
to your ho - ly hill. I come to stand be -
weep, why beg for aid? Why so dis - qui - et -

from e - vil ones. In you a - lone I can find ref - uge.
fore you with joy, to bring the songs of my thanks-giv - ing.
ed, so dis-turbed? Go to the LORD of your sal - va - tion.

Why are you deaf to all my pleas a - bout my en - e - mies?
To you, my LORD, I bring my praise for all your sav - ing ways.
Put all your hope in God and praise him for his sav - ing grace.

Text: Psalm 43; vers. Marie J. Post, 1981. © 1987, CRC Publications
Tune: Genevan Psalter, 1551; harm. Claude Goudimel, 1564
Other settings of Psalm 43: 42, 165

98 99 86
GENEVAN 43

Psalm 44: Alternative arrangement with melody in the bass

3 This hap - pened though we have been faith - ful to you;
But you broke our lives, LORD; our faith seems in vain.

our feet have not strayed from the paths that are true.
All cov - ered with dark - ness, to you we com - plain.

If we had for - got - ten God's name in our woe

or wor - shiped false i - dols, then would he not know?

No se - crets from God in our hearts can re - main;

yet now we are count - ed as sheep to be slain.

Text: Psalm 44; vers. Bert Polman, 1985
Tune: Walker's Southern Harmony, 1835; arr. Roy Hopp, 1987
Text and arrangement © 1987, CRC Publications

11 11 11 11 D
STAR IN THE EAST

44

O God, We Have Heard

Unison

1 O God, we have heard what our par - ents have told,
2 But you cast us off and brought shame to our boasts;
3 This hap-pened though we have been faith - ful to you;
4 O God, we have heard what our par - ents have told,

what won - ders you did in the great days of old.
no more in - to bat - tle you go with our hosts.
our feet have not strayed from the paths that are true.
what won - ders you did in the great days of old.

The na - tions were crushed and ex - pelled by your hand;
You gave us like sheep to be slaugh - tered and slain;
But you broke our lives, LORD; our faith seems in vain.
The na - tions were crushed and ex - pelled by your hand;

you gave to your peo - ple the vic - tory, the land.
the sale of your peo - ple has brought you no gain.
All cov - ered with dark - ness, to you we com - plain.
you gave to your peo - ple the vic - tory, the land.

Text: Psalm 44; vers. Bert Polman, 1985
Tune: Walker's *Southern Harmony,* 1835; harm. Dale Grotenhuis, 1986
Text and harmonization © 1987, CRC Publications

11 11 11 11 D
STAR IN THE EAST

O Lord, you a - lone are my God and my King!
You make all our neigh - bors re - proach us in pride,
If we had for - got - ten God's name in our woe
A - wake and a - rise, Lord, for why do you sleep?

Com - mand, and your name shall the sure vic - tory bring.
and cause those a - round us to scoff and de - ride.
or wor - shiped false i - dols, then would he not know?
No lon - ger ig - nore us, but save those who weep.

I trust not in weap - ons, for you make us strong;
The peo - ple re - vile us and joke at our name;
No se - crets from God in our hearts can re - main;
Our lives are brought low; we lie crushed in the dust.

we push back our foes and then praise you in song.
our fac - es are cov - ered, dis - graced with the shame.
yet now we are count - ed as sheep to be slain.
A - rise and re - deem us; your mer - cy we trust.

45

I Praise the King with All My Verses

1 I praise the king with all my vers - es; with bless - ings
2 Your en - e - mies are pierced by ar - rows; the na - tions
3 Your roy - al robes breathe myrrh and al - oes; with fra - grant
4 Lis - ten, O daugh - ter, and con - sid - er: for - get your
5 The bride, in gold - em - broi-dered gar - ment, is brought in -

on my tongue I sing. Your grace and beau - ty show God's
fall be - neath your feet. Your ho - ly throne will last for -
spic - es you are clad. Your i - vory pal - ac - es all
peo - ple and your house. The king, en - thralled by all your
side to greet the king. Her love - ly la - dies, vir - gin

fa - vor; God's rich - est gifts are for our king. Gird on your
ev - er; you love the right and hate de - ceit. A - noint-ed
ech - o with mu - sic that will make you glad. Daugh - ters of
beau - ty, will be your lord, and you his spouse. Be - fore you
es - cort, in fes - tive cel - e - bra - tion sing. Your chil-dren

sword, ride forth with might; de - fend the cause of truth and right.
with great joy - ful - ness, you are the one our God will bless.
for - eign kings be - hold the roy - al bride a-dorned with gold.
all the rich will stand, ex - pect-ing fa - vors from your hand.
will re - ceive ac - claim, the na - tions ev - er praise your name.

Text: Psalm 45; vers. Marie J. Post, 1985, and Bert Polman, 1986. © 1987, CRC Publications
Tune: Johann B. König, 1738

98 98 88
O DASS ICH TAUSEND

God Is Our Refuge and Our Strength

1 God   is   our ref - uge and our strength, our ev - er - pres-ent aid,
2 A   riv - er flows whose streams make glad the cit - y of our God,
3 The   na - tions rage, the king-doms move, but when his voice is heard,
4 O   come and see what won-drous works the hand of   God has done;
5 "Be   still and know that I   am God, the LORD whom all must claim;

and   there-fore, though the earth be moved, we   will   not be a - fraid—
the   ho - ly   place where - in the LORD Most High has his a - bode.
▸ earth melts with trem-bling fear be - fore the thun-der of his word.
come, see what des - o - la - tion great he brings be-neath the sun.
and   ev - ery   na - tion of the earth shall mag - ni - fy my name."

though hills in - to the seas be cast, though foam - ing wa - ters roar,
Since God is in the midst of her, un - moved her walls shall stand;
▸ The LORD of hosts is on our side, our safe - ty to se - cure;
In   ev - ery cor - ner of the earth he caus - es wars to cease;
The   LORD of hosts is on our side, our safe - ty to se - cure;

though all the might - y bil - lows shake the moun-tains on the shore.
for   God will has - ten to her aid when trou - ble is at hand.
▸ the God of Ja - cob is for us a ref - uge strong and sure.
the   weap-ons of the strong de-stroyed, he makes a - bid - ing peace.
the   God of Ja - cob is for us a ref - uge strong and sure.

Text: Psalm 46; vers. Psalter, 1887, alt.
Tune: Arthur S. Sullivan, 1871
Other settings of Psalm 46: 469, 610

CMD
GERARD

47

Nations, Clap Your Hands

1 Na - tions, clap your hands; shout with joy, you lands!
2 God goes up on high with a joy - ful cry,
3 God reigns o - ver all rul - ers great and small.

Awe - some is the LORD; spread his fame a - broad.
with a might - y shout; peo - ple, sing it out!
Lead - ers of the world, ser - vants of the LORD,

He rules ev - ery land with a might - y hand.
Let your voic - es bring prais - es to our King.
ral - ly round his throne; he is God a - lone.

Text: Psalm 47; vers. Psalter Hymnal, 1987. © 1987, CRC Publications
Tune: Louis Bourgeois, 1551; harm. Claude Goudimel, 1564
Another setting of Psalm 47: 166

55 55 55 D
GENEVAN 47

God brings na - tions low; he sub - dues each foe.
Praise him with a song; praise with heart and tongue;
Sing be - fore him now, in his pres - ence bow.

From his might - y throne God pro - tects his own.
praise with ev - ery skill; praise with mind and will.
God of A - bra - ham! God of ev - ery land!

Our in - her - i - tance is our sure de - fense.
God rules all the earth; mag - ni - fy his worth.
Wor - ship and a - dore God for - ev - er - more.

48 Great Is the LORD Our God

1 Great is the LORD our God, and great - ly to be praised.
2 God makes his cit - y strong by liv - ing in her halls.
3 With - in your tem - ple, LORD, in your most ho - ly place,
4 Let Zi - on now re - joice and all her peo - ple sing;
5 Ob - serve her pal - ac - es, mark her de - fens - es well,

Up - on a hill God's cit - y stands in glo - rious beau - ty raised—
When kings join forc - es and ad - vance, they mar - vel at her walls.
we on your lov - ing-kind - ness dwell, the won - ders of your grace.
let them with thank - ful - ness pro - claim the judg - ments of their King.
that to the chil - dren fol - lowing you her glo - ries you may tell.

his ho - ly moun - tain high, the cit - y of our King,
God scat - ters those a - round whose pride makes them so sure.
Your peo - ple sing your praise wher - e'er your name is known;
Mount Zi - on's walls be - hold, a - bout her ram - parts go,
For God as our own God for - ev - er will a - bide,

the joy of all the earth be - low. In praise of God we sing.
As we have heard, so have we seen: God's cit - y is se - cure.
by ev - ery deed your hand has done your right - eous - ness is shown.
and num - ber all the loft - y towers that guard her from the foe.
and till life's jour - ney close in death will be our faith - ful guide.

Text: Psalm 48; st. 1–2 vers. Psalter Hymnal, 1987; st. 3–5 vers. Psalter, 1887, rev. 1987.
© 1987, CRC Publications
Tune: George J. Elvey, 1868

SMD
DIADEMATA

Listen, All People Who Live in This World

1 Lis - ten, all peo - ple who live in this world;
2 Why should I fear when the e - vil days come,
3 We know both fool - ish and wise peo - ple die;
4 All those who trust in them - selves are like sheep:
5 Do not be awed by pos - ses - sors of wealth.

I will speak wis - dom to rich and to poor.
when those sur - round - ing me boast of their wealth?
► all of their wealth some - one else will pos - sess.
death is their shep - herd; the grave is their home.
Though they are praised and get hon - or from all,

My words will give un - der - stand - ing to you,
All the world's wealth can - not save them from death;
► Fools will re - main in their tombs ev - er - more,
But God will ran - som my life from the grave,
rich folk with - out un - der - stand - ing of God

bring you in - struc - tion with mu - sic and song:
no one can ran - som a life with much gold.
► though they had claimed man - y lands for them - selves.
and he will sure - ly take me to him - self.
are like the beasts of the for - est that die.

Text: Psalm 49; vers. Helen Otte, 1984. © 1987, CRC Publications
Tune: Martin F. Shaw, 1935. © 1935, Royal School of Church Music

10 10 10 10
JULIUS

50   The Mighty God and Sovereign LORD

1 The might-y God and sov-ereign LORD has called the earth from sea to sea. From Zi-on's beau-ty God shines forth; he comes and will not si-lent be. De-vour-ing flame be-fore him

2 God sum-mons earth and heaven a-bove to wit-ness how he tries his own: "Now gath-er all my chos-en saints, who cov-e-nant with me a-lone." His right-eous-ness the heavens de-

3 "Hear, O my peo-ple, I will speak; a-gainst you I will tes-ti-fy. Give ear to me, O Is-ra-el, for God, your faith-ful God, am I. I do not spurn your sac-ri-

4 "I do not need a goat or bull as of-fering for my ho-ly shrine. The cat-tle on a thou-sand hills and all the for-est beasts are mine. Each moun-tain bird to me is

Text: Psalm 50; vers. Psalter, 1912; rev. Marie J. Post, 1985. © 1987, CRC Publications
Tune: Dimitri S. Bortnianski, 1825

88 88 88
ST. PETERSBURG

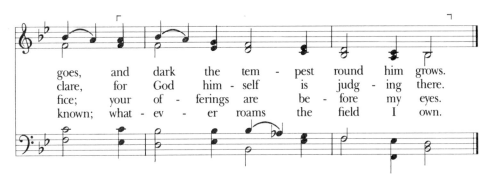

goes, and dark the tem - pest round him grows.
clare, for God him - self is judg - ing there.
fice; your of - ferings are be - fore my eyes.
known; what - ev - er roams the field I own.

5 "If I were hungry, who would know?
I would not look to you for food.
The world and all it has is mine;
I have no need of flesh or blood.
But pay your vows and call on me;
then I will set my people free."

6 But to the wicked, God declares:
"What right have you to quote my law?
Why take my covenant on your lips
when evil you will not withdraw?
My holy words you make profane;
you cast them from you in disdain.

7 "You are a scheming friend of thieves,
of those who break their marriage vows.
Your tongues speak evil and deceit;
you slander those within your house.
You thought that I was just like you,
that there was nothing I would do!

8 "Consider my rebuke and charge,
all you who have forgotten me,
or I will tear you all apart—
then what deliverance will you see?
But those who sacrifice with praise
will always know my boundless grace."

51 Be Merciful, Be Merciful, O God

1 Be mer - ci - ful, be mer - ci - ful, O God. Ac - cord-ing to your stead - fast love, have mer - cy. Blot out my sin in your a - bun - dant mer - cy. Wash all my sin a - way and make me clean.

2 You want me truth - ful in my in - most heart; you teach me in my se - cret heart your wis - dom. To wash me clean a - gain, purge me with hys - sop and make me whit - er than new - fall - en snow.

3 Cre - ate in me, O God, a new, clean heart and make my spir - it pure and right with - in me. O do not cast me help - less from your pres - ence. Your Ho - ly Spir - it must not go from me.

4 De - liv - er me from guilt of blood, O God. O God, you are the God of my sal - va - tion. My tongue will sing then that I am de - liv - ered. O - pen my lips, O Lord, to sing your praise.

5 Be good to Zi - on; LORD, in mer - cy hear. The walls a - round Je - ru - sa - lem lie bro - ken. Re - build the walls, LORD: help us to re - build them. Be good to Zi - on; LORD, in mer - cy hear.

I know my sin; it / Fill me with joy and / Re - store to me the / For you take no de - / Then you will take de -

Text: Psalm 51; vers. Stanley Wiersma, 1980. © 1987, CRC Publications
Tune: Louis Bourgeois, 1551; harm. Claude Goudimel, 1564
Other settings of Psalm 51: 167, 255

PM
GENEVAN 51

will not leave my mind. / A - gainst you, on - ly you, I
glad-ness, make me sing, / and let the bones you broke be -
▶ joy of be - ing yours. / Up - hold me with a free and
light in sac - ri - fice. / You take no plea - sure in the
light in us a - gain, / in gifts we bring to lay up -

have been sin - ning. / So you are just in judg - ing what I
gin their danc - ing. / O hide your face from sins that cause me
▶ will - ing spir - it. / Then I will teach trans - gres - sors of your
gifts I of - fer. / A bro - ken spir - it is ac - cept - a -
on your al - tar. / Then you will take de - light in us a -

did. / E - ven be - fore my birth my life was taint - ed.
shame. / Blot out the stain of all my foul trans-gres - sions.
▶ ways. / Then sin - ners will re - turn a - gain to serve you.
ble. / You will not scorn a heart con - trite and bro - ken.
gain, / in prop - er sac - ri - fice and right-eous ser - vice.

52   Mighty Mortal, Boasting Evil

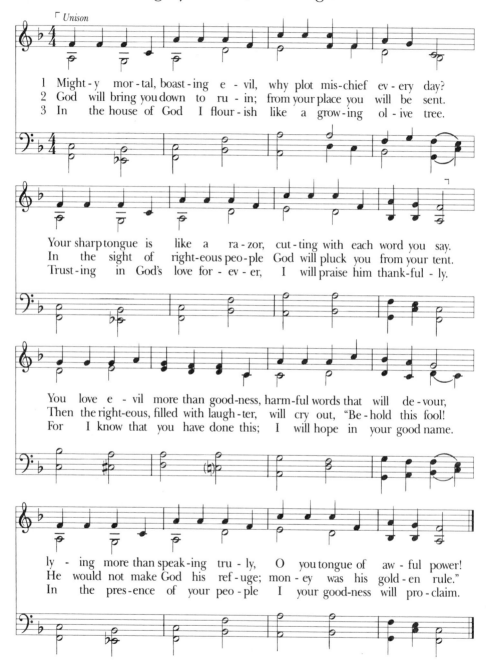

1 Might-y mor-tal, boast-ing e - vil, why plot mis-chief ev - ery day?
2 God will bring you down to ru - in; from your place you will be sent.
3 In the house of God I flour-ish like a grow-ing ol - ive tree.

Your sharp tongue is like a ra - zor, cut-ting with each word you say.
In the sight of right-eous peo-ple God will pluck you from your tent.
Trust-ing in God's love for - ev - er, I will praise him thank-ful - ly.

You love e - vil more than good-ness, harm-ful words that will de - vour,
Then the right-eous, filled with laugh-ter, will cry out, "Be - hold this fool!
For I know that you have done this; I will hope in your good name.

ly - ing more than speak-ing tru - ly, O you tongue of aw - ful power!
He would not make God his ref - uge; mon - ey was his gold - en rule."
In the pres-ence of your peo - ple I your good-ness will pro - claim.

Text: Psalm 52; vers. Helen Otte, 1985. © 1987, CRC Publications
Tune: Aubrey L. Butler, 1971. © 1971, Broadman Press. All rights reserved.
International copyright secured. Used by permission.

87 87 D
MADILL

The Foolish in Their Hearts Exclaim

1 The fool - ish in their hearts ex - claim,
2 Our God looks down from high - est heaven
3 There is not one that seeks the LORD:
4 Soon they shall all be ter - ri - fied,
5 Oh, that sal - va - tion would come out

"There is no God of might." They are cor - rupt in
on all the hu - man race to see if there are
they go their way in - stead. They nev - er learn; they
for God will put to shame, de - stroy, and scat - ter
of Zi - on to God's own! When God re - stores them,

ev - ery way; not one of them does right.
an - y wise, if an - y seek his face.
eat God's own as peo - ple eat their bread.
ev - ery - one who dis - re - gards his name.
they will sing for joy to God a - lone.

Text: Psalm 53; vers. Marie J. Post, 1982. © 1987, CRC Publications
Tune: J. Playford's The Whole Book of Psalms, 1677

CM
BRISTOL

By Your Name, O God, Now Save Me

1 By your name, O God, now save me; grant me jus - tice
2 Sure - ly God is my up - hold - er; with his help I

by your might. As I pray to you, now hear me; keep me
will not fall. God will pay back those who slan - der— in your

safe with - in your sight. Strang - ers have come up a -
truth de - stroy them all! I will sac - ri - fice with

gainst me, vi - o - lent in deed and word. They are seek - ing
glad - ness; I will praise your name, O LORD. God has saved me

to de - stroy me; they do not re - gard the LORD.
from all sad - ness, and my life he has re - stored.

Text: Psalm 54; vers. The Book of Psalms for Singing, 1975; rev. Helen Otte, 1985. © 1987, CRC Publications
Tune: Frizzoni's Canzuns Spirituaelas, 1765

87 87 D
ENGADINE

I Need Your Help, O Lord My God 55

1 I need your help, O Lord my God; do not ig-nore my plea.
2 If I had wings, I'd fly a - way in - to the wil - der - ness
3 If it had been an en - e - my who treat - ed me with scorn,
4 My trust is in the Lord my God; he hears my con - stant prayer.

For I am rest - less and dis -traught; O hear and an - swer me.
to find a qui - et, shel -tered place where I could be at rest.
in - stead of one who was my friend, that grief I could have borne.
My en - e - mies are in his hand, and I am in his care.

The wick - ed stare at me and taunt; their an - ger caus - es grief.
O Lord, de - stroy the wick - ed plans of those who stalk the streets.
But you, my close com - pan -ion, broke our cov - e - nant of trust.
Cast all your cares up - on the Lord, and he will strength-en you.

The fear of death has hold of me, and I find no re - lief.
They deal in fraud, a - buse, and lies; O Lord, con-fuse their speech.
Though smooth as but - ter, ev - ery word is like a dag-ger thrust.
He will not let the right-eous fall. I trust, O God, in you.

Text: Psalm 55; vers. Helen Otte, 1984. © 1987, CRC Publications
Tune: Danish

CMD
RELEASE

56   O God, Be Merciful to Me

1 O God, be mer - ci - ful to me; I
2 Some - times I am a - fraid, O LORD, but
3 I am sur - round - ed ev - ery day by
4 O LORD, take note of my la - ment. Do
5 To you, O LORD, I pay my vow as

am dis - tressed by en - e - mies on ev - ery
I be - lieve your prom - ised word that you are
► those who plot to take a - way my ver - y
you not list each tear I shed, up - on your
I, with thank - ful of - ferings, bow be - fore your

side. They slan - der me in what they say, at -
near. What treach - er - y can mor - tals raise? I
► life. When they con - spire to do me harm, O
scroll? What treach - er - y can mor - tals raise? I
face. For you de - liv - ered me from death and

tack - ing me from day to day in all their pride.
trust in God, whose word I praise. I will not fear.
► LORD, lift up your might - y arm and stop their strife.
trust in God, whose word I praise. He guards my soul.
set me safe - ly on the path of life and grace.

Text: Psalm 56; vers. Helen Otte, 1986. © 1987, CRC Publications
Tune: James Ward, 1984. © 1987, Music Anno Domini (A.D.). All rights reserved. Used by permission.

884 D
ROSALIE MCMILLAN

Be Merciful to Me, O God

1 Be mer - ci - ful to me, O God, bend down and hear my cry.
2 My foes are like de - vour-ing beasts, their teeth like ar - rows, spears.
3 Foes spread a net to catch my feet— a pit a - cross my path—
4 In song I thank you, O my Lord; my prais - es o - ver - flow.

With - in the shad - ow of your wings I hide while storms pass by.
Their sharp-ened tongues, like slash-ing swords, in - crease my woes and fears.
but they them-selves fell in their trap in - tend - ed for my death.
I sing of your great love, O Lord, that na - tions all may know.

You will ful - fill your pur-pos - es, will send your sav - ing power,
O be ex - alt - ed high a - bove the heavens in glo-rious might,
My heart is filled with con - fi - dence; I break out in - to song.
O be ex - alt - ed high a - bove the heavens in glo-rious might,

and put to shame my en - e - mies in this most try - ing hour.
and let your glo - ry cov - er all the earth, O LORD of light.
Rise up and play, O harp and lyre; let mu - sic greet the dawn.
and let your glo - ry cov - er all the earth, O LORD of light.

Text: Psalm 57; vers. Marie J. Post, 1982. © 1987, CRC Publications
Tune: Katherine K. Davis, 1962. © 1964, Abingdon Press. Used by permission.

CMD
MASSACHUSETTS

58

O Mighty Rulers, Can You Claim

1 O might-y rul-ers, can you claim that you speak right-eous-ness?
2 The wick-ed from their birth tell lies, they sin, they go a-stray;
3 The cry-ing vic-tims will re-joice when ven-geance is com-plete;

Do you de-fend the poor and weak in truth and up-right-ness?
they have the ven-om of a snake, they do not heed God's way.
their tri-umph is God's sov-ereign power, which saves them from de-feat.

No, in your heart you plot and scheme; in-jus-tice marks your life;
O LORD, de-stroy these en-e-mies and scat-ter all their might;
Then all will say, "The right-eous still re-ceive a sure re-ward,

you deal out vi-o-lence on earth and fa-vor hu-man strife.
let them be like a still-born child that nev-er sees the light.
for we can see there is a God who judg-es all as LORD."

Text: Psalm 58; vers. Bert Polman, 1983. © 1987, CRC Publications
Tune: Annabeth McClelland Gay, 1952; harm. Dale Grotenhuis, 1985. © 1958, 1986, Pilgrim Press.
Reprinted with permission from the Pilgrim Hymnal.

CMD
SHEPHERDS' PIPES

Protect and Save Me, O My God

1 Pro - tect and save me, O my God, from
2 The work - ers of in - iq - ui - ty a -
3 Now see their wick - ed - ness, O LORD; come
4 My en - e - mies with dead - ly rage re -

those who seek my life; and set me high, se -
gainst me lie in wait; though I am in - no -
to my help, I plead. LORD God of hosts, O
new their fierce at - tack. They think the LORD will

cure, a - bove the ris - ing tide of strife.
cent, O LORD, they gath - er in their hate.
Is - rael's God, rise, help me in my need.
not re - gard, but you will turn them back.

5 O God, my strength, on you I wait;
   to you for help I flee.
   My God with mercy will defend
   his own triumphantly.

6 O Lord our shield, let wickedness
   and pride be put to shame.
   Then all will know that you do rule,
   and all will fear your name.

7 Like dogs that prowl the city streets
   my foes slink back at night.
   They would devour my life like food,
   but God will win the fight.

8 When all the night of woe is past
   and morning dawns at length,
   then I will praise you, loving God,
   my refuge and my strength.

Text: Psalm 59; vers. Psalter, 1912, alt.
Tune: Thomas Ravenscroft, 1621; harm. Emily R. Brink, 1985. Harmonization © 1987, CRC Publications

CM
MANCHESTER

60   O God, You Have Rejected Us

1 O God, you have re-ject-ed us and torn our dwell-ing place.
2 Our God speaks from his ho-ly place: "I will give vic-to-ry.
3 Now, there-fore, who will lead us on in tri-umph on this day?

With quakes and judg-ments we are fed; LORD, save us now in grace.
For Ju-dah as my scep-ter rules; all lands will bow to me.
LORD, why have you re-ject-ed us and turned your face a-way?

LORD, you have set your ban-ners high to help your own to stand.
On E-dom I will cast my shoe, make Gil-e-ad my own.
O LORD, we plead, grant us your help a-gainst our en-e-my.

That your be-lov-ed may be saved, LORD, help us by your hand.
I use my hel-met, E-phra-im; they all are mine a-lone."
The LORD will tread down all our foes! God will give vic-to-ry!

Text: Psalm 60; vers. Marie J. Post, 1985. © 1987, CRC Publications
Tune: J. R. Tipton, 1974. © 1974, Broadman Press. All rights reserved. International copyright secured. Used by permission.

CMD
XAVIER

Listen to My Cry, LORD

1 Lis - ten to my cry, LORD; hear my hum - ble
2 From the earth's far cor - ners you will hear my
3 You are my pro - tec - tion when my foes ap -
4 In your tent for - ev - er may my dwell - ing

prayer. When my soul is trou - bled,
cry. Set me on your rock, LORD,
pear; keep me in your tow - er,
be; with your wings of mer - cy

1-6

keep me in your care.
high - er rock than I.
safe from ev - ery fear.
gent - ly shel - ter me.

Final ending

5 All my cries you've answered,
   kept me safe from shame.
I am richly blest with
   those who fear your name.

6 Bless with life forever
   your anointed king.
Through the generations
   may he always reign.

7 May your love and mercy
   keep him all his days.
Then with joy forever
   I will sing your praise.

Text: Psalm 61; vers. Henrietta Ten Harmsel, 1985. © 1987, CRC Publications
Tune: Norman L. Warren, 1969. © 1973, Hope Publishing Co. All rights reserved. Used by permission.

65 65
LISTENING

62   My Soul Finds Rest in God Alone

1 My soul finds rest in God a - lone; on him my help de - pends.
2 Find rest, my soul, in God a - lone; on him my hope de - pends.
3 The great of earth are less than dust; all mor - tal strength is vain.

He is my for - tress and my rock; sal - va - tion sure he sends.
He is my for - tress and my rock; sal - va - tion sure he sends.
And fools a - lone re - ly on wealth or prize ill - got - ten gain.

My foes con - spire to bring me down; they scorn my trou - bled state.
My aid and hon - or come from God, my ref - uge strong and sure.
I know, O God, that you are strong, a faith - ful, lov - ing Lord.

Their lips are quick to sound my praise, but in their hearts they hate.
Let all God's ser - vants trust the LORD; in him we are se - cure.
Our ev - ery deed, for good or ill, you sure - ly will re - ward.

Text: Psalm 62; vers. David J. Diephouse, 1986. © 1987, CRC Publications
Tune: Thomas Tallis, 1561
Alternative tune: BETHLEHEM, 497

CMD
THIRD MODE MELODY

O Lord, My God, Most Earnestly

1 O Lord, my God, most ear - nest - ly I seek your ho - ly face,
2 The lov - ing - kind - ness of my God is more than life to me,
3 Be - neath the shad - ow of your wings I sing my joy and praise.

with - in your house a - gain to see the glo - ries of your grace.
so I will praise you all my days and pray con - tin - ual - ly.
Your right hand is my strong sup - port through trou - bled nights and days.

A - part from you I long and thirst, and naught can sat - is - fy;
In you my soul is sat - is - fied, my dark - ness turns to light,
All those who seek my life will fall; my life is in your hand.

I wan - der in a des - ert land where all the streams are dry.
and joy - ful med - i - ta - tions fill the watch - es of the night.
God's king and peo - ple will re - joice; in vic - tory they will stand.

Text: Psalm 63; vers. Psalter, 1912; rev. Psalter Hymnal, 1987
Tune: George C. Stebbins, 1878

CMD
THE GREEN HILL

64   Hear My Voice, O God, in My Complaint

1 Hear my voice, O God, in my com-plaint; guard my life from
2 Sharp as swords the wick - ed whet their tongues and like ar - rows
3 They a - gree to form an e - vil plot; se - cret - ly they
4 They are read - y with a cun-ning plot, for the hu - man

ter - ror of the foe. Hide me from the plots of
aim their dead - ly words, shoot from am - bush at the
talk of lay - ing snares, say - ing, "Who will learn of
heart is full of guile. God will shoot an ar - row

those who hate, from the nois - y mob of e - vil ones.
in - no - cent with - out warn-ing and with - out a fear.
our de - signs?" They plan care - ful - ly their wick - ed schemes.
straight at them; with - out warn-ing they will be struck down.

5 They will all be made to trip themselves
   and undo themselves by their own tongues.
   All who see them shake their heads in scorn;
   then shall all the people fear the LORD.

6 They will ponder God's almighty deeds
   and proclaim the marvel of his works.
   Let the righteous all rejoice in God;
   praise the LORD for his protecting care!

Text: Psalm 64; vers. The Book of Psalms for Singing, 1975, alt.
Tune: Daniel Read, 1785; harm. Erik Routley, 1982, alt. © 1985, Hope Publishing Co.
*   All rights reserved. Used by permission.*

99 99
WINDHAM

Praise Is Your Right, O God, in Zion

1 Praise is your right, O God, in Zi - on. To you we
2 Your might - y acts work our sal - va - tion. All earth waits
3 You bless the earth with streams and riv - ers and with the

pay our vows. When we your peo - ple pray, you hear us.
hope - ful - ly. You have the strength to make the moun - tains,
gen - tle rain. You set - tle ridg - es, soft - en fur - rows,

All flesh to you will bow. When our trans-gres-sions o - ver -
to calm the storm - y sea. You calm the tu - mult of the
and bless the sprout - ing grain. You crown the year with am - ple

whelm us, you gra-cious-ly for - give. How sat - is - fied your
peo - ple. Such awe-some signs you do that earth, from sun - rise
har - vest; a rich a - bun-dance springs. All flocks and grains and

cho - sen ser - vants; with - in your courts they live.
to the sun - set, for joy cries out to you.
hills and mead - ows— yes, all cre - a - tion sings.

Text: Psalm 65; vers. Stanley Wiersma, 1980
Tune: Genevan Psalter, 1543; harm. Dale Grotenhuis, 1985
Text and harmonization © 1987, CRC Publications
Another setting of Psalm 65: 458

96 96 D
GENEVAN 65

66

Come, Everyone, and Join with Us

1 Come, ev - ery-one, and join with us in rous - ing songs of praise.
2 O come and see what God has done for peo - ple of his choice.
3 Come, ev - ery-one, and join with us in rous - ing songs of praise
4 With grat - i - tude and of - fer-ings I come in - to your house,

Sing out the hon - or of God's name for all his glo - rious ways.
He turned the sea to sol - id ground—come, let us all re - joice.
to God, who safe - ly holds our lives in gen - tle, stead-y ways.
for when I was in trou - ble, LORD, I spoke to you my vows.

Say to our God, "How awe - some, LORD, are you in all you do.
God rules for - ev - er by his might and his all - see - ing eye.
O God, you tried and test - ed us as sil - ver tried by flame.
I bring you now burnt of - fer - ings of fat - lings from my herd;

Your en - e - mies cringe down in fear, then rise to wor - ship you."
Let not the proud, re - bel-lious ones ex - alt them-selves on high.
You brought us low through fire and flood, but then your bless-ing came.
I of - fer you my gift of thanks, be - cause I gave my word.

Text: Psalm 66; vers. Marie J. Post, 1985. © 1987, CRC Publications
Tune: Dale Grotenhuis, 1985, ©
Another setting of Psalm 66: 242

CMD
ELEANOR

5 Come, everyone who loves the LORD,
 hear what he did for me.
My cry for help has turned to praise,
 for he has set me free.
If in my heart I'd cherished sin,
 God would have turned away.
But he has listened to my cry;
 he answers when I pray.

6 Praise be to God, who hears my prayer
 and answers my request.
His steadfast love surrounds my days;
 his name be ever blest.
Come, everyone, and join with us
 in rousing songs of praise.
Sing out the honor of God's name
 for all his glorious ways.

67

O God, to Us Show Mercy

1 O God, to us show mer - cy and bless us in your grace,
2 Let all the peo-ples praise you, let all the na-tions sing;
3 Let all the peo-ples praise you, let all the na-tions sing.

and cause to shine up - on us the bright-ness of your face,
in ev - ery land let prais - es and songs of glad-ness ring;
Then earth in rich a - bun - dance to us her fruit will bring.

so that your way most ho - ly on earth may soon be known,
for you will judge the peo - ples in truth and right - eous - ness,
The LORD our God will bless us, our God will bless - ing send,

and un - to ev - ery peo - ple your sav - ing grace be shown.
and on the earth all na - tions will your just rule con - fess.
and all the earth will fear him to its re - mot - est end.

Text: Psalm 67; vers. Psalter, 1887, alt.
Tune: J. Michael Haydn, 1737–1806, adapt.

76 76 D
OFFERTORIUM

Psalm 68: Alternative harmonization with melody in the tenor

Tune: *Genevan Psalter, 1539; harm. Claude Goudimel, 1564*

887 887 D
GENEVAN 68

68   Let God Arise and by His Might

1 Let God a-rise and by his might put all his
2 Ex-alt, ex-alt the name of God! Sing, sing his
3 LORD, when you led us on our march, the rain poured
4 God gives com-mands— a might-y host of mes-sen-
5 Proud Ba-shan, mount of man-y peaks, not from your

en-e-mies to flight with shame and con-ster-na-tion.
roy-al fame a-broad with fer-vent ex-al-ta-tion.
down from heav-en's arch and earth shook with the thun-der.
gers brings back this boast: "God's en-e-mies are flee-ing!
sum-mit our Lord speaks, nor makes you his own dwell-ing.

For when the LORD God shall ap-pear, he will con-
Cast up a high-way smooth and wide, that through the
Mount Si-nai quaked be-fore the LORD, and heav-en
Both kings and ar-mies flee a-way be-fore the
Our Lord with cap-tives in his train from Si-nai

sume, a-far and near, with fire and des-o-la-tion.
des-erts he may ride; the LORD is our sal-va-tion.
an-swered Is-rael's God; all trem-bled at the won-der.
LORD, who wins the day, God's cause and ours a-gree-ing!"
to Mount Zi-on came with char-iot host ex-cel-ling.

Text: Psalm 68; vers. Psalter Hymnal, 1987
Tune: Genevan Psalter, 1539; harm. Howard Slenk, 1985
Text and harmonization © 1987, CRC Publications

887 887 D
GENEVAN 68

As smoke be - fore his dread - ful ire, as wax is
God's might - y power sets pris - oners free; his arm of
▸ A - bun - dant show - ers blessed the way, re - freshed your
At home, mid com - mon dai - ly toil, our peo - ple
Ten thou - sand times ten thou - sand strong, ar - rayed in

mol - ten by the fire, so shall the wick - ed per - ish.
strength gains vic - to - ry, to reb - els shows no pit - y.
▸ peo - ple ev - ery day and lift - ed up their spir - it.
sort the for - eign spoil, new wealth from God re - ceiv - ing.
light and armed with song, they shamed the noise of thun - der.

But let the right - eous, blest of old, joy in their
The fa - ther of the fa - ther - less and help for
▸ You brought them to the prom - ised land, you poured forth
When God Al - might - y scat - ters foes, his glo - ry
His glo - ry filled the ho - ly place, and e - ven

God and now be - hold the vic - to - ry they cher - ish.
wid - ows in dis - tress is God in Zi - on's cit - y.
boun - ty from your hand; a home they did in - her - it.
shines like moun - tain snows and kings stop their re - bel - ling.
reb - els knew his grace; they brought him gifts and plun - der.

Stanzas 6–9 on following page

Psalm 68: stanzas 6–9

6 Give praise to God with rev - erence deep; he dai - ly
7 Pro - ces - sions come with God the King; with shouts of
8 Show us your strength, O LORD of hosts, so ev - ery
9 All na - tions of the earth, ex - ult, raise psalms of

comes our lives to keep and kind - ly bears our bur - dens.
joy the por - tals ring as God comes to his tem - ple.
king who comes to boast will hon - or and o - bey you.
praise to heav - en's vault, God's an - cient throne and dwell - ing.

Our God up - holds us in the strife; to us he
With harps and tim - brels, choirs sing, and maid - ens
LORD, for your tem - ple's sake make right those waste - land
God rides his char - iot in the height, he thun - ders

grants e - ter - nal life and saves from all that threat - ens.
dance be - fore their King, while all Mount Zi - on trem - bles.
lives now filled with blight; stop those who would de - fy you.
forth his roy - al right; God reigns, all kings ex - cel - ling.

God crush - es heads of en - e - mies; he brings them
Praise God, praise God, you ho - ly throng, with prais - es
Tram - ple to dust be - neath your feet those who de -
Pro - claim the awe - some power of God, make known his

back from far - thest seas for Is - rael's ju - bi - la - tion.
lift his name in song; bless God, O con - gre - ga - tion.
light in war's de - ceit, all those who lust for plun - der.
might - y deeds a - broad; all Is - rael shall ex - tol him.

He hears the need - y when they cry; he saves their
Here Ben - ja - min, the least, leads on; there Ju - dah's
Let plun - derers bring their ill - gained hoard; let ev - ery
For he is pow - er - ful and great: all earth and

souls when death draws nigh: this God is our sal - va - tion.
princ - es, Zeb - u - lun, and Naph - ta - li— one na - tion.
na - tion praise the LORD, lift up their hands in won - der.
skies are his es - tate; his maj - es - ty ex - cels them.

69 Save Me, O God; I Sink in Floods

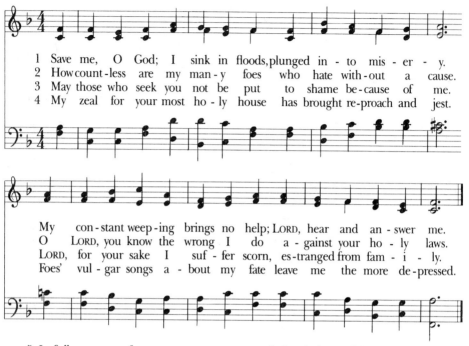

1 Save me, O God; I sink in floods, plunged in - to mis - er - y.
2 How count - less are my man - y foes who hate with - out a cause.
3 May those who seek you not be put to shame be - cause of me.
4 My zeal for your most ho - ly house has brought re - proach and jest.

My con - stant weep - ing brings no help; LORD, hear and an - swer me.
O LORD, you know the wrong I do a - gainst your ho - ly laws.
LORD, for your sake I suf - fer scorn, es - tranged from fam - i - ly.
Foes' vul - gar songs a - bout my fate leave me the more de - pressed.

5 In full assurance of your grace
   I turn to you in prayer.
   Deliver me from surging floods;
   draw near, reach out in care.

6 Your steadfast mercy, LORD, is good;
   hide not your face from me.
   Hear my distress and answer, LORD;
   make haste and set me free.

7 You know of my reproach and shame;
   my heart despairs from grief.
   I looked for pity, but I found
   no comfort or relief.

8 They gave me bitter gall for food;
   I was insulted, cursed.
   They gave me vinegar to drink
   to quench my burning thirst.

9 Let their own fullness be a snare;
   blind them with pain and strife.
   Add punishment to punishment,
   and blot them out from life.

10 Though I am poor and sorrowful,
   O LORD, attend my cry.
   Let your salvation come to me,
   and lift me up on high.

11 My song of praise to you, O God,
   is more than sacrifice.
   The LORD still hears the needy ones;
   he heeds the prisoners' cries.

12 Let heaven and earth and seas rejoice;
   let all that move give praise.
   All those that love God's name shall live
   in Zion all their days.

Text: Psalm 69; vers. Marie J. Post, 1985. © 1987, CRC Publications
Tune: J. Day's Psalter, 1562

CM
ST. FLAVIAN

Psalm 69: Alternative harmonization with melody in the alto and tenor

Tune: *J. Day's* Psalter, *1562; harm. Alan Gray, 1929*

CM
ST. FLAVIAN

Psalm 70: Alternative harmonization with melody in the alto

1 Come quick-ly, LORD, to res - cue me, and has - ten
2 May all who seek your name re - joice, your praise in
3 Yet I am poor and need - y, LORD; be quick to

to my help, I pray. May all who seek to
grat - i - tude re - cord. May those who love your
hear my ur - gent plea. You are my help, my

take my life be put to shame with - out de - lay.
sav - ing power say ev - er - more, "Ex - alt the LORD!"
Sav - ior God! Do not de - lay; re - mem - ber me.

Text: *Psalm 70; vers. Bert Polman, 1983. © 1987, CRC Publications*
Tune: *W. Walker's* Southern Harmony, *1835*

LM
DISTRESS

Come Quickly, LORD, to Rescue Me

1 Come quick-ly, LORD, to res-cue me, and has-ten
2 May all who seek your name re-joice, your praise in
3 Yet I am poor and need-y, LORD; be quick to

to my help, I pray. May all who seek to
grat-i-tude re-cord. May those who love your
hear my ur-gent plea. You are my help, my

take my life be put to shame with-out de-lay.
sav-ing power say ev-er-more, "Ex-alt the LORD!"
Sav-ior God! Do not de-lay; re-mem-ber me.

Text: Psalm 70; vers. Bert Polman, 1983. © 1987, CRC Publications
Tune: W. Walker's Southern Harmony, 1835; harm. Erik Routley, 1985.
  Harmonization © 1985, Hope Publishing Co. All rights reserved. Used by permission.

LM
DISTRESS

In You, O LORD, I Put My Trust

1 In you, O LORD, I put my trust; you are my
2 You are, O LORD, my ref - uge strong; from youth I
3 Do not re - ject me in old age; for - sake me
4 In you, O LORD, I hope once more; your love re -

rock and my de - fense. When times and tri - als are un -
have re - lied on you. Though trou - bles rise and life seems
not when strength has fled. For foes a - gainst me plot and
news my trou - bled soul. From youth to age my strength re -

just, you turn my foes from their in - tents.
long, I speak your praise the whole day through.
rage and bold - ly say, "Your God is dead."
store, and make my bat - tered spir - it whole.

5 To you, O LORD, I offer praise;
  your gracious power in me display.
  My hands in grateful thanks I raise
  and sing from dawn to close of day.

6 To you I sing unending praise;
  you scorn not age and graying hair.
  Your love encompasses my days;
  all times to come will know your care.

7 Who can compare, O LORD, with you?
  Your greatness is beyond all thought.
  And yet you come each day anew
  to comfort when I am distraught.

8 I praise the LORD with harp and song;
  I sing with shouts of joy and praise.
  For you have rescued me from wrong
  and brought me hope for all my days.

Text: Psalm 71; vers. Clarence P. Walhout, 1985. © 1987, CRC Publications
Tune: Roger W. Wischmeier, 1974, ©
Alternative tune: WAREHAM, 463

LM
JUDSON

Hail to the LORD's Anointed

1 Hail   to   the LORD's a - noint - ed, great   Da - vid's   great - er   son!
2 He   shall come down like   show - ers   up - on   the   fruit - ful   earth;
3 The   des - ert   tribes a - dore   him and   bend   to   him the   knee;
4 He   comes with   res - cue   speed - y   to   those who   suf - fer   wrong,

Hail,   in   the time ap - point - ed, his   reign on   earth be - gun!
and   love,   joy, hope, like   flow - ers, spring   in   his   path to   birth.
the   wick - ed bow be - fore   him, his   glo - ry   they will   see.
to   help   the poor and   need - y,   and   bid   the   weak be   strong.

He   comes   to   break op - pres - sion, to   set   the   cap - tive   free,
The   king   shall have   do - min - ion from   sea   to   shin - ing   sea,
With   gifts   of   ad - o - ra - tion the   for - eign kings shall   meet
He   turns   their sighs   to   sing - ing, their   dark - ness   in - to   light,

to   take   a - way   trans - gres - sion, and   rule   in   eq - ui - ty.
and   o - ver   ev - er - y   na - tion his   peace - ful rule shall   be.
to   pour the   wealth of   na - tions in   trib - ute   at   his   feet.
for   they, con - demned and   dy - ing,   are   pre - cious   in   his   sight.

Text: Psalm 72; vers. James Montgomery, 1822; rev. Bert Polman, 1985.
© 1987, CRC Publications
Tune: German
Other settings of Psalm 72: 359, 412, 541, 630

76 76 D
ES FLOG EIN KLEINS WALDVOGELEIN

5 His kingdom is increasing,
    a kingdom without end.
  For him shall prayer unceasing
    and daily praise ascend.
  The mountain dews will nourish
    a harvest from the fields;
  the grain and fruit will flourish,
    the land its bounty yields.

6 In name forever glorious,
    he on his throne shall rest,
  from age to age victorious,
    all blessing and all-blest.
  Praise God, who rules each nation;
    tell of his deeds again.
  His glory fills creation;
    sing praise to God. Amen!

73

God Loves All the Righteous

1 God loves all the right - eous; his good - ness is sure.
2 The wick - ed all pros - per, and firm is their health;
3 In gar - ments of boast - ing and vi - o - lence decked,
4 They ques - tion God's knowl - edge and bold - ly de - fy

He al - ways re - mem - bers the good and the pure.
they suf - fer no pangs as they gath - er their wealth.
with wealth more a - bun - dant than heart could ex - pect,
the might and the jus - tice of God the Most High.

Yet once my faith fal - tered; I en - vied the proud.
They nev - er are trou - bled with sick - ness or pain,
they scoff at the help - less, make fun of the poor;
The wick - ed, grown wealth - y, have com - fort and peace,

In doubt and dis - qui - et my spir - it was bowed.
but boast to all oth - ers of ill - got - ten gain.
with curs - es they charge a - gainst heav - en's own door.
while I, dai - ly chas - tened, see trou - bles in - crease.

Text: Psalm 73; vers. Psalter, 1912, alt.
Tune: Ira D. Sankey, 1877
Another setting of Psalm 73: 554

11 11 11 11
HIDING IN THEE

5 Forgetting God's children, I cried out in pain
   that clean hands are worthless and pure hearts are vain.
   But then in God's temple my doubts were dispelled;
   the end of their journey I clearly beheld.

6 In doubt and temptation, I rest, LORD, in you;
   my hand is in your hand, whatever I do.
   You always are with me; you guide with your word,
   and soon into glory will take me, O LORD.

7 Whom have I, O Savior, in heaven but you?
   On earth for none other I long but for you.
   My flesh and my heart may be weakened and sore,
   but God is the strength of my heart evermore.

8 All those who forsake you will perish and die,
   but, near to my Savior, most blessèd am I.
   I make you my refuge, my LORD and my God;
   your grace and your glory I publish abroad.

74   O God, Why Have You Cast Us All Away?

1 O God, why have you cast us all a - way?
2 The en - e - my de - stroyed your ho - ly place,
3 Yet from of old you are our might - y King;
4 The streams are yours to o - pen up or dry;

Why does your an - ger burn a - gainst your fold?
and they re - viled your wor - ship in the land.
you work sal - va - tion out up - on the earth.
the day is yours, and yours the shin - ing sun.

We are your sheep: re - mem - ber us, O LORD,
How long will e - vil ones still scoff and sneer
The seas di - vid - ed by your might - y power;
At your com - mand stars whirl in place at night,

those you re - deemed, your her - i - tage of old.
be - fore you raise, O LORD, your power - ful hand?
you crushed the heads of drag - ons in the depths.
earth's bounds are set, and chang - ing sea - sons run.

Text: Psalm 74; vers. Marie J. Post, 1985. © 1987, CRC Publications
Tune: James Langran, 1861

10 10 10 10
LANGRAN

5 Remember, LORD, how enemies have mocked,
  how they, with sneering jests, revile your name.
  Come, save your doves from those wild, raging beasts;
  do not forget us in this time of shame.

6 Remember your own covenant with us,
  for earth's dark places seethe with rage and greed.
  Do not forget the clamor of your foes,
  but come, defend yourself and us, we plead.

75   We Give Our Thanks to You, O God

1 We give our thanks to you, O God, for won-drous deeds you do.
2 No help will come from east or west; God lifts, brings low a-gain.

At your set time you judge the earth; you keep its pil-lar's true.
He pours a cup of foam-ing wine earth's wick-ed ones must drain.

"No lon-ger boast," you tell the proud, "nor flaunt your ar-ro-gance.
But as for me, I will de-clare God's judg-ments and his praise.

No lon-ger strut with pride, you fools, nor brag with in-so-lence."
The wick-ed ones he will cut off; the right-eous he will raise.

Text: Psalm 75; vers. Helen Otte, 1985. © 1987, CRC Publications
Tune: Theodore P. Ferris, 1941. © 1942, 1961, Church Pension Fund. Used by permission.

CMD
WEYMOUTH

God Is Known among His People

1 God is known a - mong his peo - ple;
2 God, most ex - cel - lent and awe - some,
3 When from heaven your judg - ment sound - ed,
4 Make your vows to God and keep them;

his name
more than
all the
pay the

shines in Is - ra - el; for of old he has es - tab - lished
moun-tains, firm and high, you have stripped the val - iant - heart - ed
earth in fear was still— when, to save the meek and low - ly,
LORD what is his own. Come and bring your gifts be - fore him;

his own house on Zi - on's hill. There he broke the
who on their own strength re - ly. Who can stand be -
you worked out your right - eous will. E - ven hu - man
wor - ship God and him a - lone. Might - y kings o -

sword and ar - row, bade the noise of war be still.
fore your an - ger or your might - y hand de - fy?
wrath shall praise you: your de - sign it shall ful - fill.
bey and fear him; lead - ers bow be - fore his throne.

Text: Psalm 76; vers. Psalter, 1912; rev. Psalter Hymnal, 1987. © 1987, CRC Publications
Tune: F. Pinder, c. 1900

87 87 87
TEMPLE BORO

I Cried Out to God to Help Me

1. I cried out to God to help me: in dis-tress and
2. I was anx-ious and be-wil-dered as, in sor-row,
3. In my grief I will re-mem-ber, Lord, your right hand
4. Through the sea a path lay o-pen when your might-y

sor-row, hear me. Day and night I sought in vain
I re-mem-bered for-mer days of peace and light;
chang-es nev-er. I will think and med-i-tate
word was spo-ken. Clouds poured wa-ter, light-ning flashed;

joy for sor-row, ease for pain. I stretched out my hands to
I re-called songs in the night. I with doubts and ques-tions
on your might-y deeds so great. All your ways, O God, are
earth then trem-bled, thun-der crashed. At your word the sea pro-

Text: Psalm 77; vers. Helen Otte, 1985. © 1987, CRC Publications
Tune: Genevan Psalter, 1551; harm. Claude Goudimel, 1564

88 77 D
GENEVAN 77

reach him; day and night my prayers be-seeched him. I was
won - dered, Am I from God's mer - cy sev - ered? Are his
ho - ly; na - tions see your power and glo - ry. You re -
vid - ed paths your un - seen foot-prints guid - ed. You your

sleep - less through the night, si - lent in the morn-ing light.
prom - is - es in vain? Will he show his love a - gain?
deemed your cho - sen folk out of E - gypt's i - ron yoke.
peo - ple safe - ly keep, might - y Shep-herd of your sheep.

78   The Mighty Deeds the LORD Has Done

1 The might - y deeds the LORD has done, God's
2 The LORD told par - ents: Teach your young God's
3 When God split E - gypt's sea in two, freed
4 The LORD rained down a spe - cial bread and

mir - a - cles of old, were known by chil - dren
law and cov - enant way, so that, un - like re -
Is - rael from de - feat, de - spite God's cloud and
blew them lus - cious quail. They ate their fill un -

long a - go and now must be re - told.
bel - lious folk, the chil - dren will o - bey.
fi - ery light, they said, "Where's bread and meat?"
grate - ful - ly; so God's grace seemed to fail.

5 In spite of blessings they rebelled;
   against the LORD they cried.
God's awesome anger burned from heaven—
   that generation died.

6 The Israelites showed fickle faith;
   repentance was not true.
But God the covenant Rock forgave
   and sent his grace anew.

Text: Psalm 78; vers. Calvin Seerveld, 1985, ©
Tune: F. William Voetberg, 1985, ©
Another setting of Psalm 78: 585

CM
ST. JAMES THE APOSTLE

7 But how could they forget the plagues—
　　the flies, the locust swarm,
　when all the rivers turned to blood,
　　when God killed all firstborn?

8 When God gushed water out of rock
　　and gave the promised land,
　complete with homes God's people lacked—
　　could they not understand?

9 Again they broke the covenant,
　　served idols, not the LORD;
　so God forsook them—ark and all
　　were captured by the sword.

10 But when God saw their heritage
　　and youth destroyed by hate,
　he woke as if from drunken sleep
　　and moved to set things straight.

11 The LORD beat back his enemies,
　　snatched victory from defeat,
　chose Jesse's son from Judah's tribe
　　as shepherd for his sheep.

12 Let us recall our LORD, who loves,
　　who saves through what is weak.
　If we obey and live in hope,
　　God will redeem the meek.

79

In Your Heritage the Nations

Capo 1:

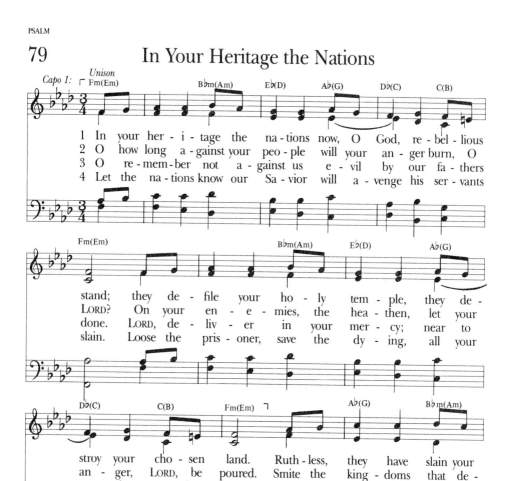

1 In your her - i - tage the na - tions now, O God, re - bel - lious
2 O how long a - gainst your peo - ple will your an - ger burn, O
3 O re - mem - ber not a - gainst us e - vil by our fa - thers
4 Let the na - tions know our Sa - vior will a - venge his ser - vants

stand; they de - file your ho - ly tem - ple, they de -
LORD? On your en - e - mies, the hea - then, let your
done. LORD, de - liv - er in your mer - cy; near to
slain. Loose the pris - oner, save the dy - ing, all your

stroy your cho - sen land. Ruth - less, they have slain your
an - ger, LORD, be poured. Smite the king - doms that de -
ru - in we have come. Help us, God of our sal -
en - e - mies re - strain. Then your flock, your cho - sen

Text: Psalm 79; *vers.* Psalter, *1912, alt.*
Tune: Geistliche Volkslieder, *Paderborn, 1850; harm. Paul Bunjes, 1982.*
Harmonization © 1982, Concordia Publishing House. Used by permission.
Another setting of Psalm 79: 254

87 87 D
O MEIN JESU

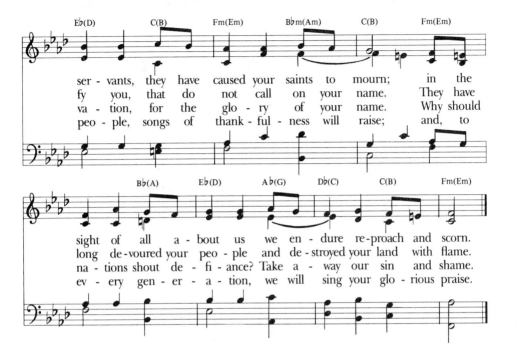

ser - vants, they have caused your saints to mourn; in the
fy you, that do not call on your name. They have
va - tion, for the glo - ry of your name. Why should
peo - ple, songs of thank - ful - ness will raise; and, to

sight of all a - bout us we en - dure re - proach and scorn.
long de - voured your peo - ple and de - stroyed your land with flame.
na - tions shout de - fi - ance? Take a - way our sin and shame.
ev - ery gen - er - a - tion, we will sing your glo - rious praise.

80   Hear Us, O Shepherd of Your Chosen Race

1 Hear us, O Shep - herd of your cho - sen race;
2 How long, O LORD, will you dis - dain our prayer?
3 You brought a vine from E - gypt with your hand;
4 Why have you bro - ken down the vine - yard wall
5 This vine once plant - ed with your own right hand

you led us like a flock with - in your care.
For you have fed us with the bread of tears.
► you drove the na - tions out to give it room.
so that its grapes are eat - en off the vine?
now burns with fire; your peo - ple cry and moan.

From out the cher - u - bim re - veal your face;
Your ho - ly an - ger brings us to de - spair;
► It took deep root and spread through-out the land;
Boars from the for - est root a - round it all;
Let your hand rest on those you cause to stand;

Text: Psalm 80; vers. Bert Polman, 1985. © 1987, CRC Publications
Tune: John Wainwright, 1750
This music in a higher key: 350

10 10 10 10 10 10
YORKSHIRE

be - fore your peo - ple let your might ap - pear.
the na - tions mock us with their scorn - ful jeers.
► the hills were cov - ered with its shade and bloom.
its fruit is rav - aged by the hun - gry swine.
then we will call on your great name a - lone.

Re - store us, LORD, your sav - ing power re - lease;
Re - store us, LORD, your sav - ing power re - lease;
► Un - der its branch - es might - y ce - dars hide;
Re - turn to us, O LORD, with power di - vine;
Re - store us, LORD, your sav - ing power re - lease;

make your face shine on us and give us peace.
make your face shine on us and give us peace.
► it sent out shoots to sea and riv - er - side.
look down from heav - en on your cho - sen vine.
make your face shine on us and give us peace.

81

Sing a Psalm of Joy

1 Sing a psalm of joy! Shout in cel - e - bra - tion.
2 Sound the fes - tal horn, your thanks - giv - ing voic - ing.
3 When in need you cried, I was near and saved you.
4 O my peo - ple, hear; when I call you, lis - ten.

Let the tam - bou - rine and the trum - pet bring
Praise the LORD your God, as he did com - mand
From the cloud I spoke, an - swered your re - quest—
Choose no for - eign god— lis - ten to my plea.

prais - es to our King for his great sal - va - tion.
when from E - gypt's land you came forth re - joic - ing.
Mer - i - bah the test— I did not for - sake you.
Have no god but me; come and be for - giv - en.

5 I, the LORD your God,
brought you out of Egypt.
I removed your yoke,
all your needs supplied.
Open your mouth wide:
surely I will fill it.

6 Oh, that Israel
would but hear my pleading!
Oh, that they would turn,
walk upon my path;
I would pour my wrath
on their foes unheeding.

7 With the finest wheat
I, your LORD, would feed you.
Honey from the rock
I would gladly give
that you all might live.
Hear me, O my people.

Text: Psalm 81; vers. Marie J. Post, 1984
Tune: Genevan Psalter, 1562; harm. Dale Grotenhuis, 1985
Text and harmonization © 1987, CRC Publications

56 55 56
GENEVAN 81

There Where the Judges Gather

1 There where the judg - es gath - er, a great-er takes his seat;
2 "Deal just - ly with the need - y, pro - tect the fa - ther - less,
3 God speaks: "I named you rul - ers, to serve the Most High God;

"How long," he asks the judg - es, "will you pro - nounce de - ceit?
de - liv - er the af - flict - ed from those who would op - press.
but you shall die as mor - tals and per - ish by my rod."

How long show spe - cial fa - vor to those of ill re - pute?
But you are whol - ly blind - ed, you do not un - der - stand;
A - rise, O God, in judg - ment, your sov-ereign - ty make known;

How long ne - glect the or - phaned, the poor and des - ti - tute?
there - fore foun-da - tions tot - ter, in - jus - tice rocks the land."
for yours are all the na - tions, the peo-ples are your own.

Text: Psalm 82; vers. Henry Zylstra, 1953, alt.
Tune: William Lloyd, 1840

76 76 D
MEIRIONYDD

83   O God, Do Not in Silence Stand

1 O God, do not in si - lence stand; do not be still, O God.
2 They say they will de - stroy our land, blot out our mem - o - ry.
3 O LORD, raise up new con - quer - ors like Jael and Gid - e - on.
4 As blaz - ing fire con - sumes the woods, as wind takes chaff from grain,

See how your en - e - mies are filled with craft - y plans and fraud.
From Mo - ab's tents to Ty - re's shore they plot con - spir - a - cy.
Wipe e - vil rul - ers from the earth; re - quite them for their sin.
so break them with tem - pes - tuous blasts and send the hur - ri - cane.

5 Pursue and terrify them, LORD,
   let them be put to shame,
that they may see their wickedness
   and call upon your name.

6 Let all who live or perish know
   that God and God alone
is LORD Most High o'er all the earth,
   the ruler on the throne.

Text: Psalm 83; vers. Clarence P. Walhout, 1982
Tune: Supplement to Kentucky Harmony, 1820; harm. Emily R. Brink, 1986
Text and harmonization © 1987, CRC Publications

CM
DETROIT

84   How Lovely Is Your House, O LORD

1 How love - ly is your house, O LORD; my soul is
2 How hap - py those who trust the LORD, whose strength is
3 O LORD Al - might - y, hear my plea; O God of
4 The LORD God is our sun and shield; his fa - vor

Text: Psalm 84; vers. Ada Roeper-Boulogne, 1979
Tune: Genevan Psalter, 1562; harm. Howard Slenk, 1985
Text and harmonization © 1987, CRC Publications
Another setting of Psalm 84: 243

889 889 88
GENEVAN 84

yearn-ing for your courts. My heart cries out, my spir - it
in the liv - ing God; they know the high-ways to his
Ja - cob, grant to me your won - drous love be - yond all
shines on all who yield their lives to him in faith - ful

fal - ters, for e - ven spar - rows find a nest
moun - tain. When they walk through the val - leys low,
mea - sure. A sin - gle day spent at your door
ser - vice. No pre - cious gift will he with - hold

near you, my God, a place to rest; the swal - low
his per - fect peace will o - ver - flow and spring with -
is bet - ter than a thou-sand more that are con -
from those be - long - ing to his fold; he hon - ors

nes - tles at your al - tar. How blest are sing - ers
in them like a foun - tain. They go from strength to
sumed in sin - ful plea - sure. O may I find my
all whose walk is blame - less. How hap - py those who

in your place who give you their un - ceas - ing praise.
strength in faith un - til they see God's ho - ly place.
true re - ward with - in the pres - ence of the LORD.
trust the LORD, who live ac - cord - ing to his word!

85

LORD, You Have Lavished on Your Land

1 LORD, you have lav-ished on your land a-maz-ing bless-ings
2 LORD, bring us back to grace a-gain; blot out your an-ger
3 To all his saints, the LORD speaks peace; his faith-ful love and
4 Then love will meet with faith-ful-ness; God's right-eous-ness and

from your hand, re-stored us from cap-tiv-i-ty
at our sin. Re-vive us, LORD, that we may raise
care in-crease. He shares his grace with o-pen hand
peace will kiss. As right-eous-ness smiles down from heaven,

and par-doned our in-iq-ui-ty. In grace you caused your
our thank-ful hymns and psalms of praise. In mer-cy, LORD, your
to spread his glo-ry through our land. Sal-va-tion from the
great har-vests to our land are given. With God all right-eous-

wrath to turn; you did not let your an-ger burn.
peo-ple bless with sav-ing love and faith-ful-ness.
LORD is near to all who trust the LORD in fear.
ness a-bides; his truth and jus-tice are our guides.

Text: Psalm 85; vers. Marie J. Post, 1985. © 1987, CRC Publications
Tune: William Hayes, 1774

88 88 88
NEW 113th

Lord, My Petition Heed

1 Lord, my pe - ti - tion heed, now help me in my need,
2 Com - fort your ser - vant now, while at your throne I bow
3 Lord, hear me when I pray; in ev - ery trou - bled day
4 By na - tions you have made, your praise will be dis - played

or else I die. I am your ser - vant, Lord; my trust is
and call to you. Your par - doning grace is free; sin - ners who
I seek your face. O Lord, you far out - shine the gods of
through earth a - broad. Your name be glo - ri - fied, your great - ness

in your word. Mer - cy to me ac - cord; to you I cry.
raise their plea your love and mer - cy see; they are made new.
our de - sign; most bright your glo - ries shine, O God of grace.
mag - ni - fied; match - less your works a - bide, for you are God!

5 Lead me to do your will,
   in me your truth instill,
      teach me your word.
   I will give thanks to you,
   your praise I will pursue;
   all glory be to you,
      O Lord my God!

6 Great is your love to me;
   from death you set me free
      when foes alarm.
   Your grace I surely know,
   your anger, Lord, is slow;
   your loving-kindness show,
      save me from harm.

7 Show me your mercy true,
   your servant's strength renew,
      salvation send.
   A sign of favor show,
   your comfort, Lord, bestow;
   let those who hate me know
      you are my friend.

Text: Psalm 86; vers. Psalter, 1912; rev. Bert Polman, 1983
Tune: William F. Sherwin, 1826–1888; harm. Dale Grotenhuis, 1985
Text and harmonization © 1987, CRC Publications

664 6664
MASON

Our Gracious God

1 Our gra - cious God has laid his firm foun - da - tions
2 What glo - rious things, O cit - y of our great God,
3 "The Cush - ite, the Phi - lis - tine, and the Tyr - ian
4 God will him - self con - firm them with his bless - ing,
5 Then will God's name with ho - ly ad - o - ra - tion

on Zi - on's mount, the courts of his de - light.
are spo - ken in me - lo - dious tones of you:
▸ will soon, O Zi - on, throng your ho - ly gate."
and on the roll of na - tions he will count
and joy - ful tones be praised by Is - rael's throng.

Her gates of splen - dor, bathed in heav - en - ly light,
"Lo, E - gypt, e - ven Ba - bel, I will view
▸ With joy - ful hearts we hear God's voice re - late,
all these as born on Zi - on's ho - ly mount,
Both harp and voice will blend in swell - ing song:

Text: Psalm 87; vers. William Kuipers, 1931, alt.
Tune: Genevan Psalter, 1562; harm. Jacobus J. Kloppers, 1985. Harmonization © 1987, CRC Publications
Another setting of Psalm 87: 168

11 10 10 11
GENEVAN 87

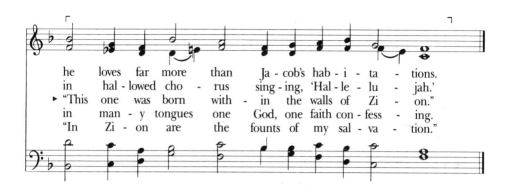

he	loves	far	more	than	Ja - cob's	hab - i - ta	- tions.
in	hal - lowed	cho	- rus	sing - ing,	'Hal - le - lu	- jah.'
▸ "This	one	was	born	with - in	the	walls of	Zi - on."
in	man - y	tongues	one	God, one	faith con - fess	- ing.
"In	Zi - on	are	the	founts of	my sal - va	- tion."

O LORD, I Call for Help by Day   88

1 O	LORD, I	call	for help by	day,	and in the	night I
2 My	soul is	trou - bled, I	am	weak,	cut off as	one whom
3 Your	wrath weighs heav	- y on	me	here.	Your an - gry	waves up -
4 I	am shut in	with - out	es - cape.	My	eyes are	dim be -

still	must	cry. Re	- gard me,	lis - ten	to	my	prayer.
you	for - sake,	for	- got - ten	near the	pit	of	death.
on	me	break. Friends	watch in	hor - ror	from	a - far.
cause	I	weep. My	hands are	lift - ed	up	to	you.

5 Do you work wonders for the dead?
   Can graves tell out your mighty deeds?
   There, who can know that you can save?

6 LORD, do not hide your face from me.
   You have afflicted me from youth.
   Your anger is destroying me.

7 Your flood of anger closes in.
   The darkness is my closest friend—
   shunned and forsaken, all alone.

8 But I, O LORD, cry out to you.
   Each morning I still pray to you.
   LORD, do not cut me off from you.

Text: Psalm 88; vers. Stanley Wiersma, 1982
Tune: Gerben Baaij, b. 1929; harm. Dale Grotenhuis, 1983. Tune © 1973, Liedboek voor de Kerken
Text and harmonization © 1987, CRC Publications

888
VERGEEF, O HEER

89 Forever I Will Sing of Your Great Love, O LORD

1 For - ev - er I will sing of your great love, O LORD,
2 The heav - ens praise, O LORD, your won - ders day and night.
3 Your faith - ful - ness and right - eous - ness for - ev - er stand.
4 Of old your vi - sion came to Da - vid, as you said:

to ev - ery chang - ing age your faith - ful - ness re - cord.
The an - gel hosts on high all trem - ble at your might.
Your jus - tice and your love reach out to all the land.
"I of - fer him the crown, my oil up - on his head.

I will de - clare how firm your stead - fast love is found - ed,
Al - might - y God, your faith - ful - ness stands round a - bout you.
You bathe in love and power the peo - ple who a - dore you.
I will a - bide with him; my hand will not for - sake him.

es - tab-lished in the skies with faith - ful - ness un - bound - ed.
You rule the rag - ing seas; no e - vil foes can rout you.
Most blest are those, O LORD, who shout their praise be - fore you,
His en - e - mies will fear; their ar - mies will not break him.

Text: Psalm 89; vers. Psalter Hymnal, 1987
Tune: Genevan Psalter, 1562; harm. Jacobus J. Kloppers, 1985
Text and harmonization © 1987, CRC Publications
Other settings of Psalm 89: 169, 593

12 12 13 13 13 13
GENEVAN 89

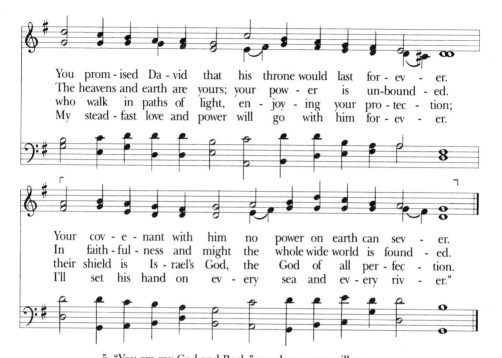

You prom - ised Da - vid that his throne would last for - ev - er.
The heavens and earth are yours; your pow - er is un-bound - ed.
who walk in paths of light, en - joy - ing your pro - tec - tion;
My stead - fast love and power will go with him for - ev - er.

Your cov - e - nant with him no power on earth can sev - er.
In faith - ful - ness and might the whole wide world is found - ed.
their shield is Is - rael's God, the God of all per - fec - tion.
I'll set his hand on ev - ery sea and ev - ery riv - er."

5 "You are my God and Rock," my chosen one will cry.
  Among the kings he'll reign, the highest of the high.
  Although his children stray, I'll fix his throne for ever.
  My covenant made with David's line I will not sever.
  As long as sun and moon shine faithfully before me,
  from his established throne King David will adore me.

6 But now, O LORD, in wrath you turn against your own.
  You have removed his crown, cast down his royal throne.
  His enemies rejoice, with scornful laughter greet him.
  Their armies lay him low; in battle they defeat him.
  You turned his scepter and his throne to desolation;
  his joy and youth are changed to shame and violation.

7 How long, O LORD, how long? Forever will you hide?
  How long before your raging flames of wrath subside?
  Whose life is more than dust? Is death not at the portal?
  Who can outwit the grave or claim to be immortal?
  LORD, note how foes now scorn the king you once appointed.
  Restore your covenant vows to David, your anointed.

Doxology:
8 Sing praises to the LORD, sing amen and amen!
  The praise we sing on earth, heaven echoes back again.
  Your faithfulness we see in mighty acts of wonder.
  Blest are all those, O LORD, whose praises rise like thunder.
  Your steadfast love goes on and on—it ceases never.
  We sing, "Blest be the LORD forever and forever."

90 Lord, You Have Been Our Dwelling Place

1 Lord, you have been our dwell-ing place through all the a - ges
2 A thou-sand years are in your sight brief as a por - tion
3 Your an - ger brings us sor - row, grief; your wrath brings fear with-
4 For three-score years and ten we wait, or four - score years if

of our race. Be - fore you gave the moun - tains birth
of the night. Short as a dream our sea - sons pass;
out re - lief. Be - fore your clear and search - ing sight
strength be great. Yet grief and toil at - tend life's day—

or by your word cre - at - ed earth, from ev - er - last -
our lives are like the ten - der grass, lux - u - riant at
our se - cret sins are brought to light. Be - neath your wrath
our lives soon pass; we fly a - way. Oh, who with true

ing you are God, to ev - er - last - ing our a - bode.
the break of day, that in the eve - ning fades a - way.
we pine and die, our life ex - pir - ing with a sigh.
and rev - erent thought can fear your an - ger as they ought?

Text: Psalm 90; vers. Psalter, 1912; rev. Psalter Hymnal, 1987. © 1987, CRC Publications
Tune: Easy Hymns, 1851; harm. Gerald H. Knight, 1950
Another setting of Psalm 90: 170

88 88 88
STELLA

5 O teach us, LORD, to count our days,
to set our hearts on wisdom's ways.
Turn, LORD, to us in our distress;
in pity now your servants bless.
Let mercy's dawn dispel our night,
let all our days with joy be bright.

6 LORD, may we with our children see
your glorious power and majesty.
O may your favor from above
come down and rest on us in love.
The work accomplished by our hand
establish, Lord—yes, make it stand.

Whoever Shelters with the LORD　91

1 Who - ev - er shel - ters with the LORD and lives with -
2 The faith - ful LORD will spare you death. God's wings will
3 Though thou - sands per - ish at your side, such pun - ish -
4 God gives his an - gels charge of you to guard from
5 "Be - cause you cleave to me in love and know my

in the Al - might - y's shade can say, "My God, in
cov - er you from harm. No ter - ror, sick - ness,
ment shall not touch you. Be - cause the LORD serves
those who per - se - cute. You shall not trip a -
name to call in need, I shall pro - tect and

whom I trust, your ref - uge makes me un - a - fraid!"
night or day, will ev - er cause you grave a - larm.
as your home, God's grace will al - ways see you through.
gainst a stone, but tram - ple ser - pents un - der - foot.
keep you safe with bless - ing, glo - ry, life in - deed."

Text: Psalm 91; vers. Calvin Seerveld, 1985, ©
Tune: Grenoble Antiphoner, 1753

LM
DEUS TUORUM MILITUM

92

How Good It Is to Thank the LORD

1 How good it is to thank the LORD, to praise your
2 O LORD, my song with joy ex - pands be - fore the
3 Though as the grass the wick - ed grow, those e - vil -
4 O LORD, you have ex - alt - ed me with roy - al
5 The right - eous all will flour - ish well and in the

name with tune - ful chord, to show your love with
won - ders of your hands. How great the works that
do - ers do not know the end - less ru - in
strength and dig - ni - ty. With your a - noint - ing
house of God will dwell. They will be plant - ed

morn - ing light and tell your faith - ful - ness each
you have wrought; how deep, O LORD, your ev - ery
they will see. But God will reign e - ter - nal -
I am blest; your grace and fa - vor on me
like a tree, will still in old age fruit - ful

night. Yes, it is good your praise to sing
thought! You make me glad; I sing your praise
ly. All foes will fall be - fore his might;
rest. My eyes have seen the wick - ed die;
be. The LORD our God is up - right, just;

Text: Psalm 92; vers. Psalter, 1912, alt.
Tune: William Matthews, 1759–1830
Another setting of Psalm 92: 171

88 88 88
MADRID

and all   our   sweet - est   mu - sic   bring.
for all   your   won - drous works and   ways.
▸ the wick - ed   shall   be   put   to   flight.
my ears   have   heard   their hope - less   cry.
he is   my   Rock;   in   him   I   trust.

The LORD Is King, Enthroned   93

1 The LORD is King, en - throned in maj - es - ty most bright,
2 The world es - tab - lished stands on its foun - da - tions broad;
3 The seas have lift - ed up their voice in maj - es - ty,
4 Your tes - ti mo - nies, LORD, in faith - ful - ness ex - cel,

ap - par - eled in om - nip - o - tence, and gird - ed round with might.
your throne is fixed, you reign su - preme, the ev - er - last - ing God.
but God on high, su-preme in might, is great - er than the sea.
and ho - ly must your ser-vants be who in your tem - ple dwell.

Text: Psalm 93; vers. Psalter, 1912, alt.
Tune: George F. Root, 1859
Another setting of Psalm 93: 172

SM
RIALTO

94   Almighty LORD God, Who Judges the Earth

1 Al - might - y LORD God, who judg - es the earth, a - rise, give the
2 They say God will not ob - serve what they do, that he will not
3 You fools, our God knows how sense - less you are! For he who made
4 The peo - ple you teach and dis - ci - pline, LORD, are hap - py and

proud just what they de - serve. How long will they boast and in
see the sins they pur - sue. The wid - ows they mur - der, the
all can see near and far. Is God who first fash - ioned your
blest to learn from your word. For you grant re - lief to all

ar - ro-gance mock, op - press - ing the peo - ple you take as your flock?
fa - ther-less snare; and strang-ers they kill, think-ing God does not care.
eye and your ear un - a - ble to see you, un - a - ble to hear?
those in de - spair, al - low - ing them peace till the wick - ed are snared.

Text: Psalm 94; vers. Patricia Haveman, 1983. © 1987, CRC Publications
Tune: Charles H. Gabriel, 1856–1932

10 10 11 11
ASPINWALL

5 O LORD, you will not abandon your own
   nor ever forsake them nor leave them alone.
   Your justice will dawn for all those who do right,
   and those who are upright will follow its light.

6 Who helps me to fight sin's mighty offense?
   Who will be my shield and my sure defense?
   Unless God had helped me when evil oppressed,
   I too would have slipped into silence and death.

7 Whenever I fall, I pleadingly cry;
   then your loving hand, LORD, holds me up high.
   If my heart should doubt and be filled with despair,
   your comfort brings joy, and I know that you care.

8 Corruption cannot be allied with you;
   injustice cannot be legal or true.
   For you, LORD, will never conspire with our foes
   who gather together, increasing our woes.

9 The LORD is my rock, invincible, strong;
   he punishes all who perpetrate wrong.
   Our God will repay them for sins they have sown,
   but he will have mercy and love for his own.

95 Now with Joyful Exultation

1 Now with joy - ful ex - ul - ta - tion let us sing to
2 For how great a God, and glo - rious, is the LORD of
3 To the LORD, such might re - veal - ing, let us come with
4 While he of - fers peace and par - don let us hear his

God our praise; to the Rock of our sal - va - tion
whom we sing; o - ver i - dol gods vic - to - rious,
rev - erence meet, and, be - fore our Mak - er kneel-ing,
voice to - day, lest, if we our hearts should hard - en,

loud ho - san - nas let us raise. Thank - ful trib - ute
great is he, our God and King. In his hand are
let us wor - ship at his feet. He is our own
we should per - ish in the way— lest to us, so

Text: Psalm 95; vers. Psalter, 1912, alt.
Tune: John Zundel, 1870
Another setting of Psalm 95: 173

87 87 D
BEECHER

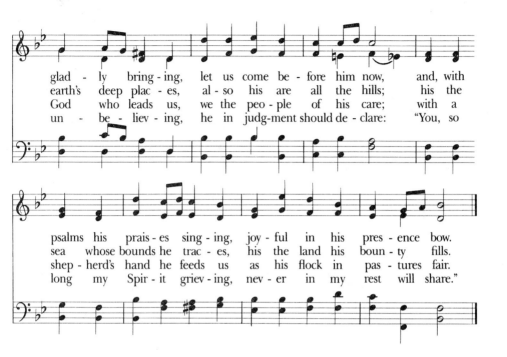

glad - ly bring - ing, let us come be - fore him now, and, with
earth's deep plac - es, al - so his are all the hills; his the
God who leads us, we the peo - ple of his care; with a
un - be - liev - ing, he in judg-ment should de - clare: "You, so

psalms his prais - es sing - ing, joy - ful in his pres - ence bow.
sea whose bounds he trac - es, his the land his boun - ty fills.
shep - herd's hand he feeds us as his flock in pas - tures fair.
long my Spir - it griev - ing, nev - er in my rest will share."

Sing to the LORD, Sing His Praise

1 Sing to the LORD, sing his praise, all you peo - ples;
2 Tell of his won - drous works, tell of his glo - ry
3 Vain are the i - dols and gods of the na - tions;
4 Give un - to God Most High glo - ry and hon - or;

new be your song as new hon - ors you pay.
till through the na - tions his name is re - vered.
God made the heavens, and his glo - ry they tell.
come with your of - ferings and hum - bly draw near.

Sing of his maj - es - ty, praise him for - ev - er,
Praise and ex - alt him, for he is al - might - y;
Splen - dor and maj - es - ty shine out be - fore him;
Wor - ship the LORD in all beau - ty and splen - dor;

show his sal - va - tion from day to day.
God o - ver all, let the LORD be feared.
glo - ry and strength in his tem - ple dwell.
trem - ble be - fore him with god - ly fear.

Text: Psalm 96; vers. Psalter, 1912, alt.
Tune: Lowell Mason, 1830

11 10 11 9
WESLEY

5 Say to the nations, "The LORD reigns forever."
   Earth is established as he did decree.
   Righteous and just is the King of the nations,
   judging the peoples with equity.

6 Let heaven and earth be glad; oceans, be joyful;
   forest and field, exultation express.
   For God is coming, the judge of the nations,
   coming to judge in his righteousness.

97

God Reigns: Let Earth Rejoice!

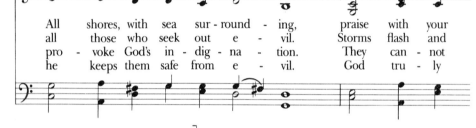

1 God reigns: let earth re - joice! Sing praise with one great voice.
2 Fire goes be - fore his path, con - sum - ing in his wrath
3 Those wor - ship - ers, un - wise, who bow to cults and lies
4 God sends de - liv - er - ance to res - cue all his saints;

All shores, with sea sur - round - ing, praise with your
all those who seek out e - vil. Storms flash and
pro - voke God's in - dig - na - tion. They can - not
he keeps them safe from e - vil. God tru - ly

voice re - sound - ing. Dark clouds of mys - ter - y
shake and rum - ble. Great moun - tains melt like wax
gain sal - va - tion. Now all in Ju - dah praise
loves be - liev - ers. Light dawns for all his own;

Text: Psalm 97; vers. Marie J. Post, 1981
Tune: Genevan Psalter, 1562; harm. Dale Grotenhuis, 1985
Text and harmonization © 1987, CRC Publications

66 77 66 66 6
GENEVAN 97

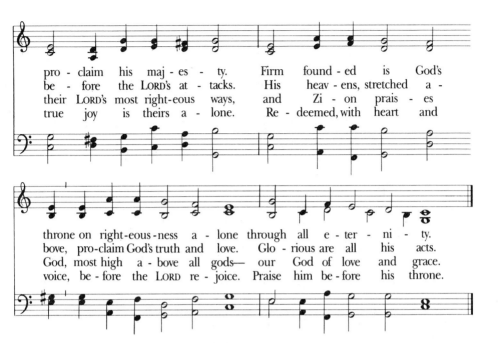

pro - claim   his   maj - es - ty.   Firm   found - ed   is   God's
be - fore   the LORD's   at - tacks.   His   heav - ens, stretched   a -
their   LORD's   most right-eous   ways,   and   Zi - on   prais - es
true   joy   is   theirs   a - lone.   Re - deemed, with   heart   and

throne on right-eous -ness   a - lone   through   all   e - ter - ni - ty.
bove,   pro-claim God's truth   and   love.   Glo - rious are   all   his   acts.
God,   most high   a - bove   all   gods—   our   God   of   love   and   grace.
voice,   be - fore   the LORD   re - joice.   Praise   him   be - fore   his   throne.

98   Sing, Sing a New Song to the LORD God

1 Sing, sing a new song to the LORD God for all the
2 Shout, make a joy - ful noise be - fore him, O all the
3 Let all the streams in joy - ous u - nion now clap their

won - ders he has wrought; his right hand and his
earth, his prais - es sing; with harp and trum - pet
hands and praise ac - cord; let moun-tains sing in

arm most ho - ly the vic - to - ry to him have brought.
sound a - dore him, make mu - sic to the LORD, the King.
glad com - mu - nion and skip for joy be - fore the LORD.

Text: Psalm 98; vers. Dewey Westra, 1931; rev. Psalter Hymnal, 1987
Tune: Genevan Psalter, 1551; harm. Dale Grotenhuis, 1985
Text and harmonization © 1987, CRC Publications
Other harmonizations: 118; in a lower key: 314
Other settings of Psalm 98: 174, 175

98 98 D
GENEVAN 98/118

The LORD has shown his great sal - va - tion, to Is - ra - el his
Let o - ceans roar with all their full - ness, the world and all who
He comes, he comes to judge the peo - ple, ar - rayed in truth and

love made known; he has re - vealed to ev - ery
dwell there - in; pro - claim the power of God with
eq - ui - ty; he shall re - deem the world from

na - tion his truth in right - eous - ness a - lone.
bold - ness, ex - alt him ev - er and a - gain.
e - vil, and right - eous shall his judg - ment be.

99

The LORD God Reigns in Majesty

1 The LORD God reigns in maj - es - ty; let all the na - tions quake.
2 The might - y King loves jus - tice well and eq - ui - ty or - dains.
3 When priests and proph-ets called on God, he their pe - ti - tions heard.

He dwells be-tween the cher - u - bim; let earth's foun-da - tions shake.
He rules his peo - ple right-eous - ly and faith - ful-ness main-tains.
His cloud - y pil - lar led them on, and they o - beyed his word.

Su - preme in Zi - on is the LORD, ex - alt - ed glo-rious - ly.
In wor - ship at his foot - stool bow, let him ex - alt - ed be.
Though send - ing judg-ments for their sins, he par-doned gra-cious - ly.

All na - tions, praise his name with awe: the Ho - ly One is he.
O mag - ni - fy the LORD our God: the Ho - ly One is he.
Ex - alt the LORD and wor - ship him: the Ho - ly One is he.

Text: Psalm 99; vers. Psalter, 1912
Tune: James McGranahan, 1840–1907
Alternative tune: ELLACOMBE, 378

CMD
NONE BUT CHRIST

All People That on Earth Do Dwell

1 All peo - ple that on earth do dwell, sing to the
2 Know that the LORD is God in - deed; he formed us
3 O en - ter then his gates with joy, with - in his
4 Be - cause the LORD our God is good, his mer - cy

LORD with cheer - ful voice. Serve him with joy, his
all with - out our aid. We are the flock he
courts his praise pro - claim. Let thank - ful songs your
is for - ev - er sure. His faith - ful - ness at

prais - es tell, come now be - fore him and re - joice!
comes to feed, the sheep who by his hand were made.
tongues em - ploy, O bless and mag - ni - fy his name.
all times stood and shall from age to age en - dure.

Text: Psalm 100; vers. William Kethe, 1561, alt.
Tune: Louis Bourgeois, 1551; harm. Dale Grotenhuis, 1985. Harmonization © 1987, CRC Publications
Alternative tune: GENEVAN 134 (OLD HUNDREDTH), 134
Another setting of Psalm 100: 176

LM
GENEVAN 100

Psalm 100: Alternative harmonization with melody in the tenor

1 All peo - ple that on earth do dwell, sing to the
2 Know that the LORD is God in - deed; he formed us
1 Vous tous qui la terre ha - bi - tez, chan - tez à
2 Sa - chez qu'il est le Sou - ve - rain qui nous a

LORD with cheer - ful voice. Serve him with joy, his
all with - out our aid. We are the flock he
hau - te voix, chan - tez; ré - jou - is - sez - vous
for - més de sa main; nous, le peu - ple qu'il

prais - es tell, come now be - fore him and re - joice!
comes to feed, the sheep who by his hand were made.
au Sei - gneur par un saint hymne à son hon - neur.
veut ché - rir et le trou - peau qu'il veut nour - rir.

3 O enter then his gates with joy,
within his courts his praise proclaim.
Let thankful songs your tongues employ,
O bless and magnify his name.

3 Entrez dans son temple aujourd'hui;
que chacun vienne devant lui;
célébrer son nom glorieux,
et qu'on l'élève jusqu'aux cieux.

4 Because the LORD our God is good,
his mercy is forever sure.
His faithfulness at all times stood
and shall from age to age endure.

4 C'est un Dieu rempli de bonté,
d'une éternelle vérité;
il nous comble de ses bienfaits,
et sa grâce dure à jamais.

Text: Psalm 100; Eng. vers. William Kethe, 1561, alt.; Fr. vers. Psaumes en Cantiques, 1891
Tune: Louis Bourgeois, 1551; harm. Claude Goudimel, 1564

LM
GENEVAN 100

I Praise Your Justice, LORD

1 I praise your jus - tice, LORD, with my thanks-giv - ing;
2 I hate the deeds of faith - less men and wom - en;
3 I will re - gard the faith - ful in your na - tion,
4 All e - vil - do - ers from my house I ban - ish;

your mer - cy and your love guide all my liv - ing.
I shrink from those who twist the truth with - in them.
that they may share my place of hab - i - ta - tion.
from God's own cit - y wick - ed ones will van - ish.

I will o - bey you, live in pu - ri - ty. Stay close to me.
All those who slan - der, those who proud-ly scoff I will cut off.
Then peo - ple who a - void all treach-er - y will serve with me.
May ev - ery shrewd de - ceiv - er be un-done: let God's rule come.

Text: Psalm 101; vers. Bert Witvoet, 1985. © 1987, CRC Publications
Tune: Louis Bourgeois, 1551; harm. Claude Goudimel, 1564, alt.

11 11 10 4
GENEVAN 101

102 LORD, Hear My Prayer and Let My Cry

1 LORD, hear my prayer and let my cry have read-y ac-cess
2 My heart is with-ered like the grass, and I for-get to
3 But you, O LORD my God, en-dure; your throne for-ev-er
4 Write down for those who are to come that they, like us, God's

to your ear. When in dis-tress to you I fly, hide
eat my bread. I groan, my bones cleave to my flesh; I
is the same. You look on Zi-on, hold her dear; you
grace may see: "The LORD has looked down from his throne, to

not your face, O LORD, be near. At-tend, O LORD, to
lie a-wake all night in bed. My drink is tears, dis-
grant her fa-vor in your time. Your ser-vants cher-ish
hear the cap-tives, set them free." How filled with mer-cy

my de-sire and quick-ly an-swer when I pray. For
tress my bread; the taunts of foes in-crease my grief. Your
Zi-on's walls; all lands will fear your glo-rious name. O
are God's ways! In Zi-on a new song is heard. God's

Text: Psalm 102; st. 1–3 vers. Psalter, 1912; st. 1–3 rev. and
st. 4–6 vers. Marie J. Post, 1985. © 1987, CRC Publications
Tune: J. Ingalls' Christian Harmony, 1805; harm. J. Harold Moyer, 1965, alt.

LMD
SOCIAL BAND

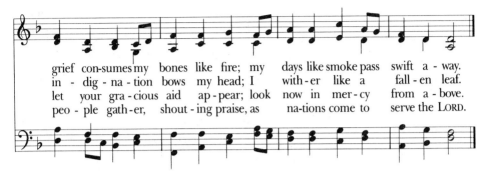

grief con-sumes my bones like fire; my days like smoke pass swift a - way.
in - dig - na - tion bows my head; I with - er like a fall - en leaf.
let your gra - cious aid ap - pear; look now in mer - cy from a - bove.
peo - ple gath - er, shout - ing praise, as na-tions come to serve the LORD.

5 When I was ill and soon to die,
I turned to God, who counts my days:
"O LORD eternal, hear my cry;
still grant me time that I may praise.
The earth's foundations you have laid,
the heavens you stretched with stars' array.
Yet, as a garment, worn and frayed,
the heavens and earth will pass away."

6 LORD, hear my prayer and let my cry
have ready access to your ear.
When in distress to you I fly,
hide not your face, O LORD, be near.
Your years, LORD, reach eternity;
you are the same, forever sure.
Our children's children too will see
that in your love they are secure.

103 Come, Praise the LORD, My Soul

1 Come, praise the LORD, my soul, and all with-in me,
2 To all the need - y God is just and faith - ful.
3 High as the heavens a - bove, so great God loves us.
4 Our days are gone as quick - ly as a flow - er;
5 God in his king - dom o - ver all is rul - ing.

praise his most ho - ly name; bring him the glo - ry.
He showed his deeds to Mo - ses and his peo - ple.
► So far has he moved our trans - gres - sions from us—
like grass, we flour - ish for the brief - est hour.
Praise him, you an - gels, you who do his bid - ding,

For - get not all his ben - e - fits to you.
The LORD is gra - cious, rich in stead - fast love.
► as far re - moved as east is from the west.
But God's love is for - ev - er - more the same;
you might - y ser - vants who o - bey his word.

Text: Psalm 103; vers. Helen Otte, 1986
Tune: Genevan Psalter, 1539; harm. Howard Slenk, 1985
Text and harmonization © 1987, CRC Publications
Other settings of Psalm 103: 297, 583, 627

11 11 10 D
GENEVAN 103

He   is   for - giv - ing,   heals   all   your   dis - eas   -   es,
He   is   com - pas - sion - ate   and   slow   to   an   -   ger.
▶ As   par - ents   have   com - pas - sion   on   their   chil   -   dren,
from   ev - er - last - ing   un - to   ev - er - last   -   ing,
Come,   praise   the LORD,   all   works   of   his   cre - a   -   tion.

re - deems   your   life,   so   sat - is - fies   and   pleas   -   es
He   will   not   keep   his   wrath   on   us   for - ev   -   er.
▶ God   is   com - pas - sion - ate   to   those   who   fear   him;
to   chil - dren's   chil - dren,   hu - man   love   sur - pass   -   ing,
Praise   God   in   ev - ery   part   of   his   do - min   -   ion.

that,   like   the   ea - gle's,   he   re - news   your   youth.
He   does   not   treat   us   as   our   sins   de - serve.
▶ he   knows   our   frame,   re - mem - bers   we   are   dust.
his   love   re - mains   with   all   who   fear   his   name.
Come,   O   my   soul,   for - ev - er   praise   the   LORD.

104 Your Spirit, O LORD, Makes Life to Abound

1 Your Spir - it, O LORD, makes life to a - bound.
2 My soul, praise the LORD! The LORD is most great,
3 He rides on the clouds and wings of the storm.
4 On moun - tains and plains the dark wa - ters lay.

The earth is re - newed, and fruit - ful the ground.
with glo - ry ar - rayed, ma - jes - tic in state.
The light - ning and wind his mis - sion per - form.
They heard his re - buke and hur - ried a - way.

To God be all glo - ry and wis - dom and might.
The light is his gar - ment, the skies form a tent,
Foun - da - tions of earth he for - ev - er has stayed;
He lift - ed the moun - tains, to val - leys gave birth,

May God in his crea - tures for - ev - er de - light.
and o - ver the wa - ters his cou - riers are sent.
to cov - er it, o - ceans like gar - ments were laid.
set bound-aries for seas that once cov - ered the earth.

Repeat stanza 1

Text: Psalm 104; vers. Psalter, 1912, alt.
Tune: Henry J. Gauntlett, 1861

10 10 11 11
HOUGHTEN

5 God causes the springs of water to flow
 in streams from the hills to valleys below.
 The LORD gives the streams for all living things there,
 while birds with their singing enrapture the air.

6 Down mountains and hills your showers are sent.
 With fruit of your work the earth is content.
 You give grass for cattle and food for our toil,
 enriching our labors with bread, wine, and oil.

7 The trees that the LORD has planted are fed,
 and over the earth their branches are spread.
 They keep in their shelter the birds of the air.
 The life of each creature God keeps in his care.   *Repeat stanza 1*

8 The seasons are fixed by wisdom divine.
 The slow-changing moon shows forth God's design.
 The sun in its circuit its Maker obeys
 and, running its journey, hastes not nor delays.

9 The LORD makes the night, when, leaving their lair,
 the lions go forth, God's bounty to share.
 The LORD makes the morning, when beasts steal away,
 when we are beginning the work of the day.

10 How many and wise the works of the LORD!
 The earth with its wealth of creatures is stored.
 The sea bears in safety the ships to and fro;
 Leviathan plays in the waters below.

11 Your creatures all look to you for their food.
 Your hand opens wide, they gather the good.
 When you hide your face, LORD, in anguish they yearn;
 when you stop their breathing, to dust they return.   *Repeat stanza 1*

12 Before the LORD's might earth trembles and quakes.
 The mountains are rent, and smoke from them breaks.
 I promise to worship the LORD all my days.
 Yes, while I have being, my God I will praise.

13 Rejoicing in God, my thought shall be sweet.
 May sinners depart in ruin complete.
 My soul, praise the LORD God—his name be adored.
 Come, praise him, all people, and worship the LORD.

105 Trumpet the Name! Praise Be to Our LORD!

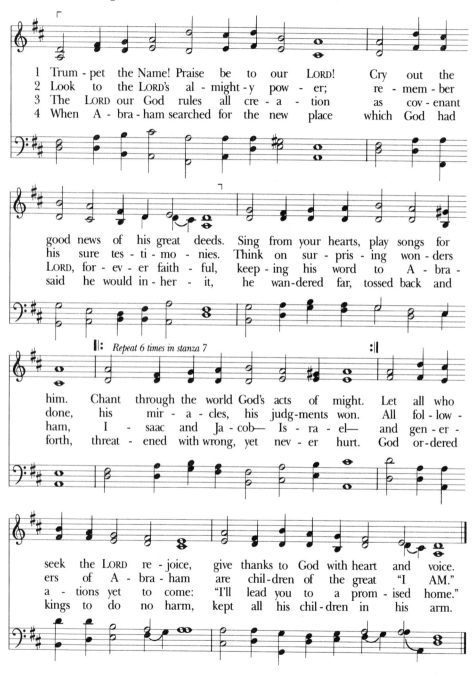

1 Trum - pet the Name! Praise be to our LORD! Cry out the
2 Look to the LORD's al - might - y pow - er; re - mem - ber
3 The LORD our God rules all cre - a - tion as cov - enant
4 When A - bra - ham searched for the new place which God had

good news of his great deeds. Sing from your hearts, play songs for
his sure tes - ti - mo - nies. Think on sur - pris - ing won - ders
LORD, for - ev - er faith - ful, keep - ing his word to A - bra -
said he would in - her - it, he wan-dered far, tossed back and

Repeat 6 times in stanza 7

him. Chant through the world God's acts of might. Let all who
done, his mir - a - cles, his judg-ments won. All fol - low -
ham, I - saac and Ja - cob— Is - ra - el— and gen - er -
forth, threat - ened with wrong, yet nev - er hurt. God or-dered

seek the LORD re - joice, give thanks to God with heart and voice.
ers of A - bra - ham are chil-dren of the great "I AM."
a - tions yet to come: "I'll lead you to a prom - ised home."
kings to do no harm, kept all his chil - dren in his arm.

Text: Psalm 105; vers. Calvin Seerveld, 1983, ©
Tune: Genevan Psalter, 1562; harm. Howard Slenk, 1985. Harmonization © 1987, CRC Publications

99 88 88
GENEVAN 105

5 All Jacob's family lodged in Canaan;
God changed their lives there with a famine.
Joseph had been sold off, a slave,
jailed, falsely maligned, lost for years,
until God providentially
made Pharaoh set poor Joseph free.

6 The king of Egypt leaned on God's slave,
made Joseph chief lord of his nation!
Princes were bound by his decree,
wise men agreed—what irony!
God's people lived as welcomed guests,
thrived better than their gentile hosts.

*7 But unleashed hate pressed down the LORD's folk;
Moses and Aaron then were chosen
to execute most fearful plagues,
curbing revolt against God's word:
pitch dark, and water turned to blood,
fish dead and frogs in Pharaoh's bed.
God spoke, and horseflies swarmed ahead!
Hail raining down instead of bread,
grasshoppers hopped, increasing dread;
God killed their firstborn sons all dead;
God rescued Israel from the foe;
Egypt was glad to see them go.

8 God hung a cloud to lead them safely;
his fiery pillar guided nightly.
When they complained, he dropped them quail,
water gushed out from solid rock!
His manna answered desert prayers:
God kept his oath to faithful heirs.

9 Exodus meant pure celebration:
the LORD's elect gained liberation!
God gave his folk rich heathen lands,
put treasures in his people's hands,
that they might demonstrate God's grace
alive before his steadfast face.

*Stanza 7 may be sung either with or without the list of plagues.
When singing the entire text, repeat the fourth melodic phrase six times.

106 O Praise the LORD, for He Is Good

1. O praise the LORD, for he is good; give thanks, re -
count his ways. What tongue can tell his might - y deeds
or ful - ly sing his praise? How blest are all who
choose the right and do God's will a - lone. O LORD, re -

2. Both we and all be - fore us sinned; re - bel - lious
is our race. In E - gypt land our par - ents walked
for - get - ful of your grace. You piled up waves like
sol - id walls, dried path - ways through the sea so that your

3. They soon for - got God's might - y acts and begged for
bread and flesh, com - plain - ing, crav - ing, test - ing God,
who sent them pain and death. They en - vied Mo - ses,
man of God, and Aa - ron, whom God sent; A - bi - ram,

4. At Ho - reb Is - rael made a calf, be - fore an
im - age kneeled, ex - changed their Glo - ry for an ox
that eats grass in the field. They soon for - got their
cov - enant God and all his sav - ing ways, but Mo - ses

Text: Psalm 106; vers. Marie J. Post, 1985. © 1987, CRC Publications
Tune: Lee Hastings Bristol, Jr., 1951

CMD
SEDGWICK

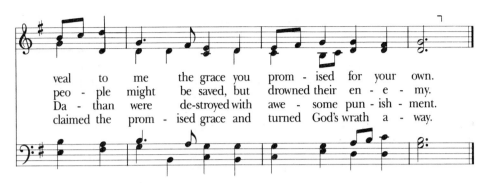

veal to me the grace you prom - ised for your own.
peo - ple might be saved, but drowned their en - e - my.
Da - than were de-stroyed with awe - some pun - ish - ment.
claimed the prom - ised grace and turned God's wrath a - way.

5 Then they despised the pleasant land,
　　the promised land of God;
　　they tempted God to make them fall
　　and scatter them abroad.
　　They even sacrificed to Baal!
　　Provoked, God sent a plague.
　　But righteous Phinehas stood up,
　　so punishment was stayed.

6 At Meribah they angered God;
　　there Moses' words were rash.
　　They sacrificed their daughters, sons,
　　provoking God's fierce wrath.
　　He gave them up to heathen foes
　　when they ignored his ways;
　　but when they cried out in despair,
　　he answered them with grace.

7 O save us, Lord, our gracious God,
　　and gather all your own,
　　that we may glory in your name
　　and sing before your throne.
　　Blest be the Lord, our covenant God;
　　all praise to him accord.
　　Let all the people say "Amen."
　　Forever praise the Lord!

107

"Thanks Be to God Our Savior"

1 "Thanks be to God our Sav - ior," let his re - deemed ones say.
2 Strang - ers with - out a cit - y, some roamed the wil - der - ness,
3 Some groaned in bit - ter an - guish, foes of the Most High's claims,
4 Slaves to pro - fane am - bi - tion, by e - vil led a - stray,

"He shows us bound - less fa - vor; his love is sure each day."
find - ing no food or pit - y, no hope in their dis - tress.
help - less, con - demned to lan - guish, cap - tives in i - ron chains.
some learned to know af - flic - tion, suf - fered, and pined a - way.

From earth's re - mot - est lands a cho - sen folk he rais - es,
Then, when they sought God's name, he made their path - ways flour - ish.
Then, when they sought God's name, he loos - ened all their fet - ters.
Then, when they sought God's name, he brought them res - to - ra - tion.

ran - somed from ty - rants' hands; join now to sound his prais - es.
Bless him, his love pro - claim: the hun - gry he will nour - ish.
Bless him, his love pro - claim: the pris - on bars he shat - ters.
Bless him, his love pro - claim; bring thanks and ad - o - ra - tion.

Text: Psalm 107; vers. David J. Diephouse, 1985
Tune: Genevan Psalter, 1551; harm. Dale Grotenhuis, 1986
Text and harmonization © 1987, CRC Publications

76 76 67 67
GENEVAN 107

5 Storms thundered forth his power
    to those who sailed the seas.
  Winds lashed them hour by hour;
    waves dashed them to their knees.
  Then, when they sought God's name,
    he calmed the raging weather.
  Bless him, his love proclaim
    where all his people gather.

6 His word brings desolation
    where evil deeds abound,
  but for his faithful nation
    springs flow from barren ground.
  Bounty he sends the meek;
    the mighty prince he plunders.
  His loving-kindness seek;
    consider all his wonders.

My Heart Is Firmly Fixed　　108

1 My heart is firm-ly fixed; to God my song I raise.
2 A - mong the na - tions, LORD, to you my song will rise.
3 How great your love, O LORD: we praise your match-less worth.
4 Stretch forth your might - y hand in an - swer to our prayer,
5 God speaks: "All lands are mine, to serve me and o - bey;

A - wake, O harp, in joy - ful strains; a - wake, my soul, to praise.
Your faith - ful - ness out - shines the heavens, your mer - cies reach the skies.
Your glo - ry be ex - alt - ed high and cov - er all the earth.
and let your own be - lov - ed ones your great sal - va - tion share.
my peo - ple and their foes will serve my glo - ry day by day."

6　O who will lead us on
      in triumph on this day?
    LORD, why do you reject your own
      and turn your face away?

7　An army's help is vain;
      to God for help we plead.
    With God we shall do valiantly;
      with God we shall succeed.

Text: Psalm 108; vers. Psalter, 1912; rev. Psalter Hymnal, 1987. © 1987, CRC Publications
Tune: Aaron Williams, 1763; harm. Lowell Mason, 1792–1872

SM
ST. THOMAS

109

Do Not Be Silent, LORD God

1 Do not be si - lent, LORD God; the wick - ed speak a -
2 I pray, dear LORD, you stop those who vi - o - late the
3 You see, my LORD, how fear - ful, how spent I am, like

gainst my life. With - out a cause they spread hate and
help - less poor. Please end the fla - grant cruel - ty that
mere de - bris. Tor - men - tors mock my frail - ty and

slan - der me both day and night. Al - though I have be -
kills the in - no - cent and pure. I pray, O God, you
aim their cru - el taunts at me. Save me, O LORD, from

friend - ed them, al - though I pray for them, they con - stant - ly ac -
short - en the life of such de - praved, up - root their nor - mal
ru - in; re - veal your stead - fast love. Con - front the haugh - ty

Text: Psalm 109; vers. Calvin Seerveld, 1985, ©
Tune: Kugelmann's Concentus Novi, 1540; harm. Psalter Hymnal, 1987

PM
NUN LOB, MEIN SEEL

cuse me and pay me ill for good. They rel - ish
liv - ing, dis - cred - it all their deeds, re - move their
god - less with your un - fail - ing might. Dis - grace the

do - ing e - vil, and ha - tred is their aim. Do
sin - ful pow - er— their names be blot - ted out. Be -
ones who hurt me, and make de - liv - erance sweet. I

not for - get their sins, LORD; e - rase from earth their name.
cause they blessed with curs - es, may curs - es be their lot.
vow my thanks to you, LORD, for you pro - tect the meek.

110 The Lord unto My Lord Has Said

1 The Lord un-to my Lord has said, "Sit here at my right hand
2 Your peo-ple will be glad-ly yours when you a-rise in might,
3 You shall sub-due the kings of earth, with God at your right hand;

un-til I make your en-e-mies sub-mit to your com-mand."
like dawn-ing day, like hope-ful youth, with ho-ly beau-ty bright.
the na-tions you shall rule in might and judge in ev-ery land.

A scep-ter pros-pered by the Lord your might-y hand shall wield;
The priest-hood of Mel-chiz-e-dek the Lord has giv-en you;
The Lord, re-freshed by liv-ing streams, shall nei-ther faint nor fall,

from Zi-on you shall rule the world, and all your foes shall yield.
it shall re-main for-ev-er-more; God's word is al-ways true.
and he shall be the glo-rious head, ex-alt-ed o-ver all.

Text: Psalm 110; vers. Psalter, 1912, alt.
Tune: Henry S. Cutler, 1872

CMD
ALL SAINTS NEW

O Give the Lord Wholehearted Praise

1 O give the Lord whole-heart-ed praise. To him thanks-
2 His saints de-light to search and trace his might-y
3 God's won-drous deeds of faith-ful-ness his peo-ple
4 God's prom-ise shall for-ev-er stand; he cares for
5 His works are true and just in-deed; his pre-cepts

giv-ing I will bring; with all his peo-ple
works and won-drous ways. Ma-jes-tic glo-ry,
▸ ev-er keep in mind. His works of love and
those who trust his word. Up-on his saints his
are for-ev-er sure. In truth and right-eous-

I will raise my voice and of his glo-ry sing.
bound-less grace, and right-eous-ness his work dis-plays.
▸ gra-cious-ness re-veal that God the Lord is kind.
might-y hand the wealth of na-tions has con-ferred.
ness de-creed, they shall for-ev-er-more en-dure.

6 From God his saints' redemption came;
his covenant sure no change can know.
Let all revere his holy name
in heaven above and earth below.

7 In reverence and in godly fear
we find the key to wisdom's ways;
the wise his holy name revere.
Through endless ages sound his praise!

Text: Psalm 111; vers. Psalter, 1912, alt.
Tune: W. Gardiner's Sacred Melodies, 1815

LM
GERMANY

112 How Blest Are Those Who Fear the LORD

1 How blest are those who fear the LORD and great - ly
2 A - bound - ing wealth shall bless their home, their right - eous -
3 The peo - ple who be - friend the weak in jus - tice
4 By e - vil tid - ings not dis - mayed, the right - eous

love God's ho - ly will. Their chil - dren share their
ness for - e'er en - dure. To them shall light a -
shall their cause main - tain. True peace shall their whole
trust in God a - lone. Their heart is stead - fast,

great re - ward, and bless - ings all their days shall fill.
rise in gloom, for they are mer - ci - ful and pure.
life at - tend, and long their mem - ory shall re - main.
un - a - fraid, for they shall see their foes o'er - thrown.

5 Dispersing gifts among the poor,
the righteous for their needs provide.
Their righteousness shall thus endure;
their strength in honor shall abide.

6 The wicked will be brought to shame,
while righteous ones will see the LORD.
Unrighteous hopes will not see gain,
for sin will find its due reward.

Text: Psalm 112; vers. Psalter, 1887; rev. Psalter Hymnal, 1987
Tune: Samuel Webbe, 1782
This music in a higher key: 274

LM
MELCOMBE

Praise God, You Servants of the LORD

1 Praise God, you ser - vants of the LORD, and bless his
2 From ris - ing un - to set - ting sun praised be the
3 On whom but God can we re - ly, the One who
4 God lifts the poor and makes them great; with joy he

name with one ac - cord. O praise the LORD, his
LORD, the Might - y One. He reigns o'er all, su -
sits en - throned on high, who con - de - scends to
fills the des - o - late. The bar - ren come to

name a - dore from this time forth for - ev - er - more.
preme in might, a - bove the heavens in glo - ry bright.
see and know the things of heaven and earth be - low?
moth - er - hood. Sing hal - le - lu - jah! God is good.

Text: Psalm 113; vers. Psalter, 1912, alt.
Tune: Geistreiches Gesangbuch, Halle, 1704, adapt.
Another setting of Psalm 113: 177

LM
FESTUS

114   When Israel Fled from Egypt Land

1 When Is-rael fled from E-gypt land, from for-eign tongue and cru-el hand, the LORD took Ju-dah for his home and Is-rael for his ver-y own.

2 The sea rolled back to form dry land, the Jor-dan fled at God's com-mand. The moun-tains skipped like joy-ful rams, the lit-tle hills like play-ful lambs.

3 What made you part, O might-y sea? Why, Jor-dan, did you turn to flee? Why, moun-tains, skip like joy-ful rams? And, lit-tle hills, like play-ful lambs?

4 Now trem-ble, earth, the Lord is near; bow down and see your God ap-pear. His might makes springs to gush and glow; from flint the cool-ing wa-ters flow.

Text: Psalm 114; vers. Henrietta Ten Harmsel, 1985. © 1987, CRC Publications
Tune: William B. Bradbury, 1816–1868, alt.
Keyboard and guitar should not sound together.

LM
ANDRE

Not unto Us, O LORD of Heaven

1 Not un-to us, O LORD of heaven, but un-to
2 The i-dol gods of hea-then lands are but the
3 O Is-rael, trust in God a-lone, the LORD, whose
4 All you that fear him and a-dore, the LORD in-
5 The heavens are God's since time be-gan, but he has

you be glo-ry given; in love and truth you do ful-fill
work of hu-man hands: they can-not see, they can-not speak,
► grace and power are known; to him your full al-le-giance yield,
crease you more and more; both great and small who God con-fess,
given the earth to man. The dead praise not the liv-ing God,

the coun-sels of your sov-ereign will. Though na-tions
their ears are deaf, their hands are weak. Like them shall
► and he will be your help and shield. All those who
you and your chil-dren he will bless. You all are
but we will sound his praise a-broad. Yes, we will

fail your power to own, you are the King— you reign a-lone.
be all those who hold to gods of sil-ver and of gold.
► fear him God will bless; his saints have proved his faith-ful-ness.
blest by him who made the heavens and earth's foun-da-tions laid.
ev-er bless his name; O praise the LORD, his praise pro-claim.

Text: Psalm 115; vers. Psalter, 1912, alt.
Tune: Ernest R. Kroeger, 1862–1934

88 88 88
GAIRNEY BRIDGE

116 I Love the LORD, for He Has Heard My Voice

1 I love the LORD, for he has heard my voice.
2 Our God is gra - cious, mer - ci - ful, and just.
3 For you, O LORD, have saved my soul from death.
4 How can I pay the LORD for all his gifts?
5 Pre - cious to God the dy - ing of his saints.

He turned to me and heard my cry for mer - cy.
He watch - es o - ver all the sim - ple - heart - ed.
► You kept my eyes from tears, my feet from stum - bling.
I will lift up the cup of full sal - va - tion.
I am your faith - ful ser - vant, freed from bond - age.

An - guished by death and o - ver - come by sor - row,
Rest, O my soul, and trust him for sal - va - tion.
► I kept my faith, though I was much af - flict - ed.
I will ful - fill my vows to God my Sav - ior.
I'll pay my vows and, with your peo - ple, thank you.

I turned in my dis - tress to God in prayer.
Re - mem - ber all his good - ness shown to you.
► Dis - mayed, I said, "All peo - ple are un - true."
With all his saints I'll call up - on his name.
Come to his house, O peo - ple, praise the LORD!

Text: Psalm 116; vers. Helen Otte, 1980. © 1987, CRC Publications
Tune: Genevan Psalter, 1562; harm. Seymour Swets, 1954
Another setting of Psalm 116: 178

10 11 11 10
GENEVAN 116

Hallelujah, Hallelujah

Hal - le - lu - jah, hal - le - lu - jah; all you peo - ples,
praise pro-claim. For God's grace and lov - ing - kind-ness O sing
prais - es to his name. For the great - ness of his mer - cy
con - stant praise to him ac - cord. For his faith - ful -
ness e - ter - nal, hal - le - lu - jah, praise the LORD!

Text: Psalm 117; vers. Psalter, 1887, alt.
Tune: Oude en Nieuwe Hollantse Boerenlities en Contradansen, 1710

87 87 D
IN BABILONE

118   Give Thanks to God for All His Goodness

1 Give thanks to God for all his good - ness: "His love for -
2 Brought low, I cried to God; he heard me. He an - swered
3 Hark! right-eous and vic - to - rious sing - ing: "The LORD's right
4 The stone the build - ers had re - ject - ed is now the
5 Our voic - es join in glad con - fes - sion: "God's love for -

ev - er is the same." Give thanks to God, O ho - ly
me and set me free. The LORD with me, no one can
hand does val - iant - ly." For life re - stored my prais - es
fore - most cor - ner - stone. The LORD has done it, we have
ev - er is the same." Most blest is he in our pro -

na - tion: "His love for - ev - er is the same."
hurt me. He is my strength, my vic - to - ry.
bring - ing: The LORD's right hand does val - iant - ly."
seen it— his ways con - found what we had known.
ces - sion who comes tri - um - phant in God's name.

Text: Psalm 118; vers. Stanley Wiersma, 1982. © 1987, CRC Publications
Tune: Genevan Psalter, 1551; harm. Claude Goudimel, 1564
Other harmonizations: 98; in a lower key: 313
Other settings of Psalm 118: 179, 241

98 98 D
GENEVAN 98/118

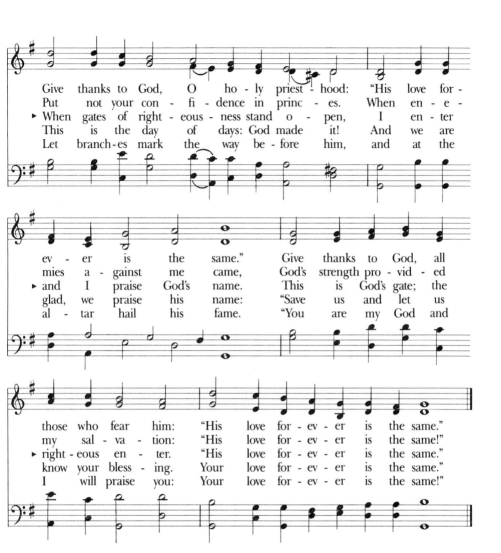

Give thanks to God, O ho - ly priest - hood: "His love for -
Put not your con - fi - dence in princ - es. When en - e -
► When gates of right - eous - ness stand o - pen, I en - ter
This is the day of days: God made it! And we are
Let branch-es mark the way be - fore him, and at the

ev - er is the same." Give thanks to God, all
mies a - gainst me came, God's strength pro - vid - ed
► and I praise God's name. This is God's gate; the
glad, we praise his name: "Save us and let us
al - tar hail his fame. "You are my God and

those who fear him: "His love for - ev - er is the same."
my sal - va - tion: "His love for - ev - er is the same!"
► right - eous en - ter. "His love for - ev - er is the same."
know your bless - ing. Your love for - ev - er is the same."
I will praise you: Your love for - ev - er is the same!"

119 Blessed Are Those Who Heed the Law of God

1 Bless - ed are those who heed the law of God,
2 How can the youth - ful keep their ac - tions pure?
3 O - pen my eyes that I may see your law.
4 Pro - tect me from the ar - ro - gant and proud;
5 Teach me, O LORD, the way that I should go;

who seek to do no e - vil or in - jus - tice.
By tak - ing care to hon - or all your stat - utes.
Your faith - ful truths are all that I de - light in;
they scorn and laugh at those who seek your plea - sure.
I will o - bey and to the end be faith - ful.

They are the LORD's who walk in all his ways.
I will not wan - der from the ways of God.
O do not hide them from my sight, O God.
Some - times I am de - pressed and sad at heart;
In - cline my heart to trust your prom - is - es.

O help us, LORD, to fol - low your com - mand - ments.
With all my heart I seek your truth and jus - tice.
I do but wan - der if you do not guide me;
re - vive my soul ac - cord - ing to your pre - cepts.
Re - new my life and turn my eyes from e - vil.

Text: Psalm 119; vers. Clarence P. Walhout, 1980
Tune: Louis Bourgeois, 1551; harm. Howard Slenk, 1985
Text and harmonization © 1987, CRC Publications
Other settings of Psalm 119: 276, 584

10 11 10 11 10 11
GENEVAN 119

With | up - right | hearts | we | strive | to | do | your | will.
I | al - ways | keep | your | word | with - in | my | heart;
▸ my | soul | is | long - ing | for | your | right - eous - ness.
Melt | sor - row; | put | false | ways | far | from | my | path.
Keep | me | from | self - ish | gain | and | van - i - ty.

For - sake | us | not; | we | want | to | learn | your | pre - cepts.
I | med - i - tate | up - on | your | per - fect | good - ness.
LORD, | be | my | coun - sel - or | and | pa - tient | teach - er.
Give | me | a - gain | your | gra - cious | un - der - stand - ing.
I | find | de - light | in | keep - ing | your | com - mand - ments.

6   Let steadfast love come ever, LORD, to me;
   send your salvation even as you promised.
      Then I can answer those who challenge me.
   I speak the truth when I uphold your precepts;
   your word gives confidence and liberty.
   I'm not ashamed to cherish your commandments.

7   Your word renews my life and gives me hope;
   it offers strength and comfort in affliction.
      I shall not turn my heart against your will.
   Hot indignation seizes my emotions
   when I see those who scorn your ancient laws.
   Your statutes fill my pilgrimage with singing.

8   You are my portion, LORD; I come to you
   with firm obedience and with bold entreaties:
      be merciful according to your word.
   I hasten and do not delay my footsteps.
   Though wicked bind with ropes, I will obey.
   I join with those who know your love and goodness.

Psalm 119 continued on following page

Psalm 119: stanzas 9–15

9 You have dealt well with me, your ser - vant, LORD;
10 Your hands have made and fash - ioned me, O LORD.
11 My soul grows faint— when will you com - fort me?
12 Your word, O LORD, is firm - ly fixed in heaven.

now give me wis - dom to re - spond up - right - ly.
Let those who fear you see in me your good - ness,
My eyes are tired from look - ing for your mer - cy.
Your faith - ful - ness en - dures through gen - er - a - tions.

I went a - stray but now would keep your law.
for I have put my trust in your com - mands.
I am a use - less wine - skin in the smoke.
You made the earth; it waits up - on your will.

The god - less smear my name with lies and slan - der.
When I have suf - fered, you have not been ab - sent.
How long be - fore you pun - ish those who harm me?
If I had not ac - knowl-edged your com - mand - ments,

Hearts filled with hate, their words are edged with gold.
Your faith - ful - ness is my de - light and stay.
Save me, O God, from those who seek my life,
the wick - ed sure - ly would have cut me off.

Bet - ter by far are all your words and stat - utes.
Let all who seek you heed your tes - ti - mo - nies.
for e - ven in dis - tress I love your pre - cepts.
I pon - der all your good and per - fect pre - cepts.

13 Oh, how I love your law, my God and King!
By day and night it is my meditation.
It makes me wise, it is my constant friend.
Sweeter than honey are your words and precepts;
sweet to my taste the laws that you have made—
they give new joy and turn me from false pathways.

14 Your statutes are a lamp to guide my feet,
your righteous laws a light upon my pathway.
Illumine me according to your word.
Accept my praise, O LORD; teach me your precepts.
Though wicked foes set snares to catch my feet,
may your word be my heritage forever.

15 I hate, O LORD, all those with double minds,
but love your law and know it will uphold me.
You are my hiding place and my defense.
Depart from me, you cunning evil doers;
you are as dross in God's refining fire.
He treasures those who follow his commandments.

Psalm 119 continued on following page

16 What I have done is just and right, O God.
17 Your law, O LORD, gives light and life to all,
18 Right - eous and just are all your stat - utes, LORD;
19 With my whole heart I call to you, O LORD;

Do not a - ban - don me to my op - pres - sors;
and to the sim - ple it gives un - der - stand - ing.
your prom - is - es have all been prov - en faith - ful.
an - swer me, save me, hear my voice of weep - ing.

be to your ser - vant cer - tain - ty for good.
With o - pen mouth I pant for your com - mands.
I am dis - tressed when foes for - get your law.
I rise be - fore the dawn and cry for help.

Act now a - gainst all those who break your stat - utes.
Keep my pace stead - y; shine your eyes up - on me.
I am de - spised and low - ly, full of an - guish;
I med - i - tate through - out the long night watch - es.

I hate the paths of those who shun the truth;
Teach me your law; be gra - cious un - to me.
yet I do not for - get your right - eous - ness.
LORD, in your gra - cious judg - ment quick - en me,

more than fine gold I cher - ish your com - mand - ments.
My eyes shed tears be - cause your law is bro - ken.
Grant me the grace to stand and walk up - right - ly.
for your com-mands are light and truth for - ev - er.

20   From my affliction, LORD, deliver me;
     defend my cause and save me from destruction.
         Renew my life according to your word.
     Salvation is denied to those who hate you,
         but those who seek your justice will be blest.
     LORD, grant me mercy, for I love your precepts.

21   When rulers persecute without a cause,
     my heart remembers all your words of promise,
         as one who, finding treasure, stands amazed.
     Seven times a day I praise you for your justice.
         Great peace have those who love your law, O God;
     they cannot stumble if they do your bidding.

22   O let my cry be heard by you, O LORD.
     My lips will speak your praise and sing your goodness.
         Be ready with your hand to strengthen me.
     Like a lost sheep I long for restoration.
         O let me live to sing your praises, LORD.
     Your law delights me; LORD, be my salvation.

120

In My Distress I Cry to God

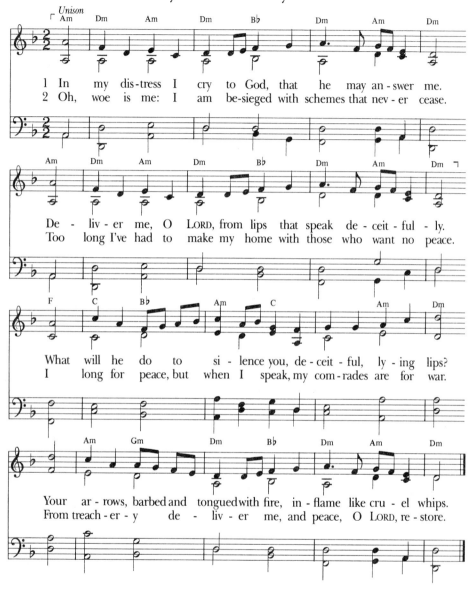

1 In my dis-tress I cry to God, that he may an-swer me.
2 Oh, woe is me: I am be-sieged with schemes that nev-er cease.

De - liv-er me, O LORD, from lips that speak de-ceit-ful - ly.
Too long I've had to make my home with those who want no peace.

What will he do to si - lence you, de-ceit-ful, ly - ing lips?
I long for peace, but when I speak, my com-rades are for war.

Your ar - rows, barbed and tongued with fire, in - flame like cru - el whips.
From treach-er - y de - liv - er me, and peace, O LORD, re - store.

Text: Psalm 120; vers. Clarence P. Walhout, 1982. © 1987, CRC Publications
Tune: Kentucky Harmony, 1816; harm. Songs for Liturgy and More Hymns and Spiritual Songs, 1971

CMD
SALVATION

To the Hills I Lift My Eyes

1 To the hills I lift my eyes; whence shall help for
2 Your pro - tec - tor is the LORD; shade for you he

me a - rise? From the LORD comes all my aid,
will af - ford. Nei - ther sun nor moon shall smite;

who the heavens and earth has made. He will guard through
God shall guard by day and night. He will ev - er

dan - gers all, will not let you slip or fall. He who
keep your soul; what would harm he will con - trol. In the

safe his peo - ple keeps nev - er slum - bers, nev - er sleeps.
home and by the way God will keep you day by day.

Text: Psalm 121; vers. Psalter, 1912, alt.
Tune: Marcus M. Wells, 1858
Other settings of Psalm 121: 180, 448

77 77 D
GUIDE

122   I Was Glad They Came to Call Me

1 I was glad they came to call me, "Let us
2 Let us pray for good in Zi - on: "May those

go to where God rests." O Je - ru - sa -
lov - ing you find peace. Let your dwell - ers

lem, we praise you; here we stand, your pil - grim guests.
live se - cure - ly; may their health and strength in - crease."

Text: Psalm 122; vers. Calvin Seerveld, 1982, ©
Tune: Johann Schop, 1600–1665; harm. after Johann S. Bach, 1685–1750, from Cantata 147

87 87 D
JESU JOY

Love - ly meet - ing place for wor - ship, sign to
On be - half of all your peo - ple, hear my

Is - rael of God's trust: thank you, LORD, for
plea, "God's will be done." Since the LORD God

Da - vid's cit - y, where the judg - ments all are just.
lives a - mong us, I will pray, "Your king - dom come."

123   To You, O Lord, I Lift My Eyes

1 To you, O Lord, I lift my eyes, to you en-throned a-
2 O Lord our God, your mer-cy show, for hu-man pride and

bove the skies. As ser-vants watch their mas-ter's hand,
scorn we know. Re-proach and shame your saints en-dure

or maid-ens by their mis-tress stand, so to the Lord our
from sin-ners who ap-pear se-cure. To you, O Lord, I

eyes we raise, un-til his mer-cy he dis-plays.
lift my eyes, to you en-throned a-bove the skies.

Text: Psalm 123; vers. Psalter, 1912, alt.
Tune: Hughes M. Huffman, 1976. © 1976, InterVarsity Christian Fellowship of the USA.
Used by permission of InterVarsity Press.

88 88 88
SARAH

If God the LORD Were Not Our Constant Help   124

1 If God the LORD were not our con - stant help—
2 Praise to the LORD God, who did not for - sake—

if God the LORD would leave us all a - lone—
we slipped like birds free from the hunt - er's trap!

then an - gry foes would swal - low us a - live!
God did not let their teeth tear us like prey—

En - gulfed by hate, we would be tossed and drowned!
the trap is smashed! Yes, we a - lone es - caped!

Yes, with - out God we would be sure to die.
Our help is in the name of God the LORD.

Text: Psalm 124; vers. Calvin Seerveld, 1981, ©
Tune: Genevan Psalter, 1551; harm. Dale Grotenhuis, 1985. Harmonization © 1987, CRC Publications

10 10 10 10 10
GENEVAN 124

125 All Who, with Heart Confiding

1 All who, with heart con - fid - ing, de - pend on God a - lone,
2 No scep - ter of op - pres - sion shall hold un - bro - ken sway,
3 All those who e - vil cher - ish, for - sak - ing truth and right,

like Zi - on's mount a - bid - ing, shall not be o - ver - thrown.
lest un - to base trans - gres - sion the right-eous turn a - way.
with wick - ed ones shall per - ish; God will their sin re - quite.

Like Zi - on's cit - y, bound - ed by guard-ing moun - tains broad,
Your fa - vor be im - part - ed to god - ly peo - ple, LORD;
From sin your saints de - fend - ing, their joy, O LORD, in - crease,

his peo - ple are sur - round - ed for - ev - er by their God.
bless all that are pure - heart - ed, the good with good re - ward.
with mer - cy nev - er end - ing and ev - er - last - ing peace.

Text: Psalm 125; vers. Psalter, 1912, alt.
Tune: Charles H. Gabriel, 1856–1932, alt.

76 76 D
KNOWHEAD

When God Brought Zion's Remnant Band 126

1 When God brought Zi-on's rem-nant band back to the land, we felt like
2 Please bless our new be-gin-nings, Lord, as you re-filled the Neg-ev's

we were dream - ing. Why, e - ven un - be - liev - ers
dried - out ba - sin; so those who suf - fered sow - ing

said, "The Lord has led with might - y works, re - deem - ing."
seed will now be freed to reap with deep e - la - tion.

Come, laugh for joy! our songs em-ploy— the Lord has won, great
Who sows with tears, but per - se - veres, comes home a - gain with

things be - gun, has filled our lives with mean - ing!
sheaves of grain, sur - prised by God's sal - va - tion.

Text: Psalm 126; vers. Calvin Seerveld, 1985, ©
Tune: J. Klug's Geistliche Lieder, 1535; harm. Dale Grotenhuis, 1985.
Harmonization © 1987, CRC Publications

847 847 887
MAG ICH UNGLÜCK

127   If God Does Not Build Up the House

1 If God does not build up the house, the build-ers la - bor
2 The LORD re-stores his folk with sleep. God gives us chil-dren

hard in vain. If God the LORD does not stand guard, your
to make sure that god - ly par - ents shall be spared when

cit - y watch-men can - not save. Ear - ly to work and
ad - ver - sar - ies crowd the door. Strong sons and daugh-ters

late to rest will prof - it you but wea - ri - ness.
raised in faith be - come like ar - rows from the LORD.

Text: Psalm 127; vers. Calvin Seerveld, 1980, ©
Tune: John Stainer, 1875

88 88 88
CREDO

How Blest Are All the People

1 How blest are all the peo - ple who fear and trust the LORD.
2 Yes, God will bless the peo - ple who glad - ly serve the LORD.

Your faith - ful work will bring you rich fruit as your re - ward.
From heav - en may he pros - per your days with rich re - ward,

Rich as a bud - ding vine - yard your wife will grace the home;
so that your hap - py eyes see the new Je - ru - sa - lem

like ol - ive shoots your chil - dren will grow both wise and strong.
and see your chil - dren's chil - dren! Sha - lom be rich on them.

Text: Psalm 128; vers. Calvin Seerveld, 1981, ©
Tune: Genevan Psalter, 1543; harm. Claude Goudimel, 1564, alt.

13 13 13 13
GENEVAN 128

129 Those Hating Zion Have Afflicted Me

1 Those hat - ing Zi - on have af - flict - ed me—
2 The plow - er gouged long fur - rows down my back,
3 May they be like the grass on house - tops sown,

let Is - rael say, "Yes, e - ven from my youth."
but from the scourge the LORD has set me free.
left there to with - er, nev - er reaped or stored.

Yet they have not pre - vailed a - gainst God's own,
He cut the cords and turned them all a - side.
No friend in pass - ing shall in greet - ing say,

his cov - enant ones who wor - ship him in truth.
Those hat - ing Zi - on on - ly shame will see.
"To you the rich - est bless - ings of the LORD."

Text: Psalm 129; vers. Marie J. Post, 1985. © 1987, CRC Publications
Tune: Erik Routley, 1943. © 1977, Hope Publishing Co. All rights reserved. Used by permission.

10 10 10 10
CLIFF TOWN

Out of the Depths I Cry, LORD

1 Out of the depths I cry, LORD. O Lord, please hear my call.
2 My hope is in the LORD's word, and for the Lord I wait

Let your ears be at - ten - tive; I beg for mer - cy, LORD.
more ea - ger - ly than watch - men yearn for the morn - ing light.

If you marked our of - fens - es, O Lord, who then could stand?
Hope in the LORD, O peo - ple, in his un - fail - ing love.

But you grant us for - give - ness; there - fore we stand in awe.
With him is full re - demp - tion; he will re - deem his own.

Text: Psalm 130; vers. Robert D. Swets, 1981. © 1987, CRC Publications
Tune: Genevan Psalter, 1539; harm. Claude Goudimel, 1564
Another setting of Psalm 130: 256

76 76 D
GENEVAN 130

131

LORD, My Heart Is Humbled Now

1 LORD, my heart is hum - bled now: I have stopped my haugh - ty frown, curbed my dreams to fit my gifts; yes, at last I have calmed down.

2 Like a child near moth - er's breast I have found con - tent - ment, rest. All God's folk, hope in the LORD; soon God's rule will be re - stored.

Text: Psalm 131; vers. Calvin Seerveld, 1982, ©
Tune: attr. Martin Herbst, 1676

77 77
AUS DER TIEFE

132

God of Jacob, Please Remember

1 God of Ja - cob, please re - mem - ber Da - vid vowed to

2 When God's foot - stool was dis - cov - ered left in Eph - ra -

3 Nev - er leave whom you a - noint - ed; LORD, take care of

4 God the LORD has cho - sen Zi - on for his dwell - ing

5 "Here in Da - vid's roy - al cit - y I will make a

Text: Psalm 132; vers. Calvin Seerveld, 1983, ©
Tune: William P. Rowlands, 1915

87 87 D
BLAENWERN

give his due, and he suf - fered man - y trou - bles when he
thah a - lone, we re - solved to march and wor - ship with the
▶ Da - vid's line. Yes, the LORD has sworn to Da - vid, gra - cious-
place and throne: "I will rest here now for - ev - er, where I
branch to sprout and pre - pare for the Mes - si - ah light to

made his oath to you: "I will not en - joy my lei - sure,
ark that we had known. "Rise, O LORD, and choose the cit - y
▶ ly has given a sign: "I will build a roy - al house-hold
longed to make my home. I will bless the ho - ly cit - y,
lead the true de - vout. En - e - mies of my a - noint - ed

close my eyes in sleep ca - ressed, till I build the
where your ark of strength shall rest. Clothe your priests with
▶ from the child you brought to birth; if your chil - dren
feed its poor and give them place; I will dress its
I will shame with sure dis - grace. God's a - noint - ed

LORD a tem - ple where the Might - y One may rest."
ho - ly ser - vice; let our joy be man - i - fest."
▶ keep my cov - enant, they will al - ways rule the earth."
priest - ly ser - vants with the clothes of sav - ing grace.
shines with judg - ment!" Make us, LORD, a rest - ing place.

133 Behold, How Good, How Pleasant Is the Union

1 Be - hold, how good, how pleas - ant is the u - nion
2 It is as if re - fresh - ing dew from Her - mon

when broth - ers, sis - ters live in sweet com - mu - nion
were fall - ing like a rain up - on Mount Zi - on,

and serve the LORD in cheer - ful - ness. It is like pre - cious
when God his ben - e - dic - tion sends. The LORD his boun - teous

oil on Aa - ron's head, which on his beard and priest - ly
bless - ings will re - lease on those who live in u - ni -

robe would spread, a - noint - ing him to ho - li - ness.
ty and peace; God gives them life that nev - er ends.

Text: Psalm 133; vers. Bert Polman, 1986
Tune: Louis Bourgeois, 1551; harm. Howard Slenk, 1985
Text and harmonization © 1987, CRC Publications
Another setting of Psalm 133: 514

11 11 8 10 10 8
GENEVAN 133

You Servants of the LORD Our God

1 You ser - vants of the LORD our God who work and
2 The LORD God bless you from his throne, the LORD show

pray both day and night, in God's own house lift
you his gra - cious face. He who cre - at - ed

up your hands and praise the LORD with all your might.
heaven and earth give you his ev - er - last - ing peace.

Text: Psalm 134; vers. Calvin Seerveld, 1981, ©
Tune: Louis Bourgeois, 1551

LM
GENEVAN 134 (OLD HUNDREDTH)

Psalm 134: Alternative harmonization with melody in the tenor

1 You   ser - vants of   the   LORD   our   God   who   work and
2 The   LORD God bless you   from   his   throne, the   LORD show

pray both   day   and   night, in   God's own house lift   up
you his   gra - cious   face. He   who   cre - at - ed   heaven

your   hands and   praise the   LORD with   all   your might.
and   earth give   you   his   ev - er - last - ing   peace.

Text: Psalm 134; vers. Calvin Seerveld, 1981, ©
Tune: Louis Bourgeois, 1551; harm. John Dowland, 1621, alt.

LM
GENEVAN 134 (OLD HUNDREDTH)

Sing Praise to the LORD God Almighty 135

1 Sing praise to the LORD God Al-might-y, pro-claim all his
2 Give praise to the LORD for his good-ness; 'tis pleas-ant his
3 I know that the LORD is al-might-y; su-preme in do-
4 His hand guides the clouds in their cours-es; the light-ning flames
5 To ran-som his peo-ple from bond-age, great won-ders and

glo-ry a-broad. O praise him, you ser-vants ap-
prais-es to sing. His peo-ple, his cho-sen and
min-ion is he, per-form-ing his will and good
forth at his will. The wind and the rain he re-
signs he dis-played. He smote all the first-born of

point-ed to stand in the house of our God.
pre-cious, your prais-es with grat-i-tude bring.
plea-sure in heaven, on the earth, in the sea.
leas-es his sov-ereign de-signs to ful-fill.
E-gypt, till Pha-raoh gave in and o-beyed.

6 Great nations and kings that opposed him
were smitten by God's mighty hand.
Their riches he gave to his people;
he made them inherit the land.

7 The name of the LORD stands forever,
through all generations renowned.
The LORD brings relief to his people;
his mercies forever abound.

8 The idols of gold and of silver
can speak not nor listen nor see.
Their makers shall also be helpless;
like them shall their worshipers be.

9 Praise God, every son, every daughter;
in worship your gladness proclaim.
His servants, and all you who fear him,
sing praise to his glorious name.

Text: Psalm 135; vers. Psalter, 1912, alt.
Tune: George C. Stebbins, 1846–1945
Another setting of Psalm 135: 181

98 98
JANET

136   Let Us with a Gladsome Mind

1 Let us with a glad-some mind   praise the LORD, for he is kind. Sound a - gain his name a - broad, for of gods he is the God.

2 Lord of lords he rules a - bove,   show - ing us his power and love: for his mer - cies shall en - dure, ev - er faith - ful, ev - er sure.

3 Heavens and earth with seas he made;   still his won - ders are dis - played. He, with all - com - mand-ing might, filled his new - made world with light—

4 sun to stride a - cross the day,   moon and stars in vast ar - ray: for his mer - cies shall en - dure, ev - er faith - ful, ev - er sure.

5 He with thunder-clasping hand
smote the sons of Egypt land,
split the Red Sea floods in two,
guided Israel safely through.

6 He brought walls of water down,
made the hosts of Pharaoh drown:
for his mercies shall endure,
ever faithful, ever sure.

7 Flowing springs and manna blessed
Israel in the wilderness.
Og and Sihon, heathen kings,
found what wicked action brings.

8 Then the land of heavy yoke
God gave to his chosen folk:
for his mercies shall endure,
ever faithful, ever sure.

9 He remembered us when low,
rescued us from every foe.
His love feeds all living things,
shelters them beneath his wings.

10 Let us, then, with thankful mind,
praise the LORD, for he is kind:
for his mercies shall endure,
ever faithful, ever sure.

Text: Psalm 136; vers. John Milton, 1623; rev. Marie J. Post, 1985. © 1987, CRC Publications
Tune: Genevan Psalter, 1562; harm. Claude Goudimel, 1564
Alternative tune: MONKLAND, 223
Another setting of Psalm 136: 182

77 77
GENEVAN 136

Babylon Streams Received Our Tears

1 Bab - y - lon streams re - ceived our tears: Zi - on, the
2 Our cap - tors laughed, "Per - form your praise! Mer - ri - ly
3 So help us, God, you may de - stroy our work - ing
4 Re - mem - ber, LORD, the aw - ful day vi - o - lent
5 God give you e - vil for re - ward. Blest be the

ho - ly cit - y, gone. Ex - iles, we cried be -
dance, Je - ru - sa - lem!" How could we chant the
▸ hands if we de - ny— strike our mouths mute if
E - dom cursed your folk: "Bab - y - lon, break Je -
one who brings your fall. Bab - y - lon great— your

neath the trees. Harps hung in si - lence man - y years.
LORD God's songs while we were crushed by hea - thens' ways?
▸ we ne - glect to make your cit - y our chief joy.
ru - sa - lem! Raze to the ground, strip her a - way!"
seed be smashed! Ven - geance shall come from God our LORD.

Text: Psalm 137; vers. Calvin Seerveld, 1982, ©
Tune: Griffith Hugh Jones, 1890

LM
LLEF

138 With All My Heart I Thank You, LORD

1 With all my heart I thank you, LORD. I wor - ship
2 The kings of earth shall praise you, LORD. They all have
3 When I must walk a trou - bled way, when I am

you with song and prais - ing. Be - fore the "gods" I
heard your won - drous sto - ry. Now they will sing what
weak, O LORD, re - vive me. Stretch out your hand a -

bless your name and praise you for your love un - fail - ing.
they have heard: "Great is the LORD and great his glo - ry."
gainst all hate. From sin and all things harm - ful save me.

Your stead - fast love, your faith - ful - ness, your name, your
The LORD is high in maj - es - ty, yet he re -
Your right hand gives me vic - to - ry. Work in my

Text: Psalm 138; vers. Stanley Wiersma, 1981
Tune: Genevan Psalter, 1551; harm. Dale Grotenhuis, 1985
Text and harmonization © 1987, CRC Publications
Another setting of Psalm 138: 183

89 89 D
GENEVAN 138

word are high ex - alt - ed. The day I cried, you
spects the meek and low - ly. The LORD is high in
life your full in - ten - tion. Your stead - fast love can

an - swered me. Your strength has made my soul un - daunt - ed.
maj - es - ty; he keeps his dis - tance from the haugh - ty.
nev - er die. Bring what you start - ed to per - fec - tion.

Psalm 138: Alternative harmonization with melody in the tenor

Tune: *Genevan Psalter, 1551; harm. Claude Goudimel, 1564*

89 89 D
GENEVAN 138

139 LORD, You Have Searched My Life and Know

1 LORD, you have searched my life and know each move I make, each
2 Where can I hide, where can I flee? There is no place you
3 You formed me in my moth-er's womb, you braid-ed me with
4 O LORD, de - stroy the vi - o - lent who speak of you with

step I go; my half - framed talk, my in - most thought— you
do not see. No dis - tant grave, no for - eign place can
awe - some care; my flesh, my un - formed bones grew there in -
ill in - tent. I shrink from those who hate your name, from

watch and note my to - tal walk. Your hand keeps hold of
bar me from your strong em - brace. I can - not be ob -
vis - i - ble, yet seen by you. Your won - ders make me
en - e - mies who feel no shame. LORD, search my heart, teach

me al - ways; your knowl - edge leaves me mute, a - mazed.
scured by night: your Spir - it pierc - es dark with light.
catch my breath, sur - round - ing me in life, in death.
me, I pray, to walk the ev - er - last - ing way.

Text: Psalm 139; vers. Calvin Seerveld, 1985, ©
Tune: John Bishop, 1711; harm. Harry E. Wooldridge, 1845–1917
Another setting of Psalm 139: 184

88 88 88
LEICESTER

Deliver Me from Evil

Unison

1 De - liv - er me from e - vil; de - fend me, LORD, from wrong.
2 O LORD, I have con-fessed you to be my God a - lone.
3 Let their own e - vil strike them and cause their o - ver - throw,

The vi - o - lent have gath-ered, with poi - son on their tongue.
Now hear my cry for mer - cy and make your pow - er known.
so that the poor see jus - tice when e - vil is brought low.

From those who plot to hurt me or catch me in their snare,
O sov - ereign LORD and Sav - ior, my ar - mor in the strife,
The right - eous will sing prais - es, pro-claim your name and grace;

pro - tect me, LORD, and keep me safe-guard - ed in your care.
let not the wick - ed tri - umph who wish to take my life.
the up - right will live safe - ly with - in your sure em - brace.

Text: Psalm 140; vers. Psalter, 1912; rev. Bert Witvoet, 1985. © 1987, CRC Publications
Tune: John Ness Beck, 1977. © 1977, Hope Publishing Co. All rights reserved. Used by permission.
Alternative tune: MUNICH, 279

76 76 D
ACCEPTANCE

141   O LORD, Come Quickly; Hear Me Pray

1 O LORD, come quick - ly; hear me pray with lift - ed
2 Guard lips and heart, with - out, with - in, so that I
3 O right - eous LORD, your chas - tise - ment, through friend or
4 When e - vil deeds dis - rupt my days, my prayers con -
5 Keep me from traps that sin - ners set; may they be

hands at close of day. May all my eve - ning
do not rel - ish sin. LORD, let my foot - steps
▸ foe, in love is sent. Though griev - ous, it will
demn those e - vil ways. The wick - ed heed my
caught in their own net. Though I am bur - dened

prayers a - rise like in - cense from the sac - ri - fice.
nev - er stray where e - vil - do - ers point the way.
▸ prof - it me; a heal - ing oint - ment it will be.
words too late, when they are faced with death's dark gate.
and dis - tressed, I look, O LORD, to you for rest.

Text: Psalm 141; vers. Marie J. Post, 1985. © 1987, CRC Publications
Tune: Henry Baker, 1854

LM
QUEBEC

Hear My Cry and Supplication

1 Hear my cry and sup - pli - ca - tion; LORD, I
2 When my path is filled with dan - gers, no one
3 LORD, I am op - pressed and low - ly; I de -
4 When you lead me from this pris - on, right - eous

pour out my com - plaint. Heed my tale of
comes to res - cue me. When I am en -
pend up - on your care. Save me now, O
friends will gath - er round. When from depths I

trib - u - la - tion; lead the way when I am faint.
snared by strang - ers, no one comes to set me free.
God most ho - ly, hear me in my deep de - spair.
have a - ris - en, I will make your praise re - sound.

Text: Psalm 142; vers. Clarence P. Walhout, 1982. © 1987, CRC Publications
Tune: Johann Crüger, 1649; adapt. Service Book and Hymnal, 1958

87 87
HERR, ICH HABE MISGEHANDELT

143   LORD, Hear My Prayer, My Supplication

1 LORD, hear my prayer, my sup-pli-ca-tion; in truth and
2 O LORD, the en-e-my pur-sues me; my life lies
3 When I re-mem-ber days of old, LORD, I med-i-
4 Make haste, O LORD, and give your an-swer. My spir-it

right-eous-ness, now an-swer. But do not judge your
bro-ken where I've fall-en. I know the dark-ness
tate on all your do-ings, on all the works your
fails; do not for-sake me, or I will be like

ser-vant, LORD, for who could stand be-fore your
of the grave. There-fore my spir-it faints with-
hands have wrought. I stretch my hands out to im-
those who die. Let morn-ing bring your lov-ing-

judg-ment? No one is right-eous in your sight.
in me; my heart with-in me is dis-mayed.
plore you: my soul thirsts like a des-ert land.
kind-ness, for I have put my trust in you.

5 Teach me to walk where you have led me,
   for I lay all my cares before you.
   Deliver me from all my foes,
   for I have fled to you for refuge.
   You are my God: teach me your will.

6 May your good Spirit lead me safely.
   For your name's sake, O LORD, protect me;
   in righteousness preserve my life.
   In love destroy all those who hate me:
   I am a servant of the LORD.

Text: Psalm 143; vers. James Vanden Bosch, 1981   99 898
Tune: Genevan Psalter, 1539; harm. Howard Slenk, 1985   GENEVAN 143
Text and harmonization © 1987, CRC Publications

All Praise to the Lord

1 All praise to the LORD, who pre - pares me to fight;
2 O LORD, part the heav - ens, reach down from on high;
3 I'll sing a new song on a harp of ten strings.
4 Our chil - dren will blos - som in beau - ty and grace.

for he is my for - tress, the rock of my might.
touch moun - tains with smoke, flash your fire in the sky.
LORD, you are the One who gives vic - tory to kings.
Our barns will be filled, sheep and cat - tle in - crease.

LORD, why care for mor - tals, whose brief earth - ly stay
LORD, save me from those who deal on - ly in lies;
Your hand keeps me safe from the foes' dead - ly sword.
No cry of dis - tress in our streets will be heard.

is like fleet - ing shad - ows, soon pass - ing a - way?
their hands are de - ceit - ful, your ways they de - spise.
De - liv - er me from the de - ceit - ful, O LORD.
How bless - ed the peo - ple whose God is the LORD!

Text: Psalm 144; vers. Helen Otte, 1985. © 1987, CRC Publications
Tune: Welsh, from Caniadau y Cyssegr, *1839*

11 11 11 11
ST. DENIO

145 I Will Exalt My God and King

Introduction

Unison

1 I will ex - alt my God and King, and I will
2 On your most glo - rious maj - es - ty and on your
3 The LORD our God is rich in grace, ten - der to
4 All you have made will praise you, LORD; your might - y

ev - er praise your name. I will ex - tol you ev - ery
deeds my mind will dwell. Your deeds will fill the world with
us, com - pas - sion - ate. His an - ger is most slow to
acts your saints will show, till all the peo - ples on the

day and ev - er - more your praise pro - claim. You, LORD, are
awe, and all your great - ness I will tell. Your match-less
rise; his love and kind - ness are most great. The LORD is
earth the splen-dor of your king - dom know. E - ter - nal

great - ly to be praised; your great-ness is be - yond all
good - ness and your grace your peo - ple will com - mem - o -
good in all his ways; his crea-tures know his con-stant
is your king - dom, LORD, for - ev - er strong and ev - er

Text: Psalm 145; vers. Psalter, 1912, alt.
Tune: C. Hubert H. Parry, 1916; arr. Janet Wyatt, 1977. © 1916, 1944, 1977, Roberton Publications.
Reprinted by permission of the publisher, Theodore Presser Co., sole representative, U.S.A.
Other settings of Psalm 145: 185, 186

LMD
JERUSALEM

thought. From age to age your peo - ple tell the might - y
rate; and all your truth and right-eous - ness our joy - ful
care. To all his works his love ex - tends; all crea - tures
sure; while gen - er - a - tions rise and die, your glo - rious

Interlude

won - ders you have wrought.
song will cel - e - brate.
in his mer - cies share.
reign will still en - dure.

Final ending

5 The LORD is faithful to his word;
   he will extend his gracious hand.
The LORD upholds the faltering feet
   and makes the weak securely stand.
The eyes of all look up to you
   for food and drink, which you supply;
your open hand is bountiful,
   and every need you satisfy.

6 The LORD is just in all his ways;
   in all his works the LORD is kind,
and all who call on him in truth
   in him a present helper find.
He will fulfill the heart's desire
   of those who fear him and obey.
The LORD will surely hear their cry,
   will save them when to him they pray.

7 The LORD in grace preserves his saints,
   redeeming those who love his name.
The wicked he will overthrow
   and put his enemies to shame.
My mouth will sing the glorious praise
   of God, whom earth and heaven adore.
Let every creature praise his name
   forever and forevermore!

146

Praise the LORD! Sing Hallelujah!

1 Praise the LORD! Sing hal - le - lu - jah! Come, our
2 Hap - py is the one who choos - es Ja - cob's
3 Food he dai - ly gives the hun - gry, sets the
4 Praise the LORD! Sing hal - le - lu - jah! Come, our

great Re - deem - er praise. I will sing the glo - rious
God to be his aid. They are blest whose hope of
mourn-ing pris - oner free, rais - es those bowed down with
great Re - deem - er praise. I will sing the glo - rious

prais - es of my God through all my days. Put no
bless - ing on the LORD their God is stayed. Heaven and
an - guish, makes the sight - less eyes to see. God our
prais - es of my God through all my days. O - ver

Text: Psalm 146; vers. Psalter, 1887, alt.
Tune: Lowell Mason, 1839

87 87 D
RIPLEY

Sing Praise to Our Creator

1 Sing praise to our Cre - a - tor. How good his name to praise! God bless - es all his peo - ple in count - less lov - ing ways. He builds the walls of

2 He num - bers stars and plan - ets, gives each a name and place. How wide and deep his pow - er through all of time and space! He lifts the meek to

3 With clouds God fills the heav - ens; he sends the wel - come rain. The slopes and hills are fer - tile with spring - ing grass and grain. God feeds the beasts and

4 Ex - tol the LORD, O Zi - on: he bless - es you with peace. He bless - es all your chil - dren; his gra - cious gifts in - crease. He speaks and makes the

5 He speaks to all his peo - ple; they know his law and word. No oth - er land is fa - vored, nor is their con - science stirred. Let all who know his

Text: Psalm 147; vers. Marie J. Post, 1985. © 1987, CRC Publications
Tune: John B. Dykes, 1877
Another setting of Psalm 147: 187

76 76 D
HARTFORD

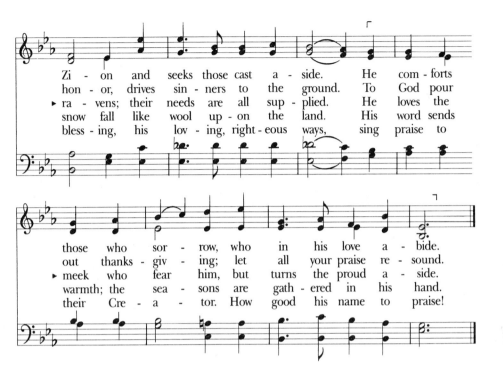

Zi - on and seeks those cast a - side. He com - forts
hon - or, drives sin - ners to the ground. To God pour
ra - vens; their needs are all sup - plied. He loves the
snow fall like wool up - on the land. His word sends
bless - ing, his lov - ing, right - eous ways, sing praise to

those who sor - row, who in his love a - bide.
out thanks - giv - ing; let all your praise re - sound.
meek who fear him, but turns the proud a - side.
warmth; the sea - sons are gath - ered in his hand.
their Cre - a - tor. How good his name to praise!

148   Praise the Lord! O Heavens, Adore Him

1 Praise the Lord! O heavens, a - dore him; praise him,
2 In the earth let all things praise him: seas and
3 All you na - tions, come be - fore him: earth - ly

an - gels in the height. Sun and moon, re -
all that they con - tain, storm - y winds that
rul - ers and all kings, men and wom - en,

joice be - fore him; praise him, shin - ing stars of
do his plea - sure, hail and light - ning, snow and
par - ents, chil - dren, join with all cre - at - ed

Text: Psalm 148; st. 1 vers. Foundling Hospital Collection, 1796, alt.; st. 2–3 vers. Psalter, 1912, alt.
Tune: Richard Dirksen, 1973. © 1977, Hope Publishing Co. All rights reserved. Used by permission.
Alternative tune: HYFRYDOL, 568
Another setting of Psalm 148: 188

87 87 D
CHRIST CHURCH: SYDNOR

light. Praise the LORD, for he has spo - ken; worlds his
rain. Hills and moun - tains, praise your Mak - er; praise him,
things. Praise the God of our sal - va - tion, who re -

might - y voice o - beyed. Laws which nev - er shall be
all you flocks and herds. Fields and or - chards, sing his
stores from sin and shame. Heaven and earth and all cre -

bro - ken for their guid - ance he has made.
glo - ry; praise him, creep - ing things and birds.
a - tion, praise and mag - ni - fy his name!

149

Sing Praise to the LORD

Descant

4 For this is God's word: his saints shall not fail,

1 Sing praise to the LORD; come, sing a new song.
2 With tim-brel and harp and joy-ful ac-claim,
3 In glo-ry ex-ult, you saints of the LORD;
4 For this is God's word: his saints shall not fail,

but o-ver the earth their power shall pre-vail.

A - mid all his saints his prais-es pro-long.
with danc-ing and song give praise to his name.
with songs in the night high prais-es ac-cord.
but o-ver the earth their power shall pre-vail.

Text: Psalm 149; vers. Psalter, 1912, alt.
Tune: William Croft, 1708; desc. Alan Gray, 1855–1935

10 10 11 11
HANOVER

All king-doms and na-tions shall yield to their sword—

Let Is - rael be glad in their Mak - er and sing;
For God in his peo - ple his plea - sure will seek,
Go forth in his ser - vice, be strong in his might
All king - doms and na - tions shall yield to their sword—

thus God shows his glo - ry. Sing praise to the LORD!

let all Zi - on's peo - ple re - joice in their King.
with robes of sal - va - tion a - dorn - ing the meek.
to con - quer all e - vil and stand for the right.
thus God shows his glo - ry. Sing praise to the LORD!

150

Hallelu the LORD Our God

1 Hal - le - lu the LORD our God! Praise him in his
2 Praise God with the trum - pet blast! Crash your cym - bals,

ho - ly place. Praise him in the skies he rules; praise him
laugh with dance! Praise with flute, with drums and strings! Ev - ery

for his sov - ereign - ty; praise his o - ver-whelm - ing
crea - ture that has breath, cel - e - brate un - til the

gran - deur. Ev - ery crea-ture far and near, make your joy - ful
earth rings: Hal - le - lu the great I AM! Hal - le - lu the

noise and cheer: hon - or, glo - ry, praise the LORD God!
wor - thy Lamb! Hal - le - lu the LORD our Sav - ior!

Text: Psalm 150; vers. Calvin Seerveld, 1981, ©
Tune: Genevan Psalter, 1562; harm. Dale Grotenhuis, 1985. Harmonization © 1987, CRC Publications
Other settings of Psalm 150: 189, 466, 628

77 778 778
GENEVAN 150

BIBLE
SONGS

151 In the Beginning

1 In the be-gin-ning the whole world was gloom-y; in the be-
2 In the be-gin-ning came clouds, fog, and wa-ter; in the be-
3 In the be-gin-ning good soil was cre-at-ed so that the
4 In the be-gin-ning the stars lit the heav-ens, moon-light at

gin-ning the earth was void. God spoke his word and the
gin-ning came sky a-bove. God spoke his word and the
bush-es and grass could root. In the be-gin-ning came
night and by day the sun, o-ver the land and the

light was cre-at-ed, mar-vel-ous light we have long en-joyed.
wa-ters di-vid-ed; up came the won-der-ful land we love.
blos-som-ing flow-ers, all kinds of trees that can give us fruit.
sea and the shore-line, so that the sea-sons and years could run.

Text: based on Genesis 1; st. 1–6, Hanna Lam, 1966; tr. and st. 7, Sietze Buning, 1982
Tune: Wim ter Burg, 1966; harm. Bert Polman, 1982
Text and music © 1982, Paideia Press

11 9 11 9
IN HET BEGIN

5 In the beginning the birds were sent flying;
   in the beginning God heard their song.
 Fish in the water and beasts on the dry land—
   God made them all, both the weak and strong.

6 In the beginning God chose to make people;
   in the beginning he spoke his word.
 Pleasant and good was our life in creation.
   All things were perfect: so said the LORD.

7 Then our Creator enjoyed his creation;
   each of his creatures he loved and blessed.
 Loving Creator, grant all of your children
   joy in their labor and in their rest.

152   I Will Sing unto the LORD

I will sing un-to the LORD, for he has tri-umphed glo-rious-ly, the horse and rid-er

thrown in-to the sea. I will sing un-to the LORD, for

he has tri-umphed glo-rious-ly, the horse and rid-er thrown in-to the sea.

The LORD, my God, my strength and song, has now be-

come my vic-to-ry. The LORD, my God, my

Text: from the Song of Moses and Miriam, Exodus 15:1–2
Tune: Israeli folk song; harm. Emily R. Brink, 1986. Harmonization © 1987, CRC Publications

PM
TZENA

strength and song, has now be - come my vic - to - ry.

The LORD is God, and I will praise him, our cov - enant

God, and I will ex - alt him. The LORD is God, and

I will praise him, our cov-enant God, and I will ex - alt him!

An optional stanza for use at Easter:

I will sing unto the LORD,
for he has triumphed gloriously:
the grave is empty. Won't you come and see? *Repeat*

The LORD, my God, my strength and song,
has now become my victory. *Repeat*

The LORD is God, and I will praise him,
our covenant God, and I will exalt him. *Repeat*

153 The Ten Commandments

1 My soul, re-call with rev-erent won-der how God a-
2 "I am the LORD, your God and Sov-ereign, who out of
3 "You shall not bow to grav-en i-dols, for I, a
4 "The LORD is God; his name is ho-ly. Do not his
5 "Re-mem-ber, keep the Sab-bath ho-ly, the day God

mid the fire and smoke pro-claimed his ho-ly law with
bond-age set you free, who saved you from the land of
▸ jeal-ous God, your LORD, shall pun-ish sin in those who
ho-li-ness pro-fane. God sure-ly will not hold them
sanc-ti-fied and blessed. Six days you shall do all your

thun-der from Si-nai's moun-tain when he spoke:
E-gypt. Then serve no oth-er gods but me.
▸ hate me, but love all those who keep my Word.
guilt-less who take his ho-ly name in vain.
la-bor, but on the sev-enth you shall rest.

6 "Honor your father and your mother;
obey the LORD your God's command,
that you may dwell secure and prosper
with length of days upon the land.

7 "You shall not hate or kill your neighbor.
Do not commit adultery.
You shall not steal from one another
nor testify untruthfully.

8 "You shall not covet the possessions
your neighbors value as their own;
home, wife or husband, all their treasures
you shall respect as theirs alone."

9 Teach us, LORD God, to love your precepts,
the good commandments of your law.
Give us the grace to keep your statutes
with thankfulness and proper awe.

Text: Exodus 20:1–17; vers. Dewey Westra, 1899–1979; rev. Psalter Hymnal, 1987.
© 1987, CRC Publications
Tune: Genevan Psalter, 1547; harm. Claude Goudimel, 1564, alt.

98 98
LES COMMANDEMENS

Alternative accompaniment with melody in the tenor

1 My soul, re - call with rev - erent won - der how God a -
9 Teach us, LORD God, to love your pre - cepts, the good com -

mid the fire and smoke pro - claimed his ho - ly law with
mand-ments of your law. Give us the grace to keep your

thun - der from Si - nai's moun - tain when he spoke:
stat - utes with thank - ful - ness and prop - er awe.

Text: Exodus 20:1–17; vers. Dewey Westra, 1899–1979; rev. Psalter Hymnal, 1987.
© *1987, CRC Publications*
Tune: Genevan Psalter, 1547; harm. Claude Goudimel, 1564

98 98
LES COMMANDEMENS

154   Be Just in Judgment, Fair to All

1 Be just in judg-ment, fair to all, be-have re-spon-si-bly.
2 Do not dis-tort your neigh-bor's deed or har-bor se-cret hate.
3 No ven-geance is with-in your right; you may not bear a grudge.

De-fer to nei-ther poor nor great: act with in-teg-ri-ty.
Deal o-pen-ly with those at fault so your own life is straight.
But love your neigh-bor as your-self; hear me, the right-eous Judge.

1-2
I am the LORD.

Final ending
I am the LORD!

Text: *Leviticus 19:15–18; vers. Calvin Seerveld, 1985*
Tune: *Calvin Seerveld, 1985; harm. Dale Grotenhuis, 1986*
Text and music © 1987, Calvin Seerveld

86 86 4
TORONTO

155   Love God with All Your Soul and Strength

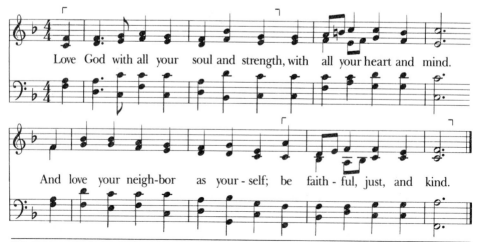

Love God with all your soul and strength, with all your heart and mind.

And love your neigh-bor as your-self; be faith-ful, just, and kind.

Text: *Deuteronomy 6:5; Leviticus 19:18; vers. Isaac Watts, 1715*
Tune: *English, 16th cent.; adapt. Edward Hodges, c. 1835*

CM
FARRANT

The LORD Bless You and Keep You

The LORD bless you and keep you; the LORD lift his
coun-te-nance up-on you and give you
and give you peace,
peace, and give you peace; the LORD make his
and give you peace;
the LORD make his
face to shine up-on you, and be gra - cious un-to
and be gra-cious,
you, be gra-cious, the LORD be gra-cious, gra-cious un-to you.
and be gra-cious,

Text: Numbers 6:24–26
Tune: Peter C. Lutkin, 1900

PM
BENEDICTION

157   Give Ear, O Earth, Attend My Songs

1 Give ear, O earth, at - tend my songs; you
2 When peo - ple serve the gods they make, di -
3 No god gives help like God the LORD, our

heav - ens, hear where praise be - longs. I will pro -
sas - ter fol - lows in their wake. Be - fore God's
ev - er - last - ing shield and sword. God's arms keep

claim God's ho - ly name, and praise our LORD's ma -
eye those god - less die; their i - dols can - not
safe all those with faith, pro - tect - ing them from

jes - tic reign. God is the Rock whose ways are
sat - is - fy. When strength is gone and sin - ners
those who hate. Take cour - age, all in God's em -

just, the cov - enant LORD in whom we trust.
faint, God vin - di - cates the con - trite saint.
brace: your Sav - ior comes with con - quering grace!

Text: from the Song of Moses, Deuteronomy 32:1, 3–4, 34–38; 33:26–29; vers. Calvin Seerveld, 1985, ©
Tune: William Hayes, 1774
Alternative tune: ST. PETERSBURG, 50

88 88 88
NEW 113th

Song of Hannah

1 My soul is filled with joy in God my Sav - ior,
2 All those who talk with pride now see who God is:
3 The strong have fall - en, but the weak are strength-ened;
4 The LORD has set the earth on sure foun - da - tions;

for he has lift - ed me and set me high.
he weighs our deeds and knows our ev - ery word.
those who were hun - gry have e - nough to spare.
help for his saints is found in God a - lone.

There is no Ho - ly One, no Rock like our God;
Proud ones are hum - bled, but the poor are lift - ed;
She who was bar - ren sees her chil - dren's chil - dren;
Those who op - pose the LORD will fall in judg - ment,

he an - swered my re - quest, he heard my cry.
all might and power be - long to God the LORD.
all things are in the LORD's con - trol - ling care.
but he will strength-en his a - noint - ed one.

Text: 1 Samuel 2:1–10; vers. Emily R. Brink, 1986. © 1987, CRC Publications
Tune: Hughes M. Huffman, 1976. © 1976, Hughes M. Huffman, assigned to
  InterVarsity Christian Fellowship of the U.S.A. By permission of InterVarsity Press.

11 10 11 10
VIOLA

159   Lord God of Israel, Come among Us

1 Lord God of Is - ra - el, come a - mong us,
2 Lord God Cre - a - tor, all things tran - scend - ing,
3 When we your peo - ple, sub - dued in bat - tle,
4 Lord, hear the strang - er who comes for bless - ing,

sov - ereign of earth and fir - ma - ment, faith - ful - ly lov - ing the
how small this house we ded - i - cate; yet hear in heav - en our
suf - fer be - cause we've gone a - stray, when we live proud - ly and
so all may know who is the Lord. Re - lease all cap - tives who

old and youn - gest who hear and keep your cov - e - nant.
prayers as - cend - ing, look at the hearts we con - se - crate.
waste your boun - ty, teach us a - gain to walk your way.
are con - fess - ing that they have sinned a - gainst your Word.

Text: Solomon's Prayer of Dedication, 1 Kings 8:23–53; vers. Calvin Seerveld, 1985, ©
Tune: Seelen-Harfe, *Ansbach, 1664; harm.* Psalter Hymnal, *1987*

10 8 10 8 888
LOBE DEN HERREN, O MEINE SEELE

We know your grace ac - com-plish - es   each word of all   your
Al - though we sin,   please, LORD, for - give;   bless our re - pen - tance,
In   sick - ness, trou - ble,   heav - y   care,   re - store us in   this
Since you chose us   your spe - cial   folk,   your last-ing mer - cy

prom - is - es: we praise you, God;   you are the   LORD.
let   us live: we praise you, God;   you are the   LORD.
house   of prayer: we praise you, God;   you are the   LORD.
we   in - voke: we praise you, God;   you are the   LORD.

160 In the Presence of Your People

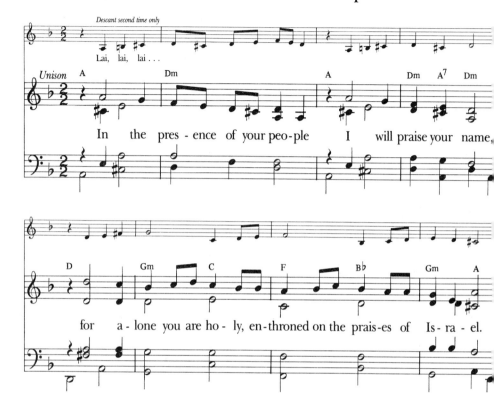

Descant second time only

Lai, lai, lai . . .

Unison

In the pres - ence of your peo-ple I will praise your name,

for a - lone you are ho - ly, en-throned on the prais-es of Is - ra - el.

Text: Psalm 22:3, 22; 145:7; para. Brent Chambers, 1977
Tune: Brent Chambers, 1977

CELEBRATI

Let us cel - e - brate your good - ness   and   your stead - fast love;

may your   name be ex - alt - ed   here   on earth and in heaven a - bove.

161 The LORD's My Shepherd

1 The LORD's my shep - herd; I'll not want. He makes me down to lie in pas - tures green; he lead - eth me the qui - et wa - ters by; he lead - eth me, he lead - eth me the qui - et wa - ters by.

2 My soul he doth re - store a - gain, and me to walk doth make with - in the paths of right - eous - ness, e'en for his own name's sake; with - in the paths of right-eous-ness, e'en for his own name's sake.

3 Yea, though I walk in death's dark vale, yet will I fear no ill; for thou art with me, and thy rod and staff me com - fort still; for thou art with me, and thy rod and staff me com - fort still.

4 My ta - ble thou hast fur - nish - ed in pres - ence of my foes; my head thou dost with oil a - noint, and my cup o - ver - flows; my head thou dost with oil a - noint, and my cup o - ver - flows.

5 Good - ness and mer - cy all my life shall sure - ly fol - low me, and in God's house for - ev - er - more my dwell - ing place shall be; and in God's house for - ev - er - more my dwell-ing place shall be.

Text: Psalm 23; vers. Scottish Psalter, 1650
Tune: J. L. Macbeth Bain, c. 1840–1925; harm. Gordon Jacob, 1934, alt.
Harmonization by permission of Oxford University Press.

86 86 86
BROTHER JAMES' AIR

My Shepherd Is the LORD
El Señor Es Mi Pastor

Refrain

My__ shep-herd is the LORD; noth-ing in-deed shall I want.
El Se-ñor es mi pas - tor; na - da me pue - de fal - tar.

1 The__ LORD__ is my shep-herd; there is noth - ing I want.__
2 The__ LORD re-stores my soul,__ and__ guides me in the right;__

1 El Se-ñor es mi pas - tor.__ ¿Qué me pue - de fal - tar?__
2 El me guí-a en sus sen - de - ros por a - mor__ de su nom-bre.

God__ leads me in green pas-tures and be - side__ qui - et wa - ters.
e - ven though I walk near death,__ noth-ing e - vil shall I fear.__

En pra - de - ras des - cu - bier - tas él me lle-va a des-can - sar.__
aun-que cru - ce a os - cu - ras nin-gún mal__ te - me - ré.__

3 In the sight of my foes
you prepare a feast for me.
You anoint my head with oil,
and my cup overflows.

3 Tú preparas una mesa
frente a mis enemigos;
tú perfumas mi cabeza
y mi copa rebosa.

Text: Psalm 23:1–5; vers. Ricardo Villarreal, 1975; tr. Psalter Hymnal, 1987
Tune: Ricardo Villarreal, 1975; harm. Delbert Asay, 1975

irregular
PASTOR

163 Lift Up Your Heads, O Gates

1 Lift up your heads, O gates; the King of
2 Who is this glo - rious King whose praise the
3 Lift up your heads, O gates; the King of
4 Who is this glo - rious King whose praise the

glo - ry waits. Lift high, O an - cient doors, o - bey;
na - tions sing? The LORD, the Might - y, Ho - ly One,
glo - ry waits. Lift high, O an - cient doors, o - bey;
na - tions sing? The LORD Al-might - y is his name;

Refrain

pre - pare the roy - al way.
whose strength the vic - tory won. Ho - san - na,
pre - pare the roy - al way.
his glo - rious might pro - claim:

ho - san - na! Re - joice, give thanks, and sing!

Text: Psalm 24:7–10; vers. Bert Polman, 1986. © 1987, CRC Publications
Tune: Richard Dirksen, 1974. © 1974, 1987, Harold Flammer, Inc. All rights reserved. Used by permission.

SM with refrain
VINEYARD HAVEN

O Lord, You Are My Light

164

1 O Lord, you are my light and my sal - va - tion near:
2 My one re - quest has been and still this prayer I raise:
3 When trou - bles round me swell, when fears and dan - gers throng,
4 Up - lift - ed on a rock a - bove my foes a - round,

then who will cause me fright or fill my heart with fear?
that I may live with - in God's house for all my days,
se - cure - ly I will dwell in his pa - vil - ion strong.
a - mid the bat - tle shock my song shall still re - sound.

While God my strength, my life sus - tains,
God's glo - rious beau - ty to ad - mire,
With - in the shel - ter of his tent
Then joy - ful of - ferings I will bring;

se - cure from fear my soul re - mains.
and in his tem - ple to in - quire.
he hides me till the storm is spent.
the Lord God's praise my heart shall sing.

Text: Psalm 27:1–6; st. 1 vers. Psalter, 1887; st. 2–4 vers. Psalter, 1912; alt.
Tune: John Goss, 1800–1880; arr. Uzziah C. Burnap, 1874

66 66 88
ARTHUR'S SEAT

165 Send Out Your Light and Your Truth

1 Send out your light and your truth, let them lead me;
2 Lead me, O LORD, in the way ev - er - last - ing;

O let them bring me to your ho - ly hill.
O lead and guide me to your ho - ly hill.

Send out your light and your truth, let them lead me;
Lead me, O LORD, in the way ev - er - last - ing;

O let them bring me to your ho - ly hill.
O lead and guide me to your ho - ly hill.

Text: Psalm 43:3; 139:24; vers. Psalter, 1912
Tune: Charles F. Gounod, 1818–1893

11 10 11 10
LUX FIAT

Clap Your Hands

Text: Psalm 47:1; para. Jimmy Owens, 1972
Tune: Jimmy Owens, 1972; harm. Dale Grotenhuis, 1986
Text and music © 1972, Lexicon Music, Inc. All rights reserved.
International copyright secured. Used by permission.

PM
CLAP YOUR HANDS

167   O God, Be Gracious to Me in Your Love

1 O God, be gra - cious to me in your love,
2 A - gainst you, LORD, you on - ly, have I sinned,
3 Fill me with glad - ness and re - joic - ing, LORD,
4 Drive me not from your pres - ence, gra - cious LORD,

and in your mer - cy par - don my mis - deeds;
and what to you is e - vil have I done;
and let my bro - ken frame know joy once more;
nor keep your Ho - ly Spir - it far from me;

wash me from guilt and cleanse me from my sin,
take hys - sop, sprin - kle me and make me clean,
cre - ate a clean and con - trite heart in me,
re - store my life with your sal - va - tion's joy,

for well I know the e - vil I have done.
wash me and make me whit - er than the snow.
re - new my life in faith - ful - ness and love.
and with a will - ing spir - it strength - en me.

Text: Psalm 51:1–12; vers. Ian Pitt-Watson, 1973, alt., ©
Tune: Orlando Gibbons, 1623
This music in a higher key: 308

10 10 10 10
SONG 24

Zion, Founded on the Mountain

1 Zi - on, found - ed on the moun - tain, God, your
2 Glo - rious things of you are spo - ken, Zi - on,
3 When the LORD shall count the na - tions, sons and

Mak - er, loves you well; he has cho - sen
cit - y of our LORD: peo - ple of all
daugh - ters shall be - long, born to end - less

you most pre - cious, he de - lights in you to dwell;
tribes and na - tions know sal - va - tion from the Word.
life in Zi - on; God him - self will keep them strong.

God's own cit - y, who can all your glo - ry tell?
God Al - might - y shall him - self their names re - cord.
"All my foun - tains are in you!" shall be their song.

Text: Psalm 87; st. 1 vers. Psalter, 1912; st. 2–3 vers. Psalter Hymnal, 1987. © 1987, CRC Publications
Tune: Walter G. Whinfield, 1865–1919; harm. Paul Bunjes, b. 1914.
Harmonization © 1982, Concordia Publishing House. Used by permission.

87 87 47
WORCHESTER

169 I Will Sing of the Mercies of the LORD

1 I will sing of the mer-cies of the LORD for - ev - er, I will
2 All the hosts of the an - gels sing God's praise for - ev - er for the

sing, I will sing. I will sing of the mer-cies of the
things he has done. All the hosts of the an - gels sing God's

LORD for - ev - er, I will sing of the mer-cies of the LORD.
praise for - ev - er, all the hosts of the an - gels sing God's praise.

With my mouth will I make known your faith - ful-ness, your
Who can be com-pared to God in faith - ful-ness, in

Text: Psalm 89:1, 5, 8; st. 1 vers. James H. Fillmore, 1849–1936; st. 2 vers. Marie J. Post, 1983
Tune: James H. Fillmore, 1849–1936

PM
FILLMORE

faith - ful - ness;   with   my   mouth   will   I   make   known   your
faith - ful - ness?   Who   can   be   com-pared   to   God   in

faith - ful - ness to   all   gen - er - a - tions.   I   will   sing   of   the
faith - ful - ness to   all   gen - er - a - tions?   I   will   sing   of   the

mer-cies of the LORD for - ev - er, I   will   sing   of the mer-cies of the LORD.
mer-cies of the LORD for - ev - er, I   will   sing   of the mer-cies of the LORD.

170 O God, Our Help in Ages Past

1 O God, our help in a - ges past, our hope for years to come,
2 un - der the shad-ow of your throne your saints have dwelt se - cure;
3 Be - fore the hills in or - der stood or earth re - ceived its frame,
4 A thou-sand a - ges in your sight are like an eve - ning gone,

our shel - ter from the storm - y blast, and our e - ter - nal home:
suf - fi - cient is your arm a - lone, and our de - fense is sure.
from ev - er - last - ing you are God, to end - less years the same.
short as the watch that ends the night be - fore the ris - ing sun.

5 Time, like an ever-rolling stream,
　　soon bears us all away;
　we fly forgotten, as a dream
　　dies at the opening day.

6 O God, our help in ages past,
　　our hope for years to come,
　still be our guard while troubles last,
　　and our eternal home!

Text: Psalm 90:1–2, 4–5; vers. Isaac Watts, 1719, alt.　　　　CM
Tune: William Croft, 1708　　　　ST. ANNE

Alternative accompaniment

Tune: William Croft, 1708; alt. accomp. David Johnson, in Free Organ Accompaniments to Festival Hymnals,　　CM
Vol. 1, 1963. Alternative accompaniment © 1963, Augsburg Publishing House. Reprinted by permission.　　　ST. ANNE

It Is Good to Sing Your Praises

1 It is good to sing your prais - es and to thank you,
2 You have filled my heart with glad - ness through the works your
3 But the good shall live be - fore you, plant - ed in your

O Most High, show - ing forth your lov - ing - kind - ness
hands have wrought; you have made my life vic - to - rious;
dwell - ing place, fruit - ful trees and ev - er ver - dant,

when the morn - ing lights the sky. It is good when
great your works and deep your thought. You, O Lord, on
nour - ished by your bound - less grace. In his good - ness

night is fall - ing of your faith - ful - ness to tell,
high ex - alt - ed, reign for - ev - er - more in might;
to the right - eous God his right - eous - ness dis - plays;

while with sweet, me - lo - dious prais - es songs of ad - o - ra - tion swell.
all your en - e - mies shall per - ish, sin be ban - ished from your sight.
God, my rock, my strength and ref - uge, just and true are all your ways.

Text: Psalm 92; vers. Psalter, 1912
Tune: J. Leavitt's Christian Lyre, 1831

87 87 D
ELLESDIE

172 The LORD Is King

1 The LORD is King; he reigns in maj - es - ty;
2 The seas have lift - ed up their voice, O LORD;
3 Your stat - utes are for - ev - er fixed and sure;

the LORD is robed and gird - ed up with strength.
the seas have lift - ed up their pound - ing waves.
a - bove the thun - der your de - crees en - dure.

The world shall not be moved; he holds it firm;
Might - ier than thun - dering wa - ters is the LORD;
Hon - or a - dorns your house, O LORD our God;

his throne is fixed from all e - ter - ni - ty.
the LORD is stron - ger than the break - ing sea.
ho - li - ness fills your house for - ev - er - more.

Text: Psalm 93; vers. Clarence P. Walhout, 1982. © 1987, CRC Publications
Tune: Genevan Psalter, 1562; harm. Claude Goudimel, 1564, alt.

10 10 10 10
GENEVAN 93

Come, Sing for Joy to the LORD God

1 Come, sing for joy to the LORD God; make joy - ful
2 The LORD is King o - ver all gods; the earth and
3 Come near to - day: God is speak - ing; o - pen your

nois - es to our King; shout to the Rock of our sal - va - tion!
sea be-long to him; he made the moun-tains and the o - ceans.
hearts to hear his word; do not re - bel a - gainst his fa - vor.

Come and re - joice with thanks-giv - ing; let fes - tive mu - sic
He is our God, we his peo - ple; come, let us wor - ship
God's judg-ment fell in the des - ert on those whose hearts had

fill the air, for God has set us free from bond - age.
and bow down and kneel be - fore the LORD our Mak - er.
gone a - stray; come, find your rest in God, your Sav - ior.

Text: Psalm 95; vers. Psalter Hymnal, 1987
Tune: Genevan Psalter, 1542; harm. Dale Grotenhuis, 1985
Text and harmonization © 1987, CRC Publications

174 Sing a New Song to the LORD God

1 Sing a new song to the LORD God for the won - ders
2 Truth and mer - cy toward his peo - ple he has ev - er
3 Seas and all your full - ness, thun - der, all earth's peo - ples,

he has wrought; his right hand and arm most ho - ly
kept in mind, and his full and free sal - va - tion
now re - joice; floods and hills, in praise u - nit - ing,

tri - umph to his cause have brought. In his love and
he has shown to all man - kind. Sing, O earth, to
to the LORD lift up your voice. For, be - hold, our

Text: Psalm 98; vers. Psalter, 1912, alt.
Tune: Charles V. Pilcher, 1935; harm. Walter MacNutt, 1968, ©

87 87 D
HERMON

ten - der mer - cy   he has made sal - va - tion known;
God sing prais - es,   let your songs of prais - es ring;
God is com - ing,   robed in jus - tice and in might;

in the sight of ev - ery na - tion   he his right-eous - ness has shown.
with the swell-ing notes of mu - sic   shout be - fore the LORD, the King.
he a - lone will judge the na - tions,   and his judg-ment shall be right.

175 Unto God Our Savior

1 Un - to God our Sav - ior sing a joy - ful song;
2 Joy - ful, all you peo - ple, sing be - fore the LORD;
3 Waves of might - y o - cean, earth with full - ness stored,

won - drous are his do - ings, for his arm is strong.
shout and sing his prais - es now in glad ac - cord;
floods and fields and moun - tains, sing be - fore the LORD;

He has wrought sal - va - tion, he has made it known,
with the harp and trum - pet joy - ful prais - es bring;
for he comes with jus - tice, e - vil to re - dress,

and be - fore the na - tions is his jus - tice shown.
come, re - joice be - fore him, God, the LORD, your King.
and to judge the na - tions in his right - eous - ness.

Text: Psalm 98; vers. Psalter, 1912
Tune: F. W. Blunt, 1839–1921

65 65 D
MERRIAL

All the Earth, Proclaim the LORD

176

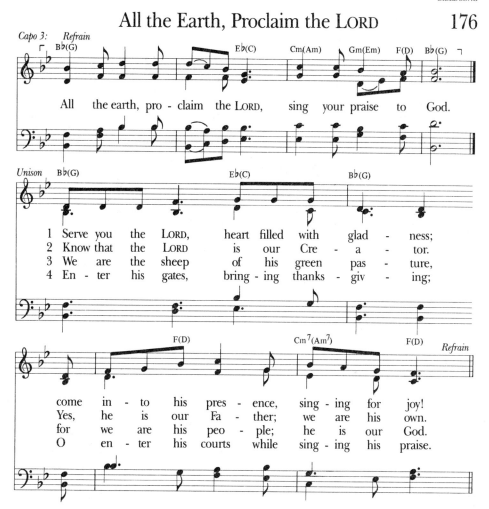

All the earth, pro - claim the LORD, sing your praise to God.

1 Serve you the LORD, heart filled with glad - ness;
2 Know that the LORD is our Cre - a - tor.
3 We are the sheep of his green pas - ture,
4 En - ter his gates, bring - ing thanks - giv - ing;

come in - to his pres - ence, sing - ing for joy!
Yes, he is our Fa - ther; we are his own.
for we are his peo - ple; he is our God.
O en - ter his courts while sing - ing his praise.

5 Our LORD is good,
   his love is lasting;
   his word is abiding
   now and always. *Refrain*

6 Honor and praise
   be to the Father,
   the Son, and the Spirit,
   world without end. *Refrain*

Text: Psalm 100; vers. Lucien Deiss, 1965
Tune: Lucien Deiss, 1965
Text and music © 1965, World Library Publications, Inc. Used by permission.

45 64 with refrain
DEISS 100

177　　Praise the LORD!

1 Praise the LORD! Praise, you ser-vants of the LORD, praise the
2 Praise the LORD! Thanks and prais-es sing to God, day by
3 Praise the LORD! Praise and glo-ry give to God: who is
4 Praise the LORD! Praise, you ser-vants of the LORD, praise the

name of the LORD! Bless-ed be the name of the LORD!
day to the LORD! High a-bove the na-tions is God,
like un-to him? Rais-ing up the poor from the dust,
love of the LORD. Giv-ing to the home-less a home,

Bless-ed be the name of the LORD from this time
high a-bove the na-tions is God, his glo-ry
rais-ing up the poor from the dust, he makes them
giv-ing to the home-less a home, he fills their

forth and for-ev-er-more. Praise the LORD! Praise the LORD!
high o-ver earth and sky. Praise the LORD! Praise the LORD!
dwell in his heart and home. Praise the LORD! Praise the LORD!
hearts with new hope and joy. Praise the LORD! Praise the LORD!

Text: Psalm 113; vers. Marjorie Jillson, 1970
Tune: Heinz W. Zimmermann, 1973
Text and music © 1973, Concordia Publishing House. Used by permission.

PM
LAUDATE PUERI

What Shall I Render to the LORD

1 What shall I ren - der to the LORD for all his
2 Sal - va - tion's cup of bless - ing now I take and
3 His saints the LORD de - lights to save; their death is
4 With thank-ful heart I of - fer now my gift and
5 With - in his house, the house of prayer, I ded - i -

ben - e - fits to me? How shall my life, by grace re -
call up - on God's name. Be - fore his saints I pay my
▸ pre - cious in his sight. He has re-deemed me from the
call up - on God's name. Be - fore his saints I pay my
cate my - self to God. Let all his saints his grace de -

stored, give wor - thy thanks, O LORD, to thee?
vow and here my grat - i - tude pro - claim.
▸ grave, and in his ser - vice I de - light.
vow and here my grat - i - tude pro - claim.
clare and join to sound his praise a - broad.

Text: Psalm 116:12–19; vers. Psalter, 1912
Tune: Second Supplement to Psalmody in Miniature, c. 1780; adapt. Edward Miller, 1790

LM
ROCKINGHAM

179   The Glorious Gates of Righteousness

1 The glo - rious gates of right - eous - ness throw o - pen un - to me, and I will come to them with praise and en - ter thank - ful - ly, and I will come to them with praise and en - ter thank - ful - ly.

2 This is your tem - ple gate, O LORD: the just shall en - ter there. My Sav - ior, I will give you thanks, for you have heard my prayer; my Sav - ior, I will give you thanks, for you have heard my prayer.

3 The stone re - ject - ed and de - spised is now the cor - ner - stone. How won - drous are the ways of God, un - fath - omed and un - known; how won - drous are the ways of God, un - fath - omed and un - known.

4 Ho - san - na! Ev - er blest is he who comes in God's own name. The bless - ing of God's ho - ly house up - on you we pro - claim; the bless - ing of God's ho - ly house up - on you we pro - claim.

5 O praise the LORD, for he is good; let all in heaven a - bove and all his saints on earth pro - claim his ev - er - last - ing love; let all his saints on earth pro - claim his ev - er - last - ing love.

Text: Psalm 118:19–23, 26, 29; vers. Psalter, 1912, alt.
Tune: Lowell Mason, 1837

CM with repeat
ZERAH

I Lift My Eyes Up to the Hills

180

1 I lift my eyes up to the hills— where shall my help a - rise?
2 The LORD God watch - es o - ver you— your shade at your right hand;
3 The LORD will keep you from all harm— he watch - es o - ver you,

Our LORD a - lone pro - vides. God, who cre - at - ed heaven and earth,
you shall se - cure - ly stand. The moon by night, the sun by day
pro - tects your whole life through. The LORD our God takes care of you,

will keep your foot from stum - bling, for God will nev - er slum - ber.
shall not af - flict or smite you, but with their ra - diance light you.
your com - ing and your go - ing, for - ev - er grace be - stow - ing.

Text: Psalm 121; vers. Psalter Hymnal, 1987
Tune: Genevan Psalter, 1551; harm. Howard Slenk, 1985
Text and harmonization © 1987, CRC Publications

866 877
GENEVAN 121

181   Exalt the LORD, His Praise Proclaim

1 Ex - alt the LORD, his praise pro - claim; all
2 I know the LORD is high in state; a -
3 Ex - alt the LORD, his praise pro - claim; all

you his ser - vants, praise his name, who
bove all gods our Lord is great. The
you his ser - vants, praise his name, who

in the LORD's house ev - er stand and
LORD per - forms what he de - crees, in
in the LORD's house ev - er stand and

hum - bly serve at his com - mand. The
heaven and earth, in depths and seas. He
hum - bly serve at his com - mand. For -

Text: Psalm 135:1–7, 19–21; vers. Psalter, 1887; rev. Psalter, 1912, alt.
Tune: Franz J. Haydn, 1798

LMD
CREATION

LORD is good, his praise pro - claim; since
makes the va - pors to as - cend in
ev - er praise and bless his name, and

it is pleas - ant, praise his name. His
clouds from earth's re - mot - est end; the
in the church his praise pro - claim. In

peo - ple for his own he takes and
light - nings flash at his com - mand; he
Zi - on is his dwell - ing place; O

his own spe - cial trea - sure makes.
holds the tem - pest in his hand.
praise the LORD, show forth his grace.

182 Give Thanks to God, for Good Is He

1 Give thanks to God, for good is he:
2 His wis-dom made the heavens to be: his love a-bides for - ev - er.
3 He helped us in our deep-est woes:

To him all praise and glo - ry be:
He spread the earth up - on the sea: his mer-cy lasts for - ev-er.
He ran-somed us from all our foes:

His won-drous works with praise re - cord:
Praise him whose sun a - wakes the day: his love a-bides for - ev-er.
Each crea-ture's need he will sup - ply:

The on - ly God, the sov-ereign Lord:
The moon and stars his might dis - play: his mer-cy lasts for - ev-er.
Give thanks to God, en - throned on high:

Text: Psalm 136:1–9, 23–26; vers. Psalter, 1912, alt.
Tune: Arthur S. Sullivan, 1875

87 87 D
CONSTANCE

Alternative harmonization

Tune: Arthur S. Sullivan, 1875; harm. Emily R. Brink, 1987
Harmonization © 1987, CRC Publications

87 87 D
CONSTANCE

183 With Grateful Heart My Thanks I Bring

1 With grate - ful heart my thanks I bring, be - fore the great your
2 I cried to you, and you did save; your word of grace new
3 O LORD, en-throned in glo - ry bright, you reign a - lone in
4 You will stretch forth your might - y arm to save me when my

praise I sing. I wor - ship in your ho - ly place and
cour - age gave. The kings of earth shall thank you, LORD, for
heav-enly height; the proud in vain your fa - vor seek, but
foes a - larm. The work you have for me be - gun shall

praise you for your truth and grace; for truth and grace to -
they have heard your won-drous word; yes, they shall come with
you have mer - cy for the meek. Through trou - ble though my
by your grace be ful - ly done. Your love for - ev - er

Text: Psalm 138; vers. Psalter, 1912, alt.
Tune: William B. Bradbury, 1863

88 88 88 with repeat
SOLID ROCK

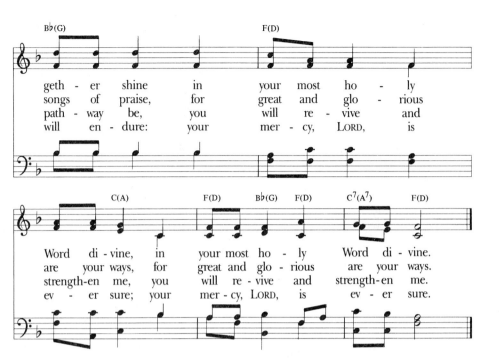

184　Lord, You Have Searched Me

1 Lord, you have searched me, and you know
2 If I the wings of morn - ing take
3 All that I am I owe to you;
4 When I was formed with - in the earth,
5 Search me, O God, my heart dis - cern;

where I take rest and where I go.
and far a - way my dwell - ing make,
► you knit me, Lord, with - in the womb.
you knew my frame be - fore my birth.
try me, my in - most thoughts to learn;

Lord, you know all that I have planned,
if I should sink in deep - est sea,
► I give my Mak - er thank - ful praise,
My life in all your per - fect plan
and lead me, if in sin I stray,

and all my ways are in your hand.
your right hand keeps its hold on me.
► whose won - drous works my soul a - maze.
was known be - fore my days be - gan.
to choose the ev - er - last - ing way.

Text: Psalm 139; vers. Psalter, 1912; rev. Marie J. Post, 1986. © 1987, CRC Publications
Tune: Henry K. Oliver, 1832
Alternative tune: MELCOMBE, 274

LM
FEDERAL STREET

I Will Extol You, O My God

1 I will ex - tol you, O my God, and praise you, O my King;
2 Each gen - er - a - tion to the next shall tes - ti - mo - ny bear,
3 Your might - y acts and glo - rious deeds we shall with awe con - fess

yes, ev - ery day and ev - er - more your prais-es I will sing.
and to your praise, from age to age, your won-drous acts de - clare.
and sing of your great good-ness and your per - fect right-eous - ness.

Great is the LORD, our might - y God, and great - ly to be praised;
Up - on your glo - rious maj - es - ty and hon - or I will dwell,
Most gra - cious and com - pas - sion-ate is God, who reigns a - bove;

his great-ness is un - search-a - ble, a - bove all glo - ry raised.
and all your grand and glo - rious works and great-ness I will tell.
his wrath is ev - er slow to rise, un - bound-ed is his love.

Text: Psalm 145:1–8; vers. Psalter, 1912, alt.
Tune: English; adapt. Arthur S. Sullivan, 1874

CMD
NOEL

I Will Exalt My God, My King
Te Exaltaré Mi Dios, Mi Rey

I will ex - alt my God, my King;
I will praise your name for - ev - er.
I will ex - alt your name for - ev - er;
ev-ery day I'll praise your ho - ly name.
I will praise your name for - ev - er;

Te_e -xal - ta - ré, mi Dios, mi Rey,
y ben - de - ci - ré tu nom - bre.
E - ter - na - men - te_y pa - ra siem - pre,
ca-da dí - a te ben - de - ci - ré.
Y a - la - ba - ré tu nom - bre

Text: Psalm 145:1–3; vers. Casiodoro Cardenas, 1979; tr. composite
Tune: Casiodoro Cardenas, 1979; arr. Raquel Mora Martínez, 1979

irregular
ECUADOR

187   O Praise the Lord, for It Is Good

3 No hu - man might, no earth - ly pride de - lights the Lord a - bove;

1 O praise the Lord, for it is good to sing un - to our God;
2 Our Lord is great: he calls by name and counts the stars of night;
3 No hu - man might, no earth - ly pride de - lights the Lord a - bove;

in those who fear him he de - lights, in those who trust his love.

'tis right and pleas-ant for his saints to tell his praise a - broad.
his wis - dom is un - search - a - ble, and won-drous is his might.
in those who fear him he de-lights, in those who trust his love.

Text: Psalm 147:1–13; vers. Psalter, 1912, alt.
Tune: John H. Stockton, 1874; desc. Dale Grotenhuis, 1976. Descant © 1976, Dale Grotenhuis

CMD
MINERVA

O Zi - on, praise the LORD your God, his won - drous love con - fess;

C   G   D

The LORD our God builds up his church, finds those who draw a - part;
The LORD up - holds the poor and meek but brings the wick - ed low;
O Zi - on, praise the LORD your God, his won - drous love con - fess;

he is your glo - ry and your strength, he will your chil - dren bless.

D⁷ G   C   G   G/D   D⁷ G

he binds their wounds and gent - ly leads, he heals the bro - ken heart.
sing praise to him who sends the rain, whose care the cat - tle know.
he is your glo - ry and your strength, he will your chil - dren bless.

188 Praise the LORD, Sing Hallelujah

1 Praise the LORD, sing hal - le - lu - jah, from the heav - ens
2 Let them praise the LORD their Mak - er: they were made at
3 All you fruit - ful trees and ce - dars, ev - ery hill and

praise his name; praise the LORD, our great Cre - a - tor;
his com - mand. God es - tab - lished them for - ev - er;
moun - tain high, creep - ing things and beasts and cat - tle,

all his an - gels, praise pro - claim. All his hosts, to - geth - er
his de - cree shall ev - er stand. Let the earth sing hal - le -
birds that in the heav - ens fly, kings of earth and all you

praise him, sun and moon and stars on high; praise the
lu - jah: rag - ing seas, you mon - sters all, fire and
peo - ple, princ - es great, earth's judg - es all; praise his

Text: Psalm 148; vers. Bible Songs Hymnal, 1927, alt.
Tune: William J. Kirkpatrick, 1838–1921

87 87 D with refrain
PRAISE JEHOVAH

LORD, O heavens of heav - ens, and the floods a - bove the sky.
hail and snow and va - pors, storm - y winds that hear his call.
name, young men and maid - ens, a - ged men, and chil - dren small.

Refrain (may be sung after stanza 3 only)

Praise the LORD, sing hal - le - lu - jah, for his
Praise the LORD,

name a - lone is high, and his glo - ry is ex -
and his glo - ry

alt - ed, and his glo - ry is ex - alt - ed, and his
and his glo - ry

glo - ry is ex - alt - ed, far a - bove the earth and sky.
and his glo - ry

189 Hallelujah, Praise the LORD

1 Hal - le - lu - jah, praise the LORD. Praise him with each
2 Praise him in his ho - ly place. Shout his power through
3 Praise him with the pluck - ing string, cym - bal clang and
4 Praise with in - stru - ments of wood, for the LORD is

note and word. Praise him for his might - y ways,
out - er space. Ev - ery - thing that breathes, pro - claim
trum - pet ring, tap - ping foot and clap - ping hand;
just and good. Praise with u - ni - son and chord.

who with love ex - alts our days. Hal - le - lu - jah.
praise and hon - or to God's name. Hal - le - lu - jah.
praise the LORD through all the land. Hal - le - lu - jah.
Hal - le - lu - jah, praise the LORD! Hal - le - lu - jah.

Text: based on Psalm 150; vers. Marie J. Post, 1974, alt. © 1974, CRC Publications
Tune: French, 13th cent.

77 77 4
ORIENTIS PARTIBUS

God's Gift It Is to Eat and Drink

1 God's gift it is to eat and drink, to find true joy in
2 In days of glad pros - per - i - ty give thanks that God en -
3 Our dai - ly deeds are in God's hands, their out - come on the

la - bor. No mat - ter what some - one may think, what
folds you. In days of hard ad - ver - si - ty,
mor - row. At times God o - ver - rules our plans to

Refrain

God does lasts for - ev - er.
mem-ber, God still holds you. God's prov - i - dence is
teach us trust through sor - row.

good and wise: God holds to - geth - er all our lives.

Text: based on Ecclesiastes 3:13–15; 7:14; vers. Calvin Seerveld, 1985, ©
Tune: Bartholomäus Gesius, 1605; adapt. and harm. Dale Grotenhuis, 1985. © 1987, CRC Publications

87 87 88
MACHS MIT MIR

191   Hear Us, O People, Hear Our Plea

1 Hear us, O peo - ple, hear our plea; so help us
2 Now like a seal up - on your heart, and like a
3 Can wa - ters quench the fire of love? No floods shall
4 With all who hear our sol - emn vow, we pray, dear

God, who makes us new: let no one rouse e - rot - ic
ring up - on your hand, take me in love as strong as
ev - er put it out! If oth - ers tried to buy our
God, who makes us new, bless the e - rot - ic love and

joy un - til the bond of love holds true.
death, with pas - sion pure as blaz - ing fire.
love, they would be ut - ter - ly de - spised.
joy of all whose bond of love holds true.

Text: based on Song of Songs 2:7; 3:5; 8:4, 6–7; vers. Calvin Seerveld, 1984, ©
Tune: Ralph Harrison, 1784

LM
WARRINGTON

The People Who in Darkness Walked   192

1 The peo-ple who in dark-ness walked have seen a glo-rious
2 To greet you, Sun of Right-eous-ness, the gath-ering na-tions
3 To us the prom-ised child is born, to us a son is
4 His name shall be the Prince of Peace for - ev - er - more a-
5 His peace and right-eous gov - ern - ment shall o - ver all ex-

light; the heav - enly dawn broke forth on those who
come, re - joic - ing as when reap - ers bring their
► given; and on his shoul - ders ev - er rests all
dored, the Won - der - ful, the Coun - sel - or, the
tend; on judg - ment and on jus - tice based, his

dwelt in death and night, who dwelt in death and night.
har - vest trea - sures home, their har - vest trea sures home.
► power in earth and heaven, all power in earth and heaven.
Might - y God and Lord, the Might - y God and Lord.
reign shall nev - er end, his reign shall nev - er end.

Text: Isaiah 9:2–3, 6–7; vers. John Morrison, 1781, alt.
Tune: Nikolaus Herman, 1554; harm. Johann S. Bach, c. 1738, in Cantata 151

CM with repeat
LOBT GOTT, IHR CHRISTEN

193 Surely It Is God Who Saves Me

1 Sure - ly it is God who saves me; trust-ing him, I shall not fear.
2 Make his deeds known to the peo-ples; tell out his ex - alt - ed name.

For the LORD de - fends and shields me, and his sav-ing help is near.
Praise the LORD, who has done great things; all his works his might pro-claim.

So re-joice as you draw wa - ter from sal - va -tion's liv - ing spring;
Zi - on, lift your voice in sing-ing, for with you has come to dwell,

in the day of your de - liv - erance thank the LORD, his mer-cies sing.
in your ver - y midst, the great and Ho - ly One of Is - ra - el.

Text: Isaiah 12; vers. Carl P. Daw, Jr., 1982, ©
Tune: early American; harm. Dale Grotenhuis, 1985. Harmonization © 1987, CRC Publications

87 87 D
LORD, REVIVE US

Comfort, Comfort Now My People

1 Com - fort, com - fort now my peo - ple; speak of peace: so
2 For the her - ald's voice is cry - ing in the des - ert
3 Then make straight what long was crook - ed; make the rough - er

says our God. Com - fort those who sit in dark - ness, mourn - ing
far and near, call - ing all to true re - pen - tance, since the
plac - es plain. Let your hearts be true and hum - ble, as be -

un - der sor - row's load. Cry out to Je - ru - sa - lem
king - dom now is here. Oh, that warn - ing cry o - bey!
fits his ho - ly reign. For the glo - ry of the Lord

of the peace that waits for them; tell her that her
Now pre - pare for God a way! Let the val - leys
now on earth is shed a - broad, and all flesh shall

sins I cov - er and her war - fare now is o - ver.
rise to meet him and the hills bow down to greet him.
see the to - ken that God's word is nev - er bro - ken.

Text: Isaiah 40:1–5; vers. Johannes G. Olearius, 1671; tr. Catherine Winkworth, 1863, alt.
Tune: Louis Bourgeois, 1551; harm. Claude Goudimel, 1564
Another harmonization with descant: 42

87 87 77 88
GENEVAN 42

195   Our God Reigns

How love-ly on the moun-tains are the feet of him
who brings good news, good news,
an-nounc-ing peace, pro-claim-ing news of hap-pi-ness:
our God reigns, our God reigns.
Our God reigns, our God reigns,
our God reigns, our God reigns.

Text: Isaiah 52:7; vers. Leonard E. Smith, Jr., 1974
Tune: Leonard E. Smith, Jr., 1974; harm. Dale Grotenhuis, 1984
Text and music © 1974, 1978, L. E. Smith, Jr., New Jerusalem Music. Used by permission.
Full five-verse version available from New Jerusalem Music.

PM
OUR GOD REIGNS

See, Christ Was Wounded for Our Sake 196

1 See, Christ was wound - ed for our sake, and bruised and
2 Look on his face, come close to him, but you will
3 Like sheep that stray, we leave God's path, to choose our
4 Cast out to die by those he loved, re - viled by
5 For on his shoul - ders God has laid the weight of

beat - en for our sin; so by his suf - ferings
find no beau - ty there. De - spised, re - ject - ed—
▸ own and not his will; like sheep to slaugh - ter
those he died to save, see how sin's pride has
sin that we should bear; so by his pas - sion

we are healed, for God has laid our guilt on him.
who can tell the grief and sor - row he must bear?
▸ he has gone, o - be - dient to his Fa - ther's will.
sought his death, see how sin's hate has made his grave.
we have peace, through his o - be - dience and his prayer.

Text: Isaiah 53:2–9; vers. Brian Foley, 1971. © 1971, Faber Music, Ltd.
Reprinted by permission from New Catholic Hymnal.
Tune: Joyce Recker, 1983. © 1987, CRC Publications

LM
KABODE

197 The Trees of the Field

You shall go out with joy and be led forth with peace; the moun-tains and the hills will break forth be-fore you; there'll be shouts of joy, and all the trees of the field will clap, will clap their hands!

Text: Isaiah 55:12; para. Steffi G. Rubin, 1975
Tune: Stuart Dauermann, 1975

irregular
TREES OF THE FIELD

And all the trees of the field will clap their hands,

the trees of the field will clap their hands,

the trees of the field will clap their hands

while you go out with joy.

✗ = *hand clapping*

198 Arise, Shine, for Your Light Is Come

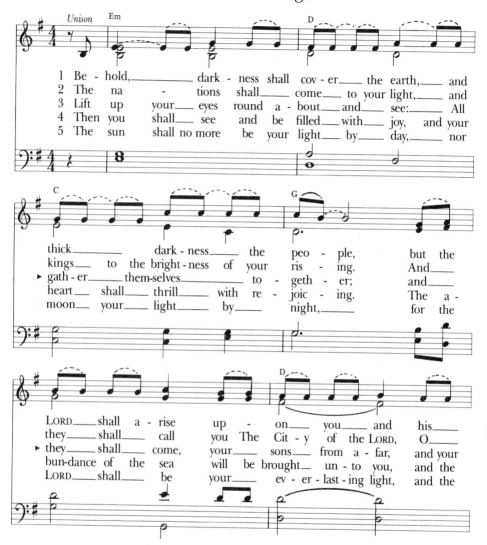

Unison · Em · D

1 Be - hold,_____ dark - ness shall cov - er_____ the earth,_____ and
2 The na - tions shall_____ come_____ to your light,_____ and
3 Lift up your_____ eyes round a - bout_____ and_____ see:_____ All
4 Then you shall_____ see and be filled_____ with_____ joy, and your
5 The sun shall no more be your light_____ by_____ day,_____ nor

C · G

thick_____ dark - ness_____ the peo - ple, but the
kings_____ to the bright - ness of your ris - ing. And_____
▸ gath - er_____ them-selves_____ to - geth - er; and_____
heart_____ shall_____ thrill_____ with re - joic - ing. The a -
moon_____ your_____ light_____ by_____ night,_____ for the

D

LORD_____ shall a - rise up - on_____ you_____ and his_____
they_____ shall_____ call you The Cit - y of the LORD, O_____
▸ they_____ shall_____ come, your_____ sons_____ from a - far, and your
bun-dance of the sea will be brought_____ un - to you, and the
LORD_____ shall_____ be your_____ ev - er - last - ing light, and the

Text: Isaiah 60:1–5, 14, 20; para. Eric Glass, 1974, alt.
Tune: Eric Glass, 1974; arr. Dale Grotenhuis, 1986
Text and music © 1974, Eric Glass

irregular
ARISE, SHINE

glo - ry shall be seen_____ up - on you._____
Zi - on of the Ho - ly One of Is - ra - el.
▸ daugh-ters shall be car - ried at your side._____
wealth____ of the na - tions un - to you._____
days____ of your mourn-ing shall be end - ed.____

Refrain
A - rise, shine, for your light is come, and the glo - ry of the

LORD is ris - en. O a - rise, shine, for your light is

come, and the glo - ry of the LORD is up - on you.

199

I Am the LORD Your God

1 I am the LORD your God; you are my peo - ple.
2 Sing praise to God the LORD, gath - ering his peo - ple,
3 God will es - tab - lish us, keep - ing his cov - enant,

I am your Sav - ior, pre - serv - er, and rock.
bring - ing them in from all parts of the earth.
which will ex - tend to each na - tion and race:

I am your God, keep - ing watch like a shep - herd,
Blind, lame, and weak he will lead all to - geth - er,
God's law will dwell in the hearts of his peo - ple;

car - ing for Is - rael, my peo - ple, my flock.
gent - ly ex - chang - ing their weep - ing for mirth.
they will be blessed with his fa - vor and grace.

Text: based on Jeremiah 31; vers. Helen Otte, 1985. © 1987, CRC Publications
Tune: Alexey Lvov, 1833

11 10 11 10
RUSSIA

O My People, Turn to Me

1 O my peo - ple, turn to me, says the LORD, your gra - cious God.
2 O my peo - ple, turn to me, says the LORD, your gra - cious God.

I will heal your faith-less - ness, I will love you and will bless.
You shall spread roots like a tree, love - ly as an ol - ive tree.

I will be like dew on flowers; like a lil - y you shall bloom.
You shall blos - som like a vine, fra-grant with the scent of wine.

O my peo - ple, turn to me, says the LORD, your gra - cious God.
O my peo - ple, turn to me, says the LORD, your gra - cious God.

Text: Hosea 14:1, 4–7; vers. Marie J. Post, 1981
Tune: Norm Jonkman, 1984
Text and music © 1987, CRC Publications

77 77 D
HOSEA

201 Fear Not, Rejoice and Be Glad

Refrain Unison

Fear not, re-joice and be glad: the LORD has done a great thing,

has poured out his Spir-it on all who live, on those who con-fess his name.

1 The fig tree is bud-ding, the vine bear - ing fruit, the
2 We shall eat in plen - ty and be sat - is - fied, the
3 "My peo - ple will know____ that I am the LORD; their

Text: based on Joel 2–3; vers. Priscilla Wright, 1971, alt.
Tune: Priscilla Wright, 1971; harm. Dale Grotenhuis, 1986
Text and music © 1971, 1975, Celebration/administered by Maranatha! Music. All rights reserved.
International copyright secured. Used by permission.

irregular
CLAY

wheat fields are gold-en with   grain.   Thrust in   the sick-le, the
moun-tains will drip with new   wine.   "My   chil-dren will drink of the
shame   I   have tak-en a - way.   My Spir - it   will lead them to -

har - vest is   ripe; the LORD ___ has giv-en   us   rain.
foun-tain of   life,   my   chil-dren will know they are   mine."
geth - er a - gain, my   Spir - it will show them the way."

Refrain

202   Song of Jonah

1 In the fish for three days bur - ied, I kept call - ing,
2 Down to death the waves had pulled me, down, en-tombed where
3 In de - spair, a - fraid of dy - ing, I im - plored you
4 In the tomb for three days bur - ied, Christ had gone to

"Save me, LORD! Keep me from the hell - ish grave - yard,
none sur - vive. Sea - weed round my head was tan - gled;
anx - ious - ly. Un - like those who shirk their prom - ise,
face the worst. Just as God took care of Jo - nah,

lost at sea, by you ig - nored." Tossed and turned be -
wa - ter swal - lowed me a - live. "Is God's face now
I bring of - ferings thank - ful - ly. Take my life I
God raised Je - sus as the first. All who know the

Text: st. 1–3, Jonah 2; st. 1–4 vers. Calvin Seerveld, 1982, ©
Tune: John Ambrose Lloyd, 1815–1874

87 87 D
EIFIONYDD

neath rough wa - ters, chok - ing in your whirl-pool sea, I cried out,
gone for - ev - er? Have I for - feit - ed God's care?" No! You saved
vowed to give you; bless my joy, and make it known. Let all know
Ho - ly Spir - it shall de - feat the grip of sin. Christ has con -

"My life is fin - ished!" But, O LORD, you an - swered me.
me from de - struc - tion, raised me, LORD, and heard my prayer.
that sure de - liv - erance comes from God the LORD a lone.
quered death and Sa - tan: let the ju - bi - lee be - gin!

203   The Day Is Coming—God Has Promised

1 The day is com - ing— God has prom-ised— when man - y
2 The God of Ja - cob shall speak jus - tice; the LORD shall
3 God's day is com - ing for each na - tion to put down

na - tions say good news has come. The LORD God's word is
judge the might - y of the earth. Strong na - tions shall beat
arms and go no more to war. The LORD shall give us

heard in Zi - on; God's ho - ly law comes from Je - ru - sa - lem!
swords to plow-shares and turn their spears to prun-ing hooks for work.
vine and fig tree, so we, in peace, shall be a - fraid no more.

Refrain

"Come, let us go to God, the source of life, so

Text: Micah 4:1–4; vers. Calvin Seerveld, 1985, ©
Tune: Musikalisches Handbuch, Hamburg, 1690; harm. Dale Grotenhuis, 1986.
Harmonization © 1987, CRC Publications

9 10 9 10 with refrain
DIR, DIR, JEHOVA

we may walk the LORD's way, end - ing strife."

Little Bethlehem of Judah — 204

1 Lit - tle Beth - le - hem of Ju - dah, what good news you bring!
2 Though your peo - ple suf - fer trou - ble wait - ing for the child,
3 Like a shep - herd he will nour - ish those who love his birth.

Out of you will come the An - cient One as King.
af - ter he has come they will be rec - on - ciled.
All who serve his rule will flour - ish on the earth.

Text: Micah 5:2–4; vers. Calvin Seerveld, 1986, ©
Tune: Martin F. Shaw, 1929. By permission of Oxford University Press.

85 83
WESTRIDGE

205 The LORD Is Saying

Unison

1 The LORD is say - ing, "I will make all things
2 The LORD is say - ing, "These things will soon be
3 The LORD is say - ing, "I love you one and

new. I will be stay - ing right in the midst of
true. I will be sav - ing those who be - long to
all. I heard you pray - ing that I should heed your

you. My cit - y will be safe and ho - ly—
you. My rem-nant will be - lieve with won - der—
call. My jeal - ous love will guard you sure - ly—

old peo - ple sit - ting re - laxed and joy - ful."
while boys and girls in the streets are play - ing."
you are my peo - ple and I am your God."

Text: Zechariah 8:2–8; vers. Calvin Seerveld, 1984, ©
Tune: Dale Grotenhuis, 1986, ©

11 11 9 10
THOMAS

Blest Are the Contrite Hearts

1 Blest are the con - trite hearts: God's king - dom
2 Blest are the gen - tle meek: they shall re -
3 Blest are the mer - ci - ful: mer - cy they
4 Blest, those who rec - on - cile: chil - dren of
5 Blest, you who suf - fer harm when it is

comes for them. Blest are the wronged and
ceive the earth. Blest are those hun - gry
▸ shall re - ceive. Blest are the ones whose
God are they. Blest are those hurt for
for Christ's sake. Bear with the per - se -

griev - ing ones: they shall be com - fort - ed.
for the right: they shall be sat - is - fied.
▸ hearts are pure: they sure - ly shall see God.
Je - sus' sake: God's rule shall make them whole.
cut - ing ones: God shall give you great joy.

6   Act like the salt of earth:
     salt without taste is waste.
   Shine like a lighthouse in the night;
   hide not your lamp of love.

7   Point to our covenant Lord
     with every word and deed;
   then all may see the works you do
   and praise the Lord our God.

Text: Matthew 5:3–16; vers. Calvin Seerveld, 1984, ©
Tune: J. Chetham's A Book of Psalmody, 1718; harm. Samuel S. Wesley, 1872

SM
WIRKSWORTH

207 The Lord's Prayer

Our Fa - ther in heaven, hal-lowed be your name, your king-dom come, your will be done on earth as it is in heaven. Give us to-day our dai - ly bread, and for - give us our debts, as we al - so

Text: Matthew 6:9–13
Tune: Richard Langdon, 1774, alt.
Other settings of the Lord's Prayer: 208, 562

PM
LANGDON

have for - given our debt - ors. And lead us not in - to temp-

ta - tion, but de - liv-er us from the e-vil one. For yours is the

king-dom and the power and the glo-ry for - ev-er. A - men.

208   Our Father, Lord of Heaven and Earth

1 Our Fa-ther, Lord of heaven and earth, let praise and hon-or
2 For-give us, Lord, our sins and debts as we to debt-ors

clothe your name. Your king-dom come, your will be done;
show your grace. Re-move us from all tempt-ing paths

through-out the world com-plete your reign. Teach us, O Lord,
and guard us from the dev-il's ways; for glo-ry, strength,

to trust in you for bread and breath each day a-new.
and heav-en's throne be-long to you, and you a-lone. A-men.

Text: Matthew 6:9–13; vers. Henry J. de Jong, 1982. © 1987, CRC Publications
Tune: V. Schumann's Geistliche Lieder, 1539; harm. Johann S. Bach, 1723, in the St. John Passion
Other settings of the Lord's Prayer: 207, 562

88 88 88
VATER UNSER

Seek Ye First the Kingdom

1 Seek ye___ first the___ king - dom of God and his
2 Ask and it shall be giv-en un - to you; seek and
3 We do not live by bread___ a - lone, but by

right - eous - ness, and all these things shall be
you shall find; knock and the door shall be
ev - ery word that pro - ceeds from the

add - ed un - to you. Al - le - lu, al - le - lu - ia.
o - pened un - to you. Al - le - lu, al - le - lu - ia.
mouth___ of___ God. Al - le - lu, al - le - lu - ia.

Text: Matthew 6:33; 7:7; 4:4; para. Karen Lafferty, 1972
Tune: Karen Lafferty, 1972

irregular
LAFFERTY

210 Whatsoever You Do to the Least

Refrain ⌐ *Unison*

What-so - ev - er you do to the least of my peo - ple,
that you do un - to me.

1 When I was hun-gry, you
2 When I was wea - ry, you

gave me to eat; when I was thirst - y, you
helped me find rest; when I was anx - ious, you

Text: Matthew 25:35–36, 40; para. Willard F. Jabusch, 1966, ©
Tune: Willard F. Jabusch, 1966, ©

irregular
WHATSOEVER YOU DO

gave   me   to   drink.   When   I   was   home - less,   you
calmed all   my   fears.   When   in   a   pris - on,   you

o - pened your   door;   when   I   was   na - ked,   you
came   to   my   cell;   when   on   a   sick - bed,   you

gave   me your   coat.   Now en - ter   in - to the home of my   Fa - ther.
cared   for   my   needs.   Now en - ter   in - to the home of my   Fa - ther.

211 The Lord Is Risen Indeed

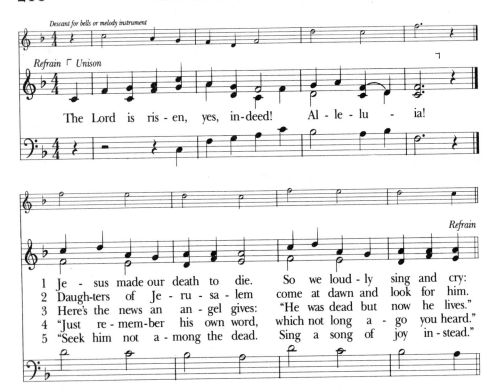

Descant for bells or melody instrument

Refrain ⌐ Unison

The Lord is ris - en, yes, in-deed! Al - le - lu - ia!

Refrain

1 Je - sus made our death to die.   So we loud - ly sing and cry:
2 Daugh-ters of Je - ru - sa - lem   come at dawn and look for him.
3 Here's the news an an - gel gives: "He was dead but now he lives."
4 "Just re - mem-ber his own word,   which not long a - go you heard."
5 "Seek him not a - mong the dead.   Sing a song of joy in - stead."

Text: based on Matt. 28:1–6; vers. Alles wordt nieuw, 1966, 1971; tr. Sietze Buning, 1982
Tune: Wim ter Burg, 1971
Text and music © 1982, Paideia Press

77 with refrain
OPGESTAAN

Song of Mary

1 My spir - it glo - ri - fies the Lord, in God my
2 All gen - er - a - tions from now on shall call me
3 His mer - cy shall ex - tend to those who fear the
4 He brought down rul - ers from their thrones, but lift - ed
5 He helped his ser - vant Is - ra - el, re - mem-bering

Sav - ior I re - joice, for he be - held my
blest and spread my fame, for he has done great
Lord from age to age; he has re - vealed his
those of low de - gree. He filled the hun - gry
to be mer - ci - ful, keep - ing his word to

hum - ble state and in his love made me his choice.
things for me— might - y and ho - ly is his name.
might - y arm, scat-tering the proud in all their rage.
with good things, but emp - ty sent the rich a - way.
A - bra - ham and to his seed for - ev - er - more.

Text: Luke 1:46–55; vers. Dewey Westra, 1931; rev. Psalter Hymnal, 1987. © 1987, CRC Publications
Tune: William Boyd, 1868
Alternative tune: PUER NOBIS, 327
Other settings of the Song of Mary: 478, 622

LM
PENTECOST

Song of Zechariah

213

1 Praised be the God of Is - ra - el, who has re-deemed his
2 My child, you will pre - pare God's way as proph-et of the

peo - ple; through Da - vid's house God will ex - cel and tri-umph
Most High, an - nounce to peo - ple that the day of sav - ing

o - ver e - vil. As told by proph - ets long a - go,
knowl - edge is nigh. In ten - der mer - cy God be - gins

Text: Luke 1:68–79; vers. Bert Polman, 1986. © 1987, CRC Publications
Tune: Wolfgang Dachstein, 1525

87 87 887 887
AN WASSERFLUSSEN BABYLON

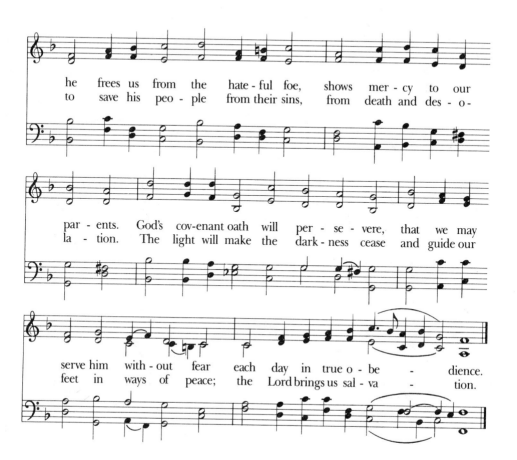

he   frees us   from   the   hate - ful foe,   shows mer - cy   to   our
to   save   his peo - ple   from their sins,   from   death and des - o -

par - ents.   God's   cov-enant oath   will   per - se - vere,   that   we may
la - tion.   The   light will make   the   dark - ness cease   and   guide our

serve him   with - out   fear   each   day   in true o - be   -   dience.
feet   in   ways   of   peace;   the   Lord brings us sal - va   -   tion.

Glory to God
Ere zij God

Glo - ry to God! Glo - ry to God in the high-est, in the
E - re zij God! E - re zij God in den ho - ge, in den

high-est, in the high - est! Peace be on earth,___
ho - ge, in den ho - ge! Vre - de op aar - de,

Peace be on earth,___ to the peo - ple whom God de - lights
vre - de op aar - de, in de men - sen een wel - be - ha -

in. Glo - ry to God in the high - est! Glo - ry to
gen. E - re zij God in den ho - ge! E - re zij

Text: Luke 2:14; para. F. A. Schultz, c. 1870; tr. Psalter Hymnal, 1987. © 1987, CRC Publications
Tune: F. A. Schultz, c. 1870

God in the high - est! Peace be on earth,____
God in den ho - ge! Vre - de op aar - de,

peace be on earth,____ peace be on earth,____ peace be on
vre - de op aar - de, vre - de op aar - de, vre - de op

earth,____ to the peo - ple, to the peo - ple whom God de -
aar - de, in de men - sen, in de men - sen een wel - be -

lights in, to the peo - ple whom God de - lights in, whom God de -
ha - gen, in de men - sen, een wel - be - ha - gen, een wel - be -

lights in. Glo - ry to God! Glo - ry to God in the
ha - gen. E - re zij God! E - re zij God in den

high-est, in the high - est, in the high - est! Peace be on
ho - ge, in den ho - ge, in den ho - ge! Vre - de op

earth,___ peace be on earth,_ to the peo - ple whom God de -
aar - de, vre - de op aar - de, in de men - sen een wel - be -

lights in. A - men. A - men.
ha - gen. A - men. A - men.

While Shepherds Watched Their Flocks   215

Descant
6 "All glo - ry be to God on high, and to the earth be peace;

1 While shep-herds watched their flocks by night, all seat - ed on the ground,
2 "Fear not," said he— for might - y dread had seized their trou-bled mind—
3 "To you, in Da - vid's town, this day is born of Da-vid's line
4 "The heav - en-ly babe you there shall find to hu - man view dis - played,

to those on whom his fa - vor rests good - will shall nev - er cease."

an an - gel of the Lord came down, and glo - ry shone a - round.
"glad tid - ings of great joy I bring to you and all man - kind.
a Sav - ior, who is Christ the Lord; and this shall be the sign:
all sim - ply wrapped in swad-dling clothes and in a man - ger laid."

5 Thus spoke the angel. Suddenly
   appeared a shining throng
   of angels praising God, who thus
   addressed their joyful song:

6 "All glory be to God on high,
   and to the earth be peace;
   to those on whom his favor rests
   goodwill shall never cease."

Text: Luke 2:8–14; vers. Nahum Tate, 1700, alt.
Tune: T. Este's The Whole Book of Psalmes, 1592; desc. Alan Gray, 1923

CM
WINCHESTER OLD

216

Song of Simeon

1 Now may your ser - vant, Lord, ac - cord-ing to your word,
2 You did for all pre - pare this gift so great, so rare,

de - part in ex - ul - ta - tion. My peace shall be se - rene,
ful - fill - ing proph-ets' sto - ry— a light to show the way

for now my eyes have seen your won-der - ful sal - va - tion.
to Gen - tiles gone a - stray, and un - to Is - rael's glo - ry.

Text: Luke 2:29–32; vers. Dewey Westra, 1931, alt.
Tune: Louis Bourgeois, 1551; harm. Claude Goudimel, 1564

667 D
NUNC DIMITTIS

Jesus, Remember Me

217

Je - sus, re-mem-ber me when you come in - to your king - dom.

Je - sus, re-mem-ber me when you come in - to your king - dom.

Instrumental descant

(second time)

Text: Luke 23:42
Tune: Jacques Berthier, 1978
Text and music © 1978, 1980, 1981, Les Presses de Taizé. Used by permission of G. I. A. Publications, Inc., exclusive agent. All rights reserved.

PM
JESUS, REMEMBER ME

218   In the Beginning Was the Word Eternal

1 In the be - gin - ning was the Word e - ter - nal;
2 The light is shin - ing in a world of dark - ness,
3 Yet those who wel - come him, his name be - liev - ing,
4 Be - com - ing flesh, the Word has dwelt a - mong us;

the Word was with God, and the Word was God.
but dark-ness has not o - ver-come the light.
re - ceive the rights of chil-dren of the Lord;
we saw his glo - ry, full of grace and truth.

Through him all things ex - ist that were cre - at - ed;
The light of God, true source of all cre - a - tion,
those who re - ceive him trust in him as chil - dren—
Law came through Mo - ses, grace and truth through Je - sus;

in him was life, the light of hu - man - kind.
came to his own, but they re - ceived him not.
not born of hu - man will, but born of God.
the Son of God has made the Fa - ther known.

Text: John 1:1–5, 9–14, 17–18; vers. Bert Polman, 1985. © 1987, CRC Publications
Tune: Israeli; arr. Francesca Leftley, 1983. © Kevin Mayhew, Ltd. Used by permission.

11 10 11 10
LINDESFARNE

As Moses Raised the Serpent Up

1 As Moses raised the serpent up, so must God's Son be lifted high, that whosoever will believe in him may live eternally.

2 For God so loved the world he made, he gave his own beloved Son; all who believe in him will live— not die, but live forevermore.

3 God did not send Christ to the world that he might then condemn us all, but that the world by Christ's own death might then be ransomed from the fall.

4 For God so loved the world he made, he gave his own beloved Son; all who believe in him will live— not die, but live forevermore.

Text: John 3:14–17; vers. Marie J. Post, 1985. © 1987, CRC Publications
Tune: English; arr. Hal Hopson, 1972. Arrangement © 1972,
    Hope Publishing Co. All rights reserved. Used by permission.

LM
O WALY WALY

220   I Am the Holy Vine

1 I am the ho - ly vine which God my Fa - ther
2 If you a - bide in me, I will in you a -
3 I am the fruit - ful vine, and you my branch - es

tends. Each branch that yields no fruit my Fa - ther
bide. Each branch to yield its fruit must with the
are. If you a - bide in me, I will in

cuts a - way. Each fruit - ful branch he
vine be one. So you shall fail to
you a - bide. So shall you yield much

prunes with care to make it yield a - bun - dant fruit.
yield your fruit if you are not with me one vine.
fruit, but none if you re - main a - part from me.

Text: John 15:1–5; vers. James Quinn, 1969, alt. © 1969, James Quinn, SJ.
Reprinted by permission of Geoffrey Chapman, a division of Cassell Publishers, Ltd.
Tune: John Ireland, 1918. By permission of the John Ireland Trust.

66 66 44 44
LOVE UNKNOWN

We Know That God Works Things for Good 221

1 We know that God works things for good with
2 Pre - des - tined to be like the Christ who
3 If God is for us day and night, and
4 What en - e - my shall sep - a - rate us
5 In Christ's firm love we con - quer all— in

those who love the Lord; each one God calls to
lived on earth and died, be - liev - ers claim his
▸ Christ now in - ter - cedes, who can with-stand us
from our lov - ing Lord? Not sick - ness, per - se -
life and death se - cure. No e - vil power can

ser - vant - hood has found that sure re - ward.
sac - ri - fice, which makes us jus - ti - fied.
▸ in the fight to fol - low where God leads?
cu - tion, hate, not hun - ger or the sword.
make us fall; in Christ God's love is sure!

Text: Romans 8:28–39; vers. Calvin Seerveld, 1985
Tune: Calvin Seerveld, 1985; harm. Dale Grotenhuis, 1986
Text and music © 1986, Calvin Seerveld

CM
LESTER

222   If I Speak a Foreign Tongue

1 If   I speak a for-eign tongue, if   I sing the   an - gels' song,
2 If   all learn-ing I   ap - prove and my faith can moun-tains move,
3 If   I give a - way all   gain,   suf - fer mar - tyr - dom in pain,
4 Love is pa-tient, love is   kind;   love re - jects an   e - vil mind.
5 Love is end - less in its   reign, though all tongues and knowl-edge wane.

I   am still   a   nois - y gong   if I have not   love.
all   these gifts still noth - ing prove   if I have not   love.
▸ noth - ing yet do   I   at - tain   if I have not   love.
Jeal - ous - y is   left   be - hind   if I have this love.
Faith and hope and love re - main;   great - est still is   love.

Text: 1 Corinthians 13; vers. Bert Polman, 1986. © 1987, CRC Publications
Tune: Frederich Filitz, 1847

77 75
CAPETOWN

For the Glories of God's Grace

1 For the glo-ries of God's grace let us bring un-ceas-ing praise.
2 Strang-ers once to what is good, bound in Sa-tan's ser-vi-tude,
3 Christ the Lord, un-stained and pure, took our sin, made us se-cure,
4 Sin-less and im-mor-tal, he paid our debt on Cal-va-ry.
5 God's good news of love we bring to the lost and wan-der-ing.

From our fall-en, sin-ful ways we are rec-on-ciled to God.
pur-chased by our Sav-ior's blood, we are rec-on-ciled to God.
► named us his am-bas-sa-dors— we are rec-on-ciled to God.
Raised from slaves to roy-al-ty, we are rec-on-ciled to God.
Come, be-lieve, re-joice, and sing: we are rec-on-ciled to God.

Text: based on 2 Corinthians 5:18–21; vers. Marie J. Post, 1985. © 1987, CRC Publications
Tune: J. Freylinghausen's Geistreiches Gesangbuch, 1704; adapt. John Antes, c. 1800; arr. John Wilkes, 1861

77 77
MONKLAND

224   The Fruit of the Spirit

The fruit of the Spir - it is love, joy, peace,

pa - tience, kind - ness, good - ness,

faith-ful -ness, gen - tle - ness, and self - con - trol.

This is the fruit of the Spir - it.

Text: Galatians 5:22–23
Tune: Dale Grotenhuis, 1985, ©

PM
ROBERT

Give Thanks to God, the Father

225

1 Give thanks to God, the Fa-ther of Je-sus Christ, our Lord,
2 He chose us as his chil-dren through Je-sus Christ, his Son,
3 How rich the grace God gives us, how gra-cious wis-dom's gift:
4 In Christ the Fa-ther made us a peo-ple set a-part,
5 You too re-ceived the Spir-it, who marks you as his own,

for all the Spir-it's bless-ings, come down from heaven in Christ.
that all might praise the glo-ry of God's great gift of grace.
▸ in Christ his lov-ing pur-pose is now at last re-vealed.
that all might praise the glo-ry re-vealed to us in Christ.
the gift of God's own prom-ise, the first-fruits of his love.

Be-fore the world was found-ed, God chose us in his Son
What fa-vor he has shown us in his be-lov-ed Son,
▸ When time would reach its full-ness, God planned to make all one—
In Christ you too have lis-tened to God's good news of truth,
The Spir-it seals God's prom-ise in us who are the heirs

to be his ho-ly peo-ple, un-blem-ished, full of love.
whose blood has won our free-dom, the par-don of our sins.
▸ all things on earth, in heav-en— in Christ, their on-ly head.
the gos-pel of sal-va-tion: in Christ you have be-lieved.
of ev-er-last-ing glo-ry— to God be all the praise.

Text: Ephesians 1:3–14; vers. James Quinn, 1980, alt. From Resource Collection of Hymns
and Service Music for the Liturgy. © 1981, International Commission on English
in the Liturgy, Inc. All rights reserved.
Tune: Johann G. Ebeling, 1666; harm. Jacobus J. Kloppers, 1987. Harmonization © 1987, CRC Publications

76 76 D
DU MEINE SEELE SINGE

226 O Father, from Your Glorious Riches

1 O Fa - ther, from your glo - rious rich - es,
2 Grant us the power to un - der - stand, Lord,
3 Un - mea - sured is your power so might - y,
4 Lord, give your love to all your peo - ple

make strong our in - ner selves with power;
how deep and wide, how high and long,
at work in us from day to day—
till all your full - ness dwells with - in;

dwell in our hearts through faith, Christ Je - sus;
how great your love sur - pass - ing knowl - edge!
be - yond all thought, im - ag - i - na - tion,
to God through Je - sus be the glo - ry

give strength, O Spir - it, hour by hour.
Root us in love and make us strong.
more than we ask or hope or pray.
now and for - ev - er - more. A - men!

Text: Ephesians 3:14–21; vers. Trudy Vander Veen, 1984
Tune: Roy Hopp, 1985
Text and music © 1987, CRC Publications

98 98
DENVER

Christ, Who Is in the Form of God 227

1 Christ, who is in the form of God, did not re-
2 And be - ing found in hu - man form, hum - bly he
3 There - fore has God ex - alt - ed him and raised him
4 that at the name of Je - sus Christ should ev - ery

tain his loft - y place, but, tak - ing on a
suf - fered fur - ther loss by will - ing - ly ac -
to the high - est place and giv - en him that
crea - ture bend the knee, and ev - ery tongue con -

ser - vant's role, be - came a mem - ber of our race.
cept - ing death— yes, e - ven death up - on a cross.
match - less name, wor - thy of all names to be praised;
fess him Lord, to God's own glo - ry end - less - ly.

Text: Philippians 2:6–11; vers. David T. Koyzis, 1985, ©
Tune: Joseph P. Holbrook, 1874

LM
BISHOP

228   Rejoice in the Lord Always

May be sung as a round

Re - joice in the Lord al - ways, and a - gain I say, Re - joice!

Re - joice in the Lord al - ways, and a - gain I say, Re - joice!

Re - joice!   Re - joice!   And a - gain I say, Re - joice!

Re - joice!   Re - joice!   And a - gain I say, Re - joice!

Text: Philippians 4:4
Tune: traditional; arr. Dale Grotenhuis, 1985. Arrangement © 1987, CRC Publications

PM
REJOICE

Christ, You Are the Fullness

Unison

1 Christ, you are the full - ness of God, first - born of ev - ery-thing.
2 Since we have been raised with you, Lord, help keep our hearts and minds
3 Help us live in peace as true mem - bers of your bod - y.

For by you____ all things were____made; you hold them up.
pure and set on things that build your rule o'er all the earth.
Let your word dwell rich - ly in us as we teach and sing.

You are head of the church, which is your bod - y.
All our life is now hid - den with____ you in God.
Thanks and praise be to God through you, Lord Je - sus.

First - born from the dead, you in all things are su - preme!
When you come a - gain, we will share your glo - ry.
In what - e'er we do let your name re - ceive the praise!

Text: Colossians 1:15–18; 3:1–4, 15–17; vers. Bert Polman, 1986
Tune: Korean; harm. Dale Grotenhuis, 1986
Text and harmonization © 1987, CRC Publications

irregular
ARIRANG

230 Since Our Great High Priest, Christ Jesus

1 Since our great high priest, Christ Je - sus, bears the name a -
2 Since we have a priest who suf - fered, know - ing weak - ness,
3 Sac - ri - fice and suf - fering o - ver, now he sits at
4 Love's ex - am - ple, hope's at - trac - tion, faith's be - gin - ning

bove all names, reign - ing Son of God, sur - pass - ing
tears, and pain; who, like us, was tried and tempt - ed;
God's right hand, crowned with praise, no more an out - cast,
and its end, pi - o - neer of our sal - va - tion,

oth - er ti - tles, powers, and claims— since to heaven our
un - like us, with - out a stain— since he shared our
his pre - em - i - nence long planned; such a great high
might - y ad - vo - cate and friend: Je - sus, now in

Lord has passed, let us hold our wit - ness fast!
low - ly place, let us bold - ly seek his grace!
priest we have, strong to help, su - preme to save!
glo - ry raised, our as - cend - ed Lord, be praised!

Text: based on Hebrews 1:3–4; 4:14–16; 12:2; vers. Christopher Idle, 1973.
© 1973, Hope Publishing Co. All rights reserved. Used by permission.
Tune: Gesangbuch, Darmstadt, 1698; adapt. William H. Monk, 1861

87 87 77
ALL SAINTS

How Great Is the Love of the Father

231

1 How great is the love of the Fa - ther, the love he has
2 The world with-out God does not know us be - cause it did
3 What we are to be in the fu - ture as yet has not

shown to us— so great that he calls us his chil - dren, and
not know Christ. Lord, help us to be pure and spot - less, for
been made known, but when Christ re-turns, we shall see him, and

chil - dren of God we are, and chil-dren of God we are!
chil - dren of God we are, for chil-dren of God we are.
then we shall be like him, and then we shall be like him.

Text: 1 John 3:1–3; vers. Edna W. Sikkema, 1986. © 1987, CRC Publications
Tune: James C. Ward, 1985. © 1987, Music Anno Domini (A.D.). All rights reserved. Used by permission.

97 97 with repeat
ANNO DOMINI

232   You Are Worthy

You are wor-thy, you are wor-thy, you are wor-thy, O Lord; you are wor-thy to re-ceive glo-ry, glo-ry and hon-or and power: for you have cre-at-ed, have all things cre-at-ed, for you have cre-at-ed all things, and by your plea-sure they were cre-at-ed; you are wor-thy, O Lord!

Text: *Revelation 4:11; para. Pauline Michael Mills, 1963, alt.*
Tune: *Pauline Michael Mills, 1963*
Text and music © *1963, 1975, Fred Bock Music Co. All rights reserved. Used by permission.*

PM
WORTHY

Heavenly Hosts in Ceaseless Worship 233

1 Heav-enly hosts in cease-less wor-ship "Ho-ly, ho-ly, ho-ly!" cry;
2 All cre-a-tion, all re-demp-tion, join to sing the Sav-ior's worth;

"He who is, who was and will be, God Al-might-y, Lord Most High."
Lamb of God whose blood has bought us, kings and priests, to reign on earth.

Praise and hon-or, power and glo-ry be to him who reigns a-lone;
Wealth and wis-dom, power and glo-ry, hon-or, might, do-min-ion, praise

we, with all his hands have fash-ioned, fall be-fore the Fa-ther's throne.
now be his from all his crea-tures and to ev-er-last-ing days.

Text: *Revelation 4:8–11; 5:9–13; vers. Timothy Dudley-Smith, 1972.*
© *1975, Hope Publishing Co. All rights reserved. Used by permission.*
Tune: *Henry Smart, 1867*

87 87 D
BETHANY

Alleluia
Alabaré

Text: *Revelation 5:11–14; Span. vers. anonymous; Eng. vers. Bert Polman, 1986.*
English text © 1987, CRC Publications
Tune: *Spanish*

11 10 10 10 with refrain
ALABARE

songs to praise the Lord.
ré a mi Se - ñor.

Final ending
Lord.
ñor.

1 John saw the an - gels___ and the saints in glo - ry; he
2 They sing to - geth - er___ a new song of heav - en to
3 Then all the crea - tures___ of the earth and heav - en re -

1 Juan vio el nú - me - ro de los re - di - mi - dos, y
2 To - dos u - ni - dos___ a - le - gres can - te - mos
3 So - mos tus hi - jos,___ Dios___ Pa - dre e - ter - no,

heard the song they sing to praise the Lamb.
praise the Lamb who gave his life for us:
peat the cho - rus, prais - ing God in song:

to - dos a - la - ba - ban al Se - ñor.
glo - ria y a - la - ban - zas al Se - ñor.
Tú nos has cre - a - do por a - mor.

Thou - sands   are   pray - ing,   mil - lions   are   sing - ing;   a -
pow - er   and   glo - ry,   wis - dom   and   hon - or   be
bless - ing   and   hon - or,   glo - ry   and   pow - er   be

U - nos   o - ra - ban,   o - tros   can - ta - ban,   y
Glo - ria   al   Pa - dre,   glo - ria   al   Hi - jo,   y
Te   a - do - ra - mos,   te   ben - de - ci - mos,   y

loud   they   raise   their   voice   to   praise   the   Lamb.
to   the   Lamb   who   gave   his   life   for   us.
to   the   Lord   for -   ev - er - more,   A - men!

to - dos   a - la -   ba - ban   al   Se - ñor.
glo - ria   al   Es -   pí - ri - tu   de a - mor.
to - dos____   can -   ta - mos   en   tu ho - nor.

F   Refrain

Here from All Nations

1 Here from all nations, all tongues, and all peo - ples,
2 These have come out of the great trib - u - la - tion;
3 Gone is their thirst and no more shall they hun - ger;
4 He will go with them to clear liv - ing wa - ter
5 Bless - ing and glo - ry and wis - dom and pow - er

count - less the crowd but their voic - es are one.
now they may stand in the pres - ence of God,
► God is their shel - ter, his power at their side.
flow - ing from springs which his mer - cy sup - plies.
be to the Sav - ior a - gain and a - gain.

Vast is the sight and ma - jes - tic their sing - ing:
serv - ing their Lord day and night in his tem - ple,
► Sun shall not pain them, no burn - ing will tor - ture;
Gone is their grief, and their tri - als are o - ver.
Might and thanks - giv - ing and hon - or for - ev - er

"God has the vic - tory: he reigns from the throne!"
ran - somed and cleansed by the Lamb's pre - cious blood.
► Je - sus the Lamb is their shep - herd and guide.
God wipes a - way ev - ery tear from their eyes.
be to our God: Al - le - lu - ia! A - men.

Text: *Revelation 7:9–17; vers. Christopher Idle, 1973.* © 1973, *Hope Publishing Co.*
All rights reserved. Used by permission.
Tune: *Antiphoner, Paris, 1681; harm. John B. Dykes, 1868, adapt.*

11 10 11 10
O QUANTA QUALIA

236   Then I Saw a New Heaven and Earth

1 Then I saw a new heaven and earth, for the first had passed a - way; and the ho - ly cit - y came down from God like a bride on her

2 He will wipe a - way ev - ery tear; e - ven death shall die at last. There'll be no more cry - ing or grief or pain— they be - long to the

3 So the thirst - y can drink their fill at the foun - tain giv - ing life. But the gates are shut on all e - vil things, on de - ceit and de -

4 As they mea - sured its length and breadth I could see no tem - ple there, for its on - ly tem - ple is God the Lord and the Lamb in that

5 And I saw by the sa - cred throne flow - ing wa - ter, crys - tal clear, and the tree of life with its heal - ing leaves and its fruit grow - ing

Text: Revelation 21:1–23; 22:1–5; vers. Christopher Idle, 1973
Tune: Norman L. Warren, 1973
Text and music © 1973, Hope Publishing Co. All rights reserved. Used by permission.

PM
NEW HEAVEN

HYMNS

237 We Praise You, O God

1 We praise you, O God, our Re - deem - er, Cre - a - tor;
2 We wor - ship you, God of our fa - thers and moth - ers;
3 With voic - es u - nit - ed our prais - es we of - fer;

in grate - ful de - vo - tion our trib - ute we bring.
through life's storm and tem - pest our guide you have been.
our songs of thanks - giv - ing to you we now raise.

We lay it be - fore you, we kneel and a - dore you;
When per - ils o'er - take us, you nev - er for - sake us.
Your strong arm will guide us, our God is be - side us.

we bless your ho - ly name, glad prais - es we sing.
And with your help, O Lord, our bat - tles we win.
To you, our great Re - deem - er, for - e'er be praise!

Text: Julia C. Cory, 1902, alt.
Tune: A. Valerius, Nederlandtsch Gedenckclanck, 1626

12 11 12 11
KREMSER

We Come, O Christ, to You

238

1 We come, O Christ, to you, true Son of God and
2 You are the way to God, your blood our ran - som
3 You are the liv - ing truth; all wis - dom dwells in
4 You on - ly are true life— to know you is to
5 We wor - ship you, Lord Christ, our Sav - ior and our

man, by whom all things con - sist, in whom all
paid; in you we face our Judge and Mak - er
► you, the source of ev - ery skill, the one e -
live the more a - bun - dant life that earth can
King; to you our youth and strength a - dor - ing -

life be - gan. In you a - lone we live and
un - a - fraid. Be - fore the throne ab - solved we
► ter - nal True! O great I AM! in you we
nev - er give. O ris - en Lord! we live in
ly we bring: so fill our hearts that all may

move and have our be - ing in your love.
stand; your love has met your law's de - mand.
► rest, sure an - swer to our ev - ery quest.
you: in us each day your life re - new!
view your life in us and turn to you!

Text: Margaret Clarkson, 1946, rev. 1984. © 1957, 1985, InterVarsity Press.
Assigned 1987 to Hope Publishing Co. All rights reserved. Used by permission.
Tune: James V. Lee, 1892–1959. © 1959, United Reformed Church
Alternative tune: DARWALL'S 148th, 408

66 66 88
EASTVIEW

239 Amid the Thronging Worshipers

1 A-mid the throng-ing wor-ship-ers the Lord, our God, I bless;
2 The bur-den of the sor-row-ful the Lord will not de-spise;
3 He feeds with good the hum-ble soul and sat-is-fies the meek,

be-fore his peo-ple gath-ered here his name will I con-fess.
he has not turned from those who mourn, he lis-tens to their cries.
and they shall live and praise the Lord who for his mer-cy seek.

Come, praise him, all who fear the Lord, the chil-dren of his grace;
His good-ness makes me join the throng where saints his praise pro-claim,
The ends of all the earth will hear, the na-tions seek the Lord;

with rev-erence sound his glo-ries forth and bow be-fore his face.
and there will I ful-fill my vows with those who fear his name.
they wor-ship him, the King of kings, in earth and heaven a-dored.

Text: Psalm 22:22–28; vers. Psalter, 1912
Tune: Laura A. Tate, 1912

CMD
BOVINA

Come, All Who Fear the Lord God

240

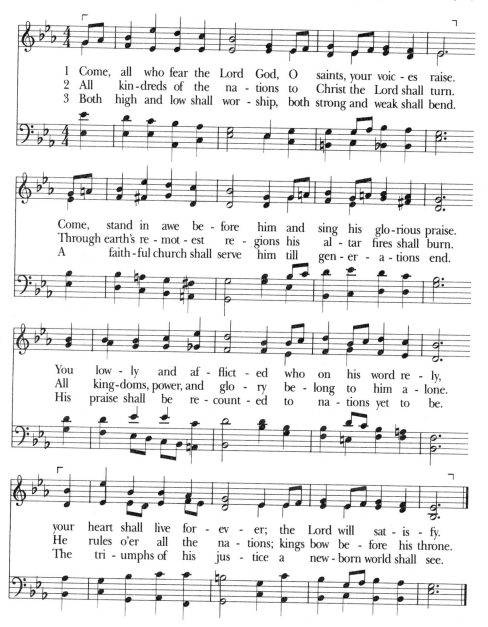

1 Come, all who fear the Lord God, O saints, your voic - es raise.
2 All kin-dreds of the na - tions to Christ the Lord shall turn.
3 Both high and low shall wor - ship, both strong and weak shall bend.

Come, stand in awe be - fore him and sing his glo-rious praise.
Through earth's re - mot - est re - gions his al - tar fires shall burn.
A faith-ful church shall serve him till gen - er - a - tions end.

You low - ly and af - flict - ed who on his word re - ly,
All king-doms, power, and glo - ry be - long to him a - lone.
His praise shall be re - count - ed to na - tions yet to be.

your heart shall live for - ev - er; the Lord will sat - is - fy.
He rules o'er all the na - tions; kings bow be - fore his throne.
The tri - umphs of his jus - tice a new - born world shall see.

Text: Psalm 22:23–31; vers. Psalter, 1912
Tune: Berthold Tours, 1872

76 76 D
TOURS

241

This Is the Day

Capo 1: E♭(D) *May be sung antiphonally*

1 This is the day, this is the day that the Lord has made, that the
2 This is the day, this is the day when he rose a-gain, when he
3 This is the day, this is the day when the Spir-it came, when the

Lord has made; we will re-joice, we will re-joice and be
rose a-gain; we will re-joice, we will re-joice and be
Spir-it came; we will re-joice, we will re-joice and be

glad in it, and be glad in it. This is the day that the
glad in it, and be glad in it. This is the day when he
glad in it, and be glad in it. This is the day when the

Lord has made, we will re-joice and be glad in it;
rose a-gain, we will re-joice and be glad in it;
Spir-it came, we will re-joice and be glad in it;

PM
THIS IS THE DAY

this is the day, this is the day that the Lord has made.
this is the day, this is the day when he rose a - gain.
this is the day, this is the day when the Spir - it came.

Come, All You People, Praise Our God   242

1 Come, all you peo - ple, praise our God and tell his glo-rious works a-broad,
2 We come with of - ferings to his house, and here we pay the sol-emn vows
3 Come, lis - ten, all who fear the Lord, while I with grate-ful heart re - cord

who holds our souls in life; he nev - er lets our feet be moved
we ut - tered in dis - tress; to him our all we ded - i - cate,
what God has done for me; I cried to him in deep dis - tress,

and, though our faith he of - ten proved, up-holds us in the strife.
to him we whol - ly con - se - crate the lives his mer - cies bless.
and now his won - drous grace I bless, for he has set me free.

Text: Psalm 66:8–20; vers. Psalter, 1912   886 D
Tune: Charles H. Gabriel, 1856–1932   ADOWA

243   How Lovely Is Your Dwelling

1 How love-ly is your dwell-ing, O Lord of hosts, to me;
2 Be-neath your care the spar-row finds place for peace-ful rest;
3 Blest they who love and serve you, whose joy and strength you are.

my soul is long-ing, faint-ing, the courts of God to see.
to keep her young in safe-ty the swal-low finds a nest.
For-ev-er they will praise you, your ways are in their heart.

The beau-ty of your dwell-ing will bring me joy a-new.
So, Lord, my King Al-might-y, your love will shel-ter me;
Though tried, their tears like show-ers shall fill the springs of peace;

My heart and flesh are cry-ing, O liv-ing God, for you.
be-neath your wings of mer-cy my dwell-ing place will be.
and all the way to Zi-on their strength shall still in-crease.

Text: Psalm 84:1–7; vers. Psalter, 1912, alt.
Tune: Justin H. Krecht, 1799, and Edward Husband, 1871

76 76 D
ST. EDITH

God Himself Is with Us

244

1 God him-self is with us; let us now a - dore him,
2 God him-self is with us; hear the harps re - sound - ing!
3 Fount of ev - ery bless - ing, pu - ri - fy my spir - it,

and with awe ap - pear be - fore him. God is in his
See the crowds the throne sur - round - ing! "Ho - ly, ho - ly,
trust-ing on - ly in your mer - it. Like the ho - ly

tem - ple; all with - in keep si - lence, pros - trate lie with
ho - ly," hear the hymn as - cend - ing, an - gels, saints, their
an - gels who be - hold your glo - ry, may I cease - less -

deep-est rev - erence. Him a - lone do we own
voic - es blend - ing! Bow your ear to us here;
ly a - dore you, and in all, great and small,

as our God and Sav - ior; praise his name for - ev - er.
hear, O Christ, the prais - es that your church now rais - es.
seek to do most near - ly what you love so dear - ly.

Text: Gerhardt Tersteegen, 1729; tr. composite
Tune: Joachim Neander, 1680

668 668 666
ARNSBERG

245

Jesus, We Love to Meet

1 Je - sus, we love to meet on this, your ho - ly day;
2 We dare not tri - fle now on this, your ho - ly day;
3 We lis - ten to your word on this, your ho - ly day.

we wor - ship round your seat on this, your ho - ly day.
In si - lent awe we bow on this, your ho - ly day.
bless all that we have heard on this, your ho - ly day;

O ten - der heav - enly Friend, to you our prayers as - cend;
Check ev - ery wan - dering thought, and let us all be taught
Go with us when we part, and to each long - ing heart

O - ver our spir - its bend on this, your ho - ly day.
to serve you as we ought on this, your ho - ly day.
your sav - ing grace im - part on this, your ho - ly day.

Optional drum pattern:

Text: Elizabeth Parson, c. 1842
Tune: A. T. Olajide Olude, 1949

irregular
JESU A FE PADE

Come, Thou Almighty King

246

1 Come, thou al - might - y King, help us thy
2 Come, thou in - car - nate Word, gird on thy
3 Come, ho - ly Com - fort - er, thy sa - cred
4 To thee, great One in Three, e - ter - nal

name to sing; help us to praise. Fa - ther all -
might - y sword; scat - ter thy foes. Let thine al -
wit - ness bear in this glad hour. Thou who al -
prais - es be hence ev - er - more! Thy sov - ereign

glo - ri - ous, o'er all vic - to - ri - ous,
might - y aid our sure de - fense be made,
might - y art, rule now in ev - ery heart,
maj - es - ty may we in glo - ry see,

come and reign o - ver us, An - cient of Days.
our souls on thee be stayed; thy won - ders show.
and ne'er from us de - part, Spir - it of power.
and to e - ter - ni - ty love and a - dore.

Text: anonymous, 1757, alt.
Tune: Felice de Giardini, 1769

664 6664
ITALIAN HYMN

247 All Glory Be to God on High

1 All glo - ry be to God on high, and peace on
2 O Lamb of God, Lord Je - sus Christ, whom God the
3 You on - ly are the Ho - ly One who came for

earth from heav - en, and God's good - will un - fail - ing -
Fa - ther gave us, who for the world was sac - ri -
our sal - va - tion, and on - ly you are God's true

ly be to his peo - ple giv - en. Al - might - y
ficed up - on the cross to save us, at God's right
Son who was be - fore cre - a - tion. You on - ly,

God, you are our King: we wor - ship you, our thanks we
hand you in - ter - cede for those who for your mer - cy
Christ, as Lord we own, and with the Spir - it you a -

bring, we praise you for your glo - ry.
plead; re - ceive the prayer we of - fer.
lone share in the Fa - ther's glo - ry.

Text: Latin: Gloria in excelsis Deo, 4th cent.; vers. Nikolaus Decius, 1525; tr. F. Bland Tucker, 1977, alt.
© 1985, The Church Pension Fund. Used by permission.
Tune: attr. Nikolaus Decius, 1539

87 87 887
ALLEIN GOTT

I Greet My Sure Redeemer

248

Text: French, 1545; tr. Elizabeth L. Smith, 1868, alt.
Tune: Louis Bourgeois, 1551, adapt. from his melody for Psalm 101; harm. after Claude Goudimel, 1564
Alternative tune: TOULON, 521

10 10 10 10
JE TU SALUE

249   Holy, Holy, Holy! Lord God Almighty

Text: Reginald Heber, 1827, alt.
Tune: John B. Dykes, 1861; desc. David McK. Williams, 1887–1978. Descant © 1948, 1976, H. W. Gray Co.,
a division of Belwin Mills Publishing Corp. All rights reserved. Used by permission.

11 12 12 10
NICAEA

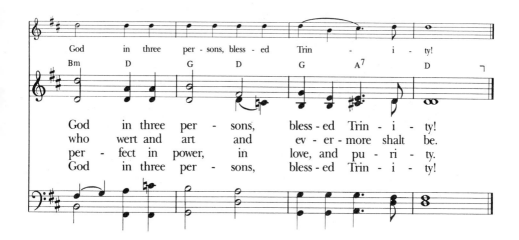

God   in   three   per - sons, bless - ed   Trin -   i - ty!

Bm   D   G   D   G A^7 D

God   in   three   per - sons,   bless - ed Trin - i - ty!
who   wert and   art   and   ev - er - more shalt be.
per - fect in power,   in   love, and pu - ri - ty.
God   in   three   per - sons,   bless - ed Trin - i - ty!

I've Come to Tell
Te Vengo a Decir

250

I've come____ to tell, I've come____ to tell, O Sav-ior di-vine,
Te ven-go_a de-cir, te ven go_a de-cir, oh buen Sal-va-dor,

how much I love you, how much I love you, with all of my heart.
que yo te_a-mo_a ti, que yo te_a-mo_a ti, con el co-ra-zón.

I've come____ to tell, I've come____ to tell, to tell you the truth:
Te ven-go_a de-cir, te ven-go_a de-cir to-da la ver-dad:

I love you, O Lord, I wor-ship you, Lord, with all of my heart.
te quie-ro, Se-ñor, te_a-do-ro, Se-ñor, con el co-ra-zón.

Text: Juan M. Isáis, 1979; tr. Frank Sawyer, 1984
Tune: Juan M. Isáis, 1979; harm. Dale Grotenhuis, 1984
Text and music © 1979, Juan M. Isáis

irregular
TE VENGO

I want___ to sing, I want___ to sing from hap - pi - ness;
Yo quie-ro can - tar, yo quie-ro can - tar de fe - li - ci - dad;

I want___ to cry, I want___ to cry from joy___ and peace.
yo quie-ro llo - rar, yo quie-ro llo - rar de go-zo_y de paz.

I've come___ to tell, I've come___ to tell, to tell you the truth:
Te ven-go_a de - cir, te ven-go_a de - cir to-da la ver - dad:

I love you, O Lord, I wor-ship you, Lord, with all of my heart.
te quie-ro, Se - ñor, te_a-do-ro, Se - ñor, con el co - ra - zón.

251 Here, O Lord, Your Servants Gather

1 Here, O Lord, your ser-vants gath-er, hand we link with hand;
2 Man-y are the tongues we speak, scat-tered are the lands;
3 Na-ture's se-crets o-pen wide, chang-es nev-er cease;
4 Grant, O God, an age re-newed, filled with death-less love;

look-ing toward our Sav-ior's cross, joined in love we stand.
yet our hearts are one in God, one in love's de-mands.
where, O where, can wea-ry souls find the source of peace?
help us as we work and pray. Send us from a-bove

As we seek the realm of God, we u-nite to pray:
E'en in dark-ness hope ap-pears, call-ing age and youth;
Un-to all those sore dis-tressed, torn by end-less strife,
truth and cour-age, faith and power need-ed in our strife:

Text: Tokuo Yamaguchi, 1958; tr. Everett M. Stowe, 1958, 1972, ©
Tune: Japanese Gagaku mode; arr. Isao Koizumi, 1958, ©

75 75 D
TOKYO

Je - sus, Sav - ior, guide our steps, for you are the way.
Je - sus, Teach-er, dwell with us, for you are the truth.
Je - sus, Heal - er, bring your balm, for you are the life.
Je sus, Mas ter, be our way, be our truth, our life.

Father in Heaven

252

Unison

1 Fa - ther in heav - en, grant to your chil - dren mer - cy and
2 Je - sus, Re-deem - er, may we re - mem - ber your gra-cious
3 Spir - it de -scend - ing, grant us your bless - ing, strength for the

bless - ing, songs nev - er ceas - ing, love to u - nite us,
pas - sion, your res - ur - rec - tion; wor - ship we bring you,
wea - ry, help for the need - y; sealed by a - dop - tion,

grace to re - deem us; Fa -ther in heav - en, Fa - ther, our God.
praise we shall sing you, Je - sus, Re - deem - er, Je - sus, our Lord.
we are God's chil - dren; Spir - it de - scend - ing, Spir - it a - dored.

Text: Daniel Thambyrapah Niles, 1964, alt.
Tune: W. Walker's Southern Harmony, 1835; harm. Gary Warmink, 1974.
    Harmonization © 1974, CRC Publications
Keyboard and guitar should not sound together.

55 55 55 54
RESTORATION

253   Praise to the Lord, the Almighty

Text: Joachim Neander, 1680; tr. Catherine Winkworth, 1863, alt.
Tune: Ernewerten Gesangbuch, Stralsund, 1665; desc. Craig S. Lang, 1891–1971.
   Descant © Novello and Co., Ltd.

14 14 478
LOBE DEN HERREN

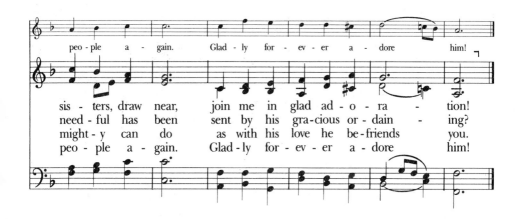

sis - ters, draw near,   join me in glad ad - o - ra - tion!
need - ful has been   sent by his gra-cious or - dain - ing?
might - y can do   as with his love he be - friends you.
peo - ple a - gain.   Glad - ly for - ev - er a - dore him!

Remember Not, O God   254

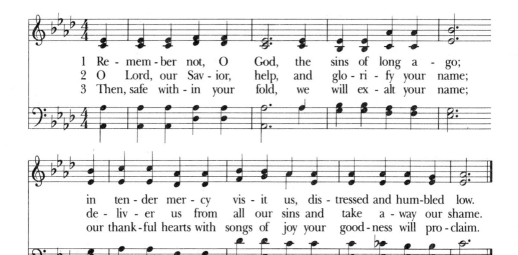

1 Re - mem - ber not, O   God,   the   sins of long a - go;
2 O   Lord, our Sav - ior,   help,   and   glo - ri - fy your name;
3 Then, safe with - in your   fold,   we   will ex - alt your name;

in ten - der mer - cy   vis - it   us, dis - tressed and hum - bled low.
de - liv - er us from   all our   sins and   take a - way our shame.
our thank - ful hearts with   songs of   joy your   good - ness will pro - claim.

Text: Psalm 79:8–9, 13; vers. Psalter, 1912
Tune: Ludwig van Beethoven, 1807, adapt.

SM
GORTON

255 God, Be Merciful to Me

1 God, be mer-ci-ful to me; on your grace I rest my plea.
2 I have sinned a-gainst your grace and pro-voked you to your face.
3 Gra-cious God, my heart re-new, make my spir-it right and true.
4 Con-trite spir-it, plead-ing cries, you, O God, will not de-spise.

My trans-gres-sions I con-fess; grief and guilt my soul op-press.
I con-fess your judg-ment just; speech-less, I your mer-cy trust.
Do not cast me from your sight nor re-move your Spir-it's light.
Sin-ful ways I will re-prove, and my tongue shall sing your love.

Wash me, make me pure with-in; cleanse, O cleanse me from my sin.
Let my con-trite heart re-joice and in glad-ness hear your voice.
Your sal-va-tion's joy re-store, make me stead-fast ev-er-more.
Let my right-eous sac-ri-fice then de-light your ho-ly eyes.

Text: from Psalm 51; vers. Psalter, 1912, alt.
Tune: Richard Redhead, 1853

77 77 77
REDHEAD 76

Out of the Depths I Cry

256

1 Out of the depths I cry to you on high; Lord, hear my call.
2 I wait for God, I trust his ho - ly word; he hears my sighs.
3 Hope in the Lord: un - fail - ing is his love; in him con - fide.

Bend down your ear and lis - ten to my sigh,
My soul still waits and looks un - to the Lord;
Mer - cy and full re - demp - tion from a - bove

for - giv - ing all. If you should mark our sins, who then could stand?
my prayers a - rise. I look for him to drive a - way my night—
he does pro - vide. From sin and e - vil, might - y though they seem,

But grace and mer - cy dwell at your right hand.
yes, more than those who watch for morn - ing light.
his arm al - might - y will his saints re - deem.

Text: Psalm 130; vers. Psalter, 1912, alt.
Tune: Charles H. Purday, 1860

10 4 10 4 10 10
SANDON

257   O Christ, the Lamb of God

Women and children

O Christ, the Lamb of God, who takes a - way the sin of the world,

have mer - cy up - on us. O Christ, the Lamb of God, who

Men

takes a - way the sin of the world, have mer - cy up - on us.

Text: Agnus Dei, *based on John 1:29*
Tune: Kirchenordnung, *Braunschweig, 1528; harm. Dale Grotenhuis, 1984.*
   Harmonization © 1987, CRC Publications

PM
CHRISTE, DU LAMM GOTTES

O Christ, the Lamb of God, who takes a-way the sin of the world, grant us your peace. A - men.

Lord, Have Mercy upon Us 258

Lord, have mer-cy up-on us. Christ, have mer-cy up-on us. Lord, have mer-cy up-on us.

Text: Kyrie, *from early Christian liturgies*
Tune: *Healey Willan, 1928. © 1928, Oxford University Press*

PM
WILLAN KYRIE

259 Out of Need and out of Custom

1 Out of need and out of cus - tom we have gath - ered
2 We now come our masks dis - play - ing, fear - ing that we
3 We have heard the glow - ing sto - ries of the things that

here a - gain. To the gath - ering we are bring - ing
shall be known, fool - ish games for - ev - er play - ing,
God has done, of his pow - er and his glo - ry,

love and laugh - ter, grief and pain. Some be - liev - ing,
feel - ing mean - while so a - lone. Let pre - ten - sion's
of his love in Christ, his Son. God of hu - man

some re - joic - ing, some a - fraid, and some in doubt; now we
power be bro - ken, to be o - pen let us dare; let the
trans - for - ma - tion, for your pres - ence now we pray; lead us

come our ques - tions voic - ing, we would search these mat - ters out.
truth in love be spo - ken, let us now the search - ing share.
ev - er on the jour - ney as we gath - er here to - day.

Text and Tune: Ken Medema, 1972. © 1977, Word Music (a division of WORD, Inc.).
All rights reserved. International copyright secured. Used by permission.

87 87 D
GATHERING

Not What My Hands Have Done

1 Not what my hands have done can save my guilt-y soul;
2 Your voice a-lone, O Lord, can speak to me of grace;
3 I praise the Christ of God; I rest on love di - vine;

not what my toil - ing flesh has borne can make my spir - it whole.
your power a - lone, O Son of God, can all my sin e - rase.
and with un - fal-tering lip and heart I call this Sav - ior mine.

Not what I feel or do can give me peace with God;
No oth - er work but yours, no oth - er blood will do;
My Lord has saved my life and free - ly par - don gives;

not all my prayers and sighs and tears can bear my aw - ful load.
no strength but that which is di - vine can bear me safe - ly through.
I love be - cause he first loved me, I live be-cause he lives.

Text: Horatius Bonar, 1861, alt.
Tune: George William Martin, 1862

SMD
LEOMINSTER

261 Lord, We Cry to You for Help

1 Lord, we cry to you for help. On - ly you can heal our pain. Out of deep dis - tress we call. Help us, Lord, send peace a - gain.

2 We have sinned a - gainst your law. We have failed to do your will, dis - o - beyed your ho - ly Word. Lord, have mer - cy on us still.

3 Purge our souls of self - ish - ness. Cleanse our hearts of bit - ter - ness. Lead us back to right - eous - ness. Save us, Lord, O save us still.

4 Lord, ex - alt your ho - ly name. Con - quer e - vil by your power. Let your right - eous will pre - vail. Reign vic - to - rious ev - er - more.

Text: Ulrich Zwingli, 1529; tr. Helen A. Dickinson, 1940, alt.
Tune: Ulrich Zwingli, 1529; harm. Clarence Dickinson, 1940, alt.
Text and harmonization © 1940, 1968, H. W. Gray Co., Inc.

77 77
HERR, NUN HEB

My Faith Looks Up to Thee

262

1 My faith looks up to thee, thou Lamb of Cal - va - ry,
2 May thy rich grace im - part strength to my faint - ing heart,
3 While life's dark maze I tread and griefs a - round me spread,
4 When life's swift race is run, death's cold work al - most done,

Sav - ior di - vine! Now hear me while I pray, take all my
my zeal in - spire. As thou hast died for me, O may my
be thou my guide. Bid dark - ness turn to day, wipe sor - row's
be near to me. Blest Sav - ior, then in love fear and dis -

guilt a - way. O let me from this day be whol - ly thine!
love to thee pure, warm, and change - less be, a liv - ing fire!
tears a - way, nor let me ev - er stray from thee a - side.
trust re - move. O bear me safe a - bove, re - deemed and free!

Text: Ray Palmer, 1830, alt.
Tune: Lowell Mason, 1832

664 6664
OLIVET

263   Just as I Am, without One Plea

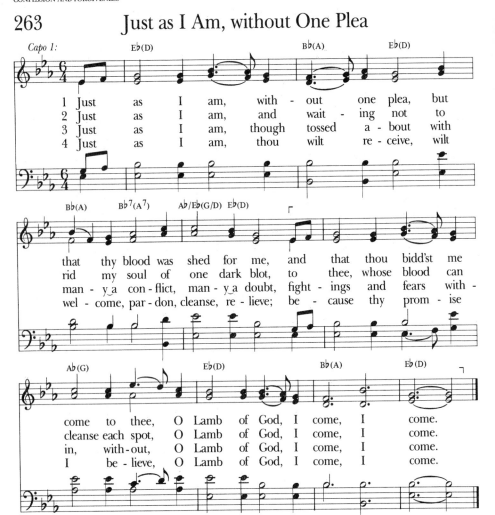

1 Just as I am, with - out one plea, but
2 Just as I am, and wait - ing not to
3 Just as I am, though tossed a - bout with
4 Just as I am, thou wilt re - ceive, wilt

that thy blood was shed for me, and that thou bidd'st me
rid my soul of one dark blot, to thee, whose blood can
man - y a con - flict, man - y a doubt, fight - ings and fears with -
wel - come, par - don, cleanse, re - lieve; be - cause thy prom - ise

come to thee, O Lamb of God, I come, I come.
cleanse each spot, O Lamb of God, I come, I come.
in, with - out, O Lamb of God, I come, I come.
I be - lieve, O Lamb of God, I come, I come.

Text: Charlotte Elliott, 1836
Tune: William B. Bradbury, 1849

LM
WOODWORTH

Lord, I Want to Be a Christian

264

1 Lord, I want to be a Chris-tian in my heart, in my heart.
2 Lord, I want to be more lov-ing in my heart, in my heart.
3 Lord, I want to be more ho-ly in my heart, in my heart.
4 Lord, I want to be like Je-sus, in my heart, in my heart.

Lord, I want to be a Chris-tian in my heart.
Lord, I want to be more lov-ing in my heart.
Lord, I want to be more ho-ly in my heart.
Lord, I want to be like Je-sus in my heart.

In my heart,   in my heart,
        in my heart,   in my heart,

Lord, I want to be a Chris-tian in my heart.
Lord, I want to be more lov-ing in my heart.
Lord, I want to be more ho-ly in my heart.
Lord, I want to be like Je-sus in my heart.

Text and Tune: Afro-American spiritual

PM
LORD, I WANT TO BE A CHRISTIAN

265   Standing in the Need of Prayer

1 Not my broth-er, nor my sis-ter, but it's me, O Lord,
2 Not the el-der, nor the dea-con, but it's me, O Lord,
3 Not my fa-ther, nor my moth-er, but it's me, O Lord,
4 Not the strang-er, nor my neigh-bor, but it's me, O Lord,

stand-ing in the need of prayer; not my broth-er, nor my sis-ter,
stand-ing in the need of prayer; not the el-der, nor the dea-con,
stand-ing in the need of prayer; not my fa-ther, nor my moth-er,
stand-ing in the need of prayer; not the strang-er, nor my neigh-bor,

but it's me, O Lord, stand-ing in the need of prayer.
but it's me, O Lord, stand-ing in the need of prayer.
but it's me, O Lord, stand-ing in the need of prayer.
but it's me, O Lord, stand-ing in the need of prayer.

Refrain

It's me, it's me, O Lord, stand-ing in the need of prayer;
it's me,

Text and Tune: Afro-American spiritual

it's me, it's me, O Lord, stand-ing in the need of prayer.
it's me,

"Forgive Our Sins As We Forgive" 266

1 "For - give our sins as we for - give," you
2 How can your par - don reach and bless the
3 In blaz - ing light your cross re - veals the
4 Lord, cleanse the depths with - in our souls and

taught us, Lord, to pray. But you a - lone can
un - for - giv - ing heart that broods on wrongs and
truth we dim - ly knew— what triv - ial debts are
bid re - sent - ment cease. Then, bound to all in

grant us grace to live the words we say.
will not let old bit - ter - ness de - part?
owed to us, how great our debt to you.
bonds of love, our lives will spread your peace.

Text: Rosamond E. Herklots, 1969. By permission of Oxford University Press.
Tune: Scottish Psalter, 1615

CM
DUNFERMLINE

267 And Can It Be

1 And can it be that I should gain an
2 He left his Fa - ther's throne a - bove— so
3 Long my im - pris - oned spir - it lay fast
4 No con - dem - na - tion now I dread, for

in - terest in the Sav - ior's blood? Died he for
free, so in - fi - nite his grace— emp - tied him -
bound in sin and na - ture's night. Your sun - rise
Christ, and all in him, is mine! A - live in

me, who caused his pain— for me, who caused his
self of all but love, and bled for Ad - am's
turned that night to day; I woke— the dun - geon
him, my liv - ing Head, and clothed in right - eous -

bit - ter death? A - maz - ing love! How can it
help - less race! What mer - cy this, im - mense and
flamed with light! My chains fell off, your voice I
ness di - vine, bold I ap - proach the_e - ter - nal

Text: Charles Wesley, 1738, alt.
Tune: Thomas Campbell, 1825

LMD
SAGINA

be   that   you,   my   Lord,   should   die   for   me?
free,   for,   O   my   God,   it   found   out   me!
knew;   I   rose,   went   out,   and   fol - lowed   you.
throne   and   claim   the   crown,   through   Christ,   my   own.

Refrain

A - maz - ing   love!   How   can   it   be   that
A - maz - ing   love!   How   can   it   be

you,   my   Lord,   should   die   for   me?!
that   you,   my   Lord,

268   Lord, I Pray

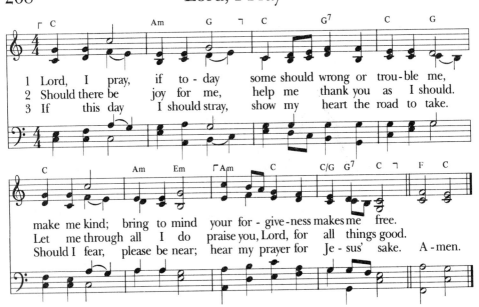

1 Lord, I pray, if to-day some should wrong or trou-ble me,
2 Should there be joy for me, help me thank you as I should.
3 If this day I should stray, show my heart the road to take.

make me kind; bring to mind your for-give-ness makes me free.
Let me through all I do praise you, Lord, for all things good.
Should I fear, please be near; hear my prayer for Je-sus' sake. A-men.

Text: Jean C. Keegstra-De Boer, 1949, alt.
Tune: Dutch; harm. AnnaMae Meyer Bush, 1985. Harmonization © 1987, CRC Publications
Keyboard and guitar should not sound together.

67 67
KLOKJE KLINGT

269   Baptized in Water

Unison

1 Bap-tized in wa - ter, sealed by the Spir - it, cleansed by the
2 Bap-tized in wa - ter, sealed by the Spir - it, dead in the
3 Bap-tized in wa - ter, sealed by the Spir - it, marked with the

blood of Christ, our King; heirs of sal - va - tion, trust-ing his
tomb with Christ, our King; one with his ris - ing, freed and for -
sign of Christ, our King; born of one Fa - ther, we are his

Text: Michael Saward, 1981. © 1982, Hope Publishing Co. All rights reserved. Used by permission.
Tune: Gaelic; harm. Dale Grotenhuis, 1985. © 1987, CRC Publications

558 D
BUNESSAN

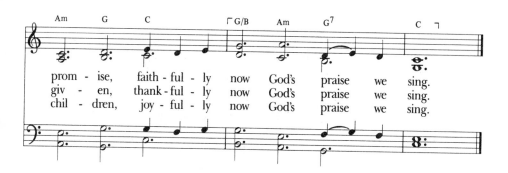

prom - ise, faith - ful - ly now God's praise we sing.
giv - en, thank - ful - ly now God's praise we sing.
chil - dren, joy - ful - ly now God's praise we sing.

Our Children, Lord, in Faith and Prayer 270

1 Our chil - dren, Lord, in faith and prayer, we
2 Such chil - dren you did once em - brace while
3 In all their days their hearts se - cure from

bap - tize in your name. Let them your cov - enant
dwell - ing here be - low; to us and ours, O
sin - ful snares, we pray. Through - out their lives let

mer - cies share as we our faith pro - claim.
Lord of grace, the same com - pas - sion show.
them en - dure in ev - ery right - eous way.

Text: Thomas Haweis, 1732–1820, alt.
Tune: arr. Lowell Mason, 1836
Alternative tune: ST. PETER, 487

CM
NAOMI

271 We Know That Christ Is Raised

1 We know that Christ is raised and dies no more.
2 We share by wa - ter in his sav - ing death.
3 The Fa - ther's splen - dor clothes the Son with life.
4 A new cre - a - tion comes to life and grows

Em - braced by death, he broke its fear - ful hold,
Re - born, we share with him an Eas - ter life
The Spir - it's pow - er shakes the church of God.
as Christ's new bod - y takes on flesh and blood.

and our de - spair he turned to blaz - ing joy.
as liv - ing mem - bers of a liv - ing Christ.
Bap - tized, we live with God, the Three in One.
The u - ni - verse, re - stored and whole, will sing:

Al - le - lu - ia! Al - le - lu - ia!

Text: John B. Geyer, 1967, alt. Used by permission.
Tune: Keith Landis, 1977; harm. Jeffrey Rickard, 1977.
Alternative tune: SINE NOMINE, 505

10 10 10 with alleluias
WALLACE

You Are Our God; We Are Your People

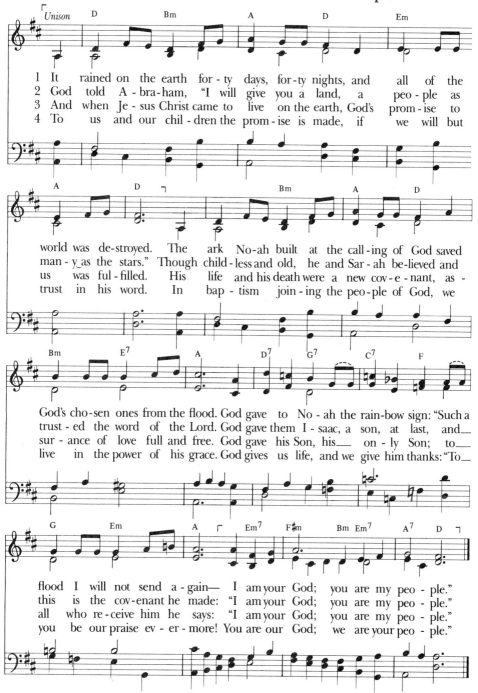

1 It rained on the earth for-ty days, for-ty nights, and all of the
2 God told A-bra-ham, "I will give you a land, a peo-ple as
3 And when Je-sus Christ came to live on the earth, God's prom-ise to
4 To us and our chil-dren the prom-ise is made, if we will but

world was de-stroyed. The ark No-ah built at the call-ing of God saved
man-y as the stars." Though child-less and old, he and Sar-ah be-lieved and
us was ful-filled. His life and his death were a new cov-e-nant, as-
trust in his word. In bap-tism join-ing the peo-ple of God, we

God's cho-sen ones from the flood. God gave to No-ah the rain-bow sign: "Such a
trust-ed the word of the Lord. God gave them I-saac, a son, at last, and—
sur-ance of love full and free. God gave his Son, his— on-ly Son; to—
live in the power of his grace. God gives us life, and we give him thanks: "To—

flood I will not send a-gain— I am your God; you are my peo-ple."
this is the cov-e-nant he made: "I am your God; you are my peo-ple."
all who re-ceive him he says: "I am your God; you are my peo-ple."
you be our praise ev-er-more! You are our God; we are your peo-ple."

Text and Tune: David A. Hoekema, 1978. © 1985, CRC Publications

irregular
JANNA

273 Almighty Father, Covenant God

1 Al - might - y Fa - ther, cov - enant God, we
2 We are en - graft - ed in - to Christ. You
3 We now pre - sent our chil - dren, Lord, as
4 They are the seed of A - bra - ham: in
5 To God the Fa - ther, God the Son, and

praise your love so free - ly given; for - give - ness through the
help us live our lives for him. Your cov - enant, sealed to
your own lambs for your em - brace. Bind lives and hearts to
ear - ly days keep them se - cure. As wa - ter seals the
God the Spir - it, Three in One, praise, hon - or, might, and

blood of Christ that names us in the book of heaven.
us, con - firms a - dop - tion through the three - fold name.
live for you a life of ser - vice and of praise.
prom - ise now, bless them with faith that shall en - dure.
glo - ry be from age to age, e - ter - nal - ly.

Text: Marie J. Post, 1975. © 1987, CRC Publications
Tune: Dale Grotenhuis, 1984, ©

LM
WYATT

O God, Great Father, Lord and King 274

1 O God, great Fa - ther, Lord and King, our chil - dren
2 Your cov - enant bless - ing did of old our par - ents
3 Look down up - on us while we pray and vis - it
4 They now the out - ward sign re - ceive; your prom - ised
5 Di - rect their feet in ho - ly ways and shine on

un - to you we bring. We come in faith and
and their seed en - fold. That an - cient prom - ise
► us in grace to - day. These lit - tle ones you
Ho - ly Spir - it give. O keep and help them
them through dark - est days. Up - hold them till their

hope and love; we dare your stead - fast word to prove.
stands se - cure and shall while heaven and earth en - dure.
► did re - ceive; your pre - cious prom - ise we be - lieve.
by your power in ev - ery hard and try - ing hour.
life is past and bring them all to heaven at last.

Text: E. Embree Hoss, 1905, alt.
Tune: Samuel Webbe, 1782
This music in a lower key: 112

LM
MELCOMBE

275 The Lord Our God in Mercy Spoke

1 The Lord our God in mer - cy spoke:
2 That prom - ise A - bra - ham be - lieved
3 How faith - ful are the ways of God;
4 So to the par - ents and their seed

"A God to you I'll be;
and pledged his child to God,
his love en - dures the same.
shall God's sal - va - tion come,

I'll bless your nu - merous race and they
but wa - ter seals the bless - ing now
He keeps the prom - ise of his grace:
and nu - merous house - holds meet at last

shall be a seed to me."
that once was sealed with blood.
pre - serves his chil - dren's name.
in one e - ter - nal home.

Text: Isaac Watts, 1707, alt.
Tune: George T. Thalben-Ball, 1951. By permission of Oxford University Press.
Alternative tune: DUNDEE, 434

CM
ARDEN

Teach Me, O Lord, Your Way of Truth   276

1 Teach me, O Lord, your way of truth, and from it
2 In your com - mand-ments make me walk, for in your
3 Your word sheds light up - on my path; a shin - ing
4 Your won-drous tes - ti - mo - nies, Lord, my soul will
5 I thirst for your com - mand-ments, Lord, and for your

I will not de - part; that I may stead - fast -
law my joy shall be; give me a heart that
light, it guides my feet; your right-eous judg - ments
keep and great - ly praise; your word, by faith - ful
mer - cy press my claim; O look on me and

ly o - bey, give me an un - der - stand - ing heart.
loves your will, from dis - con - tent and en - vy free.
to ob - serve, my sol - emn vow I now re - peat.
lips pro - claimed, to sim - plest minds the truth con - veys.
show the grace dis - played to all who love your name.

Text: Psalm 119:33–36, 105–106, 129–132; vers. Psalter, 1912, alt.
Tune: George J. Elvey, 1862

LM
ST. CRISPIN

277 God Who Spoke in the Beginning

1 God who spoke in the be - gin - ning, form - ing rock and
2 God who spoke through peo - ple, na - tions, through e - vents long
3 God whose speech be - comes in - car - nate— Christ is ser - vant,

shap - ing spar, set all life and growth in mo - tion,
past and gone, show - ing still to - day his pur - pose,
Christ is Lord!— calls us to a life of ser - vice,

earth - ly world and dis - tant star; he who calls the
speaks su - preme - ly through his Son; he who calls the
heart and will to ac - tion stirred; he who u - ses

earth to or - der is the ground of what we are.
earth to or - der gives his word, and it is done.
our o - be - dience has the first and fi - nal word.

Text: Fred H. Kaan, 1968. © 1968, Hope Publishing Co. All rights reserved. Used by permission.
Tune: Gesangbuch, Darmstadt, 1698

87 87 87
ALL SAINTS

Holy Spirit, Mighty God

1 Ho - ly Spir - it, might - y God, tune our ears to
2 Ho - ly Spir - it, might - y God, move our will, de -
3 Ho - ly Spir - it, gra - cious God, source of Sab - bath

hear the Word; o - pen our hearts, con - vert our lives;
spite our sin, in - to new deeds of truth, not lies;
rest and joy, gen - tle our hurts and still our cries;

mold us strong, sound; make us wise.
teach us love, peace; make us wise.
com - fort, heal, bless; make us wise.

Text: Calvin Seerveld, 1983, ©
Tune: John Wilson, 1967. © 1979, Hope Publishing Co. All rights reserved. Used by permission.

77 87
LAUDS

279   O Word of God Incarnate

1 O Word of God in - car - nate, O Wis - dom from on high,
2 The church from you, dear Mas - ter, re - ceived this gift di - vine;
3 O make your church, dear Sav - ior, a lamp of bur-nished gold

O Truth un-changed, un - chang - ing, O Light of our dark sky:
and still that light is lift - ed o'er all the earth to shine.
to bear be - fore the na - tions your true light as of old.

we praise you for the ra - diance that from the Scrip - ture's page,
It is the chart and com - pass that all life's voy - age through,
O teach your trav - eling pil - grims by this their path to trace

a lan - tern to our foot - steps, shines on from age to age.
mid mists and rocks and quick-sands, still guides, O Christ, to you.
till, clouds and dark - ness end - ed, we see you face to face.

Text: William W. How, 1867, alt.
Tune: Neu-vermehrtes Gesangbuch, Meiningen, 1693; adapt. and harm. Felix Mendelssohn, 1847

76 76 D
MUNICH

Blessed Jesus, at Your Word

280

1 Bless - ed Je - sus, at your word we are gath - ered
2 All our knowl-edge, sense, and sight lie in deep - est
3 Glo - rious Lord, your-self im - part; Light of Light, from

all to hear you. Let our hearts and souls be stirred
dark-ness shroud - ed, till your Spir - it breaks our night
God pro - ceed - ing, o - pen lips and ears and heart;

now to seek and love and fear you. By your gos - pel
with your beams of truth un - cloud - ed. You a - lone to
help us by your Spir - it's lead - ing. Hear the cry your

pure and ho - ly, teach us, Lord, to love you sole - ly.
God can win us; you must work all good with - in us.
church now rais - es; Lord, ac - cept our prayers and prais - es.

Text: Tobias Clausnitzer, 1663; tr. Catherine Winkworth, 1858, alt.
Tune: Johann R. Ahle, 1664

78 78 88
LIEBSTER JESU

281 Thanks to God Whose Word Was Spoken

1 Thanks to God whose word was spo - ken in the deed that
2 Thanks to God whose Word in - car - nate hu - man flesh has
3 Thanks to God whose word was writ - ten on the Bi - ble's
4 Thanks to God whose word is pub - lished in the tongues of
5 Thanks to God whose word is an - swered by the Spir - it's

made the earth; his the voice that called a na - tion,
glo - ri - fied, who by life and death and ris - ing
sa - cred page, rec - ord of the rev - e - la - tion
ev - ery race; see its glo - ry un - di - min - ished
voice with - in; here we drink of joy un - mea - sured,

his the fires that tried her worth. God has spo - ken,
grace a - bun - dant has sup - plied. God has spo - ken,
show - ing God to ev - ery age. God has spo - ken,
by the change of time or place. God is speak - ing,
life re - deemed from death and sin. God is speak - ing,

God has spo - ken:
God has spo - ken:
God has spo - ken: praise him for his o - pen word!
God is speak - ing:
God is speak - ing:

Text: R. T. Brooks, 1954. © 1954, 1982, Hope Publishing Co. All rights reserved. Used by permission.
Tune: Paul Langston, 1974. © 1975, Broadman Press. All rights reserved. International copyright secured. Used by permission.

87 87 447
ERIN

Break Now the Bread of Life

282

1 Break now the bread of life, dear Lord, to me, as once you
2 Bless your own word of truth, dear Lord, to me, as when you
3 You are the bread of life, dear Lord, to me; your ho - ly
4 O send your Spir - it now, dear Lord, to me, that he may

broke the loaves be - side the sea. Be - yond the sa - cred page
blessed the bread by Gal - i - lee. Then shall all bond-age cease,
word the truth that res - cues me. Give me to eat and live
touch my eyes and make me see. Show me the truth made plain

I seek you, Lord; my spir - it waits for you, O liv - ing Word.
all fet - ters fall; and I shall find my peace, my All in all!
with you a - bove; teach me to love your truth, for you are love.
with - in your Word, for in your book re - vealed I see you, Lord.

Text: st. 1–2, Mary A. Lathbury, 1877, alt.; st. 3–4, Alexander Groves, 1842–1909
Tune: William F. Sherwin, 1877
Keyboard and guitar should not sound together.

64 64 D
BREAD OF LIFE

283   The Lord Almighty Spoke the Word

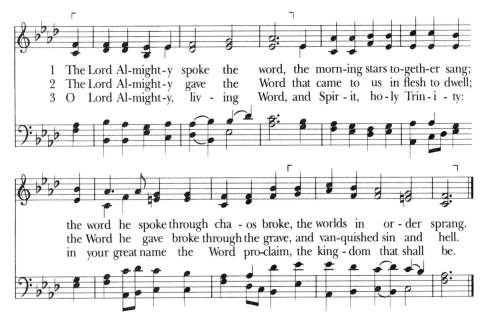

1 The Lord Al-might-y spoke the word, the morn-ing stars to-geth-er sang;
2 The Lord Al-might-y gave the Word that came to us in flesh to dwell;
3 O Lord Al-might-y, liv - ing Word, and Spir - it, ho-ly Trin-i - ty:

the word he spoke through cha - os broke, the worlds in or - der sprang.
the Word he gave broke through the grave, and van-quished sin and hell.
in your great name the Word pro-claim, the king - dom that shall be.

Text: Charles E. Watson, 1964. © Rodborough Tabernacle United Reformed Church
Tune: T. Zavorka's Kancional, 1602; harm. Dale Grotenhuis, 1984. Harmonization © 1987, CRC Publications
Another harmonization in a higher key: 444

88 86
ROK NOVY

284   Father, I Adore You

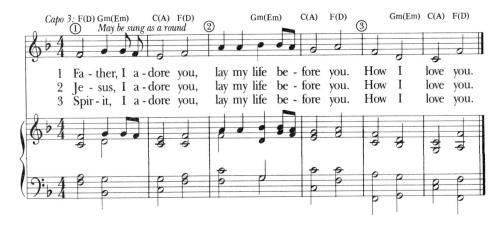

Capo 3: F(D) Gm(Em)   C(A) F(D)   Gm(Em)   C(A)   F(D)   Gm(Em) C(A) F(D)

May be sung as a round

1 Fa - ther, I a - dore you, lay my life be - fore you. How I love you.
2 Je - sus, I a - dore you, lay my life be - fore you. How I love you.
3 Spir - it, I a - dore you, lay my life be - fore you. How I love you.

Text and Tune: Terrye Coelho, 1972. © 1972, Maranatha! Music. All rights reserved.
International copyright secured. Used by permission.

664
MARANATHA

O Jesus, I Have Promised

285

1 O Je-sus, I have prom-ised to serve you to the end;
2 O let me feel you near me; the world is ev-er near:
3 O let me hear you speak-ing in ac-cents clear and still,
4 O Je-sus, you have prom-ised to all who fol-low you

be now and ev-er near me, my Mas-ter and my Friend.
I see the sights that daz-zle, the tempt-ing sounds I hear.
a-bove the storms of pas-sion, the mur-murs of self-will.
that where you are in glo-ry your ser-vants shall be too.

I shall not fear the bat-tle if you are by my side,
My foes are ev-er near me, a-round me and with-in;
O speak to re-as-sure me, to has-ten or con-trol;
O guide me, call me, draw me, up-hold me to the end,

nor wan-der from the path-way if you will be my guide.
but, Je-sus, draw still near-er and shield my soul from sin!
and speak to make me lis-ten, O Guard-ian of my soul.
when you in glo-ry take me, my Sav-ior and my Friend.

Text: John E. Bode, 1869, alt.
Tune: Finnish; harm. David Evans, 1927. Harmonization by permission of Oxford University Press.

76 76 D
NYLAND

286 Lord of Creation, to You Be All Praise

1 Lord of cre - a - tion, to you be all praise!
2 Lord of all pow - er, I give you my will,
3 Lord of all wis - dom, I give you my mind;
4 Lord of all boun - ty, I give you my heart;
5 Lord of all be - ing, I give you my all,

Most might - y your work - ing, most won - drous your ways!
in joy - ful o - be - dience your tasks to ful - fill.
▶ en - rich it with truths that ex - press your de - sign.
I praise and a - dore you for all you im - part:
for if I dis - own you, I stum - ble and fall;

Your glo - ry and might are be - yond us to tell,
Your bond - age is free - dom, your ser - vice is song,
▶ What eye has not seen and what ear has not heard
your love to in - spire me, your coun - sel to lead,
but sworn in glad ser - vice your word to o - bey,

and yet in the heart of the hum - ble you dwell.
and, held in your keep - ing, my weak - ness is strong.
▶ is taught by your Spir - it and shines from your Word.
your pres - ence to shield me, what - ev - er my need.
I walk in your free - dom the rest of the way.

Text: John C. Winslow, 1961, alt. By permission of Mrs. J. Tyrrell.
Tune: Cyril Taylor, 1951. © 1978, Hope Publishing Co. All rights reserved. Used by permission.
Alternative tune: SLANE, 558

10 11 11 11
MINIVER

Have Thine Own Way, Lord

287

1 Have thine own way, Lord! Have thine own way! Thou art the
2 Have thine own way, Lord! Have thine own way! Search me and
3 Have thine own way, Lord! Have thine own way! Wound-ed and
4 Have thine own way, Lord! Have thine own way! Hold o'er my

pot - ter, I am the clay. Mold me and make me
try me, Mas-ter, to - day. O - pen mine eyes, my
wea - ry, help me, I pray. Pow - er, all pow - er,
be - ing ab - so - lute sway. Fill with thy Spir - it

af - ter thy will, while I am wait - ing, yield-ed and still.
sin show me now, as in thy pres - ence hum-bly I bow.
sure - ly is thine. Touch me and heal me, Sav - ior di - vine.
till all shall see Christ on - ly, al - ways, liv - ing in me.

Text: Adelaide A. Pollard, 1901
Tune: George C. Stebbins, 1907

99 99
ADELAIDE

288   Take My Life and Let It Be

1 Take my life and let it be con - se - crat - ed,
2 Take my hands and let them move at the im - pulse
3 Take my voice and let me sing al - ways, on - ly,
4 Take my sil - ver and my gold; not a mite would

Lord, to thee. Take my mo - ments and my days; let them
of thy love. Take my feet and let them be swift and
for my King. Take my lips and let them be filled with
I with-hold. Take my in - tel - lect and use ev - ery

flow in end - less praise, let them flow in end - less praise.
beau - ti - ful for thee, swift and beau - ti - ful for thee.
mes - sag - es from thee, filled with mes - sag - es from thee.
power as thou shalt choose, ev - ery power as thou shalt choose.

5 Take my will and make it thine;
it shall be no longer mine.
Take my heart—it is thine own;
it shall be thy royal throne,
it shall be thy royal throne.

6 Take my love; my Lord, I pour
at thy feet its treasure store.
Take myself, and I will be
ever, only, all for thee,
ever, only, all for thee.

Text: Frances R. Havergal, 1874
Tune: H. A. Cesar Malan, 1827

77 77 with repeat
HENDON

Take My Life That It May Be

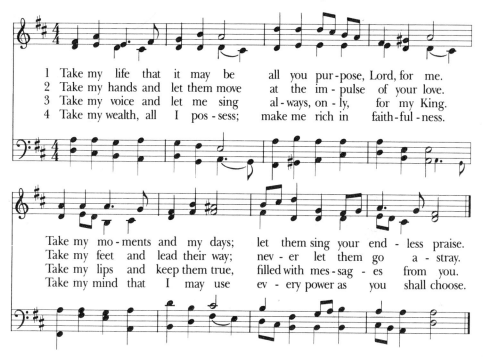

1 Take my life that it may be all you pur-pose, Lord, for me.
2 Take my hands and let them move at the im-pulse of your love.
3 Take my voice and let me sing al-ways, on-ly, for my King.
4 Take my wealth, all I pos-sess; make me rich in faith-ful-ness.

Take my mo-ments and my days; let them sing your end-less praise.
Take my feet and lead their way; nev-er let them go a-stray.
Take my lips and keep them true, filled with mes-sag-es from you.
Take my mind that I may use ev-ery power as you shall choose.

5 Take my motives and my will,
all your purpose to fulfill.
Take my heart—it is your own;
it shall be your royal throne.

6 Take my love; my Lord, I pour
at your feet its treasure store.
Take myself, and I will be
yours for all eternity.

Text: Frances R. Havergal, 1874; rev. Psalter Hymnal, 1987
Tune: Timothy Hoekman, 1979. © 1985, CRC Publications
This music in a lower key: 5

77 77
TEBBEN

290   Give Us This Day Our Daily Bread

1 Give us this day our dai - ly bread: this is our prayer.
2 We thank you, Lord, for joy and peace, for lov - ing care.

If by your grace you give us more, Lord, help us share.
As you have loved us, help us, Lord, your love to share.

We are your voice, your hands, your feet; use us to show in
Then we will tell of liv - ing bread: of Je - sus Christ, whose

word and deed com - pas - sion to a world in need.
blood was shed that hun - gry peo - ple might be fed.

Text: Helen Otte, 1986. © 1987, CRC Publications
Tune: Harold W. Friedell, 1905–1958. © 1961, Concordia Publishing House. Used by permission.

84 84 888
BARBARA

May the Mind of Christ, My Savior 291

4 May the love of Je-sus fill me as the wa-ters fill the sea.
5 May we run the race be-fore us, strong and brave to face the foe,

1 May the mind of Christ, my Sav-ior, live in me from day to day,
2 May the word of God dwell rich-ly in my heart from hour to hour,
3 May the peace of God, my Fa-ther, rule my life in ev-ery-thing,
4 May the love of Je-sus fill me as the wa-ters fill the sea.
5 May we run the race be-fore us, strong and brave to face the foe,

Him ex-alt-ing, self a-bas-ing: this is vic-to-ry.
look-ing on-ly un-to Je-sus as we on-ward go.

by his love and power con-trol-ling all I do and say.
so that all may see I tri-umph on-ly through his power.
▸ that I may be calm to com-fort sick and sor-row-ing.
Him ex-alt-ing, self a-bas-ing: this is vic-to-ry.
look-ing on-ly un-to Je-sus as we on-ward go.

Text: Kate B. Wilkinson, 1925
Tune: A. Cyril Barham-Gould, 1925; desc. Emily R. Brink, 1986.
Tune by permission of the estate of A. C. Barham-Gould. Descant © 1987, CRC Publications

87 85
ST. LEONARDS

292 Living for Jesus

1 Liv - ing for Je - sus a life that is true,
striv - ing to please him in all that I do,
yield - ing al - le - giance glad - heart - ed and free—
this is the path - way of bless - ing for me.

2 Liv - ing for Je - sus, who died in my place,
bear - ing on Cal - vary my sin and dis - grace:
such love con - strains me to an - swer his call,
fol - low his lead - ing, and give him my all.

3 Liv - ing for Je - sus wher - ev - er I am,
do - ing each du - ty in his ho - ly name,
seek - ing the lost ones he died to re - deem,
bring - ing the wea - ry to find rest in him.

Text: Thomas O. Chisholm, 1917, alt.
Tune: C. Harold Lowden, 1915
Text and music © 1917, Heidelberg Press, © renewed 1945, C. Harold Lowden. Assigned to
    The Rodenheaver Co. (a division of WORD, Inc.) All rights reserved. International copyright secured. Used by permission.
Keyboard and guitar should not sound together.

10 10 10 10 with refrain
LIVING FOR JESUS

Refrain
(may be sung after stanza 3 only)

O Je-sus, Lord and Sav-ior, I give my-self to you,

for you in your a - tone-ment did give your-self for me.

I own no oth-er mas-ter— my heart shall be your throne:

my life I give, hence-forth to live, O Christ, for you a - lone.

293   What Does the Lord Require

1 What does the Lord re - quire for praise and of - fer - ing?
2 Rul - ers of earth, give ear! Should you not jus - tice know?
3 All who gain wealth by trade, for whom the work - er toils,
4 Still down the a - ges ring the proph-et's stern com-mands;
5 How shall our life ful - fill God's law so hard and high?

What sac - ri - fice de - sire, or trib - ute bid you
Will God your plead - ing hear while crime and cruel - ty
► think not to win God's aid if greed your com - merce
to mer-chant, work - er, king he brings God's high de -
Let Christ en - due our will with grace to for - ti -

bring? Do just - ly, love mer - cy, walk
grow? Do just - ly, love mer - cy, walk
► soils: Do just - ly, love mer - cy, walk
mands: Do just - ly, love mer - cy, walk
fy. Then just - ly, in mer - cy, we'll

1-4

hum - bly with your God.
hum - bly with your God.
► hum - bly with your God.
hum - bly with your God.

Final ending

hum - bly walk with God.

Text: Albert F. Bayly, 1949, alt.; based on Micah 6:6–8. By permission of Oxford University Press.
Tune: Erik Routley, 1968. © 1969, Hope Publishing Co. All rights reserved. Used by permission.

12 12 12
SHARPTHORNE

As Saints of Old Their Firstfruits Brought 294

1 As saints of old their first-fruits brought of or-chard,
2 A world in need now sum-mons us to la-bor,
3 In grat-i-tude and hum-ble trust we bring our

flock, and field to God, the giv - er of all good,
love, and give; to make our life an of - fer - ing
best to - day to serve your cause and share your love

the source of boun - teous yield; so we to-day first-
that oth - ers too may live. The church of Christ is
with all a - long life's way. O God, who gave your-

fruits would bring: the wealth of this good land, of farm and
call - ing us to keep this end in view: a world re -
self to us in Je - sus Christ, your Son, teach us to

mar - ket, shop and home, of mind and heart and hand.
deemed, your king - dom come, all life in Christ made new.
give our - selves each day un - til life's work is done.

Text: Frank von Christierson, 1960, alt. © 1961, The Hymn Society of America. Used by permission.
Tune: Leland B. Sateren, 1963. © 1963, Augsburg Publishing House. Used by permission.

CMD
REGWAL

295   Lord of All Good

1 Lord of all good, we bring our gifts to you;
2 We give our minds to un-der-stand your ways;
3 Fa - ther, whose boun - ty all cre - a - tion shows;

use them your ho - ly pur - pose to ful - fill;
hands, voic - es, eyes to serve your great de - sign;
Christ, by whose will - ing sac - ri - fice we live;

to - kens of love and pledg - es they shall be that
hearts with the flame of your own love a - blaze: thus
Spir - it, from whom all life in full - ness flows: to

our whole life is of - fered to your will.
for your glo - ry all our powers com - bine.
you with grate - ful hearts our - selves we give.

Text: Albert F. Bayly, 1950, alt. By permission of Oxford University Press.
Tune: Sydney Watson, 1964, ©

10 10 10 10
MORESTEAD

We Give You But Your Own

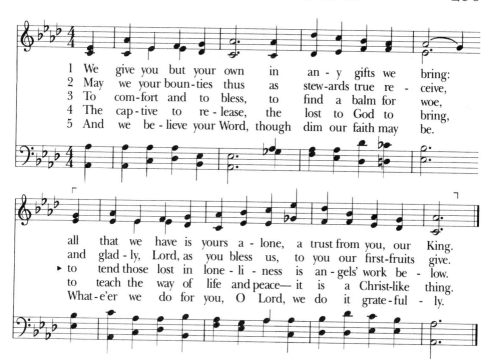

1 We give you but your own in an-y gifts we bring:
2 May we your boun-ties thus as stew-ards true re-ceive,
3 To com-fort and to bless, to find a balm for woe,
4 The cap-tive to re-lease, the lost to God to bring,
5 And we be-lieve your Word, though dim our faith may be.

all that we have is yours a-lone, a trust from you, our King.
and glad-ly, Lord, as you bless us, to you our first-fruits give.
to tend those lost in lone-li-ness is an-gels' work be-low.
to teach the way of life and peace— it is a Christ-like thing.
What-e'er we do for you, O Lord, we do it grate-ful-ly.

Text: William W. How, 1858, alt.
Tune: Mason and Webb, Cantica Laudis, 1850

SM
SCHUMANN

297 O Come, My Soul, Sing Praise to God

1 O come, my soul, sing praise to God our Mak - er,
2 Good is the Lord and full of kind com - pas - sion,
3 His love is like a fa - ther's to his chil - dren,
4 We fade and die like flowers that grow in beau - ty,
5 High in the heavens his throne is fixed for - ev - er;

and all with - in me, praise his ho - ly name.
most slow to an - ger, plen - te - ous in love.
► ten - der and kind to all who fear his name;
like ten - der grass that soon will dis - ap - pear;
his king - dom rules o'er all from pole to pole.

Sing praise to God, for - get not all his mer - cies;
Rich is his grace to all who hum - bly seek him,
► for well he knows our weak - ness and our frail - ty;
but ev - er - more the love of God is change - less,
Praise to the Lord through all his wide do - min - ion;

his par - doning grace and sav - ing love pro - claim.
bound - less and end - less as the heavens a - bove.
► he knows that we are dust, he knows our frame.
still shown to those who look to him in fear.
for - ev - er praise his ho - ly name, my soul.

Text: Psalm 103; vers. Psalter, 1912, alt.
Tune: James Walch, 1875

11 10 11 10 with refrain
TIDINGS

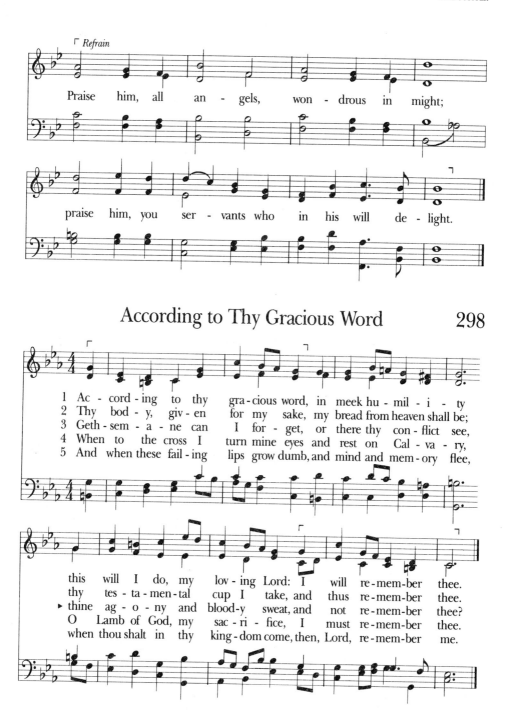

Refrain

Praise him, all an - gels, won - drous in might;

praise him, you ser - vants who in his will de - light.

According to Thy Gracious Word   298

1 Ac - cord - ing to thy gra - cious word, in meek hu - mil - i - ty
2 Thy bod - y, giv - en for my sake, my bread from heaven shall be;
3 Geth - sem - a - ne can I for - get, or there thy con - flict see,
4 When to the cross I turn mine eyes and rest on Cal - va - ry,
5 And when these fail - ing lips grow dumb, and mind and mem - ory flee,

this will I do, my lov - ing Lord: I will re - mem - ber thee.
thy tes - ta - men - tal cup I take, and thus re - mem - ber thee.
thine ag - o - ny and blood - y sweat, and not re - mem - ber thee?
O Lamb of God, my sac - ri - fice, I must re - mem - ber thee.
when thou shalt in thy king - dom come, then, Lord, re - mem - ber me.

Text: James Montgomery, 1825
Tune: William Tans'ur, 1734

CM
BANGOR

299 As We Walk Along beside You

Unison

Al - le - lu - ia, al - le - lu - ia!

1 As we walk a-long be - side you, and we hear you speak of
2 As we ask that you stay with us, and we watch what you are
3 As we reach for you be - liev - ing, and we go to love and

mer - cy, then it seems our hearts are burn-ing, for we find you in the
do - ing, then our eyes be - gin to o - pen, for we see you in the
serve you, then our lives will be pro-claim-ing that we know you in your

1-2
shar - ing of the word.
break-ing of the bread.
ris - ing from the

3
dead. Lord, al - le-lu - ia!

Text: Michael A. Perry, 1981; based on Luke 24
Tune: Norman L. Warren, 1981
Text and music © 1982, Hope Publishing Co. All rights reserved. Used by permission.

88 8 11 with alleluias
BURNING HEART

Gift of Finest Wheat

Refrain
Unison

You sat-is-fy the hun-gry heart with gift of fin-est wheat.

Come, give to us, O sav-ing Lord, the bread of life to eat.

1 As when a shep-herd calls his sheep, they know and heed his voice;
2 With joy-ful lips we sing to you our praise and grat - i - tude,
3 Is not the cup we bless and share the blood of Christ out-poured?
4 The mys-tery of your pres-ence, Lord, no mor - tal tongue can tell:
5 You give your-self to us, O Lord; then self - less let us be

Refrain

so when you call your fam-ily, Lord, we fol - low and re - joice.
that you should count us wor-thy, Lord, to share this heav-enly food.
▶ Do not one cup, one loaf de - clare our one - ness in the Lord?
whom all the world can - not con-tain comes in our hearts to dwell.
to serve each oth - er in your name in truth and char - i - ty.

Text: Omer Westendorf, 1976
Tune: Robert E. Kreutz, 1976
Text and music © 1977, Archdiocese of Philadelphia. All rights reserved.

CM with refrain
BICENTENNIAL

301

Taste and See

Unison

1 With con-trite hearts and ho-ly fear we come, with God to dine.
2 As chil-dren of this cov-e-nant we are for-ev-er blest.
3 This great sal-va-tion God has wrought is ours—but ours to share.

We taste, we touch, we see his love in this, the bread and wine.
Through Christ we are made right with God, our fears are laid to rest.
The need-y of the world must know the Sav-ior's gra-cious care.

The cup of bless-ing that we bless, the bread that we now break,
Our sins are par-doned through his blood, by grace we are re-deemed;
The home-less, hun-gry, lost, and sick may not es-cape our eyes,

are pledg-es of the cov-e-nant that God in Christ did make.
we have be-come in-her-i-tors of king-doms yet un-seen.
for Je-sus' love em-brac-es them; for them too he has died.

Refrain

Taste and see that God is good, let us ex-alt his name to-geth-er.

Text: Carol Vriend Petter, 1981, ©
Tune: Wim Mennes, 1984. © 1987, CRC Publications

CMD with refrain
ANTHEA

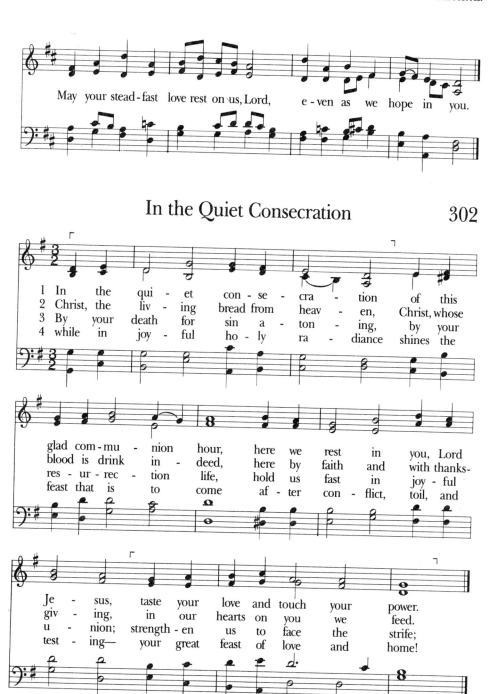

May your stead-fast love rest on us, Lord, e-ven as we hope in you.

In the Quiet Consecration 302

1 In the qui - et con - se - cra - tion of this
2 Christ, the liv - ing bread from heav - en, Christ, whose
3 By your death for sin a - ton - ing, by your
4 while in joy - ful ho - ly ra - diance shines the

glad com - mu - nion hour, here we rest in you, Lord
blood is drink in - deed, here by faith and with thanks-
res - ur - rec - tion life, hold us fast in joy - ful
feast that is to come af - ter con - flict, toil, and

Je - sus, taste your love and touch your power.
giv - ing, in our hearts on you we feed.
u - nion; strength - en us to face the strife;
test - ing— your great feast of love and home!

Text: Constance H. Coote, 1910, alt.
Tune: V. Earle Copes, 1959. © 1959, Abingdon Press. Used by permission.

87 87
KINGDOM

303   Come, Let Us Eat

Text: st. 1–3, Billema Kwillia, b. c. 1925; tr. Margaret D. Miller, 1969, alt.; st. 4, Gilbert E. Doan, b. 1930, alt.
Tune: Billema Kwillia, b. c. 1925; harm. 1972, Contemporary Worship 4
Text, st. 1–3, and tune © Lutheran World Federation. St. 4 and harmonization © 1972,
Contemporary Worship 4. Used by permission of Augsburg Publishing House.

10 10 10 10
A VA DE

Let Us Break Bread Together

304

1 Let us break bread to-geth-er on our knees;
2 Let us drink wine to-geth-er on our knees;
3 Let us praise God to-geth-er on our knees;

let us break bread to-geth-er on our knees.
let us drink wine to-geth-er on our knees.
let us praise God to-geth-er on our knees.

Refrain

When I fall on my knees, with my face to the Lord of life,

O Lord, have mer-cy on me.

Text and Tune: Afro-American spiritual; harm. Dale Grotenhuis, 1984.
Harmonization © 1987, CRC Publications

73 73 with refrain
BREAK BREAD TOGETHER

305 Clothe Yourself, My Soul, with Gladness

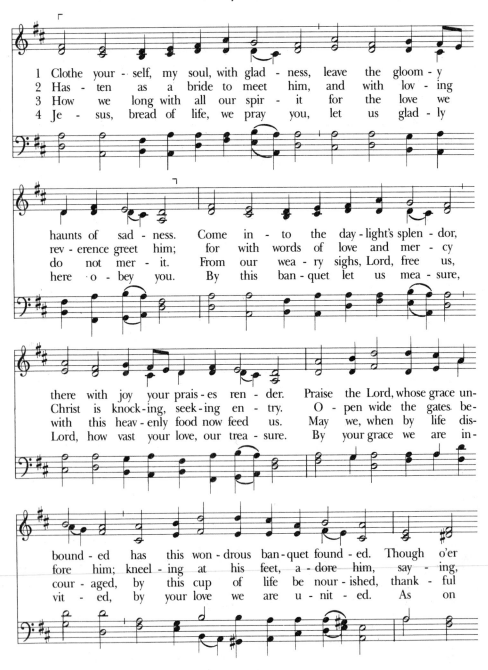

1 Clothe your-self, my soul, with glad - ness, leave the gloom - y
2 Has - ten as a bride to meet him, and with lov - ing
3 How we long with all our spir - it for the love we
4 Je - sus, bread of life, we pray you, let us glad - ly

haunts of sad - ness. Come in - to the day - light's splen - dor,
rev - erence greet him; for with words of love and mer - cy
do not mer - it. From our wea - ry sighs, Lord, free us,
here o - bey you. By this ban - quet let us mea - sure,

there with joy your prais - es ren - der. Praise the Lord, whose grace un-
Christ is knock - ing, seek - ing en - try. O - pen wide the gates be-
with this heav - enly food now feed us. May we, when by life dis-
Lord, how vast your love, our trea - sure. By your grace we are in-

bound - ed has this won - drous ban - quet found - ed. Though o'er
fore him; kneel - ing at his feet, a - dore him, say - ing,
cour - aged, by this cup of life be nour - ished, thank - ful
vit - ed, by your love we are u - nit - ed. As on

Text: Johann Franck, 1649; tr. Catherine Winkworth, 1863; rev. Psalter Hymnal, 1987.
© 1987, CRC Publications
Tune: Johann Crüger, 1649

LMD
SCHMÜCKE DICH

ev - ery power ex - cel - ling, yet he makes my heart his dwell - ing.
"Lord, let me re - ceive you, and I nev - er-more will leave you."
that our Friend in - vites us and with God him-self u - nites us.
earth you love and feed us, so in heaven, dear Lord, re - ceive us.

Now the Solemn Feast Is Done 306

1 Now the sol - emn feast is done. Thank God
2 We have kept the Lord's com-mand to re -
3 Death has lost its fear - ful sting. Now God's

for the vic - tory won. Je - sus' bod - y given in bread,
mem - ber, un - der-stand that God's Lamb took sin a - way
peo - ple laugh and sing, res - ur - rec - tion cel - e - brate—

wine poured out— his blood was shed: Christ sets us free.
so we chil -dren could o - bey: Christ sets us free.
all our lives we ded - i - cate: Christ sets us free.

Text: Calvin Seerveld, 1985, ©
Tune: Bohemian Brethren's Kirchengesang, *1566; harm.* Psalter Hymnal, *1987.*
  Harmonization © 1987, CRC Publications

77 77 4
SONNE DER GERECHTIGKEIT

307 O Jesus, Joy of Loving Hearts

1 O Jesus, joy of loving hearts, the fount of
2 Your truth unchanged has ever stood; you save all
3 We taste you, ever-living Bread, and long to
4 Our restless spirits yearn for you wher-e'er our
5 O Jesus, ever with us stay; make all our

life, the light of men, from full-est bliss that
those who on you call. To those who seek you,
feast upon you still; we drink of you, the
change-ful lot is cast; glad when you smile on
mo-ments calm and bright! Chase the dark night of

earth imparts we turn un-filled to you a-gain.
you are good; to those who find you, all in all.
foun-tain-head, our thirst to quench, our souls to fill.
us anew, blest that our faith can hold you fast.
sin away; shed o'er the world your ho-ly light!

Text: Latin, 12th cent.; tr. Ray Palmer, 1858, alt.
Tune: Henry Baker, 1854

LM
QUEBEC

Come, Risen Lord, as Guest among Your Own   308

1 Come, ris - en Lord, as guest a - mong your own!
2 We meet as in the up - per room they met;
3 One bod - y we, one bod - y who par - take—
4 One with each oth - er, Lord, and one in you—

Come and pre - side that we with you may dine.
here with your word of bless - ing now you stand.
one church u - nit - ed in com - mu - nion blest.
Je - sus, our Sav - ior and our liv - ing head.

Here at your ta - ble make your pres - ence known
This is your bod - y: you are with us yet—
One name we bear, one bread of life we break
We are your peo - ple: come, our faith re - new,

in this, our sac - ra - ment of bread and wine.
faith still re - ceives the cup as from your hand.
with all your saints on earth and saints at rest.
be known to us in break - ing of the bread.

Text: George W. Briggs, 1931, alt. By permission of Oxford University Press.
Tune: Orlando Gibbons, 1623
This music in a lower key: 167

10 10 10 10
SONG 24

309   Lift Up Your Hearts unto the Lord

Lord!

1 Lift up your hearts un - to the
2 In Christ the world has been re -
3 His res - ur - rec - tion sets us
4 There - fore we cel - e - brate the
5 Sing al - le - lu - ia to the

deemed.
free.
feast.

1 Lift up your hearts un - to the Lord,
2 In Christ the world has been re - deemed,
3 His res - ur - rec - tion sets us free,
4 There - fore we cel - e - brate the feast,
5 Sing al - le - lu - ia to the Lord,

Lord.
deemed.
free.
feast.
Lord.

Sing al - le - lu - ia,
Sing al - le - lu - ia,
Sing al - le - lu - ia,
Sing al - le - lu - ia,
Sing al - le - lu - ia,

lift up your hearts un - to the Lord.
in Christ the world has been re - deemed.
his res - ur - rec - tion sets us free.
there - fore we cel - e - brate the feast.
sing al - le - lu - ia to the Lord.

Text: st. 1–4, from early Christian liturgy; st. 5, Linda Stassen, 1974
Tune: Linda Stassen, 1974; harm. Dale Grotenhuis, 1986
Text, st. 5, and music © 1974, Linda Stassen. All rights reserved. International copyright secured. Used by permission.

PM
SING ALLELUIA

al - le - lu - ia;

Sing al - le - lu - ia, sing al - le - lu - ia;

lift	up	your hearts	un -	to	the	(Lord!)
in	Christ	the world	has	been	re -	(deemed.)
his	res -	ur - rec -	tion	sets	us	(free.)
there	fore	we cel -	e -	brate	the	(feast.)
sing	al -	le - lu -	ia	to	the	Lord.

lift up your hearts un - to the Lord!
in Christ the world has been re-deemed.
► his res - ur - rec - tion sets us free.
there-fore we cel - e - brate the feast.
sing al - le - lu - ia to the Lord.

Final ending

310   Bread of the World, in Mercy Broken

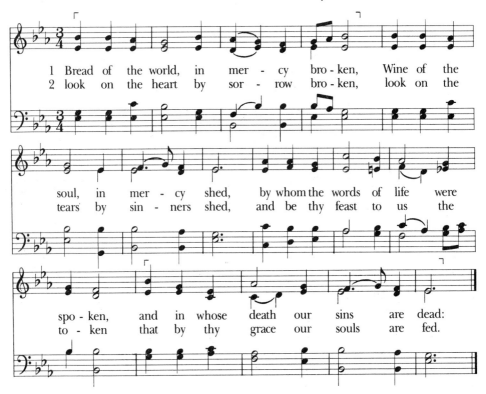

1 Bread of the world, in mer - cy bro - ken, Wine of the
2 look on the heart by sor - row bro - ken, look on the

soul, in mer - cy shed, by whom the words of life were
tears by sin - ners shed, and be thy feast to us the

spo - ken, and in whose death our sins are dead:
to - ken that by thy grace our souls are fed.

Text: Reginald Heber, 1827
Tune: John S. B. Hodges, 1868

98 98
EUCHARISTIC HYMN

I Come with Joy to Meet My Lord

311

1. I come with joy to meet my Lord, for-
2. I come with Christians far and near to
3. As Christ breaks bread and bids us share, each
4. And thus with joy we meet our Lord; his
5. To-geth-er met, to-geth-er bound, we'll

giv-en, loved, and free; in awe and won-der
find, as all are fed, the new com-mu-ni-
proud di-vi-sion ends; the love that made us,
pres-ence, al-ways near, is in such friend-ship
go our dif-ferent ways; and as his peo-ple

to re-call his life laid down for me.
ty of love in Christ's com-mu-nion bread.
makes us one, and strang-ers now are friends.
bet-ter known: we see and praise him here.
in the world, we'll live and speak his praise.

Text: Brian Wren, 1970. © 1971, Hope Publishing Co. All rights reserved. Used by permission.
Tune: American; harm. Annabel Morris Buchanan, 1938

CM
LAND OF REST

312

Eat This Bread

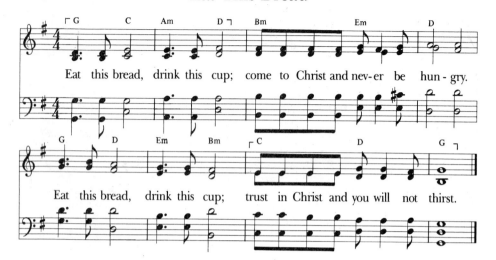

Eat this bread, drink this cup; come to Christ and nev-er be hun-gry.

Eat this bread, drink this cup; trust in Christ and you will not thirst.

Text: John 6:35; para. Robert J. Batastini and the Taizé Community, 1984, alt.
Tune: Jacques Berthier, 1984
Text and music © 1984, Les Presses de Taizé (France). Used by permission of G.I.A. Publications, Inc.,
  exclusive agent. All rights reserved.

PM
EAT THIS BREAD

Praise the Lord, Rise Up Rejoicing

1 Praise the Lord, rise up re - joic - ing, wor-ship, thanks, de - vo - tion voic-ing:
2 Scat-tered flock, one shep-herd shar-ing, lost and lone-ly, one voice hear-ing,
3 Send us forth a - lert and liv-ing, sins for - giv - en, wrongs for - giv - ing,

glo - ry be to God on high! Christ, your cross and pas-sion shar - ing,
ears are o - pen to your word. By your blood new life re - ceiv - ing,
in your Spir-it strong and free. Find - ing love in all cre - a - tion,

by this feast we are de-clar-ing your e - ter - nal vic - to - ry.
in your bod - y true be-liev-ing, we are yours and you the Lord.
bring-ing peace in ev - ery na-tion, may we faith - ful fol-lowers be.

Text: Howard C. A. Gaunt, 1969. Used by permission of Mary N. de Lande Long.
Tune: Johann Löhner, 1691, adapt.; harm. after chorale version of Johann S. Bach, 1685–1750

887 D
ALLES IST AN GOTTES SEGEN

314   Father, We Give You Thanks, Who Planted

1 Fa - ther, we give you thanks, who plant - ed your
2 Watch o'er your church, O Lord, in mer - cy, save

ho - ly name with - in our hearts; knowl - edge and faith and
it from e - vil, guard it still; per - fect it in your

life im - mor - tal Je - sus, your Son, to us im - parts.
love, u - nite it, cleansed and con-formed un - to your will.

Text: F. Bland Tucker, 1941, alt.; based on the Didache, 2nd cent.
© 1943, 1961, 1981, The Church Pension Fund. Used by permission.
Tune: Genevan Psalter, 1551; harm. Pilgrim Hymnal, 1931
Other harmonizations in a higher key: 98, 118

98 98 D
GENEVAN 98/118

Lord, you have made all for your plea - sure, and
As grain, once scat - tered on the hill - sides, was

given us food for all our days, giv - ing in Christ the
in the bro - ken bread made one, so may your world-wide

bread e - ter - nal. Yours is the power; be yours the praise.
church be gath - ered in to your king - dom by your Son.

315 Blest Be the Tie That Binds

1 Blest be the tie that binds our
2 Be - fore our Fa - ther's throne we
3 We share our mu - tual woes, our
4 When we are called to part, it

hearts in Chris - tian love; the fel - low - ship of
pour our ar - dent prayers; our fears, our hopes, our
mu - tual bur - dens bear, and of - ten for each
gives us in - ward pain; but we shall still be

kin - dred minds is like to that a - bove.
aims are one, our com - forts and our cares.
oth - er flows the sym - pa - thiz - ing tear.
joined in heart, and hope to meet a - gain.

5   This glorious hope revives
    our courage by the way;
    while each in expectation lives
    and waits to see the day.

6   From sorrow, toil, and pain,
    and sin, we shall be free;
    and perfect love and friendship reign
    through all eternity.

Text: John Fawcett, 1782
Tune: attr. Johann G. Nägeli, 1828

SM
DENNIS

God Be with You Till We Meet Again 316

1 God be with you till we meet a - gain; by his
2 God be with you till we meet a - gain; 'neath his
3 God be with you till we meet a - gain; when life's
4 God be with you till we meet a - gain; keep love's

coun - sels guide, up - hold you, with his sheep se -
wings pro - tect - ing hide you, dai - ly man - na
per - ils thick con - found you, put his arm un -
ban - ner float - ing o'er you, smite death's threat - ening

cure - ly fold you: God be with you till we meet a - gain.
still pro - vide you: God be with you till we meet a - gain.
fail - ing round you: God be with you till we meet a - gain.
wave be - fore you: God be with you till we meet a - gain.

Text: Jeremiah E. Rankin, 1880
Tune: Ralph Vaughn Williams, 1906. By permission of Oxford University Press.

98 89
RANDOLPH

317 Go Now in Peace

Text and Tune: Natalie Sleeth, 1975
Text and music © 1976, Hinshaw Music, Inc. Reprinted by permission.

The Day You Gave Us, Lord, Is Ended   318

1 The day you gave us, Lord, is end - ed,
2 We thank you that your church, un - sleep - ing
3 As o - ver con - ti - nent and is - land
4 So be it, Lord: your throne shall nev - er,

the dark - ness falls at your re - quest.
while earth rolls on - ward in - to light,
each dawn leads to an - oth - er day;
like earth's proud king - doms, pass a - way.

To you our morn - ing hymns as - cend - ed;
through all the world her watch is keep - ing,
the voice of prayer is nev - er si - lent,
Your king - dom stands and grows for - ev - er,

your praise shall sanc - ti - fy our rest.
and nev - er rests by day or night.
nor do the prais - es die a - way.
un - til there dawns your glo - rious day.

Text: John Ellerton, 1870, alt.
Tune: Clement C. Scholefield, 1874

98 98
ST. CLEMENT

319 Savior, Again to Your Dear Name We Raise

1 Sav - ior, a - gain to your dear name we raise with one ac -
2 Grant us your peace up - on our home-ward way; with you be -
3 Grant us your peace, Lord, through the com - ing night; turn all our
4 Grant us your peace through - out our earth - ly life: com - fort in

cord our part - ing hymn of praise. We give you thanks be -
gan, with you shall end the day. Guard now the lips from
dark - ness to your per-fect light. Then, while we sleep, our
sor - row, cour - age in the strife. Then, when your voice shall

fore our wor - ship cease, and now de - part - ing, wait your word of peace.
sin, the hearts from shame, that in this house have called up - on your name.
hope and strength re - new, for dark and light are both a - like to you.
make our con - flict cease, call us, O Lord, to your e - ter-nal peace.

Text: John Ellerton, 1866, alt.
Tune: Edward J. Hopkins, 1869

10 10 10 10
ELLERS

Lord, Dismiss Us with Your Blessing

320

1 Lord, dis - miss us with your bless-ing; fill our hearts with
2 Thanks we give and ad - o - ra - tion for your gos - pel's

joy and peace. Let us each, your love pos - sess - ing,
joy - ful sound. May the fruits of your sal - va - tion

tri - umph in re - deem - ing grace. O di - rect us
in our hearts and lives a - bound. Ev - er faith - ful,

and pro - tect us trav - eling through this wil - der - ness.
ev - er faith - ful to your truth may we be found.

Text: attr. John Fawcett, 1773, alt.
Tune: Sicilian, 18th cent.

87 87 87
SICILIAN MARINERS

321 Lord, Dismiss Us with Your Blessing

Descant

Ad - o - ra - tion

1 Lord, dis - miss us with your bless - ing; fill our
2 Thanks we give and ad - o - ra - tion for your

for your gos - pel's sound. Al -

hearts with joy and peace. Let us each, your love pos -
gos - pel's joy - ful sound. May the fruits of your sal -

Text: attr. John Fawcett, 1773, alt.
Tune: David Hurd, 1974. © 1983, G.I.A. Publications, Inc. All rights reserved.

87 87 87
JULION

le - lu - ia. Ev - er faith - ful

sess - ing, tri - umph in re - deem - ing grace. O di -
va - tion in our hearts and lives a - bound. Ev - er

to your truth may we be found.

rect us and pro - tect us trav-eling through this wil - der - ness.
faith-ful, ev - er faith - ful to your truth may we be found.

Final ending

322 God, the Father of Your People

1 God, the Fa-ther of your peo-ple, you have called us to be one;
2 May the grace of Christ, our Sav-ior, and the Fa-ther's bound-less love,

grant us grace to walk to-geth-er in the joy of Christ, your Son.
with the Ho-ly Spir-it's fa-vor, rest up-on us from a-bove.

Chal-lenged by your Word and Spir-it, blest with gifts from heaven a-bove,
May we now re-main in u-nion with each oth-er and the Lord,

as one bod-y we will serve you and bear wit-ness to your love.
and pos-sess, in sweet com-mu-nion, joys that earth can-not af-ford.

Text: st. 1, Alfred E. Mulder, 1978, © 1987, CRC Publications; st. 2, John Newton, 1779
Tune: W. Moore's The Columbian Harmony, 1825; harm. Norman E. Johnson, 1973.
Harmonization © 1973, Covenant Press

87 87 D
HOLY MANNA

Forth in the Peace of Christ We Go

323

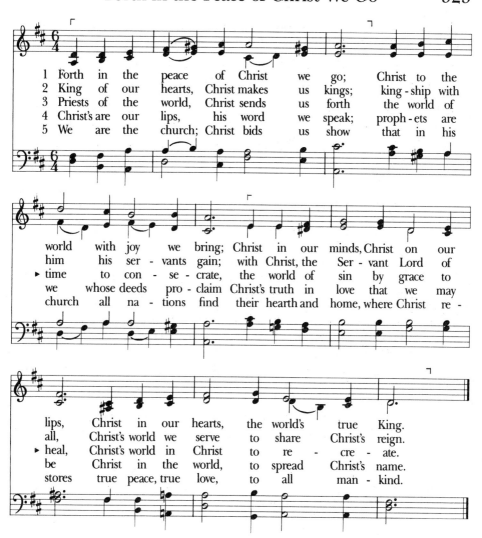

1 Forth in the peace of Christ we go; Christ to the
2 King of our hearts, Christ makes us kings; king - ship with
3 Priests of the world, Christ sends us forth the world of
4 Christ's are our lips, his word we speak; proph - ets are
5 We are the church; Christ bids us show that in his

world with joy we bring; Christ in our minds, Christ on our
him his ser - vants gain; with Christ, the Ser - vant Lord of
► time to con - se - crate, the world of sin by grace to
we whose deeds pro - claim Christ's truth in love that we may
church all na - tions find their hearth and home, where Christ re -

lips, Christ in our hearts, the world's true King.
all, Christ's world we serve to share Christ's reign.
► heal, Christ's world in Christ to re - cre - ate.
be Christ in the world, to spread Christ's name.
stores true peace, true love, to all man - kind.

Text: James Quinn, 1969, ©. Reprinted by permission of Geoffrey Chapman, a division of Cassell Publishers, Ltd.
Tune: Georg Joseph, 1657, adapt.
Alternative tune: WILDERNESS, 608

LM
ANGELUS

324 Forth in Your Name, O Lord, I Go

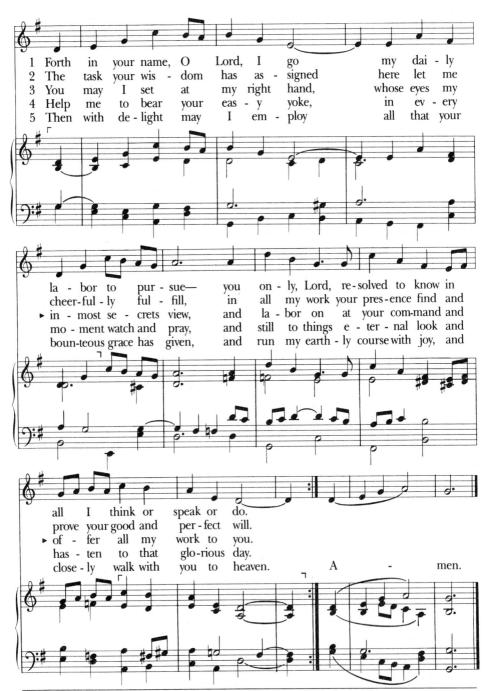

1 Forth in your name, O Lord, I go my dai - ly
2 The task your wis - dom has as - signed here let me
3 You may I set at my right hand, whose eyes my
4 Help me to bear your eas - y yoke, in ev - ery
5 Then with de - light may I em - ploy all that your

la - bor to pur - sue— you on - ly, Lord, re - solved to know in
cheer - ful - ly ful - fill, in all my work your pres - ence find and
► in - most se - crets view, and la - bor on at your com - mand and
mo - ment watch and pray, and still to things e - ter - nal look and
boun - teous grace has given, and run my earth - ly course with joy, and

all I think or speak or do.
prove your good and per - fect will.
► of - fer all my work to you.
has - ten to that glo - rious day.
close - ly walk with you to heaven. A - men.

Text: Charles Wesley, 1749, alt.
Tune: Percy C. Buck, 1913. By permission of Oxford University Press.
Alternative tune: TRURO, 539

LM
GONFALON ROYAL

Go Forth for God

325

1 Go forth for God, go to the world in peace;
2 Go forth for God, go to the world in love;
3 Go forth for God, go to the world in strength;
4 Go forth for God, go to the world in joy,

be of good cour - age, armed with heav - enly grace,
strength - en the faint, give cour - age to the weak;
hold fast the good, be ur - gent for the right;
to serve God's peo - ple ev - ery day and hour;

in God's good Spir - it dai - ly to in - crease,
help the af - flict - ed. Rich - ly from a - bove
ren - der to no one e - vil: Christ at length
and, serv - ing Christ, your ev - ery gift em - ploy,

till in the king - dom we be - hold his face.
his love sup - plies the grace and power we seek.
shall o - ver - come all dark - ness with his light.
re - joic - ing in the Ho - ly Spir - it's power.

Text: John R. Peacey, 1968, 1970; rev. English Praise, 1975, alt. By permission of M. E. Peacey.
Tune: William J. Maher, 1863
Alternative tune: WOODLANDS, 478

10 10 10 10
ANIMA CHRISTI

326 We Lift Our Hearts to God

1 We lift our hearts to God; he fills our minds with peace
2 We thank him for his word. As we de-part to serve,

that pass-es un-der-stand-ing. He stretched his arms, en-cir-cled us;
we share in his a-noint-ing: con-fess his name, pre-sent our-selves

we rise to live and love, to work in church and king-dom.
a liv-ing sac-ri-fice, fight e-vil and do jus-tice.

Text: Cor Wm. Barendrecht, 1975
Tune: Emily R. Brink, 1976
Text and music © 1987, CRC Publications

667 867
HESSEL PARK

On Jordan's Bank the Baptist's Cry

1 On Jor - dan's bank the Bap - tist's cry an - nounc - es
2 Then cleansed be ev - ery life from sin: make straight the
3 We hail you as our Sav - ior, Lord, our ref - uge
4 Stretch forth your hand, our health re - store, and make us
5 All praise to you, e - ter - nal Son, whose ad - vent

that the Lord is nigh. A - wake and hark - en,
way for God with - in, and let us all our
▶ and our great re - ward. With - out your grace we
rise to fall no more. O let your face up -
has our free - dom won, whom with the Fa - ther

for he brings glad tid - ings of the King of kings!
hearts pre - pare for Christ to come and en - ter there.
▶ waste a - way like flowers that with - er and de - cay.
on us shine and fill the world with love di - vine.
we a - dore, and Ho - ly Spir - it, ev - er - more.

Text: Charles Coffin, 1736; tr. composite
Tune: Trier manuscript, 15th cent.; adapt. Michael Praetorius, 1609; harm. George R. Woodward, 1910

LM
PUER NOBIS

328   O Come, O Come, Immanuel

1 O come, O come, Immanuel, and ransom captive
2 O come, O Wisdom from on high, who ordered all things
3 O come, O come, great Lord of might, who to your tribes on
4 O come, O Branch of Jesse's stem, unto your own and

Israel that mourns in lonely exile here
mightily; to us the path of knowledge show
Sinai's height in ancient times did give the law
rescue them! From depths of hell your people save,

un - til the Son of God ap - pear.
and teach us in its ways to go.
in cloud and maj - es - ty and awe.
and give them vic-tory o'er the grave.

Refrain

Re - joice! Re - joice! Im - man - u - el shall come to you, O Is - ra - el.

Text: Latin, 12th cent.; tr. composite
Tune: Processionale, 15th cent.; adapt. Thomas Helmore, 1854

LM with refrain
VENI IMMANUEL

5 O come, O Key of David, come
  and open wide our heavenly home.
  Make safe for us the heavenward road
  and bar the way to death's abode. *Refrain*

6 O come, O Bright and Morning Star,
  and bring us comfort from afar!
  Dispel the shadows of the night
  and turn our darkness into light. *Refrain*

7 O come, O King of nations, bind
  in one the hearts of all mankind.
  Bid all our sad divisions cease
  and be yourself our King of Peace. *Refrain*

Come, Thou Long-Expected Jesus 329

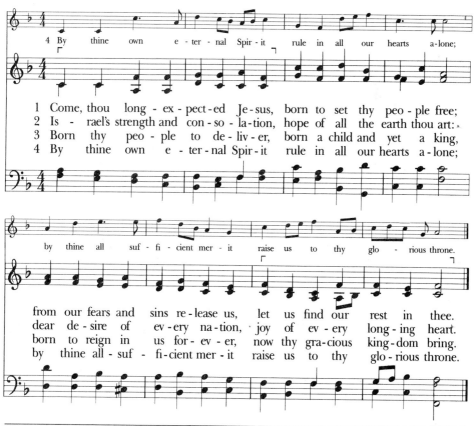

4 By thine own e-ter-nal Spir-it rule in all our hearts a-lone;

1 Come, thou long - ex-pect-ed Je-sus, born to set thy peo - ple free;
2 Is - rael's strength and con - so - la-tion, hope of all the earth thou art:
3 Born thy peo - ple to de - liv-er, born a child and yet a king,
4 By thine own e - ter-nal Spir-it rule in all our hearts a-lone;

by thine all suf - fi - cient mer - it raise us to thy glo - rious throne.

from our fears and sins re - lease us, let us find our rest in thee.
dear de - sire of ev - ery na-tion, joy of ev - ery long - ing heart.
born to reign in us for - ev - er, now thy gra-cious king-dom bring.
by thine all - suf - fi-cient mer - it raise us to thy glo - rious throne.

Text: Charles Wesley, 1744
Tune: Psalmodia Sacra, 1715; adapt. Henry J. Gauntlett, 1861; desc. John Wilson, 1983.
Descant © 1983, Hope Publishing Co. All rights reserved. Used by permission.

87 87
STUTTGART

330   O Christ! Come Back to Save Your Folk

1. O Christ! Come back to save your folk.
2. Dear God, let loose the an - gel hosts;
3. O Spir - it, give dumb - found - ing birth!
4. Dear Lord, con - vert our faith to sight.
5. O Christ! re - move our ad - vent fears.

Burst through the clouds with one clean stroke.
send them to stop all war - like boasts.
Car - pet with green a whole new earth.
Shine with the bril - liance end - ing night.
Bol - ster our hope, ex - cite our cheers.

Un - furl the glo - ry prom - ised us.
Star - tle the na - tions filled with hate.
Re - deem the rain - bows in the skies:
Win - now the wick - ed chaff from wheat.
Bring on full life both new and free.

Sur - prise with joy those keep - ing trust.
Res - cue the meek while we still wait.
wipe a - way tears from all our eyes.
Har - vest the world; make us com - plete.
Trum - pet at last the ju - bi - lee!

Text: Calvin Seerveld, 1983, ©
Tune: Gesangbuch, Augsburg, 1666; harm. Dale Grotenhuis, 1985.
Harmonization © 1987, CRC Publications

LM
O HEILAND, REISS DIE HIMMEL AUF

O Lord, How Shall I Meet You

1 O Lord, how shall I meet you, how wel - come you a - right?
2 Love caused your in - car - na - tion; love brought you down to me;
3 You come, O Lord, with glad - ness, in mer - cy and good - will,

Your peo - ple long to greet you, my hope, my heart's de - light!
your thirst for my sal - va - tion pro - cured my lib - er - ty.
to bring an end to sad - ness and bid our fears be still.

O kin - dle, Lord most ho - ly, your lamp with - in my breast,
O love be - yond all tell - ing, that led you to em - brace
In pa - tient ex - pec - ta - tion we live for that great day

to do in spir - it low - ly all that may please you best.
in love, all love ex - cel - ling, our lost and fall - en race.
when a re-newed cre - a - tion your glo - ry shall dis - play.

Text: Paul Gerhardt, 1653; tr. Catherine Winkworth, 1863, and others
Tune: Johann Crüger, 1653
Alternative tune: ST. THEODOLPH, 375

76 76 D
WIE SOLL ICH DICH EMPFANGEN

332 Hark! A Thrilling Voice Is Sounding

Descant

2 Star - tled at the sol - emn warn - ing, from the
5 Hon - or, glo - ry, might, do - min - ion to the

1 Hark! A thrill - ing voice is sound - ing! "Christ is
2 Star - tled at the sol - emn warn - ing, from the
3 See, the Lamb so long ex - pect - ed comes with
4 so when next he comes in glo - ry and the
5 Hon - or, glo - ry, might, do - min - ion to the

dark - ness we a - rise; Christ, our sun, all
Fa - ther and the Son, with the ev - er -

near," we hear it say. "Cast a - way the
dark - ness we a - rise; Christ, our sun, all
▸ par - don down from heaven. Let us haste, with
world is wrapped in fear, he will shield us
Fa - ther and the Son, with the ev - er -

ill dis - pel - ling, shines up - on the morn - ing skies.
liv - ing Spir - it while e - ter - nal a - ges run.

works of dark - ness, all you chil - dren of the day!"
ill dis - pel - ling, shines up - on the morn - ing skies.
▸ tears of sor - row, one and all, to be for - given;
with his mer - cy and with words of love draw near.
liv - ing Spir - it while e - ter - nal a - ges run.

Text: *Latin, c. 6th cent.; tr.* Hymns Ancient and Modern, *1861, alt.*
Tune: *William H. Monk, 1850; desc.* Psalter Hymnal, *1987*

87 87
MERTON

Rejoice, Rejoice, Believers

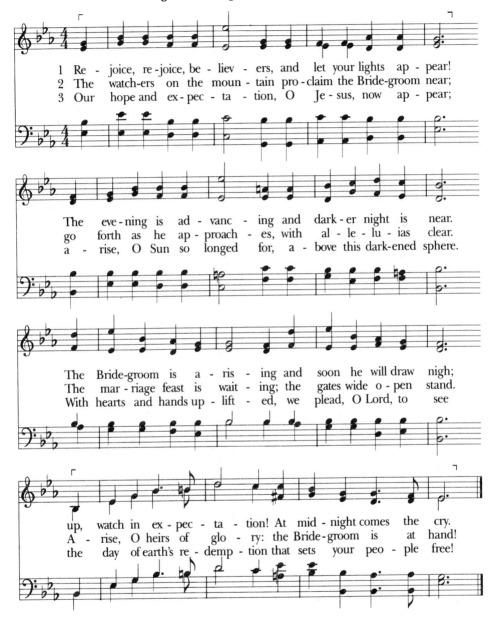

1 Re - joice, re -joice, be - liev - ers, and let your lights ap - pear!
2 The watch-ers on the moun - tain pro -claim the Bride-groom near;
3 Our hope and ex - pec - ta - tion, O Je - sus, now ap - pear;

The eve - ning is ad - vanc - ing and dark - er night is near.
go forth as he ap - proach - es, with al - le - lu - ias clear.
a - rise, O Sun so longed for, a - bove this dark-ened sphere.

The Bride-groom is a - ris - ing and soon he will draw nigh;
The mar - riage feast is wait - ing; the gates wide o - pen stand.
With hearts and hands up - lift - ed, we plead, O Lord, to see

up, watch in ex - pec - ta - tion! At mid - night comes the cry.
A - rise, O heirs of glo - ry: the Bride-groom is at hand!
the day of earth's re - demp - tion that sets your peo - ple free!

Text: Laurentius Laurenti, 1700; tr. Sarah B. Findlater, 1854, alt.
Tune: attr. J. Michael Haydn, 1737–1806; arr. in B. Jacob's National Psalmody, 1819

76 76 D
GREENLAND

334   The Prophets Came to Israel

1 The proph - ets came to Is - ra - el to tell them what to
2 In Beth - le - hem in a cat - tle stall a mir - a - cle we
3 The shep-herds watched their flocks of sheep when light broke from the
4 The an - gels sang a mid-night song, their eyes were filled with
5 It's Christ - mas Day! We cel - e - brate the com - ing of a

do.
find:
sky.
joy:
king.

They point - ed to the birth of Christ, and
that such a low - ly place should hold the
They heard a daz - zling an - gel say, "A
"The Son of God has come to earth to
He came to set his chil - dren free, and

what they said came true, and what they said came true.
Sav - ior of man - kind, the Sav - ior of man - kind!
child is born near - by, a child is born near - by."
be a lit - tle boy, to be a lit - tle boy."
that is why we sing, and that is why we sing.

Text and Tune: Bert Witvoet, 1980; harm. Bert Polman, 1981
Text and music © 1987, Bert Witvoet
Keyboard and guitar should not sound together.

CM
FIVE CANDLES

Hark, the Glad Sound! The Savior Comes 335

Descant
4 Our glad ho - san - nas, Prince of Peace, your wel - come

1 Hark, the glad sound! The Sav - ior comes, the Sav - ior
2 He comes the pris - oners to re - lease, in Sa - tan's
3 He comes the bro - ken heart to bind, the wound - ed
4 Our glad ho - san - nas, Prince of Peace, your wel - come

shall pro - claim; and heaven's e - ter - nal

prom - ised long! Let ev - ery heart pre -
bond - age held; the gates of brass be -
soul to cure; and with the trea - sures
shall pro - claim; and heaven's e - ter - nal

arch - es ring with your be - lov - ed name.

pare a throne, and ev - ery voice a song.
fore him burst, the i - ron fet - ters yield.
of his grace to en - rich the hum - bled poor.
arch - es ring with your be - lov - ed name.

Text: Philip Doddridge, 1735; based on Isaiah 61:1–2
Tune: Thomas Haweis, 1792; adapt. Samuel Webbe, 1808; desc. Craig S. Lang, 1891–1971.
Descant by permission of Novello and Company, Ltd.

CM
RICHMOND

336

Savior of the Nations, Come

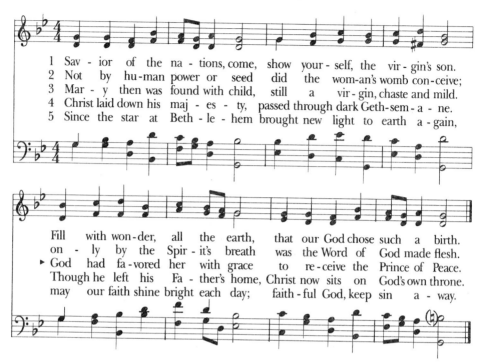

1 Sav - ior of the na - tions, come, show your - self, the vir - gin's son.
2 Not by hu-man power or seed did the wom-an's womb con-ceive;
3 Mar - y then was found with child, still a vir - gin, chaste and mild.
4 Christ laid down his maj - es - ty, passed through dark Geth-sem - a - ne.
5 Since the star at Beth - le - hem brought new light to earth a - gain,

Fill with won-der, all the earth, that our God chose such a birth.
on - ly by the Spir - it's breath was the Word of God made flesh.
► God had fa-vored her with grace to re - ceive the Prince of Peace.
Though he left his Fa - ther's home, Christ now sits on God's own throne.
may our faith shine bright each day; faith - ful God, keep sin a - way.

6 Christ in glory, intercede
for your creatures' suffering need.
Let your resurrecting power
soon complete the victory hour.

7 Praise to you, O Lord, we sing.
Praise to Christ, our newborn King!
With the Father, Spirit, one,
let your lasting kingdom come.

Text: Ambrose, 4th cent., and Martin Luther, 1523; tr. Calvin Seerveld, 1984, ©
Tune: Enchiridia, Erfurt, 1524; harm. Seth Calvisius, 1594

77 77
NUN KOMM DER HEIDEN HEILAND

Joy to the World! the Lord Is Come 337

1. Joy to the world! the Lord is come: let earth re - ceive her
2. Joy to the earth! the Sav - ior reigns: let all their songs em -
3. No more let sin and sor - row grow nor thorns in - fest the
4. He rules the world with truth and grace, and makes the na - tions

King. Let ev - ery heart pre - pare him
ploy, while fields and floods, rocks, hills, and
ground; he comes to make his bless - ings
prove the glo - ries of his right - eous -

room, and heaven and na - ture sing, and heaven and na - ture
plains re - peat the sound-ing joy, re - peat the sound-ing
flow far as the curse is found, far as the curse is
ness and won - ders of his love, and won - ders of his
and heaven and na-ture sing,

sing, and heaven, and heaven and na - ture sing.
joy, re peat, re peat the sound-ing joy.
found, far as, far as the curse is found.
love, and won - ders, won - ders of his love.

heaven and na - ture sing,

Text: Isaac Watts, 1719; based on Psalm 98
Tune: Lowell Mason, 1848

CM with repeats
ANTIOCH

338   Come and Stand Amazed, You People

1 Come and stand a-mazed, you peo - ple, see how God is rec - on - ciled!
2 See how hu-man-kind re-ceived him; see him wrapped in swad-dling bands,
3 O Lord Je - sus, God in - car - nate, who as - sumed this hum-ble form,

See his plans of love ac - com-plished, see his gift, this new-born child.
who as Lord of all cre - a - tion rules the wind by his com - mands.
coun-sel me and let my wish - es to your per-fect will con - form.

See the Might-y, weak and ten - der, see the Word who now is mute.
See him ly - ing in a man-ger with-out sign of rea - son - ing;
Light of life, dis - pel my dark-ness, let your frail - ty strength-en me;

See the Sov-ereign with-out splen-dor, see the Full-ness des - ti - tute;
Word of God to flesh sur - ren-dered, he is wis-dom's crown, our King.
let your meek-ness give me bold-ness, let your bur-den set me free;

Text: Dutch, medieval; tr. Klaas Hart, 1906–1973; rev. Psalter Hymnal, 1987
Tune: Dutch, medieval; harm. Dale Grotenhuis, 1984
Text and harmonization © 1987, CRC Publications

87 87 87 87 87
KOMT, VERWONDERT

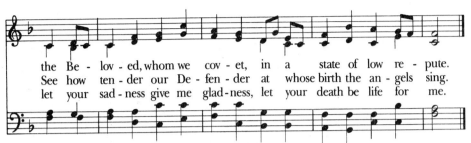

the Be - lov - ed, whom we cov - et, in a state of low re - pute.
See how ten - der our De - fen - der at whose birth the an - gels sing.
let your sad - ness give me glad - ness, let your death be life for me.

From Heaven Above to Earth I Come 339

1 "From heaven a - bove to earth I come to bring good
2 "To you this night is born a child of Mar - y,
3 "This is the Christ, God's Son most high, who hears your
4 "These are the signs which you shall mark: the swad - dling
5 We too must join the an - gel throng to sing a -

news to ev - ery home! Glad tid - ings of great
cho - sen vir - gin mild; this lit - tle child of
sad and bit - ter cry; he will him - self your
clothes and man - ger dark. There you shall find the
gain this joy - ful song: "All glo - ry be to

joy I bring to all the world, and glad - ly sing:
low - ly birth shall be the joy of all the earth.
Sav - ior be, from all your sins to set you free.
in - fant laid by whom the heavens and earth were made."
God in heaven, who un - to us his Son has given."

Text: Martin Luther, 1535; tr. composite; based on Luke 2:10–14
Tune: V. Schumann's Geistliche Lieder, 1539

LM
VOM HIMMEL HOCH

340 O Come, All Ye Faithful

Descant
4 Yea, Lord, we greet thee, born this hap-py morn - ing;

1 O come, all ye faith - ful, joy - ful and tri - um - phant! O
2 God of God, Light of Light e - ter - nal,
3 Sing, choirs of an - gels, sing in ex - ul - ta - tion,
4 Yea, Lord, we greet thee, born this hap-py morn - ing;

Je - sus, to thee be all glo - ry given;

come ye, O come ye to Beth - le - hem!
lo, he ab - hors not the vir - gin's womb;
sing, all ye bright hosts of heaven a - bove:
Je - sus, to thee be all glo - ry given;

Word of the Fa - ther, now in flesh ap - pear - ing;

Come and be - hold him, born the King of an - gels;
Son of the Fa - ther, be - got - ten, not cre - at - ed;
"Glo - ry to God, all glo - ry in the high - est!"
Word of the Fa - ther, now in flesh ap - pear - ing;

Text: attr. John F. Wade, 1743; tr. Frederick Oakeley, 1841, and others
Tune: attr. John F. Wade, 1743; desc. Hymns Ancient and Modern Revised.
Descant © 1947, Hymns Ancient and Modern, Ltd.

irregular
ADESTE FIDELES

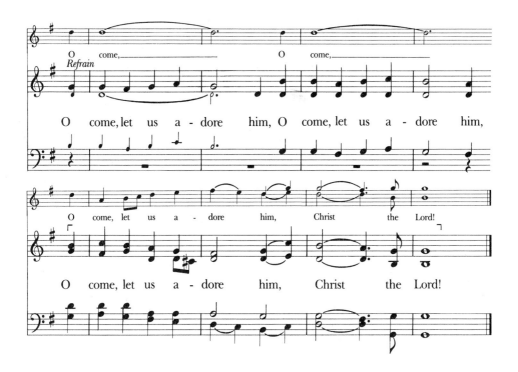

Refrain

O come,_____ O come,_____

O come, let us a - dore him, O come, let us a - dore him,

O come, let us a - dore him, Christ the Lord!

O come, let us a - dore him, Christ the Lord!

341   Let All Mortal Flesh Keep Silence

1 Let all mor-tal flesh keep si - lence, and with fear and
2 King of kings, yet born of Mar - y, once up-on the
3 Rank on rank the host of heav - en stream be-fore him
4 At his feet the six - winged ser - aph, cher - u - bim with

trem - bling stand; set your minds on things e -
earth he stood; Lord of lords we now per -
on the way, as the Light of Light, de -
sleep - less eye veil their fac - es to his

ter - nal, for with bless-ing in his hand
ceive him in the bod - y and the blood.
scend - ing from the realms of end - less day,
pres - ence, as with cease-less voice they cry:

Text: Liturgy of St. James; tr. Gerard Moultrie, 1864
Tune: French, 17th cent.

87 87 87
PICARDY

Christ our Lord to earth de - scend -
He has given to all the faith -
comes, the powers of hell to van -
"Al - le - lu - ia, al - le - lu -

ed, came our hom - age to com - mand.
ful his own self for heav - enly food.
quish, clears the gloom of hell a - way.
ia! Al - le - lu - ia, Lord Most High!"

342 Of the Father's Love Begotten

Unison

1 Of the Fa - ther's love be-got - ten ere the worlds be - gan to be,
2 O that birth for - ev - er bless - ed, when a vir - gin, blest with grace,
3 This is he whom seers in old time chant-ed of with one ac - cord,
4 Let the heights of heaven a-dore him; an - gel hosts, his prais - es sing:
5 Christ, to you, with God the Fa - ther and the Spir - it, there shall be

he is Al - pha and O - me - ga— he the source, the end - ing he,
by the Ho - ly Ghost con - ceiv - ing, bore the Sav - ior of our race;
▸ whom the voic - es of the proph-ets prom-ised in their faith - ful word;
powers, do - min - ions, bow be - fore him and ex - tol our God and King;
hymn and chant and high thanks-giv - ing and the shout of ju - bi - lee:

of the things that are, that have been, and that fu - ture years shall
and the babe, the world's Re - deem - er, first re-vealed his sa - cred
▸ now he shines, the long - ex - pect - ed; let cre - a - tion praise its
let no tongue on earth be si - lent, ev - ery voice in con - cert
hon - or, glo - ry, and do - min - ion and e - ter - nal vic - to-

see ev - er - more and ev - er - more.
face, ev - er - more and ev - er - more.
▸ Lord ev - er - more and ev - er - more.
ring ev - er - more and ev - er - more.
ry ev - er - more and ev - er - more! A - men.

Text: Marcus Aurelius C. Prudentius, 4th cent.; tr. John M. Neale, 1854, and Henry W. Baker, 1859, alt.
Tune: 12th cent. plainsong; arr. C. Winfred Douglas, 1916.
Arrangement © 1943, 1961, 1981, The Church Pension Fund

87 87 877
DIVINUM MYSTERIUM

Break Forth, O Beauteous Heavenly Light 343

1 Break forth, O beau-teous heav-enly light, and ush - er in the
2 Break forth, O beau-teous heav-enly light, to her - ald our sal -

morn - ing. O shep-herds, shud - der not with fright, but
va - tion. He stoops to earth, the God of might, our

hear the an - gel's warn - ing: this child, now weak in
hope and ex - pec - ta - tion. He comes in hu - man

in - fan - cy, our con - fi - dence and joy shall be, the
flesh to dwell, our God with us, Im - man - u - el, the

power of Sa - tan break - ing, our peace e - ter - nal mak - ing.
night of dark-ness end - ing, our fall-en race be - friend - ing.

Text: st. 1, Johann Rist, 1641; tr. John Troutbeck, 1832–1899, alt.; st. 2, Norman E. Johnson, 1973.
St. 2 © 1973, Covenant Press
Tune: Johann Schop, 1641; harm. Johann S. Bach, 1734

87 87 88 77
ERMUNTRE DICH

344   Silent Night! Holy Night!

1 Si - lent night! Ho - ly night! All is calm,
2 Si - lent night! Ho - ly night! Son of God,
3 Si - lent night! Ho - ly night! Shep - herds quake
4 Si - lent night! Ho - ly night! Son of God,

all is bright round yon vir - gin moth - er and child!
source of light, now lies cry - ing in Beth - le-hem's stall,
at the sight when they hear___ the an - gels sing
love's pure light shines a - new from your heav - en - ly face,

Ho - ly in - fant so ten - der and mild, sleep in heav - en - ly
ti - ny child,___ Cre - a - tor of all, in - fant, Sav - ior, and
al - le - lu - ia to___ the King. Christ the Sav - ior is
greets the hour of re - deem - ing grace, Je - sus, Lord, at your

peace! sleep in heav - en - ly peace!
King! in - fant, Sav - ior, and King!
born! Christ the Sav - ior is born!
birth! Je - sus, Lord, at your birth!

Text: st. 1, 3–4, Joseph Mohr, 1818, tr. John F. Young, 1818, alt.; st. 2, Henrietta Ten Harmsel, 1984   *irregular*
Tune: Franz Gruber, 1818   *STILLE NACHT*

Hark! the Herald Angels Sing

1 Hark! the her - ald an - gels sing, "Glo - ry to the new - born King;
2 Christ, by high - est heaven a - dored, Christ, the ev - er - last - ing Lord!
3 Hail the heaven-born Prince of Peace! Hail the Sun of Right-eous - ness!

peace on earth and mer - cy mild, God and sin - ners rec - on - ciled!"
Late in time be - hold him come, off - spring of the vir - gin's womb.
Light and life to all he brings, risen with heal - ing in his wings.

Joy - ful, all ye na - tions, rise; join the tri - umph of the skies;
Veiled in flesh the God-head see; hail the in - car - nate De - i - ty,
Mild, he lays his glo - ry by, born that we no more may die,

with the an - gel - ic hosts pro-claim, "Christ is born in Beth - le - hem!"
pleased as man with us to dwell, Je - sus, our Im - man - u - el.
born to raise the lost on earth, born to give them sec - ond birth.

Refrain

Hark! the her - ald an - gels sing, "Glo - ry to the new-born King!"

Text: Charles Wesley, 1739, alt.
Tune: Feliz Mendelssohn, 1840; adapt. William H. Cummings, 1856

77 77 D with refrain
MENDELSSOHN

345: Alternative arrangement with descant

3 Hail the heaven-born Prince of Peace! Hail the Sun of Right-eous-ness! Light and life to all he brings, risen with heal-ing in his wings. Mild, he lays his glo-ry by, born that we no

Text: Charles Wesley, 1739, alt.
Tune: Feliz Mendelssohn, 1840; desc. and arr. David Willcocks, 1961.
     Descant and arrangement by permission of Oxford University Press.

more may die, born to raise the lost on earth, born to give them sec - ond birth. Hark! the her - ald an - gels sing, "Glo - ry to the new - born King!"

Refrain

346 Once in Royal David's City

1 Once in roy-al Da-vid's cit-y stood a low-ly cat-tle shed,
2 He came down to earth from heav-en who is God and Lord of all;
3 For he is our child-hood's pat-tern; day by day like us he grew;
4 And our eyes at last shall see him, through his own re-deem-ing love,
5 Not in that poor low-ly sta-ble with the ox-en stand-ing by

where a moth-er laid her ba-by in a man-ger for his bed:
and his shel-ter was a sta-ble and his cra-dle was a stall:
► he was lit-tle, weak, and help-less; tears and smiles like us he knew:
for that child, so dear and gen-tle, is our Lord in heaven a-bove:
we shall see him, but in heav-en, set at God's right hand on high:

Mar-y was that moth-er mild, Je-sus Christ, her lit-tle child.
with the poor and meek and low-ly lived on earth our Sav-ior ho-ly.
► and he feels for all our sad-ness, and he shares in all our glad-ness.
and he leads his chil-dren on to the place where he has gone.
there his chil-dren gath-er round bright like stars, with glo-ry crowned.

Text: Cecil F. Alexander, 1848
Tune: Henry J. Gauntlett, 1849

87 87 77
IRBY

Alternative arrangement with descant

5 Not in that poor low - ly sta - ble with the ox - en stand - ing by

we shall see him, but in heav - en, set at God's right hand on high:

there his chil-dren gath - er round bright like stars, with glo - ry crowned.

Text: Cecil F. Alexander, 1848
Tune: Henry Gauntlett, 1849; desc. and arr. David Willcocks, 1970.
    Descant and arrangement by permission of Oxford University Press.

87 87 77
IRBY

Angels We Have Heard on High
Les Anges Dans Nos Campagnes

1 An - gels we have heard on high, sing - ing sweet - ly through the night,
2 Shep-herds, why this ju - bi - lee? Why these songs of hap - py cheer?
3 Come to Beth - le - hem and see him whose birth the an - gels sing;

and the moun-tains in re - ply, ech - o - ing their brave de - light.
What great bright-ness did you see? What glad tid - ings did you hear?
come, a - dore on bend - ed knee Christ the Lord, the new - born King.

Refrain

Glo - ri - a in ex - cel - sis De - o. Glo - ri - a in ex - cel - sis De - o.

Text: French, 18th cent.; tr. Crown of Jesus Music, 1862, alt.
Tune: French, 18th cent.; arr. Edward S. Barnes, 1937

77 77 with refrain
GLORIA

1 Les an - ges dans nos cam-pag-nes, ont en - ton-né l'hym - ne des cieux,
2 Ber - gers, pour qui cet - te fê - te? Quel est l'ob-jet de tous ces chants?
3 Cher-chons tous l'heur-eux vil - la - ge qui l'a vu naî - tre sous ses toits;

Refrain

et l'é - cho de nos mon - tag-nes, re-dit ce chant mé - lo - di - eux.
Quel vain-queur, quel - le con - quê-te mé - ri - te ces cris tri - om-phants?
of - frons - lui le ten-dre_hom-ma - ge et de nos cœurs et de nos voix!

Text and Tune: French, 18th cent.

Away in a Manger
348

Capo 3: F(D)   Bb(G)   F(D)   C7(A7)

1 A - way in a man-ger, no crib for a bed, the lit - tle Lord
2 The cat - tle are low-ing, the ba - by a - wakes, but lit - tle Lord
3 Be near me, Lord Je - sus; I ask you to stay close by me for -

F(D)

Je - sus laid down his sweet head; the stars in the bright sky looked
Je - sus, no cry - ing he makes. I love you, Lord Je - sus: look
ev - er and love me, I pray. Bless all the dear chil - dren in

Bb(G)   F(D)   C7(A7)   F(D)   Gm(Em)   C7(A7) F(D)

down where he lay; the lit - tle Lord Je - sus a - sleep on the hay.
down from on high and stay by my side un - til morn-ing is nigh.
your ten - der care; pre - pare us for heav-en to live with you there.

Text: American, 1885
Tune: James R. Murray, 1887

11 11 11 11
AWAY IN A MANGER

349 Away in a Manger

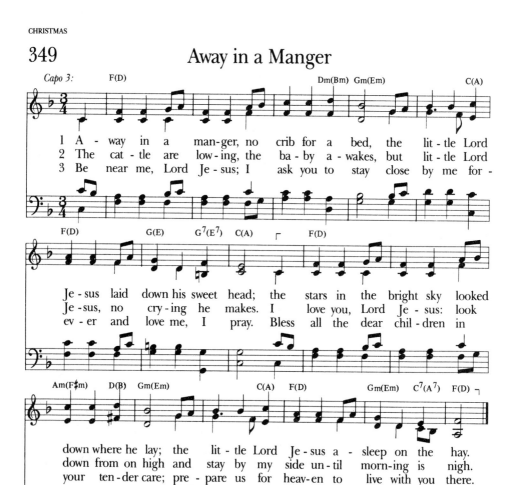

Capo 3:

1 A - way in a man-ger, no crib for a bed, the lit - tle Lord
2 The cat - tle are low - ing, the ba - by a - wakes, but lit - tle Lord
3 Be near me, Lord Je - sus; I ask you to stay close by me for -

Je - sus laid down his sweet head; the stars in the bright sky looked
Je - sus, no cry - ing he makes. I love you, Lord Je - sus: look
ev - er and love me, I pray. Bless all the dear chil - dren in

down where he lay; the lit - tle Lord Je - sus a - sleep on the hay.
down from on high and stay by my side un - til morn - ing is nigh.
your ten - der care; pre - pare us for heav - en to live with you there.

Text: American, 1885
Tune: William J. Kirkpatrick, 1895

11 11 11 11
CRADLE SONG

350 Christians, Awake

1 Chris - tians, a - wake, sa - lute the hap - py morn
2 Then to the watch - ful shep-herds it was told,
3 O may we keep and pon - der in our mind

Text: John Byrom, 1749, alt.
Tune: John Wainwright, 1750
This music in a lower key: 80

10 10 10 10 10 10
YORKSHIRE

on which the Sav - ior of the world was born.
who heard the her - ald an - gel's voice: "Be - hold,
God's won - drous love in sav - ing lost man - kind!

Rise to a - dore the mys - ter - y of love
I bring good tid - ings of a Sav - ior's birth
Christ, who was born up - on this joy - ful day,

which hosts of an - gels chant - ed from a - bove.
to you and all the na - tions on the earth.
a - round us all his glo - ry shall dis - play.

With them the joy - ful tid - ings were be - gun of
This day has God ful - filled his prom - ised word: this
Saved by his love, un - ceas - ing we shall sing e -

God in - car - nate and the vir - gin's Son.
day is born a Sav - ior, Christ the Lord!"
ter - nal praise to heaven's al - might - y King.

351　Lo, How a Rose E'er Blooming

1 Lo,　how　a　rose　e'er　bloom - ing　from　ten - der　stem　hath
2 I - sa - iah　'twas　fore - told　it,　the　rose　I　have　in
3 This flower, so　small　and　ten - der,　with　fra - grance　fills　the

sprung; of　Jes - se's　lin - eage　com - ing,　as　saints of　old　have
mind; with　Mar - y　we　be - hold　it,　the　vir - gin　moth - er
air;　his　bright-ness ends the　dark - ness　that　kept the　earth　in

sung.　It　came,　a　flower - et　bright,　a - mid　the
kind.　To　show God's love　a - right　she　bore　to
fear.　True　God and　yet true　man,　he　came　to

cold　of　win - ter　when　half spent　was　the night.
us　a　Sav - ior　when　half spent　was　the night.
save　his　peo - ple　from　earth's dark　night　of　sin.

Text: German, 15th cent.; st. 1–2 tr. Theodore Baker, 1894; st. 3 tr. Gracia Grindal, 1978.
St. 3 © 1978, Lutheran Book of Worship. Used by permission of Augsburg Publishing House.
Tune: Alte Catholische Geistliche Kirchengesäng, Cologne, 1599; harm. Michael Praetorius, 1609

76 76 676
ES IST EIN ROS

That Boy-Child of Mary

1 What shall we call him, child of the man - ger?
2 His name is Je - su, God ev - er with us,
3 He came to save us, he came to help us,
4 One with the Fa - ther, he is our Sav - ior,
5 Glad - ly we praise him, love and a - dore him,

What name is giv - en in Beth - le - hem?
God giv - en for us in Beth - le - hem.
born here a - mong us in Beth - le - hem.
heav - en - sent help - er of Beth - le - hem.
give our-selves to him of Beth - le - hem.

Text: Tom Colvin, 1967
Tune: Malawian; adapt. Tom Colvin, 1967
Text and music © 1969, Hope Publishing Co. International copyright secured. All rights reserved. Used by permission.

irregular
BLANTYRE

353　Infant Holy, Infant Lowly

1 In - fant ho - ly, in - fant low - ly, for his bed a cat - tle stall;
2 Flocks were sleep-ing, shep-herds keep-ing vig - il till the morn-ing new

ox - en low - ing, lit - tle know-ing Christ the child is Lord of all.
saw the glo - ry, heard the sto - ry, tid - ings of a gos-pel true.

Swift - ly wing-ing an - gels sing-ing, bells are ring-ing, tid-ings bring-ing:
Thus re - joic - ing, free from sor - row, prais - es voic - ing, greet the mor - row:

Christ the child is Lord of all!　Christ the child is Lord of all!
Christ the child was born for you!　Christ the child was born for you!

Text: Polish; tr. Edith M. G. Reed, 1921
Tune: Polish; harm. Psalter Hymnal, 1987

87 87 88 77
W ZLOBIE LEZY

Angels from the Realms of Glory

1 An - gels from the realms of glo - ry, wing your flight o'er
2 Shep - herds in the fields a - bid - ing, watch - ing o'er your
3 Sa - ges, leave your con - tem - pla - tions, bright - er vi - sions
4 Though an in - fant now we view him, he will share his
5 Saints and an - gels join in prais - ing God, the Fa - ther,

all the earth; ye who sang cre - a - tion's sto - ry,
flocks by night, God with us is now re - sid - ing;
beam a - far; seek the great De - sire of na - tions;
Fa - ther's throne, gath - er all the na - tions to him;
Spir - it, Son, ev - er - more their voic - es rais - ing

Refrain

now pro - claim Mes - si - ah's birth: come and wor - ship,
yon - der shines the in - fant Light:
ye have seen his na - tal star: come and wor - ship,
ev - ery knee shall then bow down:
to th' e - ter - nal Three in One:

come and wor - ship, wor - ship Christ, the new - born King!

Text: James Montgomery, 1816, alt.
Tune: Henry Smart, 1867

87 87 with refrain
REGENT SQUARE

355 Good Christian Friends, Rejoice

1 Good Chris-tian friends, re - joice with heart and soul and voice;
2 Good Chris-tian friends, re - joice with heart and soul and voice;
3 Good Chris-tian friends, re - joice with heart and soul and voice;

give ye heed to what we say: Je - sus Christ is born to-day.
now ye hear of end - less bliss: Je - sus Christ was born for this!
now ye need not fear the grave: Je - sus Christ was born to save!

Ox and ass be - fore him bow, and he is in the man - ger now.
He has o - pened heav - en's door, and we are blest for - ev - er - more.
Calls you one and calls you all to gain his ev - er - last - ing hall.

Christ is born to - day! Christ is born to - day!
Christ was born for this! Christ was born for this!
Christ was born to save! Christ was born to save!

Text: German/Latin, medieval; tr. John M. Neale, 1853, alt.
Tune: German, 14th cent.

66 77 78 55
IN DULCI JUBILO

Go, Tell It on the Mountain

Refrain Unison

Go, tell it on the moun - tain, o - ver the hills and ev - ery-where;
go, tell it on the moun - tain that Je - sus Christ is born.

1 While shep-herds kept their watch-ing o'er si - lent flocks by night, be -
2 The shep-herds feared and trem - bled when lo! a - bove the earth rang
3 Down in a low - ly sta - ble the hum-ble Christ was born, and

Refrain

hold, through-out the heav-ens there shone a ho - ly light.
out the an - gel cho-rus that hailed our Sav - ior's birth.
God sent us sal - va - tion that bless - ed Christ-mas morn.

Text and Tune: Afro-American spiritual, 19th cent.; arr. Hale Smith, 1977, alt.
Arrangement from Hymns III, © *1978, The Church Pension Fund. Used by permission.*

76 76 with refrain
GO TELL IT

357 How Bright Appears the Morning Star

1 How bright ap - pears the Morn-ing Star, with mer - cy beam-ing
2 Though cir - cled by the hosts on high, he deigned to cast a
3 Re - joice, O heavens, and earth, re - ply; with praise, O sin - ners,

from a - far; the host of heaven re - joic - es.
pit - y‿ing eye up - on his help - less crea - ture.
fill the sky for this his in - car - na - tion.

O Right-eous Branch, O Jes - se's Rod, the Son of Man and
The whole cre - a - tion's head and Lord, by high-est ser - a -
In - car - nate God, put forth your power, ride on, ride on, great

Text: William Mercer, 1859, after Philipp Nicolai, 1599, alt.
Tune: Philipp Nicolai, 1599; adapt. and harm. Johann S. Bach, 1685–1750

887 887 48 48
WIE SCHÖN LEUCHTET

Son of God! we too will lift our voic - es:
phim a - dored, as - sumed our ver - y na - ture;
Con - quer - or, till all know your sal - va - tion.

Je - sus, Je - sus, ho - ly, ho - ly, yet most low - ly,
Je - sus, grant us, through your mer - it, to in - her - it
A - men, a - men! Al - le - lu - ia, al - le - lu - ia!

come, draw near us; great Im - man - uel, come and hear us.
your sal - va - tion. Hear, O hear our sup - pli - ca - tion.
Praise be giv - en ev - er - more by earth and heav - en.

358 As with Gladness Men of Old

Descant

5 In that glo - rious cit - y bright none shall need cre - at - ed light;

1 As with glad - ness men of old did the guid - ing star be - hold,
2 As with joy - ful steps they sped to that low - ly in - fant bed,
3 As they of - fered gifts most rare at that cra - dle plain and bare,
4 Ho - ly Je - sus, ev - ery day keep us in the nar - row way,
5 In that glo - rious cit - y bright none shall need cre - at - ed light;

you its light, its joy, its crown, you its sun which goes not down;

as with joy they hailed its light, lead - ing on - ward, beam-ing bright;
there to bend the knee be - fore Christ, whom heaven and earth a - dore;
► so may we with ho - ly joy, pure and free from sin's al - loy,
and when mor - tal things are past, bring our ran-somed lives at last
you its light, its joy, its crown, you its sun which goes not down;

there for - ev - er may we sing al - le - lu - ias to our King!

so, most gra - cious Lord, may we ev - er-more your splen-dor see.
so may we with will - ing feet ev - er seek your mer - cy seat.
► all our cost - liest trea - sures bring, Christ, to you, our heav-enly King.
where they need no star to guide, where no clouds your glo - ry hide.
there for - ev - er may we sing al - le - lu - ias to our King!

Text: William C. Dix, 1860, alt.
Tune: Conrad Kocher, 1838; adapt. William H. Monk, 1861; desc. Sydney H. Nicholson, 1944.
Descant © The Royal School of Church Music

DIX
77 77 77

Christ Is the King and He Shall Reign

Descant

5 Long shall he live, so bring to him your gifts of fin - est gold;

1 Christ is the King and he shall reign from sea to ut-most sea,
2 Tribes that in far - thest des - erts dwell shall bow be - fore his throne;
3 Kings all shall come from dis - tant lands and is - lands of the sea;
4 He will de - liv - er those in need, the weak who cry in fear;
5 Long shall he live, so bring to him your gifts of fin - est gold;

to him shall con - stant prayer be made, his praise each day be told.

and un - to earth's re - mot - est bounds his peace - ful rule shall be.
his en - e - mies shall be sub - dued, and he shall rule a - lone.
▸ their of - ferings they shall bring to him and wait on bend - ed knee.
he shall re - deem them from all wrong; their life to him is dear.
to him shall con - stant prayer be made, his praise each day be told.

Text: Psalm 72:8–15; vers. Psalter, 1912, alt.
Tune: Henry Lahee, 1855; desc. Peggy Spencer Palmer, 1965

CM
NATIVITY

360   **Bright and Glorious Is the Sky**

1 Bright and glo-rious is the sky, ra-diant are the
2 Sa-ges from the East a-far, when they saw this
3 Him they found in Beth-le-hem; yet he wore no
4 Guid-ed by the star, they found him whose praise the
5 As a star, God's ho-ly Word leads us to our

heav-ens high where the gold-en star is shin-ing,
won-drous star, went to find the king of na-tions
di-a-dem. They but saw a maid-en low-ly
a-ges sound. We too have a star to guide us
King and Lord; bright-ly from its sa-cred pa-ges

all its rays to earth in-clin-ing, lead-ing to the
and to of-fer their ob-la-tions un-to him as
with an in-fant pure and ho-ly rest-ing in her
that for-ev-er will pro-vide us with the light to
shall this light through-out the a-ges shine up-on our

new-born King, lead-ing to the new-born King.
Lord and King, un-to him as Lord and King.
lov-ing arms, rest-ing in her lov-ing arms.
find our Lord, with the light to find our Lord.
path of life, shine up-on our path of life.

Text: Nikolai F. S. Grundtvig, 1810; tr. Jens C. Aaberg, 1927, and Service Book and Hymnal, *1958, alt. St. 1 and 5 © 1958, 1986. By permission of Augsburg Publishing House.*
Tune: Danish, c. 1840

77 88 77
DEJLIG ER DEN HIMMEL BLAA

Songs of Thankfulness and Praise

1 Songs of thank-ful - ness and praise, Je - sus, Lord, to you we raise,
2 Man - i - fest at Jor - dan's stream, Proph-et, Priest, and King su-preme;
3 Man - i - fest in mak - ing whole pal - sied limbs and faint-ing soul;

man - i - fest - ed by the star to the sa - ges from a - far;
and at Ca - na, wed - ding guest, in your God-head man - i - fest,
man - i - fest in val - iant fight, quell-ing all the dev - il's might;

Branch of roy - al Da - vid's stem, in your birth at Beth - le -hem;
you re - vealed your power di - vine, chang - ing wa - ter in - to wine;
man - i - fest in gra-cious will, ev - er bring-ing good from ill;

Refrain

"You are Christ," by us con-fessed— God in flesh made man - i - fest.

Text: Christopher Wordsworth, 1862, alt.
Tune: Jakob Hintze, 1678; harm. after Johann S. Bach, 1685–1750

77 77 D
SALZBURG

362   Lord of the Universe

1 Lord of the u - ni - verse, hope of the world,
2 Lord of the u - ni - verse, hope of the world,
3 Lord of the u - ni - verse, hope of the world,
4 Lord of the u - ni - verse, hope of the world,

Lord of the lim - it - less reach - es of space,
Lord of the in - fi - nite e - ons of time,
send out your light to the ends of the earth.
how your cre - a - tion cries out for re - lease!

here on this plan - et you put on our flesh,
you came a - mong us, you lived our brief years,
May we who know you o - bey your com - mand,
looks for you, longs for you, watch - es and waits,

vast - ness con - fined in the womb of a maid;
tast - ed our griefs, our a - lone - ness, our fears,
go with the grace of your gos - pel to all,
prays for your king - dom of jus - tice and peace!

10 10 10 10 10 with refrain
STONEHENGE

born   in   our   like - ness   you   ran - somed   our   race:
con - quered our   death, made   e   -   ter - ni - ty   ours:
bring - ing   sal - va - tion   and   free - dom   and   joy:
Mak   -   er,   Re - deem - er,   tri   -   um - phant One,   come!

Refrain

Sav - ior,   we   wor - ship you,   praise   and   a - dore;

help   us   to   hon - or   you   more   and   yet   more,

help   us   to   hon - or   you   more   and   yet   more!

363 Your Hands, O Lord, in Days of Old

Capo 3:

1 Your hands, O Lord, in days of old were strong to heal and save; they tri-umphed o-ver pain and death, o'er dark-ness and the grave. To you they went, the blind, the mute, the pal-sied and the lame, the lep-er set a-part and shunned, the sick and those in shame.

2 And then your touch brought life and health, gave speech and strength and sight; and youth re-newed, with health re-stored, claimed you, the Lord of light. And so, O Lord, be near to bless, al-might-y now as then, in ev-ery street, in ev-ery home, in ev-ery trou-bled friend.

3 O be our might-y heal-er still, O Lord of life and death; re-store and strength-en, soothe and bless with your al-might-y breath. On hands that work and eyes that see, your heal-ing wis-dom pour, that whole and sick and weak and strong may praise you ev-er-more.

Text: Edward H. Plumptre, 1866, alt.
Tune: W. Gawler's Hymns and Psalms, 1789

CMD
ST. MICHAEL'S

O Love, How Deep, How Broad, How High   364

Unison

1 O love, how deep, how broad, how high, be - yond all
2 For us bap - tized, for us he bore his ho - ly
3 For us he prayed; for us he taught; for us his
4 For us to e - vil power be - trayed, scourged, mocked, in

thought and fan - ta - sy, that God, the Son of
fast and hun - gered sore; for us temp - ta - tion
dai - ly works he wrought: by words and signs and
pur - ple robe ar - rayed, he bore the shame - ful

God, should take our mor - tal form for mor - tals' sake!
sharp he knew, for us the tempt - er o - ver - threw.
ac - tions thus still seek - ing not him - self, but us.
cross and death; for us gave up his dy - ing breath.

5 For us he rose from death again;
   for us he went on high to reign;
   for us he sent his Spirit here
   to guide, to strengthen, and to cheer.

6 All glory to our Lord and God
   for love so deep, so high, so broad—
   the Trinity, whom we adore
   forever and forevermore.

Text: Latin, 15th cent.; tr. Benjamin Webb, 1854, alt.
Tune: English, 15th cent.; harm. Carl Schalk, 1969.
   Harmonization © 1969, Concordia Publishing House. Used by permission.

LM
DEO GRACIAS

365

Amen

A - men, a - men, a -

Leader

1 See the lit - tle ba - by
2 See him at the tem - ple
3 See him at the sea - side
4 See him in the gar - den
5 Then they cru - ci - fied him,

men, a - men, a - men. A -

ly - ing in a man - ger on_____ Christ - mas____ morn - ing.
talk - ing to the el - ders; how they mar - veled at his wis - dom.
▸ preach - ing and heal - ing the____ blind____ and___ fee - ble.
pray - ing to his Fa - ther in____ deep - est____ sor - row.
Je - sus our Sav - ior, and he rose____ on____ Eas - ter.

men, a - men,

Final ending

a - men, a - men, a - men.

Text and Tune: Afro-American spiritual; arr. Richard Smallwood, 1981, ©

irregular
AMEN

Have No Fear, Little Flock

Unison

1 Have no fear, lit - tle flock, have no fear, lit - tle
2 Have good cheer, lit - tle flock, have good cheer, lit - tle
3 Praise the Lord high a - bove, praise the Lord high a -
4 Thank - ful hearts raise to God, thank - ful hearts raise to

flock, for the Fa - ther has cho - sen to
flock, for the Fa - ther will keep you in
bove, for he stoops down to heal you, up -
God, for he stays close be - side you, in

give you the king - dom; have no fear, lit - tle flock!
his love for - ev - er; have good cheer, lit - tle flock!
lift and re - store you; praise the Lord high a - bove!
all things works with you; thank - ful hearts raise to God!

Text: st. 1, Luke 12:32; st. 2–4, Marjorie Jillson, 1972
Tune: Heinz Werner Zimmermann, 1971
Text and music © 1972, Concordia Publishing House. Used by permission.

66 76 6
LITTLE FLOCK

367 Oh, I Know the Lord Laid His Hands on Me

Capo 1: *Refrain* Eb(D)

Oh, I know the Lord, I know the Lord,

Bb7(A7) Eb(D) Ab(G) Eb(D)

I know the Lord laid his hands on me.

Leader Eb7(D7)

1 Did ever you see the like be - fore?
2 Oh, was - n't that a hap - py day,
3 My Lord has done just what he said,

Text and Tune: Afro-American spiritual; harm. Edward Boatner

irregular
I KNOW THE LORD

All Bb⁷(A⁷)   Eb(D)   Ab(G)   Eb(D)

I know the Lord laid his hands on me,

Leader   Eb⁷(D⁷)

King Je - sus preach - ing to the poor.
when Je - sus washed my sins a - way!
he healed the sick and raised the dead.

All Bb⁷(A⁷)   Eb(D)   Ab(G)   Eb(D)   *Refrain*

I know the Lord laid his hands on me.

368   O Son of God the Father

1 O Son of God the Fa - ther, in maj - es - ty and might,
2 Yet, Lord, we see but dim - ly; O heav-enly Light, a - rise;
3 O Je - sus, shine a - round us with ra-diance of your grace;

O bright-ness of his glo - ry, e - ter - nal Light of Light:
dis - pel the mists that shroud us and hide you from our eyes.
O Je - sus, turn up - on us the bright-ness of your face.

to gloom - y haunts of dark - ness your rays are stream - ing
We long to track the foot - prints where you your - self have
We need no star to guide us, as on our way we

down; the shad - ows flee be - fore you—
trod; we long to see the path - way
press, if you will light our path - way,

Text: William W. How, 1871, alt.
Tune: Basil Harwood, 1898. Used by permission of the executors of the late Dr. Basil Harwood.

76 76 D
THORNBURY

the world's true light has come.
that leads to you, our God.
O Sun of right - eous - ness!

Christ, upon the Mountain Peak 369

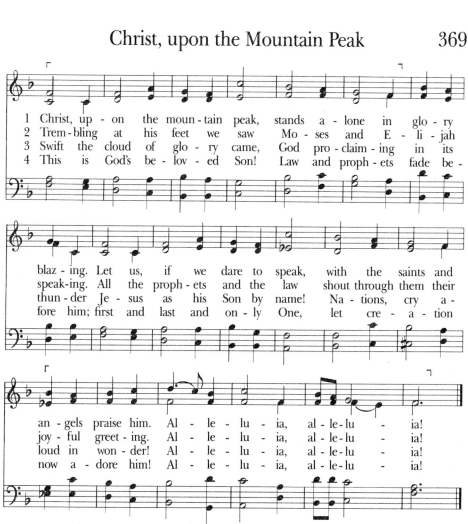

1 Christ, up - on the moun - tain peak, stands a - lone in glo - ry
2 Trem - bling at his feet we saw Mo - ses and E - li - jah
3 Swift the cloud of glo - ry came, God pro - claim - ing in its
4 This is God's be - lov - ed Son! Law and proph - ets fade be -

blaz - ing. Let us, if we dare to speak, with the saints and
speak - ing. All the proph - ets and the law shout through them their
thun - der Je - sus as his Son by name! Na - tions, cry a -
fore him; first and last and on - ly One, let cre - a - tion

an - gels praise him. Al - le - lu - ia, al - le - lu - ia!
joy - ful greet - ing. Al - le - lu - ia, al - le - lu - ia!
loud in won - der! Al - le - lu - ia, al - le - lu - ia!
now a - dore him! Al - le - lu - ia, al - le - lu - ia!

78 78 with alleluias
TRANSFIGURATION

370   The King of Glory Comes

Refrain Unison

The King of glo - ry comes, the na - tion re - joic - es.

O - pen the gates be - fore him, lift up your voic - es.

1 Who is the King of glo - ry? What shall we call him?
2 In all of Gal - i - lee, in cit - y or vil - lage,
3 He gave his life for us, the pledge of sal - va - tion;
4 He con - quered sin and death; he tru - ly has ris - en.

He is Im - man - u - el, the prom-ised of a - ges.
he goes a - mong his peo - ple, cur - ing their ill - ness.
he took up - on him-self the sin of the na - tions.
And he will share with us his heav - en - ly king - dom.

Optional instrumentation for Refrain:

Tambourine   Castanets   *Wood Block*

Text: Willard F. Jabusch, 1966, ©
Tune: Israeli; arr. John Ferguson, 1973. Arrangement from The Hymnal of the United Church of Christ,
© 1974, United Church Press. Used by permission.

12 12 with refrain
PROMISED ONE

Christ, the Life of All the Living

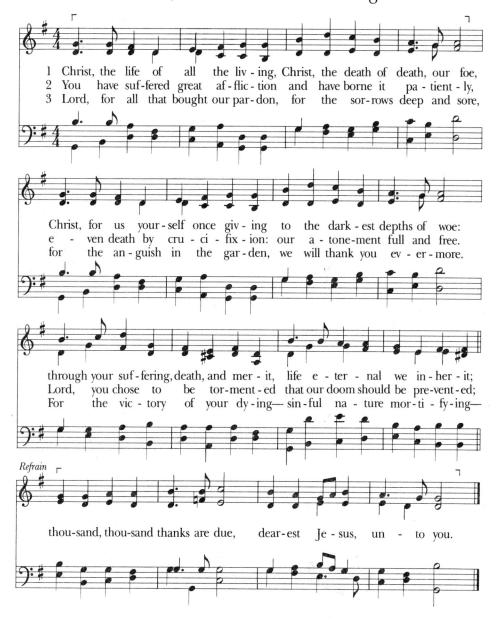

1 Christ, the life of all the liv-ing, Christ, the death of death, our foe,
2 You have suf-fered great af-flic-tion and have borne it pa-tient-ly,
3 Lord, for all that bought our par-don, for the sor-rows deep and sore,

Christ, for us your-self once giv-ing to the dark-est depths of woe:
e-ven death by cru-ci-fix-ion: our a-tone-ment full and free.
for the an-guish in the gar-den, we will thank you ev-er-more.

through your suf-fering, death, and mer-it, life e-ter-nal we in-her-it;
Lord, you chose to be tor-ment-ed that our doom should be pre-vent-ed;
For the vic-tory of your dy-ing— sin-ful na-ture mor-ti-fy-ing—

Refrain

thou-sand, thou-sand thanks are due, dear-est Je-sus, un-to you.

Text: Ernst C. Homburg, 1659; tr. Catherine Winkworth, 1863, alt.
Tune: Das grosse Cantionale, Darmstadt, 1687

87 87 88 *with refrain*
JESU, MEINES LEBENS LEBEN

372 O Christ, Our Lord, Dear Son of God

1 O Christ, our Lord, dear Son of God, we know your aw-ful death,
2 O God, our Fa-ther, source of strength, your grace fills all our needs.
3 O Spir-it of the liv-ing God, con-vict our hearts this Lent

the bru-tal shame, the kill-ing pain, which took a-way your breath.
Your word di-rects our trou-bled lives; we pray, sus-tain our deeds.
to get be-yond re-mem-bered blood and will-ing-ly re-pent!

But, thanks to God, who raised you up, the dread-ful
Pro-vide us in-sight to re-dress cre-a-tion's
So that the might-y deeds of God shall cap-ti-

grave col-lapsed. Your res-ur-rect-ed rule took shape;
groan-ing sighs, and steel us now to per-se-vere;
vate our days, make still la-ment, re-store fresh hope,

1-2
the curse of hell is past!
Lord, make us tru-ly wise.

3
and teach us shouts of praise!

Text: Calvin Seerveld, 1977, ©
Tune: William Davies, 1975, alt., ©

CMD
ORMEAU

Lift High the Cross

Descant
Lift high the cross, the love of Christ pro - claim

Refrain *Unison*
Lift high the cross, the love of Christ pro - claim

till all the world a - dore his sa - cred name.

till all the world a - dore his sa - cred name.

Harmony

1 Come, Chris - tians, fol - low where our Sav - ior led,
2 All new - born ser - vants of the Cru - ci - fied
3 From north and south, from east and west we raise
4 O Lord, once lift - ed on the tree of pain,

Refrain

our King vic - to - rious, Je - sus Christ, our Head.
bear on their brows the seal of him who died.
in grow - ing u - ni - son our song of praise.
draw all the world to seek you once a - gain.

5 Let every race and every language tell
of him who saves our lives from death and hell. *Refrain*

6 Set up your throne, that earth's despair may cease
beneath the shadow of its healing peace. *Refrain*

7 So shall our song of triumph ever be:
praise to the Crucified for victory! *Refrain*

Text: George W. Kitchin, 1887; rev. Michael R. Newbolt, 1916, alt.
Tune: Sydney H. Nicholson, 1916; desc. Richard Proulx, 1985
Text and music © Hymns Ancient and Modern, Ltd. Descant © 1985, G.I.A. Publications, Inc. All rights reserved.

10 10 with refrain
CRUCIFER

374 No Weight of Gold or Silver

1 No weight of gold or sil - ver can mea - sure hu - man worth;
2 Our sins, our griefs and trou - bles, he bore and made his own;
3 In Christ the past is o - ver; a new world now be - gins.

no soul se - cures its ran - som with all the wealth of earth;
we hid our fac - es from him, re - ject - ed and a - lone.
With him we rise to free - dom who saves us from our sins.

no sin - ners find their free - dom but by the gift un - priced:
His wounds are for our heal - ing, our peace is by his pain.
We live by faith in Je - sus to make his glo - ry known.

the Lamb of God un - blem - ished, the pre - cious blood of Christ.
Be - hold, the Man of Sor - rows, the Lamb for sin - ners slain!
Be - hold, the Man of Sor - rows, the Lamb up - on his throne!

Text: Timothy Dudley-Smith, 1972. © 1984, Hope Publishing Co. All rights reserved. Used by permission.
Tune: Adrian Hartog, 1954

76 76 D
PASTORALE

All Glory, Laud, and Honor

1 All glo-ry, laud, and hon-or to you, Re-deem-er, King,
2 The com-pa-ny of an-gels is prais-ing you on high;
3 To you be-fore your pas-sion they sang their hymns of praise;

to whom the lips of chil-dren made sweet ho-san-nas ring.
and we with all cre-a-tion in cho-rus make re-ply.
to you, now high ex-alt-ed, our mel-o-dy we raise.

You are the King of Is-ra-el and Da-vid's roy-al Son,
The peo-ple of the He-brews with palms be-fore you went;
As you re-ceived their prais-es, ac-cept the prayers we bring,

now in the Lord's name com-ing, the King and Bless-ed One.
our praise and prayer and an-thems be-fore you we pre-sent.
for you de-light in good-ness, O good and gra-cious King!

Text: Theodulph of Orleans, c. 820; tr. John M. Neale, 1851, alt.
Tune: Melchior Teschner, 1615; harm. William H. Monk, 1861

76 76 D
ST. THEODULPH

376 All Glory, Laud, and Honor

Trumpet Descant

Choir Descant

3 To you be - fore your pas - sion they sang their hymns of praise;

1 All glo - ry, laud, and hon - or to you, Re - deem - er, King,
2 The com - pa - ny of an - gels is prais - ing you on high;
3 To you be - fore your pas - sion they sang their hymns of praise;

to you, now high ex - alt - ed, our mel - o - dy we raise.

to whom the lips of chil - dren made sweet ho - san - nas ring.
and we with all cre - a - tion in cho - rus make re - ply.
to you, now high ex - alt - ed, our mel - o - dy we raise.

As you re - ceived their prais - es, ac - cept the prayers we bring,

You are the King of Is - ra - el and Da - vid's roy - al Son,
The peo - ple of the He - brews with palms be - fore you went;
As you re - ceived their prais - es, ac - cept the prayers we bring,

Text: Theodulph of Orleans, c. 820; tr. John M. Neale, 1851, alt.
Tune: Melchior Teschner, 1615; harm. Johann S. Bach, 1685–1750, alt.; desc. Randall De Bruyn, 1981.

76 76 D
ST. THEODULPH

for   you   de - light   in   good - ness,   O   good   and   gra - cious   King!

now   in   the Lord's name   com - ing,   the   King and Bless - ed   One.
our praise and prayer and   an - thems be - fore you   we   pre - sent.
for   you   de - light   in   good - ness,   O   good and gra - cious   King!

Bb *Trumpet descant*

377

Were You There

1 Were you there when they cru - ci - fied my Lord? Were you
2 Were you there when they nailed him to the tree? Were you
3 Were you there when they laid him in the tomb? Were you
4 Were you there when God raised him from the tomb? Were you

there when they cru - ci - fied my Lord? Oh,
there when they nailed him to the tree? Oh,
there when they laid him in the tomb? Oh,
there when God raised him from the tomb? Oh,

some-times it caus - es me to trem-ble, trem-ble, trem - ble.
some-times it caus - es me to trem-ble, trem-ble, trem - ble.
some-times it caus - es me to trem-ble, trem-ble, trem - ble.
some-times it caus - es me to trem-ble, trem-ble, trem - ble.

Were you there when they cru - ci - fied my Lord?
Were you there when they nailed him to the tree?
Were you there when they laid him in the tomb?
Were you there when God raised him from the tomb?

Text and Tune: Afro-American spiritual; harm. C. Winfred Douglas, 1940
Keyboard and guitar should not sound together.

10 10 14 10
WERE YOU THERE

Hosanna, Loud Hosanna

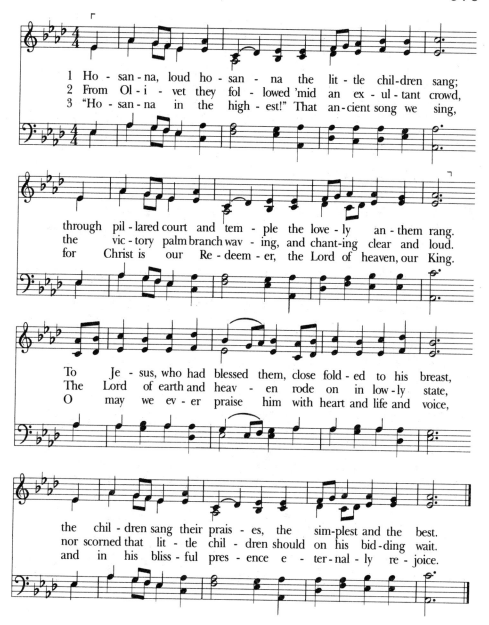

1 Ho - san - na, loud ho - san - na the lit - tle chil-dren sang;
2 From Ol - i - vet they fol - lowed 'mid an ex - ul - tant crowd,
3 "Ho - san - na in the high - est!" That an-cient song we sing,

through pil - lared court and tem - ple the love - ly an - them rang.
the vic - tory palm branch wav - ing, and chant-ing clear and loud.
for Christ is our Re - deem - er, the Lord of heaven, our King.

To Je - sus, who had blessed them, close fold - ed to his breast,
The Lord of earth and heav - en rode on in low - ly state,
O may we ev - er praise him with heart and life and voice,

the chil - dren sang their prais - es, the sim-plest and the best.
nor scorned that lit - tle chil - dren should on his bid - ding wait.
and in his bliss - ful pres - ence e - ter - nal - ly re - joice.

Text: *Jennette Threlfall, 1873*
Tune: Gesangbuch, *Wittenberg, 1784*

76 76 D
ELLACOMBE

379   What Wondrous Love

1 What won-drous love is this, O my soul, O my soul!
2 When I was sink-ing down, sink-ing down, sink-ing down,
3 To God and to the Lamb I will sing, I will sing,
4 And when from death I'm free, I'll sing on, I'll sing on,

What won-drous love is this, O my soul!
when I was sink-ing down, sink-ing down;
to God and to the Lamb I will sing;
and when from death I'm free, I'll sing on;

What won-drous love is this that caused the Lord of bliss
when I was sink-ing down be-neath God's right-eous frown,
to God and to the Lamb, who is the great I AM—
and when from death I'm free, I'll sing and joy-ful be,

to bear the dread-ful curse for my soul, for my soul,
Christ laid a-side his crown for my soul, for my soul,
while mil-lions join the theme, I will sing, I will sing,
and through e-ter-ni-ty I'll sing on, I'll sing on,

Text: S. Mead's A General Selection, *1811*
Tune: W. Walker's Southern Harmony, *1835; harm. Emily R. Brink, 1986.*
Harmonization © 1987, CRC Publications

12 9 12 9 12 9
WONDROUS LOVE

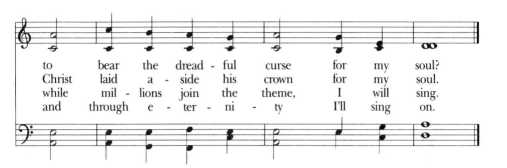

to	bear	the	dread - ful	curse	for	my	soul?
Christ	laid	a - side	his	crown	for	my	soul.
while	mil - lions	join	the	theme,	I	will	sing.
and	through	e - ter - ni - ty			I'll	sing	on.

O Perfect Life of Love 380

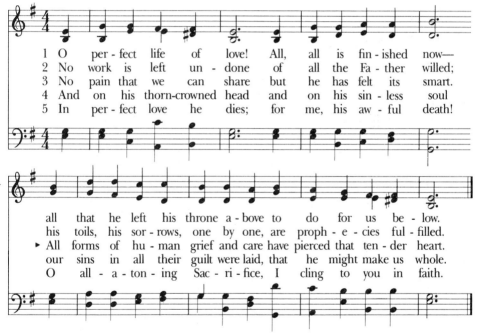

1	O	per - fect	life	of	love!	All,	all	is	fin - ished	now—
2	No	work	is	left	un - done	of	all	the	Fa - ther	willed;
3	No	pain	that	we	can	share	but	he	has felt its	smart.
4	And	on	his	thorn-crowned	head	and	on	his	sin - less	soul
5	In	per - fect	love	he	dies;	for	me,	his	aw - ful	death!

all	that	he	left	his	throne a - bove	to	do	for	us	be - low.
his	toils,	his	sor - rows,	one	by one,	are	proph - e - cies	ful - filled.
All	forms	of	hu - man	grief	and care have	pierced that	ten - der	heart.
our	sins	in	all	their	guilt were laid,	that	he	might make us	whole.
O	all - a - ton - ing	Sac - ri - fice,	I	cling	to	you	in	faith.

6 In every time of need,
   before your judgment throne
   your work, O Lamb of God, I'll plead—
   your merit, not my own.

7 Yet work your way in me,
   my self-will, Lord, remove;
   then shall my love and service be
   my answer to your love.

Text: Henry W. Baker, 1875, alt.
Tune: W. Daman's Psalmes, 1579

SM
SOUTHWELL

381 Go to Dark Gethsemane

1 Go to dark Geth-sem-a-ne, all who feel the tempt-er's power;
2 Fol-low to the judg-ment hall, view the Lord of life ar-raigned.
3 Cal-vary's mourn-ful moun-tain climb; there, a-dor-ing at his feet,

your Re-deem-er's con-flict see, watch with him one bit-ter hour:
Oh, the worm-wood and the gall! Oh, the pangs his soul sus-tained!
mark the mir-a-cle of time, God's own sac-ri-fice com-plete:

turn not from his griefs a-way— teach us, Lord, how we should pray.
Shun not suf-fering, shame, or loss— help us, Lord, to bear our cross.
"It is fin-ished!" hear him cry— save us, Lord, when death draws nigh.

Text: James Montgomery, 1825, alt.
Tune: Richard Redhead, 1853

77 77 77
REDHEAD 76

Ride On, Ride On in Majesty

382

1 Ride on, ride on in maj - es - ty as all the
2 Ride on, ride on in maj - es - ty, in low - ly
3 Ride on, ride on in maj - es - ty, the last and
4 Ride on, ride on in maj - es - ty, in low - ly

crowds "Ho - san - na!" cry; through wav - ing branch-es
pomp ride on to die; O Christ, your tri - umph
fierc - est foe de - fy; the Fa - ther on his
pomp ride on to die; bow your meek head to

slow - ly ride, O Sav - ior to be cru - ci - fied.
now be - gin o'er cap - tive death and con - quered sin!
sap - phire throne a - waits his own a - noint - ed Son.
mor - tal pain, then take, O God, your power and reign!

Text: Henry H. Milman, 1827, alt.
Tune: Henry B. Hays, 1981, alt. © 1981, Order of St. Benedict, Inc.

LM
CHICKAHOMINY

383   O Sacred Head, Now Wounded

1 O   sa - cred head, now wound - ed, with grief and shame weighed down,
2 My Lord, what you did   suf - fer was   all   for sin - ners'   gain;
3 What lan-guage shall I   bor - row to   thank you, dear - est   Friend,

now scorn-ful - ly sur - round - ed with thorns, your   on - ly   crown.
mine, mine was the trans - gres - sion, but yours   the   dead - ly   pain.
for   this, your dy - ing   sor - row, your mer - cy   with - out   end?

O   sa - cred head, what   glo - ry and bless-ing you have known!
So   here I   kneel, my   Sav - ior, for   I de - serve your place;
Lord, make me yours for - ev - er, a   loy - al ser - vant   true,

Yet,   though de - spised and gor - y, I   claim you as my   own.
look   on   me with your fa - vor and save me by your grace.
and   let   me nev - er, nev - er out - live my love for   you.

Text: Latin, medieval; German tr. Paul Gerhardt, 1656; tr. James W. Alexander, 1830, alt.
Tune: Hans L. Hassler, 1601; adapt. and harm. Johann S. Bach in St. Matthew Passion, 1729   76 76 D
HERZLICH TUT MICH VERLANGEN

When I Survey the Wondrous Cross

384

1 When I sur - vey the won - drous cross on which the
2 For - bid it, Lord, that I should boast save in the
3 See, from his head, his hands, his feet, sor - row and
4 Were the whole realm of na - ture mine, that were a

Prince of glo - ry died, my rich - est gain I
death of Christ, my God! All the vain things that
love flow min - gled down. Did e'er such love and
pres - ent far too small. Love so a - maz - ing,

count but loss, and pour con - tempt on all my pride.
charm me most, I sac - ri - fice them through his blood.
sor - row meet, or thorns com - pose so rich a crown?
so di - vine, de - mands my soul, my life, my all.

Text: Isaac Watts, 1707
Tune: Lowell Mason, 1824
Alternative tune: ROCKINGHAM, 178

LM
HAMBURG

385 Alas! and Did My Savior Bleed

1 A - las! and did my Sav - ior bleed, and did my Sov - ereign die? Would he de - vote that sa - cred head for sin - ners such as I?

2 Was it for sins that I have done he groaned up - on the tree? A - maz - ing pit - y, grace un - known, and love be - yond de - gree!

3 Well might the sun in dark - ness hide and shut its glo - ries in when Christ, the might - y Mak - er, died for his own crea - tures' sin.

4 Thus might I hide my blush - ing face while his dear cross ap - pears, dis - solve my heart in thank - ful - ness, and melt mine eyes to tears.

Text: Isaac Watts, 1707, alt.
Tune: Hugh Wilson, c. 1800; adapt. Robert Smith, 1825

CM
MARTYRDOM

Ah, Holy Jesus, How Have You Offended 386

1 Ah, ho - ly Je - sus, how have you of - fend - ed,
2 Who was the guilt - y? Who brought this up - on you?
3 For me, dear Je - sus, was your in - car - na - tion,
4 There - fore, dear Je - sus, since I can - not pay you,

that mor - tal judg - ment has on you de - scend - ed? By foes de -
It is my trea - son, Lord, that has un - done you. 'Twas I, Lord
your mor - tal sor - row, and your life's ob - la - tion; your death of
I do a - dore you and will ev - er pray you, think on your

rid - ed by your own re - ject - ed, O most af - flict - ed!
Je - sus, I it was de - nied you; I cru - ci - fied you.
an - guish and your bit - ter pas - sion, for my sal - va - tion.
pit - y and your love un - swerv - ing, not my de - serv - ing.

Text: Johann Heermann, 1630; tr. Robert Bridges, 1899, alt.
Tune: Johann Crüger, 1640

11 11 11 5
HERZLIEBSTER JESU

387

Alleluia! Alleluia!

1 Al - le - lu - ia, al - le - lu - ia! Hearts to
2 Al - le - lu - ia, Christ is ris - en! Death at
3 Christ is ris - en, Christ the first - fruits of the
4 Al - le - lu - ia, al - le - lu - ia! Glo - ry

heaven and voic - es raise. Sing to God a
last has met de - feat. See the an - cient
ho - ly har - vest field, which will all its
be to God on high; al - le - lu - ia!

hymn of glad - ness, sing to God a hymn of praise.
powers of e - vil in con - fu - sion and re - treat.
full a - bun - dance at his sec - ond com - ing yield.
to the Sav - ior, who has won the vic - to - ry;

Text: Christopher Wordsworth, 1862, alt.
Tune: Thomas J. Williams, 1890

87 87 D
EBENEZER

He who on the cross a vic - tim for the
Once he died and once was bur - ied; now he
Then the gold - en ears of har - vest will their
al - le - lu - ia! to the Spir - it, fount of

world's sal - va - tion bled, Je - sus Christ, the
lives for - ev - er - more— Je - sus Christ, the
heads be - fore him wave, rip - ened by his
love and sanc - ti - ty: al - le - lu - ia,

King of glo - ry, now is ris - en from the dead.
world's Re - deem - er, whom we wor - ship and a - dore.
glo - rious sun - shine from the fur - rows of the grave.
al - le - lu - ia! to the tri - une Maj - es - ty.

388   Christ the Lord Is Risen Today

Descant

4, 5 Ah,_____ Al - le - lu - ia! Ah

⌐ *May be sung antiphonally*

1 Christ the Lord is risen to day! Al - le - lu - ia!
2 Love's re - deem-ing work is done, Al - le - lu - ia!
3 Lives a - gain our glo - rious King; Al - le - lu - ia!
4 Soar we now where Christ has led, Al - le - lu - ia!
5 Hail the Lord of earth and heaven! Al - le - lu - ia!

Al - le - lu - ia! Ah

All cre - a - tion, join to say: Al - le - lu - ia!
Fought the fight, the bat - tle won; Al - le - lu - ia!
▸ Where, O death, is now your sting? Al - le - lu - ia!
Fol - lowing our ex - alt - ed Head; Al - le - lu - ia!
Praise to you by both be given; Al - le - lu - ia!

Text: Charles Wesley, 1739, alt.
Tune: Lyra Davidica, 1708; desc. Paul Sjolund, 1976. Descant © 1976, Paragon Music.
All rights reserved. International copyright secured. Used by permission of the Zondervan Music Group.

77 77 with alleluias
EASTER HYMN

Al - le-lu - ia! Al-

Raise your joys and tri-umphs high; Al - le - lu - ia!
Death in vain for - bids him rise; Al - le - lu - ia!
Once he died, our souls to save; Al - le - lu - ia!
Made like him, like him we rise; Al - le - lu - ia!
Ris - en Christ, tri - um-phant now; Al - le - lu - ia!

le - lu - ia! Al - le - lu - ia!

Sing, O heavens, and earth, re - ply: Al - le - lu - ia!
Christ has o - pened par - a - dise. Al - le - lu - ia!
Where your vic - to - ry, O grave? Al - le - lu - ia!
Ours the cross, the grave, the skies. Al - le - lu - ia!
Ev - ery knee to you shall bow. Al - le - lu - ia!

389   Come, You Faithful, Raise the Strain

1 Come, you faith-ful, raise the strain of tri-um-phant glad-ness;
2 'Tis the spring of life to day! Christ has burst his pris-on,
3 "Al - le - lu - ia!" now we cry to our King im-mor-tal,

God has brought his peo-ple forth in-to joy from sad-ness.
and from three days' sleep in death like the sun has ris-en.
who, tri-um-phant, burst the bars of the tomb's dark por-tal;

Now re-joice, Je - ru - sa-lem, and with true af-fec-tion
All the win-ter of our sins, long and dark, is fly-ing;
"Al - le - lu - ia!" with the Son, God the Fa-ther prais-ing;

wel-come in un - wea-ried strains Je-sus' res-ur-rec-tion.
wel-come now the light of Christ, give him praise un-dy-ing.
"Al - le - lu - ia!" yet a - gain to the Spir-it rais-ing.

Text: John of Damascus, 8th cent.; tr. John M. Neale, 1859, alt.
Tune: Arthur S. Sullivan, 1872

76 76 D
ST. KEVIN

The Day of Resurrection

1 The day of res - ur - rec - tion! Earth, tell it out a - broad,
2 Let hearts be purged of e - vil that we may see a - right
3 Now let the heavens be joy - ful, let earth its song be - gin,

the Pass - o - ver of glad - ness, the Pass - o - ver of God.
the Lord in rays e - ter - nal of res - ur - rec - tion light,
let all the world keep tri - umph and all that is there - in.

From death to life e - ter - nal, from sin's do - min - ion free,
and, lis - tening to his ac - cents, may hear so calm and plain
Let all things, seen and un - seen, their notes of glad - ness blend;

our Christ has brought us o - ver with hymns of vic - to - ry.
his own "All hail!" and, hear - ing, may raise the vic - tor strain.
for Christ the Lord has ris - en, our joy that has no end!

Text: John of Damascus, 8th cent.; tr. John M. Neale, 1862, alt.
Tune: John Farmer, 1892

76 76 D
FARMER

391   The Strife is O'er, the Battle Done

Alleluia, alleluia, alleluia!

1. The strife is o'er, the battle done;
   the victory of life is won;
   the song of triumph has begun. Alleluia!
2. The powers of death have done their worst,
   but Christ their legions has dispersed.
   Let shouts of holy joy outburst. Alleluia!
3. The three sad days are quickly sped;
   he rises glorious from the dead.
   All glory to our risen Head. Alleluia!
4. He closed the yawning gates of hell;
   the bars from heaven's high portals fell.
   Let hymns of praise his triumph tell. Alleluia!
5. Lord, by the stripes which wounded thee,
   from death's dread sting thy servants free,
   that we may live and sing to thee. Alleluia!

Final ending

Alleluia, alleluia, alleluia!

Text: Symphonia Sirenum, *Cologne, 1695; tr. Francis Pott, 1861*
Tune: Giovanni da Palestrina, *1591; adapt. and arr. William H. Monk, 1861*

888 with alleluias
VICTORY

A Shout Rings Out, a Joyful Voice
Daar juicht een toon

1 A shout rings out, a joyful voice: "Je-
2 No grave could con-quer Da-vid's Son; he

1 Daar juicht een toon, daar klinkt een stem, die
2 Geen graf hield Da-vids Zoon om kneld, hij

ru-sa-lem, a-rise, re-joice!" A glo-rious morn-ing
con-quered death and vic-tory won, rose from the grave in

galmt door gans Je-ru-za-lem; een heer-lijk mor-gen
o-ver-won, die ster-ke held, hij steeg uit 't graf door

breaks the night; the Son of God is risen with might.
heav enly power, for he is God, our strength and tower.

licht breekt aan: de Zoon van God is op-ge-staan!
ei-gen kracht, want hij is God, be-kleed met macht!

3 Now death no longer holds a sting;
Christ fully paid for all our sin.
Believers who his glory tell
need never fear the grave or hell.

4 Since Christ the Lord is risen with might,
new life begins in glorious light:
a life that triumphs over death,
eternal life with Christ, our Head.

3 Nu jaagt de dood geen angst meer aan,
want alles, alles is voldaan;
wie in geloof op Jezus ziet,
die vreest voor dood en duivel niet.

4 Want nu de Heer is opgestaan,
nu vangt het nieuwe leven aan,
een leven door zijn dood bereid,
een leven in zijn heerlijkheid!

Text: Eduard Gerdes, 1821–1898; tr. Psalter Hymnal, 1987. © 1987, CRC Publications
Tune: attr. Henri A. C. Malan, 1787–1864

LM
DAAR JUICHT EEN TOON

393   O Sons and Daughters

Al - le - lu - ia, al - le - lu - ia, al - le-lu - ia, al - le-lu - ia!

1 O sons and daugh - ters of the King, whom
2 That Eas - ter morn at break of day, the
3 An an - gel clad in white they see, who
4 When Thom - as first the tid - ings heard that

heav - enly hosts in glo - ry sing, to - day the
faith - ful wom - en went their way to seek the
sat and spoke un - to the three, "Your Lord has
some had seen the ris - en Lord, he doubt - ed

grave has lost its sting.   Al - le - lu - ia!
tomb where Je - sus lay.   Al - le - lu - ia!
gone to Gal - i - lee."   Al - le - lu - ia!
the dis - ci - ples' word.   Lord, have mer - cy!

Text: early 16th cent.; tr. John M. Neale, 1851, alt.; based on Matthew 28 and John 20
Tune: Airs sur les hymnes sacrez, odes et noëls, Paris, 1623

888 with alleluias
O FILII ET FILIAE

5 At night the apostles met in fear;
 among them came their Master dear
 and said, "My peace be with you here."
 Alleluia!

6 "My piercèd side, O Thomas, see,
 and look upon my hands, my feet;
 not faithless but believing be."
 Alleluia!

7 No longer Thomas then denied;
 he saw the feet, the hands, the side.
 "You are my Lord and God!" he cried.
 Alleluia!

8 How blest are they who have not seen
 and yet whose faith has constant been,
 for they eternal life shall win.
 Alleluia!

Final ending

Al - le - lu - ia, al - le - lu - ia, al - le-lu - ia, al - le - lu - ia!

394 These Things Did Thomas Count as Real

┌ *Unison*

1 These things did Thom-as count as real: the warmth of
2 The vi - sion of his skep - tic mind was keen e -
3 His rea - soned cer - tain - ties de-nied that one could
4 May we, O God, by grace be-lieve and thus the

blood, the chill of steel, the grain of wood, the
nough to make him blind to an - y un - ex -
live when one had died, un - til his fin - gers
ris - en Christ re - ceive, whose raw im - print - ed

heft of stone, the last frail twitch of blood and bone.
pect - ed act too large for his small world of fact.
read like braille the mark-ings of the spear and nail.
palms reached out and beck-oned Thom - as from his doubt.

Text: Thomas H. Troeger, 1983; based on John 20:24–29
Tune: Carol Doran, 1983
Text and music © 1984, Oxford University Press, NY
Alternative tune: BISHOP, 224

LM
MERLE MARIE

Hail, O Once-Despised Jesus

1 Hail, O once-despis-ed Je-sus! Hail, O Gal-i-le-an King!
2 Pas-chal Lamb, by God ap-point-ed, all our sins on you were laid;
3 Je-sus! Heav-enly hosts a-dore you, seat-ed at your Fa-ther's side.
4 Wor-ship, hon-or, power, and bless-ing you are wor-thy to re-ceive;

You have suf-fered to re-lease us, hope and joy and peace to bring.
by al-might-y love a-noint-ed, you have full a-tone-ment made.
Cru-ci-fied this world once saw you; now in glo-ry you a-bide.
loud-est prais-es, with-out ceas-ing, right it is for us to give.

Hail, O ag-o-niz-ing Sav-ior, bear-er of our sin and shame;
All your peo-ple are for-giv-en through the vir-tue of your blood;
There for sin-ners you are plead-ing, and our place you now pre-pare,
Help, O bright an-gel-ic spir-its, all your no-blest an-thems raise;

by your mer-its we find fa-vor; life is giv-en through your name.
o-pened is the gate of heav-en; we are rec-on-ciled to God.
ev-er for us in-ter-ced-ing, till in glo-ry we ap-pear.
help to sing our Sav-ior's mer-its, help to chant Im-man-uel's praise.

Text: attr. John Bakewell, 1757, alt.
Tune: Welsh; adapt. and harm. Stanley L. Osborne, 1970, ©

87 87 D
ARFON

396 Low in the Grave Christ Lay

1 Low in the grave Christ lay— Je - sus, my Sav - ior;
2 Vain - ly they watch his bed— Je - sus, my Sav - ior;
3 Death can - not keep its prey— Je - sus, my Sav - ior;

wait - ing the com - ing day—
vain - ly they seal the dead— Je - sus, my Lord.
he tore the bars a - way—

Refrain

Up from the grave he a - rose,
he a - rose!
with a might - y tri - umph o'er his

foes,
he a - rose!
He a - rose a vic - tor from the dark do - main,

and he lives for - ev - er with his saints to reign! He a - rose!

He a - rose!

Text and Tune: Robert Lowry, 1874, alt.

65 65 with refrain
CHRIST AROSE

He a - rose!
He a-rose!
Hal - le - lu - jah! Christ a - rose!

Good Christians All, Rejoice and Sing   397

1 Good Chris-tians all, re - joice and sing! Now is the
2 The Lord of life is risen to - day. Sing songs of
3 Praise we in songs of vic - to - ry that love, that
4 Your name we bless, O ris - en Lord, and sing to -

tri - umph of our King! To all the world glad news we bring:
praise a - long his way. Let all the world re - joice and say:
life which can - not die, and sing with hearts up lift - ed high:
day with one ac - cord the life laid down, the life re - stored:

Descant

Al - le - lu - ia, al - le - lu - ia, al - le - lu - ia!

Al - le - lu - ia, al - le - lu - ia, al - le - lu - ia!

Text: Cyril A. Alington, 1925, alt. © 1955, Hymns Ancient and Modern, Ltd.
Tune: Melchior Vulpius, 1609; desc. Emily R. Brink, 1986

888 with alleluias
GELOBT SEI GOTT

398   Christ Jesus Lay in Death's Strong Bands

1 Christ Je - sus lay in death's strong bands, for our of -
2 It was a strange and dread - ful strife when life and
3 Here the true pas - chal Lamb we see, whom God so
4 So let us keep the fes - ti - val to which the
5 Then let us feast this ho - ly day on Christ, the

fens - es giv - en; but now at God's right hand he stands
death con - tend - ed. The vic - to - ry re-mained with life;
free - ly gave us. He died on the ac - curs - ed tree—
Lord in - vites us. Christ is him-self the joy of all,
bread of heav - en. The Word of grace has purged a - way

and brings us life from heav - en. There - fore let us
the reign of death was end - ed. Ho - ly Scrip - ture
so strong his love— to save us. See, his blood now
the sun that warms and lights us. Now his grace to
the old and e - vil leav - en. Christ a - lone our

Text: Martin Luther, 1524; tr. Richard Massie, 1854, alt.
Tune: J. Walther's Geystliche gesangk Buchleyn, 1524

87 87 78 74
CHRIST LAG IN TODESBANDEN

joy - ful   be,   and sing   to   God   right thank - ful - ly
plain - ly   says   his death has   swal - lowed up   our   death;
▸ marks our   door;   faith points to   it,   death pass - es   o'er,
us   im - parts   e - ter - nal   sun - shine to   our   hearts;
souls will   feed;   he   is   our   meat   and   drink in   deed;

loud songs of   al - le - lu - ia!   Al - le - lu - ia!
its   sting is   lost for - ev - er.   Al - le - lu - ia!
▸ and   Sa - tan can - not harm   us.   Al - le - lu - ia!
the night of   sin   is   end - ed.   Al - le - lu - ia!
faith lives up - on   no   oth - er!   Al - le - lu - ia!

399

Jesus Lives, and So Do We

1 Je - sus lives, and so do we: Death, where is your
2 Je - sus lives: his king - dom comes o - ver earth as
3 Je - sus lives: his death a - toned for my sin; I
4 Je - sus lives: this truth is sure. What from Christ can
5 Je - sus lives: be not a - fraid! Take by faith God's

sting so threat - ening? Je - sus lives and cares for me,
well as heav - en. I shall rule with God's own Son
am for - giv - en. Rule my heart, O Lord en-throned;
sep - a - rate me? E - vil's powers I shall en-dure;
prom - ised sure - ty. All our sins in Christ are paid:

turns the grave to life un - end - ing. God shall
through the grace that shall be giv - en. God shall
may my life be Spir - it driv - en. God shall
death nor hell can thwart my safe - ty. God shall
death is swal-lowed up in vic - tory. God shall

raise me from the dust: Je - sus is my hope and trust.
raise me from the dust: Je - sus is my hope and trust.
raise me from the dust: Je - sus is my hope and trust.
raise me from the dust: Je - sus is my hope and trust.
raise us from the dust: Je - sus Christ, our hope and trust!

Text: Christian Gellert, 1757; tr. Calvin Seerveld, 1985, ©
Tune: Johann Crüger, 1653

78 78 77
JESUS, MEINE ZUVERZICHT

Praise the Savior, Now and Ever

1 Praise the Sav - ior now and ev - er; praise him, all be -
2 Our work fail - eth, Christ's a - vail - eth; he is all our
3 Sin's bonds sev - ered, we're de - liv - ered; Christ has crushed the
4 For his fa - vor, praise for - ev - er un - to God the

neath the skies; self de - ny - ing, suf - fering, dy - ing,
right - eous - ness. He, our Sav - ior, has for - ev - er
ser - pent's head. Death no lon - ger is the stron - ger;
Fa - ther sing. Praise the Sav - ior, praise him ev - er,

on the cross a sac - ri - fice. Vic - tory gain - ing,
set us free from dire dis - tress. Through his mer - it
hell it - self is cap - tive led. Christ has ris - en
Son of God, our Lord and King. Praise the Spir - it;

life ob - tain - ing, now in glo - ry he doth rise!
we in - her - it light and peace and hap - pi - ness.
from death's pris - on; o'er the tomb he light has shed.
through Christ's mer - it he doth us sal - va - tion bring.

Text: Venantius Honorius Fortunatus, 569; tr. Augustus Nelson, 1863–1949, alt.
Tune: Then Swenska Psalm-Boken, Stockholm, 1697

87 87 87
UPP, MIN TUNGA

Oh, How Good Is Christ the Lord
Oh, Qué Bueno Es Jesús

401

Oh, how good is Christ the Lord! On the cross he died for me.
Oh, qué bue - no es Je - sús. Que por mí mu - rió en la cruz.

He has par-doned all my sin. Glo-ry be to Je - sus.
Mis pe - ca - dos per-do - nó. A su nom - bre glo - ria.

Glo-ry be to Je - sus! Glo-ry be to Je - sus!
A su nom - bre glo - ria. A su nom - bre glo - ria.

In three days he rose a - gain. Glo-ry be to Je - sus.
En tres días re - su - ci - tó. A su nom - bre glo - ria.

Text and Tune: Puerto Rican folk hymn; harm. Dale Grotenhuis, 1985.
Harmonization © 1987, CRC Publications

irregular
OH QUE BUENO

Alleluia, Alleluia! Give Thanks

402

Capo 3: ⌐ Refrain

Al - le - lu - ia, al - le - lu - ia! Give thanks to the ris - en Lord. Al - le-
lu - ia, al - le - lu - ia! Give praise to his name.

Unison

1 Je - sus is Lord of all the earth;
2 Spread the good news o'er all the earth:
3 We have been cru - ci - fied with Christ;
4 God has pro - claimed the just re - ward:
5 Come, let us praise the liv - ing God,

he is the King of cre - a - tion.
Je - sus has died and has ris - en.
▸ now we shall live_____ for - ev - er.
life for his own. Al - le - lu - ia!
joy - ful - ly sing to our Sav - ior.

Refrain

Text and Tune: Donald Fishel, 1971; harm. Dale Grotenhuis, 1984
Text and music © 1973, The Word of God. All rights reserved.

irregular
CHURCH STREET

403

This Joyful Eastertide

1 This joy-ful Eas-ter-tide, a - way with sin and
2 My be-ing shall re-joice se - cure with-in God's
3 Death's wa-ters lost their chill when Je - sus crossed the

sad - ness! Our Lord, the cru-ci - fied, has
keep - ing, un - til the trum-pet voice shall
riv - er. His love shall reach me still; his

Refrain

filled our hearts with glad - ness.
wake us from our sleep - ing. Had Christ, who once was
mer-cy is for-ev - er.

Text: George R. Woodward, 1894, alt.
Tune: J. Oudaen's David's Psalmen, 1685; harm. Dale Grotenhuis, 1984.
Harmonization © 1987, CRC Publications

67 67 with refrain
VRUCHTEN

slain, not burst his three-day pris - on, our faith would be in

vain. But now has Christ a - ris - en, a - ris - en, a -

ris - en, but now has Christ a - ris - en!

404 Sing, Choirs of New Jerusalem

1 Sing, choirs of new Je - ru - sa - lem, your
2 For Ju - dah's Li - on burst his chains and
3 Tri - um - phant in his glo - ry now— to
4 All glo - ry to the Fa - ther be, all

sweet - est notes em - ploy, your sweet - est notes em - ploy
crushed the ser - pent's head, and crushed the ser - pent's head;
him all power is given, to him all power is given;
glo - ry to the Son, all glo - ry to the Son,

the pas - chal vic - to - ry to hymn
Christ cries a - loud through death's do - mains
to him in one com - mu - nion bow
all glo - ry to the Spir - it be

Text: Fulbert of Chartres, early 11th cent.; tr. Robert Campbell, 1850, alt.
Tune: Thomas Jarman, c. 1803

CM with repeats
LYNGHAM

405

I Serve a Risen Savior

Capo 1:

1 I serve a ris - en Sav - ior, he's in the world to - day;
2 In all the world a - round me I see his lov - ing care,
3 Re - joice, re - joice, O Chris - tian, lift up your voice and sing

I know that he is liv - ing, what - ev - er peo - ple say;
and though my heart grows wea - ry, I nev - er will de - spair;
e - ter - nal hal - le - lu - jahs to Je - sus Christ the King!

I see his hand of mer - cy, I hear his voice of cheer,
I know that he is lead - ing through all the storm - y blast;
The hope of all who seek him, the help of all who find;

and ev - ery time I need him he's al - ways near.
the day of his ap - pear - ing will come at last.
no oth - er is so lov - ing, so good and kind.

76 76 76 74 with refrain
ACKLEY

406

Alleluia! Sing to Jesus

1 Al - le - lu - ia! sing to Je - sus! his the scep - ter, his the throne;
2 Al - le - lu - ia! not as or - phans are we left in sor - row now;
3 Al - le - lu - ia! heav-enly High Priest, here on earth our help, our stay;

Al - le - lu - ia! his the tri-umph, his the vic - to - ry a - lone.
Al - le - lu - ia! he is near us; faith be-lieves, nor ques-tions how.
Al - le - lu - ia! hear the sin - ful cry to you from day to day.

Hark! the songs of peace-ful Zi - on thun-der like a might-y flood.
Though the cloud from sight re-ceived him when the for - ty days were o'er,
In - ter - ces - sor, Friend of sin - ners, earth's Re-deem-er, hear our plea,

Je - sus, out of ev - ery na - tion, has re-deemed us by his blood.
shall our hearts for - get his prom-ise, "I am with you ev - er-more"?
where the songs of all the sin - less sweep a - cross the crys-tal sea.

Text: William C. Dix, 1866, alt.
Tune: H. Ernest Nichol, 1905
Alternative tune: HYFRYDOL, 568

87 87 D
LOWELL

Christ the Lord Ascends to Reign

407

1 Christ the Lord as-cends to reign, Christ has bro-ken ev-ery chain;
2 Christ, who bore all pain and loss, com-fort-less up-on the cross,
3 Christ, our pas-chal Lamb in-deed, all your ran-somed peo-ple feed;
4 Christ now bids us tell a-broad how the lost may be re-stored,

hear the an-gel voic-es cry, sing-ing ev-er-more on high:
lives in glo-ry now on high, pleads for us and hears our cry:
take our sin and guilt a-way; let us sing by night and day:
how the pen-i-tent for-given, how we all may en-ter heaven:

Refrain (may be sung after last stanza only)

Al-le-lu-ia! Al-le-lu-ia, al-le-lu-ia, al-le-lu-ia! Through the u-ni-verse it rings that the Lamb is King of kings: Al-le-lu-ia!

Text: Michael Weise, 1531; tr. Catherine Winkworth, 1858, alt.
Tune: J. Klug's Geistliche Lieder, 1533; harm. Dale Grotenhuis, 1984.
Harmonization © 1987, CRC Publications

77 77 4 with refrain
CHRIST IST ERSTANDEN

408   Rejoice, the Lord Is King

Descant

4 Re - joice in glo - rious hope; for Christ, the Judge, shall come to

1 Re - joice, the Lord is King! Your Lord and King a - dore. Re -
2 His king - dom can - not fail; he rules o'er earth and heaven; the
3 He sits at God's right hand till all his foes sub - mit, bow
4 Re - joice in glo - rious hope; for Christ, the Judge, shall come to

gath - er all his saints to their e - ter - nal home. We soon shall

joice, give thanks and sing and tri - umph ev - er - more. Lift up your
keys of death and hell to Christ the Lord are given. Lift up your
down at his com - mand, and fall be - neath his feet. Lift up your
gath - er all his saints to their e - ter - nal home. We soon shall

hear the arch - an - gel's voice; the trump of God shall sound, re - joice!

heart, lift up your voice. Re - joice, a - gain I say, re - joice!
heart, lift up your voice. Re - joice, a - gain I say, re - joice!
heart, lift up your voice. Re - joice, a - gain I say, re - joice!
hear the arch - an - gel's voice; the trump of God shall sound, re - joice!

Text: Charles Wesley, 1744, alt.
Tune: John Darwall, 1770; desc. Sydney H. Nicholson, 1875–1947.
Descant © 1947, Hymns Ancient and Modern, Ltd.
Alternative tune: ARTHUR'S SEAT, 164

66 66 88
DARWALL'S 148th

Hail the Day That Sees Him Rise

1 Hail the day that sees him rise, Al - le - lu - ia!
2 There for him high tri - umph waits; Al - le - lu - ia!
3 High - est heaven its Lord re - ceives; Al - le - lu - ia!
4 Still for us he in - ter - cedes; Al - le - lu - ia!
5 There we shall with you re - main, Al - le - lu - ia!

to his throne be - yond the skies. Al - le - lu - ia!
lift your heads, e - ter - nal gates. Al - le - lu - ia!
▶ yet he loves the earth he leaves. Al - le - lu - ia!
his a - ton - ing death he pleads, Al - le - lu - ia!
part - ners of your end - less reign, Al - le - lu - ia!

Christ, the Lamb for sin - ners given, Al - le - lu - ia!
He has con-quered death and sin; Al - le - lu - ia!
▶ Though re - turn - ing to his throne, Al - le - lu - ia
near him - self pre - pares our place, Al - le - lu - ia!
see you with un - cloud - ed view, Al - le - lu - ia!

en - ters now the high - est heaven. Al - le - lu - ia!
take the King of glo - ry in. Al - le - lu - ia!
▶ still he calls us all his own. Al - le - lu - ia!
he the first - fruits of our race. Al - le - lu - ia!
find our heaven of heavens in you. Al - le - lu - ia!

Text: *Charles Wesley, 1739, and Thomas Cotterill, 1820, alt.*
Tune: *Robert Williams, 1817*

77 77 with alleluias
LLANFAIR

410   Crown Him with Many Crowns

Descant

3 Crown him the Lord of peace; his king-dom is at hand.

1 Crown him with man - y crowns, the Lamb up - on his throne,
2 Crown him the Lord of life, tri - um - phant o'er the grave,
3 Crown him the Lord of peace; his king-dom is at hand.

From pole to pole let war - fare cease and Christ rule ev - ery land! All hail,

while heaven's e - ter - nal an - them drowns all mu - sic but its own!
who rose vic - to - rious from the strife for those he came to save.
From pole to pole let war - fare cease and Christ rule ev - ery land!

Re - deem - er, hail, for you died for me. Crown him

A - wake, my soul, and sing of him who died to be your
His glo - ries now we sing who died and reigns on high; he
All hail, Re - deem - er, hail, for you have died for me. Your

---

Text: st. 1, 3, Matthew Bridges, 1851; st. 2, Godfrey Thring, 1874; alt.
Tune: George J. Elvey, 1868; desc. Hal H. Hopson, 1979. Descant © 1979, G.I.A. Publications. All rights reserved.

SMD
DIADEMATA

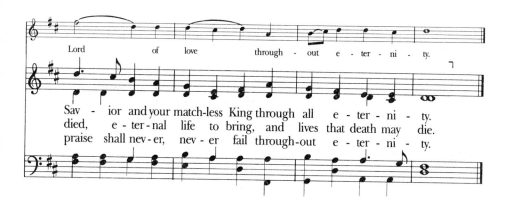

Lord of love through-out e - ter - ni - ty.

Sav - ior and your match-less King through all e - ter - ni - ty.
died, e - ter-nal life to bring, and lives that death may die.
praise shall nev-er, nev - er fail through-out e - ter - ni - ty.

The Head That Once Was Crowned with Thorns 411

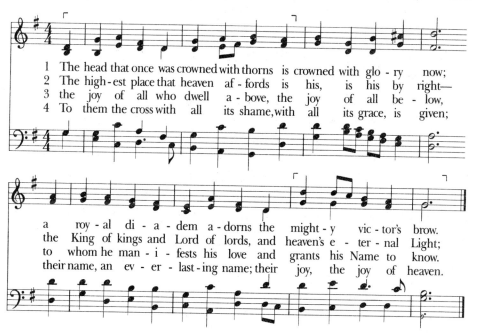

1 The head that once was crowned with thorns is crowned with glo - ry now;
2 The high-est place that heaven af - fords is his, is his by right—
3 the joy of all who dwell a - bove, the joy of all be - low,
4 To them the cross with all its shame, with all its grace, is given;

a roy - al di - a - dem a - dorns the might - y vic - tor's brow.
the King of kings and Lord of lords, and heaven's e - ter - nal Light;
to whom he man - i - fests his love and grants his Name to know.
their name, an ev - er - last-ing name; their joy, the joy of heaven.

5 They suffer with their Lord below,
  they reign with him above,
their profit and their joy to know
  the mystery of his love.

6 The cross he bore is life and health,
  though shame and death to him:
his people's hope, his people's wealth,
  their everlasting theme.

Text: Thomas Kelly, 1820
Tune: attr. Jeremiah Clark, 1707

CM
ST. MAGNUS

412   Jesus Shall Reign

1. Je-sus shall reign wher - e'er the sun does its suc -
2. To him shall end - less prayer be made, and prais - es
3. Peo - ple and realms of ev - ery tongue dwell on his
4. Bless - ings a - bound wher - e'er he reigns: the pris-oners
5. Let ev - ery crea - ture rise and bring the high - est

ces - sive jour - neys run, his king-dom stretch from
throng to crown his head. His name like sweet per -
► love with sweet - est song, and in - fant voic - es
leap to lose their chains, the wea - ry find e -
hon - ors to our King, an - gels de - scend with

shore to shore, till moons shall wax and wane no more.
fume shall rise with ev - ery morn - ing sac - ri - fice.
► shall pro - claim their ear - ly bless - ings on his name.
ter - nal rest, and all who suf - fer want are blest.
songs a - gain, and earth re - peat the loud a - men.

Text: Isaac Watts, 1719, alt.
Tune: John Hatton, 1793

LM
DUKE STREET

Christ Is Alive! Let Christians Sing

413

1 Christ is a - live! Let Chris - tians sing. His cross stands
2 Christ is a - live! No lon - ger bound to dis - tant
3 Not decked with gold, re - mote - ly high, un - touched, un -
4 In ev - ery in - sult, rift, and war where col - or,
5 Christ is a - live! His Spir - it burns through this and

emp - ty to the sky. Let streets and homes with
years in Pal - es - tine, he comes to claim the
moved by hu - man pains, but dai - ly, in the
scorn, or wealth di - vide, he suf - fers still, yet
ev - ery fu - ture age, till all cre - a - tion

prais - es ring. His love in death shall nev - er die.
here and now and con - quer ev - ery place and time.
midst of life, our Sav - ior with the Fa - ther reigns.
loves the more, with heal - ing hands and ach - ing side.
lives and learns his joy, his jus - tice, love, and praise.

Text: Brian Wren, 1968, 1978, alt. © 1975, Hope Publishing Co. All rights reserved. Used by permission.
Tune: T. Williams' Psalmodia Evangelica, 1789

LM
TRURO

414   See, the Conqueror Mounts in Triumph

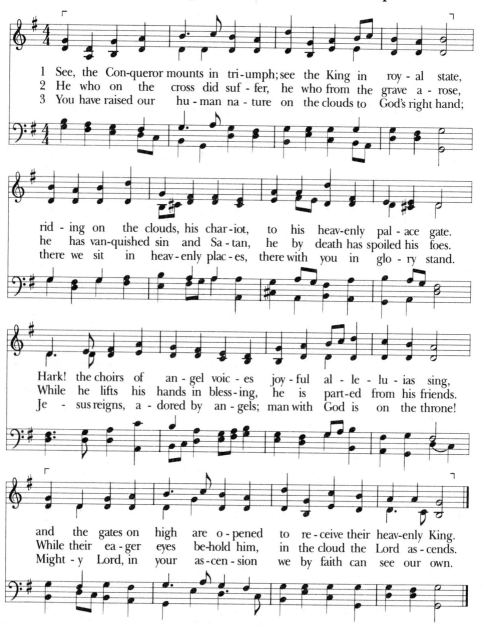

1 See, the Con-queror mounts in tri-umph; see the King in roy - al state,
2 He who on the cross did suf - fer, he who from the grave a - rose,
3 You have raised our hu - man na - ture on the clouds to God's right hand;

rid - ing on the clouds, his char-iot, to his heav-enly pal - ace gate.
he has van-quished sin and Sa - tan, he by death has spoiled his foes.
there we sit in heav-enly plac-es, there with you in glo - ry stand.

Hark! the choirs of an - gel voic - es joy - ful al - le - lu - ias sing,
While he lifts his hands in bless-ing, he is part-ed from his friends.
Je - sus reigns, a - dored by an - gels; man with God is on the throne!

and the gates on high are o - pened to re - ceive their heav-enly King.
While their ea - ger eyes be-hold him, in the cloud the Lord as - cends.
Might - y Lord, in your as - cen - sion we by faith can see our own.

Text: Christopher Wordsworth, 1862, alt.
Tune: Henry Smart, 1868

87 87 D
REX GLORIAE

Spirit, Working in Creation

415

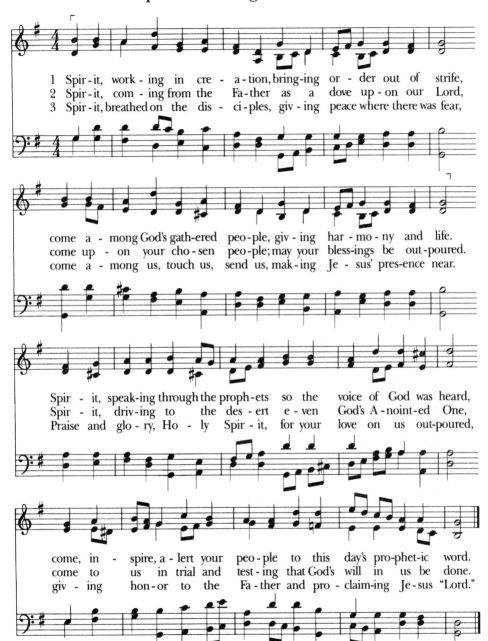

1 Spir-it, work-ing in cre - a-tion, bring-ing or - der out of strife,
2 Spir-it, com - ing from the Fa-ther as a dove up-on our Lord,
3 Spir-it, breathed on the dis - ci-ples, giv-ing peace where there was fear,

come a - mong God's gath-ered peo-ple, giv - ing har - mo - ny and life.
come up - on your cho - sen peo-ple; may your bless-ings be out-poured.
come a - mong us, touch us, send us, mak-ing Je - sus' pres-ence near.

Spir - it, speak-ing through the proph-ets so the voice of God was heard,
Spir - it, driv-ing to the des - ert e - ven God's A-noint-ed One,
Praise and glo - ry, Ho - ly Spir - it, for your love on us out-poured,

come, in - spire, a - lert your peo - ple to this day's pro-phet-ic word.
come to us in trial and test - ing that God's will in us be done.
giv - ing hon-or to the Fa - ther and pro - claim-ing Je-sus "Lord."

Text: John Richards, 1978
Tune: Kyriale, Luxembourg, 1768

87 87 D
SUNRISE

416   For Your Gift of God the Spirit

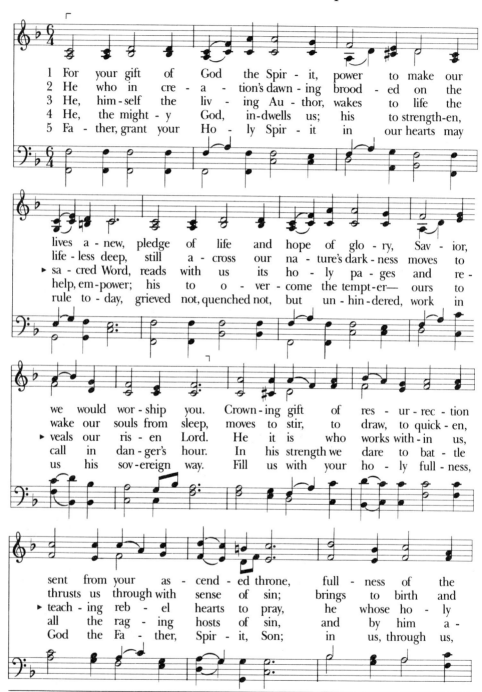

1 For your gift of God the Spir - it, power to make our
2 He who in cre - a - tion's dawn - ing brood - ed on the
3 He, him - self the liv - ing Au - thor, wakes to life the
4 He, the might - y God, in-dwells us; his to strength-en,
5 Fa - ther, grant your Ho - ly Spir - it in our hearts may

lives a - new, pledge of life and hope of glo - ry, Sav - ior,
life - less deep, still a - cross our na - ture's dark - ness moves to
sa - cred Word, reads with us its ho - ly pa - ges and re -
help, em-power; his to o - ver - come the tempt-er— ours to
rule to - day, grieved not, quenched not, but un - hin-dered, work in

we would wor - ship you. Crown-ing gift of res - ur - rec - tion
wake our souls from sleep, moves to stir, to draw, to quick - en,
veals our ris - en Lord. He it is who works with-in us,
call in dan - ger's hour. In his strength we dare to bat - tle
us his sov-ereign way. Fill us with your ho - ly full - ness,

sent from your as - cend - ed throne, full - ness of the
thrusts us through with sense of sin; brings to birth and
teach - ing reb - el hearts to pray, he whose ho - ly
all the rag - ing hosts of sin, and by him a -
God the Fa - ther, Spir - it, Son; in us, through us,

Text: Margaret Clarkson, 1959, 1976, 1984. © *1960, 1976, Margaret Clarkson. Assigned 1987 to*
Hope Publishing Co. All rights reserved. Used by permission.
Tune: William P. Rowlands, 1905

87 87 D
BLAENWERN

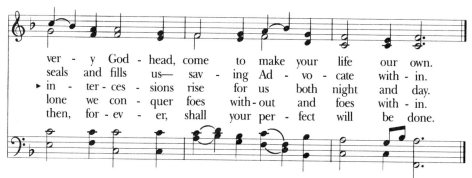

ver - y God - head, come to make your life our own.
seals and fills us— sav - ing Ad - vo - cate with - in.
in - ter - ces - sions rise for us both night and day.
lone we con - quer foes with - out and foes with - in.
then, for - ev - er, shall your per - fect will be done.

Filled with the Spirit's Power 417

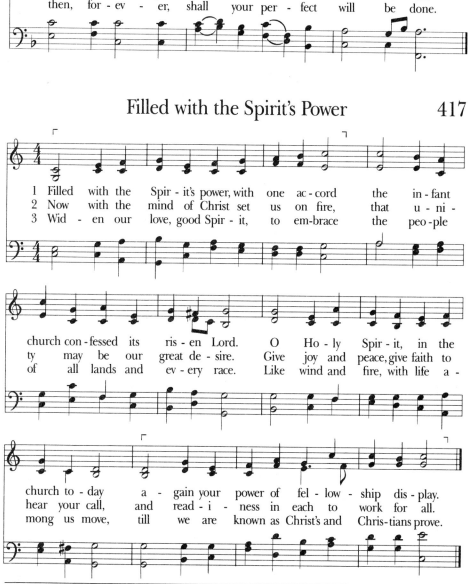

1 Filled with the Spir - it's power, with one ac - cord the in - fant
2 Now with the mind of Christ set us on fire, that u - ni -
3 Wid - en our love, good Spir - it, to em-brace the peo -ple

church con - fessed its ris - en Lord. O Ho - ly Spir - it, in the
ty may be our great de - sire. Give joy and peace, give faith to
of all lands and ev - ery race. Like wind and fire, with life a -

church to - day a - gain your power of fel - low - ship dis - play.
hear your call, and read - i - ness in each to work for all.
mong us move, till we are known as Christ's and Chris-tians prove.

Text: John. R. Peacey, 1967. By permission of Mildred E. Peacey.
Tune: Henry Lawes, 1638

10 10 10 10
FARLEY CASTLE

418 The Spirit Came, As Promised

1 The Spir - it came, as prom - ised, in God's ap-point-ed hour;
2 The Spir - it makes our bod - ies the tem - ple of the Lord.
3 He bids us live to-geth - er in u - ni - ty and peace;
4 The word, the Spir-it's weap - on, will bring all sin to light;

and now to each be - liev - er he comes in love and power.
He binds us all to - geth - er in faith and true ac - cord.
em - ploy his gifts in bless - ing, and let base pas-sions cease.
and prayer, by his di - rect - ing, will give new joy and might.

And by his Ho - ly Spir - it, God seals us as his own,
The Spir - it in his great - ness brings power from God a - bove,
We should not grieve the Spir - it by o - pen sin or shame,
Be filled then with his Spir - it, live out God's will and word;

and through the Son and Spir - it makes ac - cess to his throne.
and with the Son and Fa - ther dwells in our hearts in love.
nor let our words and ac - tions de - ny his ho - ly name.
re - joice with hymns and sing - ing, make mu - sic to the Lord.

Text: James E. Seddon, 1973; based on references to the Holy Spirit in Ephesians.
© *1973, Hope Publishing Co. All rights reserved. Used by permission.*
Tune: Johannes G. Bastiaans, 1868

76 76 D
BEFIEHL DU DEINE WEGE

Spirit of God, Who Dwells within My Heart 419

Capo 3:

1. Spir - it of God, who dwells with - in my heart,
2. I ask no dream, no proph - et ec - sta - sies,
3. Did you not bid us love you, God and King,
4. Teach me to feel that you are al - ways nigh;
5. Teach me to love you as your an - gels love,

wean it from sin, through all its puls - es move.
no sud - den rend - ing of the veil of clay,
love you with all our heart and strength and mind?
teach me the strug - gles of the soul to bear,
one ho - ly pas - sion fill - ing all my frame:

Stoop to my weak - ness, might - y as you are,
no an - gel vis - i - tant, no o - pening skies;
I see the cross— there teach my heart to cling.
to check the ris - ing doubt, the reb - el sigh;
the full - ness of the heaven - de - scend - ed Dove;

and make me love you as I ought to love.
but take the dim - ness of my soul a - way.
O let me seek you and O let me find!
teach me the pa - tience of un - ceas - ing prayer.
my heart an al - tar, and your love the flame.

Text: George Croly, 1867, alt.
Tune: Frederick C. Atkinson, 1870

10 10 10 10
MORECAMBE

420   Breathe on Me, Breath of God

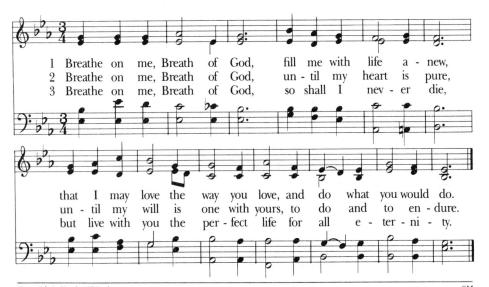

1 Breathe on me, Breath of God, fill me with life a - new,
2 Breathe on me, Breath of God, un - til my heart is pure,
3 Breathe on me, Breath of God, so shall I nev - er die,

that I may love the way you love, and do what you would do.
un - til my will is one with yours, to do and to en - dure.
but live with you the per - fect life for all e - ter - ni - ty.

Text: Edwin Hatch, 1878, alt.
Tune: Robert Jackson, 1894

SM
TRENTHAM

421   Spirit Divine, Inspire Our Prayer

1 Spir - it di - vine, in - spire our prayer and make our hearts your home;
2 Come as the light; re - veal our need, our hid - den fail - ings show,
3 Come as the fire and cleanse our hearts with pu - ri - fy - ing flame;
4 Come as the dove and spread your wings, the wings of peace and love,

de - scend with all your gra - cious power; come, Ho - ly Spir - it, come!
and lead us in those paths of life where - on the right - eous go.
let our whole life an of - fering be to our Re - deem - er's name.
un - til your church on earth be - low joins with your church a - bove.

Text: Andrew Reed, 1829, alt.
Tune: Johann Crüger, 1647

CM
GRÄFENBERG

Eternal Spirit, God of Truth

422

1 E - ter - nal Spir - it, God of truth, our con - trite hearts in - spire;
2 Sub - due the power of ev - ery sin and make our hearts your throne,

ig - nite a flame of heav-enly love and feed the pure de - sire.
that we in sin - gle - ness of heart may wor - ship God a - lone.

O come to soothe the sor - rowing mind with guilt and fear op-pressed;
Then with our spir - its wit - ness bear, O Spir - it of our God,

O come to bid the dy - ing live and give the wea - ry rest.
that we are chil-dren of the Lord, re-deemed through Christ's own blood.

Text: Thomas Cotterill, 1810, alt.
Tune: English; adapt. and harm. Ralph Vaughan Williams, 1906. By permission of Oxford University Press.

CMD
FOREST GREEN

423 Holy Spirit, Truth Divine

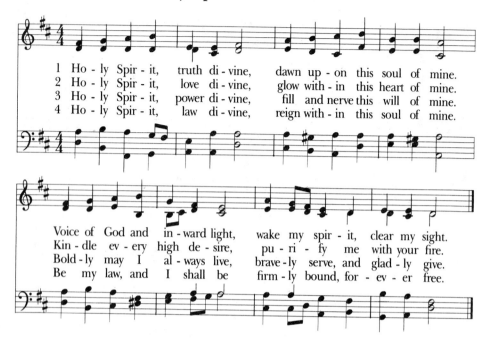

1 Ho - ly Spir - it, truth di - vine, dawn up - on this soul of mine.
2 Ho - ly Spir - it, love di - vine, glow with - in this heart of mine.
3 Ho - ly Spir - it, power di - vine, fill and nerve this will of mine.
4 Ho - ly Spir - it, law di - vine, reign with - in this soul of mine.

Voice of God and in - ward light, wake my spir - it, clear my sight.
Kin - dle ev - ery high de - sire, pu - ri - fy me with your fire.
Bold - ly may I al - ways live, brave - ly serve, and glad - ly give.
Be my law, and I shall be firm - ly bound, for - ev - er free.

5 Holy Spirit, peace divine,
still this restless heart of mine.
Speak to calm this tossing sea,
grant me your tranquility.

6 Holy Spirit, joy divine,
gladden now this heart of mine.
In the desert ways I sing—
spring, O Living Water, spring!

Text: Samuel Longfellow, 1864, alt.
Tune: Orlando Gibbons, 1623

77 77
SONG 13

Spirit of the Living God

1 Spir - it of the liv - ing God, fall a - fresh on me;
2 Spir - it of the liv - ing God, move a - mong us all;

Spir - it of the liv - ing God, fall a - fresh on me.
make us one in heart and mind, make us one in love:

Melt me, mold me, fill me, use me.
hum - ble, car - ing, self - less, shar - ing.

Spir - it of the liv - ing God, fall a - fresh on me.
Spir - it of the liv - ing God, fill our lives with love.

Text: st. 1, Daniel Iverson, 1926. © 1935, 1963, Moody Bible Institute of Chicago. Used by permission.
st. 2, Michael Baughen, 1982. © 1982, Hope Publishing Co. All rights reserved. Used by permission.
Tune: Daniel Iverson, 1926. © 1935, 1963, Moody Bible Institute of Chicago. Used by permission.

irregular
IVERSON

425   Creator Spirit, by Whose Aid

1 Cre - a - tor Spir - it, by whose aid the world's foun - da - tions
2 O source of un - cre - at - ed light, the Fa - ther's prom - ised
3 Plen - teous of grace, de - scend from high, rich in thy seven - fold

first were laid, come, vis - it ev - ery pi - ous mind;
Par - a - clete, thrice ho - ly fount, thrice ho - ly fire,
en - er - gy; make us e - ter - nal truths re - ceive

come, pour thy joys on hu - man - kind; from sin and sor - row
our hearts with heav - enly love in - spire; come and thy sa - cred
and prac - tice all that we be - lieve; give us thy - self that

set us free and make thy tem - ples wor - thy thee.
unc - tion bring to sanc - ti - fy us while we sing.
we may see the Fa - ther and the Son by thee.

Text: Latin hymn, Veni Creator Spiritus, 9th cent.; para. John Dryden, 1693
Tune: John B. Dykes, 1861

88 88 88
MELITA

O Holy Spirit, by Whose Breath

1 O Ho - ly Spir - it, by whose breath life ris - es
2 You are the seek - er's on - ly course, of burn - ing
3 In you God's en - er - gy is shown, to us your
4 Flood our dull sens - es with your light; in mu - tual

vi - brant out of death, come to cre - ate, re -
love the liv - ing source, pro - tec - tor in the
var - ied gifts made known. Teach us to speak, teach
love our hearts u - nite. Your power the whole cre -

new, in - spire; come, kin - dle in our hearts your fire.
midst of strife, the giv - er and the Lord of life.
us to hear; yours be the tongue and yours the ear.
a - tion fills; make strong our weak, un - cer - tain wills.

5 From inner strife grant us release;
turn nations to the ways of peace.
To fuller life your people bring
that as one body we may sing:

6 Praise to the Father, Christ, his Word,
and to the Spirit: God the Lord,
to whom all honor, glory be
both now and for eternity.

Text: Latin hymn, *Veni Creator Spiritus, 9th cent.; tr. John W. Grant, 1968, alt.,* ©
Tune: Melchior Vulpius, 1609; harm. Johann S. Bach, 1724

LM
DAS NEUGEBORNE KINDELEIN

427   Dwell in Me, O Blessed Spirit

1 Dwell in me, O bless-ed Spir-it! How I need your help di-vine!
2 Grant to me your sa-cred pres-ence; then my faith will ne'er de-cline.

In the way of life e-ter-nal, keep, O keep this heart of mine.
Com-fort me and help me on-ward; fill with love this heart of mine.

Refrain

Dwell in me, O bless-ed Spir-it, gra-cious Teach-er, Friend di-vine!

For the king-dom work that calls me, O pre-pare this heart of mine.

Text: Martha J. Lankton, 1929, alt.
Tune: Georgia G. Berky, 1929

87 87 with refrain
DWELL IN ME

O Worship the King

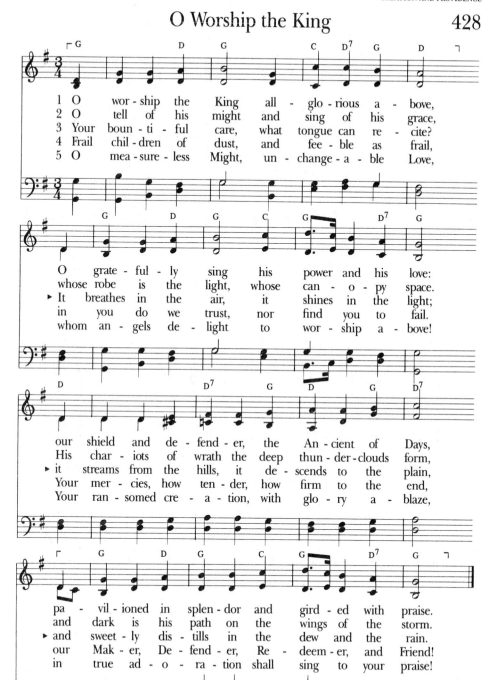

1 O wor-ship the King all - glo-rious a - bove,
2 O tell of his might and sing of his grace,
3 Your boun-ti-ful care, what tongue can re - cite?
4 Frail chil-dren of dust, and fee - ble as frail,
5 O mea-sure-less Might, un - change-a - ble Love,

O grate-ful-ly sing his power and his love:
whose robe is the light, whose can - o - py space.
▶ It breathes in the air, it shines in the light;
in you do we trust, nor find you to fail.
whom an - gels de - light to wor - ship a - bove!

our shield and de - fend - er, the An - cient of Days,
His char - iots of wrath the deep thun - der-clouds form,
▶ it streams from the hills, it de - scends to the plain,
Your mer - cies, how ten - der, how firm to the end,
Your ran - somed cre - a - tion, with glo - ry a - blaze,

pa - vil - ioned in splen - dor and gird - ed with praise.
and dark is his path on the wings of the storm.
▶ and sweet - ly dis - tills in the dew and the rain.
our Mak - er, De - fend - er, Re - deem - er, and Friend!
in true ad - o - ra - tion shall sing to your praise!

Text: Robert Grant, 1833, alt.; based on Psalm 104
Tune: W. Gardner's Sacred Melodies, 1815; attr. Haydn
Alternative tune: HANOVER, 149

10 10 11 11
LYONS

429 The Heavens Declare Your Glory

1 The heavens de - clare your glo - ry, the fir - ma-ment your power;
2 The sun with roy - al splen - dor goes forth to chant your praise,
3 All heaven on high re - joic - es to do its Mak - er's will;

day un - to day the sto - ry re - peats from hour to hour.
and moon - beams soft and ten - der their gen - tler an - them raise.
the stars with sol-emn voic - es re - sound your prais - es still.

Night un - to night re - ply - ing, pro - claims in ev - ery land,
O'er ev - ery tribe and na - tion the mu - sic is out - poured,
So let my whole be - hav - ior, each thought, each deed I do,

O Lord, with voice un - dy - ing, the won - ders of your hand.
the song of all cre - a - tion to you, cre - a - tion's Lord.
be, Lord, my strength, my Sav - ior, a cease-less song to you.

Text: Psalm 19:1–6, 14; vers. Thomas R. Birks, 1874, alt.
Tune: Johann S. Bach, 1685–1750; adapt. from "My Heart Ever Faithful," Cantata 68

76 76 D
FAITHFUL

We Sing the Mighty Power of God 430

1 We sing the might-y power of God that made the moun-tains
2 We sing the good-ness of the Lord that filled the earth with
3 There's not a plant or flower be-low but makes your glo-ries

rise, that spread the flow-ing seas a-broad and built the loft - y
food; he formed the crea-tures with his word and then pro-nounced them
known, and clouds a-rise and tem-pests blow by or-der from your

skies. We sing the wis-dom that or-dained the sun to rule the
good. Lord, how your won-ders are dis-played, wher-e'er we turn our
throne; while all that bor-rows life from you is ev-er in your

day; the moon shines full at his com-mand, and all the stars o - bey.
eyes, if we sur-vey the ground we tread or gaze up-on the skies.
care, and ev-ery-where that we can be, you, God, are pres-ent there.

Text: Isaac Watts, 1715, alt.
Tune: English; adapt. and harm. Ralph Vaughan Williams, 1906. By permission of Oxford University Press.
Alternative tune: ELLACOMBE, 378

CMD
KINGSFOLD

431   All Creatures of Our God and King

Unison

1 All crea-tures of our God and King, lift up your voice
2 O rush-ing wind so wild and strong, white clouds that sail
3 Cool flow-ing wa-ter, pure and clear, make mu-sic for
4 Earth ev-er fer-tile, day by day bring forth your bless-
5 Peo-ple and na-tions, take your part; sing praise to God

Harmony

with us and sing: al-le-lu-ia, al-le-lu-ia!
in heaven a-long, al-le-lu-ia, al-le-lu-ia!
▸ your Lord to hear; al-le-lu-ia, al-le-lu-ia!
ings on our way; al-le-lu-ia, al-le-lu-ia!
with all your heart: al-le-lu-ia, al-le-lu-ia!

Unison

O burn-ing sun with gold-en beam, and shin-ing moon
New ris-ing dawn, in praise re-joice; you lights of eve-
▸ Fierce fire, so mas-ter-ful and bright, pro-vid-ing us
All flowers and fruits that in you grow, let them his glo-
Let all things their Cre-a-tor bless and wor-ship him

Harmony

with sil-ver gleam, O praise him, O praise him,
ning, find a voice: O praise him, O praise him,
▸ with warmth and light, O praise him, O praise him,
ry al-so show: O praise him, O praise him,
in low-li-ness: O praise him, O praise him,

Text: Francis of Assisi, 1225; tr. William H. Draper, c. 1910, alt.   *LM with alleluias*
Tune: Auserlesen Catholische Geistliche Kirchengesange, Cologne, 1623;   *LASST UNS ERFREUEN*
    adapt. and harm. Ralph Vaughan Williams, 1906. By permission of Oxford University Press.

al - le - lu - ia, al le - lu - ia, al - le - lu - ia!

For the Beauty of the Earth 432

1 For the beau-ty of the earth, for the glo-ry of the skies,
2 For the won-der of each hour of the day and of the night,
3 For the joy of hu-man love, broth-er, sis-ter, par-ent, child,
4 For your-self, best gift di-vine, to the world so free-ly given,

for the love which from our birth o-ver and a-round us lies,
hill and vale and tree and flower, sun and moon and stars of light,
friends on earth, and friends a-bove, for all gen-tle thoughts and mild,
a - gent of God's grand de-sign: peace on earth and joy in heaven.

Refrain

Christ, our Lord, to you we raise this, our hymn of grate-ful praise.

Text: Folliott S. Pierpont, 1864, alt.
Tune: Conrad Kocher, 1838; adapt. William H. Monk, 1861
This music with descant: 358

77 77 77
DIX

433 Earth and All Stars

1 Earth and all stars! Come, rush - ing plan - ets!
2 Hail, wind, and rain! Come, blow - ing snow - storms!
3 Trum - pet and pipes! Come, clash - ing cym - bals!
4 En - gines and steel! Come, pound - ing ham - mers!

Sing to the Lord a new song!

Oh, vic - to - ry! Or - der from cha - os!
Flow - ers and trees! Soft rus - tling dry leaves!
Harp, lute, and lyre! Low hum - ming cel - los!
Lime - stone and beams! Strong build - ing work - ers!

Sing to the Lord a new song!

Refrain

He has done mar - vel - ous things.

Text: Herbert Brokering, 1964, alt.
Tune: David Johnson, 1968; harm. Dale Grotenhuis, 1984
Text and music © 1968, Augsburg Publishing House. Used by permission.

457 457 with refrain
EARTH AND ALL STARS

I too will praise him with a new song!

5   Classrooms and labs!
    Come, boiling test tubes!
    Sing to the Lord a new song!
    Athlete and band!
    Loud cheering people!
    Sing to the Lord a new song! *Refrain*

6   Knowledge and truth!
    Come, piercing wisdom!
    Sing to the Lord a new song!
    Children of God,
    dying and rising,
    Sing to the Lord a new song! *Refrain*

God Moves in a Mysterious Way   434

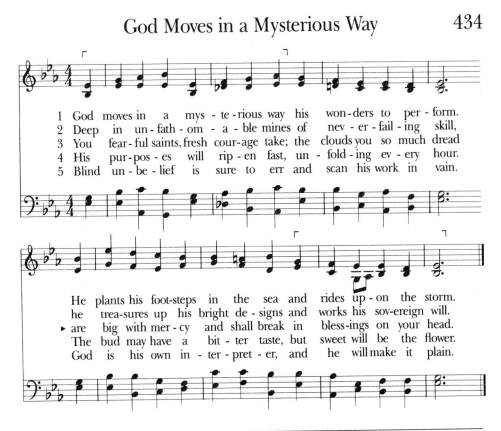

1 God moves in a mys-te-rious way his won-ders to per-form.
2 Deep in un-fath-om-a-ble mines of nev-er-fail-ing skill,
3 You fear-ful saints, fresh cour-age take; the clouds you so much dread
4 His pur-pos-es will rip-en fast, un-fold-ing ev-ery hour.
5 Blind un-be-lief is sure to err and scan his work in vain.

He plants his foot-steps in the sea and rides up-on the storm.
he trea-sures up his bright de-signs and works his sov-ereign will.
are big with mer-cy and shall break in bless-ings on your head.
The bud may have a bit-ter taste, but sweet will be the flower.
God is his own in-ter-pret-er, and he will make it plain.

Text: William Cowper, 1774
Tune: Scottish Psalter, 1615; harm. Thomas Ravenscroft, c. 1592–1635, alt.

CM
DUNDEE

435 All Things Bright and Beautiful

Unison   Refrain

All things bright and beau-ti - ful, all crea-tures great and small,

all things wise and won-der-ful— the Lord God made them all.

1 Each lit - tle flower that o - pens, each lit - tle bird that sings—
2 The pur - ple-head - ed moun-tain, the riv - er run-ning by,
3 The cold wind in the win - ter, the pleas-ant sum-mer sun,
4 He gave us eyes to see them, and lips that we might tell

he made their glow-ing col - ors, he made their ti - ny wings.
the sun - set, and the morn-ing that bright-ens up the sky.
the ripe fruits in the gar - den— he made them ev - ery one.
how great is God Al - might-y, who has made all things well.

Refrain

Text: Cecil F. Alexander, 1848
Tune: The Dancing Master, 1686; harm. John Worst, 1974, alt. Harmonization © 1987, CRC Publications

76 76 with refrain
ROYAL OAK

This Is My Father's World

Text: Maltbie D. Babcock, 1901, alt.; st. 2 rev. Mary Babcock Crawford, 1972. St. 2 used by permission.
Tune: English; adapt. Franklin L. Sheppard, 1915
Keyboard and guitar should not sound together.

SMD
TERRA BEATA

437 Thank You, God, for Water, Soil, and Air

1 Thank you, God, for wa - ter, soil, and air— large gifts sup -
2 Thank you, God, for min - er - als and ores— the ba - sis
3 Thank you, God, for price - less en - er - gy stored in each
4 Thank you, God, for weav - ing na - ture's life in - to a
5 Thank you, God, for mak - ing plan - et earth a home for

port - ing ev - ery - thing that lives. For - give our spoil - ing and a -
of all build - ing, wealth, and speed. For - give our reck - less plun - der -
at - om, gath - ered from the sun. For - give our greed and care - less -
seam - less robe, a frag - ile whole. For - give our haste that tam - pers
us and a - ges yet un - born. Help us to share, con - sid - er,

buse of them. Help us re - new the face of the earth.
ing and waste. Help us re - new the face of the earth.
ness of power. Help us re - new the face of the earth.
un - a - wares. Help us re - new the face of the earth.
save, and store. Come and re - new the face of the earth.

9 10 10 9
PENET

When Morning Gilds the Sky

438

1 When morn-ing gilds the sky, our hearts a - wak - ing cry:
2 To God, the Word on high, the hosts of an - gels cry:
3 Let earth's wide cir - cle round in joy - ful notes re - sound:
4 Be this, when day is past, of all our thoughts the last:
5 Then let us join to sing to Christ, our lov - ing King:

May Je - sus Christ be praised! In all our work and prayer
May Je - sus Christ be praised! Let mor - tals too up - raise
May Je - sus Christ be praised! Let air and sea and sky
May Je - sus Christ be praised! The night be - comes as day
May Je - sus Christ be praised! Be this the e - ter - nal song

we ask his lov - ing care: May Je - sus Christ be praised!
their voice in hymns of praise: May Je - sus Christ be praised!
from depth to height re - ply: May Je - sus Christ be praised!
when from the heart we say: May Je - sus Christ be praised!
through all the a - ges long: May Je - sus Christ be praised!

Text: German, c. 1800; tr. Edward Caswall, 1858, alt.
Tune: Joseph Barnby, 1868

666 D
LAUDES DOMINI

439 We Come to Thank You, God, by Singing

1 We come to thank you, God, by sing-ing your prais-es in our
2 You chose to safe-guard us for-ev-er; your hand has fed us,
3 We know who is our con-so-la-tion, un-chang-ing, though night

eve-ning song. The sun-light may be dis-ap-pear-ing, but
led us through. When we were trou-bled, you were ev-er our
fol-lows day. We know the Rock, our firm foun-da-tion; you

you, our light, stay bright and strong. You have sur round-ed us with
help-er near, so close and true. This eve-ning we must not be
nev-er fail, our strength and stay. Though you may call us in the

fa-vor; more than a fa-ther you have been. Our source of
anx-ious: our minds and bod-ies will be blest. We give you
eve-ning of lives made wea-ry by our strife, we rest our

Text: Herman A. Bruining, 1806; tr. Arie Verduijn, 1969
Tune: Freylinghausen's Geistreiches Gesangbuch, 1704; harm. Johanna Wagenaar, b. 1900

98 98 D
DIE TUGEND WIRD

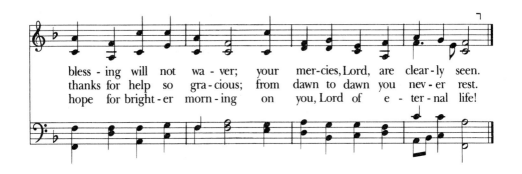

bless - ing will not wa - ver; your mer-cies, Lord, are clear-ly seen.
thanks for help so gra - cious; from dawn to dawn you nev - er rest.
hope for bright-er morn - ing on you, Lord of e - ter - nal life!

Children of the Heavenly Father 440

1 Chil-dren of the heav-enly Fa - ther safe - ly in his bo - som gath-er;
2 God his own shall tend and nour-ish; in his ho - ly courts they flour-ish.
3 Nei-ther life nor death shall ev - er from the Lord his chil-dren sev - er;
4 God has giv - en, he has tak-en, but his chil-dren ne'er for - sak - en;

nest-ling bird nor star in heav - en such a ref - uge e'er was giv - en.
From all e - vil powers he spares them; in his might - y arms he bears them.
for to them his grace re - veal - ing, he turns sor - row in - to heal - ing.
his the lov - ing pur-pose sole - ly to pre-serve them pure and ho - ly.

Text: Caroline V. Sandell Berg, 1855; tr. Ernest W. Olson, 1925, alt. © 1978,
Board of Publication of the Lutheran Church in America. Used by permission.
Tune: Swedish
Keyboard and guitar should not sound together.

LM
TRYGGARE KAN INGEN VARA

441 All Praise to You, My God, This Night

May be sung in canon

1 All praise to you, my God, this night, for all the bless-ings
2 For - give me, Lord, for this I pray, the wrong that I have
3 Lord, may I be at rest in you and sweet - ly sleep the
4 Praise God, from whom all bless - ings flow; praise him, all crea - tures

of the light. Keep me, O keep me, King of kings, be -
done this day. May peace with God and neigh - bor be, be -
whole night through. Re - fresh my strength, for your own sake, so
here be - low. Praise him a - bove, you heav - enly host; praise

for canon only

neath the shel - ter of your wings. (-ter of your wings.)
fore I sleep, re - stored to me. (re - stored to me.)
I may serve you when I wake. (you when I wake.)
Fa - ther, Son, and Ho - ly Ghost. (and Ho - ly Ghost.)

Text: Thomas Ken, 1709, alt.
Tune: Thomas Tallis, c. 1561
Keyboard and guitar should not sound together.

LM
TALLIS CANON

Abide with Me

1 A - bide with me: fast falls the e - ven - tide;
2 Swift to its close ebbs out life's lit - tle day;
3 I need your pres - ence ev - ery pass - ing hour.
4 I fear no foe with you at hand to bless,
5 Hold now your Word be - fore my clos - ing eyes.

the dark - ness deep - ens; Lord, with me a - bide.
earth's joys grow dim, its glo - ries pass a - way.
► What but your grace can foil the tempt - er's power?
though ills have weight, and tears their bit - ter - ness.
Shine through the gloom and point me to the skies.

When oth - er help - ers fail and com - forts flee,
Change and de - cay in all a - round I see.
► Who like your - self my guide and strength can be?
Where is death's sting? Where, grave, your vic - to - ry?
Heaven's morn - ing breaks and earth's vain shad - ows flee;

Help of the help - less, O a - bide with me.
O Lord who chang - es not, a - bide with me.
► Through cloud and sun - shine, O a - bide with me.
I tri - umph still, if you a - bide with me.
in life, in death, O Lord, a - bide with me.

Text: Henry F. Lyte, 1847, alt.
Tune: William H. Monk, 1861

10 10 10 10
EVENTIDE

443   Hours and Days and Years and Ages

1 Hours and days and years and a - ges swift as mov-ing shad-ows flee;
2 But from sin your mer - cy drew us, would not leave our souls a - lone.
3 Though swift time keeps march-ing on-ward, it will not de - cide our end.
4 Speed a - long, then, years and a - ges, with your glad-ness and your pain;

as we scan life's fleet-ing pa - ges, noth-ing last-ing do we see.
Gra - cious Lord, you did re - new us; in Christ's death we are your own.
You will al - ways be our Fa - ther, lov - ing God, e - ter - nal Friend.
when our deep-est sor - row ra - ges, God our Fa - ther will re - main.

On the paths our feet are walk-ing, foot-prints all will fade a - way;
Through the mer - cy of your lead-ing, each short step a - long our way
When life's dan - gers o - ver-whelm us, you will ev - er be our stay;
Though all friends on earth for - sake us and our trou-bles still in-crease,

each to - day as we en - joy it soon be - comes a yes - ter - day.
now be-comes a path to guide us to the land of end - less day.
through your Son you are our Fa - ther, al - ways change-less, come what may.
God with his right hand will take us to our ev - er - last - ing peace.

Text: Rhijnvis Feith, 1753–1824; tr. Leonard P. Brink, 1929; rev. Henrietta Ten Harmsel, 1984.
© 1987, CRC Publications
Tune: Moravian chorale book manuscript, Herrnhut, 1735
Another harmonization in a higher key: 513

87 87 D
O DU LIEBE MEINER LIEBE

Greet Now the Swiftly Changing Year

444

1 Greet now the swift-ly chang - ing year with
2 Re - mem - ber now the Son of God and
3 This Je - sus came to end sin's war; the
4 His love a - bun - dant far ex - ceeds the

joy and pen - i - tence sin - cere. Re - joice! Re - joice! With
how he shed for us his blood. Re - joice! Re - joice! With
name of names for us he bore. Re - joice! Re - joice! With
vol - ume of a whole year's needs. Re - joice! Re - joice! With

thanks em - brace an - oth - er year of grace.
thanks em - brace an - oth - er year of grace.
thanks em - brace an - oth - er year of grace.
thanks em - brace an - oth - er year of grace.

5 With him as Lord to lead our way
in want and in prosperity,
what need we fear in earth or space
in this new year of grace!

6 "All glory be to God on high,
and peace on earth!" the angels cry.
Rejoice! Rejoice! With thanks embrace
another year of grace.

7 God, Father, Son, and Spirit, hear!
To all our pleas incline your ear;
upon our lives rich blessing trace
in this new year of grace.

Text: Slovak, 1636; tr. Jaroslav J. Vajda, 1968, alt.
Tune: T. Zavorka's Kancional, 1602; harm. Theodore Beck, 1969
Text and harmonization © 1969, Concordia Publishing House. Used by permission.
Another harmonization in a lower key: 283

88 86
ROK NOVY

445 Our Faithful God

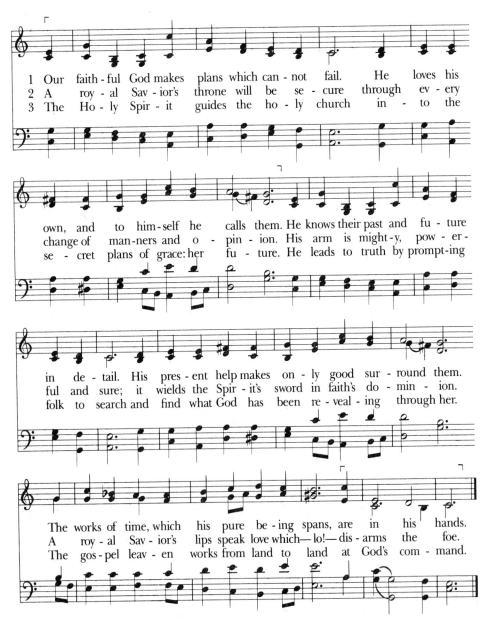

1 Our faith - ful God makes plans which can - not fail. He loves his
2 A roy - al Sav - ior's throne will be se - cure through ev - ery
3 The Ho - ly Spir - it guides the ho - ly church in - to the

own, and to him - self he calls them. He knows their past and fu - ture
change of man - ners and o - pin - ion. His arm is might - y, pow - er -
se - cret plans of grace: her fu - ture. He leads to truth by prompt - ing

in de - tail. His pres - ent help makes on - ly good sur - round them.
ful and sure; it wields the Spir - it's sword in faith's do - min - ion.
folk to search and find what God has been re - veal - ing through her.

The works of time, which his pure be - ing spans, are in his hands.
A roy - al Sav - ior's lips speak love which— lo!— dis - arms the foe.
The gos - pel leav - en works from land to land at God's com - mand.

Text: Hendrik Pierson, 1904; tr. Stanley Wiersma, 1974. © 1974, CRC Publications
Tune: Christian Gregor, 1784

10 11 10 11 10 4
GREGOR'S 112th METRE

If You But Trust in God to Guide You 446

1 If you but trust in God to guide you and place your
2 On - ly be still and wait his plea-sure in cheer - ful
3 Sing, pray, and keep his ways un - swerv-ing, of - fer your

con - fi - dence in him, you'll find him al - ways there be - side you
hope with heart con - tent. He fills your needs to full - est mea-sure
ser - vice faith - ful - ly, and trust his word; though un - de - serv-ing,

to give you hope and strength with - in; for those who trust God's
with what dis - cern - ing love has sent; doubt not our in - most
you'll find his prom - ise true to be. God nev - er will for -

change - less love build on the rock that will not move.
wants are known to him who chose us for his own.
sake in need the soul that trusts in him in - deed.

Text: Georg Neumark, 1641; tr. composite
Tune: Georg Neumark, 1657

98 98 88
WER NUR DEN LIEBEN GOTT

447 Eternal God beyond All Time

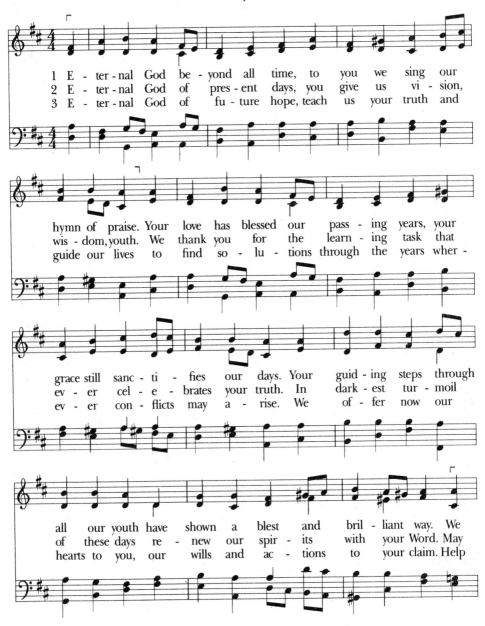

1 E - ter - nal God be - yond all time, to you we sing our
2 E - ter - nal God of pres - ent days, you give us vi - sion,
3 E - ter - nal God of fu - ture hope, teach us your truth and

hymn of praise. Your love has blessed our pass - ing years, your
wis - dom, youth. We thank you for the learn - ing task that
guide our lives to find so - lu - tions through the years wher -

grace still sanc - ti - fies our days. Your guid - ing steps through
ev - er cel - e - brates your truth. In dark - est tur - moil
ev - er con - flicts may a - rise. We of - fer now our

all our youth have shown a blest and bril - liant way. We
of these days re - new our spir - its with your Word. May
hearts to you, our wills and ac - tions to your claim. Help

Text: Marie J. Post, 1979. © 1987, CRC Publications
Tune: Joseph Barnby, 1872

LMD
JORDAN

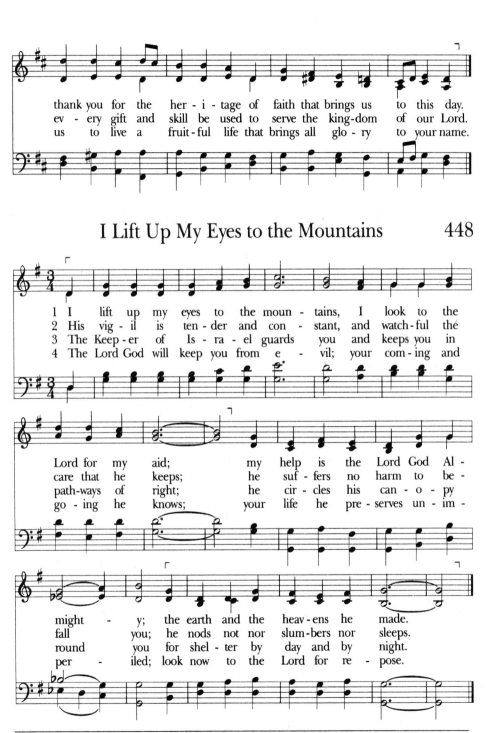

thank you for the her - i - tage of faith that brings us to this day.
ev - ery gift and skill be used to serve the king-dom of our Lord.
us to live a fruit - ful life that brings all glo - ry to your name.

I Lift Up My Eyes to the Mountains 448

1 I lift up my eyes to the moun - tains, I look to the
2 His vig - il is ten - der and con - stant, and watch-ful the
3 The Keep-er of Is - ra - el guards you and keeps you in
4 The Lord God will keep you from e - vil; your com - ing and

Lord for my aid; my help is the Lord God Al -
care that he keeps; he suf - fers no harm to be -
path-ways of right; he cir - cles his can - o - py
go - ing he knows; your life he pre - serves un - im -

might - y; the earth and the heav - ens he made.
fall you; he nods not nor slum-bers nor sleeps.
round you for shel - ter by day and by night.
per - iled; look now to the Lord for re - pose.

Text: Psalm 121; vers. Henry Zylstra, 1953, alt.
Tune: Dick L. Van Halsema, 1954, alt.

98 98
LUZON

449 O Righteous, in the Lord Rejoice

1 O right-eous, in the Lord re-joice; how pleas-ant that
2 The Lord God from his throne on high looks down with clear
3 His eye is on all those who fear; to those who hope,

with joy-ful voice God's saints his name should praise.
and search-ing eye on all that dwell be - low.
the Lord is near ac - cord-ing to his word.

With harp and hymn of glad - ness sing, your gift of
And he that fash-ioned heart and mind looks ev - er
Death can - not touch those in his hand, nor trou - ble

sweet-est mu - sic bring, to him a new song raise.
down on hu - man-kind the works of all to know.
con - quer in the land; we wait up - on the Lord.

Text: from Psalm 33; vers. Psalter, 1912, alt.
Tune: James McGranahan, 1840–1907

886 D
FRANCES

O God, Our Father, We Come

450

1 O God, our Fa - ther, we come in - to your pres - ence,
2 Not un - to us, Lord, but un - to you be giv - en
3 Your Ho - ly Spir - it has blessed our lives with free - dom,
4 O God, our Mak - er, we take our task up - on us,

here in your courts to lift our hearts in praise.
praise for the Lamb, who died up - on the tree;
strength-ened our faith, and shat-tered sin - ful pride.
to tell to all the won - der of your grace.

Vast is your mer - cy, rich your great for - give - ness,
praise for your great love, which no sin can sev - er;
In ev - ery tri - al you have been our ref - uge;
Yours is the king - dom, yours the power and glo - ry;

boun - teous your fa - vor; bless us all our days.
praise for your Son, who sets the pris - oner free!
through all our years your Word has been our guide.
ours but to walk in love be - fore your face.

Text: John H. Kromminga, 1957; rev. Psalter Hymnal, 1987
Tune: Claire Kromminga, 1957; harm. Dale Grotenhuis, 1984
Text and music © 1987, CRC Publications

12 10 11 10
CENTENNIAL PRAYER

451   What God Ordains Is Always Right

1 What God or-dains is al-ways right; his will is just and
2 What God or-dains is al-ways right, and he will not de-
3 What God or-dains is al-ways right; all that he does is
4 What God or-dains is al-ways right; he guides our joy and

ho - ly. He holds us in his per - fect might; in Christ our lives are
ceive us. He leads us in the way of light and will not ev - er
for us. He heals our souls and gives us sight and puts no ill be -
sad - ness. He is our life and bless - ed light; in him a - lone is

god - ly. He is our God and all we need, the Fa - ther
leave us. In him we rest, who makes the best of all the
fore us. Our God is true; he makes us new; our lives are
glad - ness. We see his face, the way of grace; he holds us

who pre - serves us still; to him we bend each heart and will.
stum - bling turns we take and loves us for his mer - cy's sake.
built up - on his rock, our cor - ner-stone and build - ing block.
in his might - y arm and keeps us safe from ev - ery harm.

Text: Samuel Rodigast, 1675; tr. Gracia Grindal, 1978, alt. © 1978, Lutheran Book of Worship.
By permission of Augsburg Publishing House.
Tune: attr. Severus Gastorius, c. 1675

87 87 888
WAS GOTT TUT

He Leadeth Me

1 He lead - eth me: O bless - ed thought! O
2 Some - times mid scenes of deep - est gloom, some -
3 Lord, I would clasp thy hand in mine, nor
4 And when my task on earth is done, when,

words with heav - enly com - fort fraught! What - e'er I do, wher -
times where E - den's flow - ers bloom, by wa - ters calm, o'er
ev - er mur - mur nor re - pine; con - tent, what - ev - er
by thy grace, the vic - tory's won, e'en death's cold wave I

e'er I be, still 'tis God's hand that lead - eth me.
trou - bled sea, still 'tis God's hand that lead - eth me.
lot I see, since 'tis my God that lead - eth me.
will not flee, since God through Jor - dan lead - eth me.

Refrain

He lead-eth me, he lead - eth me; by his own hand he lead-eth me:

his faith-ful fol - lower I would be, for by his hand he lead-eth me.

Text: *Joseph H. Gilmore, 1862*
Tune: *William B. Bradbury, 1864*

LM with refrain
AUGHTON

453   Let All Things Now Living

1 Let all things now liv-ing a song of thanks-giv-ing to God the Cre-a-tor tri-um-phant-ly raise, who fash-ioned and made us, pro-tect-ed and stayed us, who guides us and leads to the

2 His law he en-forc-es; the stars in their cours-es and sun in its or-bit o-be-dient-ly shine; the hills and the moun-tains, the riv-ers and foun-tains, the deeps of the o-cean pro-

Text: Katherine K. Davis, 1939
Tune: Welsh; desc. Katherine K. Davis
Text and descant © 1939, 1966, E.C. Schirmer Music Co.

66 11 66 11 D
ASH GROVE

454   Now Thank We All Our God

1 Now thank we all our God with heart and hands and voic - es,
2 O may this boun-teous God through all our life be near us,
3 All praise and thanks to God the Fa - ther now be giv - en,

who won-drous things has done, in whom his world re - joic - es;
with ev - er joy - ful hearts and bless - ed peace to cheer us,
the Son and Spir - it blest, who reign in high-est heav - en—

who from our moth-ers' arms has blessed us on our way
to keep us in his grace, and guide us when per - plexed,
the one e - ter - nal God, whom heaven and earth a - dore;

with count-less gifts of love, and still is ours to - day.
and free us from all ills of this world in the next.
for thus it was, is now, and shall be ev - er - more.

Text: Martin Rinkart, 1636; tr. Catherine Winkworth, 1863, alt.
Tune: Johann Crüger, 1647; harm. based on Felix Mendelssohn's Lobgesang, Opus 52, 1840

67 67 66 66
NUN DANKET

For the Fruits of His Creation

1 For the fruits of his cre - a - tion, thanks be to
2 In the just re - ward of la - bor, God's will be
3 For the har - vests of the Spir - it, thanks be to

God. For his gifts to ev - ery na - tion,
done. In the help we give our neigh - bor,
God. For the good we all in - her - it,

thanks be to God. For the plow - ing, sow - ing, reap - ing,
God's will be done. In our world-wide task of car - ing
thanks be to God. For the won - ders that as-tound us,

si - lent growth while we are sleep - ing, fu - ture needs in
for the hun - gry and de - spair - ing, in the har - vests
for the truths that still con-found us, most of all that

earth's safe - keep - ing, thanks be to God.
we are shar - ing, God's will be done.
love has found us, thanks be to God.

Text: Fred Pratt Green, 1970. © 1970, Hope Publishing Co. All rights reserved. Used by permission.
Tune: Francis Jackson, 1957, ©

84 84 88 84
EAST ACKLAM

456 We Plow the Fields and Scatter

1 We plow the fields and scat - ter the good seed on the land,
2 He on - ly is the mak - er of all things near and far;
3 We thank you, our Cre - a - tor, for all things bright and good:

but it is fed and wa - tered by God's al - might - y hand.
he paints the way - side flow - er, he lights the eve - ning star.
the seed - time and the har - vest, our life, our health, our food.

He sends the snow in win - ter, the warmth to swell the grain,
The wind and waves o - bey him, by him the birds are fed;
Ac - cept the gifts we of - fer for all your love im - parts;

the breez - es and the sun - shine, and soft re - fresh-ing rain.
much more to us, his chil - dren, he gives our dai - ly bread.
ac - cept what you most wel - come: our hum - ble, thank-ful hearts!

Refrain

All good gifts a - round us are sent from heaven a - bove;

Text: Matthias Claudius, 1782; tr. Jane Montgomery-Campbell, 1861, alt.
Tune: Johann A. P. Schulz, 1800; harm. John B. Dykes, 1861, alt.

76 76 D with refrain
WIR PFLÜGEN

then thank the Lord, O thank the Lord for all his love.

He's Got the Whole World in His Hands 457

1 He's got the whole world in his hands. He's got the whole world in his hands.
He's got the whole world in his hands. He's got the whole world in his hands.

2 He's got the wind and the rain in his hands. *(Sing three times)*
He's got the whole world in his hands.

3 He's got the little tiny baby in his hands. . . .
He's got the whole world in his hands.

4 He's got you and me, brother, in his hands. . . .
He's got the whole world in his hands.

5 He's got you and me, sister, in his hands. . . .
He's got the whole world in his hands.

6 He's got everybody here in his hands. . . .
He's got the whole world in his hands.

Text and Tune: Afro-American spiritual

irregular
WHOLE WORLD

458 Sing to the Lord of Harvest

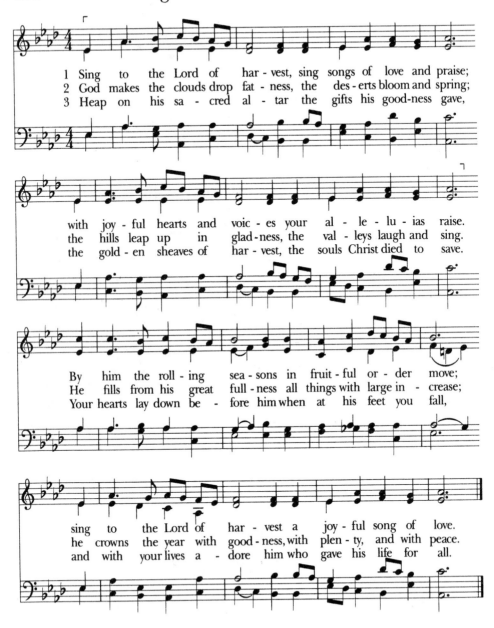

1 Sing to the Lord of har - vest, sing songs of love and praise;
2 God makes the clouds drop fat - ness, the des - erts bloom and spring;
3 Heap on his sa - cred al - tar the gifts his good-ness gave,

with joy - ful hearts and voic - es your al - le - lu - ias raise.
the hills leap up in glad - ness, the val - leys laugh and sing.
the gold - en sheaves of har - vest, the souls Christ died to save.

By him the roll - ing sea - sons in fruit - ful or - der move;
He fills from his great full - ness all things with large in - crease;
Your hearts lay down be - fore him when at his feet you fall,

sing to the Lord of har - vest a joy - ful song of love.
he crowns the year with good - ness, with plen - ty, and with peace.
and with your lives a - dore him who gave his life for all.

Text: John S. B. Monsell, 1866, alt.; based on Psalm 65:9–13
Tune: Johann Steurlein, 1575

76 76 D
WIE LIEBLICH IST DER MAIEN

Our World Belongs to God

459

1 Our world be-longs to God. He called it in-to place,
2 Our world be-longs to God. He tells us in his Word
3 Our world be-longs to God. We know that one bright day

up - holds, re - news, con - trols with sov - ereign love and grace.
of his great cov-enant love that man - y have ig - nored.
each chal-lenge to his rule will sure - ly pass a - way.

Through all our earth's long his - to - ry of God's cre - at -
Yet his great an - ger did not flame; the prom - ised right -
We wait the end - ing of all wrong. Then we will join

ed fam - i - ly, all things were done by his de - cree.
eous Sav - ior came, who paid our debt and cleared our name.
the tri - umph song to God, to whom all things be - long.

Text: Marie J. Post, 1986. © 1987, CRC Publications
Tune: John D. Edwards, c. 1840

66 66 888
RHOSYMEDRE

460   Immortal, Invisible, God Only Wise

1 Im - mor - tal, in - vis - i - ble, God on - ly wise,
2 Un - rest - ing, un - hast - ing, and si - lent as light,
3 Life - giv - ing Cre - a - tor of both great and small,
4 We wor - ship be - fore you, great Fa - ther of light,

in light in - ac - ces - si - ble hid from our eyes,
nor want - ing nor wast - ing, you rule day and night;
of all life the mak - er, the true life of all;
while an - gels a - dore you, all veil - ing their sight;

most bless - ed, most glo - rious, the An - cient of Days,
your jus - tice like moun - tains high soar - ing a - bove,
we blos - som, then with - er like leaves on the tree,
our prais - es we ren - der, O Fa - ther, to you,

al - might - y, vic - to - rious, your great name we praise.
your clouds which are foun - tains of good - ness and love.
but you are for - ev - er, who was and will be.
whom on - ly the splen - dor of light hides from view.

Text: Walter C. Smith, 1867, alt.
Tune: Welsh, in J. Roberts' Caniadau y Cyssegr, 1839

11 11 11 11
ST. DENIO

Beautiful Savior

1 Beau - ti - ful Sav - ior! King of cre - a - tion!
2 Fair are the mead - ows, fair are the wood - lands,
3 Fair is the sun - shine, fair is the moon - light,
4 Beau - ti - ful Sav - ior! Lord of the na - tions!

Son of God and Son of Man!
robed in flowers of bloom - ing spring;
bright the spar - kling stars on high;
Son of God and Son of Man!

Tru - ly I'd love thee, tru - ly I'd serve thee,
Je - sus is fair - er, Je - sus is pur - er;
Je - sus shines bright - er, Je - sus shines pur - er
Glo - ry and hon - or, praise, ad - o - ra - tion,

Light of my soul, my joy, my crown.
he makes our sor - rowing spir - it sing.
than all the an - gels in the sky.
now and for - ev - er - more be thine!

Text: Gesangbuch, Münster, 1677; tr. Joseph A. Seiss, 1873
Tune: Schleisische Volkslieder, 1842

557 558
ST. ELIZABETH

462　Amazing Grace—How Sweet the Sound

1. A - maz - ing grace— how sweet the sound—
2. 'Twas grace that taught my heart to fear,
3. The Lord has prom - ised good to me,
4. Through man - y dan - gers, toils, and snares
5. When we've been there ten thou - sand years,

that saved a wretch like me! I once was lost
and grace my fears re - lieved; how pre - cious did
his word my hope se - cures; he will my shield
I have al - read - y come; 'tis grace hath brought
bright shin - ing as the sun, we've no less days

but now am found, was blind but now I see.
that grace ap - pear the hour I first be - lieved!
and por - tion be as long as life en - dures.
me safe thus far, and grace will lead me home.
to sing God's praise than when we'd first be - gun.

Text: st. 1–4, John Newton, 1779; st. 5, John Rees, 1859
Tune: Virginia Harmony, 1831; adapt. and harm. Edwin O. Excell, 1900

CM
NEW BRITAIN

O Love of God, How Strong and True

1 O love of God, how strong and true, e - ter - nal
2 O heav - enly love, how pre - cious still in days of
3 O wide - em - brac - ing, won - drous love! we read you
4 We read you in the flowers, the trees, the fresh - ness
5 We read you best in him who came to bear for

and yet ev - er new, un - com - pre - hend - ed
wea - ri - ness and ill, in nights of pain and
in the sky a - bove; we read you in the
of the fra - grant breeze, the song of birds up -
us the cross of shame, sent by the Fa - ther

and un - bought, be - yond all knowl - edge and all thought.
help - less - ness, to heal, to com - fort, and to bless.
earth be - low, in seas that swell and streams that flow.
on the wing, the joy of sum - mer and of spring.
from on high, our life to live, our death to die.

6 We read your power to bless and save
e'en in the darkness of the grave;
still more in resurrection light
we read the fullness of your might.

7 O love of God, our shield and stay
through all the perils of our way;
eternal love, in you we rest,
forever safe, forever blest.

Text: Horatius Bonar, 1861
Tune: William Knapp, 1738

LM
WAREHAM

464   Father, Long before Creation

1 Fa - ther, long be - fore cre - a - tion you had cho - sen
2 Though the world may change its fash - ion, you will still re -
3 Your com - pas - sion is our sto - ry, is our boast - ing
4 Lov - ing Fa - ther, now be - fore you we shall ev - er

us in love, and that love so deep, so mov - ing,
main the same; your com - pas - sion and your cov - enant
all the day; mer - cy free and nev - er fail - ing
sing your grace, and our song will sound for - ev - er

draws us close to Christ a - bove. Still it
through all a - ges will re - main. Your own
moves our will, di - rects our way. God so
when we see you face to face, giv - ing

keeps us firm - ly fixed in Christ a - lone.
chil - dren shall for - ev - er praise your name.
loved us that he gave his on - ly Son.
glo - ry to the Lamb up - on the throne.

Text: Chinese, c. 1952; tr. Francis P. Jones, 1953, alt.
Tune: William H. Monk, 1871

87 87 47
CORONAE

Sing Praise to God Who Reigns Above 465

1 Sing praise to God who reigns a-bove, the God of all cre-
2 What God's al-might-y power has made, in mer-cy he is
3 We sought the Lord in our dis-tress; O God, in mer-cy
4 Let all who name Christ's ho-ly name give God the praise and

a-tion, the God of power, the God of love, the God of
keep-ing; by morn-ing glow or eve-ning shade his eye is
hear us. Our Sav-ior saw our help-less-ness and came with
glo-ry. Let all who know his power pro-claim a-loud the

our sal-va-tion. My soul with com-fort rich he fills, and
nev-er sleep-ing. And where he rules in king-ly might, there
peace to cheer us. For this we thank and praise the Lord, who
won-drous sto-ry. Cast ev-ery i-dol from its throne; the

ev-ery grief he gent-ly stills: to God all praise and glo-ry!
all is just and all is right: to God all praise and glo-ry!
is by one and all a-dored: to God all praise and glo-ry!
Lord is God, and he a-lone: to God all praise and glo-ry!

Text: Johann J. Schütz, 1675; tr. Frances Cox, 1864, alt.
Tune: Bohemian Brethren's Kirchengesänge, 1566; harm. Heinrich Reimann, 1895

87 87 887
MIT FREUDEN ZART

466   Sing Praise to the Lord

1 Sing praise to the Lord! Praise him in the height;
re - joice in his word, you an - gels of light.
You heav - ens, a - dore him by whom you were made,
and wor - ship be - fore him, in bright-ness ar - rayed.

2 Sing praise to the Lord! Praise him on the earth
in tune - ful ac - cord, you saints of new birth.
Praise him who has brought you his grace from a - bove,
praise him who has taught you to sing of his love.

3 Sing praise to the Lord! All things that give sound,
each ju - bi - lant chord, re - ech - o a - round.
Loud or - gans, his glo - ry tell forth in deep tone,
and trum - pets, the sto - ry of what he has done.

4 Sing praise to the Lord! Thanks - giv - ing and song
to him be out - poured all a - ges a - long!
For love in cre - a - tion, for heav - en re - stored,
for grace of sal - va - tion, sing praise to the Lord!

Text: Henry W. Baker, 1875, alt.; based on Psalms 148 and 150
Tune: C. Hubert H. Parry, 1894

10 10 11 11
LAUDATE DOMINUM

At the Name of Jesus

1 At the name of Je - sus ev - ery knee shall bow,
2 At his voice cre - a - tion sprang at once to sight:
3 Hum-bled for a sea - son, to re-ceive a name
4 bore it up tri - um - phant with its hu - man light,

ev - ery tongue con - fess him King of glo - ry now;
all the an - gel fac - es, all the hosts of light,
from the lips of sin - ners, un - to whom he came;
through all ranks of crea - tures, to the cen - tral height,

'tis the Fa - ther's plea - sure we should call him Lord,
thrones and dom - i - na - tions, stars up - on their way,
faith - ful - ly he bore it spot - less to the last,
to the throne of God - head, to the Fa - ther's breast;

who from the be - gin - ning was the might - y Word.
all the heav-enly or - ders in their great ar - ray.
brought it back vic - to - rious when from death he passed;
filled it with the glo - ry of that per - fect rest.

5 In your hearts enthrone him;
    there let him subdue
all that is not holy,
    all that is not true.
Look to him, your Savior,
    in temptation's hour;
let his will enfold you
    in its light and power.

6 Christians, this Lord Jesus
    shall return again,
with his Father's glory,
    o'er the earth to reign;
for all wreaths of empire
    meet upon his brow,
and our hearts confess him
    King of glory now.

Text: Caroline M. Noel, 1870, alt.
Tune: Ralph Vaughan Williams, 1925. By permission of Oxford University Press.

65 65 D
KING'S WESTON

468 God Is Our Fortress and Our Rock

1 God is our for - tress and our rock, our might - y
2 Our hope is fixed on Christ a - lone, the Man of
3 The word of God will not be slow while de - mon

help in dan - ger; he shields us from the
God's own choos - ing; with - out him noth - ing
hordes sur - round us, though e - vil strike its

bat - tle's shock and thwarts the dev - il's an - ger;
can be won and fight - ing must be los - ing;
cruel - est blow and death and hell con - found us:

Text: Martin Luther, 1529; tr. Michael A. Perry, 1981, alt.; based on Psalm 46.
© 1982, Hope Publishing Co. All rights reserved. Used by permission.
Tune: Martin Luther, 1529

87 87 55 567
EIN FESTE BURG
(rhythmic)

for   still   the   prince of night   pro - longs   e - vil's   fight;
so   let   the   powers ac -cursed come   try   do   their worst;
for   though   we   meet   dis - tress, lose   all   we   pos - sess;

he   us - es   all   skill   to work   his   wick - ed will;
Christ Je - sus   shall ride   to bat - tle   at   our side,
those plan - ning our   ill   may rav - age, wreck, or kill;

no   earth - ly force is   like   him.
and   he   shall have the   vic   -   tory.
God's king - dom is   im - mor   -   tal!

469   A Mighty Fortress Is Our God

1 A might-y for-tress is our God, a bul-wark nev-er fail-ing; our help-er he, a-mid the flood of mor-tal ills pre-vail-ing. For still our an-cient foe does seek to work us woe; his craft and power are great,

2 Did we in our own strength con-fide, our striv-ing would be los-ing, were not the right Man on our side, the Man of God's own choos-ing. You ask who that may be? Christ Je-sus, it is he; Lord Sa-ba-oth his name,

3 And though this world, with dev-ils filled, should threat-en to un-do us, we will not fear, for God has willed his truth to tri-umph through us. The prince of dark-ness grim, we trem-ble not for him; his rage we can en-dure,

4 That Word a-bove all earth-ly powers— no thanks to them— a-bid-eth; the Spir-it and the gifts are ours through him who with us sid-eth. Let goods and kin-dred go, this mor-tal life al-so; the bod-y they may kill:

Text: Martin Luther, 1529; tr. Frederick H. Hedge, 1852; based on Psalm 46
Tune: Martin Luther, 1529, alt.; harm. Johann S. Bach, 1685–1750

87 87 66 66 7
EIN FESTE BURG
(isorhythmic)

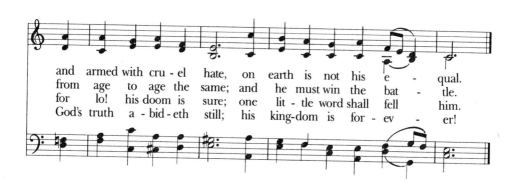

and armed with cru - el hate, on earth is not his e - qual.
from age to age the same; and he must win the bat - tle.
for lo! his doom is sure; one lit - tle word shall fell him.
God's truth a - bid - eth still; his king-dom is for - ev - er!

All Hail the Power of Jesus' Name   470

1 All hail the power of Je - sus' name! Let an - gels
2 O seed of Is - rael's cho - sen race now ran - somed
3 Let ev - ery tongue and ev - ery tribe re - spon - sive
4 Oh, that with all the sa - cred throng we at his

pros - trate fall. Bring forth the roy - al di - a - dem,
from the fall, hail him who saves you by his grace,
to his call, to him all maj - es - ty as - cribe,
feet may fall! We'll join the ev - er - last - ing song

Refrain

and crown him, crown him, crown him, crown him Lord of all!

Text: st. 1–3, Edward Perronet, 1780, alt.; st. 4, John Rippon, 1787, alt.
Tune: William Shrubsole, 1779

868 with refrain
MILES LANE

471 All Hail the Power of Jesus' Name

1 All hail the power of Je - sus' name! Let an - gels
2 O seed of Is - rael's cho - sen race now ran - somed
3 Let ev - ery tongue and ev - ery tribe re - spon - sive
4 Oh, that with all the sa - cred throng we at his

pros - trate fall. Bring forth the roy - al di - a - dem,
from the fall, hail him who saves you by his grace,
to his call, to him all maj - es - ty as - cribe,
feet may fall! We'll join the ev - er - last - ing song

and crown him Lord of all. Bring forth the roy - al
and crown him Lord of all. Hail him who saves you
and crown him Lord of all. To him all maj - es -
and crown him Lord of all. We'll join the ev - er -

di - a - dem, and crown him Lord of all!
by his grace, and crown him Lord of all!
ty as - cribe, and crown him Lord of all!
last - ing song and crown him Lord of all!

Text: st. 1–3, Edward Perronet, 1780, alt.; st. 4, John Rippon, 1787, alt.
Tune: Oliver Holden, 1793

86 86 86
CORONATION

O Jesus, We Adore You

1 O Jesus, we adore you, upon the cross, our King.
2 The world does yet disdain you, still passing by the cross;
3 O glorious King, we praise you, no longer pass you by;

We bow our hearts before you; your gracious name we sing.
Lord, may our hearts retain you; all else we count but loss.
O Jesus, we confess you the Son enthroned on high.

That name has brought salvation, that name in life our stay,
Ah, Lord, our sins arraigned you and nailed you to the tree;
Lord, grant to us forgiveness; life through your death restore;

our peace, our consolation, when life shall fade away.
our pride, O Lord, disdained you; yet you have set us free.
yes, grant to us the fullness of life forevermore.

Text: Arthur T. Russell, 1851, alt.
Tune: William Lloyd, 1840

76 76 D
MEIRIONYDD

473   To God Be the Glory

1 To God be the glo - ry, great things he has done; so loved he the
2 O per - fect re - demp-tion, the pur-chase of blood, to ev - ery be -
3 Great things he has taught us, great things he has done, and great our re -

world that he gave us his Son, who yield - ed his life an a -
liev - er the prom-ise of God; the vil - est of-fend-er who
joic - ing through Je - sus the Son; but pur - er and high-er and

tone-ment for sin, and o-pened the life-gate that we may go in.
tru - ly be - lieves, that mo-ment from Je - sus a par-don re - ceives.
great - er will be our won-der, our glad-ness, when Je - sus we see.

Refrain

Praise the Lord, praise the Lord; let the earth hear his voice! Praise the

Lord, praise the Lord; let the peo-ple re - joice! O come to the

Text: Fanny J. Crosby, 1875, alt.
Tune: William H. Doane, 1875

11 11 11 11 with refrain
TO GOD BE THE GLORY

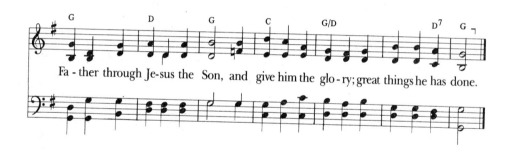

Fa-ther through Je-sus the Son, and give him the glo-ry; great things he has done.

In the Cross of Christ I Glory 474

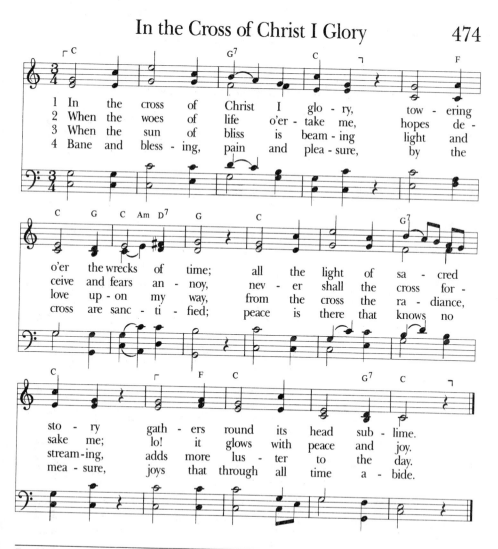

1 In the cross of Christ I glo - ry, tow - ering
2 When the woes of life o'er - take me, hopes de -
3 When the sun of bliss is beam - ing light and
4 Bane and bless - ing, pain and plea - sure, by the

o'er the wrecks of time; all the light of sa - cred
ceive and fears an - noy, nev - er shall the cross for -
love up - on my way, from the cross the ra - diance,
cross are sanc - ti - fied; peace is there that knows no

sto - ry gath - ers round its head sub - lime.
sake me; lo! it glows with peace and joy.
stream-ing, adds more lus - ter to the day.
mea - sure, joys that through all time a - bide.

Text: John Bowring, 1825
Tune: Ithamar Conkey, 1851

87 87
RATHBUN

475   Praise, My Soul, the King of Heaven

1 Praise, my soul, the King of heav - en; to his feet your
trib - ute bring. Ran - somed, healed, re - stored, for - giv - en,
ev - er - more his prais - es sing. Al - le - lu - ia,
al - le - lu - ia! Praise the ev - er - last - ing King!

Text: Henry F. Lyte, 1834, alt.; based on Psalm 103
Tune: John Goss, 1869

87 87 87
LAUDA ANIMA

2 Praise him for his grace and fa - vor to his peo - ple in dis - tress. Praise him, still the same as ev - er, slow to chide, and swift to bless. Al - le - lu - ia, al - le - lu - ia! Glo - rious in his faith - ful - ness!

The accompaniment for stanza 2 may be used for all stanzas.

Continued on following page

3 Fa - ther - like he tends and spares us; well our fee - ble frame he knows. In his hand he gent - ly bears us, res - cues us from all our foes. Al - le - lu - ia, al - le - lu - ia! Wide - ly yet his mer - cy flows!

4 An - gels, help us to a - dore him; you be - hold him

face to face. Sun and moon, bow down be - fore him,

dwell - ers all in time and space. Al - le - lu - ia,

al - le - lu - ia! Praise with us the God of grace!

476 When Israel Was in Egypt's Land

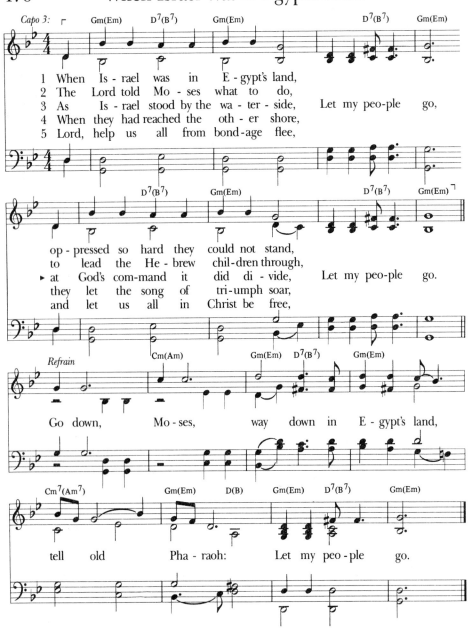

1 When Is-rael was in E-gypt's land,
2 The Lord told Mo-ses what to do,
3 As Is-rael stood by the wa-ter-side,
4 When they had reached the oth-er shore,
5 Lord, help us all from bond-age flee,

Let my peo-ple go,

op-pressed so hard they could not stand,
to lead the He-brew chil-dren through,
at God's com-mand it did di-vide,
they let the song of tri-umph soar,
and let us all in Christ be free,

Let my peo-ple go.

Refrain

Go down, Mo-ses, way down in E-gypt's land,

tell old Pha-raoh: Let my peo-ple go.

Text and Tune: Afro-American spiritual; harm. John W. Work, 1871–1925
Keyboard and guitar should not sound together.

irregular
GO DOWN, MOSES

You Servants of God, Your Master Proclaim 477

1 You ser - vants of God, your Mas - ter pro - claim,
2 God rules in the height, al - might - y to save;
3 "Sal - va - tion to God, who sits on the throne!"
4 Then let us a - dore and give him his right:

and pub - lish a - broad his won - der - ful name;
though hid from our sight, his pres - ence we have;
let all cry a - loud, and hon - or the Son;
all glo - ry and power, all wis - dom and might,

the name all - vic - to - rious of Je - sus ex - tol;
the great con - gre - ga - tion his tri - umph shall sing,
the prais - es of Je - sus the an - gels pro - claim,
all hon - or and bless - ing— with an - gels a - bove—

his king - dom is glo - rious and rules o - ver all.
as - crib - ing sal - va - tion to Je - sus, our King.
fall down on their fac - es and wor - ship the Lamb.
and thanks nev - er ceas - ing for in - fi - nite love.

Text: Charles Wesley, 1744, alt.
Tune: attr. William Croft, 1708

10 10 11 11
HANOVER

478   Tell Out, My Soul

1 Tell out, my soul, the great-ness of the Lord! Un-
2 Tell out, my soul, the great-ness of his name! Make
3 Tell out, my soul, the great-ness of his might! Powers
4 Tell out, my soul, the glo-ries of his word! Firm

num-bered bless-ings give my spir - it voice; ten-der to
known his might, the deeds his arm has done; his mer-cy
and do - min-ions lay their glo - ry by. Proud hearts and
is his prom-ise, and his mer - cy sure. Tell out, my

me the prom - ise of his word; in
sure, from age to age the same; his
stub - born wills are put to flight, the
soul, the great - ness of the Lord to

Text: Timothy Dudley-Smith, 1961; based on the Song of Mary, Luke 1:46–55.
© 1962, Hope Publishing Co. All rights reserved. Used by permission.
Tune: Walter Greatorex, 1916, alt. By permission of Oxford University Press.

10 10 10 10
WOODLANDS

God my Sav - ior shall my heart re - joice.
ho - ly name— the Lord, the Might - y One.
hun - gry fed, the hum - ble lift - ed high.
chil - dren's chil - dren and for - ev - er - more!

Alternative accompaniment

Tune: *Walter Greatorex, 1916. By permission of Oxford University Press.*

479   I Will Sing of My Redeemer

1 I will sing of my Re - deem - er and his won - drous
2 I will tell the won - drous sto - ry, how my lost es -
3 I will sing of my Re - deem - er and his heav - enly

love to me; on the cru - el cross he suf - fered, from the
tate to save, in his bound-less love and mer - cy, he the
love for me; he from death to life has brought me, Son of

curse to set me free. Sing, O sing of my Re - deem - er!
ran - som free - ly gave. I will praise my dear Re - deem - er,
God, with him to be. Sing, O sing of my Re - deem - er!

With his blood he pur - chased me; on the cross he
his tri - um - phant power I'll tell: how the vic - to -
With his blood he pur - chased me; on the cross he

Text: Philip P. Bliss, 1876
Tune: Rowland H. Prichard, 1830

87 87 D
HYFRYDOL

sealed my par - don, paid the debt, and made me free.
ry he gives me o - ver sin and death and hell.
sealed my par - don, paid the debt, and made me free.

Jesus, the Very Thought of You 480

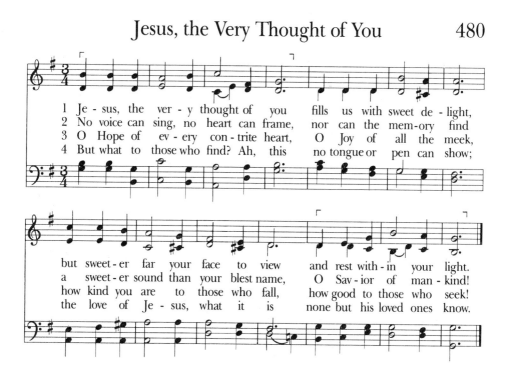

1 Je - sus, the ver - y thought of you fills us with sweet de - light,
2 No voice can sing, no heart can frame, nor can the mem-ory find
3 O Hope of ev - ery con - trite heart, O Joy of all the meek,
4 But what to those who find? Ah, this no tongue or pen can show;

but sweet - er far your face to view and rest with - in your light.
a sweet - er sound than your blest name, O Sav - ior of man - kind!
how kind you are to those who fall, how good to those who seek!
the love of Je - sus, what it is none but his loved ones know.

Text: Latin, 12th cent.; tr. Edward Caswall, 1849, alt.
Tune: John B. Dykes, 1866

CM
ST. AGNES

481   Christ, Whose Glory Fills the Skies

1 Christ, whose glo - ry fills the skies, Christ, the true and on - ly Light,
2 Dark and cheer - less is the morn un - ac - com - pa - nied by thee;
3 Vis - it, then, this soul of mine, pierce the gloom of sin and grief;

Sun of Right-eous - ness, a - rise, tri - umph o'er the shades of night;
joy - less is the day's re - turn till thy mer - cy's beams I see,
fill me, Ra - dian - cy di - vine, scat - ter all my un - be - lief;

Day - spring from on high, be near; Day - star, in my heart ap - pear.
till they in - ward light im - part, glad my eyes and warm my heart.
more and more thy - self dis - play, shin - ing to the per - fect day!

Text: Charles Wesley, 1740
Tune: Charles F. Gounod, 1872
Alternative tune: RATISBON, 34

77 77 77
LUX PRIMA

Man of Sorrows—What a Name

1 Man of sor - rows— what a name for the
2 Bear - ing shame and scoff - ing rude, in my
3 Guilt - y, help - less, lost were we; blame - less
4 He was lift - ed up to die; "It is
5 When he comes, our glo - rious King, all his

Son of God, who came ru - ined sin - ners
place con - demned he stood, sealed my par - don
Lamb of God was he, sac - ri - ficed to
fin - ished" was his cry; now in heaven ex -
ran - somed home to bring, then a - new this

to re - claim: Hal - le - lu - jah, what a Sav - ior!
with his blood: Hal - le - lu - jah, what a Sav - ior!
set us free: Hal - le - lu - jah, what a Sav - ior!
alt - ed high: Hal - le - lu - jah, what a Sav - ior!
song we'll sing: Hal - le - lu - jah, what a Sav - ior!

Text and Tune: Philip P. Bliss, 1875, alt.

77 78
HALLELUJAH! WHAT A SAVIOR

483   How Great Thou Art

1 O Lord my God, when I in awe-some won-der
2 When through the woods and for-est glades I wan-der,
3 But when I think that God, his Son not spar-ing,
4 When Christ shall come, with shout of ac-cla-ma-tion,

con-sid-er all the works thy hand hath made,
I hear the birds sing sweet-ly in the trees;
sent him to die, I scarce can take it in,
and claim his own, what joy shall fill my heart!

I see the stars, I hear the might-y thun-der,
when I look down from loft-y moun-tain gran-deur
that on the cross my bur-den glad-ly bear-ing
Then I shall bow in hum-ble ad-o-ra-tion

thy power through-out the u-ni-verse dis-played;
and hear the brook and feel the gen-tle breeze;
he bled and died to take a-way my sin;
and there pro-claim, "My God, how great thou art!"

Text: Stuart K. Hine, 1949
Tune: Swedish; harm. Stuart K. Hine, 1949
Text and music © 1953, 1981, Manna Music, Inc. International copyright secured.
  All rights reserved. Used by permission.

11 10 11 10 with refrain
O STORE GUD

Refrain

Then sings my soul, my Sav-ior God, to thee: how great thou art, how great thou art! Then sings my soul, my Sav-ior God, to thee: how great thou art, how great thou art!

484   Humble Praises, Holy Jesus

1 Hum - ble prais - es, ho - ly Je - sus, chil - dren's voic - es raise in song.
2 Gra - cious Sav - ior, stay be - side us, lead and guide us as we go.

As our shep - herd, O pro - tect us; we as lambs to you be - long.
By your Spir - it, bless - ed Je - sus, help us in your love to grow.

Refrain

Al - le - lu - ia, al - le - lu - ia, joy - ful prais - es now we sing.

Al - le - lu - ia, al - le - lu - ia, al - le - lu - ia to our King.

Text: anonymous; rev. Emily R. Brink, 1985. © 1987, CRC Publications
Tune: John A. Stevenson, 1818

87 87 *with refrain*
VESPER HYMN

O Christ, Our Hope, Our Heart's Desire 485

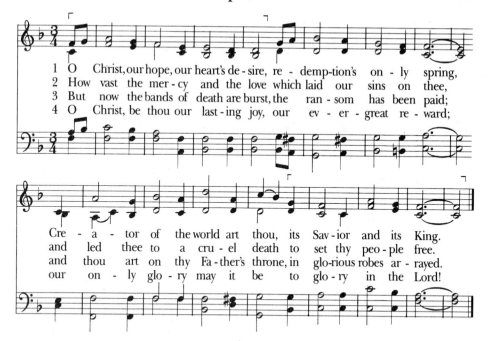

1 O Christ, our hope, our heart's de-sire, re-demp-tion's on-ly spring,
2 How vast the mer-cy and the love which laid our sins on thee,
3 But now the bands of death are burst, the ran-som has been paid;
4 O Christ, be thou our last-ing joy, our ev-er-great re-ward;

Cre - a - tor of the world art thou, its Sav-ior and its King.
and led thee to a cru-el death to set thy peo-ple free.
and thou art on thy Fa-ther's throne, in glo-rious robes ar-rayed.
our on - ly glo-ry may it be to glo-ry in the Lord!

Text: Latin, c. 8th cent.; tr. John Chandler, 1837
Tune: H. W. Greatorex's Collection, 1851

CM
MANOAH

486   Come, Thou Fount of Every Blessing

1 Come, thou Fount of ev-ery bless-ing, tune my heart to sing thy
2 Here I find my great-est trea-sure; hith-er by thy help I've
3 Oh, to grace how great a debt-or dai-ly I'm con-strained to

grace; streams of mer - cy, nev-er ceas - ing, call for
come; and I hope, by thy good plea - sure, safe-ly
be! Let thy good-ness, like a fet - ter, bind my

songs of loud-est praise. Teach me some me - lo-dious
to ar - rive at home. Je - sus sought me when a
wan - dering heart to thee: prone to wan - der, Lord, I

son - net, sung by flam - ing tongues a - bove. Praise the
strang - er, wan-dering from the fold of God; he, to
feel it, prone to leave the God I love; here's my

Text: Robert Robinson, 1758, alt.
Tune: J. Wyeth's Repository of Sacred Music, Part II, 1813

87 87 D
NETTLETON

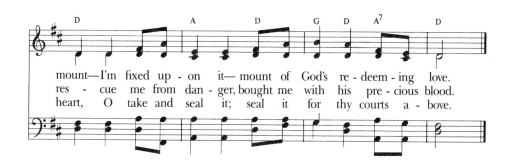

mount—I'm fixed up - on it— mount of God's re - deem - ing love.
res - cue me from dan - ger, bought me with his pre - cious blood.
heart, O take and seal it; seal it for thy courts a - bove.

How Sweet the Name of Jesus Sounds 487

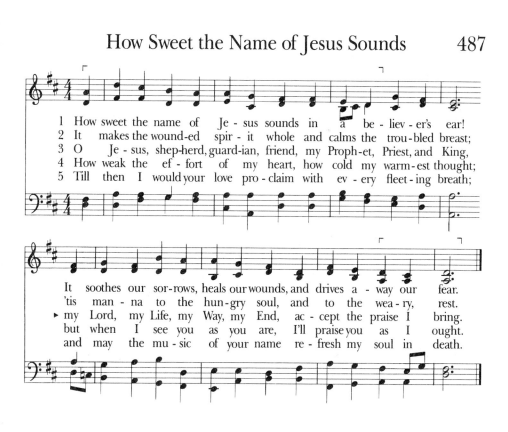

1 How sweet the name of Je - sus sounds in a be - liev - er's ear!
2 It makes the wound-ed spir - it whole and calms the trou-bled breast;
3 O Je - sus, shep-herd, guard-ian, friend, my Proph-et, Priest, and King,
4 How weak the ef - fort of my heart, how cold my warm-est thought;
5 Till then I would your love pro - claim with ev - ery fleet-ing breath;

It soothes our sor-rows, heals our wounds, and drives a - way our fear.
'tis man - na to the hun-gry soul, and to the wea - ry, rest.
my Lord, my Life, my Way, my End, ac - cept the praise I bring.
but when I see you as you are, I'll praise you as I ought.
and may the mu - sic of your name re - fresh my soul in death.

Text: John Newton, 1779
Tune: Alexander R. Reinagle, 1836

CM
ST. PETER

488   I Heard the Voice of Jesus Say

1 I heard the voice of Je-sus say, "Come un-to me and rest;
2 I heard the voice of Je-sus say, "Be-hold, I free-ly give
3 I heard the voice of Je-sus say, "I am this dark world's light;

lay down, O wea-ry one, lay down your head up-on my breast."
the liv-ing wa-ter; thirst-y one, stoop down and drink and live."
look un-to me; your morn shall rise and all your day be bright."

I came to Je-sus as I was, so wea-ry, worn, and sad;
I came to Je-sus and I drank of that life-giv-ing stream;
I looked to Je-sus and I found in him my star, my sun;

I found in him a rest-ing place, and he has made me glad.
my thirst was quenched, my soul re-vived, and now I live in him.
and in that light of life I'll walk till trav-eling days are done.

Text: Horatius Bonar, 1846
Tune: Henry Vander Werp, 1911

CMD
RESTING PLACE

When Peace like a River

1 When peace like a riv - er at - tend - eth my way, when
2 Though Sa - tan should buf - fet, though tri - als should come, let
3 My sin— oh, the bliss of this glo - ri - ous thought! —my
4 O Lord, haste the day when my faith shall be sight, the

sor - rows like sea bil - lows roll; what - ev - er my lot, thou hast
this blest as - sur - ance con - trol: that Christ has re - gard - ed my
sin, not in part, but the whole, is nailed to the cross, and I
clouds be rolled back as a scroll; the trump shall re - sound and the

taught me to say, "It is well, it is well with my soul."
help - less es - tate, and has shed his own blood for my soul.
bear it no more; praise the Lord, praise the Lord, O my soul!
Lord shall de - scend; e - ven so, it is well with my soul.

Refrain (may be sung after final stanza only)

It is well with my soul;
it is well with my soul;

it is well, it is well with my soul.

Text: Horatio G. Spafford, 1873
Tune: Philip P. Bliss, 1876

11 8 11 9 *with refrain*
VILLE DU HAVRE

490   Blessed Assurance: Jesus Is Mine

1 Bless-ed as-sur-ance: Je-sus is mine! Oh, what a fore-taste of
2 Joy-ful con-fes-sion: I am his own! Fol-low-ing Je-sus, I'm
3 Per-fect sub-mis-sion: all is at rest, I in my Sav-ior am

glo-ry di-vine! Heir of sal-va-tion, pur-chase of God,
nev-er a-lone. Born of his Spir-it, I am re-stored,
hap-py and blest; watch-ing and wait-ing, look-ing a-bove,

Refrain

born of his Spir-it, washed in his blood.
chal-lenged to serve my Sav-ior and Lord. This is my sto-ry, this is my
filled with his good-ness, kept in his love.

song, prais-ing my Sav-ior all the day long; this is my sto-ry,

this is my song, prais-ing my Sav-ior all the day long.

Text: st. 1, 3, Fanny J. Crosby, 1873; st. 2, Marie J. Post, 1985. St. 2 © 1987, CRC Publications
Tune: Phoebe P. Knapp, 1873

9 10 9 9 with refrain
ASSURANCE

Our Lives Are Filled with Sorrows

491

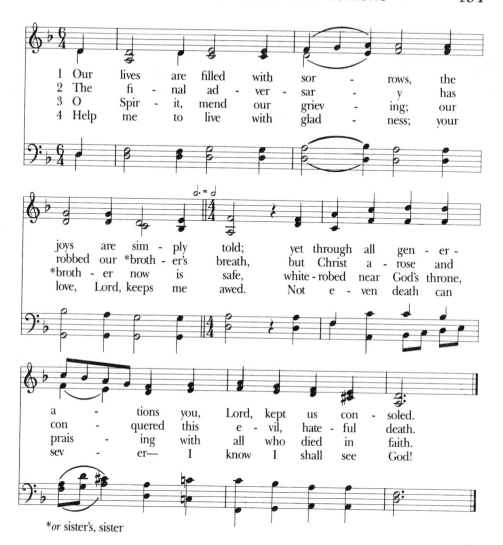

1 Our lives are filled with sor - rows, the
2 The fi - nal ad - ver - sar - y has
3 O Spir - it, mend our griev - ing; our
4 Help me to live with glad - ness; your

joys are sim - ply told;
robbed our *broth - er's breath,
*broth - er now is safe,
love, Lord, keeps me awed.

yet through all gen - er -
but Christ a - rose and
white - robed near God's throne,
Not e - ven death can

a - tions you, Lord, kept us con - soled.
con - quered this e - vil, hate - ful death.
prais - ing with all who died in faith.
sev - er— I know I shall see God!

*or sister's, sister

Text: Calvin Seerveld, 1983, ©
Tune: Andernacher Gesangbuch, 1608; harm. Emily R. Brink, 1985.
  Harmonization © 1987, CRC Publications
Alternative tune: CHRISTUS, DER IST MEIN LEBEN, 565

76 76
ES KOMMT EIN SCHIFF GELADEN

492 Our Voice Would Be a Useless Cry

1 Our voice would be a use-less cry blown down the heed-less
2 To you a-lone be prais-es now for vic-to-ries a-
3 Your Spir-it gave us ut-ter-ance that man-y might be

wind; our ev-ery ac-tion count-ed loss, our
chieved; for in-spi-ra-tion, com-fort, joy when
reached. Your Spir-it gave us el-o-quence as

work un-dis-ci-plined; our blood-bought vic-tories
e-ven one be-lieved; for match-less power in
truth a-lone was preached. Ten thou-sand times ten

turned to dust, no prize at home, a-broad— with-
trou-bled times, for calm when tem-pests came; for
thou-sand hosts have joined the heav-enly throng, and

out the con-stant pres-ence of your Spir-it, tri-une God.
peace that on-ly comes to those who la-bor in your name.
from that ran-somed ar-my comes a new and joy-ous song.

Text: Marie J. Post, 1974, alt. © 1974, CRC Publications
Tune: Guy Warrack, 1931. By permission of Oxford University Press.
Alternative tune: ALL SAINTS NEW, 110

CMD
WELLINGTON SQUARE

Precious Lord, Take My Hand

1 Pre-cious Lord, take my hand, lead me on, help me stand;
2 When my way grows_____ drear, pre-cious Lord, lin-ger near;
3 When the dark-ness ap-pears and the night draws_____ near,

I am tired, I am weak, I am worn;
when my life is_____ al-most_____ gone,
when the day is_____ past and_____ gone,

through the storm, through the night, lead me on to the light;
hear my cry, hear my call, hold my hand lest I fall;
at the riv-er I stand, guide my feet, hold my hand;

take my hand, pre-cious Lord, lead me home.

Text: Thomas A. Dorsey, 1938
Tune: George N. Allen, 1844; adapt. Thomas A. Dorsey, 1938
Text and music © 1938, 1966, Hill & Range Songs, Inc. All rights controlled by Unichappell Music, Inc.
International copyright secured. All rights reserved. Used by permission.

irregular
PRECIOUS LORD

494 There Is a Balm in Gilead

Capo 3: F(D) *Refrain*

There is a balm in Gil-e-ad to make the wound - ed whole,
there is a balm in Gil-e - ad to heal the sin - sick soul.

1 Some - times I feel dis - cour-aged and think my work's in vain,
2 If you can - not preach like Pe - ter, if you can - not pray like Paul,

but then the Ho - ly Spir - it re - vives my soul a - gain.
you can tell the love of Je - sus and say, "He died for all."

Text and Tune: Afro-American spiritual

irregular
BALM IN GILEAD

I Know Not Why God's Wondrous Grace 495

1 I know not why God's won-drous grace to me he has made known,
2 I know not how this sav - ing faith to me he did im - part,
3 I know not how the Spir - it moves, con - vinc - ing us of sin,
4 I know not what of good or ill may be re - served for me,

nor why, un-wor - thy, Christ in love re - deemed me for his own.
nor how be-liev - ing in his Word wrought peace with - in my heart.
re - veal-ing Je - sus through the Word, cre - at - ing faith in him.
of wea - ry ways or gold - en days, be - fore his face I see.

Refrain

But "I know whom I have be - liev - ed, and am per-suad - ed that he is

a - ble to keep that which I've com - mit-ted un - to him a-gainst that day."

Text: Daniel W. Whittle, 1883; based on 2 Timothy 1:12
Tune: James McGranahan, 1883

CM with refrain
EL NATHAN

496 My Lord, I Did Not Choose You

1 My Lord, I did not choose you, for that could nev-er be;
2 Un-less your grace had called me and taught my o-pening mind,

my heart would still re-fuse you, had you not cho-sen me.
the world would have en-thralled me, to heav-enly glo-ries blind.

You took the sin that stained me, you cleansed me, made me new;
My heart knows none a-bove you; for your rich grace I thirst.

of old you have or-dained me, that I should live in you.
I know that if I love you, you must have loved me first.

Text: Josiah Conder, 1836, alt.
Tune: Greek; adapt. in A. Sullivan's Church Hymns, *1874*

76 76 D
CALCUTTA

How Vast the Benefits Divine

1 How vast the ben - e - fits di - vine which we in Christ pos - sess!
2 To you, O Christ, a - lone is due all glo - ry and re - nown;
3 With - in the arms of sov-ereign love we ev - er shall re - main;

We are re-deemed from sin and shame, and called to ho - li - ness.
no mer - it of our own we claim, nor rob you of your crown.
nor shall the rage of earth or hell make God's sure coun-sel vain.

'Tis not for works that we have done—these all to him we owe;
You were our on - ly sur - e - ty in God's re - demp-tion plan;
Each one of all the cho - sen race shall sure - ly heaven at - tain;

but he of his e - lect - ing love sal - va - tion does be - stow.
in you his grace was giv - en us be - fore the world be - gan.
here they will share a - bound - ing grace, and there with Je - sus reign.

Text: Augustus M. Toplady, 1774, alt.
Tune: Gottfried W. Fink, 1842

CMD
BETHLEHEM

498   I Sought the Lord, and Afterward I Knew

1. I sought the Lord, and af-ter-ward I knew
2. Thou didst reach forth thy hand and mine en-fold;
3. I find, I walk, I love; but, oh, the whole

he moved my soul to seek him, seek-ing me;
I walked and sank not on the storm-vexed sea;
of love is but my an-swer, Lord, to thee!

it was not I that found, O Sav-ior true;
'twas not so much that I on thee took hold,
For thou wert long be-fore-hand with my soul;

no, I was found, was found of thee.
as thou, dear Lord, took hold on me.
al-ways, al-ways thou lov-edst me.

It was not I that found, O Sav-ior true;
'Twas not so much that I on thee took hold,
For thou wert long be-fore-hand with my soul;

Text: anonymous, 1878
Tune: Jean Sibelius, 1899. © Breitkopf & Härtel

10 10 10 8 10 8
FINLANDIA

no, I was found, was found of thee.
as thou, dear Lord, took hold on me.
al - ways, al - ways thou lov - edst me.

My God, How Wonderful You Are   499

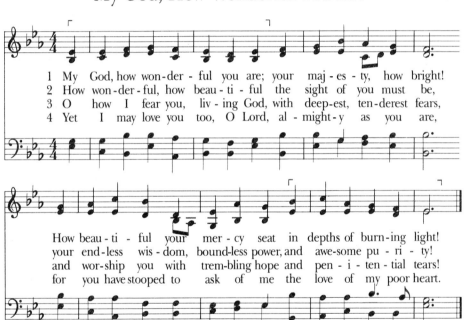

1 My God, how won-der - ful you are; your maj - es - ty, how bright!
2 How won-der-ful, how beau - ti - ful the sight of you must be,
3 O how I fear you, liv - ing God, with deep-est, ten-derest fears,
4 Yet I may love you too, O Lord, al - might-y as you are,

How beau - ti - ful your mer - cy seat in depths of burn-ing light!
your end-less wis - dom, bound-less power, and awe-some pu - ri - ty!
and wor-ship you with trem-bling hope and pen - i - ten - tial tears!
for you have stooped to ask of me the love of my poor heart.

5 No earthly father loves like you,
   no mother half so mild
bears and forbears as you have done
with me, your sinful child.

6 Father of Jesus, Love divine,
   great King upon your throne,
what joy to see you as you are
and worship you alone!

Text: Frederick W. Faber, 1849, alt.   *CM*
Tune: Thomas Turton, 1860   *ST. ETHELDREDA*

500 How Firm a Foundation

1 How firm a foun - da - tion, you saints of the Lord,
2 "Fear not, I am with you; O be not dis - mayed,
3 "When through the deep wa - ters I call you to go,
4 "When through fi - ery tri - als your path - way shall lie,
5 "The soul that on Je - sus has leaned for re - pose

is laid for your faith in his ex - cel - lent Word!
for I am your God and will still give you aid;
▸ the riv - ers of sor - row shall not o - ver - flow,
my grace all - suf - fi - cient shall be your sup - ply;
I will not, I will not de - sert to its foes;

What more can he say than to you he has said,
I'll strength - en you, help you, and cause you to stand,
▸ for I will be with you in trou - ble to bless,
the flame shall not hurt you; I on - ly de - sign
that soul, though all hell should en - deav - or to shake,

to you who for ref - uge to Je - sus have fled?
up - held by my right - eous, om - nip - o - tent hand.
▸ and sanc - ti - fy to you your deep - est dis - tress.
your dross to con - sume and your gold to re - fine.
I'll nev - er, no nev - er, no nev - er for - sake!"

Text: J. Rippon's Selection of Hymns, 1787, alt.; based on Isaiah 43:1–5
Tune: J. Funk's A Compilation of Genuine Church Music, 1832; harm. Dale Grotenhuis, 1985.
Harmonization © 1987, CRC Publications

11 11 11 11
FOUNDATION

Oh, for a Thousand Tongues to Sing

501

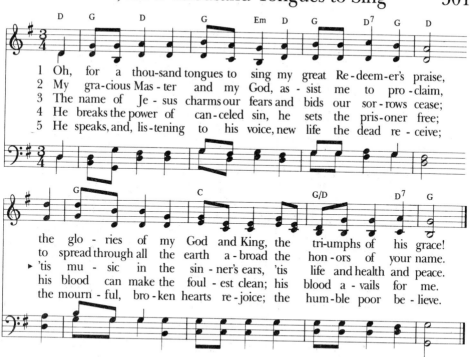

1 Oh, for a thou-sand tongues to sing my great Re-deem-er's praise,
2 My gra-cious Mas-ter and my God, as-sist me to pro-claim,
3 The name of Je-sus charms our fears and bids our sor-rows cease;
4 He breaks the power of can-celed sin, he sets the pris-oner free;
5 He speaks, and, lis-tening to his voice, new life the dead re-ceive;

the glo-ries of my God and King, the tri-umphs of his grace!
to spread through all the earth a-broad the hon-ors of your name.
'tis mu-sic in the sin-ner's ears, 'tis life and health and peace.
his blood can make the foul-est clean; his blood a-vails for me.
the mourn-ful, bro-ken hearts re-joice; the hum-ble poor be-lieve.

6 Hear him, you deaf; you voiceless ones,
  your loosened tongues employ;
  you blind, behold your Savior come;
  and leap, you lame, for joy!

7 To God all glory, praise, and love
  be now and ever given
  by saints below and saints above,
  the church in earth and heaven.

Text: Charles Wesley, 1739, alt.
Tune: Carl G. Gläser, 1828; adapt. and arr. Lowell Mason, 1839

CM
AZMON

502 The Church's One Foundation

1 The church's one foun - da - tion is Je - sus Christ, her Lord;
2 E - lect from ev - ery na - tion, yet one o'er all the earth;
3 Though with a scorn - ful won - der the world sees her op - pressed,
4 Mid toil and trib - u - la - tion, and tu - mult of her war,

she is his new cre - a - tion by wa - ter and the Word.
her char - ter of sal - va - tion: one Lord, one faith, one birth.
by schisms rent a - sun - der, by her - e - sies dis - tressed,
she waits the con - sum - ma - tion of peace for - ev - er - more,

From heaven he came and sought her to be his ho - ly bride;
One ho - ly name she bless - es, par - takes one ho - ly food,
yet saints their watch are keep - ing; their cry goes up: "How long?"
till with the vi - sion glo - rious her long - ing eyes are blest,

with his own blood he bought her, and for her life he died.
and to one hope she press - es, with ev - ery grace en - dued.
and soon the night of weep - ing shall be the morn of song.
and the great church vic - to - rious shall be the church at rest.

Text: Samuel J. Stone, 1866
Tune: Samuel S. Wesley, 1864

76 76 D
AURELIA

Built on the Rock

1 Built on the Rock, the church shall stand e - ven when
2 Not in a tem - ple made with hands God the Al -
3 We are God's house of liv - ing stones, built for his

stee - ples are fall - ing; Christ builds his church in
might - y is dwell - ing; high in the heavens his
own hab - i - ta - tion; he fills our hearts, his

ev - ery land; bells still are chim - ing and call - ing,
tem - ple stands, all earth - ly tem - ples ex - cel - ling.
hum - ble thrones, grant - ing us life and sal - va - tion.

call - ing the young and old to rest, call - ing the souls of
Yet he who dwells in heaven a - bove choos - es to live with
Yet to this place, an earth - ly frame, we come with thanks to

those dis - tressed, long - ing for life ev - er - last - ing.
us in love, mak - ing our bod - ies his tem - ple.
praise his name; God grants his peo - ple true bless - ing.

Text: Nikolai Grundtvig, 1854; tr. Carl Doving, 1909, alt.
Tune: Ludwig M. Lindeman, 1840

88 88 888
KIRKEN

504 Holy God, We Praise Your Name

Descant

4 Ho - ly Fa - ther, ho - ly Son, Ho - ly Spir - it,

1 Ho - ly God, we praise your name; Lord of all, we
2 Hark, the glad ce - les - tial hymn an - gel choirs a -
3 Lo, the ap - os - tol - ic train joins your sa - cred
4 Ho - ly Fa - ther, ho - ly Son, Ho - ly Spir - it,

three we name you, though in es - sence on - ly one;

bow be - fore you. Saints on earth your rule ac - claim;
bove are rais - ing; cher - u - bim and ser - a - phim,
name to hal - low; proph - ets swell the glad re - frain,
three we name you, though in es - sence on - ly one;

Text: Te Deum, 4th. cent.; vers. Ignaz Franz, c. 1774; tr. Clarence A. Walworth, 1853, alt.
Tune: Katholisches Gesangbuch, Vienna, 1774; desc. Emily R. Brink, 1986.
Descant © 1987, CRC Publications

78 78 77
GROSSER GOTT

un - di - vid - ed God, we claim you, and, a - dor - ing,

all in heaven a - bove a - dore you. In - fi - nite your
in un - ceas - ing cho - rus prais - ing, fill the heavens with
and the white - robed mar - tyrs fol - low; and from morn to
un - di - vid - ed God, we claim you, and, a - dor - ing,

bend the knee while we own the mys - ter - y.

vast do - main; ev - er - last - ing is your reign.
sweet ac - cord: "Ho - ly, ho - ly, ho - ly Lord!"
set of sun, through the church the song goes on.
bend the knee while we own the mys - ter - y.

505   For All the Saints

1 For all the saints who from their la - bors rest,
2 You were their rock, their for - tress, and their might;
3 May all your sol - diers, faith - ful, true, and bold,

6 But then there breaks a yet more glo - rious day:
7 From earth's wide bounds, from o - cean's far - thest coast,

who to the world by faith their Lord con - fessed, your
you, Lord, their cap - tain in the well-fought fight, and
fight as the saints who no - bly fought of old, and

the saints tri - um - phant rise in bright ar - ray; the
through gates of pearl streams in the count - less host, _____

name, O Je - sus, be for - ev - er blest.
in the dark - ness drear, their one true light.
win with them the vic - tor's crown of gold.

King of glo - ry pass - es on his way.
sing - ing to Fa - ther, Son, and Ho - ly Ghost:

Text: William W. How, 1864, alt.
Tune: Ralph Vaughan Williams, 1906. By permission of Oxford University Press.

10 10 10 with alleluias
SINE NOMINE

Al - le - lu - ia, al - le - lu - ia!

Harmony

4 O blest com - mu - nion, fel - low-ship di - vine! We fee-bly strug - gle,
5 And when the strife is fierce, the war-fare long, far off we hear the

they in glo - ry shine; yet all are one with - in your great de -
dis - tant tri - umph song; and hearts are brave a - gain, and arms are

sign.
strong. Al - le - lu - ia, al - le-lu - ia!

506 Glorious Things of You Are Spoken

1 Glo - rious things of you are spo - ken, Zi - on, cit - y
2 See, the streams of liv - ing wa - ters, spring - ing from e -
3 Round each hab - i - ta - tion hov - ering, see the cloud and
4 Sav - ior, since of Zi - on's cit - y I through grace a

of our God. He whose word can - not be bro - ken formed you
ter - nal love, well sup - ply your sons and daugh - ters and all
fire ap - pear for a glo - ry and a cov - ering, show - ing
mem - ber am, let the world de - ride or pit - y, I will

for his own a - bode. On the Rock of A - ges
fear of want re - move. Who can faint while such a
that the Lord is near. Thus de - riv - ing from their
glo - ry in your name. Fad - ing are the world's best

Text: John Newton, 1779, alt.
Tune: C. Hubert H. Parry, 1897
Alternative tune: ABBOT'S LEIGH, 523

87 87 D
RUSTINGTON

found-ed, what can shake your sure re - pose? With sal -
riv - er ev - er will their thirst as - suage? Grace which,
ban - ner light by night and shade by day, safe they
plea - sures, all its boast - ed pomp and show; sol - id

va - tion's walls sur - round-ed, you may smile at all your foes.
like the Lord, the giv - er, nev - er fails from age to age.
feed up - on the man - na which God gives them on their way.
joys and last - ing trea - sures none but Zi - on's chil - dren know.

507   The Son of God, through His Spirit

The Son of God, through his Spir-it and Word, out of the entire hu-man race, from the be-gin-ning of the world to its end,
gath-ers, pro-tects, and pre-serves for him-self a com-mu-ni-ty
cho-sen for e-ter-nal life and u-nit-ed in
true faith. Of this com-mu-ni-ty I

Text: Zacharius Ursinus and Caspar Olevianus, 1563; Heidelberg Catechism, Lord's Day 21;
tr. Christian Reformed Church, 1975
Tune: Emily R. Brink, 1977
Text and music © 1987, CRC Publications

PM
HEIDELBERG 54

am and al - ways will be a liv - ing mem - ber.

Jesus, with Your Church Abide   508

1 Je - sus, with your church a - bide; be our
2 May we guide the poor and blind, seek the
3 May our lamp of truth be bright; may we
4 Par - don us for work un - done, par - don
5 May we ho - ly tri - umphs win, o - ver -

Sav - ior, Lord, and Guide, while on earth our
lost un - til we find and the bro - ken -
bear a - loft its light through the realms of
us for fields un - won, bless the work we
throw the hosts of sin, gath - er all the

faith is tried:
heart - ed bind:
sin - ful night: Lord, our Sav - ior, hear us.
have be - gun:
na - tions in:

Text: Thomas Benson Pollock, 1871, alt.
Tune: John H. Gower, 1891

777 6
GOWER'S LITANY

509   Your Hand, O God, Has Guided

1 Your hand, O God, has guid - ed your flock from age to age;
2 Your her-alds brought the gos - pel to great - est and to least;
3 Your mer - cy will not fail us nor leave your work un - done;

your faith - ful - ness is writ - ten on his - tory's o - pen page.
they sum-moned men and wom - en to share the great King's feast.
with your right hand to help us the vic - tory shall be won.

Our par - ents knew your good - ness, and we their
And this was all their teach - ing in ev - ery
And then by earth and heav - en your name shall

deeds re - cord; and both to this bear wit - ness:
deed and word, to all a - like pro - claim - ing:
be a - dored; and this shall be our an - them:

Text: Edward H. Plumptre, 1864, alt.
Tune: Basil Harwood, 1898. By permission of the executors of the late Dr. Basil Harwood.
Alternative tune: LANCASHIRE, 555

76 76 D
THORNBURY

Refrain

one church, one faith, one Lord!

one faith, one Lord!

Organ

I Love Your Church, O Lord 510

1 I love your church, O Lord! Her saints be - fore you stand,
2 Be - yond my high - est joy I prize her heav - enly ways,
3 I love your church, O God, the peo - ple you have called,

dear as the ap - ple of your eye, and grav - en on your hand.
her sweet com · mu-nion, sol - emn vows, her hymns of love and praise.
the church our blest Re - deem - er saved with his own pre-cious blood.

Text: Timothy Dwight, 1800, alt.
Tune: Aaron Williams, 1770

SM
ST. THOMAS

511 These Are the Facts As We Have Received Them

1 These are the facts as we have re - ceived them, these are the
2 These are the facts as we have re - ceived them: Christ has ful -
3 These are the facts as we have re - ceived them: we, with our
4 These are the facts as we have re - ceived them: we shall be
5 These are the facts as we have re - ceived them, these are the

truths that the Chris - tian be-lieves, this is the ba - sis of
filled what the Scrip - tures fore-told, Ad - am's whole fam - ily in
▸ Sav - ior, have died on the cross; now, hav - ing ris - en, our
changed in the blink of an eye, trum - pets shall sound as we
truths that the Chris - tian be-lieves, this is the ba - sis of

all of our preach-ing: Christ died for sin-ners and rose from the tomb.
death had been sleep - ing, Christ through his ris - ing re - stores us to life.
▸ Je - sus lives in us, gives us his Spir - it and makes us his home.
face life im - mor - tal; this is the vic-tory through Je - sus our Lord.
all of our preach-ing: Christ died for sin-ners and rose from the tomb.

Text: Michael Saward, 1971; based on 1 Corinthians 15
Tune: Norman L. Warren, 1969
Text and music © 1973, Hope Publishing Co. All rights reserved. Used by permission.

10 10 11 10
YVONNE

When in Our Music God Is Glorified 512

Unison

1 When in our mu - sic God is glo - ri - fied, and
2 How of - ten, mak - ing mu - sic, we have found a
3 So has the church, in lit - ur - gy and song, in
4 And did not Je - sus sing a psalm that night when
5 Let ev - ery in - stru-ment be tuned for praise! Let

ad - o - ra - tion leaves no room for pride, it is as
new di - men - sion in the world of sound, as wor - ship
faith and love, through cen - tu - ries of wrong, borne wit - ness
ut - most e - vil strove a - gainst the Light? Then let us
all re - joice who have a voice to raise! And may God

though the whole cre - a - tion cried, "Al - le - lu - ia!"
moved us to a more pro - found al - le - lu - ia!
to the truth in ev - ery tongue: al - le - lu - ia!
sing, for whom he won the fight: al - le - lu - ia!
give us faith to sing al - ways, "Al - le - lu - ia!"

Accompaniment for final stanza

Text: Fred Pratt Green, 1971. © 1972, Hope Publishing Co. All rights reserved. Used by permission.
Tune: Charles V. Stanford, 1904

10 10 10 4
ENGELBERG

513   Christian Hearts in Love United

1 Chris - tian hearts in love u - nit - ed: search to know God's ho - ly will.
2 Grant, Lord, that with your di - rec - tion "Love each oth - er" we com-ply.
3 Come, then, liv - ing church of Je - sus, cov - e - nant with him a - new.

Let his love, in us ig - nit - ed, more and more your spir - its fill.
Help us live in true af - fec - tion, your love to ex - em-pli - fy.
Un - to him who con-quered for us may we pledge our ser-vice true.

Christ the head, and we his mem-bers— we re - flect the light he is.
Let our mu - tual love be glow - ing bright-ly so that all may view
May our lives re - flect the bright-ness of God's love in Je - sus shown.

Christ the mas - ter, we dis - ci - ples— he is ours and we are his.
that we, as on one stem grow-ing, liv - ing branch-es are in you.
To the world we then bear wit - ness: we be - long to God a - lone.

Text: Nicolaus L. von Zinzendorf, 1723; tr. composite
Tune: Moravian chorale book manuscript, Herrnhut, 1735
Another harmonization in a lower key: 443

87 87 D
O DU LIEBE MEINER LIEBE

How Good and Pleasant Is the Sight 514

1 How good and pleas-ant is the sight when Chris-tians
2 Such love in peace and joy dis - tills, as if from

make it their de - light to live in blest ac - cord;
heights of Her-mon's hills re - fresh-ing dew de - scends.

such love is like a - noint-ing oil that con - se -
The Lord com-mands his bless-ing there, and they that

crates for ho - ly toil the ser - vants of the Lord.
walk in love shall share in life that nev - er ends.

Text: Psalm 133; vers. Psalter, 1912, alt.
Tune: Charles H. Gabriel, 1856–1932

886 D
PRESSLY

515 Lift Your Heart to the Lord

Refrain

Lift your heart to the Lord and make this a day of re - joic - ing.

God is our strength and song: glo - ry and praise to his name!

1 Here God's life - giv - ing word once more is pro-claimed to his peo - ple,

Repeat refrain

up - lift - ing those who are down, chal - leng-ing all with its truth.

Text: John E. Bowers, 1982, alt., ©
Tune: Ralph Vaughan Williams, 1906. By permission of Oxford University Press.

irregular
SALVE FESTA DIES

2 All those bap - tized in - to Christ share the glo - ry of
3 Sum-moned by Je - sus' com - mand, all his peo - ple draw

his res - ur - rec - tion, dy - ing with him un - to
near to his ta - ble, glad - ly to meet with their

Repeat refrain

sin, walk - ing in new - ness of life.
Lord, known in the break - ing of bread.

516 God Is Here

1 God is here! As we your peo - ple meet to of - fer
2 Here are sym - bols to re - mind us of our life - long
3 Here our chil - dren find a wel - come in the Shep - herd's
4 Lord of all, of church and king - dom, in an age of

praise and prayer, may we find in full - er mea - sure what it
need of grace; here are ta - ble, font, and pul - pit, here the
flock and fold; here, as bread and wine are tak - en, Christ sus -
change and doubt, keep us faith - ful to the gos - pel, help us

is in Christ we share. Here, as in the world a - round us,
Word has cen - tral place. Here in hon - es - ty of preach-ing,
tains us as of old. Here the ser - vants of the Ser - vant
work your pur - pose out. Here, in this day's cel - e - bra - tion,

Text: Fred Pratt Green, 1977. © 1979, Hope Publishing Co. All rights reserved. Used by permission.
Tune: Peter Janson, 1982, ©

87 87 D
ST. JOHN'S QUADRA

all   our   var - ied   skills and   arts   wait   the   com - ing
here   in   si - lence   as   in   speech,   here   in   new - ness
seek   in   wor - ship   to   ex - plore   what   it   means   in
all   we   have   to   give, re - ceive;   we   who   can - not

of   your Spir - it   in - to o - pen   minds   and   hearts.
and   re - new - al   God   the Spir - it comes   to   each.
dai - ly liv - ing   to   be-lieve and   to   a - dore.
live   with - out you,   we   a - dore you!   We   be - lieve!

There's No God as Great
No Hay Dios tan Grande

There's no god as great as you, O Lord, O___ Lord, my___
No hay dios tan gran-de co-mo tú, no lo hay, no lo

God. There's no god as great as you, O Lord, O___ Lord, my___
hay. No hay dios tan gran-de co-mo tú, no lo hay, no lo

God. There's no god who works the might-y won-ders, all the
hay. No hay dios que pue-da_ha-cer las o-bras co-mo

won-ders that you do. There's no god who works the might-y
las que ha-ces tú. No hay dios que pue-da_ha-cer las

won-ders, all the won-ders that you do. Not by our
o-bras co-mo las que ha-ces tú. No_es con es-

Text and Tune: Spanish; tr. Psalter Hymnal, 1987

irregular
NO HAY DIOS

weap - ons, nor by our pow - er, but by your Spir - it we are
pa - da, ni con e - jér - ci - to, mas con tu San-to Es-pí - ri -

led. Not by our weap - ons, nor by our pow - er, but by your
tu. No es con es - pa - da, ni con e - jér - ci - to, mas con tu

Spir - it we are led. The Ho - ly Spir - it will move the
San - to Es - pí - ri - tu. Y es - ta i - gle - sia se mo - ve -

church, the Ho - ly Spir - it will move the church, the Ho - ly
rá, y es - ta i - gle - sia se mo - ve - rá, y es - ta i -

Spir - it will move the church, for by your Spir - it___ we are led.
gle - sia se mo - ve - rá con tu San - to Es-pí - ri - tu.

518   In God the Father I Believe

1 In God the Fa - ther I be - lieve, al - might - y Lord of
2 who suf - fered when he stood con-demned by Pon - tius Pi - late's
3 As - cend - ing in - to heaven a - bove, he sits at God's right
4 I do be - lieve that all the saints must now com - mune in

all, who made the heav - ens and the earth: his
code; was cru - ci - fied, was dead, as he him -
hand; from there he shall re - turn to judge the
love, and that, re - deemed by Je - sus' blood, our

name be praised in awe. And I be - lieve in Je - sus Christ,
self had long fore - told. Our Lord was bur - ied in a tomb,
liv - ing and the dead. In God the Spir - it I be - lieve,
sins are par - doned us. And at life's end my bod - y frail,

Text: Apostles' Creed; vers. Frank De Vries, 1975
Tune: Frank De Vries, 1975; harm. Bert Polman, 1975
Text and music © 1975, CRC Publications

86 86 D
CREEDAL SONG

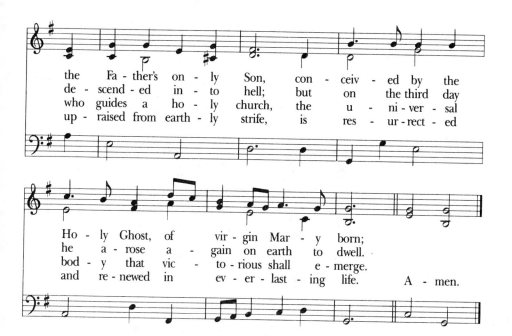

the Fa - ther's on - ly Son, con - ceiv - ed by the
de - scend - ed in - to hell; but on the third day
who guides a ho - ly church, the u - ni - ver - sal
up - raised from earth - ly strife, is res - ur - rect - ed

Ho - ly Ghost, of vir - gin Mar - y born;
he a - rose a - gain on earth to dwell.
bod - y that vic - to - rious shall e - merge.
and re - newed in ev - er - last - ing life. A - men.

519   Apostles' Creed

I be-lieve in God the Fa - ther al - might-y, Mak - er of heaven and earth.

And in Je - sus Christ, his on - ly be-got-ten Son, our Lord; who was con-

ceived by the Ho - ly Spir - it, born of the vir - gin Mar - y;

suf - fered un-der Pon-tius Pi - late; was cru - ci - fied, dead, and bur - ied;

he de-scend-ed in - to hell; the third day he rose a - gain

from the dead; he as-cend-ed in - to heav - en, and is seat - ed at the

Text: Apostles' Creed
Tune: 17th cent.; arr. M. Schouten, b. 1929; harm. John Hamersma, 1974.
Harmonization © 1974, CRC Publications

PM
SCHOUTEN

520

Nicene Creed

I be-lieve in one God, the Fa-ther al-might-y, Mak-er of heav-en and earth, and of all things vis-i-ble and in-vis-i-ble. And in one Lord Je-sus Christ, the on-ly be-got-ten Son of God, be-got-ten of the Fa-ther be-fore all worlds; God of God, Light of Light, ver-y God of ver-y

Text: Nicene Creed, 4th cent.
Tune: Herbert G. Draesel, Jr., 1964; arr. Verlyn Schultz, 1985. © 1964, Edward B. Marks Music Corp.
International copyright secured. All rights reserved. Used by permission.

PM
DRAESEL

spoke   by   the proph-ets.   And   I   be-lieve one ho - ly   cath - olic,

ap - os-tol - ic church.   I   ac-knowl-edge one   bap - tism   for the for -

give-ness of sins;   and I   look   for the   res - ur - rec - tion

of   the dead,   and the   life   of   the   world   to

come.   A   -   men.

521   God of the Prophets

Descant

5 Make us a - pos - tles, her - alds of your cross; forth may we

1 God of the proph - ets, bless the proph - ets' heirs!
2 A - noint us proph - ets! Teach us your in - tent:
3 A - noint us priests! Help us to in - ter - cede
4 A - noint us kings! Help us do jus - tice, Lord!
5 Make us a - pos - tles, her - alds of your cross;

go_____ to tell all realms your grace: by

E - li - jah's man - tle o'er E - li - sha cast:
to hu - man need, our quick - ened hearts a - wake;
▸ with all your roy - al priest - hood born of grace;
A - noint us with the Spir - it of your Son:
forth may we go to tell all realms your grace:

Text: st. 1–2, 4–5, Denis Wortman, 1884, alt.; st. 3, Carl P. Daw, Jr., 1981, alt., ©
Tune: Genevan Psalter, 1551; adapt. from GENEVAN 124; desc. Emily R. Brink, 1986.
Descant © 1987, CRC Publications

10 10 10 10
TOULON

you in - spired, may we count all but loss, and stand at

each age for your own sol - emn task pre - pares;
fill us with power, our lips make el - o - quent
▸ through us your church pre - sents in word and deed
ours not a mon - arch's crown or ty - rant's sword;
by you in - spired, may we count all but loss,

last with joy be - fore your face.

make each one stron - ger, no - bler than the last.
for right - eous - ness that shall all e - vil break.
▸ a liv - ing sac - ri - fice with thanks and praise.
ours by the love of Christ a king - dom won.
and stand at last with joy be - fore your face.

522 Onward, Christian Soldiers

1 On - ward, Chris - tian sol - diers, march - ing as to war,
2 Like a might - y ar - my moves the church of God;
3 Crowns and thrones may per - ish, king - doms rise and wane,
4 On - ward, then, O peo - ple, join our hap - py throng:

with the cross of Je - sus go - ing on be - fore.
let us bold - ly fol - low where the saints have trod.
but the church of Je - sus con - stant will re - main;
blend with ours your voic - es in the tri - umph song.

Christ, the roy - al mas - ter, leads a - gainst the foe;
We are not di - vid - ed; all one bod - y we—
gates of hell can nev - er 'gainst that church pre - vail.
Glo - ry, laud, and hon - or un - to Christ the King,

Text: Sabine Baring-Gould, 1865, alt.
Tune: Arthur S. Sullivan, 1871

65 65 D with refrain
ST. GERTRUDE

for - ward in - to bat - tle see his ban - ners go!
one in hope and doc - trine, one in char - i - ty.
We have Christ's own prom - ise, and that can - not fail.
we through count - less a - ges with the an - gels sing.

Refrain

On - ward, Chris - tian sol - diers, march - ing as to war,

with the cross of Je - sus go - ing on be - fore.

523 Lord, You Give the Great Commission

1 Lord, you give the great com - mis-sion: "Heal the sick and
2 Lord, you call us to your ser - vice: "In my name bap-
3 Lord, you make the com - mon ho - ly: "This my bod - y,
4 Lord, you show us love's true mea-sure: "Fa - ther, what they
5 Lord, you bless with words as - sur-ing: "I am with you

preach the Word." Lest the church ne - glect its mis - sion
tize and teach." That the world may trust your prom-ise—
▸ this my blood." Let us all, for earth's true glo - ry,
do, for - give." Yet we hoard as pri - vate trea-sure
to the end." Faith and hope and love re - stor - ing,

and the gos - pel go un - heard, help us wit - ness
life a - bun - dant meant for each— give us all new
▸ dai - ly lift life heav - en - ward, ask - ing that the
all that you so free - ly give. May your care and
may we serve as you in - tend, and, a - mid the

Text: Jeffery Rowthorn, 1978, ©
Tune: Cyril V. Taylor, 1941. © 1942, 1970, Hope Publishing Co. All rights reserved. Used by permission.

87 87 D
ABBOT'S LEIGH

to   your pur-pose   with   re - newed   in - teg - ri - ty;
fer - vor, draw us   clos - er   in   com - mu - ni - ty;
► world   a - round us   share   your   chil - dren's lib - er - ty;
mer - cy   lead us   to   a   just   so - ci - et - y;
cares   that claim us,   hold   in   mind   e - ter - ni - ty;

Refrain

with the Spir - it's   gifts   em-power us   for   the   work of   min - is - try.

524   Hope of the World

1 Hope of the world, O Christ of great com - pas - sion:
2 Hope of the world, God's gift from high - est heav - en,
3 Hope of the world, a - foot on dust - y high - ways,
4 Hope of the world, who by your cross did save us
5 Hope of the world, O Christ, o'er death vic - to - rious,

speak to our fear - ful hearts by con - flict rent.
bring - ing to hun - gry souls the bread of life:
show - ing to wan - dering souls the path of light:
from death and dark de - spair, from sin and guilt:
who by this sign did con - quer grief and pain:

Save us, your peo - ple, from con - sum - ing pas - sion,
still let your Spir - it un - to us be giv - en
walk now be - side us lest the tempt - ing by - ways
we ren - der back the love your mer - cy gave us;
we would be faith - ful to your gos - pel glo - rious;

who by our own false hopes and aims are spent.
to heal earth's wounds and end our bit - ter strife.
lure us a - way from you to end - less night.
take now our lives and use them as you will.
you are our Lord, and you for - ev - er reign!

Text: Georgia Harkness, 1954, alt. © 1954, 1982, The Hymn Society of America. Used by permission.
Tune: V. Earle Copes, 1963. © 1963, Abingdon Press. Used by permission.
Alternative tune: GENEVAN 12, 12

11 10 11 10
VICAR

O Christians, Haste

525

1 O Chris-tians, haste, your mis-sion high ful - fill - ing, to tell to
2 Pro- claim to ev - ery peo - ple, tongue, and na - tion that God, in
3 Send her - alds forth to bear the mes - sage glo-rious; give of your

all the world that God is light, that he who made all na - tions
whom they live and move, is love; tell how he stooped to save his
wealth to speed them on their way; pour out your soul for them in

is not will - ing one life should per - ish, lost in shades of night.
lost cre - a - tion, and died on earth that we might live in love.
prayer vic - to - rious, till God shall bring his king-dom's joy - ful Day.

Refrain

Pub - lish glad tid - ings, tid - ings of peace,

tid - ings of Je - sus, re - demp - tion, and re - lease.

Text: Mary A. Thomson, 1868, alt.
Tune: James Walch, 1875

11 10 11 10 with refrain
TIDINGS

526 Come, Labor On

1 Come, la - bor on. Who dares stand i - dle
2 Come, la - bor on. The en - e - my is
3 Come, la - bor on. A - way with gloom - y
4 Come, la - bor on. Claim the high call - ing
5 Come, la - bor on. No time for rest, till

on the har - vest plain while all a - round us
watch - ing night and day, to sow the tares, to
doubts and faith - less fear! No arm so weak but
an - gels can - not share: to young and old the
glows the west - ern sky, till the long shad - ows

Text: Jane L. Borthwick, 1859, 1863
Tune: T. Tertius Noble, 1918. © 1918, 1946, H. W. Gray Co. Used by permission of Belwin Mills Publishing Corp.
All rights reserved.

4 10 10 10 4
ORA LABORA

waves the gold - en grain?
snatch the seed a - way;
► may do ser - vice here:
gos - pel glad - ness bear.
o'er our path - way lie

And to each ser - vant
while we in sleep our
by fee - blest a - gents
Re - deem the time— its
and a glad sound comes

does the Mas - ter say, "Go work to - day."
du - ty have for - got, he slum - bers not.
► may our God ful - fill his right - eous will.
hours so swift - ly fly— the night draws nigh.
with the set - ting sun:___ "Ser - vants, well done."

527   Come, You Thankful People, Come

1 Come, you thank-ful peo - ple, come, raise the song of har-vest home;
2 All the world is God's own field, fruit un - to his praise to yield;
3 For the Lord our God shall come and shall take his har-vest home;
4 E - ven so, Lord, quick-ly come to your fi - nal har-vest home;

all is safe-ly gath - ered in ere the win-ter storms be - gin;
wheat and weeds to - geth - er sown, un - to joy or sor - row grown:
he him - self in that great day all of - fense shall take a - way,
gath - er all your peo - ple in, free from sor - row, free from sin—

Descant

4 there, for - ev - er pu - ri - fied, in your pres - ence

God, our Mak - er, does pro - vide for our needs to
first the blade and then the ear, then the full corn
give his an - gels charge at last in the fire the
there, for - ev - er pu - ri - fied, in your pres - ence

Text: Henry Alford, 1844, alt.
Tune: George J. Elvey, 1858; desc. C. S. Lang, 1953. Descant © 1953, Novello & Company, Ltd.

77 77 D
ST. GEORGE'S WINDSOR

to a - bide; come, with all your an - gels

be sup - plied; come, with all his peo - ple
shall ap - pear; Lord of har - vest, grant that
weeds to cast, but the fruit - ful ears to
to a - bide; come, with all your an - gels

come, raise the glo - rious har - vest home.

come, raise the song of har - vest home.
we whole - some grain and pure may be.
store in his gar - ner ev - er - more.
come, raise the glo - rious har - vest home.

528   Lord, Speak to Me That I May Speak

1 Lord, speak to me that I may speak in liv - ing
2 O lead me, Lord, that I may lead the wan - dering
3 O teach me, Lord, that I may teach the pre - cious
4 O use me, Lord, use e - ven me, just as you

ech - oes of your tone. As you have sought, so
and the wa - vering feet. O feed me, Lord, that
truths which you im - part. And wing my words that
will, and when, and where un - til your bless - ed

let me seek your err - ing chil - dren lost and lone.
I may feed your hun - gry ones with man - na sweet.
they may reach the hid - den depths of man - y a heart.
face I see, your rest, your joy, your glo - ry share.

Text: Frances R. Havergal, 1872, alt.
Tune: Robert A. Schumann, 1839, from Nachtstücke, *Op. 23, No. 4*

LM
CANONBURY

Speak Forth Your Word, O Father

529

1 Speak forth your word, O Fa - ther, your faith - ful peo - ple plead;
2 The se - crets of the at - om, the u - ni-verse of light,
3 In ev - ery hu - man lan - guage, to ev - ery hu-man home,
4 How shall they hear your mes - sage if there are none to preach?

the na - tions starve and per - ish and can - not name their need;
all won - ders of cre - a - tion pro - claim your bound-less might;
by man - y paths and chan - nels the faith of Christ may come:
Shall peo - ple learn your gos - pel if there are none to teach?

O Lord, you have so made us that not a - lone by bread,
but on - ly through the wit - ness of Scrip - ture's word passed on
the print - ed word on pa - per, the wave that spans the air,
Take us, then, Lord, and use us to tell what we have heard,

but by your word of com - fort our hun - ger must be fed.
do you re - veal in full - ness the gos - pel of your Son.
the screen, the stage, the pic - ture— may all your truth de - clare.
and all the man - y mil - lions shall feed up - on your Word.

Text: Charles Jeffries, 1967, alt. © 1967, Feed the Minds
Tune: Irish; harm. William France, 1971, ©

76 76 D
DURROW

530   I Love to Tell the Story

1 I love to tell the story of unseen things above, of Jesus and his glory, of Jesus and his love. I love to tell the story because I know 'tis true;

2 I love to tell the story; 'tis pleasant to repeat what seems, each time I tell it, more wonderfully sweet. I love to tell the story, for some have never heard

3 I love to tell the story, for those who know it best seem hungering and thirsting to hear it, like the rest. And when, in scenes of glory, I sing the new, new

Text: A. Catherine Hankey, 1866
Tune: William G. Fischer, 1869

76 76 D with refrain
HANKEY

true; it sat - is - fies my long-ings as noth - ing else can do.
heard the mes - sage of sal - va - tion from God's own ho - ly Word.
song, 'twill be the old, old sto - ry that I have loved so long.

Refrain

I love to tell the sto - ry; 'twill be my theme in glo - ry

to tell the old, old sto - ry of Je - sus and his love.

531 How Shall They Hear the Word of God

1 How shall they hear the word of God un - less his
2 How shall they call to God for help un - less they
3 How shall the gos - pel be pro - claimed that sin - ners

truth is told? How shall the sin - ful be set free,
have be - lieved? How shall the poor be giv - en hope,
may re - pent? How shall the world find peace at last

the sor - row - ful con - soled? To all who speak the
the pris - on - er re - prieved? To those who help the
if her - alds are not sent? So send us, Lord, for

truth to - day, im - part your Spir - it, Lord, we pray.
blind to see, give light and love and clar - i - ty.
we re - joice to speak of Christ with life and voice.

Text: Michael A. Perry, 1980; based on Romans 10:14–17.
© 1982, Hope Publishing Co. All rights reserved. Used by permission.
Tune: Evangelisches Gesangbuch, Hirschberg, 1741

86 86 88
O JESU

We Have Told the Blessed Tidings

1 We have told the bless - ed tid - ings to a dark and
2 With your bless - ing still ig - nite us, burn our lips that
3 Time and skills are ours; Lord, use them toward the great com -

trou - bled world. From the poles to the e - qua - tor Christ's own
we may speak, wit - ness - ing to friends and fam - ily, neigh-bors,
mis - sion's goals. Pour your Spir - it out up - on us in com -

ban - ner is un - furled. With the bless - ing of the
strang-ers, all we meet; al - ways dil - i - gent in
pas - sion for lost souls. May we use our gifts and

Spir - it and the pen - te - cos - tal flame, those who
ser - vice, spread - ing Je - sus' love a - broad; with the
tal - ents nev - er for our-selves a - lone; make us

else would death in - her - it now sing prais - es to God's name.
Ho - ly Spir - it's pow - er, gath-ering all the church of God.
ser - vants, work - ing al - ways, on - ly that your name be known.

Text: Marie J. Post, 1973, alt. © 1974, CRC Publications
Tune: C. Hubert H. Parry, 1897

87 87 D
RUSTINGTON

533   Church of God, Elect and Glorious

1 Church of God, e - lect and glo - rious, ho - ly na - tion,
2 God has called you out of dark - ness in - to his most
3 Once you were an a - lien peo - ple, strang - ers to God's
4 Church of God, e - lect and ho - ly, be the peo - ple

cho - sen race, called as God's own spe - cial peo - ple,
mar - velous light, brought his truth to life with - in you,
heart of love, but he brought you home in mer - cy,
he in - tends, strong in faith and swift to an - swer

roy - al priests and heirs of grace: know the pur - pose
turned your blind - ness in - to sight. Let your light so
cit - i - zens of heaven a - bove. Let his love flow
each com - mand your Mas - ter sends; roy - al priests, ful -

of your call - ing, show to all his might - y deeds; tell of
shine a - round you that God's name is glo - ri - fied, and all
out to oth - ers, let them feel the Fa - ther's care, that they
fill your call - ing through your sac - ri - fice and prayer, give your

Text: James E. Seddon, 1982; based on 1 Peter 2:9–12
Tune: Cyril V. Taylor, 1951
Text and music © 1982, Hope Publishing Co. All rights reserved. Used by permission.

87 87 D
MEAD HOUSE

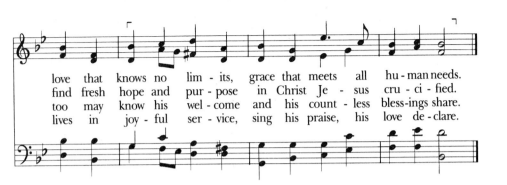

love that knows no lim - its, grace that meets all hu - man needs.
find fresh hope and pur - pose in Christ Je - sus cru - ci - fied.
too may know his wel - come and his count - less bless-ings share.
lives in joy - ful ser - vice, sing his praise, his love de - clare.

Come, You Sinners, Poor and Needy 534

1 Come, you sin - ners, poor and need - y, weak and
2 Let not con - science make you lin - ger, nor of
3 Come, you wea - ry, heav - y lad - en, lost and
4 Come, a - rise, and go to Je - sus, he will

wound - ed, sick and sore; Je - sus read - y
fit - ness fond - ly dream; all that he re -
ru - ined by the fall; if you tar - ry
take you in his arms; in the love of

stands to save you, full of pit - y, love, and power.
quires as fit - ness is to know your need of him.
till you're bet - ter, you will nev - er come at all.
your dear Sav - ior you are safe from all a - larms.

Text: Joseph Hart, 1759, alt.
Tune: W. Walker's Southern Harmony, 1835

.87 87
ARISE

535 Come to the Savior Now

1 Come to the Sav - ior now, he gent - ly calls to you;
2 Come to the Sav - ior now, all who have wan-dered far;
3 Come to the Sav - ior now, he of - fers all to you,
4 Come to the Sav - ior, all, what - e'er your bur - dens be;

in true re - pen - tance bow, let him your heart re - new.
re - new your sol - emn vow, for his by right you are;
and on his mer - its you can plead for life a - new.
hear now his lov - ing call, "Cast all your care on me."

Christ came that you may know sal - va - tion, peace and love,
come like poor, wan - dering sheep re - turn - ing to his fold;
No vain ex - cus - es frame, re - spond to Christ to - day!
Come, and for ev - ery grief, in Je - sus you will find

true joy on earth be - low, a home in heaven a - bove.
his arm will safe - ly keep, his love will ne'er grow cold.
None who to Je - sus came were ev - er sent a - way.
a sure and safe re - lief, a lov - ing friend and kind.

Text: John M. Wigner, 1871, alt.
Tune: Frederick C. Maker, 1895

66 66 D
INVITATION

Lord Jesus Is Calling to All Who Will Hear   536

1 Lord Je - sus is call - ing to all who will hear;
2 The gift of the Spir - it he wants you to own;
3 Our Sav - ior has suf - fered and gone to the cross.

to all who are thirst - y he's say - ing, "Come near;
re - freshed in your spir - it with Je - sus a - lone,
He car - ried our sor - rows and made up our loss.

I'll give you fresh wa - ter so cool and so clear.
that filled to the brim, you will soon o - ver - flow
And now he is say - ing, "You nev - er need fear!

Drink deep - ly, my peo - ple, and be of good cheer."
to oth - ers still thirst - y, so Je - sus they'll know.
Be filled with my Spir - it and be of good cheer."

Text: Vernon Luchies, 1974. © 1974, CRC Publications
Tune: Hilary P. Chadwyck-Healey, 1971. © 1971, Royal School of Church Music
Alternative tune: ST. DENIO, 144

11 11 11 11
RADWELL

537   Awake, All Who Sleep

1 A - wake, all who sleep, and a - rise from the dead,
2 A - wake, do not wait, you who sleep in your sins.
3 A - wake from the dead, O poor sin - ner, a - wake.
4 How hap - py God's peo - ple! They walk in the light,

and Christ shall be - come your new dawn - ing.
The dark - ness has van - ished al - read - y.
Let Je - sus re - move sin and er - ror.
in Christ's res - ur - rec - tion their be - ing.

God's Son and your King— not in judg - ment and dread—
The light of God's grace, which for you now be - gins,
A - wake from the dead, O poor sin - ner, and quake
No mat - ter how of - ten their day turns to night,

Text: Petro Parson, 1857; tr. Stanley M. Wiersma, 1982. © 1987, CRC Publications
Tune: Johannes G. Bastiaans, 1868

11 9 11 9 11 11
ONTWAAK

as   Sav - ior   wakes you   to   his   morn   -   ing.
through a - ges   has   kept the   world stead   -   y.
lest   Je - sus   as   Judge in - voke   ter   -   ror.
no   dark - ness can   keep them from   see   -   ing.

A - wake   and   a - rise,   for   the   dan - ger is   great:
Your call - ing is   no - ble, your du - ties are vast;
The   Sav - ior   com - pels you: a - wake and de - cide;
A - wake, you   who   sleep, and   a - rise from the dead;

choose Christ as   your life   or choose death as   your fate.
a - wake, you   who   sleep, or   your time will be   past.
a - wake   and   be - lieve or   be   ev - er   de - nied.
Christ calls as   your Sav - ior, your Lord, and   your Head!

538 Come, You Disconsolate

1 Come, you dis-con-so-late, wher-e'er you lan-guish;
2 Joy of the des-o-late, light of the stray-ing,
3 Here see the bread of life; see wa-ters flow-ing

come to the mer-cy seat, fer-vent-ly kneel.
hope of the pen-i-tent, fade-less and pure!
forth from the throne of God, pure from a-bove.

Here bring your wound-ed hearts, here tell your an-guish;
Here speaks the Com-fort-er, in mer-cy say-ing,
Come to the feast pre-pared; come, ev-er know-ing

earth has no sor-rows that heaven can-not heal.
"Earth has no sor-rows that heaven can-not cure."
earth has no sor-rows but heaven can re-move.

Text: st. 1–2, Thomas Moore, 1824; st. 1–2 rev. and st. 3, Thomas Hastings, 1831
Tune: arr. from Samuel Webbe, 1792

11 10 11 10
CONSOLATION

Shout, for the Blessed Jesus Reigns

539

1 Shout, for the bless - ed Je - sus reigns; through dis - tant
2 He calls his cho - sen from a - far; they all at
3 Gen - tiles and Jews his laws o - bey. All lands and
4 Oh, may his ho - ly church in - crease, his Word and
5 Loud hal - le - lu - jahs to the Lamb from all be -

lands his tri - umphs spread. And sin - ners, freed from
Zi - on's gates ar - rive. Those who were dead in
na - tions of - ferings bring and, un - con - strained, their
Spir - it still pre - vail, while an - gels cel - e -
low and all a - bove! In loft - y songs ex -

end - less pains, own him their Sav - ior and their Head.
sin be - fore by sov - ereign grace are made a - live.
hom - age pay to their ex - alt - ed God and King.
brate his praise and saints his grow - ing glo - ries hail.
alt his name, in songs as last - ing as his love.

Text: Benjamin Beddome, 1769
Tune: T. Williams' Psalmodia Evangelica, 1789

LM
TRURO

540 In Christ There Is No East or West

1 In Christ there is no east or west, in
2 For God in Christ has made us one from
3 It is by grace we are as - sured that
4 So, broth - ers, sis - ters, praise his name who
5 In Christ there is no east or west— he

him no pride of birth; the cho - sen fam - ily
ev - ery land and race; he rec - on - ciled us
▸ we be - long to him; the love we share in
died to set us free from sin, di - vi - sion,
breaks all bar - riers down; by Christ re - deemed, by

God has blessed now spans the whole wide earth.
through his Son and met us with his grace.
▸ Christ our Lord, the Spir - it works with - in.
hate, and shame, from spite and en - mi - ty.
Christ pos - sessed, in Christ we live as one.

Text: Michael A. Perry, 1982; after a line by John Oxenham, 1905. © 1982, Hope Publishing Co.
All rights reserved. Used by permission.
Tune: Afro-American spiritual; adapt. and harm. Harry T. Burleigh, 1939

CM
MC KEE

Christ Shall Have Dominion

541

1 Christ shall have do - min - ion o - ver land and sea;
2 When the need - y seek him, he will mer - cy show;
3 Ev - er and for - ev - er shall his name en - dure;
4 Un - to God Al - might - y joy - ful Zi - on sings;

earth's re - mot - est re - gions shall his em - pire be.
all the weak and help - less shall his pit - y know.
long as suns con - tin - ue it shall stand se - cure.
he a - lone is glo - rious, do - ing won-drous things.

They that wilds in - hab - it shall their wor - ship bring;
He will sure - ly save them from op - pres - sion's might,
And in him for - ev - er na - tions shall be blest,
Ev - er - more, O peo - ple, bless his glo - rious name,

kings shall bring their trib - ute, na - tions serve our King.
for their lives are pre - cious in his ho - ly sight.
and all peo - ples hail him King of kings con - fessed.
his e - ter - nal glo - ry through the earth pro - claim.

Text: Psalm 72:8–19; *vers.* Psalter, 1912
Tune: Albert Piersma, 1933

65 65 D
KING OF GLORY

542   The Ends of All the Earth Shall Hear

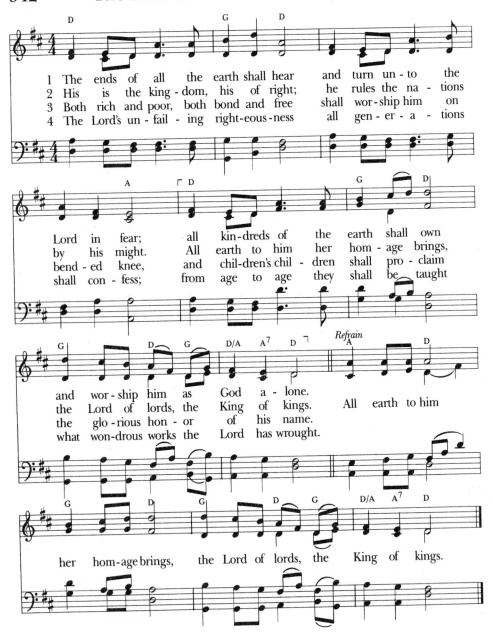

1 The ends of all the earth shall hear and turn un - to the
2 His is the king - dom, his of right; he rules the na - tions
3 Both rich and poor, both bond and free shall wor - ship him on
4 The Lord's un - fail - ing right-eous-ness all gen - er - a - tions

Lord in fear; all kin-dreds of the earth shall own
by his might. All earth to him her hom - age brings,
bend - ed knee, and chil-dren's chil - dren shall pro - claim
shall con - fess; from age to age they shall be taught

and wor - ship him as God a - lone.
the Lord of lords, the King of kings. All earth to him
the glo - rious hon - or of his name.
what won-drous works the Lord has wrought.

her hom-age brings, the Lord of lords, the King of kings.

Text: Psalm 22:27–31; *vers.* Psalter, *1912*
Tune: William H. Doane, *1832–1915*

LM with refrain
VISION

Guide Me, O My Great Redeemer

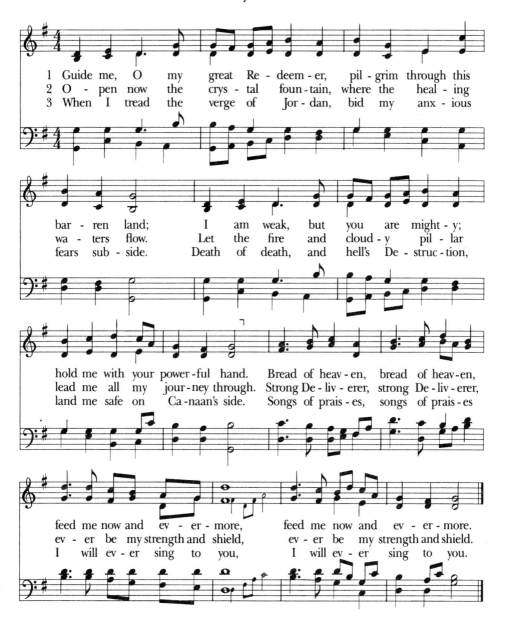

1 Guide me, O my great Re - deem - er, pil - grim through this
2 O - pen now the crys - tal foun - tain, where the heal - ing
3 When I tread the verge of Jor - dan, bid my anx - ious

bar - ren land; I am weak, but you are might - y;
wa - ters flow. Let the fire and cloud - y pil - lar
fears sub - side. Death of death, and hell's De - struc - tion,

hold me with your power - ful hand. Bread of heav - en, bread of heav - en,
lead me all my jour - ney through. Strong De - liv - erer, strong De - liv - erer,
land me safe on Ca - naan's side. Songs of prais - es, songs of prais - es

feed me now and ev - er - more, feed me now and ev - er - more.
ev - er be my strength and shield, ev - er be my strength and shield.
I will ev - er sing to you, I will ev - er sing to you.

Text: William Williams, 1745; st. 1 tr. Peter Williams, 1771, alt.; st. 2–3 tr. William Williams, 1772, alt.
Tune: John Hughes, 1907

87 87 877
CWM RHONDDA

544

Lead Me, Guide Me

Refrain

Lead me, guide me, a-long the way,

for if you lead me, I can-not stray.

Lord, let me walk each day with you,

lead me my whole life through.

irregular
LEAD ME

1 I am weak and I need your strength and power to en-
2 Help me walk in the paths of right - eous - ness; be my
3 I am lost if you take your hand from me, I am

dure with grace____ my weak - est hour. Help me
aid when Sa - tan and sin op - press. I am
blind with - out____ your light to see. Lord, for -

through the dark - ness your face to see.
trust - ing you____ what - e'er may be.
ev - er may I your ser - vant be.

Refrain

Lead me, O Lord, lead me.

545 Make Me a Channel of Your Peace

1 Make me a chan-nel of your peace. Where there is ha-tred,
2 Make me a chan-nel of your peace. Where there's de-spair in
3 Make me a chan-nel of your peace. It is in par-don-

let me bring your love;_____ where there is in-ju-ry, your par-don,
life, let me bring hope;_____ where there is dark-ness, let me bring your
ing that we are par-doned; in giv-ing to all peo-ple, we re-

Lord; and where there's doubt, true faith in you.
light; and where there's sad-ness, ev-er joy.
ceive; and in dy-ing that we're born to e-ter-nal life.

O Mas-ter, grant that I may nev-er seek so

Text: Francis of Assisi, 13th cent.
Tune: Sebastian Temple, 1967. © 1967, Franciscan Communications Center

irregular
TEMPLE

much to be con - soled as to con - sole, to be un-der-stood as to un-der - stand, to be loved as to love with all my soul.

Make Me a Captive, Lord 546

1 Make me a cap - tive, Lord, and then I shall be free;
2 I sink in life's a - larms when by my - self I stand;
3 My will is not my own till thou hast made it thine;
4 I on - ly stand un - bent a - mid the clash-ing strife

force me to ren - der up my sword, and I shall con-queror be.
im - pris - on me with - in thine arms, and strong shall be my hand.
if it would reach a mon-arch's throne, it must its crown re - sign.
when on thy bo - som I have leaned and found in thee my life.

Text: George Matheson, 1890, alt.
Tune: Samuel Howard, 1762

SM
ST. BRIDE

547 Fill Thou My Life, O Lord, My God

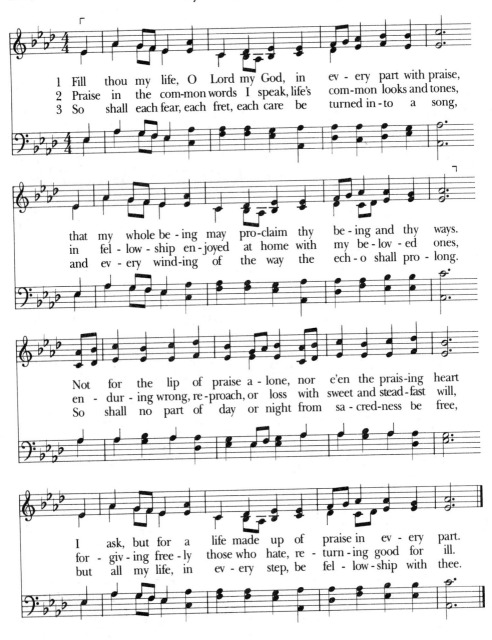

1 Fill thou my life, O Lord my God, in ev - ery part with praise,
2 Praise in the com-mon words I speak, life's com-mon looks and tones,
3 So shall each fear, each fret, each care be turned in - to a song,

that my whole be - ing may pro-claim thy be - ing and thy ways.
in fel - low - ship en - joyed at home with my be - lov - ed ones,
and ev - ery wind-ing of the way the ech - o shall pro - long.

Not for the lip of praise a - lone, nor e'en the prais-ing heart
en - dur - ing wrong, re-proach, or loss with sweet and stead-fast will,
So shall no part of day or night from sa - cred-ness be free,

I ask, but for a life made up of praise in ev - ery part.
for - giv - ing free - ly those who hate, re - turn-ing good for ill.
but all my life, in ev - ery step, be fel - low-ship with thee.

Text: Horatius Bonar, 1863, alt.
Tune: Gesangbuch, Wittenberg, 1784

CMD
ELLACOMBE

When We Walk with the Lord

548

1 When we walk with the Lord in the light of his Word,
2 But we nev-er can prove the de-lights of his love
3 Then in fel-low-ship sweet we will sit at his feet,

what a glo-ry he sheds on our way! While we do his good
un-til all on the al-tar we lay; for the fa-vor he
or we'll walk by his side in the way; what he says we will

will he a-bides with us still, and with all who will
shows and the joy he be-stows are for those who will
do, where he sends we will go— nev-er fear, on-ly

trust and o-bey. *Refrain* Trust and o-bey, for there's no oth-er

way to be hap-py in Je-sus but to trust and o-bey.

Text: John H. Sammis, 1887
Tune: Daniel B. Towner, 1887

669 D with refrain
TRUST AND OBEY

549

My Only Comfort

1 My only comfort in life and in death is
2 He fully has paid for all my sins
3 He also watches over me in

that I am not my own, but be-long— bod-y and soul, in
with his pre-cious blood, and has set me free from the
such a way that not a hair can fall from my head with-

life and in death— to my faith-ful Sav-ior Je-sus Christ.
tyr-an-ny of the dev-il.
out the will of my Fa-ther in heav-en:

4 in fact, all things must work to-geth-er for my sal-va-tion.

Text: Zacharius Ursinus and Caspar Olevianus, 1563; Heidelberg Catechism, Lord's Day 1;
tr. Christian Reformed Church, 1975
Tune: Emily R. Brink, 1975
Text and music © 1987, CRC Publications

irregular
HEIDELBERG 1

5 Be - cause I be - long to him, Christ, by his Ho - ly Spir - it,

as - sures me of e - ter - nal life and makes me whole-heart-ed-ly

will - ing and read - y from now on to live for him.

550

My Shepherd Will Supply My Need

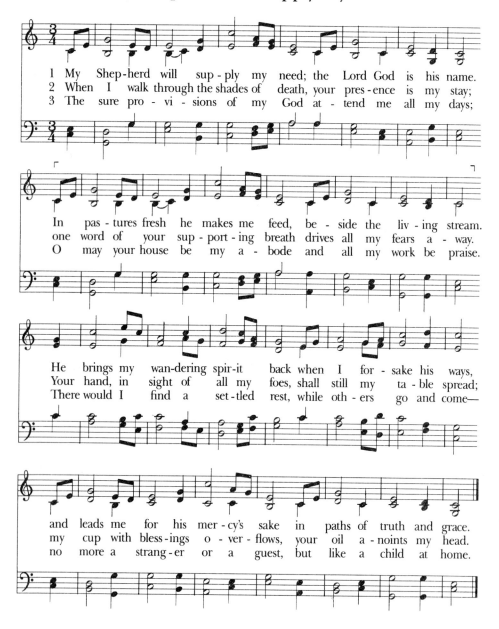

1 My Shep-herd will sup-ply my need; the Lord God is his name.
2 When I walk through the shades of death, your pres-ence is my stay;
3 The sure pro-vi-sions of my God at-tend me all my days;

In pas-tures fresh he makes me feed, be-side the liv-ing stream.
one word of your sup-port-ing breath drives all my fears a-way.
O may your house be my a-bode and all my work be praise.

He brings my wan-dering spir-it back when I for-sake his ways,
Your hand, in sight of all my foes, shall still my ta-ble spread;
There would I find a set-tled rest, while oth-ers go and come—

and leads me for his mer-cy's sake in paths of truth and grace.
my cup with bless-ings o-ver-flows, your oil a-noints my head.
no more a strang-er or a guest, but like a child at home.

Text: Isaac Watts, 1719; based on Psalm 23, alt.
Tune: W. Walker's Southern Harmony, 1835; harm. Hymnal for Colleges and Schools, 1956.
Harmonization © 1956, Yale University Press

CMD
RESIGNATION

Oh, for a Closer Walk with God

1 Oh, for a clos - er walk with God,
2 Where is the bless - ed - ness I knew
3 What peace - ful hours I once en - joyed!
4 The dear - est i - dol I have known,
5 So shall my walk be close with God,

a calm and heav - enly frame,
when first I sought the Lord?
How sweet their mem - ory still!
what - e'er that i - dol be,
calm and se - rene my frame;

a light to shine up -
Where is the soul - re -
But they have left an
help me to tear it
so pur - er light shall

on the road that leads me to the Lamb!
fresh - ing view of Je - sus and his Word?
ach - ing void the world can nev - er fill.
from thy throne and wor - ship on - ly thee.
mark the road that leads me to the Lamb.

Text: William Cowper, 1772
Tune: John B. Dykes, 1875

CM
BEATITUDO

552 The Blood Will Never Lose Its Power

1 The blood that Je - sus shed for me way back on
2 It soothes my doubts and calms my fears, and it dries

Cal - va - ry, the blood that gives me strength from day to
all my tears; the blood that gives me strength from day to

day— it will nev - er lose its power.
day— it will nev - er lose its power.

Refrain

It reach-es to the high - est moun - tain. It flows to the

low - est val - ley. The blood that gives me strength from

86 10 7 with refrain
THE BLOOD

Jesus Calls Us; O'er the Tumult   553

day to day— it will nev - er lose its power.

1 Je - sus calls us; o'er the tu - mult of our
2 Long a - go a - pos - tles heard it by the
3 In our joys and in our sor - rows, days of
4 Je - sus calls us; by your mer - cies, Sav - ior,

life's wild, rest - less sea, day by day his
Gal - i - le - an lake, turned from home and
work and hours of ease, still he calls, in
may we hear your call, give our hearts to

voice is sound - ing, say - ing, "Chris - tian, fol - low me."
work and fam - i - ly, leav - ing all for his dear sake.
cares and plea - sures, "Chris - tian, love me more than these."
your o - be - dience, serve and love you best of all.

Text: Cecil F. Alexander, 1852
Tune: William Boyce, c. 1765

87 87
HALTON HOLGATE

554   In Sweet Communion, Lord, with You

1 In sweet com - mu - nion, Lord, with you I
2 Your coun - sel through my earth - ly way shall
3 Whom have I, Lord, in heaven but you, to
4 Though flesh and heart should faint and fail, the
5 To live a - part from God is death; 'tis

con - stant - ly a - bide; my hand you hold with -
guide me and con - trol, and then to glo - ry
whom my thoughts as - pire? And, hav - ing you, what
Lord will ev - er be the strength and por - tion
good his face to seek. My ref - uge is the

in your own to keep me near your side.
af - ter - ward you will re - ceive my soul.
more on earth is there I can de - sire?
of my heart, my God e - ter - nal - ly.
liv - ing God; his praise I long to speak.

Text: Psalm 73:23–28; vers. Psalter, *1912, alt.*
Tune: William U. Butcher, 1860

CM
PRAYER

Lead On, O King Eternal

1 Lead on, O King e - ter - nal, the day of march has come;
2 Lead on, O King e - ter - nal, till sin's fierce war shall cease,
3 Lead on, O King e - ter - nal; we fol - low, not with fears,

hence - forth in fields of con - quest your tents will be our home.
and ho - li - ness shall whis - per the sweet a - men of peace.
for glad - ness breaks like morn - ing wher - e'er your face ap - pears.

Through days of prep - a - ra - tion your grace has made us strong;
For not with swords' loud clash - ing or roll of stir - ring drums—
Your cross is lift - ed o'er us, we jour - ney in its light;

and now, O King e - ter - nal, we lift our bat - tle song.
with deeds of love and mer - cy the heav - enly king - dom comes.
the crown a - waits the con - quest; lead on, O God of might.

Text: Ernest W. Shurtleff, 1888, alt.
Tune: Henry T. Smart, 1836

76 76 D
LANCASHIRE

556   Great Is Thy Faithfulness

1 Great is thy faith - ful-ness, O God my Fa - ther; there is no
2 Sum - mer and win - ter and spring-time and har - vest, sun, moon, and
3 Par - don for sin and a peace that en - dur - eth, thy own dear

shad - ow of turn - ing with thee; thou chang-est not, thy com -
stars in their cours - es a - bove join with all na - ture in
pres - ence to cheer and to guide, strength for to - day and bright

pas - sions, they fail not; as thou hast been thou for - ev - er wilt be.
man - i - fold wit-ness to thy great faith - ful-ness, mer - cy, and love.
hope for to - mor-row— bless-ings all mine, with ten thou-sand be - side!

Refrain (may be sung after stanza 3 only)

Great is thy faith - ful-ness! Great is thy faith - ful-ness! Morn - ing by

morn-ing new mer - cies I see; all I have need - ed thy

Text: Thomas O. Chisholm, 1923
Tune: William M. Runyan, 1923

11 10 11 10 *with refrain*
FAITHFULNESS

hand hath pro - vid - ed. Great is thy faith - ful-ness, Lord, un - to me!

My Jesus, I Love Thee 557

1 My Je - sus, I love thee, I know thou art mine; for thee all the
2 I love thee be - cause thou hast first lov - ed me and pur-chased my
3 I'll love thee in life, I will love thee in death, and praise thee as
4 In man-sions of glo - ry and end - less de - light, I'll ev - er a -

fol - lies of sin I re - sign; my gra - cious Re - deem - er, my
par - don on Cal - va - ry's tree; I love thee for wear - ing the
long as thou lend - est me breath, and say when the death - dew lies
dore thee in heav - en so bright; I'll sing with the glit - ter - ing

Sav - ior art thou; if ev - er I loved thee, my Je - sus, 'tis now.
thorns on thy brow; if ev - er I loved thee, my Je - sus, 'tis now.
cold on my brow: If ev - er I loved thee, my Je - sus, 'tis now.
crown on my brow: If ev - er I loved thee, my Je - sus, 'tis now.

Text: William R. Featherstone, c. 1862
Tune: Adoniram J. Gordon, 1876

11 11 11 11
GORDON

558 Lord of All Hopefulness

1 Lord of all hope - ful - ness, Lord of all joy,
2 Lord of all ea - ger - ness, Lord of all faith,
3 Lord of all kind - li - ness, Lord of all grace,
4 Lord of all gen - tle - ness, Lord of all calm,

whose trust, ev - er child - like, no cares could de - stroy:
whose strong hands were skilled at the plane and the lathe:
your hands swift to wel - come, your arms to em - brace:
whose voice is con - tent - ment, whose pres - ence is balm:

be there at our wak - ing, and give us, we pray,
be there at our la - bors, and give us, we pray,
be there at our hom - ing, and give us, we pray,
be there at our sleep - ing, and give us, we pray,

your bliss in our hearts, Lord, at the break of the day.
your strength in our hearts, Lord, at the noon of the day.
your love in our hearts, Lord, at the eve of the day.
your peace in our hearts, Lord, at the end of the day.

Text: Jan Struther, 1931. By permission of Oxford University Press.
Tune: Irish; harm. Hymnal 1982
Keyboard and guitar should not sound together.

10 11 11 12
SLANE

Stand Up, Stand Up for Jesus

1 Stand up, stand up for Je - sus as sol - diers of the cross;
2 Stand up, stand up for Je - sus, the trum - pet call o - bey;
3 Stand up, stand up for Je - sus, stand in his strength a - lone;
4 Stand up, stand up for Je - sus; the fight will not be long—

lift high his roy - al ban - ner, it must not suf - fer loss.
then join the might - y con - flict in this, his glo - rious day.
the arm of flesh will fail you, you dare not trust your own.
this day the noise of bat - tle, the next the vic - tor's song.

From vic - tory un - to vic - tory his ar - my shall he lead,
Be strong in faith and serve him a - gainst un - num - bered foes;
Put on the gos - pel ar - mor, each piece put on with prayer;
To ev - ery one who con - quers, a crown of life shall be;

till ev - ery foe is van - quished and Christ is Lord in - deed.
let cour - age rise with dan - ger, and all God's foes op - pose.
where du - ty calls, or dan - ger, be nev - er fail - ing there.
we with the King of glo - ry shall reign e - ter - nal - ly.

Text: George Duffield, 1858, alt.
Tune: George J. Webb, 1837

76 76 D
WEBB

560 Like a River Glorious

1 Like a riv-er glo-rious is God's per-fect peace,
2 Hid-den in the hol-low of his might-y hand,

o-ver all vic-to-rious in its bright in-crease:
where no harm can fol-low, in his strength we stand.

per-fect, yet still flow-ing full-er ev-ery day;
We may trust him ful-ly all for us to do;

per-fect, yet still grow-ing deep-er all the way.
those who trust him whol-ly find him whol-ly true.

Refrain

Trust-ing in the Fa-ther, hearts are ful-ly blest,

find-ing, as he prom-ised, per-fect peace and rest.

Text: Frances R. Havergal, 1878, alt.
Tune: James Mountain, 1876

65 65 D with refrain
WYE VALLEY

Rejoice, O Pure in Heart

1 Re - joice, O pure in heart, re - joice, give thanks, and sing;
2 Bright youth and snow-crowned age, both men and wom - en, raise
3 Still lift your stan - dard high, still chant-ing as you go,
4 At last the march shall end; the wea - ried ones shall rest,
5 Praise God, who reigns on high, the Lord whom we a - dore:

your fes - tal ban - ner wave on high, the cross of Christ your King.
on high your free, ex - ult - ing song, de - clare God's won -drous praise.
from youth to age, by night and day, in glad-ness and in woe.
the pil - grims reach their home at last, Je - ru - sa - lem the blest.
the Fa - ther, Son, and Ho - ly Ghost, one God for - ev - er - more.

Refrain

Re - joice, re - joice, re - joice, give thanks, and sing!
re - joice, re - joice,

Text: Edward H. Plumptre, 1865, alt.
Tune: Arthur H. Messiter, 1883

SM with refrain
MARION

562

Our Father, Clothed with Majesty

1 Our Fa - ther, clothed with maj - es - ty, pro - vid - er from e -
2 Your name be hal - lowed, might - y Lord; your name be wor-shiped
3 Your king-dom come, O Lord, with haste; lay Sa - tan's dark do -
4 Your will be done, your will a - lone, on earth be - low as

ter - ni - ty, with power be - yond all thought and sight,
and a - dored. Help us to bring your name all praise
main to waste. And rule us by your pre - cious Word
round your throne. Help us to turn from our own way,

in Christ a - lone we have the right to know that you, O
for all your splen-did works and ways. Lord, may we nev - er
till ev - ery-where your praise is heard. Your church keep strong, your
re - ject our will and yours o - bey, then do the tasks that

God, will give what we most need so we can live.
share the blame of blas - phem-ing your ho - ly name.
rule com - plete un - til we wor - ship at your feet.
we are given with joy, as an - gels do in heaven.

Text: Marie J. Post, 1984; based on Dewey Westra's 1931 versification and the Heidelberg Catechism's section on the Lord's Prayer. © 1987, CRC Publications
Tune: V. Schumann's Geistliche lieder, 1539; harm. Johann S. Bach, 1723, in the St. John Passion

88 88 88
VATER UNSER

5 Give us our daily bread, we pray,
   and grant your faithful care today.
   You are the only source of good;
   help us to show our gratitude.
   Our work and effort, we confess,
   will do no good unless you bless.

6 Our sin and guilt do not record,
   but freely pardon them, dear Lord,
   as we forgive the debts owed us
   by others who have been unjust.
   Because of Christ's redeeming blood,
   may we all seek each other's good.

7 Into temptation do not lead;
   deliver us from sin, we plead.
   Uphold us, Lord, and make us strong,
   resisting evil, ending wrong.
   Against the darkness help us fight
   and, by your Spirit, do the right.

8 O Lord, your kingdom, glory, power
   go far beyond this temporal hour.
   Your holy name be ever praised
   in all we do, through all our days,
   in this world and eternally.
   Amen, Amen, so shall it be!

God Works His Purposes in Us   563

1 God works his pur-pos-es in us, per-sist-ing toward his goal:
2 God works his pur-pos-es in us, gives cour-age in our pain;
3 God works his pur-pos-es in us, to im-i-tate his Son;
4 God works his pur-pos-es in us; our pride re-cedes to dust.
5 God works his pur-pos-es in us; be joy-ful, calm, con-tent.

a   love that knows, a   fruit that grows; he works to make us whole.
in   Christ we   live, for   him   we give; con-fess and praise his name.
► Christ emp-tied all, gives us his   call our race on earth to run.
With Christ a-rise! Press toward the prize with self-less faith and trust.
Give up all fears: your prayers he hears; his strength is nev-er spent.

Text: Dale Topp, 1981; based on phrases from Philippians. © 1987, CRC Publications
Tune: Llyfr y Psalmau, *1621*

CM
SONG 67

564 Fount of Love, Our Savior God

1 Fount of love, our Savior God, light on baffling
2 In this age of sore distress hidden dangers
3 In this changing world of care dreams like bubbles
4 Many paths before us lie, many voices
5 To this earth of gloom and night you did bring true

ways we've trod, your cross is our compass sure,
round us press; life's true way we cannot find,
burst in air; human hopes are empty things,
to us cry: Which of all these shall we choose?
freedom's light. While life's winding roads we tread,

your love keeps our vision pure. Lord, we thank you
disillusion fills the mind. Savior, give us
like dead trees and dried-up springs. Help us, Christ our
Here find peace or there all lose? Jesus, take our
shepherd Christ, lead on ahead. Guide us through the

for your grace; darkness flees before your face.
eyes to see your great kingdom that will be.
Lord, we pray, send us new life every day.
hands, we pray, show us your divine, true way.
narrow door to your joy forevermore.

Text: Ernest Y. L. Yang, 1934; tr. Frank W. Price, 1953, alt. © 1977, Chinese Christian Literature Council, Ltd.
Tune: ancient Chinese; arr. I-to Loh, 1983, ©

77 77 77 with refrain
MAN-CHIANG-HUNG

Refrain

Fount of love, our Sav - ior God, be our guide.

Abide with Us, Our Savior

565

1 A - bide with us, our Sav - ior, let not your mer - cy cease;
2 A - bide with us, our Help - er, sus - tain us by your Word;
3 A - bide with us, Re - deem - er, O Light, e - ter - nal Light;
4 To Fa - ther, Son, and Spir - it all praise and glo - ry be,

from Sa - tan's might de - fend us, and give our hearts your peace.
let us and all your peo - ple to liv - ing faith be stirred.
your truth di - rect and guide us to flee from er - ror's night.
who were and are for - ev - er the e - ter - nal One in Three.

Text: Josua Stegmann, 1628; tr. composite
Tune: Melchior Vulpius, 1609

76 76
CHRISTUS, DER IST MEIN LEBEN

566 In You Is Gladness

1 In you is glad - ness a - mid all sad - ness, Je - sus,
2 If he is ours,_____ we fear no pow - ers— not of

sun - shine of my heart. By you are giv - en the gifts of
sin or death or night. He knows our trou - bles, our pain and

heav - en, you the true Re - deem - er are. Our hearts you
strug - gles; he up - holds us by his might. Where-fore the

wak - en, we're not for - sak - en; who trusts you sure - ly
sto - ry— tell of his glo - ry with heart and voic - es;

Text: Johann Lindemann, 1598; tr. Catherine Winkworth, 1858, alt.
Tune: Giovanni G. Gastoldi, 1591

PM
IN DIR IST FREUDE

has built se - cure - ly   and stands for - ev - er: Al - le - lu - ia!
all heaven re - joic - es   in him for - ev - er: Al - le - lu - ia!

Our hearts are plead - ing, your pres - ence need - ing, liv - ing or   dy - ing,
We shout for glad - ness— a - way, all   sad - ness!— love him and praise him,

on Christ re - ly - ing now and for - ev - er: Al - le - lu - ia!
and still shall raise him glad hymns for - ev - er: Al - le - lu - ia!

567

We've Come This Far by Faith

We've come this far by faith, lean-ing on the Lord, trust-ing in his ho-ly Word— he's nev-er failed us yet. Oh, I can't turn a-round, we've come this far by faith.

Don't be dis-cour-aged with trou-ble in your life; he'll bear your bur-dens and re-move all mis-er-y and strife.

Text and Tune: Albert A. Goodson, 1963; arr. Richard Smallwood, 1981
Text and music © 1963, Manna Music, Inc. International copyright secured.
All rights reserved. Used by permission.

irregular
WE'VE COME THIS FAR

Love Divine, All Loves Excelling

568

1 Love di - vine, all loves ex - cel - ling, Joy of heaven, to
2 Come, Al - might - y to de - liv - er, let us all thy
3 Fin - ish, then, thy new cre - a - tion; pure and spot - less

earth come down; fix in us thy hum - ble dwell - ing, all thy
life re - ceive; sud - den - ly re - turn, and nev - er, nev - er -
let us be; let us see thy great sal - va - tion per - fect -

faith - ful mer - cies crown. Je - sus, thou art all com - pas - sion,
more thy tem - ples leave. Thee we would be al - way bless - ing,
ly re - stored in thee: changed from glo - ry in - to glo - ry,

pure, un - bound - ed love thou art; vis - it us with
serve thee with thy hosts a - bove, pray and praise thee
till in heaven we take our place, till we cast our

thy sal - va - tion, en - ter ev - ery trem - bling heart.
with - out ceas - ing, glo - ry in thy per - fect love.
crowns be - fore thee, lost in won - der, love, and praise.

Text: Charles Wesley, 1747
Tune: Rowland H. Prichard, 1831

87 87 D
HYFRYDOL

569 Praise the Lord with the Sound of Trumpet

Stanza 2 may be sung in canon

1 Praise the Lord with the sound of trum - pet, praise the Lord with the
2 Praise the Lord with the crash - ing cym - bal, praise the Lord with the

harp and lute, praise the Lord with the gen - tle-sound - ing flute.
pipe and string, praise the Lord with the joy - ful songs you sing.

Praise the Lord in the field and for - est, praise the Lord in the
Praise the Lord on a week-day morn - ing, praise the Lord on a

cit - y square, praise the Lord an - y - time and an - y - where.
Sun-day noon, praise the Lord by the light of sun or moon.

Praise the Lord in the wind and sun-shine, praise the Lord in the
Praise the Lord in the time of sor - row, praise the Lord in the

Text and Tune: Natalie Sleeth, 1975, from Sunday Songbook
Text and music © 1976, Hinshaw Music, Inc. Used by permission.

PM
PRAISE THE LORD

570 Soldiers of Christ, Arise

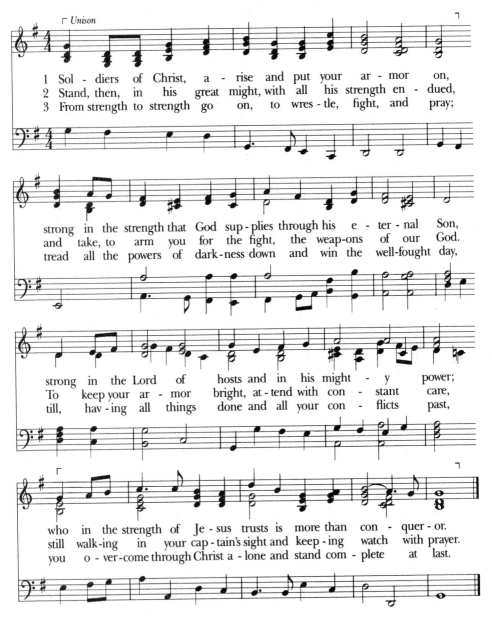

1 Sol - diers of Christ, a - rise and put your ar - mor on,
2 Stand, then, in his great might, with all his strength en - dued,
3 From strength to strength go on, to wres - tle, fight, and pray;

strong in the strength that God sup - plies through his e - ter - nal Son,
and take, to arm you for the fight, the weap-ons of our God.
tread all the powers of dark-ness down and win the well-fought day,

strong in the Lord of hosts and in his might - y power;
To keep your ar - mor bright, at - tend with con - stant care,
till, hav - ing all things done and all your con - flicts past,

who in the strength of Je - sus trusts is more than con - quer - or.
still walk-ing in your cap - tain's sight and keep - ing watch with prayer.
you o - ver-come through Christ a - lone and stand com - plete at last.

Text: Charles Wesley, 1749, alt.
Tune: Edward W. Naylor, 1902
Alternative tune: DIADEMATA, 48

SMD
FROM STRENGTH TO STRENGTH

Jesus Loves Me, This I Know

1 Je - sus loves me, this I know, for the Bi - ble tells me so.
2 Je - sus loves me— he who died heav - en's gate to o - pen wide.
3 Je - sus loves me, this I know, as he loved so long a - go,

Lit - tle ones to him be - long; they are weak, but he is strong.
He will wash a - way my sin, let his lit - tle child come in.
tak - ing chil - dren on his knee, say - ing, "Let them come to me."

Refrain

Yes, Je - sus loves me! Yes, Je - sus loves me!

Yes, Je - sus loves me! The Bi - ble tells me so.

Text: st. 1–2, Anna B. Warner, 1859; st. 3, David K. McGuire, 1971.
St. 3 by permission of the Anglican Church of Canada.
Tune: William B. Bradbury, 1861

77 77 with refrain
JESUS LOVES ME

572 Jesus, Priceless Treasure

1 Je - sus, price - less trea - sure, source of pur - est plea - sure,
friend most sure and true: long my heart was burn - ing,
faint - ing much and yearn - ing, thirst - ing, Lord, for
you. Yours I am, O spot - less Lamb, so will I let

2 Let your arms en - fold me: those who try to wound me
can - not reach me here. Though the earth be shak - ing,
ev - ery heart be quak - ing, Je - sus calms my
fear. Fires may flash and thun - der crash; yea, though sin and

3 Hence, all world - ly trea - sure! Je - sus is my plea - sure,
Je - sus is my choice. Hence, all emp - ty glo - ry!
What to me your sto - ry told with tempt - ing
voice? Pain or loss or shame or cross shall not from my

4 Ban - ish thoughts of sad - ness, for the Lord of glad - ness,
Je - sus, en - ters in; though the clouds may gath - er,
those who love the Sav - ior still have peace with -
in. Though I bear much sor - row here, still in you lies

Text: Johann Franck, 1653; tr. Catherine Winkworth, 1863, alt.
Tune: Johann Crüger, 1653

665 665 786
JESU, MEINE FREUDE

noth - ing hide you, seek no joy be - side you!
hell as - sail me, Je - sus will not fail me.
Sav - ior move me, since he chose to love me.
pur - est plea - sure, Je - sus, price - less trea - sure!

O Master, Let Me Walk with Thee   573

1 O   Mas - ter,   let   me   walk   with   thee   in   low - ly
2 Help   me   the   slow   of   heart   to   move   by   some   clear,
3 Teach   me   thy   pa - tience;   still   with   thee   in   clos - er,
4 In   hope   that   sends   a   shin - ing   ray   far   down   the

paths   of   ser - vice   free;   tell   me   thy   se - cret;   help   me
win - ning   word   of   love;   teach   me   the   way - ward   feet   to
dear - er   com - pa - ny,   in   work   that   keeps   faith   sweet   and
fu - ture's   broad - ening   way,   in   peace   that   on - ly   thou   canst

bear   the   strain   of   toil,   the   fret   of   care.
stay,   and   guide   them   in   the   home - ward   way.
strong,   in   trust   that   tri - umphs   o - ver   wrong.
give,   with   thee,   O   Mas - ter,   let   me   live.

Text: Washington Gladden, 1879
Tune: H. Percy Smith, 1874

LM
MARYTON

574   O God, My Faithful God

1 O God, my faith-ful God, true foun-tain ev - er flow - ing,
2 Give me the strength to do with read - y heart and will - ing
3 Keep me from say - ing words that lat - er need re - call - ing;
4 When dan-gers gath - er round, O keep me calm and fear - less;

with - out whom noth - ing is, all per - fect gifts be - stow - ing:
what - ev - er you com - mand, my call - ing here ful - fill - ing.
guard me lest i - dle speech may from my lips be fall - ing;
help me to bear the cross when life seems dark and cheer - less.

give me a health - y frame, and may I have with - in
Help me do what I should in all that comes my way;
but when with - in my place I must and ought to speak,
Help me, as you have taught, to love both great and small,

a con-science free from blame, a soul un - stained by sin.
I know that you are good, you bless those who o - bey.
then to my words give grace lest I of - fend the weak.
and by your Spir - it's might to live at peace with all.

Text: Johann Heermann, 1630; tr. Catherine Winkworth, 1863, alt.
Tune: Ahasuerus Fritsch, 1679; harm. Johann S. Bach, 1685–1750, in Cantata 45

67 67 66 66
DARMSTADT

Christian, Do You Struggle

1 Chris - tian, do you strug - gle on the bat - tle - ground,
2 Chris - tian, do you bat - tle Sa - tan's power with - in,
3 Chris - tian, do you wres - tle those who taunt and claim,

'gainst the powers of dark - ness clos - ing in a - round?
all his striv - ing, lur - ing, tempt-ing you to sin?
"Why keep fast and vig - il? Prayer is said in vain!"

Chris - tian, rise, take ar - mor, sol - dier of the cross;
Chris - tian, do not trem - ble, do not be down - cast;
Chris - tian, an - swer bold - ly: "While I breathe I pray!"

for the sake of Je - sus count your gain but loss.
arm your - self for bat - tle, watch and pray and fast.
Peace shall fol - low bat - tle, night shall end in day.

Text: attr. Andrew of Crete, c. 660–732; tr. John M. Neale, 1862; rev. Bert Polman, 1985.
© 1987, CRC Publications
Tune: John B. Dykes, 1868

65 65 D
ST. ANDREW OF CRETE

576 A Congregational Lament

1 Why, Lord, must e - vil seem to get its way? We do con -
2 Why, Lord, must he be sen-tenced, locked a - way? True, he has
3 Why, Lord, must she be left to waste a - way? Do you not
4 Why, Lord, must bro - ken vows cut like a knife? How can one

fess our sin is deep - ly shame - ful; but now the
wronged his neigh - bor and has failed you. Yet none of
see how pain - ful - ly she suf - fers? Could you not
wed - ded bod - y break in piec - es? We all have

wick - ed o - pen - ly are scorn - ful— they mock your
us is in - no - cent and sin - less; on - ly by
change the curse of this di - sas - ter? A - maze us
failed at be - ing pure and faith - ful; on - ly by

name and laugh at our dis - may. We know your prov - i -
grace we fol - low in your way. We plead: Re - pair the
by your might - y sov - ereign - ty. We plead: Re - pair the
grace we keep our sol - emn vows. We plead: Re - pair the

Note: In stanzas 2, 3, and 5 the words *he/she* and *brother/sister* are interchangeable; also, *they* may
be substituted for both *he* and *she*. Ordinarily, two stanzas will be sung—the first introduc-
tory stanza and one other according to the particular need:
    imprisonment (st. 2)   untimely death (st. 5)
    illness (st. 3)   other times of deep hurt (st. 6)
    divorce (st. 4)

Text: Calvin Seerveld, 1986, ©
Tune: Genevan Psalter, 1551; harm. Claude Goudimel, 1564

10 11 11 10 10 11 10 11
GENEVAN 51

den - tial love holds true: noth - ing can curse us end - less -
bro - ken - ness we share. Chas - tise no more lest it de -
bro - ken - ness we share. Chas - tise no more lest it de -
bro - ken - ness we share. Chas - tise no more lest it de -

ly with sor - row. Trans - form, dear Lord, this dam - age in - to
stroy your crea - tures. Hear this la - ment as in - ter - ces - sory
stroy your crea - tures. Hear this la - ment as in - ter - ces - sory
stroy your crea - tures. Hear this la - ment as in - ter - ces - sory

good; show us your glo - ry, hid - den by this e - vil.
prayer, and speak your power - ful word to make us hope - ful.
prayer, and speak your power - ful word to make us hope - ful.
prayer, and speak your power - ful word to make us hope - ful.

5 Why, Lord, did you abruptly take him home?
Could you not wait to summon him before you?
Why must we feel the sting of death's old cruelty?
Come quickly, Lord, do not leave us alone.
We plead: Repair the brokenness we share.
Chastise no more lest it destroy your creatures.
Hear this lament as intercessory prayer,
and speak your powerful word to make us hopeful.

6 Why, Lord, must any child of yours be hurt?
Does all our pain and sorrow somehow please you?
You are a God so jealous for our praises—
hear this lament as prayer that fills the earth.
We plead: Repair the brokenness we share.
Chastise no more lest it destroy your creatures.
Hear this lament as intercessory prayer,
and speak your powerful word to make us hopeful.

577   Beams of Heaven

1 Beams of heav-en, as I go through this wil-der-ness be-low,
2 Of-ten-times my sky is clear, joy a-bounds with-out a tear;
3 Bur-dens now may crush me down, dis-ap-point-ments all a-round,

guide my feet in peace-ful ways, turn my mid-nights in-to days.
though a day's so bright be-gun, clouds may hide to-mor-row's sun.
trou-bles speak in mourn-ful sigh, sor-row through a tear-stained eye.

When in the dark-ness I would grope, faith al-ways
There'll be a day that's al-ways bright, a day that
There is a world where plea-sure reigns, no mourn-ing

sees a star of hope, and soon from all life's grief and
nev-er yields to night, and in its light the streets of
soul shall roam its plains, and to that land of peace and

Text: Charles A. Tindley, 1851–1933
Tune: Charles A. Tindley; harm. Dale Grotenhuis, 1985. Harmonization © 1987, CRC Publications

77 77 88 96 with refrain
SOME DAY

dan - ger   I   shall   be   free   some - day.
glo - ry   I   shall   be - hold   some - day.
glo - ry   I   want   to   go   some - day.

Refrain

I do not know how long 'twill be, nor what the fu - ture holds for me,

but this I   know: if Je - sus leads me, I shall get home   some - day.

578 Jesus, Lover of My Soul

1 Je - sus, lov - er of my soul, let me to thy bo - som fly,
2 Oth - er ref - uge have I none; hangs my help - less soul on thee;
3 Plen - teous grace with thee is found, grace to cov - er all my sin;

while the near - er wa - ters roll, while the tem - pest still is high;
leave, ah! leave me not a - lone, still sup - port and com - fort me.
let the heal - ing streams a - bound; make and keep me pure with - in.

hide me, O my Sav - ior, hide, till the storm of life is past;
All my trust on thee is stayed, all my help from thee I bring;
Thou of life the foun - tain art; free - ly let me take of thee;

safe in - to the ha - ven guide, O re - ceive my soul at last!
cov - er my de - fense-less head with the shad - ow of thy wing.
spring thou up with - in my heart, rise to all e - ter - ni - ty.

Text: Charles Wesley, 1738
Tune: Joseph Parry, 1879
This music and an alternative arrangement in a lower key: 18

77 77 D
ABERYSTWYTH

What a Friend We Have in Jesus

579

1 What a friend we have in Je - sus, all our sins and griefs to bear!
2 Have we tri - als and temp - ta - tions? Is there trou - ble an - y-where?
3 Are we weak and heav - y lad - en, cum bered with a load of care?

What a priv - i - lege to car - ry ev - ery - thing to God in prayer!
We should nev - er be dis - cour-aged; take it to the Lord in prayer.
Pre - cious Sav - ior, still our ref - uge! Take it to the Lord in prayer.

Oh, what peace we of - ten for - feit, oh, what need - less pain we bear,
Can we find a friend so faith - ful, who will all our sor - rows share?
Do your friends de - spise, for - sake you? Take it to the Lord in prayer!

all be - cause we do not car - ry ev - ery - thing to God in prayer.
Je sus knows our ev - ery weak-ness; take it to the Lord in prayer.
In his arms he'll take and shield you; you will find a so - lace there.

Text: Joseph M. Scriven, 1855
Tune: The Sacred Harp, Philadelphia, 1844; harm. A. Royce Eckhardt, 1972.
Harmonization © 1972, Covenant Press

87 87 D
BEACH SPRING

580   O Perfect Love

1 O per-fect Love, all hu-man thought tran-scend-ing,
2 O per-fect Life, be thou their full as-sur-ance
3 Grant them the joy which bright-ens earth-ly sor-row;

low-ly we kneel in prayer be-fore thy throne,
of-ten-der char-i-ty and stead-fast faith,
grant them the peace which calms all earth-ly strife;

that theirs may be the love which knows no end-ing,
of pa-tient hope and qui-et, brave en-dur-ance,
grant them the vi-sion of the glo-rious mor-row

whom thou in sa-cred vow dost join in one.
with child-like trust that fears no pain or death.
that will re-veal e-ter-nal love and life.

Text: Dorothy F. Gurney, 1883, alt.
Tune: Joseph Barnby, 1889

11 10 11 10
O PERFECT LOVE

Lord, Today Bless This New Marriage

1 Lord, to - day bless this new mar - riage, guide this
2 Fill their lives with love and ser - vice where their
3 May the home they are pre - par - ing be a

u - nion in your way. With the bless - ing
dai - ly walk may be. Grant them hum - ble
place of faith and prayer, fruit - ful for this

of your Spir - it may they walk from day to day.
hearts when pros - pered, pa - tience in ad - ver - si - ty.
life and fruit - ful for your king - dom, which they share.

Text: Marie J. Post, 1974. © 1987, CRC Publications
Tune: John Stainer, 1887

87 87
CROSS OF JESUS

582

Praised Be the Father

1 Praised be the Fa - ther, Lord, our God of grace,
2 Praised be the Christ, the ris - en Lord of light,
3 Praised be the Spir - it, pres - ent ev - ery - where.

sov - ereign in your faith - ful cov - e - nant em - brace.
ho - ly rev - e - la - tion, God's and our de - light.
Pour out all your bless - ings: wis - dom, truth, and prayer.

From this day to - geth - er, make our love en - dure,
Lov - er of your peo - ple, close as hus-band, wife:
Soft - ly breathe the pow - er bind-ing two to one;

ev'r - er self - ef - fac - ing, pas - sion - ate, and pure.
work in us the se - cret— re - cre - at - ed life.
com - fort, strength-en, pros - per this new home be - gun.

Text: Calvin Seerveld, 1957. © 1974, CRC Publications
Tune: George F. Handel, 1748

55 65 65 65 with refrain
JUDAS MACCABEUS

Praised be the Fa - ther, Son, and Ho - ly Ghost.

Glo - ri - ous the won - der prom - ised us to - day.

The Tender Love a Father Has 583

1 The ten - der love a fa - ther has for all his chil - dren dear—
2 The Lord re - mem - bers we are dust, and all our frail - ty knows;
3 The flower is with - ered by the wind that smites with blight - ing breath;
4 Un - chang - ing is the love of God, from age to age the same,
5 Those who his gra cious cov - enant keep the Lord will ev - er bless;

such love the Lord be - stows on those who wor - ship him in fear.
our life is like the ten - der grass, and as the flower it grows.
so we are quick - ly swept a - way be - fore the blast of death.
dis - played to all who do his will and rev - er - ence his name.
their chil - dren's chil - dren shall re - joice to see his right - eous - ness.

Text: Psalm 103:13–18; vers. Psalter, 1912, alt.
Tune: Thomas Tallis, c. 1567

CM
TALLIS' ORDINAL

584   How Shall the Young Direct Their Way?

1 How shall the young direct their way?
2 Sin - cere - ly I have sought you, Lord,
3 O bless - ed Lord, teach me your law,
4 Up - on your pre - cepts and your ways

What light shall be their per - fect guide?
O let me not from you de - part;
your right - eous judg - ments I de - clare;
my heart will med - i - tate with awe;

Your Word, O Lord, will safe - ly lead
to know your will and keep from sin,
your tes - ti - mo - nies make me glad,
your Word shall be my chief de - light,

if in its wis - dom they con - fide.
your Word I cher - ish in my heart.
for they are wealth be - yond com - pare.
and I will not for - get your law.

Text: Psalm 119:9–16; vers. Psalter, 1912
Tune: Roy Hopp, 1981. © 1987, CRC Publications

LM
BROOKSIDE

Let Children Hear the Mighty Deeds

585

1 Let chil-dren hear the might-y deeds which God per-formed of old,
2 Our lips shall tell them to our young, and they a-gain to theirs,

which in our youn-ger years we heard, and which our par-ents told.
that gen-er-a-tions yet un-born may teach them to their heirs;

He bids us make his glo-ries known, his works of power and grace;
thus shall they learn, in God a-lone their hope se-cure-ly stands,

and we'll con-vey his won-ders down through ev-ery ris-ing race.
that they may not for-get his works, but hon-or his com-mands.

Text: Psalm 78:1–7; vers. Isaac Watts, 1719, alt.
Tune: Theodore P. Ferris, 1941. © 1942, 1961, The Church Pension Fund. Used by permission.

CMD
WEYMOUTH

586   In Our Households, Heavenly Father

1 In our house-holds, heav-enly Fa - ther, bless the
2 Send your Spir - it to in - spire us and to
3 Help us make our homes a ha - ven, quick with

bonds that make us one. May our love re - flect your
teach your dis - ci - pline. May our acts and con - ver -
hos - pi - tal - i - ty. Move us, Lord, to serve each

lov - ing, may your will be al - ways done.
sa - tions show your peace and joy with - in.
oth - er with true love and char - i - ty.

Text: Marie J. Post, 1974, 1986
Tune: Latvian; harm. Dale Grotenhuis, 1986
Text and harmonization © 1987, CRC Publications

87 87
CAPTIVITY

O God in Heaven

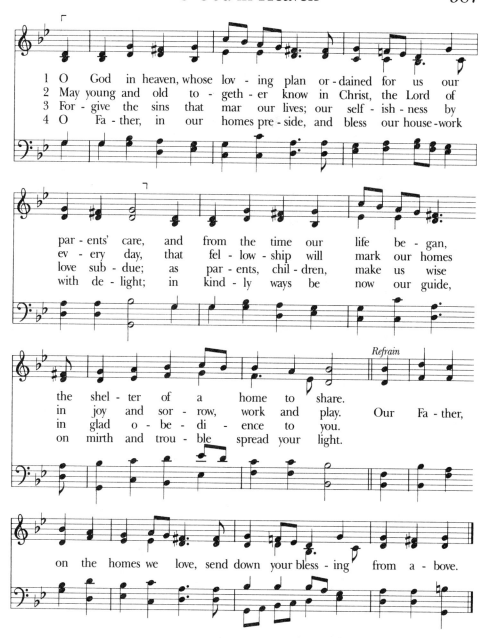

1 O God in heaven, whose lov - ing plan or - dained for us our
2 May young and old to - geth - er know in Christ, the Lord of
3 For - give the sins that mar our lives; our self - ish - ness by
4 O Fa - ther, in our homes pre - side, and bless our house - work

par - ents' care, and from the time our life be - gan,
ev - ery day, that fel - low - ship will mark our homes
love sub - due; as par - ents, chil - dren, make us wise
with de - light; in kind - ly ways be now our guide,

Refrain

the shel - ter of a home to share.
in joy and sor - row, work and play. Our Fa - ther,
in glad o - be - di - ence to you.
on mirth and trou - ble spread your light.

on the homes we love, send down your bless - ing from a - bove.

Text: Hugh Martin, 1961, alt. © 1961, The Hymn Society of America. Used by permission.
Tune: John Bishop, 1711; harm. Harry E. Wooldridge, 1845–1917
Alternative tune: MELITA, 425

88 88 88
LEICESTER

588 Tell Your Children

1 God the Fa-ther, God of glo-ry, mir-a-cles, and
2 Lift the fall-en, feed the hun-gry; God pro-vides for
3 Awe-in-spir-ing deeds of splen-dor— these pro-claim his

mys-ter-y; gen-er-a-tions all a-dore him,
ev-ery-thing. He is fair and full of kind-ness,
might-y power; in-ter-wo-ven with com-pas-sion

God the same through his-to-ry.
sav-ing those who call him King. Par-ents, tell your chil-dren,
is his strength for ev-ery hour.

age to age the same. Glo-ri-fy the liv-ing Lord a-bove, mag-ni-

fy his ho-ly name, mag-ni-fy his ho-ly name.

Text: Grace Hawthorne, 1980, alt.; based on Psalm 145
Tune: Tom Fettke, 1980
Text and music © 1980, Lillenas Publishing Co. All rights reserved. Used by permission.

87 87 with refrain
TELL YOUR CHILDREN

Our Father, Whose Creative Love

1 Our Fa - ther, whose cre - a - tive love the
2 Grant those en - trust - ed with the care of
3 Teach them to meet the grow - ing needs of
4 All par - ents need your wis - dom's light, your

gift of life be - stows, each child of earth - ly
pre - cious life from you, your grace, that faith - ful
in - fant, child, and youth; to build the bod - y,
love with - in their heart; then bless their home, and

u - nion born your heav - enly like - ness shows.
they will prove and strong in all they do.
train the mind to know and love the truth.
for their task your Spir - it's grace im - part.

Text: Albert F. Bayly, 1966, alt.
Tune: Gordon Slater, 1929
Text and music by permission of Oxford University Press.

CM
ST. BOTOLPH

590
Jesus, Our Mighty Lord

1 Je - sus, our might - y Lord, our strength in sad - ness,
2 Good shep - herd of your sheep, your own de - fend - ing,
3 Glo - rious their life who sing, with glad thanks - giv - ing,

the Fa - ther's con - quering Word, true source of glad-ness;
in love your chil - dren keep to life un - end - ing.
true hymns to Christ the King in all their liv - ing:

your name we glo - ri - fy, O Je - sus, throned on high;
You are your - self the Way: lead us then day by day
all who con - fess his Name, come then with hearts a -flame;

you gave your - self to die for our sal - va - tion.
in your own steps, we pray, O Lord most ho - ly.
the God of peace ac-claim as Lord and Sav - ior.

Text: Clement of Alexandria, c. 200; para. F. Bland Tucker, 1982.
© 1982, The Church Pension Fund. Used by permission.
Tune: Wim Mennes, 1984. © 1987, CRC Publications

65 65 66 65
ROSE-MARIE

Savior, Like a Shepherd Lead Us

1 Sav - ior, like a shep - herd lead us; much we need your
2 We are yours; in love be - friend us, be the guard - ian
3 You have prom - ised to re - ceive us, poor and sin - ful
4 Ear - ly let us seek your fa - vor, ear - ly let us

ten - der care. In your pleas - ant pas - tures feed us,
of our way; keep your flock, from sin de - fend us,
though we be; you have mer - cy to re - lieve us,
do your will; bless - ed Lord and on - ly Sav - ior,

for our use your folds pre - pare. Bless - ed Je - sus,
seek us when we go a - stray. Bless - ed Je - sus,
grace to cleanse, and power to free. Bless - ed Je - sus,
with your love our spir - its fill. Bless - ed Je - sus,

bless - ed Je - sus, you have bought us: yours we are.
bless - ed Je - sus, hear your chil - dren when we pray.
bless - ed Je - sus, ear - ly let us turn to you.
bless - ed Je - sus, you have loved us; love us still.

Text: D. Thrupp's Hymns for the Young, *1836, alt.*
Tune: Welsh
Alternative tune: PICARDY, 341

87 87 87
RHUDDLAN

592 O God, Your Constant Care and Love

1 O God, your con - stant care and love are
2 We thank you, Lord, for dreams of youth, for
3 All time is yours, O Lord, to give; may
4 Let not the pass - ing of the years rob

shed up - on us from a - bove, through - out our lives in
wis - dom lead - ing on to truth, for mem - ories gath - ered
we, in all the years we live, find that each day of
us of joy or cause us fears; and make our faith, O

ev - ery stage, from in - fan - cy to lat - er age.
through the years, and faith that grows from joys and tears.
life is new, a cel - e - bra - tion, Lord, with you.
Lord, hold true, that we may al - ways rest in you.

Text: H. Glen Lanier, 1976, alt. © 1976, The Hymn Society of America. Used by permission.
Tune: François H. Barthélémon, 1785
Alternative tune: WINCHESTER NEW, 593

LM
MORNING HYMN

My Song Forever Shall Record

1 My song for - ev - er shall re - cord the ten - der
2 I sing of mer - cies that en - dure, for - ev - er
3 Al - might - y God, your loft - y throne has jus - tice
4 With bless - ing is the na - tion crowned whose peo - ple
5 All glo - ry un - to God we yield, who is our

mer - cies of the Lord; your faith - ful - ness will
build - ed firm and sure, of faith - ful - ness that
for its cor - ner - stone, and shin - ing bright be -
know the joy - ful sound; they in the light, O
con - stant help and shield; all praise and hon - or

I pro - claim, and ev - ery age shall know your name.
nev - er dies, es - tab - lished change - less in the skies.
fore your face are truth and love and bound - less grace.
Lord, shall live, the light your face and fa - vor give.
we will bring to you, the Ho - ly One, our King.

Text: based on Psalm 89; vers. Psalter, 1912, alt.

Tune: Musikalisches Hand-buch, Hamburg, 1690

LM

WINCHESTER NEW

594   God Is Working His Purpose Out

May be sung in canon

1   God is___ work - ing his pur - pose out as___ year___ suc - ceeds___ to year:___
2 From ut - most___ east to___ ut - most west, wher - e'er the church has gone, by the
3 March we___ forth in the strength of God, with the ban - ner of Christ___ un - furled, that the
4 All we can do is___ done in vain un - less___ God bless - es the deed;___

Text: Arthur C. Ainger, 1894
Tune: Martin F. Shaw, 1931. By permission of Oxford University Press.

irregular
PURPOSE

595 Praise to God in the Highest!

1 Praise to God in the high - est! Bless us, O
2 May the truth in its beau - ty flour - ish tri -
3 May the good be o - beyed and e - vil be
4 Peace on earth and good - will be ev - er a -

Fa - ther: praise to you! Guide and pros - per the
um - phant: praise to you! May the mills bring us
con - quered: praise to you! Give us laugh - ter, and
mong us: praise to you! A - men, al - le -

na - tions, rul - ers, and peo - ples: praise to you!
bread, for food and for giv - ing: praise to you!
set us dai - ly re - joic - ing: praise to you!
lu - ia, al - le - lu - ia, a - men.

Text: Russian, 19th cent.; tr. Percy Dearmer, 1928
Tune: Russian; arr. Dale Grotenhuis, 1984. Arrangement © 1987, CRC Publications

753 D
SLAVA BOGU

From Ocean unto Ocean

1 From o-cean un-to o-cean our land shall name you Lord,
2 O Christ, for your own glo-ry and for our coun-try's weal,
3 Where er-ror smites with blind-ness, en-slaves, and leads a-stray,
4 Our Sav-ior King, de-fend us and guide where we should go;

and, filled with true de-vo-tion, o-bey your sov-ereign Word.
we hum-bly plead be-fore you: your-self in us re-veal.
pro-claim in lov-ing-kind-ness your joy-ful gos-pel day,
forth with your mes-sage send us, your love and light to show,

Our prai-ries and our moun-tains, the for-est, fer-tile field,
And may we know, Lord Je-sus, the touch of your dear hand,
till all the tribes and rac-es that dwell in this fair land,
till, fired with true de-vo-tion and kin-dled by your Word,

our riv-ers, lakes, and foun-tains to you shall trib-ute yield.
and, healed of our dis-eas-es, the tempt-er's power with-stand.
a-dorned with Chris-tian grac-es, with-in your courts shall stand.
from o-cean un-to o-cean our land shall name you Lord.

Text: Robert Murray, 1880, alt.
Tune: Bohemian Brethren's Hemmets Koral Bok, 1921; harm. C. Winfred Douglas, 1940.
Harmonization © 1943, 1961, The Church Pension Fund. Used by permission.
Alternative tune: LANCASHIRE, 555

76 76 D
FAR OFF LANDS

597

The City Is Alive, O God

1 The cit-y is a-live, O God, with sound of hus-tling
2 Is it your will, O lov-ing God, that rac-es live in
3 In Gal-i-lee the peo-ple heard your ser-vant Christ de-
4 O God, in-spire your church to-day to take Christ's ser-vant

feet, with rap-id change and flash-ing lights that
strife? that lone-li-ness and greed and hate should
clare through heal-ing touch, through word and cross, the
role, to love the world, to hear its claims, to

pulse through ev-ery street; but oft there's in-hu-
mark a cit-y's life? Do you de-sire one
good news of your care. He said your heart touched
sense its yearn-ing soul, to live with-in the

man-i-ty be-hind the bright fa-cade, and
per-son's wealth to keep an-oth-er poor? Must
ev-ery heart that longed for peace and right, that
mar-ket-place, to serve both weak and strong, to

Text: William W. Reid, Jr., alt. © 1969, The Hymn Society of America. Used by permission.
Tune: Eric H. Thiman, 1923. © Novello and Co., Ltd.

CMD
STOKESAY CASTLE

throngs with emp - ty, hun-gering hearts cry out for help, O God.
crime and slums and lust a - bound? O Lord, is there no cure?
those bowed down by bur-dens borne could find your life, your light.
lose it - self, to share its dream, to give the world its song.

Lord, Keep Us Steadfast in Your Word   598

1 Lord, keep us stead-fast in your word; curb those who
2 Lord Je - sus Christ, your power make known, for you are
3 O Com - fort - er of price - less worth, send peace and

by de - ceit or sword would wrest the king-dom from your
Lord of lords a - lone; de - fend your ho - ly church, that
u - ni - ty on earth; sup - port us in our fi - nal

Son and bring to naught all he has done.
we may sing your praise tri - um - phant - ly.
strife and lead us out of death to life.

Text: Martin Luther, 1542; tr. Catherine Winkworth, 1863, alt.
Tune: J. Klug's Geistliche Lieder, 1543

LM
ERHALT UNS, HERR

599 God of All Ages, Whose Almighty Hand

Trumpets, before each stanza (optional)

1 God of all a - ges, whose al-might-y
2 Thy love di - vine hath led us in the
3 From war's a - larms, from dead - ly pes - ti -
4 Re - fresh thy peo - ple on their toil-some

hand leads forth in beau - ty all the star - ry band
past; in this free land by thee our lot is cast;
lence, be thy strong arm our ev - er sure de - fense;
way, lead us from night to nev - er-end-ing day;

of shin - ing worlds in splen - dor through the skies:
be thou our rul - er, guard-ian, guide, and stay;
may true re - li - gion in our hearts in - crease,
fill all our lives with love and grace di - vine;

our grate - ful songs be - fore thy throne a - rise.
thy Word our law, thy paths our cho - sen way.
thy boun-teous good - ness nour - ish us in peace.
all glo - ry, laud, and praise be ev - er thine.

Text: Daniel C. Roberts, 1876, alt.
Tune: George W. Warren, 1892

10 10 10 10
NATIONAL HYMN

Christ Is the World's True Light

1 Christ is the world's true light, its cap-tain of sal-va-tion,
2 In Christ all rac-es meet, their an-cient feuds for-get-ting,
3 One Lord, in one great name u-nite us all who own you.

the day-star clear and bright of ev-ery race and na-tion.
the whole round world com-plete, from sun-rise to its set-ting.
Cast out our pride and shame that hin-der to en-throne you.

New life, new hope a-wakes for all who own his sway.
When Christ is throned as Lord, all shall for-sake their fear,
The world has wait-ed long, has la-bored long in pain.

Free-dom her bond-age breaks, and night is turned to day.
to plow-share beat the sword, to prun-ing hook the spear.
To heal its an-cient wrong, come, Prince of Peace, and reign.

Text: George W. Briggs, 1931, alt. By permission of Oxford University Press.
Tune: Percy E. B. Coller, 1941. © 1941, 1969, The Church Pension Fund. Used by permission.
Alternative tune: DARMSTADT, 574

67 67 66 66
ST. JOAN

601   Jesu, Jesu, Fill Us with Your Love

Refrain

Je - su, Je - su, fill us with your love, show us how to serve the neigh-bors we have from you.

1 Kneels at the feet of his friends, si - lent - ly wash - es their feet, Mas - ter who acts as a slave to them.
2 Neigh-bors are rich folk and poor, neigh-bors are black, brown, and white, neigh-bors are near - by and far a - way.
3 These are the ones we should serve, these are the ones we should love; all these are neigh-bors to us and you.
4 Lov - ing puts us on our knees, serv - ing as though we are slaves: this is the way we should live with you.

779 with refrain
CHEREPONI

Text: Tom Colvin, 1963
Tune: Ghanaian; adapt. Tom Colvin, 1963; arr. Jane Marshall, 1982
Text and music © 1969, 1982, Hope Publishing Co. International copyright secured. All rights reserved. Used by permission.

Where Cross the Crowded Ways of Life

1 Where cross the crowd - ed ways of life, where sound the
2 In haunts of wretch - ed - ness and need, on shad - owed
3 The cup of wa - ter given for you still holds the
4 O Mas - ter, from the moun-tain - side make haste to
5 till all the world shall learn your love and fol - low

cries of race and clan, a - bove the noise of
thresh - olds dark with fears, from paths where hide the
fresh - ness of your grace; yet long these mul - ti -
heal these hearts of pain; a - mong these rest - less
where your feet have trod, till glo - rious from your

self - ish strife, we hear your voice, O Son of Man.
lures of greed, we catch the vi - sion of your tears.
tudes to see the true com - pas - sion of your face.
throngs a - bide, and tread the cit - y's streets a - gain—
heaven a - bove shall come the cit - y of our God.

Text: Frank M. North, 1905, alt.
Tune: W. Gardiner's Sacred Melodies, 1815

LM
GERMANY

603 Lord, Whose Love in Humble Service

1 Lord, whose love in hum-ble ser-vice bore the weight of
2 Still your chil-dren wan-der home-less; still the hun-gry
3 As we wor-ship, grant us vi-sion till your love's re-
4 Called from wor-ship in-to ser-vice, for-ward in your

hu-man need, who up-on the cross, for-sak-en,
cry for bread; still the cap-tives long for free-dom;
veal-ing light in its height and depth and great-ness
name we go, to the child, the youth, the a-ged,

worked your mer-cy's per-fect deed, we, your ser-vants, bring the
still in grief we mourn our dead. As you, Lord, in deep com-
dawns up-on our quick-ened sight, mak-ing known the needs and
love in liv-ing deeds to show. Hope and health, good-will and

Text: *Albert F. Bayly, 1961, alt.*
Tune: *J. Leavitt's* Christian Lyre, *1830; harm. Ralph Vaughan Williams, 1906*
Text and harmonization by permission of Oxford University Press.

87 87 D
PLEADING SAVIOR

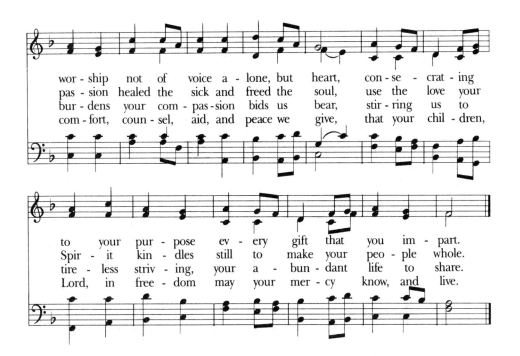

wor - ship   not   of   voice a - lone, but   heart,   con - se - crat - ing
pas - sion healed the   sick and freed the   soul,   use   the   love   your
bur - dens   your com - pas - sion bids us   bear,   stir - ring   us   to
com - fort, coun - sel,   aid, and peace we   give,   that   your   chil - dren,

to   your   pur - pose   ev - ery   gift   that   you   im - part.
Spir - it   kin - dles   still   to   make   your   peo - ple   whole.
tire - less   striv - ing,   your   a - bun - dant   life   to   share.
Lord,   in   free - dom   may   your   mer - cy   know,   and   live.

604

God of All Living

1 God of all liv - ing, we make our con - fes - sion:
2 Broth - ers and sis - ters of mine are the hun - gry
3 Strang - ers and neigh - bors, they claim my at - ten - tion,
4 Peo - ple are they, men and wom - en and chil - dren,
5 God of all liv - ing, we make our con - fes - sion:

too long we have wast - ed the wealth of our lands.
who sigh in their sor - row and weep in their pain.
they sleep by my door - step, they sit by my bed.
and each has a heart keep - ing time with my own.
too long we have wast - ed the wealth of our lands.

God of all lov - ing, re - new our com - pas - sion
Sis - ters and broth - ers of mine are the home - less
Neigh-bors and strang - ers, their an - guish con - cerns me,
Peo - ple are they, per - sons made in God's im - age;
God of all lov - ing, re - new our com - pas - sion

and o - pen our hearts while we reach out our hands.
who wait with - out shel - ter from wind and from rain.
and I must not feast till the hun - gry are fed.
so what shall I of - fer them— bread or a stone?
and o - pen our hearts while we reach out our hands.

Text: Kenneth I. Morse, 1974, alt. © 1974, Church of the Brethren General Board
Tune: Emily R. Brink, 1987. © 1987, CRC Publications

11 11 11 11
COMPASSION

Creating God, Your Fingers Trace

1 Cre - at - ing God, your fin - gers trace
2 Sus - tain - ing God, your hands up - hold
3 Re - deem - ing God, your arms em - brace
4 In - dwell - ing God, your gos - pel claims

the bold de - signs of far - thest space.
earth's mys - teries known or yet un - told.
all those op - pressed for creed or race.
one fam - ily with a bil - lion names.

Let sun and moon and stars and light and what lies
Let wa - ter's frag - ile blend with air, en - a - bling
Let peace, de - scend - ing like a dove, make known on
Let ev - ery life be touched by grace un - til we

1-3

hid - den praise your might.
life, pro - claim your care.
earth your heal - ing love.

Final stanza

praise you face to face.

Text: Jeffery W. Rowthorn, 1979, alt. © *1979, The Hymn Society of America. Used by permission.*
Tune: William Davies, 1975, ©
Alternative tune: WILDERNESS, 608

LM
KILLIBEGS

606   O God of Every Nation

1 O God of ev - ery na - tion, of ev - ery race and land,
2 From search for wealth and pow - er and scorn of truth and right,
3 Lord, strength-en all who la - bor that we may find re - lease
4 Keep bright in us the vi - sion of days when war shall cease,

re - deem the whole cre - a - tion with your al - might-y hand.
from trust in bombs that show - er de - struc-tion through the night,
from fear of rat - tling sa - ber, from dread of war's in - crease.
when ha - tred and di - vi - sion give way to love and peace,

Where hate and fear di - vide us and bit - ter threats are hurled,
from pride of race and na - tion and blind-ness to your way,
When hope and cour-age fal - ter, Lord, let your voice be heard;
till dawns the morn-ing glo - rious when truth and jus - tice reign,

in love and mer - cy guide us, and heal our strife-torn world.
de - liv - er ev - ery na - tion, e - ter - nal God, we pray!
with faith that none can al - ter, your ser - vants un - der - gird.
and Christ shall rule vic - to - rious o'er all the world's do - main.

Text: William W. Reid, Jr., 1958, alt. © *1958, The Hymn Society of America. Used by permission.*
Tune: Welsh, 19th cent.

76 76 D
LLANGLOFFAN

Father, Help Your People

1 Fa - ther, help your peo - ple in this world to build
2 Lord of desk and al - tar, bind our lives in one,
3 Ho - ly is the set - ting of each room and yard,
4 Strength-en, Lord, for ser - vice, hand and heart and brain;

some - thing of your king - dom and to do your will.
that in work and wor - ship love may set the tone.
lec - ture hall and kitch - en, of - fice, shop, and ward.
help us good re - la - tions dai - ly to main - tain.

Lead us to dis - cov - er part - ner-ship in love;
Give us grace to lis - ten, clar - i - ty of speech;
Ho - ly is the rhy - thm of our work-ing hours;
Let the liv - ing pres - ence of the Ser - vant-Christ

bless our ways of shar - ing, and our pride re - move.
make us tru - ly thank - ful for the gifts of each.
hal - low then our pur - pose, en - er - gy, and powers.
height-en our de - vo - tion, make our lives a feast.

Text: Fred Kaan, 1966. © 1972, Hope Publishing Co. All rights reserved. Used by permission.
Tune: Walter MacNutt, 1967. © 1970, Waterloo Music Co., Ltd. All rights reserved. Used by permission.

65 65 D
WHITWORTH

608   O God of Love, O King of Peace

1 O God of love, O King of peace,
   make wars throughout the world to cease;
   the wrath of nations now restrain.

2 Remember, Lord, your works of old,
   the wonders that our parents told;
   remember not our sins' dark stain.

3 Whom shall we trust but you, O Lord?
   Where rest but on your faithful word?
   None ever called on you in vain.

Refrain
Give peace, O God, give peace again!

Text: Henry W. Baker, 1861, alt.
Tune: Reginald S. Thatcher, 1936. By permission of Oxford University Press.

LM
WILDERNESS

How Would the Lord Be Worshiped

1 How would the Lord be wor - shiped by those who
2 How would the Lord be wor - shiped by those who
3 How would the Lord be wor - shiped by those who
4 Then shall the Lord be wor - shiped, and light shall
5 Then shall the Lord be wor - shiped: our light will

seek to serve him? Let us loose ev - ery chain
seek to serve him? Let us find those in need,
► seek to serve him? Re - move the heav - y yoke.
break like dawn - ing, as heal - ing quick - ly springs.
rise in dark - ness; our night will shine like day.

of all who still are bur - dened by sin and by op -
di - vide bread with the hun - gry, give wel - come to the
► No lon - ger point the fin - ger or speak de - ceit and
God's glo - ry shall sur - round us, pro - tect - ing us from
The Lord will guide us al - ways, give strength to those who

pres - sion, and break a - part each yoke and bond.
home - less, and clothe the cold and nak - ed ones.
► e - vil, but sat - is - fy our neigh - bor's need.
dan - ger. The Lord will an - swer when we call.
seek him. God makes our lives a - bound with joy.

Text: Marie J. Post, 1982; based on Isaiah 58:6–11
Tune: Brent Assink, 1984
Text and music © 1987, CRC Publications

776 778
HELDER

610 God Is My Rock/ El Señor Es Mi Fuerza

God is my rock and my sal - va - tion, the strength of my life. life.
El Se - ñor es mi fuer - za, mi ro - ca_y sal - va - ción. ción.

1 You still call us to walk in paths of jus - tice, you
2 In the midst of our fears and dark - ening shad - ows you

1 Tú me guí - as por sen - das de jus - ti - cia, me_en -
2 I - lu - mi - nas las som - bras de mi vi - da, al

help us see the way. As you give us the
bring us hope and light. In your pres - ence we

se - ñas la ver - dad. Tú me das el va -
mun - do das la luz. Aun - que pa - se por

cour - age for life's tri - als, we shall not be a - fraid.
go through death's dark val - leys; we shall not be a - fraid.

lor pa - ra la lu - cha, sin mie - do_a - van - za - ré.
va - lles de ti - nie - blas, yo nun - ca te - me - ré.

Text and Tune: Juan A. Espinosa, 1978

11 6 11 6 with refrain
FUERZA

3 We will trust you, the God of our salvation
      for all the future holds.
    Guide, protect, and defend the poor and helpless;
      you are their rock and shield. *Refrain*

4 Lord Almighty, protector of your people,
      our strong deliverer,
    our Redeemer, secure us in your power;
      we trust in you alone. *Refrain*

3 Yo confío_el destino de mi vida
      al Dios de mi salud.
    A los pobres enseñas el camino;
      su_escudo eres tú. *Refrain*

4 El Señor es la fuerza de su pueblo,
      su gran libertador;
    tú le haces vivir en la confianza,
      seguro_en tu poder. *Refrain*

611 As Stewards of a Vineyard

1 As stew-ards of a vine-yard and keep-ers of the land,
2 We search in new di-rec-tions for jus-tice and for peace,

we wish to serve our Mak-er and fol-low his com-mand:
re-joic-ing in our la-bors: God's bless-ings will not cease.

to ev-er love our neigh-bor and jus-tice to main-tain.
We wish to heal what's bro-ken; we seek to ease the pain.

Refrain
If in the Lord we la-bor, our work is not in vain.

Text and Tune: Frank De Vries, 1970; harm. Dale Grotenhuis, 1986
Text and music © 1970, Christian Labour Association of Canada

76 76 D
WORKERS' SONG

Lo! He Comes, with Clouds Descending 612

1 Lo! he comes, with clouds de - scend - ing, once for our sal -
2 Ev - ery eye shall now be - hold him, robed in dread - ful
3 Those dear to - kens of his pas - sion still his daz - zling
4 Yea, a - men! let all a - dore thee, high on thine e -

va - tion slain; thou - sand thou - sand saints at - tend - ing
maj - es - ty; those who set at naught and sold him,
bod - y bears, cause of end - less ex - ul - ta - tion
ter - nal throne; Sav - ior, take the power and glo - ry,

swell the tri - umph of his train: Al - le - lu - ia!
pierced, and nailed him to the tree, deep - ly wail - ing,
to his ran - somed wor - ship - ers; with what rap - ture,
claim the king - dom for thine own: Al - le - lu - ia!

Al - le - lu - ia! Christ the Lord re - turns to reign.
deep - ly wail - ing, shall the true Mes - si - ah see.
with what rap - ture gaze we on those glo - rious scars!
Al - le - lu - ia! Thou shalt reign, and thou a - lone.

Text: Charles Wesley, 1758
Tune: Henry Purcell, c. 1692

87 87 87
WESTMINSTER ABBEY

613   "Wake, Awake, for Night Is Flying"

1 "Wake, a-wake, for night is fly - ing," the watch-men on the
2 Zi - on hears the watch-men sing - ing, and in her heart new
3 Lamb of God, the heavens a - dore you, the saints and an - gels

heights are cry - ing; "A-wake, Je - ru - sa - lem, a - rise!"
joy is spring - ing. She wakes, she ris - es from her gloom.
sing be - fore you with harp and cym - bals' clear-est tone.

Mid-night hears the wel-come voic - es and at the thrill-ing
For her Lord comes down all - glo - rious and strong in grace, in
Of one pearl each shin-ing por - tal, where, join-ing with the

cry re - joic - es: "Where are the vir - gins pure and wise?
truth vic - to - rious. Her star is risen, her light is come!
choir im - mor - tal, we gath - er round your ra - diant throne.

Text: Philipp Nicolai, 1599; tr. Catherine Winkworth, 1858; rev. Lutheran Worship, 1982, alt.
Tune: Hans Sachs, c. 1513; adapt. Philipp Nicolai, 1599; harm. Johann S. Bach, 1685–1750, in Cantata 140

PM
WACHET AUF

The   Bride - groom comes: A - wake! Your   lamps   with glad - ness take!
Now   come,   O   Bless - ed   One, Lord   Je - sus, God's   own   Son.
No   eye   has   seen that   light,   no   ear   the ech - oed   might

Al - le - lu - ia! With   brid - al   care   and   faith's bold prayer,
Sing   ho - san - na! We   an - swer   all   in   joy   your   call;
of   your glo - ry;   yet   there shall we   in   vic - to - ry

to   meet   the   Bride - groom,   come,   pre - pare!"
we   fol - low   to   the   wed - ding   hall.
sing   shouts   of   joy   e - ter - nal - ly!

614   Day of Judgment! Day of Wonders!

1 Day of judg-ment! Day of won-ders! Hark! the trum-pet's
2 See the Judge, our na-ture wear-ing, clothed in maj-es-
3 At his call the dead a-wak-en, rise to life from
4 But to those who have con-fess-ed, loved, and served the

awe-some sound, loud-er than a thou-sand thun-ders,
ty di-vine. You who long for his ap-pear-ing
earth and sea. All the powers of na-ture, shak-en
Lord be-low, he will say, "Come near, you bless-ed,

shakes the vast cre-a-tion round. How the
then shall say, "This God is mine!" Gra - cious
by his looks, pre-pare to flee. Care - less
see the king-dom I be-stow; you for -

sum - mons will the sin-ner's heart con-found!
Sav - ior, own me on that day as thine.
sin - ner, what will then be-come of thee?
ev - er shall my love and glo - ry know."

Text: John Newton, 1774; based on Dies Irae, Latin, 13th cent.
Tune: J. Neander's Alpha und Omega, 1680; adapt. and harm. Johann S. Bach, 1685–1750, in Cantata 40
Alternative tune: CORONAE, 464

87 87 47
MEINE HOFFNUNG

The King Shall Come When Morning Dawns 615

1 The King shall come when morning dawns and
2 not, as of old, a lit - tle child, to
3 Oh, bright - er than the ris - ing morn when
4 oh, bright - er than that glo - rious morn shall
5 The King shall come when morn - ing dawns and

light tri - um - phant breaks, when beau - ty gilds the
bear and fight and die, but crowned with glo - ry
► Christ, vic - to - rious, rose and left the lone - some
dawn up - on our race the day when Christ in
light and beau - ty brings. Hail, Christ the Lord! Your

east - ern hills and life to joy a - wakes—
like the sun that lights the morn - ing sky.
► place of death, de - spite the rage of foes—
splen - dor comes and we shall see his face.
peo - ple pray: come quick - ly, King of kings.

Text: Greek; tr. John Brownlie, 1907, alt.
Tune: J. Wyeth, Repository of Sacred Music, 1813; harm. Jack Grotenhuis, 1983.
  Harmonization © 1987, CRC Publications

CM
~~CONSOLATION~~
Morning Song

616   Isaiah the Prophet Has Written of Old

1 I - sa - iah the proph - et has writ - ten of old how
2 Yet na - tions still prey on the meek of the world, and

God's earth - ly king - dom shall come. In - stead of the thorn tree the
con - flict turns par - ent from child. Your peo - ple de - spoil all the

fir tree shall grow; the wolf shall lie down with the
sweet - ness of earth; the brier and the thorn grow___

lamb. The moun - tains and hills shall break forth in - to song, the
wild. Lord, has - ten to bring in your king - dom on earth, when

Text: Joy F. Patterson, 1982; based on Isaiah 11. © 1982, The Hymn Society of America. Used by permission.
Tune: American; harm. AnnaMae Meyer Bush, 1984. Harmonization © 1987, CRC Publications

irregular
SAMANTHRA

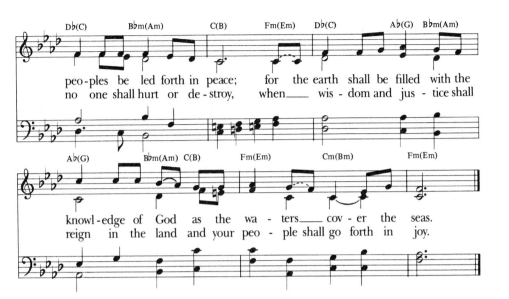

peo-ples be led forth in peace; for the earth shall be filled with the
no one shall hurt or de-stroy, when___ wis - dom and jus - tice shall

knowl-edge of God as the wa - ters___ cov - er the seas.
reign in the land and your peo - ple shall go forth in joy.

617 Swing Low, Sweet Chariot

Text and Tune: Afro-American spiritual

irregular
SWING LOW

Jerusalem the Golden

1 Je - ru - sa - lem the gold - en, de - scend - ing from a - bove,
2 They stand, those halls of Zi - on, all ju - bi - lant with song,
3 There is the throne of Da - vid, and there, from pain re - leased,
4 How love - ly is that cit - y, the home of God's e - lect!

the cit - y of God's pres - ence, the vi - sion of God's love—
so bright with man - y an an - gel and all the mar - tyr throng.
the shout of those who tri - umph, the song of those who feast.
How beau - ti - ful the coun - try that ea - ger hearts ex - pect!

I know not, oh, I know not what joys a - wait us there,
The Prince is ev - er in them, the day - light is se - rene;
And all who with their lead - er have con - quered in the fight,
O Christ, in mer - cy bring us to that e - ter - nal shore

what ra - dian - cy of glo - ry, what bliss be - yond com - pare!
the tree of life and heal - ing has leaves of rich - est green.
for - ev - er and for - ev - er are robed in pur - est white.
where Fa - ther, Son, and Spir - it are wor - shiped ev - er - more.

Text: Bernard of Cluny, 12th cent.; tr. John M. Neale, 1858, alt.
Tune: Alexander Ewing, 1853

76 76 D
EWING

619 Ten Thousand Times Ten Thousand

1 Ten thou - sand times ten thou - sand give glo - ry
2 O day, for which cre - a - tion and all its
3 Bring near your great sal - va - tion, O Lord, re -

to the Lamb; the an - gel hosts a - round the
tribes were made! O joy, for all its for - mer
turn a - gain to gath - er all your cho - sen

throne praise God, the great I AM. Tri - um - phant al - le -
grief a thou - sand - fold re - paid! The ar - mies of the
flock— then take your power and reign! Ap - pear, De - sire of

lu - ias fill earth and sea and sky, as count - less
ran - somed have fought with death and sin: fling o - pen
Na - tions; your ex - iles long for home. Show in the

voic - es join the song and wor - ship God on high.
wide the might - y gates to let the vic - tors in!
heavens your prom - ised sign, then, Prince and Sav - ior, come!

Text: Henry Alford, 1867; rev. Jubilate Hymns, 1982. © 1982, Hope Publishing Co. All rights reserved. Used by permission.
Tune: John B. Dykes, 1875

76 86 D
ALFORD

By the Sea of Crystal

1 By the sea of crys - tal saints in glo - ry stand,
2 Out of trib - u - la - tion, death, and Sa - tan's hand,
3 "Un - to God Al - might - y, sit - ting on the throne,

myr - i - ads in num - ber, drawn from ev - ery land.
they have been trans - lat - ed at the Lord's com - mand.
and the Lamb, vic - to - rious, be the praise a - lone."

Robed in white ap - par - el, washed in Je - sus' blood,
In their hands they're hold - ing palms of vic - to - ry.
God has wrought sal - va - tion; he did won-drous things.

they now reign in heav - en with the Lamb of God.
Hark! the ju - bilant cho - rus shouts tri - um-phant-ly:
Who shall not ex - tol thee, ho - ly King of kings!

Text: William Kuipers, 1933; based on Revelation 4–5
Tune: John Vanderhoven, 1933

65 65 D
CRYSTAL

621   The God of Abraham Praise

1 The God of A-braham praise, who reigns en-throned a - bove,
2 He by his name has sworn, on this we shall de - pend,
3 The good - ly land I see, with peace and plen - ty blest,
4 There rules the Lord our King, the Lord our Right- eous - ness,
5 Tri - um-phant hosts on high give thanks to God and sing,

the An - cient of e - ter - nal days, the God of love!
and as on ea - gles' wings up-borne to heaven as - cend.
a land of sa - cred lib - er - ty and end - less rest.
vic - to - rious o - ver death and sin, the Prince of Peace.
and "Ho - ly, ho - ly, ho - ly" cry, "Al - might - y King!"

The Lord, the great I AM, by earth and heaven con - fessed—
There we shall see his face, his power we shall a - dore
There milk and hon - ey flow, and oil and wine a - bound;
On Zi - on's sa - cred height his king - dom he main - tains,
Hail, A-braham's God and ours! One might-y hymn we raise.

we bow be - fore his ho - ly name for - ev - er blest.
and sing the won - ders of his grace for - ev - er - more.
the tree of life for - ev - er grows with mer - cy crowned.
and glo - rious with his saints in light for - ev - er reigns.
All power and maj - es - ty be yours and end - less praise!

Text: Thomas Olivers, c. 1770, alt.; based on a Hebrew doxology
Tune: Hebrew; adapt. Meyer Lyon, c. 1770

66 84 D
LEONI

Magnify the Lord

Text: from the Song of Mary, Luke 1:46–49; para. Bert Polman, 1985
Tune: Jacques Berthier, 1984

PM
MAGNIFICAT

623   Unto Christ, Who Loved Us

Un - to Christ, who loved us   and washed us

from our sins   in   his   own blood,   and has made us

kings and priests   un - to God   and   his   Fa - ther—

un - to him be   glo - ry   and do - min - ion

Text: Revelation 1:5–6
Tune: Ralph Vaughan Williams, 1936. By permission of Oxford University Press.

PM
UNTO HIM THAT LOVED US

for - ev - er and ev - er. A - men.

Hear Our Prayer, O Lord 624

Hear our prayer, O Lord, hear our prayer, O Lord,

in - cline your ear to us, and grant us your peace. A - men.

Text: anonymous
Tune: George Whelpton, 1897

PM
WHELPTON

625   Lord, Listen to Your Children Praying

Lord, lis-ten to your chil-dren pray-ing,

Lord, send your Spir-it in this place;

Lord, lis-ten to your chil-dren pray-ing, send us

love, send us power, send us grace!

Text and Tune: Ken Medema, 1970, ©

PM
CHILDREN PRAYING

"Holy, Holy, Holy"/ "Santo, Santo, Santo" 626

"Ho - ly, ho - ly, ho - ly," an - gel hosts are sing - ing.
"San - to, san - to, san - to," can - tan se - ra - fi - nes.

"Ho - ly, ho - ly, ho - ly is the Lord our God.
"San - to, san - to, san - to, Dios es el Se - ñor.

Ho - ly, ho - ly, ho - ly is God, the Lord of might. Your
San - to, san - to, san - to es fuer - te nue - stro Dios. Tu

glo - ry fills the heav - ens, your glo - ry fills the earth." Ho -
glo - ria lle - na los cie - los, la tie - rra lle - na es - tá." Ho -

san - na in the high - est, ho - san - na is our song.
sa - na en las al - tu - ras, ho - sa - na la can - ción.

Text: Isaiah 6:3; Spanish; Eng. para. Bert Polman, 1985
Tune: Spanish; harm. AnnaMae Meyer Bush, 1985
Text and harmonization © 1987, CRC Publications

irregular
MERENGUE

627   Bless His Holy Name

Bless the Lord, O my soul, and all that is with-in me, bless his ho - ly name.

He has done great things, he has done great things,

Text: Psalm 103:1; para. Andraé Crouch, 1973
Tune: Andraé Crouch, 1973; arr. Richard Smallwood, 1981
Text and music © 1973, Lexicon Music, Inc. All rights reserved. International copyright secured. Used by permission.

PM
BLESS THE LORD

628   Praise God, You Angel Hosts Above

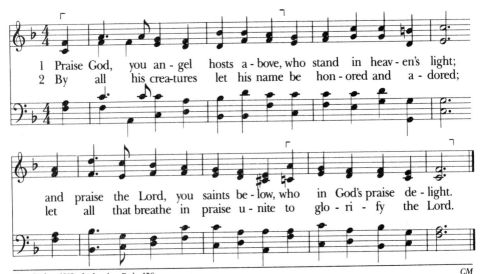

1 Praise God, you an-gel hosts a-bove, who stand in heav-en's light;
2 By all his crea-tures let his name be hon-ored and a-dored;

and praise the Lord, you saints be-low, who in God's praise de-light.
let all that breathe in praise u-nite to glo-ri-fy the Lord.

Text: Psalter, 1912, alt.; based on Psalm 150
Tune: attr. George Kirbye, 1592

CM
WINCHESTER OLD

629   Worthy Is Christ/Digno Es Jesús

1 Wor - thy is Christ, wor - thy is Christ;
2 He gave his life, he died for me;
1 Dig - no es Je - sús, dig - no es Je - sús;
2 Su vi - da dio, por mí mu - rió;

to him be praise and glo - ry: wor - thy is the Lord.
de re - ci - bir la glo - ria, dig - no es Je - sús.

Text and Tune: traditional Spanish

irregular
DIGNO ES JESUS

Now Blessed Be the Lord Our God

630

1 Now bless - ed be the Lord our God, the God of
2 And bless - ed be his glo - rious name through all e -

Is - ra - el, for he a - lone does won - drous works:
ter - ni - ty; the whole earth let his glo - ry fill:

his glo - rious deeds ex - cel; for he a - lone does
A - men! so shall it be; the whole earth let his

won - drous works: his glo - rious deeds ex - cel.
glo - ry fill: A - men! so shall it be.

Text: Psalm 72:18–19; Scottish Psalter, 1650, alt.
Tune: Oliver Holden, 1793

86 86 86
CORONATION

631 Praise and Thanksgiving

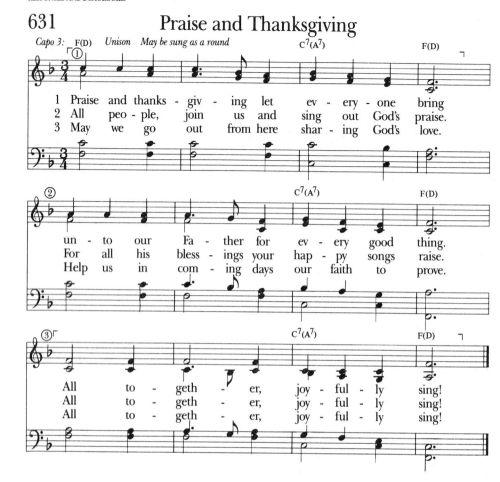

1 Praise and thanks - giv - ing let ev - ery - one bring
2 All peo - ple, join us and sing out God's praise.
3 May we go out from here shar - ing God's love.

un - to our Fa - ther for ev - ery good thing.
For all his bless - ings your hap - py songs raise.
Help us in com - ing days our faith to prove.

All to - geth - er, joy - ful - ly sing!
All to - geth - er, joy - ful - ly sing!
All to - geth - er, joy - ful - ly sing!

Text: st. 1, Alsatian; tr. Edith Lowell Thomas, 1950; st. 2–3, Marie J. Post, 1974
Tune: Alsatian round; harm. Dale Grotenhuis, 1985
Text, st. 2–3, and harmonization © 1987, CRC Publications

10 10 8
LOBET UND PREISET

To God Be the Glory

To God be the glo - ry, to God be the glo - ry,
to God be the glo - ry for the things he has done:
with his blood he has saved me; with his power he has raised me.
To God be the glo - ry for the things he has done.

*Text and Tune: Andraé Crouch, 1971, from "My Tribute." © 1971, Lexicon Music, Inc.
All rights reserved. International copyright secured. Used by permission.*

PM
MY TRIBUTE

633

He Is Lord

He is Lord, he is Lord, he is ris - en from the
dead, and he is Lord! Ev - ery knee shall bow, ev - ery
tongue con - fess that Je - sus Christ is Lord.

Text: Philippians 2:10–11
Tune: traditional; harm. Dale Grotenhuis, 1986. Harmonization © 1987, CRC Publications

PM
HE IS LORD

Father, We Love You

634

1 Fa - ther,
2 Je - sus, we love you, we wor - ship, we a - dore you,
3 Spir - it,

glo - ri - fy your name in all the earth,

glo - ri - fy your name, glo - ri - fy your name,

glo - ri - fy your name in all the earth.

Text and Tune: Donna Adkins, 1976; harm. Dale Grotenhuis, 1985. © 1976, 1981, Maranatha! Music.
All rights reserved. International copyright secured. Used by permission.

PM
GLORIFY THY NAME

635 Glory Be to the Father

Glo - ry be to the Fa - ther and to the
Son and to the Ho - ly Ghost, as it
was in the be - gin - ning, is now, and ev - er
shall be, world with - out end. A - men, a - men.

Text: Gloria Patri, *the Lesser Doxology, 2nd cent.*
Tune: *Charles Meineke, 1844*

PM
MEINEKE

Glory to the Father

Glo-ry to the Fa - ther, glo-ry to the Son,

glo - ry to the Ho - ly Spir - it, three in one— as it

was in the be - gin - ning, is now, and shall be,

world with-out end. A - men.

Text: Gloria Patri, *the Lesser Doxology*, 2nd cent.
Tune: John Erickson, 1984, ©

PM
BETHEL PARK

637 Praise God, from Whom All Blessings Flow

Praise God, from whom all bless - ings flow;

praise him, all crea - tures here be - low;

praise him a - bove, ye heav - enly host;

praise Fa - ther, Son, and Ho - ly Ghost.

A - men. A - men.

Text: Thomas Ken, 1709
Tune: traditional Black gospel

LM
NEW DOXOLOGY

Praise God, from Whom All Blessings Flow   638

Praise God, from whom all bless - ings flow; praise him, all
crea - tures here be - low; praise him a - bove, ye
heav - enly host; praise Fa - ther, Son, and Ho - ly Ghost. A - men.

Text: Thomas Ken, 1709
Tune: Louis Bourgeois, 1551
Another harmonization: 134

LM
GENEVAN 134 (OLD HUNDREDTH)

639   Alleluia

Al - le - lu - ia, al - le - lu - ia, al - le - lu - ia.

Al - le - lu - ia, al - le - lu - ia, al - le - lu - ia.

Tune: Jacques Berthier, 1982. © 1982, 1983, 1984, G.I.A. Publications. All rights reserved.

PM
TAIZÉ ALLELUIA

640   Alleluia

Al - le - lu - ia, al - le - lu - ia, al - le - lu - ia, al - le - lu - ia.

Al - le - lu - ia, al - le - lu - ia, al - le - lu - ia, al - le - lu - ia.

Text and Tune: Jerry Sinclair, 1972. © 1972, Manna Music, Inc. International copyright secured.
All rights reserved. Used by permission.

PM
SINCLAIR

Twofold Amen

Tune: *Dresden Amen; attr. Johann G. Naumann, 1741–1801*

Threefold Amen

Tune: *Danish*

Fourfold Amen

Tune: *John Stainer, 1873*

ECUMENICAL CREEDS AND DOCTRINAL STANDARDS

---

*Article 9 of the Belgic Confession names three writings, dating from the first centuries of the Christian church, that we willingly accept as creeds; the Apostles' Creed, the Nicene Creed, and the Athanasian Creed. The adoption of the Belgic Confession by the synods of the Reformed churches in the Netherlands during the late sixteenth and early seventeenth centuries implicitly approved the three creeds mentioned above. They are called *ecumenical* (general, universal) because they have been approved and accepted by nearly all Christian churches.

Apostles' Creed

I believe in God the Father almighty,
>   Maker of heaven and earth.

And in Jesus Christ, his only begotten Son, our Lord;
who was conceived by the Holy Spirit,
>   born of the virgin Mary;
suffered under Pontius Pilate;
>   was crucified, dead, and buried;
>   he descended into hell;
the third day he rose again from the dead;
he ascended into heaven,
>   and is seated at the right hand of God the Father almighty;
from there he shall come to judge the living and the dead.

I believe in the Holy Spirit.
I believe a holy catholic church,
>   the communion of saints;
the forgiveness of sins;
the resurrection of the body;
and the life everlasting.
AMEN.

This creed is called the *Apostles' Creed* not because it was produced by the apostles themselves but because it contains a brief summary of their teachings. It sets forth their doctrine "in sublime simplicity, in unsurpassable brevity, in beautiful order, and with liturgical solemnity." In its present form it is dated no later than the fourth century. More than any other Christian creed, it may justly be called an ecumenical symbol of faith.

Nicene Creed

I believe in one God,
the Father almighty,
Maker of heaven and earth
and of all things visible and invisible.

And in one Lord Jesus Christ,
the only begotten of the Father before all worlds;
God of God,
Light of light,
very God of very God;
begotten, not made,
being of one substance with the Father,
by whom all things were made.
Who, for us and our salvation,
came down from heaven,
and was incarnate by the Holy Spirit of the virgin Mary,
and was made man;
and was crucified also for us under Pontius Pilate;
he suffered and was buried;
and the third day he rose again,
according to the Scriptures;
and ascended into heaven,
and is seated at the right hand of the Father;
and he shall come again, with glory,
to judge the living and the dead;
whose kingdom shall have no end.

And I believe in the Holy Spirit, the Lord and Giver of life;
who proceeds from the Father and the Son;
who with the Father and the Son together is worshiped and
glorified;
who spoke by the prophets.
And I believe one holy catholic and apostolic church.
I acknowledge one baptism for the forgiveness of sins;
and I look for the resurrection of the dead,
and the life of the world to come.
AMEN.

The Nicene Creed, also called the Nicaeno-Constantinopolitan Creed, is a statement of the orthodox faith of the early Christian church in opposition to certain heresies, especially Arianism. These heresies, which disturbed the church during the fourth century, concerned the doctrine of the Trinity and of the person of Christ. Both the Greek (Eastern) and the Latin (Western) church held this creed in honor, though with one important difference: the Western church insisted on the inclusion of the phrase *and the Son* (known as the *filioque*) in the article on the procession of the Holy Spirit; this phrase still is repudiated by the Eastern church. In its present form this creed goes back neither to the Council of Nicea (A.D. 325) nor to the Council of Constantinople (A.D. 381), but is in substance an accurate and majestic formulation of the Nicene faith.

Athanasian Creed

Whosoever will be saved, before all things it is necessary that he hold the catholic Faith;

which faith except everyone do keep whole and undefiled, without doubt he shall perish everlastingly.

And the catholic faith is this: That we worship one God in Trinity, and Trinity in Unity,

neither confounding the persons, nor dividing the substance.

For there is one person of the Father, another of the Son, and another of the Holy Spirit.

But the Godhead of the Father, of the Son, and of the Holy Spirit is all one, the glory equal, the majesty co-eternal.

Such as the Father is, such is the Son, and such is the Holy Spirit.

The Father uncreate, the Son uncreate, and the Holy Spirit uncreate.

The Father incomprehensible, the Son incomprehensible, and the Holy Spirit incomprehensible.

The Father eternal, the Son eternal, and the Holy Spirit eternal.

And yet they are not three eternals, but one eternal.

As also there are not three uncreates, nor three incomprehensibles, but one uncreated, and one incomprehensible.

So likewise the Father is almighty, the Son almighty, and the Holy Spirit almighty;

and yet they are not three Almighties, but one Almighty.

So the Father is God, the Son is God, and the Holy Spirit is God;

and yet they are not three Gods, but one God.

So likewise the Father is Lord, the Son Lord, and the Holy Spirit Lord;

and yet not three Lords, but one Lord.

For like as we are compelled by the Christian verity to acknowledge every person by himself to be both God and Lord;

so we are forbidden by the catholic religion, to say: There be three Gods, or three Lords.

The Father is made of none, neither created, nor begotten.

The Son is of the Father alone, not made, nor created, but begotten.

The Holy Spirit is of the Father and of the Son, neither made, nor created, nor begotten, but proceeding.

So there is one Father, not three Fathers; one Son, not three Sons; one Holy Spirit, not three Holy Spirits.

And in this Trinity none is afore, or

This creed is named after Athanasius (293–373 A.D.), the champion of orthodoxy against Arian attacks on the doctrine of the Trinity. Although Athanasius did not write this creed and it is improperly named after him, the name persists because until the seventeenth century it was commonly ascribed to him. Another name for it is the *Symbol Quicunque,* taken from its opening word in the Latin original. Its author is unknown, but in its present form it probably does not date back farther than the sixth century. It is not from Greek (Eastern), but from Latin (Western) origin, and is not recognized by the Greek church today. Apart from the opening and closing sentences, this creed consists of two parts, the first setting forth the orthodox doctrine of the Trinity (3–28), and the second dealing chiefly with the incarnation and the two natures doctrine (29–43). This creed, though more explicit and advanced theologically than the Apostles' and the Nicene Creeds, does not possess the simplicity, spontaneity, and majesty of these.

after other; none is greater, or less than another;

but the whole three persons are coeternal together and coequal.

So that in all things, as is aforesaid, the Unity in Trinity and the Trinity in Unity is to be worshipped.

He therefore that will be saved must thus think of the Trinity.

Furthermore it is necessary to everlasting salvation that he also believe rightly the incarnation of our Lord Jesus Christ.

For the right faith is that we believe and confess that our Lord Jesus Christ, the Son of God, is God and man.

God of the substance of the Father, begotten before the worlds; and man of the substance of his mother, born in the world.

Perfect God and perfect man, of a reasonable soul and human flesh subsisting.

Equal to the Father, as touching his Godhead; and inferior to the Father, as touching his manhood.

Who although he is God and man, yet he is not two, but one Christ.

One, not by conversion of the Godhead into flesh, but by taking of the manhood into God.

One, altogether, not by confusion of substance, but by unity of person.

For as the reasonable soul and flesh is one man, so God and man is one Christ;

who suffered for our salvation, descended into hell, rose again the third day from the dead;

he ascended into heaven, he sitteth on the right hand of the Father, God Almighty; from thence he shall come to judge the living and the dead.

At whose coming all men shall rise again with their bodies and shall give account for their own works.

And they that have done good shall go into life everlasting, and they that have done evil into everlasting fire.

This is the catholic faith, which except a man believe faithfully, he cannot be saved.

The Belgic Confession

Article 1: *The Only God*

We all believe in our hearts
and confess with our mouths
that there is a single
and simple
spiritual being,
whom we call God—

> eternal,
> incomprehensible,
> invisible,
> unchangeable,
> infinite,
> almighty;

> completely wise,
> just,
> and good,
> and the overflowing source
>   of all good.

The oldest of the doctrinal standards of the Christian Reformed Church is the *Belgic Confession*, so called because it originated in the Southern Netherlands, now know as Belgium. Its chief author was *Guido de Brès* a preacher of the Reformed Churches of the Netherlands, who died a martyr to the faith in the year 1567. During the sixteenth century the churches in this country were exposed to the most terrible persecution by the Roman Catholic government. To protest against this cruel oppression, and to prove to the persecutors that the adherents of the Reformed faith were no rebels, as was laid to their charge, but law-abiding citizens who professed the true Christian doctrine according to the Holy Scriptures, de Brès prepared this confession in the year 1561. In the following year a copy was sent to King Philip II, together with an address in which the petitioners declared that they were ready to obey the government in all lawful things, but that they would "offer their backs to stripes, their tongues to knives, their mouths to gags, and their whole bodies to the fire," rather than deny the truth expressed in this confession.

Although the immediate purpose of securing freedom from persecution was not attained, and de Brès himself fell as one of the many thousands who sealed their faith with their lives, his work has endured and will continue to endure. In its composition the author availed himself to some extent of a confession of the Reformed churches in France, written chiefly by John Calvin, published two years earlier. The work of de Brès, however, is not a mere revision of Calvin's work, but an independent composition. In 1566 the text of this confession was revised at a synod held at Antwerp. In the Netherlands it was at once gladly received by the churches, and adopted by the national synods held during the last three decades of the sixteenth century. The text, not the contents, was revised again at the great Synod of Dort in 1618–19 and adopted as one of the doctrinal standards of the Reformed churches, to which all officebearers of the churches were required to subscribe. It stands as one of the best symbolical statements of Reformed doctrine.

Article 2: *The Means by Which We Know God*

We know him by two means:

First, by the creation, preservation, and government
of the universe,
since that universe is before our eyes
like a beautiful book
  in which all creatures,
  great and small,
  are as letters
  to make us ponder
  the invisible things of God:
    his eternal power
    and his divinity,
    as the apostle Paul says in Romans 1:20.

All these things are enough to convict men
and to leave them without excuse.

Second, he makes himself known to us more openly
by his holy and divine Word,
as much as we need in this life,
  for his glory
  and for the salvation of his own.

Article 3: *The Written Word of God*

We confess that this Word of God
was not sent nor delivered by the will of men,
but that holy men of God spoke,
being moved by the Holy Spirit,
  as Peter says.[1]

Afterwards our God—
  because of the special care he has
  for us and our salvation—
commanded his servants,
the prophets and apostles,
to commit this revealed Word to writing.
He himself wrote
with his own finger
the two tables of the law.

Therefore we call such writings
holy and divine Scriptures.

[1] 2 Pet. 1:21

Article 4: *The Canonical Books*

We include in the Holy Scripture the two volumes
of the Old and New Testaments.
They are canonical books
with which there can be no quarrel at all.

In the church of God the list is as follows:
In the Old Testament,
    the five books of Moses—
        Genesis, Exodus, Leviticus, Numbers, Deuteronomy;
    the books of Joshua, Judges, and Ruth;
    the two books of Samuel, and two of Kings;
    the two books of Chronicles, called Paralipomenon;
    the first book of Ezra; Nehemiah, Esther, Job;
    the Psalms of David;
    the three books of Solomon—
    Proverbs, Ecclesiastes, and the Song;
the four major prophets—
    Isaiah, Jeremiah, Ezekiel, Daniel;
and then the other twelve minor prophets—
    Hosea, Joel, Amos, Obadiah,
    Jonah, Micah, Nahum, Habakkuk,
    Zephaniah, Haggai, Zechariah, Malachi.

In the New Testament,
    the four gospels—
    Matthew, Mark, Luke, and John;
    the Acts of the Apostles;
    the fourteen letters of Paul—
    to the Romans;
    the two letters to the Corinthians;
    to the Galatians, Ephesians, Philippians, and Colossians;
    the two letters to the Thessalonians;
    the two letters to Timothy;
    to Titus, Philemon, and to the Hebrews;
    the seven letters of the other apostles—
    one of James;
    two of Peter;
    three of John;
    one of Jude;
    and the Revelation of the apostle John.

Article 5: *The Authority of Scripture*

We receive all these books
and these only
as holy and canonical,
for the regulating, founding, and establishing
of our faith.

And we believe
without a doubt
all things contained in them—
    not so much because the church
    receives and approves them as such
    but above all because the Holy Spirit
    testifies in our hearts
    that they are from God,
    and also because they
    prove themselves
    to be from God.

For even the blind themselves are able to see
that the things predicted in them
do happen.

Article 6: *The Difference Between Canonical*
                and Apocryphal Books

We distinguish between these holy books
and the apocryphal ones,
    which are the third and fourth books of Esdras;
    the books of Tobit, Judith, Wisdom, Jesus Sirach, Baruch;
    what was added to the Story of Esther;
    the Song of the Three Children in the Furnace;
    the Story of Susannah;
    the Story of Bell and the Dragon;
    the Prayer of Manasseh;
    and the two books of Maccabees.

The church may certainly read these books
and learn from them
as far as they agree with the canonical books.
But they do not have such power and virtue
that one could confirm
from their testimony
any point of faith or of the Christian religion.
Much less can they detract
from the authority
of the other holy books.

Article 7: *The Sufficiency of Scripture*

We believe
that this Holy Scripture contains
the will of God completely
and that everything one must believe
to be saved
is sufficiently taught in it.
For since the entire manner of service
which God requires of us
is described in it at great length,
no one—
  even an apostle
  or an angel from heaven,
  as Paul says—[2]
ought to teach other than
what the Holy Scriptures have
already taught us.
For since it is forbidden
to add to or subtract from the Word of God,[3]
this plainly demonstrates
that the teaching is perfect
and complete in all respects.

Therefore we must not consider human writings—
  no matter how holy their authors may have been—
  equal to the divine writings;
  nor may we put custom,
  nor the majority,
  nor age,
  nor the passage of time or persons,
  nor councils, decrees, or official decisions
  above the truth of God,
  for truth is above everything else.

For all human beings are liars by nature
and more vain than vanity itself.

Therefore we reject with all our hearts
everything that does not agree
with this infallible rule,
as we are taught to do by the apostles
when they say,
"Test the spirits
to see if they are of God,"[4]
and also,

"If anyone comes to you
and does not bring this teaching,
do not receive him
into your house."[5]

[2] Gal. 1:8
[3] Deut. 12:32; Rev. 22:18–19
[4] 1 John 4:1
[5] 2 John 10

Article 8: *The Trinity*

In keeping with this truth and Word of God
we believe in one God,
who is one single essence,
in whom there are three persons,
really, truly, and eternally distinct
according to their incommunicable properties—
    namely,
        Father,
        Son,
        and Holy Spirit.
The Father
    is the cause,
    origin,
    and source of all things,
        visible as well as invisible.

The Son
    is the Word,
    the Wisdom,
    and the image
        of the Father.

The Holy Spirit
    is the eternal power
    and might,
        proceeding from the Father and the Son.

Nevertheless,
this distinction does not divide God into three,
    since Scripture teaches us
    that the Father, the Son, and the Holy Spirit
    each has his own subsistence
    distinguished by characteristics—
    yet in such a way
    that these three persons are
    only one God.

It is evident then
that the Father is not the Son
and that the Son is not the Father,
and that likewise the Holy Spirit is
neither the Father nor the Son.

Nevertheless,
these persons,
thus distinct,
are neither divided
nor fused or mixed together.

> For the Father did not take on flesh,
> nor did the Spirit,
> but only the Son.

> The Father was never
> without his Son,
> nor without his Holy Spirit,
> since all these are equal from eternity,
> in one and the same essence.

There is neither a first nor a last,
for all three are one
in truth and power,
in goodness and mercy.

Article 9: *The Scriptural Witness on the Trinity*

All these things we know
from the testimonies of Holy Scripture
as well as from the effects of the persons,
especially from those we feel within ourselves.

The testimonies of the Holy Scriptures,
which teach us to believe in this Holy Trinity,
are written in many places of the Old Testament,
which need not be enumerated
but only chosen with discretion.

> In the book of Genesis God says,
> "Let us make man in our image,
> according to our likeness."
> So "God created man in his own image"—
> indeed, "male and female he created them."[6]
> "Behold, man has become like one of us."[7]

It appears from this
that there is a plurality of persons
within the Deity,
  when he says,
  "Let us make man in our image"—
and afterwards he indicates the unity
  when he says,
  "God created."

It is true that he does not say here
how many persons there are—
but what is somewhat obscure to us
in the Old Testament
is very clear in the New.

For when our Lord was baptized in the Jordan,
the voice of the Father was heard saying,
  "This is my dear Son";[8]
the Son was seen in the water;
and the Holy Spirit appeared in the form of a dove.

So, in the baptism of all believers
this form was prescribed by Christ:
  "Baptize all people in the name
  of the Father,
  and of the Son,
  and of the Holy Spirit."[9]

In the Gospel according to Luke
the angel Gabriel says to Mary,
the mother of our Lord:
  "The Holy Spirit will come upon you,
  and the power of the Most High will overshadow you;
  and therefore that holy one to be born of you
  shall be called the Son of God."[10]

And in another place it says:
  "The grace of our Lord Jesus Christ,
  and the love of God,
  and the fellowship of the Holy Spirit
  be with you."[11]

  "There are three who bear witness in heaven—
  the Father, the Word, and the Holy Spirit—
  and these three are one."[12]

In all these passages we are fully taught
that there are three persons
in the one and only divine essence.
And although this doctrine surpasses human understanding,
we nevertheless believe it now,
     through the Word,
waiting to know and enjoy it fully
     in heaven.

Furthermore,
we must note the particular works and activities
of these three persons in relation to us.
     The Father is called our Creator,
          by reason of his power.
     The Son is our Savior and Redeemer,
          by his blood.
     The Holy Spirit is our Sanctifier,
          by his living in our hearts.

This doctrine of the holy Trinity
has always been maintained in the true church,
     from the time of the apostles until the present,
     against Jews, Muslims, and certain false Christians
     and heretics,
          such as Marcion, Mani,
          Praxeas, Sabellius, Paul of Samosata, Arius,
          and others like them,
          who were rightly condemned by the holy fathers.

And so,
     in this matter we willingly accept
     the three ecumenical creeds—
     the Apostles', Nicene, and Athanasian—
     as well as what the ancient fathers decided
     in agreement with them.

6 Gen. 1:26–27
7 Gen. 3:22
8 Matt. 3:17
9 Matt. 28:19
10 Luke 10:35
11 2 Cor. 13:14
12 1 John 5:7 (KJV)

Article 10: *The Deity of Christ*

We believe that Jesus Christ,
according to his divine nature,
is the only Son of God—
    eternally begotten,
    not made nor created,
        for then he would be a creature.

He is one in essence with the Father;
coeternal;
the exact image of the person of the Father
and the "reflection of his glory,"[13]
    being in all things like him.

He is the Son of God
not only from the time he assumed our nature
but from all eternity,
    as the following testimonies teach us
    when they are taken together.

Moses says that God "created the world";[14]
and John says that "all things were created by the Word,"[15]
    which he calls God.
    The apostle says that "God made the world by his Son."[16]
He also says that "God created all things by Jesus Christ."[17]

And so it must follow
that he who is called God, the Word, the Son, and Jesus Christ
already existed when all things were created by him.

Therefore the prophet Micah says
that his origin is "from ancient times,
    from eternity."[18]
And the apostle says
that he has "neither beginning of days
    nor end of life."[19]

    So then,
    he is the true eternal God,
    the Almighty,
    whom we invoke,
    worship,
    and serve.

[13] Col. 1:15; Heb. 1:3
[14] Gen. 1:1
[15] John 1:3
[16] Heb. 1:2
[17] Col. 1:16
[18] Mic. 5:2
[19] Heb. 7:3

Article 11: *The Deity of the Holy Spirit*

We believe and confess also
that the Holy Spirit proceeds eternally
from the Father and the Son—
    neither made,
    nor created,
    nor begotten,
    but only proceeding
    from the two of them.

In regard to order,
he is the third person of the Trinity—
    of one and the same essence,
    and majesty,
    and glory,
    with the Father and the Son.

He is true and eternal God,
    as the Holy Scriptures teach us.

Article 12: *The Creation of All Things*

We believe that the Father
created heaven and earth and all other creatures
from nothing,
when it seemed good to him,
by his Word—
    that is to say,
    by his Son.

He has given all creatures
their being, form, and appearance,
and their various functions
    for serving their Creator.

Even now
he also sustains and governs them all,
according to his eternal providence,
and by his infinite power,
    that they may serve man,
    in order that man may serve God.

He has also created the angels good,
that they might be his messengers
and serve his elect.

Some of them have fallen
   from the excellence in which God created them
   into eternal perdition;
and the others have persisted and remained
   in their orginal state,
   by the grace of God.

The devils and evil spirits are so corrupt
that they are enemies of God
and of everything good.
They lie in wait for the church
and every member of it
like thieves,
   with all their power,
to destroy and spoil everything
   by their deceptions.

So then,
by their own wickedness
they are condemned to everlasting damnation,
   daily awaiting their torments.

For that reason
we detest the error of the Sadducees,
   who deny that there are spirits and angels,
and also the error of the Manicheans,
   who say that the devils originated by themselves,
   being evil by nature,
      without having been corrupted.

Article 13: *The Doctrine of God's Providence*

We believe that this good God,
   after he created all things,
did not abandon them to chance or fortune
but leads and governs them
   according to his holy will,
in such a way that nothing happens in this world
without his orderly arrangement.

Yet God is not the author of,
nor can he be charged with,
the sin that occurs.
For his power and goodness
are so great and incomprehensible
that he arranges and does his work very well and justly
even when the devils and wicked men act unjustly.

We do not wish to inquire
 with undue curiosity
into what he does that surpasses human understanding
 and is beyond our ability to comprehend.
But in all humility and reverence
we adore the just judgments of God,
which are hidden from us,
 being content to be Christ's disciples,
  so as to learn only what he shows us in his Word,
   without going beyond those limits.

This doctrine gives us unspeakable comfort
since it teaches us
that nothing can happen to us by chance
but only by the arrangement of our gracious
heavenly Father.
He watches over us with fatherly care,
keeping all creatures under his control,
so that not one of the hairs on our heads
(for they are all numbered)
nor even a little bird
can fall to the ground[20]
without the will of our Father.

In this thought we rest,
knowing that he holds in check
the devils and all our enemies,
 who cannot hurt us
 without his permission and will.

 For that reason we reject
 the damnable error of the Epicureans,
 who say that God involves himself in nothing
 and leaves everything to chance.

[20] Matt. 10:29–30

Article 14: *The Creation and Fall of Man*

We believe
that God created man from the dust of the earth
and made and formed him in his image and likeness—
    good, just, and holy;
    able by his own will to conform
    in all things
    to the will of God.

But when he was in honor
he did not understand it[21]
and did not recognize his excellence.
But he subjected himself willingly to sin
and consequently to death and the curse,
    lending his ear to the word of the devil.

For he transgressed the commandment of life,
    which he had received,
and by his sin he separated himself from God,
    who was his true life,
having corrupted his entire nature.

So he made himself guilty
and subject to physical and spiritual death,
    having become wicked,
    perverse,
    and corrupt in all his ways.
He lost all his excellent gifts
    which he had received from God,
and he retained none of them
except for small traces
    which are enough to make him
    inexcusable.

Moreover, all the light in us is turned to darkness,
as the Scripture teaches us:
    "The light shone in the darkness,
    and the darkness did not receive it."[22]
Here John calls men "darkness."

Therefore we reject everything taught to the contrary
concerning man's free will,
since man is nothing but the slave of sin
and cannot do a thing
unless it is "given him from heaven."[23]

For who can boast of being able
to do anything good by himself,
since Christ says,
    "No one can come to me
    unless my Father who sent me
    draws him"?[24]

Who can glory in his own will
    when he understands that "the mind of the flesh
    is enmity against God"?[25]
Who can speak of his own knowledge
    in view of the fact that "the natural man
    does not understand the things of the Spirit of God"?[26]

In short,
who can produce a single thought,
    since he knows that we are "not able to think a thing"
    about ourselves,
    by ourselves,
    but that "our ability is from God"?[27]

And therefore,
what the apostle says
ought rightly to stand fixed and firm:
    "God works within us both to will and to do
    according to his good pleasure."[28]

For there is no understanding nor will
conforming to God's understanding and will
apart from Christ's involvement,
    as he teaches us when he says,
    "Without me you can do nothing."[29]

[21] Ps. 49:20
[22] John 1:5
[23] John 3:27
[24] John 6:44
[25] Rom. 8:7
[26] 1 Cor. 2:14
[27] 2 Cor. 3:5
[28] Phil. 2:13
[29] John 15:5

Article 15: *The Doctrine of Original Sin*

We believe
that by the disobedience of Adam
original sin has been spread
through the whole human race.

It is a corruption of all nature—
an inherited depravity which even infects small infants
    in their mother's womb,
and the root which produces in man
    every sort of sin.
It is therefore so vile and enormous in God's sight
that it is enough to condemn the human race,
and it is not abolished
    or wholly uprooted
    even by baptism,
        seeing that sin constantly boils forth
        as though from a contaminated spring.

Nevertheless,
it is not imputed to God's children
for their condemnation
but is forgiven
by his grace and mercy—
    not to put them to sleep
    but so that the awareness of this corruption
    might often make believers groan
    as they long to be set free
    from the "body of this death."[30]

Therefore we reject the error of the Pelagians
who say that this sin is nothing else than a matter of
imitation.

[30] Rom. 7:24

Article 16: *The Doctrine of Election*

We believe that—
   all Adam's descendants having thus fallen
   into perdition and ruin
   by the sin of the first man—
God showed himself to be as he is:
merciful and just.

He is merciful
in withdrawing and saving from this perdition those whom he,
   in his eternal and unchangeable counsel,
has elected and chosen in Jesus Christ our Lord
   by his pure goodness,
   without any consideration of their works.

He is just
   in leaving the others in their ruin and fall
   into which they plunged themselves.

Article 17: *The Recovery of Fallen Man*

We believe that our good God,
   by his marvelous wisdom and goodness,
   seeing that man had plunged himself in this manner
   into both physical and spiritual death
   and made himself completely miserable,
set out to find him,
though man,
   trembling all over,
was fleeing from him.

And he comforted him,
promising to give him his Son,
   "born of a woman,"[31]
to crush the head of the serpent,[32]
and to make him blessed.

[31] Gal. 4:4
[32] Gen. 3:15

Article 18: *The Incarnation*

So then we confess
that God fulfilled the promise
   which he had made to the early fathers
   by the mouth of his holy prophets
when he sent his only and eternal Son
into the world
at the time set by him.

The Son took the "form of a servant"
and was made in the "likeness of man,"[33]
   truly assuming a real human nature,
   with all its weaknesses,
   except for sin;
   being conceived in the womb of the blessed virgin Mary
   by the power of the Holy Spirit,
   without male participation.

And he not only assumed human nature
   as far as the body is concerned
but also a real human soul,
   in order that he might be a real human being.
For since the soul had been lost as well as the body
he had to assume them both
to save them both together.

Therefore we confess,
   against the heresy of the Anabaptists
   who deny that Christ assumed human flesh from
   his mother,
that he "shared the very flesh and blood of children";[34]
that he is "fruit of the loins of David" according to the flesh;[35]
"born of the seed of David" according to the flesh;[36]
"fruit of the womb of the virgin Mary";[37]
"born of a woman";[38]
"the seed of David";[39]
"a shoot from the root of Jesse";[40]
"the offspring of Judah,"[41]
   having descended from the Jews according to the flesh;
"from the seed of Abraham"—
   for he "assumed Abraham's seed"
   and was "made like his brothers
      except for sin."[42]

In this way he is truly our Immanuel—
   that is: "God with us."[43]

[33] Phil. 2:7
[34] Heb. 2:14
[35] Acts 2:30
[36] Rom. 1:3
[37] Luke 1:42
[38] Gal. 4:4
[39] 2 Tim. 2:8
[40] Rom. 15:12
[41] Heb. 7:14
[42] Heb. 2:17; 4:15
[43] Matt. 1:23

Article 19: *The Two Natures of Christ*

We believe that by being thus conceived
the person of the Son has been inseparably united
and joined together
with human nature,
in such a way that there are not two Sons of God,
nor two persons,
but two natures united in a single person,
with each nature retaining its own distinct properties.

Thus his divine nature has always remained uncreated,
without beginning of days or end of life,[44]
filling heaven and earth.

His human nature has not lost its properties
but continues to have those of a creature—
it has a beginning of days;
it is of a finite nature
and retains all that belongs to a real body.
And even though he,
by his resurrection,
gave it immortality,
that nonetheless did not change
the reality of his human nature;
for our salvation and resurrection
depend also on the reality of his body.

But these two natures
are so united together in one person
that they are not even separated by his death.

So then,
what he committed to his Father when he died
was a real human spirit which left his body.
But meanwhile his divine nature remained
united with his human nature
even when he was lying in the grave;
and his deity never ceased to be in him,
just as it was in him when he was a little child,
though for a while it did not show itself as such.

These are the reasons why we confess him
to be true God and true man—
true God in order to conquer death
by his power,
and true man that he might die for us
in the weakness of his flesh.

[44] Heb. 7:3

Article 20: *The Justice and Mercy of God in Christ*

We believe that God—
  who is perfectly merciful
  and also very just—
sent his Son to assume the nature
in which the disobedience had been committed,
  in order to bear in it the punishment of sin
  by his most bitter passion and death.

So God made known his justice toward his Son,
  who was charged with our sin,
and he poured out his goodness and mercy on us,
  who are guilty and worthy of damnation,
giving to us his Son to die,
  by a most perfect love,
and raising him to life
  for our justification,
    in order that by him
    we might have immortality
    and eternal life.

Article 21: *The Atonement*

We believe
that Jesus Christ is a high priest forever
according to the order of Melchizedek—
  made such by an oath—
and that he presented himself
in our name
before his Father,
to appease his wrath
with full satisfaction
  by offering himself
    on the tree of the cross
  and pouring out his precious blood
    for the cleansing of our sins,
    as the prophets had predicted.

For it is written
that "the chastisement of our peace"
was placed on the Son of God
and that "we are healed by his wounds."
He was "led to death as a lamb";
he was "numbered among sinners"[45]
and condemned as a criminal by Pontius Pilate,
  though Pilate had declared
  that he was innocent.

So he paid back
what he had not stolen,[46]
and he suffered—
    the "just for the unjust,"[47]
    in both his body and his soul—
in such a way that
when he senses the horrible punishment
required by our sins
his sweat became like "big drops of blood
falling on the ground."[48]
He cried, "My God, my God,
why have you abandoned me?"[49]

And he endured all this
for the forgiveness of our sins.

Therefore we rightly say with Paul that
we "know nothing but Jesus and him crucified";[50]
we consider all things as "dung
for the excellence of the knowledge
of our Lord Jesus Christ."[51]
We find all comforts in his wounds
and have no need to seek or invent any other means
to reconcile ourselves with God
than this one and only sacrifice,
once made,
which renders believers perfect
forever.

This is also why
the angel of God called him Jesus—
that is, "Savior"—
    because he would save his people
    from their sins.[52]

[45] Isa. 53:4–12
[46] Ps. 69:4
[47] 1 Pet. 3:18
[48] Luke 22:44
[49] Matt. 27:46
[50] 1 Cor. 2:2
[51] Phil. 3:8
[52] Matt. 1:21

Article 22: *The Righteousness of Faith*

We believe that
for us to acquire the true knowledge of this great mystery
the Holy Spirit kindles in our hearts a true faith
that embraces Jesus Christ,
    with all his merits,
and makes him its own,
and no longer looks for anything
    apart from him.

For it must necessarily follow
that either all that is required for our salvation
is not in Christ or,
if all is in him,
then he who has Christ by faith
has his salvation entirely.

Therefore,
to say that Christ is not enough
but that something else is needed as well
is a most enormous blasphemy against God—
    for it then would follow
    that Jesus Christ is only half a Savior.
And therefore we justly say with Paul
that we are justified "by faith alone"
or by faith "apart from works."[53]

However,
we do not mean,
properly speaking,
that it is faith itself that justifies us—
    for faith is only the instrument
    by which we embrace Christ,
    our righteousness.

But Jesus Christ is our righteousness
    in making available to us all his merits
    and all the holy works he has done
    for us and in our place.
And faith is the instrument
    that keeps us in communion with him
    and with all his benefits.

When those benefits are made ours
they are more than enough to absolve us
of our sins.

[53] Rom. 3:28

Article 23: *The Justification of Sinners*

We believe
that our blessedness lies in the forgiveness of our sins
because of Jesus Christ,
and that in it our righteousness before God is contained,
    as David and Paul teach us
    when they declare that man blessed
    to whom God grants righteousness
    apart from works.[54]

And the same apostle says
that we are justified "freely" or "by grace"
through redemption in Jesus Christ.[55]
And therefore we cling to this foundation,
which is firm forever,
    giving all glory to God,
    humbling ourselves,
    and recognizing ourselves as we are;
    not claiming a thing for ourselves or our merits
    and leaning and resting on the sole obedience of Christ
crucified,
    which is ours when we believe in him.

That is enough to cover all our sins
and to make us confident,
freeing the conscience from the fear, dread, and terror
    of God's approach,
without doing what our first father, Adam, did,
    who trembled as he tried to cover himself
        with fig leaves.

In fact,
if we had to appear before God relying—
    no matter how little—
on ourselves or some other creature,
then, alas, we would be swallowed up.

Therefore everyone must say with David:
"Lord, do not enter into judgment with your servants,
    for before you no living person shall be justified."[56]

[54] Ps. 32:1; Rom. 4:6
[55] Rom. 3:24
[56] Ps. 143:2

Article 24: *The Sanctification of Sinners*

We believe that this true faith,
   produced in man by the hearing of God's Word
   and by the work of the Holy Spirit,
regenerates him and makes him a "new man,"[57]
   causing him to live the "new life"[58]
   and freeing him from the slavery of sin.

Therefore,
far from making people cold
toward living in a pious and holy way,
this justifying faith,
quite to the contrary,
so works within them that
   apart from it
they will never do a thing out of love for God
but only out of love for themselves
and fear of being condemned.

So then, it is impossible
for this holy faith to be unfruitful in a human being,
seeing that we do not speak of an empty faith
but of what Scripture calls
"faith working through love,"[59]
   which leads a man to do by himself
   the works that God has commanded
     in his Word.

These works,
   proceeding from the good root of faith,
are good and acceptable to God,
   since they are all sanctified by his grace.
Yet they do not count toward our justification—
   for by faith in Christ we are justified,
even before we do good works.
   Otherwise they could not be good,
     any more than the fruit of a tree could be good
     if the tree is not good in the first place.

So then, we do good works,
but nor for merit—
    for what would we merit?
Rather, we are indebted to God for the good works we do,
    and not he to us,
since it is he who "works in us both to will and do
    according to his good pleasure"[60]—
thus keeping in mind what is written:
    "When you have done all that is commanded you,
    then you shall say, 'We are unworthy servants;
    we have done what it was our duty to do.' "[61]

Yet we do not wish to deny
that God rewards good works—
but it is by his grace
that he crowns his gifts.

Moreover,
although we do good works
we do not base our salvation on them;
    for we cannot do any work
    that is not defiled by our flesh
    and also worthy of punishment.
And even if we could point to one,
    memory of a single sin is enough
    for God to reject that work.

So we would always be in doubt,
    tossed back and forth
    without any certainty,
and our poor consciences would be tormented constantly
    if they did not rest on the merit
of the suffering and death of our Savior.

[57] 2 Cor. 5:17
[58] Rom. 6:4
[59] Gal. 5:6
[60] Phil. 2:13
[61] Luke 17:10

Article 25: *The Fulfillment of the Law*

We believe
that the ceremonies and symbols of the law have ended
     with the coming of Christ,
and that all foreshadowings have come to an end,
so that the use of them ought to be abolished
     among Christians.
Yet the truth and substance of these things
remain for us in Jesus Christ,
     in whom they have been fulfilled.

Nevertheless,
we continue to use the witnesses
drawn from the law and prophets
to confirm us in the gospel
and to regulate our lives with full integrity
     for the glory of God,
according to his will.

Article 26: *The Intercession of Christ*

We believe that we have no access to God
except through the one and only Mediator and Intercessor:
Jesus Christ the Righteous.[62]

He therefore was made man,
uniting together the divine and human natures,
so that we human beings might have access to the divine Majesty.
Otherwise we would have no access.

But this Mediator,
     whom the Father has appointed between himself and us,
ought not terrify us by his greatness,
     so that we have to look for another one,
     according to our fancy.
For neither in heaven nor among the creatures on earth
is there anyone who loves us
more than Jesus Christ does.
     Although he was "in the form of God,"
     he nevertheless "emptied himself,"
     taking the form of "a man" and "a servant" for us;[63]
     and he made himself "completely like his brothers."[64]

Suppose we had to find another intercessor.
　Who would love us more than he who gave his life for us,
　　even though "we were his enemies"?[65]
And suppose we had to find one who has prestige and power.
　Who has as much of these as he who is seated
　　"at the right hand of the Father,"[66]
　and who has all power
　　"in heaven and on earth"?[67]
　And who will be heard more readily
　　than God's own dearly beloved Son?

So then, sheer unbelief has led to the practice
of dishonoring the saints,
instead of honoring them.
That was something the saints never did nor asked for,
but which in keeping with their duty,
　as appears from their writings,
they consistently refused.

We should not plead here
that we are unworthy—
　for it is not a question of offering our prayers
　on the basis of our own dignity
　but only on the basis of the excellence and dignity
　of Jesus Christ,
　　whose righteousness is ours
by faith.

Since the apostle for good reason
wants us to get rid of this foolish fear—
　or rather, this unbelief—
he says to us that Jesus Christ
was "made like his brothers in all things,"
　that he might be a high priest
　　who is merciful and faithful
　to purify the sins of the people.[68]
For since he suffered,
being tempted,
he is also able to help those
who are tempted.[69]

And further,
to encourage us more
to approach him
he says,
"Since we have a high priest,
Jesus the Son of God,
who has entered into heaven,
we maintain our confession.
For we do not have a high priest
who is unable to have compassion for our weaknesses,
but one who was tempted in all things,
just as we are,
except for sin.
Let us go then
with confidence
to the throne of grace
that we may obtain mercy
and find grace,
in order to be helped."[70]

The same apostle says that
we "have liberty to enter into the holy place
by the blood of Jesus.
Let us go, then, in the assurance
of faith. . . ."[71]

Likewise,
"Christ's priesthood is forever.
By this he is able to save completely
those who draw near to God through him
who always live to intercede
for them."[72]

What more do we need?
For Christ himself declares:
"I am the way, the truth, and the life;
no one comes to my Father
but by me."[73]
Why should we seek
another intercessor?

Since it has pleased God
to give us his Son as our Intercessor,
let us not leave him for another—
    or rather seek, without ever finding.
For when God gave him to us
he knew well that we were sinners.

Therefore,
in following the command of Christ
we call on the heavenly Father
through Christ,
our only Mediator,
as we are taught by the Lord's Prayer,
   being assured that we shall obtain
   all we ask of the Father
   in his name.

[62] 1 John 2:1
[63] Phil. 2:6–8
[64] Heb. 2:17
[65] Rom. 5:10
[66] Rom. 8:34; Heb. 1:3
[67] Matt. 28:18
[68] Heb. 2:17
[69] Heb. 2:18
[70] Heb. 4:14–16
[71] Heb. 10:19, 22
[72] Heb. 7:24–25
[73] John 14:6

Article 27: *The Holy Catholic Church*

We believe and confess
one single catholic or universal church—
   a holy congregation and gathering
   of true Christian believers,
      awaiting their entire salvation in Jesus Christ
      being washed by his blood,
      and sanctified and sealed by the Holy Spirit.

This church has existed from the beginning of the world
and will last until the end,
   as appears from the fact
   that Christ is eternal King
   who cannot be without subjects.

And this holy church is preserved by God
against the rage of the whole world,
   even though for a time
   it may appear very small
   in the eyes of men—
   as though it were snuffed out.

For example,
during the very dangerous time of Ahab
the Lord preserved for himself seven thousand men
who did not bend their knees to Baal.[74]

And so this holy church
is not confined,
bound,
or limited to a certain place or certain persons.
But it is spread and dispersed
throughout the entire world,
    though still joined and united
      in heart and will,
      in one and the same Spirit,
      by the power of faith.

[74] 1 Kings 19:18

Article 28: *The Obligations of Church Members*

We believe that
    since this holy assembly and congregation
    is the gathering of those who are saved
    and there is no salvation apart from it,
no one ought to withdraw from it,
    content to be by himself,
    regardless of his status or condition.

But all people are obliged
to join and unite with it,
keeping the unity of the church
    by submitting to its instruction and discipline,
    by bending their necks under the yoke of Jesus Christ,
    and by serving to build up one another,
according to the gifts God has given them
as members of each other
in the same body.

And to preserve this unity more effectively,
it is the duty of all believers,
    according to God's Word,
to separate themselves
from those who do not belong to the church,
    in order to join this assembly
    wherever God has established it,
      even if civil authorities and royal decrees forbid
      and death and physical punishment result.

And so,
all who withdraw from the church
or do not join it
act contrary to God's ordinance.

Article 29: *The Marks of the True Church*

We believe that we ought to discern
   diligently and very carefully,
   by the Word of God,
what is the true church—
   for all sects in the world today
claim for themselves the name of "the church."

We are not speaking here of the company of hypocrites
who are mixed among the good in the church
and who nonetheless are not part of it,
even though they are physically there.
But we are speaking of distinguishing
the body and fellowship of the true church
from all sects that call themselves "the church."

The true church can be recognized
if it has the following marks:
   The church engages in the pure preaching
      of the gospel;
   it makes use of the pure administration of the sacraments
      as Christ instituted them;
   it practices church discipline
      for correcting faults.
In short, it governs itself
according to the pure Word of God,
   rejecting all things contrary to it
   and holding Jesus Christ as the only Head.
By these marks one can be assured
of recognizing the true church—
   and no one ought to be separated from it.

As for those who can belong to the church,
we can recognize them by the distinguishing marks of Christians:
   namely by faith,
   and by their fleeing from sin and pursuing righteousness,
      once they have received the one and only Savior,
      Jesus Christ.
They love the true God and their neighbors,
   without turning to the right or left,
and they crucify the flesh and its works.

Though great weakness remains in them,
   they fight against it
   by the Spirit
all the days of their lives,
   appealing constantly
to the blood, suffering, death, and obedience of the Lord Jesus,

in whom they have forgiveness of their sins,
through faith in him.

As for the false church,
it assigns more authority to itself and its ordinances
    than to the Word of God;
it does not want to subject itself
    to the yoke of Christ;
it does not administer the sacraments
    as Christ commanded in his Word;
it rather adds to them or subtracts from them
    as it pleases;
it bases itself on men,
    more than on Jesus Christ;
it persecutes those
    who live holy lives according to the Word of God
and who rebuke it for its faults, greed, and idolatry.

These two churches
are easy to recognize
and thus to distinguish
from each other.

Article 30: *The Government of the Church*

We believe that this true church
ought to be governed according to the spiritual order
that our Lord has taught us in his Word.
    There should be ministers or pastors
        to preach the Word of God
and adminster the sacraments.
    There should also be elders and deacons,
        along with the pastors,
to make up the council of the church.

By this means
true religion is preserved;
true doctrine is able to take its course;
and evil men are corrected spiritually and held in check,
    so that also the poor
    and all the afflicted
    may be helped and comforted
    according to their need.

By this means
everything will be done well
and in good order
in the church,
    when such persons are elected

who are faithful
and are chosen according to the rule
that Paul gave to Timothy.[75]

[75] 1 Tim. 3

Article 31: *The Officers of the Church*

We believe that
ministers of the Word of God, elders, and deacons
ought to be chosen to their offices
by a legitimate election of the church,
with prayer in the name of the Lord,
and in good order,
    as the Word of God teaches.

So everyone must be careful
not to push himself forward improperly,
but he must wait for God's call,
    so that he may be assured of his calling
    and be certain that he is
    chosen by the Lord.

As for the ministers of the Word,
they all have the same power and authority,
    no matter where they may be,
since they are all servants of Jesus Christ,
    the only universal bishop,
    and the only head of the church.

Moreover,
to keep God's holy order
from being violated or despised,
we say that everyone ought,
as much as possible,
to hold the ministers of the Word and elders of the church
in special esteem,
    because of the work they do,
and be at peace with them,
    without grumbling, quarreling, or fighting.

Article 32: *The Order and Discipline of the Church*

We also believe that
although it is useful and good
for those who govern the churches
to establish and set up
a certain order among themselves
for maintaining the body of the church,

they ought always to guard against deviating
from what Christ,
our only Master,
has ordained
for us.

Therefore we reject all human innovations
and all laws imposed on us,
in our worship of God,
which bind and force our consciences
in any way.

So we accept only what is proper
to maintain harmony and unity
and to keep all in obedience
to God.

To that end excommunication,
with all it involves,
according to the Word of God,
is required.

Article 33: *The Sacraments*

We believe that our good God,
mindful of our crudeness and weakness,
had ordained sacraments for us
    to seal his promises in us,
        to pledge his good will and grace toward us,
        and also to nourish and sustain our faith.

He has added these to the Word of the gospel
to represent better to our external senses
both what he enables us to understand by his Word
and what he does inwardly in our hearts,
    confirming in us
    the salvation he imparts to us.

For they are visible signs and seals
of something internal and invisible,
    by means of which God works in us
    through the power of the Holy Spirit.
So they are not empty and hollow signs
to fool and deceive us,
    for their truth is Jesus Christ,
    without whom they would be nothing.

Moreover,
we are satisfied with the number of sacraments
that Christ our Master has ordained for us.

There are only two:
  the sacrament of baptism
  and the Holy Supper of Jesus Christ.

Article 34: *The Sacrament of Baptism*

We believe and confess that Jesus Christ,
in whom the law is fulfilled,
has by his shed blood
put an end to every other shedding of blood,
  which anyone might do or wish to do
  in order to atone or satisfy for sins.

Having abolished circumcision,
which was done with blood,
he established in its place
the sacrament of baptism.
  By it we are received into God's church
    and set apart from all other people and alien religions,
  that we may be dedicated entirely to him,
    bearing his mark and sign.
  It also witnesses to us
  that he will be our God forever,
    since he is our gracious Father.

Therefore he has commanded
that all those who belong to him
be baptized with pure water
  in the name of the Father,
  and the Son,
  and the Holy Spirit.[76]

In this way he signifies to us
that just as water washes away the dirt of the body
when it is poured on us
and also is seen on the body of the baptized
when it is sprinkled on him,
so too the blood of Christ does the same thing internally,
in the soul,
by the Holy Spirit.
  It washes and cleanses it from its sins
    and transforms us from being the children of wrath
    into the children of God.

This does not happen by the physical water
but by the sprinkling of the precious blood of the Son of God,
who is our Red Sea,
through which we must pass
  to escape the tyranny of Pharoah,

who is the devil,
and to enter the spiritual land
of Canaan.

So ministers,
as far as their work is concerned,
give us the sacrament and what is visible,
but our Lord gives what the sacrament signifies—
namely the invisible gifts and graces;
washing, purifying, and cleansing our souls
of all filth and unrighteousness;
renewing our hearts and filling them
with all comfort;
giving us true assurance
of his fatherly goodness;
clothing us with the "new man" and stripping off the "old,"
with all its works.

For this reason we believe that
anyone who aspires to reach eternal life
ought to be baptized only once
without ever repeating it—
for we cannot be born twice.
Yet this baptism is profitable
not only when the water is on us
and when we receive it
but throughout our
entire lives.

For that reason we detest the error of the Anabaptists
who are not content with a single baptism
once received
and also condemn the baptism
of the children of believers.
We believe our children ought to be baptized
and sealed with the sign of the covenant,
as little children were circumcised in Israel
on the basis of the same promises
made to our children.

And truly,
Christ has shed his blood no less
for washing the little children of believers
than he did for adults.

Therefore they ought to receive the sign and sacrament
of what Christ has done for them,
just as the Lord commanded in the law that
by offering a lamb for them

the sacrament of the suffering and death of Christ
would be granted them
shortly after their birth.
This was the sacrament of Jesus Christ.

Furthermore,
baptism does for our children
what circumcision did for the Jewish people.
That is why Paul calls baptism
the "circumcision of Christ."[77]

[76] Matt. 28:19
[77] Col. 2:11

Article 35: *The Sacrament of the Lord's Supper*

We believe and confess
that our Savior Jesus Christ
has ordained and instituted the sacrament of the Holy Supper
to nourish and sustain those
who are already born again and ingrafted
into his family:
his church.

Now those who are born again have two lives in them.
The one is physical and temporal—
they have it from the moment of their first birth,
and it is common to all.
The other is spiritual and heavenly,
and is given them in their second birth;
it comes through the Word of the gospel
in the communion of the body of Christ;
and this life is common to God's elect only.

Thus, to support the physical and earthly life
God has prescribed for us
an appropriate earthly and material bread,
which is as common to all
as life itself also is.
But to maintain the spiritual and heavenly life
that belongs to believers
he has sent a living bread
that came down from heaven:
namely Jesus Christ,
who nourishes and maintains
the spiritual life of believers
when eaten—
that is, when appropriated
and received spiritually
by faith.

To represent to us
this spiritual and heavenly bread
Christ has instituted
an earthly and visible bread as the sacrament of his body
and wine as the sacrament of his blood.
He did this to testify to us that
just as truly as we take and hold the sacraments in our hands
and eat and drink it in our mouths,
    by which our life is then sustained,
so truly we receive into our souls,
    for our spiritual life,
the true body and true blood of Christ,
    our only Savior.
We receive these by faith,
    which is the hand and mouth of our souls.

Now it is certain
that Jesus Christ did not prescribe
his sacraments for us in vain,
since he works in us all he represents
by these holy signs,
    although the manner in which he does it
    goes beyond our understanding
    and is uncomprehensible to us,
        just as the operation of God's Spirit
        is hidden and incomprehensible.

Yet we do not go wrong when we say
that what is eaten is Christ's own natural body
and what is drunk is his own blood—
but the manner in which we eat it
is not by the mouth but by the Spirit,
through faith.

In that way Jesus Christ remains always seated
at the right hand of God the Father
in heaven—
but he never refrains on that account
to communicate himself to us
through faith.

This banquet is a spiritual table
at which Christ communicates himself to us
with all his benefits.
At that table he makes us enjoy himself
as much as the merits of his suffering and death,
as he nourishes, strengthens, and comforts
our poor, desolate souls
    by the eating of his flesh,

and relieves and renews them
   by the drinking of his blood.

Moreover,
though the sacraments and thing signified are joined together,
not all receive both of them.
The wicked person certainly takes the sacrament,
to his condemnation,
but does not receive the truth of the sacrament,
   just as Judas and Simon the Sorcerer both indeed
   received the sacrament,
   but not Christ,
   who was signified by it.
   He is communicated only to believers.

Finally,
with humility and reverence
we receive the holy sacrament
in the gathering of God's people,
   as we engage together,
   with thanksgiving,
   in a holy remembrance
   of the death of Christ our Savior,
   and as we thus confess
   our faith and Christian religion.
Therefore no one should come to this table
without examining himself carefully,
   lest "by eating this bread
   and drinking this cup
   he eat and drink to his own judgment."[78]

In short,
by the use of this holy sacrament
we are moved to a fervent love
of God and our neighbors.

Therefore we reject
as desecrations of the sacraments
all the muddled ideas and damnable inventions
that men have added and mixed in with them.
And we say that we should be content with the procedure
that Christ and the apostles have taught us
and speak of these things
as they have spoken of them.

[78] 1 Cor. 11:27

Article 36: *The Civil Government*

We believe that
because of the depravity of the human race
our good God has ordained kings, princes, and civil officers.
He wants the world to be governed by laws and policies
so that human lawlessness may be restrained
and that everything may be conducted in good order
among human beings.

For that purpose he has placed the sword
in the hands of the government,
to punish evil people
and protect the good.

And being called in this manner
to contribute to the advancement of a society
that is pleasing to God,
the civil rulers have the task,
    subject to God's law,
of removing every obstacle
    to the preaching of the gospel
    and to every aspect of divine worship.

They should do this
while completely refraining from every tendency
    toward exercising absolute authority,
and while functioning in the sphere entrusted to them,
    with the means belonging to them.

They should do it in order that
    the Word of God may have free course;
    the kingdom of Jesus Christ may make progress;
    and every anti-Christian power may be resisted.*

---

*The Synod of 1958, in line with 1910 and 1938, substituted the above statement for the following (which it
judged unbiblical): And the government's task is not limited
to caring for and watching over the public domain
but extends also to upholding the sacred ministry,
    with a view to removing and destroying
        all idolatry and false worship of the Antichrist;
to promoting the kingdom of Jesus Christ;
and to furthering the preaching of the gospel everywhere;
to the end that God may be honored and served by everyone,
as he requires in his Word.

Moreover everyone,
regardless of status, condition, or rank,
must be subject to the government,
and pay taxes,
and hold its representatives in honor and respect,
and obey them in all things that are not in conflict
    with God's Word,
praying for them
    that the Lord may be willing to lead them
        in all their ways
    and that we may live a peaceful and quiet life
        in all piety and decency.*

Article 37: *The Last Judgment*

Finally we believe,
according to God's Word,
that when the time appointed by the Lord is come
(which is unknown to all creatures)
and the number of the elect is complete,
our Lord Jesus Christ will come from heaven,
    bodily and visibly,
as he ascended,
    with great glory and majesty,
to declare himself the judge
    of the living and the dead.
He will burn this old world,
    in fire and flame,
    in order to cleanse it.

Then all human creatures will appear in person
before the great judge—
    men, women, and children,
    who have lived from the beginning until the end
    of the world.

---

*The Synod of 1985 directed that the following paragraph be taken from the body of the text and be placed in a footnote: For that reason we detest the Anabaptists and other anarchists,
and in general all those who want
to reject the authorities and civil officers
and to subvert justice
    by introducing common ownership of goods
    and corrupting the moral order
        that God has established among human beings.

They will be summoned there
by the voice of the archangel
and by the sound of the divine trumpet.[79]

For all those who died before that time
will be raised from the earth,
   their spirits being joined and united
   with their own bodies
   in which they lived.
And as for those who are still alive,
they will not die like the others
but will be changed "in the twinkling of an eye"
from "corruptible to incorruptible."[80]

Then "the books" (that is, the consciences) will be opened,
and the dead will be judged
   according to the things they did in the world,[81]
   whether good or evil.
Indeed, all people will give account
of all the idle words they have spoken,[82]
   which the world regards
   as only playing games.
And then the secrets and hypocrisies of men
will be publicly uncovered
in the sight of all.

Therefore,
with good reason
the thought of this judgment
is horrible and dreadful
to wicked and evil people.
But it is very pleasant
and a great comfort
to the righteous and elect,
   since their total redemption
   will then be accomplished.
They will then receive the fruits of their labor
   and of the trouble they have suffered;
   their innocence will be openly recognized by all;
   and they will see the terrible vengeance
      that God will bring on the evil ones
      who tyrannized, oppressed, and tormented them
         in this world.

The evil ones will be convicted
   by the witness of their own consciences,
and shall be made immortal—
   but only to be tormented
   in the everlasting fire

prepared for the devil and his angels.[83]

In contrast,
the faithful and elect will be crowned
    with glory and honor.
The Son of God will "confess their names"[84]
    before God his Father and the holy and elect angels;
all tears will be "wiped from their eyes";[85]
and their cause—
    at present condemned as heretical and evil
    by many judges and civil officers—
will be acknowledged as the "cause of the Son of God."

And as a gracious reward
the Lord will make them possess a glory
such as the heart of man
could never imagine.

So we look forward to that great day with longing
in order to enjoy fully
the promises of God in Christ Jesus,
our Lord.

[79] 1 Thess. 4:16
[80] 1 Cor. 15:51–53
[81] Rev. 20:12
[82] Matt. 12:36
[83] Matt. 25:14
[84] Matt. 10:32
[85] Rev. 7:17

The Heidelberg Catechism was composed in Heidelberg at the request of Elector Frederick III, who ruled the Palatinate, an influential German province, from 1559 to 1576. An old tradition credits Zacharius Ursinus and Caspar Olevianus with being coauthors of the new catechism. Both were certainly involved in its composition, although one of them may have had primary responsibility. All we know for sure is reported by the Elector in his preface of January 19, 1563. It was, he writes, "with the advice and cooperation of our entire theological faculty in this place, and of all superintendents and distinguished servants of the church" that he secured the preparation of the Heidelberg Catechism. The catechism was approved by a synod in Heidelberg in January 1563. A second and third German edition, each with small additions, as well as a Latin translation were published the same year in Heidelberg. Soon the catechism was divided into fifty-two sections so that one Lord's Day could be explained in preaching each Sunday of the year.

The great Synod of Dort (1618–1619) approved the Heidelberg Catechism, and it soon become the most ecumenical of the Reformed catechisms and confessions. The catechism has been translated into many European, Asian, and African languages and is the most widely used and most warmly praised catechism of the Reformation period.

The translation of the Heidelberg Catechism here presented was prepared by a committee appointed by the 1968 Synod of the Christian Reformed Church. The final text of the new translation was adopted by the Synod of 1975. Synod requested the committee to produce "a modern and accurate translation . . . which will serve as the official text of the Heidelberg Catechism and as a guide for catechism preaching."

The English translation follows the first German edition of the Catechism except in two instances explained in footnotes to questions 57 and 80. The result of those inclusions is that the translation therefore actually follows the German text of the third edition as it was included in the Palatinate Church Order of November 15, 1563. This is the "received text" used throughout the world.

Biblical passages quoted in the catechism are now taken from the New International Version. In the German editions, biblical quotations sometimes include additional words not found in the Greek text and therefore not included in such recent translations as the NIV. The additions from the German are indicated in footnotes in questions 4, 71, and 119.

The Heidelberg Catechism

LORD'S DAY 1

**1 Q. What is your only comfort
in life and in death?**

A. That I am not my own,[1]
but belong—
body and soul,
in life and in death—[2]
to my faithful Savior Jesus Christ.[3]

He has fully paid for all my sins with his precious
blood,[4]
and has set me free from the tyranny of the devil.[5]
He also watches over me is such a way[6]
that not a hair can fall from my head
without the will of my Father in heaven:[7]
in fact, all things must work together for my
salvation.[8]

Because I belong to him,
Christ, by his Holy Spirit,
assures me of eternal life[9]
and makes me whole-heartedly willing and ready
from now on to live for him.[10]

[1] 1 Cor. 6:19–20.
[2] Rom. 14:7–9.
[3] 1 Cor. 3:23; Titus 2:14.
[4] 1 Pet. 1:18–19; 1 John 1:7–9; 2:2.
[5] John 8:34–36; Heb. 2:14–15; 1 John 3:1–11.
[6] John 6:39–40; 10:27–30; 2 Thess. 3:3; 1 Pet. 1:5.
[7] Matt. 10:29–31; Luke 21:16–18.
[8] Rom. 8:28.
[9] Rom. 8:15–16; 2 Cor. 1:21–22; 5:5; Eph. 1:13–14.
[10] Rom. 8:1–17.

**2 Q. What must you know
to live and die in the joy of this comfort?**

A. Three things:
first, how great my sin and misery are;[1]
second, how I am set free from all my sins and
misery;[2]
third, how I am to thank God for such
deliverance.[3]

[1] Rom. 3:9–10; 1 John 1:10.
[2] John 17:3; Acts 4:12; 10:43.
[3] Matt. 5:16; Rom. 6:13; Eph. 5:8–10; 2 Tim. 2:15; 1 Pet. 2:9–10.

Part I: Man's Misery

LORD'S DAY 2

3 Q. How do you come to know your misery?

    A. The law of God tells me.[1]

    [1] Rom. 3:20; 7:7–25.

4 Q. What does God's law require of us?

    A. Christ teaches us this in summary in Matthew 22—

> Love the Lord your God
> with all your heart
> and with all your soul
> and with all your mind
> and with all your strength.[1]*
> This is the first and greatest commandment.

> And the second is like it:
> Love your neighbor as yourself.[2]

> All the Law and the Prophets hang
> on these two commandments.

    [1] Deut. 6:5.
    [2] Lev. 19:18.

5 Q. Can you live up to all this perfectly?

    A. No.[1]
    I have a natural tendency
    to hate God and my neighbor.[2]

    [1] Rom. 3:9–20; 1 John 1:8, 10.
    [2] Gen. 6:5; Jer. 17:9; Rom. 7:23–24; 8:7; Eph. 2:1–3; Titus 3:3.

    *Earlier and better manuscripts of Matthew 22 omit the words "and with all your strength." They are found in Mark 12:30.

LORD'S DAY 3

**6 Q. Did God create man
so wicked and perverse?**

A. No.
God created man good[1] and in his own image,[2]
   that is, in true righteousness and holiness,[3]
so that he might
   truly know God his creator,[4]
   love him with all his heart,
   and live with him in eternal happiness
for his praise and glory.[5]

[1] Gen. 1:31.
[2] Gen. 1:26–27.
[3] Eph. 4:24.
[4] Col. 3:10.
[5] Ps. 8.

**7 Q. Then where does man's corrupt nature
come from?**

A. From the fall and disobedience of our first parents,
   Adam and Eve, in Paradise.[1]
This fall has so poisoned our nature[2]
   that we are born sinners—
   corrupt from conception on.[3]

[1] Gen. 3.
[2] Rom. 5:12, 18–19.
[3] Ps. 51:5.

**8 Q. But are we so corrupt
that we are totally unable to do any good
and inclined toward all evil?**

A. Yes,[1] unless we are born again,
by the Spirit of God.[2]

[1] Gen. 6:5; 8:21; Job 14:4; Isa. 53:6.
[2] John 3:3–5.

LORD'S DAY 4

**9 Q. But doesn't God do man an injustice
by requiring in his law
what man is unable to do?**

A. No, God created man with the ability to keep the law.[1]
Man, however, tempted by the devil,[2]
in reckless disobedience,[3]
robbed himself and his descendants of these gifts.[4]

[1] Gen. 1:31; Eph. 4:24.
[2] Gen. 3:13; John 8:44.
[3] Gen. 3:6.
[4] Rom. 5:12, 18, 19.

**10 Q. Will God permit
such disobedience and rebellion
to go unpunished?**

A. Certainly not.
He is terribly angry
about the sin we are born with
as well as the sins we personally commit.

As a just judge
he punishes them now and in eternity.[1]

He has declared:
"Cursed is the man who does not uphold
the words of this law,
by carrying them out."[2]

[1] Ex. 34:7; Ps. 5:4–6; Nah. 1:2; Rom. 1:18; Eph. 5:6; Heb. 9:27.
[2] Deut. 27:26; Gal. 3:10.

11 Q. But isn't God also merciful?

A. God is certainly merciful,[1]
but he is also just.[2]
His justice demands
that sin, committed against his supreme majesty,
be punished with the supreme penalty—
eternal punishment of body and soul.[3]

[1] Ex. 34:6–7; Ps. 103:8–9.
[2] Ex. 34:7; Deut. 7:9–11; Ps. 5:4–6; Heb. 10:30–31.
[3] Matt. 25:35–46.

Part II: Man's Deliverance

LORD'S DAY 5

**12 Q. According to God's righteous judgment
we deserve punishment
both in this world and forever after:
how then can we escape this punishment
and return to God's favor?**

A. God requires that his justice be satisfied.[1]
Therefore the claims of his justice
must be paid in full,
either by ourselves or another.[2]

[1] Ex. 23:7; Rom. 2:1–11.
[2] Isa. 53:11; Rom. 8:3–4.

13 Q. Can we pay this debt ourselves?

A. Certainly not.
Actually, we increase our guilt every day.[1]

[1] Matt. 6:12; Rom. 2:4–5.

**14 Q. Can another creature—any at all—
pay this debt for us?**

A. No.
To begin with,
God will not punish another creature
for man's guilt.[1]
Besides,
no mere creature can bear the weight
of God's eternal anger against sin
and release others from it.[2]

[1] Ezek. 18:4, 20; Heb. 2:14–18.
[2] Ps. 49:7–9; 130:3.

**15 Q. What kind of mediator and deliverer
should we look for then?**

A. He must be truly human[1] and truly righteous,[2]
yet more powerful than all creatures,
that is, he must also be true God.[3]

[1] Rom. 1:3; 1 Cor. 15:21; Heb. 2:17.
[2] Isa. 53:9; 2 Cor. 5:21; Heb. 7:26.
[3] Isa. 7:14; 9:6; Jer. 23:6; John 1:1.

LORD'S DAY 6

**16 Q. Why must he be truly human
and truly righteous?**

A. God's justice demands it:
man has sinned,
man must pay for his sin,[1]
but a sinner can not pay for other.[2]

[1] Rom. 5:12, 15; 1 Cor. 15:21; Heb. 2:14–16.
[2] Heb. 7:26–27; 1 Pet. 3:18.

17 Q. Why must he also be true God?

A. So that,
by the power of his divinity,
he might bear the weight of God's anger in his
humanity
and earn for us
and restore to us
righteousness and life.[1]

[1] Isa. 53; John 3:16; 2 Cor. 5:21.

**18 Q. And who is this mediator—
true God and at the same time
truly human and truly righteous?**

A. Our Lord Jesus Christ,[1]
who was given us
to set us completely free
and to make us right with God.[2]

[1] Matt. 1:21–23; Luke 2:11; 1 Tim. 2:5.
[2] 1 Cor. 1:30.

19 Q. How do you come to know this?

A. The holy gospel tells me.
God himself began to reveal the gospel already in
Paradise;[1]
later, he proclaimed it
by the holy patriarchs[2] and prophets,[3]
and portrayed it
by the sacrifices and other ceremonies of the law;[4]
finally, he fulfilled it
through his own dear Son.[5]

[1] Gen. 3:15.
[2] Gen. 22:18; 44:10.
[3] Isa. 53; Jer. 23:5–6; Mic. 7:18–20; Acts 10:43; Heb. 1:1–2.
[4] Lev. 1–7; John 5:46; Heb. 10:1–10.
[5] Rom. 10:4; Gal. 4:4–5; Col. 2:17.

LORD'S DAY 7

**20 Q. Are all men saved through Christ
just as we all were lost through Adam?**

A. No.
Only those are saved
who by true faith
are grafted into Christ
and accept all his blessings.[1]

[1] Matt. 7:14; John 3:16, 18, 36; Rom. 11:16–21.

21 Q. What is true faith?

A. True faith is
not only a knowledge and conviction
that everything God reveals in his Word is true;[1]
it is also a deep-rooted assurance,[2]
created in me by the Holy Spirit[3] through the
gospel[4]
that, out of sheer grace earned for us by Christ,[5]
not only others, but I too,[6]
have had my sins forgiven,
have been made forever right with God,
and have been granted salvation.[7]

[1] John 17:3, 17; Heb. 11:1–3; James 2:19.
[2] Rom. 4:18–21; 5:1; 10:10; Heb. 4:14–16.
[3] Matt. 16:15–17; John 3:5; Acts 16:14.
[4] Rom. 1:16; 10:17; 1 Cor. 1:21.
[5] Rom. 3:21–26; Gal. 2:16; Eph. 2:8–10.
[6] Gal. 2:20.
[7] Rom. 1:17; Heb. 10:10.

22 Q. What then must a Christian believe?

A. Everything God promises us in the gospel.[1]
That gospel is summarized for us
in the articles of our Christian faith—
a creed beyond doubt,
and confessed throughout the world.

[1] Matt. 28:18–20; John 20:30–31.

23 Q. What are these articles?

A. I believe in God the Father almighty,
   Maker of heaven and earth.

And in Jesus Christ, his only begotten Son,
   our Lord;
who was conceived by the Holy Spirit,
   born of the virgin Mary;
suffered under Pontius Pilate;
   was crucified, dead, and buried;
   he descended into hell;
the third day he rose again from the dead;
he ascended into heaven,
   and is seated at the right hand of God the Father
      almighty;
from there he shall come
   to judge the living and the dead.

I believe in the Holy Spirit;
I believe a holy catholic church,
   the communion of saints;
the forgiveness of sins;
the resurrection of the body;
and the life everlasting.

LORD'S DAY 8

24 Q. How are these articles divided?

A. Into three parts:
  God the Father and our creation;
  God the Son and our deliverance;
  God the Holy Spirit and our sanctification.

**25 Q. Since there is but one God,[1]
  why do you speak of three:
  Father, Son, and Holy Spirit?**

A. Because that is how
  God has revealed himself in his Word:[2]
  these three distinct persons
  are one, true, eternal God.

[1] Deut. 6:4; 1 Cor. 8:4, 6.
[2] Matt. 3:16–17; 28:18–19; Luke 4:18 (Isa. 61:1); John 14:16; 15:26; 2 Cor. 13:14;
  Gal. 4:6; Tit. 3:5–6.

God the Father

LORD'S DAY 9

**26 Q. What do you believe when you say:
"I believe in God the Father almighty,
Maker of heaven and earth"?**

A. That the eternal Father of our Lord Jesus Christ,
who out of nothing created heaven and earth
and everything in them,[1]
who still upholds and rules them
by his eternal counsel and providence,[2]
is my God and Father
because of Christ his Son.[3]

I trust him so much that I do not doubt
he will provide
whatever I need
for body and soul,[4]
and he will turn to my good
whatever adversity he sends me
in this sad world.[5]

He is able to do this because he is almighty God;[6]
he desires to do this because he is a faithful Father.[7]

[1] Gen. 1 & 2; Ex. 20:11; Ps. 33:6; Isa. 44:24; Acts 4:24; 14:15.
[2] Ps. 104; Matt. 6:30; 10:29; Eph. 1:11.
[3] John 1:12–13; Rom. 8:15–16; Gal. 4:4–7; Eph. 1:5.
[4] Ps. 55:22; Matt. 6:25–26; Luke 12:22–31.
[5] Rom. 8:28.
[6] Gen. 18:14; Rom. 8:31–39.
[7] Matt. 7:9–11.

LORD'S DAY 10

**27 Q. What do you understand
by the providence of God?**

A. Providence is
the almighty and ever present power of God[1]
by which he upholds, as with his hand,
heaven
and earth
and all creatures,[2]
and so rules them that
leaf and blade,
rain and drought,
fruitful and lean years,
food and drink,
health and sickness,
prosperity and poverty—[3]
all things, in fact, come to us
not by chance[4]
but from his fatherly hand.[5]

[1] Jer. 23:23–24; Acts 17:24–28.
[2] Heb. 1:3.
[3] Jer. 5:24; Acts 14:15–17; John 9:3; Prov. 22:2.
[4] Prov. 16:33.
[5] Matt. 10:29.

**28 Q. How does the knowledge
of God's creation and providence
help us?**

A. We can be patient when things go against us,[1]
thankful when things go well,[2]
and for the future we can have
good confidence in our faithful God and Father
that nothing will separate us from his love.[3]
All creatures are so completely in his hand
that without his will
they can neither move nor be moved.[4]

[1] Job 1:21–22; James 1:3.
[2] Deut. 8:10; 1 Thess. 5:18.
[3] Ps. 55:22; Rom. 5:3–5; 8:38–39.
[4] Job 1:12; 2:6; Prov. 21:1; Acts 17:24–28.

God the Son

LORD'S DAY 11

29 Q. Why is the Son of God called "Jesus" meaning "Savior"?

A. Because he saves us from our sins.[1]
Salvation cannot be found in anyone else;
it is futile to look for any salvation elsewhere.[2]

[1] Matt. 1:21; Heb. 7:25.
[2] Isa. 43:11; John 15:5; Acts 4:11–12; 1 Tim. 2:5.

30 Q. Do those who look for their salvation and security in saints, in themselves, or elsewhere really believe in the only Savior Jesus?

A. No.
Although they boast of being his,
by their deeds they deny
the only savior and deliverer, Jesus.[1]

Either Jesus is not a perfect savior,
or those who in true faith accept this savior
have in him all they need for their salvation.[2]

[1] 1 Cor. 1:12–13; Gal. 5:4.
[2] Col. 1:19–20; 2:10; 1 John 1:7.

LORD'S DAY 12

31 Q. Why is he called "Christ" meaning "Anointed"?

A. Because he has been ordained by God the Father
and has been anointed with the Holy Spirit[1]
to be
our chief prophet and teacher[2]
who perfectly reveals to us
the secret counsel and will of God for our
deliverance;[3]
our only high priest[4]
who has set us free by the one sacrifice of his body,[5]
and who continually pleads our cause with the
Father;[6]
and our eternal king[7]
who governs us by his Word and Spirit,
and who guards us and keeps us
in the freedom he has won for us.[8]

[1] Luke 3:21–22; 4:14–19 (Isa. 61:1); Heb. 1:9 (Ps. 45:7).
[2] Acts 3:22 (Deut. 18:15).
[3] John 1:18; 15:15.
[4] Heb. 7:17 (Ps. 110:4).
[5] Heb. 9:12; 10:11–14.
[6] Rom. 8:34; Heb. 9:24.
[7] Matt. 21:5 (Zech. 9:9).
[8] Matt. 28:18–20; John 10:28; Rev. 12:10–11.

32 Q. But why are you called a Christian?

A. Because by faith I am a member of Christ[1]
and so I share in his anointing.[2]
I am anointed
to confess his name,[3]
to present myself to him as a living sacrifice
of thanks,[4]
to strive with a good conscience against sin and
the devil
in this life,[5]
and afterward to reign with Christ
over all creation
for all eternity.[6]

[1] 1 Cor. 12:12–27.
[2] Acts 2:17 (Joel 2:28); 1 John 2:27.
[3] Matt. 10:32; Rom. 10:9–10; Heb. 13:15.
[4] Rom. 12:1; 1 Pet. 2:5, 9.
[5] Gal. 5:16–17; Eph. 6:11; 1 Tim. 1:18–19.
[6] Matt. 25:34; 2 Tim. 2:12.

LORD'S DAY 13

**33 Q. Why is he called God's "only begotten son"
when we also are God's children?**

A. Because Christ alone is the eternal, natural Son
of God.[1]
We, however, are adopted children of God—
adopted by grace through Christ.[2]

[1] John 1:1–3, 14, 18; Heb. 1.
[2] John 1:12; Rom. 8:15–17; Eph. 1:5–6.

34 Q. Why do you call him "our Lord"?

A. Because—
not with gold or silver,
but with his precious blood—[1]
he has set us free
from sin and from the tyranny of the devil,[2]
and has bought us,
body and soul,
to be his very own.[3]

[1] 1 Pet. 1:18–19.
[2] Col. 1:13–14; Heb. 2:14–15.
[3] 1 Cor. 6:20; 1 Tim. 2:5–6.

LORD'S DAY 14

**35 Q. What does it mean that he
"was conceived by the Holy Spirit,
born of the virgin Mary"?**

A. That the eternal Son of God,
who is and remains
true and eternal God,[1]
took to himself,
through the working of the Holy Spirit,[2]
from the flesh and blood of the virgin Mary,[3]
a truly human nature
so that he might become David's true descendant,[4]
in all things like us his brothers[5]
except for sin.[6]

[1] John 1:1; 10:30–36; Acts 13:33 (Ps. 2:7); Col. 1:15–17; 1 John 5:20.
[2] Luke 1:35.
[3] Matt. 1:18–23; John 1:14; Gal. 4:4; Heb. 2:14.
[4] 2 Sam. 7:12–16; Ps. 132:11; Matt. 1:1; Rom. 1:3.
[5] Phil. 2:7; Heb. 2:17.
[6] Heb. 4:15; 7:26–27.

**36 Q. How does the holy conception and birth of Christ
benefit you?**

A. He is our mediator,[1]
and with his innocence and perfect holiness
he removes from God's sight
my sin—mine since I was conceived.[2]

[1] 1 Tim. 2:5–6; Heb. 9:13–15.
[2] Rom. 8:3–4; 2 Cor. 5:21; Gal. 4:4–5; 1 Pet. 1:18–19.

LORD'S DAY 15

**37 Q. What do you understand
by the word "suffered"?**

A. That during his whole life on earth,
but especially at the end,
Christ sustained
in body and soul
the anger of God against the sin of the whole
human race.[1]

This he did in order that,
by his suffering as the only atoning sacrifice,[2]
he might set us free, body and soul,
from eternal condemnation,[3]
and gain for us
God's grace,
righteousness,
and eternal life.[4]

[1] Isa. 53; 1 Pet. 2:24; 3:18.
[2] Rom. 3:25; Heb. 10:14; 1 John 2:2; 4:10.
[3] Rom. 8:1–4; Gal. 3:13.
[4] John 3:16; Rom. 3:24–26.

**38 Q. Why did he suffer
"under Pontius Pilate" as judge?**

A. So that he,
though innocent,
might be condemned by a civil judge,[1]
and so free us from the severe judgment of God
that was to fall on us.[2]

[1] Luke 23:13–24; John 19:4, 12–16.
[2] Isa. 53:4–5; 2 Cor. 5:21; Gal. 3:13.

**39 Q. Is it significant
that he was "crucified"
instead of dying some other way?**

A. Yes.
This death convinces me
that he shouldered the curse
which lay on me,
since death by crucifixion was accursed by God.[1]

[1] Gal. 3:10–13 (Deut. 21:23).

LORD'S DAY 16

40 Q. Why did Christ have to go all the way to death?

A. Because God's justice and truth demand it:[1]
only the death of God's Son could pay for our sin.[2]

[1] Gen. 2:17.
[2] Rom. 8:3–4; Phil. 2:8; Heb. 2:9.

41 Q. Why was he "buried"?

A. His burial testifies
that he really died.[1]

[1] Isa. 53:9; John 19:38–42; Acts 13:29; 1 Cor. 15:3–4.

**42 Q. Since Christ has died for us,
why do we still have to die?**

A. Our death does not pay the debt of our sins.[1]
Rather, it puts an end to our sinning
and is our entrance into eternal life.[2]

[1] Ps. 49:7.
[2] John 5:24; Phil. 1:21–23; 1 Thess. 5:9–10.

**43 Q. What further advantage do we receive
from Christ's sacrifice and death on the cross?**

A. Through Christ's death
our old selves are crucified, put to death, and buried
with him,[1]
so that the evil desires of the flesh
may no longer rule us,[2]
but that instead we may dedicate ourselves
as an offering of gratitude to him.[3]

[1] Rom. 6:5–11; Col. 2:11–12.
[2] Rom. 6:12–14.
[3] Rom. 12:1; Eph. 5:1–2.

**44 Q. Why does the creed add:
"He descended into hell"?**

A. To assure me in times of personal crisis and
temptation
that Christ my Lord,
by suffering unspeakable anguish, pain, and terror
of soul,
especially on the cross but also earlier,
has delivered me from the anguish and torment
of hell.[1]

[1] Isa. 53; Matt. 26:36–46; 27:45–46; Luke 22:44; Heb. 5:7–10.

LORD'S DAY 17

**45 Q. How does Christ's resurrection
benefit us?**

A. First, by his resurrection he has overcome death,
so that he might make us share in the
righteousness
he won for us by his death.[1]

Second, by his power we too
are already now resurrected to a new life.[2]

Third, Christ's resurrection
is a guarantee of our glorious resurrection.[3]

[1] Rom. 4:25; 1 Cor. 15:16–20; 1 Pet. 1:3–5.
[2] Rom. 6:5–11; Eph. 2:4–6; Col. 3:1–4.
[3] Rom. 8:11; 1 Cor. 15:12–23; Phil. 3:20–21.

LORD'S DAY 18

**46 Q. What do you mean by saying:
"he ascended into heaven"?**

A. That Christ,
   while his disciples watched,
   was lifted up from the earth into heaven[1]
   and will be there for our good[2]
   until he comes again
      to judge the living and the dead.[3]

[1] Luke 24:50–51; Acts 1:9–11.
[2] Rom. 8:34; Eph. 4:8–10; Heb. 7:23–25; 9:24.
[3] Acts 1:11.

**47 Q. But isn't Christ with us
until the end of the world
as he promised us?**

A. Christ is true man and true God.
   In his human nature Christ is not now on earth;[2]
   but in his divinity, majesty, grace, and Spirit
   he is not absent from us for a moment.[3]

[1] Matt. 28:20.
[2] Acts 1:9–11; 3:19–21.
[3] Matt. 28:18–20; John 14:16–19.

**48 Q. If his humanity is not present
wherever his divinity is,
then aren't the two natures of Christ
separated from each other?**

A. Certainly not.
   Since divinity
      is not limited
      and is present everywhere,[1]
   it is evident that
      Christ's divinity is surely beyond the bounds of
      the humanity he has taken on,
   but at the same time his divinity is in
   and remains personally united to
      his humanity.[2]

[1] Jer. 23:23–24; Acts 7:48–49 (Isa. 66:1).
[2] John 1:14; 3:13; Col. 2:9.

49 Q. How does Christ's ascension into heaven benefit us?

A. First, he pleads our cause
    in heaven
    in the presence of his Father.[1]

Second, we have our own flesh in heaven—
    a guarantee that Christ our head
    will take us, his members,
    to himself in heaven.[2]

Third, he sends his Spirit to us on earth
    as a further guarantee.[3]
By the Spirit's power
    we make a goal of our lives,
        not earthly things,
        but the things above where Christ is,
        sitting at God's right hand.[4]

[1] Rom. 8:34; 1 John 2:1.
[2] John 14:2; 17:24; Eph. 2:4–6.
[3] John 14:16; 2 Cor. 1:21–22; 5:5.
[4] Col. 3:1–4.

LORD'S DAY 19

**50 Q. Why the next words:
"and is seated at the right hand of God"?**

A. Christ ascended to heaven,
there to show that he is head of his church,[1]
and that the Father rules all things through him.[2]

[1] Eph. 1:20–23; Col. 1:18.
[2] Matt. 28:18; John 5:22–23.

**51 Q. How does this glory of Christ our head
benefit us?**

A. First, through his Holy Spirit
he pours out his gifts from heaven
upon us his members.[1]

Second, by his power
he defends us and keeps us safe
from all enemies.[2]

[1] Acts 2:33; Eph. 4:7–12.
[2] Ps. 110:1–2; John 10:27–30; Rev. 19:11–16.

**52 Q. How does Christ's return
"to judge the living and the dead"
comfort you?**

A. In all my distress and persecution
I turn my eyes to the heavens
and confidently await as judge the very One
who has already stood trial in my place before God
and so has removed the whole curse from me.[1]
All his enemies and mine
he will condemn to everlasting punishment:
but me and all his chosen ones
he will take along with him
into the joy and the glory of heaven.[2]

[1] Luke 21:28; Rom. 8:22–25; Phil. 3:20–21; Tit. 2:13–14.
[2] Matt. 25:31–46; 2 Thess. 1:6–10.

God the Holy Spirit

LORD'S DAY 20

**53 Q. What do you believe
concerning "the Holy Spirit"?**

A. First, he, as well as the Father and the Son,
is eternal God.[1]

Second, he has been given to me personally,[2]
so that, by true faith,
he makes me share in Christ and all his blessings,[3]
comforts me,[4]
and remains with me forever.[5]

[1] Gen. 1:1–2; Matt. 28:19; Acts 5:3–4.
[2] 1 Cor. 6:19; 2 Cor. 1:21–22; Gal. 4:6.
[3] Gal. 3:14.
[4] John 15:26; Acts 9:31.
[5] John 14:16–17; 1 Pet. 4:14.

LORD'S DAY 21

**54 Q. What do you believe
concerning the "holy catholic church"?**

A. I believe that the Son of God
through his Spirit and Word,[1]
out of the entire human race,[2]
from the beginning of the world to its end,[3]
gathers, protects, and preserves for himself
a community chosen for eternal life[4]
and united in true faith.[5]
And of this community I am[6] and always will be[7]
a living member.

[1] John 10:14–16; Acts 20:28; Rom. 10:14–17; Col. 1:18.
[2] Gen. 26:3b–4; Rev. 5:9.
[3] Isa. 59:21; 1 Cor. 11:26.
[4] Matt. 16:18; John 10:28–30; Rom. 8:28–30; Eph. 1:3–14.
[5] Acts 2:42–47; Eph. 4:1–6.
[6] 1 John 3:14, 19–21.
[7] John 10:27–28; 1 Cor. 1:4–9; 1 Pet. 1:3–5.

**55 Q. What do you understand by
"the communion of saints"?**

A. First, that believers one and all,
as members of this community,
share in Christ
and in all his treasures and gifts.[1]

Second, that each member
should consider it his duty
to use his gifts
readily and cheerfully
for the service and enrichment
of the other members.[2]

[1] Rom. 8:32; 1 Cor. 6:17; 12:4–7, 12–13; 1 John 1:3.
[2] Rom. 12:4–8; 1 Cor. 12:20–27; 13:1–7; Phil. 2:4–8.

56 Q. What do you believe
concerning "the forgiveness of sins"?

A. I believe that God,
   because of Christ's atonement,
   will never hold against me
   any of my sins[1]
   nor my sinful nature
   which I need to struggle against all my life.[2]

Rather, in his grace
   God grants me the righteousness of Christ
   to free me forever from judgment.[3]

[1] Ps. 103:3–4, 10, 12; Mic. 7:18–19; 2 Cor. 5:18–21; 1 John 1:7; 2:2.
[2] Rom. 7:21–25.
[3] John 3:17–18; Rom. 8:1–2.

LORD'S DAY 22

57 Q. How does "the resurrection of the body" comfort you?

A. Not only my soul
  will be taken immediately after this life
  to Christ its head,[1]
but even my very flesh, raised by the power
of Christ,
  will be reunited with my soul
  and make like Christ's glorious* body.[2]

[1] Luke 23:43; Phil. 1:21–23.
[2] 1 Cor. 15:20, 42–46, 54; Phil. 3:21; 1 John 3:2.

58 Q. How does the article concerning "life everlasting" comfort you?

A. Even as I already now
  experience in my heart
  the beginning of eternal joy,[1]
so after this life I will have
  perfect blessedness such as
    no eye has seen,
    no ear has heard,
    no man has ever imagined:
  a blessedness in which to praise God eternally.[2]

[1] Rom. 14:17.
[2] John 17:3; 1 Cor. 2:9.

*The first edition had here the German word for holy. This was later corrected to the German word for glorious.

LORD'S DAY 23

**59 Q. What good does it do you, however,
to believe all this?**

A. In Christ I am right with God
and heir to life everlasting.[1]

[1] John 3:36; Rom. 1:17 (Hab. 2:4); Rom. 5:1–2.

60 Q. How are you right with God?

A. Only by true faith in Jesus Christ

Even though my conscience accuses me
of having grievously sinned against all God's
commandments
and of never having kept any of them,[2]
and even though I am still inclined toward all evil,[3]
nevertheless,
without my deserving it at all,[4]
out of sheer grace,[5]
God grants and credits to me
the perfect satisfaction, righteousness, and holiness
of Christ,[6]
as if I had never sinned nor been a sinner,
as if I had been as perfectly obedient
as Christ was obedient for me.[7]

All I need to do
is to accept this gift of God with a believing heart.[8]

[1] Rom. 3:21–28; Gal. 2:16; Eph. 2:8–9; Phil 3:8–11.
[2] Rom. 3:9–10.
[3] Rom. 7:23.
[4] Tit. 3:4–5.
[5] Rom. 3:24; Eph. 2:8.
[6] Rom. 4:3–5 (Gen. 15:6); 2 Cor. 5:17–19; 1 John 2:1–2.
[7] Rom. 4:24–25; 2 Cor. 5:21.
[8] John 3:18; Acts 16:30–31.

**61 Q. Why do you say that
by faith alone
you are right with God?**

A. It is not because of any value my faith has
that God is pleased with me.
Only Christ's satisfaction, righteousness, and
holiness
make me right with God.[1]
And I can receive this righteousness and make it
mine
in no other way than
by faith alone.[2]

[1] 1 Cor. 1:30–31.
[2] Rom. 10:10; 1 John 5:10–12.

LORD'S DAY 24

**62 Q. Why can't the good we do
make us right with God,
or at least help make us right with him?**

A. Because the righteousness
which can pass God's scrutiny
must be entirely perfect
and must in every way measure up to the
divine law.[1]
Even the very best we do in this life
is imperfect
and stained with sin.[2]

[1] Rom. 3:20; Gal. 3:10 (Deut. 27:26).
[2] Isa. 64:6.

**63 Q. How can you say that the good we do
doesn't earn anything
when God promises to reward it
in this life and the next?[1]**

A. This reward is not earned;
it is a gift of grace.[2]

[1] Matt. 5:12; Heb. 11:6.
[2] Luke 17:10; 2 Tim. 4:7–8.

**64 Q. But doesn't this teaching
make people indifferent and wicked?**

A. No.
It is impossible
for those grafted into Christ by true faith
not to produce fruits of gratitude.[1]

[1] Luke 6:43–45; John 15:5.

The Sacraments

LORD'S DAY 25

**65 Q. You confess that by faith alone
you share in Christ and all his blessings:
where does that faith come from?**

A. The Holy Spirit produces it in our hearts[1]
by the preaching of the holy gospel,[2]
and confirms it
through our use of the holy sacraments.[3]

[1] John 3:5; 1 Cor. 2:10–14; Eph. 2:8.
[2] Rom. 10:17; 1 Pet. 1:23–25.
[3] Matt. 28:19–20; 1 Cor. 10:16.

66 Q. What are sacraments?

A. Sacraments are holy signs and seals for us to see.
They were instituted by God so that
by our use of them
he might make us understand more clearly
the promise of the gospel,
and might put his seal on that promise.[1]

And this is God's gospel promise:
to forgive our sins and give us eternal life
by grace alone
because of Christ's one sacrifice
finished on the cross.[2]

[1] Gen. 17:11; Deut. 30:6; Rom. 4:11.
[2] Matt. 26:27–28; Acts 2:38; Heb. 10:10.

**67 Q. Are both the word and the sacraments then
intended to focus our faith
on the sacrifice of Jesus Christ on the cross
as the only ground of our salvation?**

A. Right!
In the gospel the Holy Spirit teaches us
and through the holy sacraments he assures us
that our entire salvation
rests on Christ's one sacrifice for us on the cross.[1]

[1] Rom. 6:3; 1 Cor. 11:26; Gal. 3:27.

**68 Q. How many sacraments
did Christ institute in the New Testament?**

A. Two: baptism and the Lord's Supper.[1]

[1] Matt. 28:19–20; 1 Cor. 11:23–26.

Baptism

LORD'S DAY 26

**69 Q. How does baptism
remind you and assure you
that Christ's one sacrifice on the cross
is for you personally?**

A. In this way:
Christ instituted this outward washing[1]
and with it gave the promise that,
as surely as water washes away the dirt from the body,
so certainly his blood and his Spirit
wash away my soul's impurity,
in other words, all my sins.[2]

[1] Acts 2:38.
[2] Matt. 3:11; Rom. 6:3–10; 1 Pet. 3:21.

**70 Q. What does it mean
to be washed with Christ's blood and spirit?**

A. To be washed with Christ's blood means
that God, by grace, has forgiven my sins
because of Christ's blood
poured out for me in his sacrifice on the cross.[1]

To be washed with Christ's Spirit means
that the Holy Spirit has renewed me
and set me apart to be a member of Christ
so that more and more I become dead to sin
and increasingly live a holy and blameless life.[2]

[1] Zech. 13:1; Eph. 1:7–8; Heb. 12:24; 1 Pet. 1:2; Rev. 1:5.
[2] Ezek. 36:25–27; John 3:5–8; Rom. 6:4; 1 Cor. 6:11; Col. 2:11–12.

**71 Q. Where does Christ promise
that we are washed with his blood and spirit
as surely as we are washed
with the water of baptism?**

A. In the institution of baptism where he says:
"Therefore go and make disciples of all nations,
baptizing them in the name of the Father
and of the Son
and of the Holy Spirit."[1]

"Whoever believes and is baptized will be saved,
but whoever does not believe will be condemned."[2]*

This promise is repeated when Scripture calls
baptism
the washing of rebirth[3] and
the washing away of sins.[4]

[1] Matt. 28:19.
[2] Mark 16:16.
[3] Tit. 3:5.
[4] Acts 22:16.

*Earlier and better manuscripts of Mark 16 omit the words "Whoever believes and is
baptized . . . condemned."

LORD'S DAY 27

**72 Q. Does this outward washing with water
itself wash away sins?**

A. No, only Jesus Christ's blood and the Holy Spirit
cleanse us from all sins.[1]

[1] Matt. 3:11; 1 Pet. 3:21; 1 John 1:7.

**73 Q. Why then does the Holy Spirit call baptism
the washing of regeneration and
the washing away of sins?**

A. God has good reason for these words.
He wants to teach us that
the blood and Spirit of Christ wash away our sins
just as water washes away dirt from our bodies.[1]

But more important,
he wants to assure us, by this divine pledge and sign,
that the washing away of our sins spiritually
is as real as physical washing with water.[2]

[1] 1 Cor. 6:11; Rev. 1:5; 7:14.
[2] Acts 2:38; Rom. 6:3–4; Gal. 3:27.

74 Q. Should infants, too, be baptized?

A. Yes.
Infants as well as adults
are in God's covenant and are his people.[1]
They, no less than adults, are promised
the forgiveness of sin through Christ's blood
and the Holy Spirit who produces faith.[2]

Therefore, by baptism, the mark of the covenant,
infants should be received into the Christian church
and should be distinguished from the children of
unbelievers.[3]
This was done in the Old Testament by circumcision,[4]
which was replaced in the New Testament by
baptism.[5]

[1] Gen. 17:7; Matt. 19:14.
[2] Isa. 44:1–3; Acts 2:38–39; 16:31.
[3] Acts 10:47; 1 Cor. 7:14.
[4] Gen. 17:9–14.
[5] Col. 2:11–13.

The Lord's Supper

LORD'S DAY 28

**75 Q. How does the Lord's Supper
remind you and assure you
that you share in
Christ's one sacrifice on the cross
and in all his gifts?**

A. In this way:
Christ has commanded me and all believers
to eat this broken bread and to drink this cup.
With this command he gave this promise:[1]

First,
    as surely as I see with my eyes
        the bread of the Lord broken for me
        and the cup given to me,
    so surely
        his body was offered and broken for me
        and his blood poured out for me
            on the cross.

Second,
    as surely as
        I receive from the hand of him who serves,
        and taste with my mouth
            the bread and cup of the Lord,
            given me as sure signs of Christ's body and blood,
    so surely
        he nourishes and refreshes my soul for eternal life
        with his crucified body and poured-out blood.

[1] Matt. 26:26–28; Mark 14:22–24; Luke 22:19–20; 1 Cor. 11:23–25.

**76 Q. What does it mean
to eat the crucified body of Christ
and to drink his poured-out blood?**

A. It means
    to accept with a believing heart
      the entire suffering and death of Christ
    and by believing
      to receive forgiveness of sins and eternal life.[1]

But it means more.
    Through the Holy Spirit, who lives both in Christ
      and in us,
    we are united more and more to Christ's blessed body.[2]
      And so, although he is in heaven[3] and we are on
        earth,
      we are flesh of his flesh and bone of his bone.[4]
      And we forever live on and are governed by one
        Spirit,
      as members of our body are by one soul.[5]

[1] John 6:35, 40, 50–54.
[2] John 6:55–56; 1 Cor. 12:13.
[3] Acts 1:9–11; 1 Cor. 11:26; Col. 3:1.
[4] 1 Cor. 6:15–17; Eph. 5:29–30; 1 John 4:13.
[5] John 6:56–58; 15:1–6; Eph. 4:15–16; 1 John 3:24.

**77 Q. Where does Christ promise
to nourish and refresh believers
with his body and blood
as surely as
they eat this broken bread
and drink this cup?**

A. In the institution of the Lord's Supper:

"The Lord Jesus, on the night he was betrayed,
took bread, and when he had given thanks,
he broke it and said,
  'This is my body, which is for you;
  do this in remembrance of me.'
In the same way, after supper he took the cup, saying,
  'This cup is the new covenant in my blood;
  do this, whenever you drink it,
  in remembrance of me.'
For whenever you eat this bread and drink this cup,
you proclaim the Lord's death
until he comes."[1]

This promise is repeated by Paul in these words:
"Is not the cup of thanksgiving for which we give
  thanks
  a participation in the blood of Christ?
And is not the bread that we break
  a participation in the body of Christ?
Because there is one loaf, we, who are many, are
  one body,
for we all partake of the one loaf."[2]

[1] 1 Cor. 11:23–26.
[2] 1 Cor. 10:16–17.

LORD'S DAY 29

**78 Q. Are the bread and wine changed into
the real body and blood of Christ?**

A. No.

Just as the water of baptism
  is not changed into Christ's blood
  and does not itself wash away sins
  but is simply God's sign and assurance,[1]
so too the bread of the Lord's Supper
  is not changed into the actual body of Christ[2]
  even though it is called the body of Christ[3]
    in keeping with the nature and language of
      sacraments.[4]

[1] Eph. 5:26; Tit. 3:5.
[2] Matt. 26:26–29.
[3] 1 Cor. 10:16–17; 11:26–28.
[4] Gen. 17:10–11; Ex. 12:11, 13; 1 Cor. 10:1–4.

**79 Q. Why then does Christ call
the bread his body
and the cup his blood,
or the new covenant in his blood?
(Paul uses the words,
a participation in Christ's body and blood.)**

A. Christ has good reason for these words.
He wants to teach us that
  as bread and wine nourish our temporal life,
  so too his crucified body and poured-out blood
  truly nourish our souls for eternal life.[1]

But more important,
he wants to assure us, by this visible sign and pledge,
  that we, through the Holy Spirit's work,
    share in his true body and blood
    as surely as our mouths
    receive these holy signs in his remembrance,[2]
  and that all of his suffering and obedience
    are as definitely ours
    as if we personally
    had suffered and paid for our sins.[3]

[1] John 6:51, 55.
[2] 1 Cor. 10:16–17; 11:26.
[3] Rom. 6:5–11.

LORD'S DAY 30

*80 Q. How does the Lord's Supper differ from the Roman Catholic Mass?

A. The Lord's Supper declares to us
that our sins have been completely forgiven
through the one sacrifice of Jesus Christ
which he himself finished on the cross once for all.[1]
It also declares to us
that the Holy Spirit grafts us into Christ,[2]
who with his very body
is now in heaven at the right hand of the Father[3]
where he wants us to worship him.[4]

But the Mass teaches
that the living and the dead
do not have their sins forgiven
through the suffering of Christ
unless Christ is still offered for them daily by
the priests.
It also teaches
that Christ is bodily present
in the form of bread and wine
where Christ is therefore to be worshiped.
Thus the Mass is basically
nothing but a denial
of the one sacrifice and suffering of Jesus Christ
and a condemnable idolatry.

[1] John 19:30; Heb. 7:27; 9:12, 25–26; 10:10–18.
[2] 1 Cor. 6:17; 10:16–17.
[3] Acts 7:55–56; Heb. 1:3; 8:1.
[4] Matt. 6:20–21; John 4:21–24; Phil. 3:20; Col. 3:1–3.

*Question and answer 80 were altogether absent from the first edition of the catechism
and were present in a short form in the second edition. The translation here given is of
the text of the third edition.

81 Q. **Who are to come
to the Lord's table?**

A. Those who are displeased with themselves
because of their sins,
but who nevertheless trust
that their sins are pardoned
and that their continuing weakness is covered
by the suffering and death of Christ,
and who also desire more and more
to strengthen their faith
and to lead a better life.

Hypocrites and those who are unrepentant, however,
eat and drink judgment on themselves.[1]

[1] 1 Cor. 10:19–22; 11:26–32.

82 Q. **Are those to be admitted
to the Lord's Supper
who show by what they say and do
that they are unbelieving and ungodly?**

A. No, that would dishonor God's covenant
and bring down God's anger upon the entire
congregation.[1]
Therefore, according to the instruction of Christ and
his apostles,
the Christian church is duty-bound to exclude
such people,
by the official use of the keys of the kingdom,
until they reform their lives.

[1] 1 Cor. 11:17–32; Ps. 50:14–16; Isa. 1:11–17.

LORD'S DAY 31

83 Q. What are the keys of the kingdom?

A. The preaching of the holy gospel
and Christian discipline toward repentance.
Both preaching and discipline
open the kingdom of heaven to believers
and close it to unbelievers.[1]

[1] Matt. 16:19; John 20:22–23.

**84 Q. How does preaching the gospel
open and close the kingdom of heaven?**

A. According to the command of Christ:

The kingdom of heaven is opened
by proclaiming and publicly declaring
to each and every believer that,
as often as he accepts the gospel promise in
true faith,
God, because of what Christ has done,
truly forgives all his sins.

The kingdom of heaven is closed, however,
by proclaiming and publicly declaring
to unbelievers and hypocrites that,
as long as they do not repent,
the anger of God and eternal condemnation
rest on them.

God's judgment, both in this life and in the life to come,
is based on this gospel testimony.[1]

[1] Matt. 16:19; John 3:31–36; 20:21–23.

85 Q. How is the kingdom of heaven
closed and opened by Christian discipline?

A. According to the command of Christ:

If anyone, though called a Christian,
    professes unchristian teachings or lives an
      unchristian life,
if after repeated brotherly counsel,
    he refuses to abandon his errors and
      wickedness, and,
if after being reported to the church, that is, to its
    officers,
    he fails to respond also to their admonition—
such a one the officers exclude from the Christian
    fellowship
    by withholding the sacraments from him,
and God himself excludes him from the kingdom
    of Christ.[1]

Such a person,
    when he promises and demonstrates genuine reform,
is received again
    as a member of Christ
    and of his church.[2]

[1] Matt. 18:15–20; 1 Cor. 5:3–5, 11–13; 2 Thess. 3:14–15.
[2] Luke 15:20–24; 2 Cor. 2:6–11.

Part III: Man's Gratitude

LORD'S DAY 32

**86 Q. We have been delivered
from our misery
by God's grace alone through Christ
and not because we have earned it:
why then must we still do good?**

A. To be sure, Christ has redeemed us by his blood.
But we do good because
Christ by his Spirit is also renewing us to be like
himself,
so that in all our living
we may show that we are thankful to God
for all he has done for us,[1]
and so that he may be praised through us.[2]

And we do good
so that we may be assured of our faith by its fruits,[3]
and so that by our godly living
our neighbors may be won over to Christ.[4]

[1] Rom. 6:13; 12:1–2; 1 Pet. 2:5–10.
[2] Matt. 5:16; 1 Cor. 6:19–20.
[3] Matt. 7:17–18; Gal. 5:22–24; 2 Pet. 1:10–11.
[4] Matt. 5:14–16; Rom. 14:17–19; 1 Pet. 2:12; 3:1–2.

**87 Q. Can those be saved
who do not turn to God
from their ungrateful
and impenitent ways?**

A. By no means.
Scripture tells us that
no unchaste person,
no idolater, adulterer, thief,
no covetous person,
no drunkard, slanderer, robber,
or the like
is going to inherit the kingdom of God.[1]

[1] 1 Cor. 6:9–10; Gal. 5:19–21; Eph. 5:1–20; 1 John 3:14.

LORD'S DAY 33

**88 Q. What is involved
in genuine repentance or conversion?**

A. Two things:
the dying-away of the old self,
and the coming-to-life of the new.[1]

[1] Rom. 6:1–11; 2 Cor. 5:17; Eph. 4:22–24; Col. 3:5–10.

89 Q. What is the dying-away of the old self?

A. It is to be genuinely sorry for sin,
to hate it more and more,
and to run away from it.[1]

[1] Ps. 51:3–4, 17; Joel 2:12–13; Rom. 8:12–13; 2 Cor. 7:10.

90 Q. What is the coming-to-life of the new self?

A. It is wholehearted joy in God through Christ[1]
and a delight to do every kind of good
as God wants us to.[2]

[1] Ps. 51:8, 12; Isa.57:15; Rom. 5:1; 14:17.
[2] Rom. 6:10–11; Gal. 2:20.

91 Q. What do we do that is good?

A. Only that which
arises out of true faith,[1]
conforms to God's law,[2]
and is done for his glory;[3]
and not that which is based
on what we think is right
or on established human tradition.[4]

[1] John 15:5; Heb. 11:6.
[2] Lev. 18:4; 1 Sam. 15:22; Eph. 2:10.
[3] 1 Cor. 10:31.
[4] Deut. 12:32; Isa. 29:13; Ezek. 20:18–19; Matt. 15:7–9.

LORD'S DAY 34

92 Q. What does the Lord say in his law?

    A. God spoke all these words:

The First Commandment
I am the LORD your God,
  who brought you out of Egypt,
  out of the land of slavery.
You shall have no other gods before me.

The Second Commandment
You shall not make for yourself an idol
  in the form of anything in heaven above
  or on the earth beneath
  or in the waters below.
You shall not bow down to them or worship them;
  for I, the LORD your God, am a jealous God,
  punishing the children for the sin of the fathers
    to the third and fourth generation
    of those who hate me,
  but showing love to a thousand generations of those
    who love me and keep my commandments.

The Third Commandment
You shall not misuse the name of the LORD your God,
  for the LORD will not hold anyone guiltless
  who misuses his name.

The Fourth Commandment
Remember the Sabbath day by keeping it holy.
Six days you shall labor and do all your work,
  but the seventh day is a Sabbath to the LORD your God.
On it you shall not do any work,
  neither you, nor your son or daughter,
  nor your manservant or maidservant,
  nor your animals,
  nor the alien within your gates.
For in six days the LORD made the heavens and
  the earth,
  the sea, and all that is in them,
  but he rested on the seventh day.
Therefore the LORD blessed the Sabbath day
and made it holy.

The Fifth Commandment
Honor your father and your mother,
so that you may live long
in the land the LORD your God is giving you.

The Sixth Commandment
You shall not murder.

The Seventh Commandment
You shall not commit adultery.

The Eighth Commandment
You shall not steal.

The Ninth Commandment
You shall not give false testimony against your
neighbor.

The Tenth Commandment
You shall not covet your neighbor's house.
You shall not covet your neighbor's wife,
or his manservant or maidservant,
his ox or donkey,
or anything that belongs to your neighbor.[1]

[1] Ex. 20:1–17; Deut. 5:6–21.

93 Q. How are these commandments divided?

A. Into two tables.
The first has four commandments,
teaching us what our relation to God should be.
The second has six commandments,
teaching us what we owe our neighbor.[1]

[1] Matt. 22:37–39.

**94 Q. What does the Lord require
in the first commandment?**

A. That I, not wanting to endanger my very salvation,
avoid and shun
all idolatry,[1] magic, superstitious rites,[2]
and prayer to saints or to other creatures.[3]

That I sincerely acknowledge the only true God,[4]
trust him alone,[5]
look to him for every good thing[6]
humbly[7] and patiently,[8]
love him,[9] fear him,[10] and honor him[11]
with all my heart.

In short,
That I give up anything
rather than go against his will in any way.[12]

[1] 1 Cor. 6:9–10; 10:5–14; 1 John 5:21.
[2] Lev. 19:31; Deut. 18:9–12.
[3] Matt. 4:10; Rev. 19:10; 22:8–9.
[4] John 17:3.
[5] Jer. 17:5, 7.
[6] Ps. 104:27–28; James 1:17.
[7] 1 Pet. 5:5–6.
[8] Col. 1:11; Heb. 10:36.
[9] Matt. 22:37 (Deut. 6:5).
[10] Prov. 9:10; 1 Pet. 1:17.
[11] Matt. 4:10 (Deut. 6:13).
[12] Matt. 5:29–30; 10:37–39.

95 Q. What is idolatry?

A. Idolatry is
having or inventing something in which one trusts
in place of or alongside of the only true God,
who has revealed himself in his Word.[1]

[1] 1 Chron. 16:26; Gal. 4:8–9; Eph. 5:5; Phil. 3:19.

LORD'S DAY 35

96 Q. What is God's will for us
in the second commandment?

A. That we in no way make any image of God[1]
nor worship him in any other way
than he has commanded in his Word.[2]

[1] Deut. 4:15–19; Isa. 40:18–25; Acts 17:29; Rom. 1:23.
[2] Lev. 10:1–7; 1 Sam. 15:22–23; John 4:23–24.

97 Q. May we then not make
any image at all?

A. God can not and may not
be visibly portrayed in any way.

Although creatures may be portrayed,
yet God forbids making or having such images
if one's intention is to worship them
or to serve God through them.[1]

[1] Ex. 34:13–14, 17; 2 Kings 18:4–5.

98 Q. But may not images be permitted in the churches
as teaching aids for the unlearned?

A. No, we shouldn't try to be wiser than God.
He wants his people instructed
by the living preaching of his Word—[1]
not by idols that cannot even talk.[2]

[1] Rom. 10:14–15, 17; 2 Tim. 3:16–17; 2 Pet. 1:19.
[2] Jer. 10:8; Hab. 2:18–20.

LORD'S DAY 36

**99 Q. What is God's will for us
in the third commandment?**

A. That we neither blaspheme nor misuse the name
of God
by cursing,[1] perjury,[2] or unnecessary oaths,[3]
nor share in such horrible sins
by being silent bystanders.[4]

In a word, it requires
that we use the holy name of God
only with reverence and awe,[5]
so that we may properly
confess him,[6]
pray to him,[7]
and praise him in everything we do and say.[8]

[1] Lev. 24:10–17.
[2] Lev. 19:12.
[3] Matt. 5:37; James 5:12.
[4] Lev. 5:1; Prov. 29:24.
[5] Ps. 99:1–5; Jer. 4:2.
[6] Matt. 10:32–33; Rom. 10:9–10.
[7] Ps. 50:14–15; 1 Tim. 2:8.
[8] Col. 3:17.

**100 Q. Is blasphemy of God's name by swearing and cursing
really such serious sin
that God is angry also with those
who do not do all they can
to help prevent it and forbid it?**

A. Yes, indeed.[1]
No sin is greater,
no sin makes God more angry
than blaspheming his name.
That is why he commanded the death penalty for it.[2]

[1] Lev. 5:1.
[2] Lev. 24:10–17.

LORD'S DAY 37

**101 Q. But may we swear an oath in God's name
if we do it reverently?**

A. Yes, when the government demands it,
or when necessity requires it,
in order to maintain and promote truth and
trustworthiness
for God's glory and our neighbor's good.

Such oaths are approved in God's Word[1]
and were rightly used by Old and New Testament
believers.[2]

[1] Deut. 6:13; 10:20; Jer. 4:1–2; Heb. 6:16.
[2] Gen. 21:24; Josh. 9:15; 1 Kings 1:29–30; Rom. 1:9; 2 Cor. 1:23.

102 Q. May we swear by saints or other creatures?

A. No.
A legitimate oath means calling upon God
as the one who knows my heart
to witness to my truthfulness
and to punish me if I swear falsely.[1]
No creature is worthy of such honor.[2]

[1] Rom. 9:11; 2 Cor. 1:23.
[2] Matt. 5:34–37; 23:16–22; James 5:12.

LORD'S DAY 38

**103 Q. What is God's will for us
in the fourth commandment?**

A. First,
that the gospel ministry and education for it be
maintained,[1]
and that, especially on the festive day of rest,
I regularly attend the assembly of God's people[2]
to learn what God's Word teaches,[3]
to participate in the sacraments,[4]
to pray to God publicly,[5]
and to bring Christian offerings for the poor.[6]

Second,
that every day of my life
I rest from my evil ways,
let the Lord work in me through his Spirit,
and so begin in this life
the eternal Sabbath.[7]

[1] Deut. 6:4–9, 20–25; 1 Cor. 9:13–14; 2 Tim. 2:2; 3:13–17; Tit. 1:5.
[2] Deut. 12:5–12; Ps. 40:9–10; 68:26; Acts 2:42–47; Heb. 10:23–25.
[3] Rom. 10:14–17; 1 Cor. 14:31–32; 1 Tim. 4:13.
[4] 1 Cor. 11:23–24.
[5] Col. 3:16; 1 Tim. 2:1.
[6] Ps. 50:14; 1 Cor. 16:2; 2 Cor. 8 & 9.
[7] Isa. 66:23; Heb. 4:9–11.

LORD'S DAY 39

**104 Q. What is God's will for us
in the fifth commandment?**

A. That I honor, love, and be loyal to
my father and mother
and all those in authority over me;
that I obey and submit to them, as is proper,
when they correct and punish me;[1]
and also that I be patient with their failings—[2]
for through them God chooses to rule us.[3]

[1] Ex. 21:17; Prov. 1:8; 4:1; Rom. 13:1–2; Eph. 5:21–22; 6:1–9; Col. 3:18–4:1.
[2] Prov. 20:20; 23:22; 1 Pet. 2:18.
[3] Matt. 22:21; Rom. 13:1–8; Eph. 6:1–9; Col. 3:18–21.

LORD'S DAY 40

**105 Q. What is God's will for us
in the sixth commandment?**

A. I am not to belittle, insult, hate, or kill my
neighbor—
not by my thoughts, my words, my look or
gesture,
and certainly not by actual deeds—
and I am not to be party to this in others;[1]
rather, I am to put away all desire for revenge.[2]

I am not to harm or recklessly endanger myself
either.[3]

Prevention of murder is also why
government is armed with the sword.[4]

[1] Gen. 9:6; Lev. 19:17–18; Matt. 5:21–22; 26:52.
[2] Prov. 25:21–22; Matt. 18:35; Rom. 12:19; Eph. 4:26.
[3] Matt. 4:7; 26:52; Rom. 13:11–14.
[4] Gen. 9:6; Ex. 21:14; Rom. 13:4.

106 Q. Does this commandment refer only to killing?

A. By forbidding murder God teaches us
that he hates the root of murder:
envy, hatred, anger, vindictiveness.[1]

In God's sight all such are murder.[2]

[1] Prov. 14:30; Rom. 1:29; 12:19; Gal. 5:19–21; 1 John 2:9–11.
[2] 1 John 3:15.

**107 Q. Is it enough then
that we do not kill our neighbor
in any such way?**

A. No.
By condemning envy, hatred, and anger
God tells us
to love our neighbor as ourselves,[1]
to be patient, peace-loving, gentle,
merciful, and friendly to him,[2]
to protect him from harm as much as we can,
and to do good even to our enemies.[3]

[1] Matt. 7:12; 22:39; Rom. 12:10.
[2] Matt. 5:3–12; Luke 6:36; Rom. 12:10, 18; Gal. 6:1–2; Eph. 4:2; Col. 3:12; 1 Pet. 3:8.
[3] Ex. 23:4–5; Matt. 44–45; Rom. 12:20–21 (Prov. 25:21–22).

LORD'S DAY 41

**108 Q. What is God's will for us
in the seventh commandment?**

A. God condemns all unchastity.[1]
We should therefore thoroughly detest it[2]
and, married or single,
live decent and chaste lives.[3]

[1] Lev. 18:30; Eph. 5:3–5.
[2] Jude 22–23.
[3] 1 Cor. 7:1–9; 1 Thess. 4:3–8; Heb. 13:4.

**109 Q. Does God, in this commandment,
forbid only such scandalous sins as adultery?**

A. We are temples of the Holy Spirit, body and soul,
and God wants both to be kept clean and holy.
That is why he forbids
everything which incites unchastity,[1]
whether it be actions, looks, talk, thoughts, or
desires.[2]

[1] 1 Cor. 15:33; Eph. 5:18.
[2] Matt. 5:27–29; 1 Cor. 6:18–20; Eph. 5:3–4.

LORD'S DAY 42

**110 Q. What does God forbid
in the eighth commandment?**

A. He forbids not only outright theft and robbery,
punishable by law.[1]

But in God's sight theft also includes
cheating and swindling our neighbor
by schemes made to appear legitimate,[2]
such as:
inaccurate measurements of weight, size, or
volume;
fraudulent merchandising;
counterfeit money;
excessive interest;
or any other means forbidden by God.[3]

In addition he forbids all greed[4]
and pointless squandering of his gifts.[5]

[1] Ex. 22:1; 1 Cor. 5:9–10; 6:9–10.
[2] Mic. 6:9–11; Luke 3:14; James 5:1–6.
[3] Deut. 25:13–16; Ps. 15:5; Prov. 11:1; 12:22; Ezek. 45:9–12; Luke 6:35.
[4] Luke 12:15; Eph. 5:5.
[5] Prov. 21:20; 23:20–21; Luke 16:10–13.

**111 Q. What does God require of you
in this commandment?**

A. That I do whatever I can
for my neighbor's good,
that I treat him
as I would like others to treat me,
and that I work faithfully
so that I may share with those in need.[1]

[1] Isa. 58:5–10; Matt. 7:12; Gal. 6:9–10; Eph. 4:28.

LORD'S DAY 43

**112 Q. What is God's will for us
in the ninth commandment?**

A. God's will is that I
never give false testimony against anyone,
twist no one's words,
not gossip or slander,
nor join in condemning anyone
without a hearing or without a just cause.[1]

Rather, in court and everywhere else,
I should avoid lying and deceit of every kind;
these are devices the devil himself uses,
and they would call down on me God's intense anger.[2]
I should love the truth,
speak it candidly,
and openly acknowledge it.[3]
And I should do what I can
to guard and advance my neighbor's good name.[4]

[1] Ps. 15; Prov. 19:5; Matt. 7:1; Luke 6:37; Rom. 1:28–32.
[2] Lev. 19:11–12; Prov. 12:22; 13:5; John 8:44; Rev. 21:8.
[3] 1 Cor. 13:6; Eph. 4:25.
[4] 1 Pet. 3:8–9; 4:8.

LORD'S DAY 44

**113 Q. What is God's will for us
in the tenth commandment?**

A. That not even the slightest thought or desire
contrary to any one of God's commandments
should ever arise in my heart.

Rather, with all my heart
I should always hate sin
and take pleasure in whatever is right.[1]

[1] Ps. 19:7-14; 139:23-24; Rom. 7:7-8.

**114 Q. But can those converted to God
obey these commandments perfectly?**

A. No.
In this life even the holiest
have only a small beginning of this obedience.[1]

Nevertheless, with all seriousness of purpose,
they do begin to live
according to all, not only some,
of God's commandments.[2]

[1] Eccles. 7:20; Rom. 7:14-15; 1 Cor. 13:9; 1 John 1:8-10.
[2] Ps. 1:1-2; Rom. 7:22-25; Phil. 3:12-16.

**115 Q. No one in this life
can obey the ten commandments perfectly:
why then does God want them
preached so pointedly?**

A. First, so that the longer we live
the more we may come to know our sinfulness
and the more eagerly look to Christ
for forgiveness of sins and righteousness.[1]

Second, so that,
while praying to God for the grace of the
Holy Spirit,
we may never stop striving
to be renewed more and more after God's image,
until after this life we reach our goal:
perfection.[2]

[1] Ps. 32:5; Rom. 3:19-26; 7:7, 24-25; 1 John 1:9.
[2] 1 Cor. 9:24; Phil. 3:12-14; 1 John 3:1-3.

Prayer

LORD'S DAY 45

116 Q. Why do Christians need to pray?

A. Because prayer is the most important part
of the thankfulness God requires of us.[1]
And also because God gives his grace and
Holy Spirit
only to those who pray continually and groan
inwardly,
asking God for these gifts
and thanking him for them.[2]

[1] Ps. 50:14–15; 116:12–19; 1 Thess. 5:16–18.
[2] Matt. 7:7–8; Luke 11:9–13.

117 Q. How does God want us to pray
so that he will listen to us?

A. First, we must pray from the heart
to no other than the one true God,
who has revealed himself in his Word,
asking for everything he has commanded us to
ask for.[1]

Second, we must acknowledge our need and misery,
hiding nothing,
and humble ourselves in his majestic presence.[2]

Third, we must rest on this unshakable foundation:
even though we do not deserve it,
God will surely listen to our prayer
because of Christ our Lord.
That is what he promised us in his Word.[3]

[1] Ps. 145:18–20; John 4:22–24; Rom. 8:26–27; James 1:5; 1 John 5:14–15.
[2] 2 Chron. 7:14; Ps. 2:11; 34:18; 62:8; Isa. 66:2; Rev. 4.
[3] Dan. 9:17–19; Matt. 7:8; John 14:13–14; 16:23; Rom. 10:13; James 1:6.

118 Q. What did God command us to pray for?

A. Everything we need, spiritually and physically,[1]
as embraced in the prayer
Christ our Lord himself taught us.

[1] James 1:17; Matt. 6:33.

119 Q. What is this prayer?

A. Our Father in heaven,
    hallowed be your name,
    your kingdom come,
    your will be done
        on earth as it is in heaven.
    Give us today our daily bread.
    Forgive us our debts,
        as we also have forgiven our debtors.
    And lead us not into temptation,
        but deliver us from the evil one,
    for yours is the kingdom
        and the power
        and the glory forever.
    Amen.[1]*

[1] Matt. 6:9–13; Luke 11:2–4.

*Earlier and better manuscripts of Matthew 6 omit the words "For yours is . . . Amen."

LORD'S DAY 46

**120 Q. Why did Christ command us
to call God "Our Father"?**

A. At the very beginning of our prayer
Christ wants to kindle in us
what is basic to our prayer—
the childlike awe and trust
that God through Christ has become
our Father.

Our fathers do not refuse us
the things of this life;
God our Father will even less refuse to give us
what we ask in faith.[1]

[1] Matt. 7:9–11; Luke 11:11–13.

**121 Q. Why the words
"in heaven"?**

A. These words teach us
not to think of God's heavenly majesty
as something earthly,[1]
and to expect everything
for body and soul
from his almighty power.[2]

[1] Jer. 23:23–24; Acts 17:24–25.
[2] Matt. 6:25–34; Rom. 8:31–32.

LORD'S DAY 47

122 Q. What does the first request mean?

A. *Hallowed be your name* means,

Help us to really know you,[1]
to bless, worship, and praise you
    for all your works
    and for all that shines forth from them:
        your almighty power, wisdom, kindness,
        justice, mercy, and truth.[2]

And it means,

Help us to direct all our living—
    what we think, say, and do—
so that your name will never be blasphemed
    because of us
but always honored and praised.[3]

[1] Jer. 9:23–24; 31:33–34; Matt. 16:17; John 17:3.
[2] Ex. 34:5–8; Ps. 145; Jer. 32:16–20; Luke 1:46–55, 68–75; Rom. 11:33–36.
[3] Ps. 115:1; Matt. 5:16.

LORD'S DAY 48

123 Q. What does the second request mean?

A. *Your kingdom come* means,

Rule us by your Word and Spirit in such a way
that more and more we submit to you.[1]

Keep your church strong, and add to it.[2]

Destroy the devil's work;
destroy every force which revolts against you
and every conspiracy against your Word.[3]

Do this until your kingdom is so complete
and perfect
that in it you are
all in all.[4]

[1] Ps. 119:5, 105; 143:10; Matt. 6:33.
[2] Ps. 122:6–9; Matt. 16:18; Acts 2:42–47.
[3] Rom. 16:20; 1 John 3:8.
[4] Rom. 8:22–23; 1 Cor. 15:28; Rev. 22:17, 20.

LORD'S DAY 49

124 Q. What does the third request mean?

A. *Your will be done on earth as it is in heaven* means,

Help us and all men
   to reject our own wills
   and to obey your will without any back talk.
   Your will alone is good.[1]

Help everyone carry out the work he is called to[2]
   as willingly and faithfully as the angels in heaven.[3]

[1] Matt. 7:21; 16:24–26; Luke 22:42; Rom. 12:1–2; Tit. 2:11–12.
[2] 1 Cor. 7:17–24; Eph. 6:5–9.
[3] Ps. 103:20–21.

LORD'S DAY 50

125 Q. What does the fourth request mean?

A. *Give us today our daily bread* means,

Do take care of all our physical needs[1]
so that we come to know
that you are the only source of everything good,[2]
and that neither our work and worry
nor your gifts
can do us any good without your blessing.[3]

And so help us to give up our trust in creatures
and to put trust in you alone.[4]

[1] Ps. 104:27–30; 145:15–16; Matt. 6:25–34.
[2] Acts 14:17; 17:25; James 1:17.
[3] Deut. 8:3; Ps. 37:16; 127:1–2; 1 Cor. 15:58.
[4] Ps. 55:22; 62; 146; Jer. 17:5–8; Heb. 13:5–6.

LORD'S DAY 51

126 Q. What does the fifth request mean?

A. *Forgive us our debts,*
as we also have forgiven our debtors means,

Because of Christ's blood,
do not hold against us, poor sinners that we are,
    any of the sins we do
    or the evil that constantly clings to us.[1]

Forgive us just as we are fully determined,
    as evidence of your grace in us,
to forgive our neighbors.[2]

[1] Ps. 51:1–7; 143:2; Rom. 8:1; 1 John 2:1–2.
[2] Matt. 6:14–15; 18:21–35.

LORD'S DAY 52

127 Q. What does the sixth request mean?

A. *And lead us not into temptation,*
but deliver us from the evil one means,

By ourselves we are too weak
to hold our own even for a moment.[1]

And our sworn enemies—
the devil,[2] the world,[3] and our own flesh—[4]
never stop attacking us.

And so, Lord,
uphold us and make us strong
with the strength of your Holy Spirit,
so that we may not go down to defeat
in this spiritual struggle,[5]
but may firmly resist our enemies
until we finally win the complete victory.[6]

[1] Ps. 103:14–16; John 15:1–5.
[2] 2 Cor. 11:14; Eph. 6:10–13; 1 Pet. 5:8.
[3] John 15:18–21.
[4] Rom. 7:23; Gal. 5:17.
[5] Matt. 10:19–20; 26:41; Mark 13:33; Rom. 5:3–5.
[6] 1 Cor. 10:13; 1 Thess. 3:13; 5:23.

128 Q. What does your conclusion to this prayer mean?

A. *For yours is the kingdom*
and the power
and the glory forever means,

We have made all these requests of you
because, as our all-powerful king,
you not only want to,
but are able to give us all that is good;[1]
and because your holy name,
and not we ourselves,
should receive all the praise, forever.[2]

[1] Rom. 10:11–13; 2 Pet. 2:9.
[2] Ps. 115:1; John 14:13.

129 Q. What does that little word "Amen" express?

A. *Amen* means,

This is sure to be!

It is even more sure
   that God listens to my prayer,
than that I really desire
   what I pray for.[1]

[1] Isa. 65:24; 2 Cor. 1:20; 2 Tim. 2:13.

The Decision of the Synod of Dort on the Five Main Points of Doctrine in Dispute in the Netherlands is popularly known as the *Canons of Dort.* It consists of statements of doctrine adopted by the great Synod of Dort which met in the city of Dordrecht in 1618–19. Although this was a national synod of the Reformed churches of the Netherlands, it had an international character, since it was composed not only of Dutch delegates but also of twenty-six delegates from eight foreign countries.

The Synod of Dort was held in order to settle a serious controversy in the Dutch churches initiated by the rise of Arminianism. Jacob Arminius, a theological professor at Leiden University, questioned the teaching of Calvin and his followers on a number of important points. After Arminius's death, his own followers presented their views on five of these points in the Remonstrance of 1610. In this document or in later more explicit writings, the Arminians taught election based on foreseen faith, universal atonement, partial depravity, resistible grace, and the possibility of a lapse from grace. In the Canons the Synod of Dort rejected these views and set forth the Reformed doctrine on these points, namely, unconditional election, limited atonement, total depravity, irresistible grace, and the perseverance of saints.

The Canons have a special character because of their original purpose as a judicial decision on the doctrinal points in dispute during the Arminian controversy. The original preface called them a "judgment, in which both the true view, agreeing with God's Word, concerning the aforesaid five points of doctrine is explained, and the false view, disagreeing with God's Word, is rejected." The Canons also have a limited character in that they do not cover the whole range of doctrine, but focus on the five points of doctrine in dispute.

Each of the main points consists of a positive and a negative part, the former being an exposition of the Reformed doctrine on the subject, the latter a repudiation of the corresponding errors. Although in form there are only four points, we speak properly of five points, because the Canons were structured to correspond to the five articles of the 1610 Remonstrance. Main Points 3 and 4 were combined into one, always designated as Main Point III/IV.

The new translation of the Canons, based on the only extant Latin manuscript among those signed at the Synod of Dort, was adopted by the 1986 Synod of the Christian Reformed Church. The biblical quotations are translations from the original Latin and so do not always correspond to current versions. Though not in the original text, subheadings have been added to the positive articles and to the conclusion in order to facilitate study of the Canons.

The Canons of Dort

Formally Titled
The Decision of the Synod of Dort on the Five Main Points of Doctrine
in Dispute in the Netherlands

The First Main Point of Doctrine

Divine Election and Reprobation

The Judgment Concerning Divine Predestination
Which the Synod Declares to Be in Agreement with the Word of God
and Accepted Till Now in the Reformed Churches,
Set Forth in Several Articles

Article 1: *God's Right to Condemn All People*
Since all people have sinned in Adam and have come under the sentence of the curse and eternal death, God would have done no one an injustice if it had been his will to leave the entire human race in sin and under the curse, and to condemn them on account of their sin. As the apostle says: *The whole world is liable to the condemnation of God* (Rom. 3:19), *All have sinned and are deprived of the glory of God* (Rom. 3:23), and *The wages of sin is death* (Rom. 6:23).*

Article 2: *The Manifestation of God's Love*
But this is how God showed his love: he sent his only begotten Son into the world, so that whoever believes in him should not perish but have eternal life.

Article 3: *The Preaching of the Gospel*
In order that people may be brought to faith, God mercifully sends proclaimers of this very joyful message to the people he wishes and at the time he wishes. By this ministry people are called to repentance and faith in Christ crucified. For *how shall they believe in him of whom they have not heard? And how shall they hear*

without someone preaching? And how shall they preach unless they have been sent? (Rom. 10:14-15).

Article 4: *A Twofold Response to the Gospel*
God's anger remains on those who do not believe this gospel. But those who do accept it and embrace Jesus the Savior with a true and living faith are delivered through him from God's anger and from destruction, and receive the gift of eternal life.

Article 5: *The Sources of Unbelief and of Faith*
The cause or blame for this unbelief, as well as for all other sins, is not at all in God, but in man. Faith in Jesus Christ, however, and salvation through him is a free gift of God. As Scripture says, *It is by grace you have been saved, through faith, and this not from yourselves; it is a gift of God* (Eph. 2:8). Likewise: *It has been freely given to you to believe in Christ* (Phil. 1:29).

Article 6: *God's Eternal Decision*
The fact that some receive from God the gift of faith within time, and that others do not, stems from his eternal

---

*All quotations from Scripture are translations of the original Latin manuscript.

decision. For *all his works are known to God from eternity* (Acts 15:18; Eph. 1:11). In accordance with this decision he graciously softens the hearts, however hard, of his chosen ones and inclines them to believe, but by his just judgment he leaves in their wickedness and hardness of heart those who have not been chosen. And in this especially is disclosed to us his act—unfathomable, and as merciful as it is just—of distinguishing between people equally lost. This is the well-known decision of election and reprobation revealed in God's Word. This decision the wicked, impure, and unstable distort to their own ruin, but it provides holy and godly souls with comfort beyond words.

Article 7: *Election*
Election [or choosing] is God's unchangeable purpose by which he did the following:

Before the foundation of the world, by sheer grace, according to the free good pleasure of his will, he chose in Christ to salvation a definite number of particular people out of the entire human race, which had fallen by its own fault from its original innocence into sin and ruin. Those chosen were neither better nor more deserving than the others, but lay with them in the common misery. He did this in Christ, whom he also appointed from eternity to be the mediator, the head of all those chosen, and the foundation of their salvation.

And so he decided to give the chosen ones to Christ to be saved, and to call and draw them effectively into Christ's fellowship through his Word and Spirit. In other words, he decided to grant them true faith in Christ, to justify them, to sanctify them, and finally, after powerfully preserving them in the fellowship of his Son, to glorify them.

God did all this in order to demonstrate his mercy, to the praise of the riches of his glorious grace.

As Scripture says, *God chose us in Christ, before the foundation of the world, so that we should be holy and blameless before him with love; he predestined us whom he adopted as his children through Jesus Christ, in himself, according to the good pleasure of his will, to the praise of his glorious grace, by which he freely made us pleasing to himself in his beloved* (Eph. 1:4–6). And elsewhere, *Those whom he predestined, he also called; and those whom he called, he also justified; and those whom he justified, he also glorified* (Rom. 8:30).

Article 8: *A Single Decision of Election*
This election is not of many kinds; it is one and the same election for all who were to be saved in the Old and the New Testament. For Scripture declares that there is a single good pleasure, purpose, and plan of God's will, by which he chose us from eternity both to grace and to glory, both to salvation and to the way of salvation, which he prepared in advance for us to walk in.

Article 9: *Election Not Based on Foreseen Faith*
This same election took place, not **on the basis of** foreseen faith, of the obedience of faith, of holiness, or of any other good quality and disposition, as though it were based on a prerequisite cause or condition in the person to be chosen, but rather **for the purpose of** faith, of the obedience of faith, of holiness, and so on. Accordingly, election is the source of each of the benefits of salvation. Faith, holiness, and the other saving gifts, and at last eternal life itself,

flow forth from election as its fruits and effects. As the apostle says, *He chose us* (not because we were, but) *so that we should be holy and blameless before him in love* (Eph. 1:4).

Article 10: *Election Based on God's Good Pleasure*

But the cause of this undeserved election is exclusively the good pleasure of God. This does not involve his choosing certain human qualities or actions from among all those possible as a condition of salvation, but rather involves his adopting certain particular persons from among the common mass of sinners as his own possession. As Scripture says, *When the children were not yet born, and had done nothing either good or bad. . . , she* (Rebecca) *was told, "The older will serve the younger."* *As it is written, "Jacob I loved, but Esau I hated"* (Rom. 9:11–13). Also, *All who were appointed for eternal life believed* (Acts 13:48).

Article 11: *Election Unchangeable*

Just as God himself is most wise, unchangeable, all-knowing, and almighty, so the election made by him can neither be suspended nor altered, revoked, or annulled; neither can his chosen ones be cast off, nor their number reduced.

Article 12: *The Assurance of Election*

Assurance of this their eternal and unchangeable election to salvation is given to the chosen in due time, though by various stages and in differing measure. Such assurance comes not by inquisitive searching into the hidden and deep things of God, but by noticing within themselves, with spiritual joy and holy delight, the unmistakable fruits of election pointed out in God's Word—such as a true faith in Christ, a childlike fear of God, a godly sorrow for their sins, a hunger and thirst for righteousness, and so on.

Article 13: *The Fruit of This Assurance*

In their awareness and assurance of this election God's children daily find greater cause to humble themselves before God, to adore the fathomless depth of his mercies, to cleanse themselves, and to give fervent love in return to him who first so greatly loved them. This is far from saying that this teaching concerning election, and reflection upon it, make God's children lax in observing his commandments or carnally self-assured. By God's just judgment this does usually happen to those who casually take for granted the grace of election or engage in idle and brazen talk about it but are unwilling to walk in the ways of the chosen.

Article 14: *Teaching Election Properly*

Just as, by God's wise plan, this teaching concerning divine election has been proclaimed through the prophets, Christ himself, and the apostles, in Old and New Testament times, and has subsequently been committed to writing in the Holy Scriptures, so also today in God's church, for which it was specifically intended, this teaching must be set forth—with a spirit of discretion, in a godly and holy manner, at the appropriate time and place, without inquisitive searching into the ways of the Most High. This must be done for the glory of God's most holy name, and for the lively comfort of his people.

Article 15: *Reprobation*

Moreover, Holy Scripture most especially highlights this eternal and undeserved grace of our election and brings it out more clearly for us, in that it further bears witness that not all people have been chosen but that some have not been chosen or have been passed by in God's eternal election—those, that is, concerning whom God, on the basis of his entirely free, most just, irreproachable, and unchangeable good pleasure, made the following decision:

to leave them in the common misery into which, by their own fault, they have plunged themselves;
not to grant them saving faith and the grace of conversion;
but finally to condemn and eternally punish them (having been left in their own ways and under his just judgment), not only for their unbelief but also for all their other sins, in order to display his justice.

And this is the decision of reprobation, which does not at all make God the author of sin (a blasphemous thought!) but rather its fearful, irreproachable, just judge and avenger.

Article 16: *Responses to the Teaching of Reprobation*
Those who do not yet actively experience within themselves a living faith in Christ or an assured confidence of heart, peace of conscience, a zeal for childlike obedience, and a glorying in God through Christ, but who nevertheless use the means by which God has promised to work these things in us— such people ought not to be alarmed at the mention of reprobation, nor to count themselves among the reprobate; rather they ought to continue diligently in the use of the means, to desire fervently a time of more abundant grace, and to wait for it in reverence and humility. On the other hand, those who seriously desire to turn to God, to be pleasing to him alone, and to be delivered from the body of death, but are not yet able to make such progress along the way of godliness and faith as they would like—such people

ought much less to stand in fear of the teaching concerning reprobation, since our merciful God has promised that he will not snuff out a smoldering wick and that he will not break a bruised reed. However, those who have forgotten God and their Savior Jesus Christ and have abandoned themselves wholly to the cares of the world and the pleasures of the flesh—such people have every reason to stand in fear of this teaching, as long as they do not seriously turn to God.

Article 17: *The Salvation of the Infants of Believers*
Since we must make judgments about God's will from his Word, which testifies that the children of believers are holy, not by nature but by virtue of the gracious covenant in which they together with their parents are included, godly parents ought not to doubt the election and salvation of their children whom God calls out of this life in infancy.

Article 18: *The Proper Attitude Toward Election and Reprobation*
To those who complain about this grace of an undeserved election and about the severity of a just reprobation, we reply with the words of the apostle, *Who are you, O man, to talk back to God?* (Rom. 9:20), and with the words of our Savior, *Have I no right to do what I want with my own?* (Matt. 20:15). We, however, with reverent adoration of these secret things, cry out with the apostle: *Oh, the depths of the riches both of the wisdom and the knowledge of God! How unsearchable are his judgments, and his ways beyond tracing out! For who has known the mind of the Lord? Or who has been his counselor? Or who has first given to God, that God should repay him? For from him and through him and to him are all things. To him be the glory forever! Amen* (Rom. 11:33–36).

*Rejection of the Errors
by Which the Dutch Churches
Have for Some Time Been Disturbed*

Having set forth the orthodox teaching concerning election and reprobation, the Synod rejects the errors of those

I

Who teach that the will of God to save those who would believe and persevere in faith and in the obedience of faith is the whole and entire decision of election to salvation, and that nothing else concerning this decision has been revealed in God's Word.

For they deceive the simple and plainly contradict Holy Scripture in its testimony that God does not only wish to save those who would believe, but that he has also from eternity chosen certain particular people to whom, rather than to others, he would within time grant faith in Christ and perseverance. As Scripture says, *I have revealed your name to those whom you gave me* (John 17:6). Likewise, *All who were appointed for eternal life believed* (Acts 13:48), and *He chose us before the foundation of the world so that we should be holy. . .* (Eph. 1:4).

II

Who teach that God's election to eternal life is of many kinds: one general and indefinite, the other particular and definite; and the latter in turn either incomplete, revocable, nonperemptory (or conditional), or else complete, irrevocable, and peremptory (or absolute). Likewise, who teach that there is one election to faith and another to salvation, so that there can be an election to justifying faith apart from a peremptory election to salvation.

For this is an invention of the human brain, devised apart from the Scriptures, which distorts the teaching concerning election and breaks up this golden chain of salvation: *Those whom he predestined, he also called; and those whom he called, he also justified; and those whom he justified, he also glorified* (Rom. 8:30).

III

Who teach that God's good pleasure and purpose, which Scripture mentions in its teaching of election, does not involve God's choosing certain particular people rather than others, but involves God's choosing, out of all possible conditions (including the works of the law) or out of the whole order of things, the intrinsically unworthy act of faith, as well as the imperfect obedience of faith, to be a condition of salvation; and it involves his graciously wishing to count this as perfect obedience and to look upon it as worthy of the reward of eternal life.

For by this pernicious error the good pleasure of God and the merit of Christ are robbed of their effectiveness and people are drawn away, by unprofitable inquiries, from the truth of undeserved justification and from the simplicity of the Scriptures. It also gives the lie to these words of the apostle: *God called us with a holy calling, not in virtue of works, but in virtue of his own purpose and the grace which was given to us in Christ Jesus before the beginning of time* (2 Tim. 1:9).

IV

Who teach that in election to faith a prerequisite condition is that man should rightly use the light of nature, be upright, unassuming, humble, and disposed to eternal life, as though election depended to some extent on these factors.

For this smacks of Pelagius, and it clearly calls into question the words of the apostle: *We lived at one time in the passions of our flesh, following the will of our flesh and thoughts, and we were by nature children of wrath, like everyone else. But God, who is rich in mercy, out of the great love with which he loved us, even when we were dead in transgressions, made us alive with Christ, by whose grace you have been saved. And God raised us up with him and seated us with him in heaven in Christ Jesus, in order that in the coming ages we might show the surpassing riches of his grace, according to his kindness toward us in Christ Jesus. For it is by grace you have been saved, through faith (and this not from yourselves; it is the gift of God) not by works, so that no one can boast* (Eph. 2:3–9).

V

Who teach that the incomplete and nonperemptory election of particular persons to salvation occurred on the basis of a foreseen faith, repentance, holiness, and godliness, which has just begun or continued for some time; but that complete and peremptory election occurred on the basis of a foreseen perseverance to the end in faith, repentance, holiness, and godliness. And that this is the gracious and evangelical worthiness, on account of which the one who is chosen is more worthy than the one who is not chosen. And therefore that faith, the obedience of faith, holiness, godliness, and perseverance are not fruits or effects of an unchangeable election to glory, but indispensable conditions and causes, which are prerequisite in those who are to be chosen in the complete election, and which are foreseen as achieved in them.

This runs counter to the entire Scripture, which throughout impresses upon our ears and hearts these sayings among others: *Election is not by works, but by him who calls* (Rom. 9:11–12); *All who were appointed for eternal life believed* (Acts 13:48); *He chose us in himself so that we should be holy* (Eph. 1:4); *You did not choose me, but I chose you* (John 15:16); *If by grace, not by works* (Rom. 11:6); *In this is love, not that we loved God, but that he loved us and sent his Son* (1 John 4:10).

VI

Who teach that not every election to salvation is unchangeable, but that some of the chosen can perish and do in fact perish eternally, with no decision of God to prevent it.

By this gross error they make God changeable, destroy the comfort of the godly concerning the steadfastness of their election, and contradict the Holy Scriptures, which teach that *the elect cannot be led astray* (Matt. 24:24), that *Christ does not lose those given to him by the Father* (John 6:39), and that *those whom God predestined, called, and justified, he also glorifies* (Rom. 8:30).

VII

Who teach that in this life there is no fruit, no awareness, and no assurance of one's unchangeable election to glory, except as conditional upon something changeable and contingent.

For not only is it absurd to speak of an uncertain assurance, but these things also militate against the experience of the saints, who with the apostle rejoice from an awareness of their election and sing the praises of this gift of God; who, as Christ urged, *rejoice* with his disciples *that their names have been written in heaven* (Luke 10:20); and finally who hold up against the flaming arrows of the devil's temptations the awareness of their election, with the question *Who will bring any charge against those whom God has chosen?* (Rom. 8:33).

VIII

Who teach that it was not on the basis of his just will alone that God decided to leave anyone in the fall of Adam and in the common state of sin and condemnation or to pass anyone by in the imparting of grace necessary for faith and conversion.

For these words stand fast: *He has mercy on whom he wishes, and he hardens whom he wishes* (Rom. 9:18). And also: *To you it has been given to know the secrets of the kingdom of heaven, but to them it has not been given* (Matt. 13:11). Likewise: *I give glory to you, Father, Lord of heaven and earth, that you have hidden these things from the wise and understanding, and have revealed them to little children; yes, Father, because that was your pleasure* (Matt. 11:25–26).

IX

Who teach that the cause for God's sending the gospel to one people rather than to another is not merely and solely God's good pleasure, but rather that one people is better and worthier than the other to whom the gospel is not communicated.

For Moses contradicts this when he addresses the people of Israel as follows: *Behold, to Jehovah your God belong the heavens and the highest heavens, the earth and whatever is in it. But Jehovah was inclined in his affection to love your ancestors alone, and chose out their descendants after them, you above all peoples, as at this day* (Deut. 10:14–15). And also Christ: *Woe to you, Korazin! Woe to you, Bethsaida! for if those mighty works done in you had been done in Tyre and Sidon, they would have repented long ago in sackcloth and ashes* (Matt. 11:21).

The Second Main Point of Doctrine

Christ's Death and Human Redemption Through It

Article 1: *The Punishment Which God's Justice Requires*

God is not only supremely merciful, but also supremely just. His justice requires (as he has revealed himself in the Word) that the sins we have committed against his infinite majesty be punished with both temporal and eternal punishments, of soul as well as body. We cannot escape these punishments unless satisfaction is given to God's justice.

Article 2: *The Satisfaction Made by Christ*

Since, however, we ourselves cannot give this satisfaction or deliver ourselves from God's anger, God in his boundless mercy has given us as a guarantee his only begotten Son, who was made to be sin and a curse for us, in our place, on the cross, in order that he might give satisfaction for us.

Article 3: *The Infinite Value of Christ's Death*

This death of God's Son is the only and entirely complete sacrifice and satisfaction for sins; it is of infinite value and worth, more than sufficient to atone for the sins of the whole world.

Article 4: *Reasons for This Infinite Value*

This death is of such great value and worth for the reason that the person who suffered it is—as was necessary to be our Savior—not only a true and perfectly holy man, but also the only begotten Son of God, of the same eternal and infinite essence with the Father and the Holy Spirit. Another reason is that this death was accompanied by the experience of God's anger and curse, which **we** by our sins had fully deserved.

Article 5: *The Mandate to Proclaim the Gospel to All*

Moreover, it is the promise of the gospel that whoever believes in Christ crucified shall not perish but have eternal life. This promise, together with the command to repent and believe, ought to be announced and declared without differentiation or discrimination to all nations and people, to whom God in his good pleasure sends the gospel.

Article 6: *Unbelief Man's Responsibility*

However, that many who have been called through the gospel do not repent or believe in Christ but perish in unbelief is not because the sacrifice of Christ offered on the cross is deficient or insufficient, but because they themselves are at fault.

Article 7: *Faith God's Gift*

But all who genuinely believe and are delivered and saved by Christ's death from their sins and from destruction receive this favor solely from God's grace—which he owes to no one—given to them in Christ from eternity.

Article 8: *The Saving Effectiveness of Christ's Death*

For it was the entirely free plan and very gracious will and intention of God the Father that the enlivening and saving effectiveness of his Son's costly death should work itself out in all his chosen ones, in order that he might grant justifying faith to them only and thereby lead them without fail to salvation. In other words, it was God's will that Christ through the blood of the cross (by which he confirmed the new covenant) should effectively redeem from every people, tribe, nation, and language all those and only those who were chosen from eternity to salvation and given to him by the Father; that he should grant them faith (which, like the Holy Spirit's other saving gifts, he acquired for them by his death); that he should cleanse them by his blood from all their sins, both original and actual, whether committed before or after their coming to faith; that he should faithfully preserve them to the very end; and that he should finally present them to himself, a glorious people, without spot or wrinkle.

Article 9: *The Fulfillment of God's Plan*

This plan, arising out of God's eternal love for his chosen ones, from the beginning of the world to the present time has been powerfully carried out and will also be carried out in the future, the gates of hell seeking vainly to prevail against it. As a result the chosen are gathered into one, all in their own time, and there is always a church of believers founded on Christ's blood, a church which steadfastly loves, persistently worships, and—here and in all eternity—praises him as her Savior who laid down his life for her on the cross, as a bridegroom for his bride.

Rejection of the Errors

Having set forth the orthodox teaching, the Synod rejects the errors of those

I

Who teach that God the Father appointed his Son to death on the cross without a fixed and definite plan to save anyone by name, so that the necessity, usefulness, and worth of what Christ's death obtained could have stood intact and altogether perfect, complete and whole, even if the redemption that was obtained had never in actual fact been applied to any individual.

For this assertion is an insult to the wisdom of God the Father and to the merit of Jesus Christ, and it is contrary to Scripture. For the Savior speaks as follows: *I lay down my life for the sheep, and I know them* (John 10:15, 27). And Isaiah the prophet says concerning the Savior: *When he shall make himself an offering for sin, he shall see his offspring, he shall prolong his days, and the will of Jehovah shall prosper in his hand* (Isa. 53:10). Finally, this undermines the article of the creed in which we confess what we believe concerning the Church.

II

Who teach that the purpose of Christ's death was not to establish in actual fact a new covenant of grace by his blood, but only to acquire for the Father the mere right to enter once more into a covenant with men, whether of grace or of works.

For this conflicts with Scripture, which teaches that Christ *has become the guarantee and mediator of a better—that is, a new—covenant* (Heb. 7:22; 9:15), and that *a will is in force only when someone has died* (Heb. 9:17).

III

Who teach that Christ, by the satisfaction which he gave, did not certainly merit for anyone salvation itself and the faith by which this satisfaction of Christ is effectively applied to salvation, but only acquired for the Father the authority or plenary will to relate in a new way with men and to impose such new conditions as he chose, and that the satisfying of these conditions depends on the free choice of man; consequently, that it was possible that either all or none would fulfill them.

For they have too low an opinion of the death of Christ, do not at all acknowledge the foremost fruit or benefit which it brings forth, and summon back from hell the Pelagian error.

IV

Who teach that what is involved in the new covenant of grace which God the Father made with men through the intervening of Christ's death is not that we are justified before God and saved through faith, insofar as it accepts Christ's merit, but rather that God, having withdrawn his demand for perfect obedience to the law, counts faith itself, and the imperfect obedience of faith, as perfect obedience to the law, and graciously looks upon this as worthy of the reward of eternal life.

For they contradict Scripture: *They are justified freely by his grace through the redemption that came by Jesus Christ, whom God presented as a sacrifice of atonement, through faith in his blood* (Rom. 3:24–25). And along with the ungodly Socinus, they introduce a new and foreign justification of man before God, against the consensus of the whole church.

V

Who teach that all people have been received into the state of reconciliation and into the grace of the covenant, so that no one on account of original sin is liable to condemnation, or is to be condemned, but that all are free from the guilt of this sin.

For this opinion conflicts with Scripture which asserts that we are by nature children of wrath.

VI

Who make use of the distinction between obtaining and applying in order to instill in the unwary and inexperienced the opinion that God, as far as he is concerned, wished to bestow equally upon all people the benefits which are gained by Christ's death; but that the distinction by which some rather than others come to share in the forgiveness of sins and eternal life depends on their own free choice (which applies itself to the grace offered indiscriminately) but does not depend on the unique gift of mercy which effectively works in them, so that they, rather than others, apply that grace to themselves.

For, while pretending to set forth this distinction in an acceptable sense, they attempt to give the people the deadly poison of Pelagianism.

VII

Who teach that Christ neither could die, nor had to die, nor did die for those whom God so dearly loved and chose to eternal life, since such people do not need the death of Christ.

For they contradict the apostle, who says: *Christ loved me and gave himself up for me* (Gal. 2:20), and likewise: *Who will bring any charge against those whom God has chosen? It is God who justifies. Who is he that condemns? It is Christ who died,* that is, for them (Rom. 8:33–34). They also contradict the Savior, who asserts: *I lay down my life for the sheep* (John 10:15), and *My command is this: Love one another as I have loved you. Greater love has no one than this, that one lay down his life for his friends* (John 15:12–13).

The Third and Fourth Main Points of Doctrine

Human Corruption, Conversion to God, and the Way It Occurs

Article 1: *The Effect of the Fall on Human Nature*

Man was originally created in the image of God and was furnished in his mind with a true and salutary knowledge of his Creator and things spiritual, in his will and heart with righteousness, and in all his emotions with purity; indeed, the whole man was holy. However, rebelling against God at the devil's instigation and by his own free will, he deprived himself of these outstanding gifts. Rather, in their place he brought upon himself blindness, terrible darkness, futility, and distortion of judgment in his mind; perversity, defiance, and hardness in his heart and will; and finally impurity in all his emotions.

Article 2: *The Spread of Corruption*

Man brought forth children of the same nature as himself after the fall. That is to say, being corrupt he brought forth corrupt children. The corruption spread, by God's just judgment, from Adam to all his descendants—except for Christ alone—not by way of imitation (as in former times the Pelagians would have it) but by way of the propagation of his perverted nature.

Article 3: *Total Inability*

Therefore, all people are conceived in sin and are born children of wrath, unfit for any saving good, inclined to evil, dead in their sins, and slaves to sin; without the grace of the regenerating Holy Spirit they are neither willing nor able to return to God, to reform their distorted nature, or even to dispose themselves to such reform.

Article 4: *The Inadequacy of the Light of Nature*

There is, to be sure, a certain light of nature remaining in man after the fall, by virtue of which he retains some notions about God, natural things, and the difference between what is moral and immoral, and demonstrates a certain eagerness for virtue and for good outward behavior. But this light of nature is far from enabling man to come to a saving knowledge of God and conversion to him—so far, in fact, that man does not use it rightly even in matters of nature and society. Instead, in various ways he completely distorts this light, whatever its precise character, and suppresses it in unrighteousness. In doing so he renders himself without excuse before God.

Article 5: *The Inadequacy of the Law*

In this respect, what is true of the light of nature is true also of the Ten Commandments given by God through Moses specifically to the Jews. For man cannot obtain saving grace through the Decalogue, because, although it does expose the magnitude of his sin and increasingly convict him of his guilt, yet it does not offer a remedy or enable him to escape from his misery, and, indeed, weakened as it is by the flesh, leaves the offender under the curse.

Article 6: *The Saving Power of the Gospel*

What, therefore, neither the light of nature nor the law can do, God accomplishes by the power of the Holy Spirit, through the Word or the ministry of reconciliation. This is the gospel about the Messiah, through which it has pleased

God to save believers, in both the Old and the New Testament.

Article 7: *God's Freedom in Revealing the Gospel*

In the Old Testament, God revealed this secret of his will to a small number; in the New Testament (now without any distinction between peoples) he discloses it to a large number. The reason for this difference must not be ascribed to the greater worth of one nation over another, or to a better use of the light of nature, but to the free good pleasure and undeserved love of God. Therefore, those who receive so much grace, beyond and in spite of all they deserve, ought to acknowledge it with humble and thankful hearts; on the other hand, with the apostle they ought to adore (but certainly not inquisitively search into) the severity and justice of God's judgments on the others, who do not receive this grace.

Article 8: *The Serious Call of the Gospel*

Nevertheless, all who are called through the gospel are called seriously. For seriously and most genuinely God makes known in his Word what is pleasing to him: that those who are called should come to him. Seriously he also promises rest for their souls and eternal life to all who come to him and believe.

Article 9: *Human Responsibility for Rejecting the Gospel*

The fact that many who are called through the ministry of the gospel do not come and are not brought to conversion must not be blamed on the gospel, nor on Christ, who is offered through the gospel, nor on God, who calls them through the gospel and even bestows various gifts on them, but on the people themselves who are called. Some in self-assurance do not even entertain the Word of life; others do entertain it but do not take it to heart, and for that reason, after the fleeting joy of a temporary faith, they relapse; others choke the seed of the Word with the thorns of life's cares and with the pleasures of the world and bring forth no fruits. This our Savior teaches in the parable of the sower (Matt. 13).

Article 10: *Conversion as the Work of God*

The fact that others who are called through the ministry of the gospel do come and are brought to conversion must not be credited to man, as though one distinguishes himself by free choice from others who are furnished with equal or sufficient grace for faith and conversion (as the proud heresy of Pelagius maintains). No, it must be credited to God: just as from eternity he chose his own in Christ, so within time he effectively calls them, grants them faith and repentance, and, having rescued them from the dominion of darkness, brings them into the kingdom of his Son, in order that they may declare the wonderful deeds of him who called them out of darkness into this marvelous light, and may boast not in themselves, but in the Lord, as apostolic words frequently testify in Scripture.

Article 11: *The Holy Spirit's Work in Conversion*

Moreover, when God carries out this good pleasure in his chosen ones, or works true conversion in them, he not only sees to it that the gospel is proclaimed to them outwardly, and enlightens their minds powerfully by the Holy Spirit so that they may rightly understand and discern the things of the Spirit of God, but, by the effective operation of the same regenerating Spirit, he also penetrates into the inmost being of man, opens the closed heart, softens the hard heart, and circumcises the heart that is uncircumcised. He infuses new qualities into the will, making the dead will alive, the evil one good, the unwilling one willing, and the stubborn one compliant; he activates and strengthens the will so that, like a good tree, it may be enabled to produce the fruits of good deeds.

Article 12: *Regeneration a Supernatural Work*

And this is the regeneration, the new creation, the raising from the dead, and the making alive so clearly proclaimed in the Scriptures, which God works in us without our help. But this certainly does not happen only by outward teaching, by moral persuasion, or by such a way of working that, after God has done his work, it remains in man's power whether or not to be reborn or converted. Rather, it is an entirely supernatural work, one that is at the same time most powerful and most pleasing, a marvelous, hidden, and inexpressible work, which is not lesser than or inferior in power to that of creation or of raising the dead, as Scripture (inspired by the author of this work) teaches. As a result, all those in whose hearts God works in this marvelous way are certainly, unfailingly, and effectively reborn and do actually believe. And then the will, now renewed, is not only activated and motivated by God but in being activated by God is also itself active. For this reason, man himself, by that grace which he has received, is also rightly said to believe and to repent.

Article 13: *The Incomprehensible Way of Regeneration*

In this life believers cannot fully understand the way this work occurs; meanwhile, they rest content with knowing and experiencing that by this grace of God they do believe with the heart and love their Savior.

Article 14: *The Way God Gives Faith*

In this way, therefore, faith is a gift of God, not in the sense that it is offered by God for man to choose, but that it is in actual fact bestowed on man, breathed and infused into him. Nor is it a gift in the sense that God bestows only the potential to believe, but then awaits assent—the act of believing—from man's choice; rather, it is a gift in the sense that he who works both willing and acting and, indeed, works all things in all people produces in man both the will to believe and the belief itself.

Article 15: *Responses to God's Grace*

God does not owe this grace to anyone. For what could God owe to one who has nothing to give that can be paid back? Indeed, what could God owe to one who has nothing of his own to give but sin and falsehood? Therefore the person who receives this grace owes and gives eternal thanks to God alone; the person who does not receive it either does not care at all about these spiritual things and is satisfied with himself in his condition, or else in self-assurance foolishly boasts about having something which he lacks. Furthermore, following the example of the apostles, we are to think and to speak in the most favorable way about those who outwardly profess their faith and better their lives, for the inner chambers of the heart are unknown to us. But for others who have not yet been called, we are to pray to the God who calls things that do not exist as though they did. In no way, however, are we to pride ourselves as better than they, as though we had distinguished ourselves from them.

Article 16: *Regeneration's Effect*

However, just as by the fall man did not cease to be man, endowed with intellect and will, and just as sin, which has spread through the whole human race, did not abolish the nature of the human race but distorted and spiritually killed it, so also this divine grace of regeneration does not act in people as if they were blocks and stones; nor does it abolish the will and its properties or coerce a reluctant will by force, but spiritually revives, heals, reforms, and—in a manner at once pleasing and powerful—bends it back. As a result, a ready and sincere obedience of the Spirit now begins to prevail where before the rebellion and resistance of the flesh were completely dominant. It is in this that the true and spiritual restoration and freedom of our will consists. Thus, if the marvelous Maker of every good thing were not dealing with us, man would have no hope of getting up from his fall by his free choice, by which he plunged himself into ruin when still standing upright.

Article 17: *God's Use of Means in Regeneration*

Just as the almighty work of God by which he brings forth and sustains our natural life does not rule out but requires the use of means, by which God, according to his infinite wisdom and goodness, has wished to exercise his power, so also the aforementioned supernatural work of God by which he regenerates us in no way rules out or cancels the use of the gospel, which God in his great wisdom has appointed to be the seed of regeneration and the food of the soul. For this reason, the apostles and the teachers who followed them taught the people in a godly manner about this grace of God, to give him the glory and to humble all pride, and yet did not neglect meanwhile to keep the people, by means of the holy admonitions of the gospel, under the administration of the Word, the sacraments, and discipline. So even today it is out of the question that the teachers or those taught in the church should presume to test God by separating what he in his good pleasure has wished to be closely joined together. For grace is bestowed through admonitions, and the more readily we perform our duty, the more lustrous the benefit of God working in us usually is and the better his work advances. To him alone, both for the means and for their saving fruit and effectiveness, all glory is owed forever. Amen.

Rejection of the Errors

Having set forth the orthodox teaching, the Synod rejects the errors of those

I

Who teach that, properly speaking, it cannot be said that original sin in itself is enough to condemn the whole human race or to warrant temporal and eternal punishments.

For they contradict the apostle when he says: *Sin entered the world through one man, and death through sin, and in this way death passed on to all men because all sinned* (Rom. 5:12); also: *The guilt followed one sin and brought condemnation* (Rom. 5:16); likewise: *The wages of sin is death* (Rom. 6:23).

II

Who teach that the spiritual gifts or the good dispositions and virtues such as goodness, holiness, and righteousness could not have resided in man's will when he was first created, and therefore could not have been separated from the will at the fall.

For this conflicts with the apostle's description of the image of God in Ephesians 4:24, where he portrays the image in terms of righteousness and holiness, which definitely reside in the will.

III

Who teach that in spiritual death the spiritual gifts have not been separated from man's will, since the will in itself has never been corrupted but only hindered by the darkness of the mind and the unruliness of the emotions, and since the will is able to exercise its innate free capacity once these hindrances are removed, which is to say, it is able of itself to will or choose whatever good is set before it—or else not to will or choose it.

This is a novel idea and an error and has the effect of elevating the power of free choice, contrary to the words of Jeremiah the prophet: *The heart itself is deceitful above all things and wicked* (Jer. 17:9); and of the words of the apostle: *All of us also lived among them* (the sons of disobedience) *at one time in the passions of our flesh, following the will of our flesh and thoughts* (Eph. 2:3).

IV

Who teach that unregenerate man is not strictly or totally dead in his sins or deprived of all capacity for spiritual good but is able to hunger and thirst for righteousness or life and to offer the sacrifice of a broken and contrite spirit which is pleasing to God.

For these views are opposed to the plain testimonies of Scripture: *You were dead in your transgressions and sins* (Eph. 2:1, 5); *The imagination of the thoughts of man's heart is only evil all the time* (Gen. 6:5; 8:21). Besides, to hunger and thirst for deliverance from misery and for life, and to offer God the sacrifice of a broken spirit is characteristic only of the regenerate and of those called blessed (Ps. 51:17; Matt. 5:6).

V

Who teach that corrupt and natural man can make such good use of common grace (by which they mean the light of nature) or of the gifts remaining after the fall that he is able thereby gradually to obtain a greater grace—evangelical or saving grace—as well as salvation itself; and that in this way God, for his part, shows himself ready to reveal Christ to all people, since he provides to all, to a sufficient extent and in an effective manner, the means necessary for the revealing of Christ, for faith, and for repentance.

For Scripture, not to mention the experience of all ages, testifies that this is false: *He makes known his words to Jacob, his statutes and his laws to Israel; he has done this for no other nation, and they do not know his laws* (Ps. 147:19–20); *In the past God let all nations go their own way* (Acts 14:16); *They* (Paul and his companions) *were kept by the Holy Spirit from speaking God's word in Asia;* and *When they had come to Mysia, they tried to go to Bithynia, but the Spirit would not allow them to* (Acts 16:6–7).

VI

Who teach that in the true conversion of man new qualities, dispositions, or gifts cannot be infused or poured into his will by God, and indeed that the faith [or believing] by which we first come to conversion and from which we receive the name "believers" is not a quality or gift infused by God, but only an act of man, and that it cannot be called a gift except in respect to the power of attaining faith.

For these views contradict the Holy Scriptures, which testify that God does infuse or pour into our hearts the new qualities of faith, obedience, and the experiencing of his love: *I will put my law in their minds, and write it on their hearts* (Jer. 31:33); *I will pour water on the thirsty land, and streams on the dry ground; I will pour out my Spirit on your offspring* (Isa. 44:3); *The love of God has been poured out in our hearts by the Holy Spirit, who has been given to us* (Rom. 5:5). They also conflict with the continuous practice of the Church, which prays with the prophet: *Convert me, Lord, and I shall be converted* (Jer. 31:18).

VII

Who teach that the grace by which we are converted to God is nothing but a gentle persuasion, or (as others explain it) that the way of God's acting in man's conversion that is most noble and suited to human nature is that which happens by persuasion, and that nothing prevents this grace of moral suasion even by itself from making natural men spiritual; indeed, that God does not produce the assent of the will except in this manner of moral suasion, and that the effectiveness of God's work by which it surpasses the work of Satan consists in the fact that God promises eternal benefits while Satan promises temporal ones.

For this teaching is entirely Pelagian and contrary to the whole of Scripture, which recognizes besides this persuasion also another, far more effective and divine way in which the Holy Spirit acts in man's conversion. As Ezekiel 36:26 puts it: *I will give you a new heart and put a new spirit in you; and I will remove your heart of stone and give you a heart of flesh. . . .*

VIII

Who teach that God in regenerating man does not bring to bear that power of his omnipotence whereby he may powerfully and unfailingly bend man's will to faith and conversion, but that even when God has accomplished all the works of grace which he uses for man's conversion, man nevertheless can, and in actual fact often does, so resist God and the Spirit in their intent and will to regenerate him, that man completely thwarts his own rebirth; and, indeed, that it remains in his own power whether or not to be reborn.

For this does away with all effective functioning of God's grace in our conversion and subjects the activity of Almighty God to the will of man; it is contrary to the apostles, who teach that *we believe by virtue of the effective working of God's mighty strength* (Eph. 1:19), and that *God fulfills the undeserved good will of his kindness and the work of faith in us with power* (2 Thess. 1:11), and likewise that *his divine power has given us everything we need for life and godliness* (2 Pet. 1:3).

IX

Who teach that grace and free choice are concurrent partial causes which cooperate to initiate conversion, and that grace does not precede—in the order of causality—the effective influence of the will; that is to say, that God does not effectively help man's will to come to conversion before man's will itself motivates and determines itself.

For the early church already condemned this doctrine long ago in the Pelagians, on the basis of the words of the apostle: *It does not depend on man's willing or running but on God's mercy* (Rom. 9:16); also: *Who makes you different from anyone else?* and *What do you have that you did not receive?* (1 Cor. 4:7); likewise: *It is God who works in you to will and act according to his good pleasure* (Phil. 2:13).

The Fifth Main Point of Doctrine

The Perseverance of the Saints

Article 1: *The Regenerate Not Entirely Free from Sin*

Those people whom God according to his purpose calls into fellowship with his Son Jesus Christ our Lord and regenerates by the Holy Spirit, he also sets free from the reign and slavery of sin, though in this life not entirely from the flesh and from the body of sin.

Article 2: *The Believer's Reaction to Sins of Weakness*

Hence daily sins of weakness arise, and blemishes cling to even the best works of God's people, giving them continual cause to humble themselves before God, to flee for refuge to Christ crucified, to put the flesh to death more and more by the Spirit of supplication and by holy exercises of godliness, and to strain toward the goal of perfection, until they are freed from this body of death and reign with the Lamb of God in heaven.

Article 3: *God's Preservation of the Converted*

Because of these remnants of sin dwelling in them and also because of the temptations of the world and Satan, those who have been converted could not remain standing in this grace if left to their own resources. But God is faithful, mercifully strengthening them in the grace once conferred on them and powerfully preserving them in it to the end.

Article 4: *The Danger of True Believers' Falling into Serious Sins*

Although that power of God strengthening and preserving true believers in grace is more than a match for the flesh, yet those converted are not always so activated and motivated by God that in certain specific actions they cannot

by their own fault depart from the leading of grace, be led astray by the desires of the flesh, and give in to them. For this reason they must constantly watch and pray that they may not be led into temptations. When they fail to do this, not only **can** they be carried away by the flesh, the world, and Satan into sins, even serious and outrageous ones, but also by God's just permission they sometimes **are** so carried away—witness the sad cases, described in Scripture, of David, Peter, and other saints falling into sins.

Article 5: *The Effects of Such Serious Sins*

By such monstrous sins, however, they greatly offend God, deserve the sentence of death, grieve the Holy Spirit, suspend the exercise of faith, severely wound the conscience, and sometimes lose the awareness of grace for a time—until, after they have returned to the way by genuine repentance, God's fatherly face again shines upon them.

Article 6: *God's Saving Intervention*

For God, who is rich in mercy, according to his unchangeable purpose of election does not take his Holy Spirit from his own completely, even when they fall grievously. Neither does he let them fall down so far that they forfeit the grace of adoption and the state of justification, or commit the sin which leads to death (the sin against the Holy Spirit), and plunge themselves, entirely forsaken by him, into eternal ruin.

Article 7: *Renewal to Repentance*

For, in the first place, God preserves in those saints when they fall his imperishable seed from which they have been born again, lest it perish or be dislodged. Secondly, by his Word and

Spirit he certainly and effectively renews them to repentance so that they have a heartfelt and godly sorrow for the sins they have committed; seek and obtain, through faith and with a contrite heart, forgiveness in the blood of the Mediator; experience again the grace of a reconciled God; through faith adore his mercies; and from then on more eagerly work out their own salvation with fear and trembling.

Article 8: *The Certainty of This Preservation*

So it is not by their own merits or strength but by God's undeserved mercy that they neither forfeit faith and grace totally nor remain in their downfalls to the end and are lost. With respect to themselves this not only easily could happen, but also undoubtedly would happen; but with respect to God it cannot possibly happen, since his plan cannot be changed, his promise cannot fail, the calling according to his purpose cannot be revoked, the merit of Christ as well as his interceding and preserving cannot be nullified, and the sealing of the Holy Spirit can neither be invalidated nor wiped out.

Article 9: *The Assurance of This Preservation*

Concerning this preservation of those chosen to salvation and concerning the perseverance of true believers in faith, believers themselves can and do become assured in accordance with the measure of their faith, by which they firmly believe that they are and always will remain true and living members of the church, and that they have the forgiveness of sins and eternal life.

Article 10: *The Ground of This Assurance*

Accordingly, this assurance does not derive from some private revelation beyond or outside the Word, but from faith in the promises of God which he has very plentifully revealed in his Word for our comfort, from the testimony of *the Holy Spirit testifying with our spirit that we are God's children and heirs* (Rom. 8:16–17), and finally from a serious and holy pursuit of a clear conscience and of good works. And if God's chosen ones in this world did not have this well-founded comfort that the victory will be theirs and this reliable guarantee of eternal glory, they would be of all people most miserable.

Article 11: *Doubts Concerning This Assurance*

Meanwhile, Scripture testifies that believers have to contend in this life with various doubts of the flesh and that under severe temptation they do not always experience this full assurance of faith and certainty of perseverance. But God, the Father of all comfort, *does not let them be tempted beyond what they can bear, but with the temptation he also provides a way out* (1 Cor. 10:13), and by the Holy Spirit revives in them the assurance of their perseverance.

Article 12: *This Assurance as an Incentive to Godliness*

This assurance of perseverance, however, so far from making true believers proud and carnally self-assured, is rather the true root of humility, of childlike respect, of genuine godliness, of endurance in every conflict, of fervent prayers, of steadfastness in crossbearing and in confessing the truth, and of well-founded joy in God. Reflecting on this benefit provides an incentive to a serious and continual practice of thanksgiving and good works, as is evident from the testimonies of Scripture and the examples of the saints.

Article 13: *Assurance No Inducement to Carelessness*

Neither does the renewed confidence of perseverance produce immorality or lack of concern for godliness in those put back on their feet after a fall, but it produces a much greater concern to observe carefully the ways of the Lord which he prepared in advance. They observe these ways in order that by walking in them they may maintain the assurance of their perseverance, lest, by their abuse of his fatherly goodness, the face of the gracious God (for the godly, looking upon his face is sweeter than life, but its withdrawal is more bitter than death) turn away from them again, with the result that they fall into greater anguish of spirit.

Article 14: *God's Use of Means in Perseverance*

And, just as it has pleased God to begin this work of grace in us by the proclamation of the gospel, so he preserves, continues, and completes his work by the hearing and reading of the gospel, by meditation on it, by its exhortations, threats, and promises, and also by the use of the sacraments.

Article 15: *Contrasting Reactions to the Teaching of Perseverance*

This teaching about the perseverance of true believers and saints, and about their assurance of it—a teaching which God has very richly revealed in his Word for the glory of his name and for the comfort of the godly and which he impresses on the hearts of believers—is something which the flesh does not understand, Satan hates, the world ridicules, the ignorant and the hypocrites abuse, and the spirits of error attack. The bride of Christ, on the other hand, has always loved this teaching very tenderly and defended it steadfastly as a priceless treasure; and God, against whom no plan can avail and no strength can prevail, will ensure that she will continue to do this. To this God alone, Father, Son, and Holy Spirit, be honor and glory forever. Amen.

Rejection of the Errors
Concerning the Teaching of
the Perseverance of the Saints

Having set forth the orthodox teaching, the Synod rejects the errors of those

I

Who teach that the perseverance of true believers is not an effect of election or a gift of God produced by Christ's death, but a condition of the new covenant which man, before what they call his "peremptory" election and justification, must fulfill by his free will.

For Holy Scripture testifies that perseverance follows from election and is granted to the chosen by virtue of Christ's death, resurrection, and intercession: *The chosen obtained it; the others were hardened* (Rom. 11:7); likewise, *He who did not spare his own son, but gave him up for us all—how will he not, along with him, grant us all things? Who will bring any charge against those whom God has chosen? It is God who justifies. Who is he that condemns? It is Christ Jesus who died—more than that, who was raised—who also sits at the right hand of God, and is also interceding for us. Who shall separate us from the love of Christ?* (Rom. 8:32–35).

II

Who teach that God does provide the believer with sufficient strength to persevere and is ready to preserve this strength in him if he performs his duty, but that even with all those things in place which are necessary to persevere in faith and which God is pleased to use to preserve faith, it still always depends on the choice of man's will whether or not he perseveres.

For this view is obviously Pelagian; and though it intends to make men free it makes them sacrilegious. It is against the enduring consensus of evangelical teaching which takes from man all cause for boasting and ascribes the praise for this benefit only to God's grace. It is also against the testimony of the apostle: *It is God who keeps us strong to the end, so that we will be blameless on the day of our Lord Jesus Christ* (1 Cor. 1:8).

III

Who teach that those who truly believe and have been born again not only can forfeit justifying faith as well as grace and salvation totally and to the end, but also in actual fact do often forfeit them and are lost forever.

For this opinion nullifies the very grace of justification and regeneration as well as the continual preservation by Christ, contrary to the plain words of the apostle Paul: *If Christ died for us while we were still sinners, we will therefore much more be saved from God's wrath through him, since we have now been justified by his blood* (Rom. 5:8–9); and contrary to the apostle John: *No one who is born of God is intent on sin, because God's seed remains in him, nor can he sin, because he has been born of God* (1 John 3:9); also contrary to the words of Jesus Christ: *I give eternal life to my sheep, and they shall never perish; no one can snatch them out of my hand. My Father, who has given them to me, is greater than all; no one can snatch them out of my Father's hand* (John 10:28–29).

IV

Who teach that those who truly believe and have been born again can commit the sin that leads to death (the sin against the Holy Spirit).

For the same apostle John, after making mention of those who commit the sin that leads to death and forbidding prayer for them (1 John 5:16–17), immediately adds: *We know that anyone born of God does not commit sin* (that is, that kind of sin), *but the one who was born of God keeps himself safe, and the evil one does not touch him* (v. 18).

V

Who teach that apart from a special revelation no one can have the assurance of future perseverance in this life.

For by this teaching the well-founded consolation of true believers in this life is taken away and the doubting of the Romanists is reintroduced into the church. Holy Scripture, however, in many places derives the assurance not from a special and extraordinary revelation but from the marks peculiar to God's children and from God's completely reliable promises. So especially the apostle Paul: *Nothing in all creation can separate us from the love of God that is in Christ Jesus our Lord* (Rom. 8:39); and John: *They who obey his commands remain in him and he in them. And this is how we know that he remains in us: by the Spirit he gave us* (1 John 3:24).

VI

Who teach that the teaching of the assurance of perseverance and of salvation is by its very nature and character an opiate of the flesh and is harmful to godliness, good morals, prayer, and other holy exercises, but that, on the contrary, to have doubt about this is praiseworthy.

For these people show that they do not know the effective operation of God's grace and the work of the indwelling Holy Spirit, and they contradict the apostle John, who asserts the opposite in plain words: *Dear friends, now we are children of God, but what we will be has not yet been made known. But we know that when he is made known, we shall be like him, for we shall see him as he is. Everyone who has this hope in him purifies himself, just as he is pure* (1 John 3:2–3). Moreover, they are refuted by the examples of the saints in both the Old and the New Testament, who though assured of their perseverance and salvation yet were constant in prayer and other exercises of godliness.

VII

Who teach that the faith of those who believe only temporarily does not differ from justifying and saving faith except in duration alone.

For Christ himself in Matthew 13:20 ff. and Luke 8:13 ff. clearly defines these further differences between temporary and true believers: he says that the former receive the seed on rocky ground, and the latter receive it in good ground, or a good heart; the former have no root, and the latter are firmly rooted; the former have no fruit, and the latter produce fruit in varying measure, with steadfastness, or perseverance.

VIII

Who teach that it is not absurd that a person, after losing his former regeneration, should once again, indeed quite often, be reborn.

For by this teaching they deny the imperishable nature of God's seed by which we are born again, contrary to the testimony of the apostle Peter: *Born again, not of perishable seed, but of imperishable* (1 Pet. 1:23).

IX

Who teach that Christ nowhere prayed for an unfailing perseverance of believers in faith.

For they contradict Christ himself when he says: *I have prayed for you, Peter, that your faith may not fail* (Luke 22:32); and John the gospel writer when he testifies in John 17 that it was not only for the apostles, but also for all those who were to believe by their message that Christ prayed: *Holy Father, preserve them in your name* (v. 11); and *My prayer is not that you take them out of the world, but that you preserve them from the evil one* (v. 15).

Conclusion

Rejection of False Accusations

And so this is the clear, simple, and straightforward explanation of the orthodox teaching on the five articles in dispute in the Netherlands, as well as the rejection of the errors by which the Dutch churches have for some time been disturbed. This explanation and rejection the Synod declares to be derived from God's Word and in agreement with the confessions of the Reformed churches. Hence it clearly appears that those of whom one could hardly expect it have shown no truth, equity, and charity at all in wishing to make the public believe:

—that the teaching of the Reformed churches on predestination and on the points associated with it by its very nature and tendency draws the minds of people away from all godliness and religion, is an opiate of the flesh and the devil, and is a stronghold of Satan where he lies in wait for all people, wounds most of them, and fatally pierces many of them with the arrows of both despair and self-assurance;

—that this teaching makes God the author of sin, unjust, a tyrant, and a hypocrite; and is nothing but a refurbished Stoicism, Manicheism, Libertinism, and Mohammedanism;

—that this teaching makes people carnally self-assured, since it persuades them that nothing endangers the salvation of the chosen, no matter how they live, so that they may commit the most outrageous crimes with self-assurance; and that on the other hand nothing is of use to the reprobate for salvation even if they have truly performed all the works of the saints;

—that this teaching means that God

predestined and created, by the bare and unqualified choice of his will, without the least regard or consideration of any sin, the greatest part of the world to eternal condemnation; that in the same manner in which election is the source and cause of faith and good works, reprobation is the cause of unbelief and ungodliness; that many infant children of believers are snatched in their innocence from their mothers' breasts and cruelly cast into hell so that neither the blood of Christ nor their baptism nor the prayers of the church at their baptism can be of any use to them;

and very many other slanderous accusations of this kind which the Reformed churches not only disavow but even denounce with their whole heart.

Therefore this Synod of Dort in the name of the Lord pleads with all who devoutly call on the name of our Savior Jesus Christ to form their judgment about the faith of the Reformed churches, not on the basis of false accusations gathered from here or there, or even on the basis of the personal statements of a number of ancient and modern authorities—statements which are also often either quoted out of context or misquoted and twisted to convey a different meaning—but on the basis of the churches' own official confessions and of the present explanation of the orthodox teaching which has been endorsed by the unanimous consent of the members of the whole Synod, one and all.

Moreover, the Synod earnestly warns the false accusers themselves to consider how heavy a judgment of God awaits those who give false testimony against so many churches and their confessions, trouble the consciences of the weak, and seek to prejudice the minds of many against the fellowship of true believers.

Finally, this Synod urges all fellow ministers in the gospel of Christ to deal with this teaching in a godly and reverent manner, in the academic institutions as well as in the churches; to do so, both in their speaking and writing, with a view to the glory of God's name, holiness of life, and the comfort of anxious souls; to think and also speak with Scripture according to the analogy of faith; and, finally, to refrain from all those ways of speaking which go beyond the bounds set for us by the genuine sense of the Holy Scriptures and which could give impertinent sophists a just occasion to scoff at the teaching of the Reformed churches or even to bring false accusations against it.

May God's Son Jesus Christ, who sits at the right hand of God and gives gifts to men, sanctify us in the truth, lead to the truth those who err, silence the mouths of those who lay false accusations against sound teaching, and equip faithful ministers of his Word with a spirit of wisdom and discretion, that all they say may be to the glory of God and the building up of their hearers. Amen.

LITURGICAL FORMS AND RESOURCES

The liturgy of the Christian Reformed Church has been substantially revised since the Synod of 1964 appointed a Liturgical Committee "to review all our liturgical literature in the light of its history, its theological content, and the contemporary needs of the churches; and to recommend such revisions or substitutions as the results of the review might recommend" (*Acts of Synod*, 1964, p. 60). This committee developed new liturgical forms (sacramental and nonsacramental), services of the Word and sacraments, responsive readings of the law, and prayers. After provisional approval by synod, these liturgical materials were referred to the church for several years of trial use, study, and reactions before they were officially approved.

The Synods of 1984 and 1986 selected from among these traditional, revised, and newly developed liturgical materials, the forms, services, and responsive readings that are now being included in this 1987 edition of the *Psalter Hymnal* (*Acts of Synod*, 1984, p. 631; 1986, pp. 722–723).

The Synod of 1979 appointed a contemporary testimony committee "to move in the direction of formulating a contemporary testimony in view of the secularization of modern life and culture" (*Acts of Synod*, 1979, pp. 75–76). A draft of this testimony was provisionally approved by Synod 1983 and referred to the churches for discussion and response. The Synod of 1986 approved a final version of the testimony and authorized its inclusion in the liturgical section of the 1987 edition of the *Psalter Hymnal* (*Acts of Synod*, pp. 679–80).

Liturgical Forms and Resources

Note: The dates appended indicate the year synod adopted each form. The forms adopted in 1912 were revised in 1934. Synod of 1986 approved editorial revisions of all the above forms for the purpose of stylistic consistency.

Service for Baptism

*The Beginning of Worship

Call to Worship

Minister: Give thanks to the Lord, call on his name; make known among the nations what he has done.

People: He remembers his covenant forever, the word he commanded, for a thousand generations.

Minister: Glory in his holy name; let the hearts of those who seek the Lord rejoice.

People: That they might keep his precepts and observe his laws. Praise the Lord. *(Ps. 105:1, 8, 3, 45)*

Greeting

Minister: The Lord be with you.

People: And the Lord be with you.

Minister: Grace, mercy, and peace be to you, from God the Father and from his Son, Jesus Christ.

People: Amen.

All sing: *[Hymn of praise]*

The Institution of Baptism

Minister: Congregation of our Lord Jesus Christ: Let us hear the Lord's command concerning the sacrament of holy baptism. After he had risen victorious from the grave, Jesus said to his disciples: "All authority in heaven and on earth has been given to me. Therefore go and make disciples of all nations, baptizing them in the name of the Father and of the Son and of the Holy Spirit, and teaching them to obey everything I have commanded you. And surely I am with you always, to the very end of the age" *(Matt. 28:18–20)*. In obedience to this command the church baptizes believers and their children.

Confession and Assurance

Minister: Before we proceed with the baptism, let us hear what the law of God requires of us, that it may convince us of our sin and incite us to seek his mercy. Christ teaches this in summary: " 'Love the Lord your God with all your heart, and with all your soul and with all your mind.' This is the first and greatest commandment. And the second is like it: 'Love your neighbor as yourself.' All the Law and the Prophets hang on these two commandments" *(Matt. 22:37–40)*.

All: We confess to you, our God, and before one another that we have sinned greatly, in thought, word, and deed. We have offended your holiness. We have failed to love our neighbor. We have followed the devices of our own hearts, and have spurned the promptings of your Spirit. Through our own fault, we have deserved your judgment. O Lord God, Lamb of God, Son of the Father, who takes away the sin of the world, have mercy on us and hear our prayer. Amen.

Minister: Let us hear the promises of God which are confirmed in baptism. The Lord made this great promise to Abraham: "I will establish my covenant as an everlasting covenant between me and you and your descendants after you for the

*indicates congregation stands

This service was approved by the Synod of 1981 as a model order of worship that may be adapted to local needs. The "Confession and Assurance" and "The Sacrament of Baptism," however, have the status of a synodically approved form; these components are always to be read complete and unchanged.

generations to come, to be your God and the God of your descendants after you" *(Gen. 17:7)*. In later years, though Israel was unfaithful, God renewed his promise through the prophet: " 'This is the covenant I will make with the house of Israel after that time,' declares the Lord. 'I will put my law in their minds and write it on their hearts. I will be their God, and they will be my people. . . . For I will forgive their wickedness and will remember their sins no more' " *(Jer. 31:33–34)*. In the fullness of time God came in Jesus Christ to give pardon and peace through the blood of the cross, the "blood of the covenant, which is poured out for many for the forgiveness of sins" *(Matt. 26:28)*. After Jesus had risen from the dead, the apostles proclaimed: "Repent and be baptized, every one of you, in the name of Jesus Christ for the forgiveness of your sins. And you will receive the gift of the Holy Spirit. The promise is for you and your children and for all whom the Lord our God will call" *(Acts 2:38–39)*. Anticipating the fulfillment of God's promises, Paul assures us, "If we died with him, we will also live with him; if we endure, we will also reign with him" *(2 Tim. 2:11–12)*. These are the unfailing promises of our Lord to those who are baptized.

*All sing: *[Hymn of thanksgiving]*

The Sacrament of Baptism

Minister: Let us recall the teaching of Scripture concerning the sacrament of baptism. The water of baptism signifies the washing away of our sin by the blood of Christ and the renewal of our lives by the Holy Spirit *(Titus 3:5)*. It also signifies that we are buried with Christ *(Rom. 6:4)*. From this we learn that our sin has been condemned by God, that we are to hate it and consider ourselves as having died to it. Moreover, the water of baptism signifies that we are raised with Christ *(Col. 2:12)*. From this we learn that we are to walk with Christ in newness of life. All this tells us that God has adopted us as his children: "Now if we are children, then we are heirs—heirs of God and co-heirs with Christ" *(Rom. 8:17)*. Thus in baptism God seals the promises he gave when he made his covenant with us, calling us and our children to put our trust for life and death in Christ our Savior, deny ourselves, take up our cross, and follow him in obedience and love. God graciously includes our children in his covenant; and all his promises are for them as well as us *(Gen. 17:7; Acts 2:39)*. Jesus himself embraced little children, and blessed them *(Mark 10:16)*; and the apostle Paul said that children of believers are holy *(1 Cor. 7:14)*. So, just as children of the old covenant received the sign of circumcision, our children are given the sign of baptism. We are therefore always to teach our little ones that they have been set apart by baptism as God's own children.

The Prayer of Preparation

Minister: Father in heaven, we pray that you willl never destroy us in our sin as with the flood, but save us as you saved believing Noah and his family and spare us as you spared the Israelites who walked safely through the sea. We pray that Christ, who went down into the Jordan and came up to receive the Spirit, who sank deep into death and was raised up Lord of life, will always keep us and our little ones in the grip of his hand. We pray, O holy Father, that your Spirit will separate us from sin and openly mark us with a faith that can stand the light of day and endure the dark of night. Prepare us now, O Lord, to respond with glad hope to your promises so that we, and all entrusted to our care, may drink deeply from the well of living water. We pray in the name of Christ our Lord. Amen.

The Vows
Minister: Since you have presented these children for holy baptism, you are asked to answer the following questions before God and his people:

First, do you confess Jesus Christ as your Lord and Savior, accept the promises of God, and affirm the truth of the Christian faith which is proclaimed in the Bible and confessed in this church of Christ?

Second, do you believe that your children, though sinful by nature, are received by God in Christ as members of his covenant, and therefore ought to be baptized?

Third, do you promise, in reliance on the Holy Spirit and with the help of the Christian community, to do all in your power to instruct these children in the Christian faith and to lead them by your example into the life of Christian discipleship?
Parents: We do, God helping us.
Minister: Do you, the people of the Lord, promise to receive these children in love, pray for them, help instruct them in the faith, and encourage and sustain them in the fellowship of believers?
People: We do, God helping us.

[The minister may say: Our Lord said: "Let little children come to me, and do not hinder them, for the kingdom of God belongs to such as these" (Mark 10:14).]

Minister: *[In administering the sacrament the minister shall say]:*
  (name), I baptize you into the name of the Father and of the Son and of the Holy Spirit.

All sing: [Hymn (optional)]

The Baptismal Prayer
Minister: Lord our God, forever faithful to your promises, we thank you for assuring us again that you will forgive us and receive us as children in Christ. Grant wisdom and love to the parents and to us all as we carry out the vows we have just made. We pray that you will govern these children by your Spirit and guide them throughout their lives. Help them see your fatherly goodness which surrounds us all and enable them to respond in faith to Jesus Christ, our chief teacher, eternal king, and only high priest. Give them strength to fight sin and endure trials. And when Christ returns, let them celebrate with all the people of God your greatness and goodness forever, in the joy of your new creation. Amen.

All sing: [Hymn]

The Word of God
Prayer for Illumination
Minister: O God of all truth, be pleased to grant us your Spirit as we attend to your Word. Open our minds that we may understand what you have revealed to us. Release us from self-will that we may be ready to obey. And open our lips that our mouths may show forth your praise. Through Jesus Christ our Lord. Amen.

Minister: *[Reading of the Scriptures]*
  [Sermon]
  [Post-sermon prayer (optional)]

The Response

*All sing: [Hymn]

Minister: [Intercessory prayer]

All: [Lord's Prayer in unison]

*All: [The Creed (optional)]

All: [Offering of gifts]

Minister: [Dedication prayer (optional)]

*All sing: [Doxology hymn]

*The Dismissal

Minister: Go in peace. The grace of our Lord Jesus Christ, the love of God the Father, and the fellowship of the Holy Spirit be with you all.

People: Amen.

Baptism of Children

Congregation of our Lord Jesus Christ:

What the Lord has revealed to us in his Word about holy baptism can be summarized in this way:

First, Scripture teaches that we and our children are sinners from birth, sinful from the time our mothers conceived us (*Ps. 51:5*). This means that we are all under the judgment of God and for that reason cannot be members of his kingdom unless we are born again. Baptism, whether by immersion or sprinkling, teaches that sin has made us so impure that we must undergo a cleansing which only God can accomplish. Therefore, we ought to be displeased with ourselves, humble ourselves, and turn to God for our salvation.

Second, baptism is a sign and seal that our sins are washed away through Jesus Christ. For this reason we are baptized into the name of God, the Father, the Son, and the Holy Spirit.

Our baptism into the name of God the Father is his assurance to us that he makes an everlasting covenant of grace with us and adopts us as his children and heirs. Therefore, he surrounds us with his goodness and protects us from evil or turns it to our profit.

When we are baptized into the name of the Son, we are assured by Christ himself that he washes us in his blood from all our sins. Christ joins us to himself so that we share in his death and resurrection. Through this union with Christ we are liberated from our sins and regarded as righteous before God.

Baptism into the name of the Holy Spirit is the assurance that the Spirit of God will make his home within us. While living within us, the Spirit will continually work to strengthen and deepen our union with Christ. He will make real in our lives Christ's work of washing away our sins. He will also help us each day to live the new life we have in Christ. As a result of his work within us, we shall one day be presented without the stain of sin among the assembly of the elect in life eternal.

Third, because all covenants have two sides, baptism also places us under obligation to live in obedience to God. We must cling to this one God, Father, Son, and Holy Spirit. We must trust him and love him with all our heart, soul, mind, and strength. We must abandon the sinful way of life, put to death our old nature, and show by our lives that we belong to God. If we through weakness should fall into sin, we must not despair of God's grace, nor use our weakness as an excuse to keep sinning. Baptism is a seal and totally reliable witness that God is always faithful to his covenant.

Our children should not be denied the sacrament of baptism because of their inability to understand its meaning. Without their knowledge, our children not only share in Adam's condemnation but are also received into God's favor in Christ. God's gracious attitude toward us and our children is revealed in what he said to Abraham, the father of all believers: "I will establish my covenant as an everlasting covenant between me and you and your descendants after you for the generations to come, to be your God and the God of your descendants after you" (*Gen. 17:7*). The apostle Peter also testifies to this with these words: "The promise is for you and your children and

This form for the baptism of children is one of the oldest in our liturgy. The earliest Dutch version of 1566 is an abbreviation and translation of a German form used in Heidelberg. An earlier English translation was approved by the Synod of 1912. The present translation was adopted by the Synod of 1976.

for . . . all whom the Lord our God will call" *(Acts 2:39)*. Therefore God formerly commanded circumcision as a seal of the covenant and as a declaration that righteousness comes by faith. Christ also recognized that children are members of the covenant people when he embraced them, laid his hands on them, and blessed them *(Mark 10:16)*. Since baptism has replaced circumcision, our children should be baptized as heirs of God's kingdom and of his covenant. As the children mature, their parents are responsible for teaching them the meaning of baptism.

Let us turn to God, asking that in this baptism his name may be glorified, we may be comforted, and the church may be edified.

Almighty, eternal God, long ago you severely punished an unbelieving and unrepentant world by sending a flood. But you showed your great mercy when you saved and protected believing Noah and his family. Your judgment upon sin and your great mercy toward us were again shown when the obstinate pharoah and his whole army were drowned in the Red Sea, and you brought your people Israel through the same sea on dry ground.

We pray that in this baptism you will again be merciful. Look upon these your children with favor by bringing them into union with your Son, Jesus Christ, through your Holy Spirit. May they be buried with Christ into death and be raised with him to new life. Give them true faith, firm hope, and ardent love so that they may joyfully bear their cross as they daily follow Christ.

Give these children the full assurance of your grace so that when they leave this life and its constant struggle against the power of sin they may appear before the judgment seat of Christ without fear. We ask this in the name of our Lord Jesus Christ, who with the Father and the Holy Spirit, one only God, lives and reigns forever. Amen.

Address to the Parents

People of God, as you have now heard, baptism is given to us by God as proof that he does make a covenant with us and our children. We must, therefore, use the sacrament for the purpose that God intended and not out of custom or superstition. You are asked to give an honest answer to these questions as a testimony that you are doing what God commands.

First, do you acknowledge that our children, who are sinful from the time of conception and birth and therefore subject to the misery which sin brings, even the condemnation of God, are made holy by God in Christ and so as members of his body ought to be baptized?

Second, do you acknowledge that the teaching of the Old and New Testaments, summarized in the Apostles' Creed, and taught in this Christian church, is the true and complete doctrine of salvation?

Third, do you sincerely promise to do all you can to teach these children, and to have them taught, this doctrine of salvation?

Answer: We do.

____(name)____, I baptize you into the name of the Father and of the Son and of the Holy Spirit.

Prayer of Thanksgiving

Almighty God and merciful Father, we thank you and praise your name for having forgiven our sins through the blood of your dear Son, Jesus Christ. We thank you for uniting us with Christ through your Holy Spirit and adopting us as your children, and we thank you for sealing and confirming these blessings to us and our children in the sacrament of baptism.

govern these children by your Holy Spirit. May they, through your guidance, be so nurtured in the Christian faith and godliness as to grow and develop in Jesus Christ. Help them see your fatherly goodness and mercy which surrounds us all. Make them champions of righteousness under the direction of Jesus Christ, our chief teacher, eternal king, and only high priest. Give them the courage to fight against and overcome sin, the devil, and his whole dominion. May their lives become an eternal song of praise to you, the one only true God, Father, Son, and Holy Spirit. Amen.

We pray, O Lord, that you will always

Baptism of Children

The Institution

Congregation of our Lord Jesus Christ:

Let us hear our Lord's command concerning the sacrament of holy baptism. After he had risen victorious from the grave, Jesus said to his disciples: "All authority in heaven and on earth has been given to me. Therefore go and make disciples of all nations, baptizing them in the name of the Father and of the Son and of the Holy Spirit, and teaching them to obey everything I have commanded you. And surely I am with you always, to the very end of the age" *(Matt. 28:18–20).*

In obedience to this command the church baptizes believers and their children.

The Promises

Let us hear the promises of God which are confirmed in baptism.

The Lord made this great promise to Abraham: "I will establish my covenant as an everlasting covenant between me and you and your descendants after you for the generations to come, to be your God and the God of your descendants after you" *(Gen. 17:7).*

In later years, though Israel was unfaithful, God renewed his promise through the prophet: " 'This is the covenant I will make with the house of Israel after that time,' declares the LORD. 'I will put my law in their minds and write it on their hearts. I will be their God, and they will be my people. No longer will a man teach his neighbor, or a man his brother, saying, "Know the LORD," because they will all know me, from the least of them to the greatest,' declares the LORD. 'For I will forgive their wickedness and will remember their sins no more' " *(Jer. 31:33–34).*

In the fullness of time God came in Jesus Christ to give pardon and peace through the blood of the cross, the "blood of the covenant, which is poured out for many for the forgiveness of sins" *(Matt. 26:28).*

After Jesus had risen from the dead, the apostles proclaimed: "Repent and be baptized, every one of you, in the name of Jesus Christ for the forgiveness of your sins. And you will receive the gift of the Holy Spirit. The promise is for you and your children and for all who are far off— for all whom the Lord our God will call" *(Acts 2:38–39).*

Anticipating the fulfillment of God's promises, Paul assures us, "If we died with him, we will also live with him; if we endure, we will also reign with him" *(2 Tim. 2:11–12).*

These are the unfailing promises of our Lord to those who are baptized.

The Instruction

Let us also recall the teaching of Scripture concerning the sacrament of baptism.

The water of baptism signifies the washing away of our sin by the blood of Christ and the renewal of our lives by the Holy Spirit *(Titus 3:5).* It also signifies that we are buried with Christ *(Rom. 6:4).* From this we learn that our sin has been condemned by God, that we are to hate it and consider ourselves as having died to it. Moreover, the water of baptism signifies that we are raised with Christ *(Col. 2:12).* From this we learn that we are to walk with Christ in newness of life. All this tells us that God has adopted us as his children, "Now if we are children, then we are heirs—heirs of God and co-heirs with Christ" *(Rom. 8:17).*

Thus in baptism God seals the promises he gave when he made his covenant with us, calling us and our children to put our trust for life and death in Christ our Savior, deny ourselves, take up our cross, and follow him in obedience and love.

God graciously includes our children in his covenant, and all his promises are for them as well as us *(Gen. 17:7; Acts 2:39).* Jesus himself embraced little children and blessed them *(Mark 10:16);* and the apostle Paul said that children of believers are holy *(1 Cor. 7:14).* So, just as children of the old covenant received the sign of circumcision, our children are given the sign of baptism. We are therefore always to teach our little ones that they have been set apart by baptism as God's own children.

The Prayer of Preparation

Father in heaven, we pray that you will never destroy us in our sin as with the flood, but save us as you saved believing Noah and his family, and spare us as you spared the Israelites who walked safely through the sea.

We pray that Christ, who went down into the Jordan and came up to receive the Spirit, who sank deep into death and was raised up Lord of life, will always keep us and our little ones in the grip of his hand.

We pray, O holy Father, that your Spirit will separate us from sin and openly mark us with a faith that can stand the light of day and endure the dark of night.

Prepare us now, O Lord, to respond with glad hope to your promises so that we, and all entrusted to our care, may drink deeply from the well of living water. We pray in the name of Jesus Christ our Lord. Amen!

The Vows

[The minister addresses the parents]:

Since you have presented these children for holy baptism, you are asked to answer the following questions before God and his people:

First, do you confess Jesus Christ as your Lord and Savior, accept the promises of God, and affirm the truth of the Christian faith which is proclaimed in the Bible and confessed in this church of Christ?

Second, do you believe that your children, though sinful by nature, are received by God in Christ as members of his covenant, and therefore ought to be baptized?

Third, do you promise, in reliance on the Holy Spirit and with the help of the Christian community, to do all in your power to instruct these children in the Christian faith and to lead them by your example to be Christ's disciples?

[The parents respond]: We do, God helping us.

[The minister addresses the congregation]: Do you, the people of the Lord, promise to receive these children in love, pray for them, help instruct them in the faith, and encourage and sustain them in the fellowship of believers?

[The congregation responds]: We do, God helping us.

The Sacrament

[The minister may say]:

Our Lord said: "Let the little children come to me, and do not hinder them, for the kingdom of God belongs to such as these" *(Mark 10:14).*

[In administering the sacrament the minister shall say]:

_____(name)_____, I baptize you into the name of the Father and of the Son and of the Holy Spirit.

A Triumphant Hymn

The Baptismal Prayer

Lord our God, forever faithful to your promise, we thank you for assuring us again that you will forgive us and receive us as children in Christ.

Grant wisdom and love to the parents and to us all as we carry out the vows we have just made.

We pray that you will guide our little ones throughout their lives. Enable them to respond in faith to the gospel. Fill them with your Spirit and make their lives fruitful. Give them strength to endure trials. And when Christ returns, let them celebrate with all the people of God your greatness and goodness forever in the joy of your new creation. Amen.

Public Profession of Faith

Beloved in the Lord Jesus Christ:

We thank our God for the grace that he gave you through Christ Jesus that made you desire to profess your faith publicly, here in the presence of God and his holy church, and to obtain the privileges of full communion with the people of God.

You are now requested to answer sincerely the following questions:

First, do you declare that you love the Lord, and that you desire to serve him according to his Word—to forsake the world, to put to death your old nature, and to lead a godly life?

Second, do you openly accept God's covenant promise, which has been signified and sealed to you in your baptism, and do you humbly confess that you are sinful and that you seek life not in yourselves but only in Jesus Christ your Savior?

Third, do you sincerely believe the doctrine contained in the Old and the New Testaments, and in the articles of the Christian faith, and taught in this Christian church, to be the true and complete doctrine of salvation, and do you promise by the grace of God steadfastly to continue in this profession?

Fourth, do you promise to submit to the government of the church and also, if you should become delinquent either in doctrine or in life, to submit to its admonition and discipline?

_____(name)_____, what is your answer?

Answer: I do *[to be given by each individually]*.

I charge you, then, beloved, that you, by the diligent use of the means of grace and with the assistance of your God, continue in the profession you have just made. In the name of Christ Jesus our Lord, I now welcome you to full communion with the people of God. Rest assured that all the privileges of such communion are now yours. "And the God of all grace, who called you to his eternal glory in Christ, after you have suffered a little while, will himself restore you and make you strong, firm and steadfast. To him be the power for ever and ever. Amen" *(1 Pet. 5:10–11).*

Prayer [optional]

Heavenly Father, we thank you that you have from the beginning embraced in your covenant the children together with their parents. We thank you that you from the first cast the lot of these your servants in the Christian church and granted them all the many blessings of Christian culture. We bless you that in their case you added the special grace of your Holy Spirit, so that of their own will they come here today to profess your truth and to consecrate their lives to your service. We earnestly pray that you will continue to carry on the good work you have begun in them until the day of complete redemption. Increase in them daily the many gifts of your grace, the spirit of wisdom and understanding, the spirit of knowledge and of the fear of the Lord. Grant them the happiness of promoting the glory of their Lord and the edification of his people. Deliver them in the temptations of this life and in the final trial of death. And in that day when you make up your jewels, set also these servants in your crown, that they may shine as stars, to your praise, forever and ever. Amen.

This form was prepared between 1924 and 1932. Prior to this, churches used a generally agreed upon series of questions that allowed great flexibility of style and custom.

Public Profession of Faith

Congregation of our Lord Jesus Christ:

Today we are privileged to welcome into the full life of the church's fellowship those who wish to confess their faith in Christ as Lord and Savior. When they were baptized God made clear his claim on them as his own, and they were received into the church. Now they wish to share fully in the life of this congregation and of the whole church of God. And so today they will publicly accept and confirm what was sealed in their baptism, confess their faith in the Lord Jesus, and offer themselves to God as his willing servants. We thank God for having given them this desire and pray that as we now hear their confession, he will favor us with the presence and guidance of his Holy Spirit.

The Vows *

_____(name)_____, will you stand now, and in the presence of God and his people respond to the following questions:

1. Do you believe that Jesus Christ is the Son of God sent to redeem the world, do you love and trust him as the one who saves you from your sin, and do you with repentance and joy embrace him as Lord of your life?

Answer: I do.

2. Do you believe that the Bible is the Word of God revealing Christ and his redemption, and that the confessions of this church faithfully reflect this revelation?

Answer: I do.

3. Do you accept the gracious promises of God sealed to you in your baptism and do you affirm your union with Christ and his church which your baptism signifies?

Answer: I do.

4. Do you promise to do all you can, with the help of the Holy Spirit, to strengthen your love and commitment to Christ by sharing faithfully in the life of the church, honoring and submitting to its authority; and do you join with the people of God in doing the work of the Lord everywhere?

Answer: I do.

The Reception
[The minister asks the congregation to rise.]

Minister: In the name of our Lord Jesus Christ I now welcome you to all the privileges of full communion. I welcome you to full participation in the life of the church. I welcome you to its responsibilities, its joys, and its sufferings. "May the God of peace, who through the blood of the eternal covenant brought back from the dead our Lord Jesus, that great Shepherd of the sheep, equip you with everything good for doing his will, and may he work in us what is pleasing to him, through Jesus Christ, to whom be glory for ever and ever. Amen" *(Heb. 13:20–21).*

Congregation: Thanks be to God! We promise you our love, encouragement, and prayers.

Minister: Let us together say what we believe:

[Here follows the Apostles' Creed in unison.]

The Prayer

Lord, our God, we thank you for your Word and Spirit through which we know Jesus Christ as Lord and Savior. May those who confessed your name today never cease to wonder at what you have done for them. Help them to continue firmly in the faith, to bear witness to your love, and to let the Holy Spirit shape their

---

*The questions may be changed into statements and said by the confessors. Opportunity may also be given here for additional self-expression on the part of the confessors. The response may be asked after the last question only.

lives. Take them, good Shepherd, into your care that they may loyally endure opposition in serving you.

May we, with all your children, live together in the joy and power of your Holy Spirit. We ask this, Lord Jesus, in the hope of your coming. Amen.

Baptism of Adults

Congregation of our Lord Jesus Christ:

What the Lord has revealed to us in his Word about holy baptism can be summarized in this way:

First, Scripture teaches that we and our children are sinners from birth, from the time our mothers conceived us (*Ps. 51:5*). This means that we are all under the judgment of God and for that reason cannot be members of his kingdom unless we are born again. Baptism, whether by immersion or sprinkling, teaches that sin has made us so impure that we must undergo a cleansing which only God can accomplish. Therefore, we ought to be displeased with ourselves, humble ourselves, and turn to God for our salvation.

Second, baptism is a sign and seal that our sins are washed away through Jesus Christ. For this reason we are baptized into the name of God, the Father, the Son, and the Holy Spirit.

Our baptism into the name of God the Father is his assurance to us that he makes an everlasting covenant of grace with us and adopts us as his children and heirs. Therefore, he surrounds us with his goodness and protects us from evil or turns it to our profit.

When we are baptized into the name of the Son, we are assured by Christ himself that he washes us in his blood from all our sins. Christ joins us to himself so that we share in his death and resurrection. Through this union with Christ we are liberated from our sins and regarded as righteous before God.

Baptism into the name of the Holy Spirit is the assurance that the Spirit of God will make his home within us. While living within us, the Spirit will continually work to strengthen and deepen our union with Christ. He will make real in our lives Christ's work of washing away our sins. He will also help us each day to live the new life we have in Christ. As a result of his work within us, we shall one day be presented without the stain of sin among the assembly of the elect in life eternal.

Third, because all covenants have two sides, baptism also places us under obligation to live in obedience to God. We must cling to this one God, Father, Son, and Holy Spirit. We must trust him and love him with all our heart, soul, mind, and strength. We must abandon the sinful way of life, put to death our old nature, and show by our lives that we belong to God. If we through weakness should fall into sin, we must not despair of God's grace, nor use our weakness as an excuse to keep on sinning. Baptism is a seal and totally reliable witness that God is always faithful to his covenant.

On the basis of the covenant the children of believers are to be baptized despite their inability to understand its meaning. Adults, however, should not be baptized unless they have felt their sins and confess repentance and faith in Christ. This is why John the Baptist followed God's command by preaching the baptism of repentance for the forgiveness of sins and why he baptized those who confessed their sins (*Mark 1:4–5; Luke 3:3*). Similarly, our Lord Jesus Christ commissioned his apostles to make disciples of all nations, baptizing them in the name of the Father and of the Son and of the Holy Spirit (*Matt. 28:19*). To these instructions he added the promise that he who believes and is baptized will be saved (*Mark 16:16*). And, as the book

---

The Synod of Dort (1618–19) drew from two earlier adult baptism forms to produce this form. An earlier English translation was approved by the Synod of 1912. The present translation was adopted by the Synod of 1978.

of Acts clearly shows, the apostles accordingly followed the rule of baptizing only those adults who confessed their penitence and faith. Also today, therefore, only those adults are to be baptized who have come to understand the meaning of baptism through the preaching of the gospel, and who are able to give an account both of baptism and of their own faith.

Let us turn to God, asking that in this baptism his name may be glorified, we may be comforted, and the church may be edified.

Almighty, eternal God, long ago you severely punished an unbelieving and unrepentant world by sending a flood. But you showed your great mercy when you saved and protected believing Noah and his family. Your judgment upon sin and your great mercy toward us were again shown when the obstinate pharaoh and his whole army were drowned in the Red Sea, and you brought your people Israel through the same sea on dry ground.

We pray that in this baptism you will again be merciful. Look with favor upon these brothers and sisters who are about to be baptized by bringing them into union with your Son, Jesus Christ, through your Holy Spirit. May they be buried with Christ into death and be raised with him to new life.

Give them true faith, firm hope, and ardent love so that they may joyfully bear their cross as they daily follow him. Give them the full assurance of your grace so that when they leave this life and its constant struggle against the power of sin, they may appear before the judgment seat of Christ without fear. We ask this in the name of our Lord Jesus Christ, who with the Father and the Holy Spirit, one only God, lives and reigns forever. Amen.

Address to the Adults to Be Baptized

____(name)____, since you want to be baptized as a seal of your incorporation into God's church, you are asked here in the presence of God and his people to respond without reservation to the following questions.

Your response will demonstrate that you accept the Christian faith as taught to you and professed by you, and it will also confirm your intention, by God's grace, to live according to that faith.

First, do you believe in the only true God, who is distinct in three Persons: Father, Son, and Holy Spirit? Do you believe that he has created out of nothing heaven, earth, and everything in them, and that he still upholds and rules them so that nothing happens outside his divine will?

Second, do you believe that you are sinful from the time of conception and birth, that therefore you are under the judgment of God, and that you are by nature entirely incapable of doing good and inclined to all kinds of evil? Do you declare that you have often broken the Lord's commands in your thoughts, your words, and your actions, and that with your whole heart you repent of these sins?

Third, do you believe that Jesus Christ, who is both true and eternal God and true man, and who assumed his human nature from the virgin Mary's flesh and blood, has been given you by God as your Savior; that through this faith you receive forgiveness of sins in his blood; and that by the power of the Holy Spirit you have become a member of Jesus Christ and his church?

Fourth, do you agree with all the articles of the Christian faith as taught from God's Word in this church and do you intend to continue steadfastly in this teaching? Do you also reject all heresies and errors conflicting with this doctrine? And do you promise to continue in the fellowship of this church both by listening to the preached Word and by celebrating the Lord's Supper?

Fifth, do you genuinely intend always to live as a Christian and to reject the world and its evil attractions, as a member of Christ and his church should; and do you promise to submit gladly to all Christian admonitions?

Answer: I do.

May our great and good God mercifully crown with his grace and blessing the sacred commitment that you have just made, through Jesus Christ. Amen.

The Sacrament

[The minister shall say]:

I baptize you,___(name)___, into the name of the Father and of the Son and of the Holy Spirit.

Prayer of Thanksgiving

Almighty God and merciful Father, we thank you and praise your name for forgiving our sins through the blood of your dear Son, Jesus Christ. We thank you for uniting us with Christ through your Holy Spirit and adopting us as your children, and we thank you for sealing and confirming these blessings to us and our children in the sacrament of baptism.

We pray, O Lord, that you will so govern these new members of your church by your Holy Spirit, that they will live a devout Christian life, growing and developing in Jesus Christ. Help them see your fatherly goodness and mercy surrounding us all. Make them champions of righteousness under the direction of Jesus Christ, our chief teacher, eternal king, and only high priest. Give them the courage to fight against and overcome sin, the devil, and his whole dominion. May their lives become an eternal song of praise to you, the only true God, Father, Son, and Holy Spirit. Amen.

Baptism of Adults

Congregation of our Lord Jesus Christ:

It is always a joy for the church to receive new believers into its fellowship. At our last consistory meeting ___(names)___ declared their faith in Christ and expressed their desire to receive the sacrament of baptism. Today we are happy that they will confess their faith before us all and receive the sacrament.

The Vows

___(names)___, will you stand now, and in the presence of God and his people respond to the following questions:

1. Do you believe that Jesus Christ is the Son of God sent to redeem the world, do you love and trust him as the one who saves you from your sin, and do you with repentance and joy embrace him as Lord of your life?

Answer: I do.

2. Do you believe that the Bible is the Word of God, revealing Christ and his redemption, and that the confessions of this church faithfully reflect this revelation?

Answer: I do.

3. Do you promise to do all you can, with the help of the Holy Spirit, to strengthen your love and commitment to Christ by sharing faithfully in the life of the church, honoring and submitting to its authority; and do you join with the people of God in doing the work of the Lord everywhere?

Answer: I do.

[The questions may be changed into statements and said by the confessors. Opportunity may also be given here for additional self-expression on the part of the confessors. The response may be given after the last question only.]

The Institution

Congregation of our Lord Jesus Christ:

Let us hear our Lord's command concerning the sacrament of holy baptism. After he had risen victoriously from the grave, Jesus said to his disciples: "All authority in heaven and on earth has been given to me. Therefore go and make disciples of all nations, baptizing them in the name of the Father and of the Son and of the Holy Spirit, and teaching them to obey everything I have commanded you. And surely I will be with you always, to the very end of the age" *(Matt. 28:18–20)*. In obedience to this command the church baptizes believers and their children.

The Promises

These are the promises God confirms to his people through baptism.

The Lord made this great promise to Abraham: "I will establish my covenant as an everlasting covenant between me and you and your descendants after you for the generations to come, to be your God and the God of your descendants after you" *(Gen. 17:7)*.

In later years, though Israel was unfaithful, God renewed his promise through the prophet: " 'This is the covenant I will make with the house of Israel after that time,' declares the LORD. 'I will put my law in their minds and write it on their hearts. I will be their God, and they will be my people . . . . For I will forgive their wickedness and will remember their sins no more' " *(Jer. 31:33–34)*.

In the fullness of time God came in Jesus Christ to give pardon and peace through the blood of the cross, the "blood of the covenant, which is poured out for many for the forgiveness of sins" *(Matt. 26:28)*.

After Jesus had risen from the dead, the apostles proclaimed: "Repent and be baptized, every one of you, in the name of Jesus Christ for the forgiveness of your sins. And you will receive the gift of the Holy Spirit. The promise is for you and your children and for all whom the Lord our God will call" *(Acts 2:38–39).*

Anticipating the fulfillment of God's promises, Paul assures us, "If we died with him, we will also live with him; if we endure, we will also reign with him" *(1 Tim. 2:11–12).*

These are the unfailing promises of our Lord to those who are baptized.

The Instruction

And this is what Scripture teaches concerning the sacrament of baptism.

The water of baptism signifies the washing away of our sin by the blood of Christ and the renewal of our lives by the Holy Spirit *(Titus 3:5).* It also signifies that we are buried with Christ *(Rom. 6:4).* From this we learn that our sin has been condemned by God, that we are to hate it and consider ourselves as having died to it. Moreover, the water of baptism signifies that we are raised with Christ *(Col. 2:12).* From this we learn that we are to walk with Christ in newness of life. All this tells us that God has adopted us as his children: "Now if we are children, then we are heirs—heirs of God and co-heirs with Christ" *(Rom. 8:17).*

Thus in baptism God seals the promises he gave when he made his covenant with us, calling us and our children to put our trust for life and death in Christ our Savior, deny ourselves, take up our cross, and follow him in obedience and love.

*God graciously includes our children in his covenant, and all his promises are for them as well as for us *(Gen. 17:7; Acts 2:39).* Jesus himself embraced little children and blessed them *(Mark 10:16),* and the apostle Paul said that children of believers are holy *(1 Cor. 7:14).* So, just as the children of the old covenant received the sign of circumcision, our children are given the sign of baptism. We are therefore always to teach our little ones that they have been set apart by baptism as God's own children.

The Prayer of Preparation

Father in heaven, we pray that you will never destroy us in our sin as with the flood, but save us as you saved believing Noah and his family, and spare us as you spared the Israelites who walked safely through the sea.

We pray that Christ, who went down into the Jordan and came up to receive the Spirit, who sank deep into death and was raised up Lord of life, will always keep us and our little ones in the grip of his hand.

We pray, O holy Father, that your Spirit will separate us from sin and openly mark us with a faith that can stand the light of day and endure the dark of night.

Prepare us now, O Lord, to respond with glad hope to your promises so that we, and all entrusted to our care, may drink deeply from the well of living water. We pray in the name of Jesus Christ our Lord. Amen!

The Sacrament
[The minister addresses the confessors (standing)]:

Do you now wish to be baptized in the name of the triune God, and will you receive your baptism as a sign and seal that God accepts you in Christ, forgives all your sins, and incorporates you into his church?

[Each confessor responds]: I do, with all my heart.

*Second, do you believe that your

---

*This paragraph should be read in instances of family baptism.

children, though sinful by nature, are received by God in Christ as members of this covenant, and therefore ought to be baptized?

*Third, do you promise, in reliance on the Holy Spirit and with the help of the Christian community, to do all in your power to instruct these children in the Christian faith and to lead them by your example into the life of Christian discipleship?

*The parents respond: We do, God helping us.

[The minister addresses the congregation]:

Do you, the people of the Lord, promise to receive ____(names)____ into your fellowship as members of the body of Christ, and do you promise to encourage them in the Christian faith and help them in doing the work of the Lord?

Congregation: We do, God helping us.

[In administering the sacrament the minister shall say]:

____(name)____, I baptize you into the name of the Father and of the Son and of the Holy Spirit.

Minister: In the name of our Lord Jesus Christ I now welcome you to all the privileges of full communion. I welcome you to full participation in the life of the church. I welcome you to its responsibilities, its privileges, its sufferings, and its joys.

A Triumphant Hymn

The Baptismal Prayer

Our Father in heaven, we thank you for Jesus Christ, for the new life given in him, and for the one faith, one hope, and one baptism which your people have shared through the ages. We rejoice that ____(names)____ are now one with your church and that we may receive them as members of this congregation. Guide them in the Christian way and sustain us all in the fellowship and service of our Lord. Amen.

---

*In case of family baptism, questions 2 and 3 for children's baptism should be asked.

Service of Word and Sacrament

*The Opening

Minister: In the name of the Father, and the Son, and the Holy Spirit.

People: Our help is in the name of the Lord, who made heaven and earth.

Minister: Grace be to you, and peace, from God our Father and our Lord Jesus Christ.

People: Amen.

Minister: [optional]
And now as our Lord gives to us his peace, so let us pass the peace to each other, saying, "The peace of the Lord be with you."

[Here the people express their unity by greeting each other with these or similar words.]

All: [Hymn]

Confession and Assurance

The Call to Confession

Minister: God is light; in him there is no darkness at all.
If we claim to have fellowship with him
    yet walk in darkness,
we lie and do not live by the truth.
But if we walk in the light, as he is in the light,
we have fellowship with one another,
and the blood of Jesus, his Son,
    purifies us from all sin.
If we claim to be without sin, we deceive ourselves
    and the truth is not in us.
(1 John 1:5b–8)

The Confession

All: Most holy and merciful Father,
We confess to you and to one another,
    that we have sinned against you
    by what we have done,
    and by what we have left undone.
We have not loved you with our
    whole heart and mind and strength.
We have not fully loved our neighbors
    as ourselves.
We have not always had in us the
    mind of Christ.
You alone know how often we have grieved you
    by wasting your gifts,
    by wandering from your ways,
    by forgetting your love.
Forgive us, we pray you, most merciful Father,
    and free us from our sin.
Renew in us the grace and strength of your Holy Spirit,
    for the sake of Jesus Christ your Son,
        our Savior.
        Amen.

The Declaration of Pardon

Minister: To all who confess themselves to be sinners, humbling themselves before God and believing in the Lord Jesus Christ for their salvation, I declare this sure promise: "If we confess our sins, he is faithful and just and will forgive us our sins and purify us from all unrighteousness" (1 John 1:9).

*indicates congregation stands

This service, approved by the Synod of 1981, contains portions of a synodically approved Lord's Supper form. These components, which should be read in their entirety and not changed in any way, are the following: the introduction spoken by the minister (Brothers and sisters in Christ. . ."); the first part of the thanksgiving (through "Christ our Lord"); the institution; the memorial; the preparation of the elements; and the communion.

The Response
All Sing: Glory be to the Father,
and to the Son, and to the Holy
Ghost;
as it was in the beginning,
is now, and ever shall be,
world without end. Amen. Amen.

The Dedication
Minister: Let us, God's forgiven people,
now listen to his law for our lives.
[Here the minister proclaims God's covenant
law as a guide for our lives, as it is found
in the Decalogue or some other scriptural
passage.]
*All: Hymn

Communion
Proclamation of the Word
Minister: Let us pray:
Almighty God, grant us your Spirit,
that we may rightly understand and
truly obey your
Word of truth.
Open our hearts that we may love
what you command
and desire what you promise.
Set us free from private distractions
that we may hear
and from selfish pride that we
may receive
the promise of your grace.
Through Jesus Christ our Lord.
Amen.
Minister or other member: [Scripture
readings]
Minister: [Sermon]
Minister or other member: [Prayer for
blessing on the Word]

The Response
*All: [Hymn]

*The Creed
Minister: Let us together confess the
faith of the church at all times and in
all places:

All: [Say or sing the Apostles' Creed or the
Nicene Creed.]

The Intercessory Prayer
[Prayers led by the minister or by some other
member.]

The Offertory
Minister: Let us present our gifts to
God. [Here the offerings are received. At
the conclusion the people sing.]
*All sing: Praise God from whom all
blessings flow.
Praise him all creatures here below.
Praise him above ye heavenly host.
Praise Father, Son, and Holy Ghost.
Amen.

The Lord's Supper
Minister: Brothers and sisters in Christ,
the gospels tell us that on the first day
of the week, the day on which our
Lord rose from the dead, he
appeared to some of his disciples and
was made known to them in the
breaking of bread. Come, then, to the
joyful feast of our Lord.
[If the communion elements are not already
on the table, they may be brought forward
at this point.]

The Thanksgiving
Minister: Lift up your hearts.
People: We lift them up to the Lord.
Minister: Let us give thanks to the Lord
our God.
People: It is right for us to give thanks.
It is our joy and our peace,
At all times and in all places
To give thanks to you,
holy Father,
almighty, everlasting God,
through Christ our Lord.
Minister: We bless you for your continual
love and care for every creature.
We praise you for forming us in
your image and calling us to be your
people.

We thank you that you did not abandon us in our rebellion against your love, but sent prophets and teachers to lead us into the way of salvation.

Above all we thank you for sending Jesus, your Son, to deliver us from the way of sin and death by the obedience of his life, by his suffering upon the cross, and by his resurrection from the dead. We praise you that he now reigns with you in glory and ever lives to pray for us.

We thank you for the Holy Spirit, who leads us into truth, defends us in adversity, and out of every people unites us into one holy church.

Therefore with the whole company of saints in heaven and on earth we worship and glorify you, God most holy, and we sing with joy.

All sing: Holy, holy, holy! Lord God Almighty!
All thy works shall praise thy name, in earth and sky and sea.
Holy, holy, holy! Merciful and mighty!
God in three persons, blessed Trinity!

The Institution
Minister: We give thanks to God the Father that our Savior, Jesus Christ, before he suffered, gave us this memorial of this sacrifice, until he comes again. "The Lord Jesus, on the night when he was betrayed, took bread, and when he had given thanks, he broke it and said, 'This is my body, which is for you; do this in remembrance of me.' In the same way, he took the cup, after supper, saying, 'This cup is the new covenant in my blood; do this, whenever you drink it, in remembrance of me.' For whenever you eat this bread and

drink this cup, you proclaim the Lord's death until he comes."
(1 Cor. 11:23–26)

The Memorial
All: We shall do as our Lord commands.
We proclaim that our Lord Jesus was sent by the Father into the world,
that he took upon himself our flesh and blood,
and bore the wrath of God against our sin.
We confess that he was condemned to die that we might be pardoned,
and suffered death that we might live.
We proclaim that he is risen to make us right with God,
and that he shall come again in the glory of his new creation.
This we do now, and until he comes again.

Prayer of Consecration
Minister: Heavenly Father, show forth among us the presence of your life-giving Word and Holy Spirit, to sanctify us and your whole church through this sacrament. Grant that all who share the body and blood of our Savior Jesus Christ may be one in him and may remain faithful in love and hope. And as this grain has been gathered from many fields into one loaf and these grapes from many hills into one cup, grant, O Lord, that your whole church may soon be gathered from the ends of the earth into your kingdom. Now, as our Savior Christ has taught us, we pray:
All: Our Father in heaven, hallowed be . . .

Preparation of the Elements
[as the minister breaks the bread and pours the cup]

Minister: The bread which we break
is a sharing in the body of Christ.
People: We who are many are one body,
for we all share the same loaf.
Minister: The cup for which we give thanks
is a sharing in the blood of Christ.
People: The cup which we drink
is our participation in the blood of Christ.

The Invitation
Minister: Congregation in the Lord Jesus Christ, the Lord has prepared his table for all who love him and trust in him alone for their salvation. All who are truly sorry for their sins, who sincerely believe in the Lord Jesus as their Savior, and who desire to live in obedience to him, are now invited to come with gladness to the table of the Lord.

The Dedication
All: Holy Father, in thanks for the sacrifice of Jesus Christ,
in the joy of his resurrection,
in the hope of his coming again,
we present ourselves a living sacrifice
and come to the table of our Lord.
[as the minister indicates the elements]
Minister: The gifts of God for the people of God.

The Communion
[when the people are ready to eat the bread]
Minister: Take, eat, remember and believe that the body of our Lord Jesus Christ was given for the complete forgiveness of all our sins.
[when the people are ready to drink the cup]

Minister: Take, drink, remember and believe that the precious blood of our Lord Jesus Christ was shed for the complete forgiveness of all our sins.

The Thanksgiving
Minister: Congregation in Christ, since the Lord has fed us at his table, let us praise his holy name with thanksgiving.
[Sing together Psalm 103 or say in unison]:
All: Praise the Lord, O my soul;
all my inmost being, praise his holy name.
Praise the Lord, O my soul,
and forget not all his benefits.
He forgives all my sins
and heals all my diseases;
he redeems my life from the pit
and crowns me with love and compassion.
He satisfies my desires with good things,
so that my youth is renewed like the eagle's *(Ps. 103:1–5)*.
*All: [Hymn—optional]

*The Dismissal
Minister: The peace of God which passes all understanding keep your hearts and minds in the knowledge and love of God, and of his Son Jesus Christ, our Lord; and the blessing of God almighty, Father, Son, and Holy Spirit, be among you and remain with you always.
People: Amen.
Minister: Go in peace to love and serve the Lord.
All: *[Hymn—optional]*

Preparatory Exhortation for the Lord's Supper

Minister: As we prepare to celebrate holy communion, let us remember that Scripture calls us to examine ourselves before God. We are taught that eating and drinking unworthily brings judgment upon ourselves *(1 Cor. 11:28–29)*. Let us therefore ask God for the proper spirit in which to celebrate the sacrament.

Almighty God, before whom can be neither secret thought nor hidden deed, grant us your Spirit that we may know our hearts, our lives, and our inmost thoughts as you know them.

Grant us your grace that we may repent sincerely of all sin, find peace with you through our Lord Jesus Christ, and grow in assurance of salvation in him.

May the celebration of our Savior's infinite love in his redeeming death bring joy to us and glory to you.

All: We thank you, heavenly Father, for the atoning power of our Savior's death and for our share in his victory over sin. Open our hearts as we prepare for this celebration, that it may strengthen us in our faith, establish us in our hope, and confirm us in our love. In his name, Amen.

Minister: Brothers and sisters, let us first examine our faith. We all confess the truth of God as taught by Scripture and summarized in the creeds of the church. By this faith we take to ourselves Christ and all his benefits, so that for us to live is Christ.

All: Lord God, author and finisher of all true believing, confirm our faith as we prepare for the holy sacrament.

Minister: Let us, further, examine our hope. All Christian hope rests upon the finished work of Christ as Savior. The holy gospel teaches that all our righteousness is in him alone.

God's children rely wholly upon the merits of Christ, find in him their strength and victory, and confidently expect his return in glory. They look forward to celebrating this holy supper anew with him in the kingdom. They will surely be received by God at his table.

All: Most merciful Father, fill us with all joy and peace in believing, so that by the power of the Holy Spirit we may abound in hope.

Minister: Let us also examine our love, both for God and our neighbors. Remember the great and first commandment to love the Lord our God with all our heart, soul, mind, and strength. Let us consciously determine to live a life of loving service to him, through Christ our Lord.

Let us also search ourselves to determine whether we love our neighbors as Christ commands. Do we unselfishly live for the welfare of others? Do our lives reflect the godly virtues of obedience, fidelity, integrity, justice, humility, and contentment? Do we seek reconciliation with our neighbors in all cases of offense?

All: Dear Father, daily increase in us the greatest gift of all, our Christian love.

The Synod of 1981 approved this material as an option to the preparatory sections of the forms for the celebration of the Lord's Supper. It may be read at the service prior to the Sunday on which communion is celebrated.

Minister: If these marks of spiritual life are not evident in us, we may not presume to approach his table. Those, therefore, who live in self-righteousness, who hope in works or virtues of their own, and who do not show love to God and neighbor, have no true place at the Lord's supper.

Yet we should not be deterred by any sin lingering within against our will. As we find faith, hope, and love within us, we ought gladly to obey our Lord's command and come with full expectation to God's open house of mercy.

All: Gracious God, we love and adore you in Christ our Lord. We thank you for reconciling us to yourself in him. We rejoice in being received as your children.

Prepare us by your Holy Spirit for the sacrament. Help us to come in the assurance that by it we shall be spiritually revived, and strengthened in faith, hope, and love, through Christ our Lord. Amen.

[An appropriate hymn may be sung.]

Celebration of the Lord's Supper

Preparatory Exhortation

Beloved in Jesus Christ, since we hope next Lord's Day (*or:* since it is our privilege this day) to celebrate the blessed sacrament of the Lord's Supper, we are called to prepare our hearts by rightly examining ourselves. For the apostle Paul has written: "Therefore, whoever eats the bread or drinks the cup of the Lord in an unworthy manner will be guilty of sinning against the body and blood of the Lord. A man ought to examine himself before he eats of the bread and drinks of the cup" (*1 Cor. 11:27–28*).

Let all of us, then, examine our lives and, considering our own sin and the wrath of God on it, be sure that we humble ourselves in repentance before God.

Let us examine our hearts to be sure that we trust in Jesus Christ alone for our salvation, and that we believe our sins are forgiven wholly by grace, for the sake of our Lord's sacrifice on the cross.

Finally, let us examine our consciences to be sure that we resolve to live in faith and obedience before our Lord, and in love and peace with our neighbors.

God will surely receive at the table of his Son all who truly repent of their sins, believe in Jesus Christ as their Savior, and desire to do his will. All those, however, who do not repent, who do not put their trust in the Lord Jesus, and who have no desire to lead a godly life, are warned, according to the command of God, to keep themselves from the holy sacrament. If we are living in disobedience to Christ and in enmity with our neighbors, we must repent of our sin and reconcile ourselves to our neighbors before we come to the Lord's table. For if we partake of the sacrament in unbelief and willful disobedience, we eat and drink judgment to ourselves.

This solemn warning is not designed, however, to discourage penitent sinners from coming to the holy sacrament. We do not come to the supper as though we were righteous in ourselves but rather to testify that we are sinners and that we look to Jesus Christ for our salvation. Although we do not have perfect faith and do not serve and love God with all our hearts, and though we do not love our neighbors as we ought, we are confident that the Savior accepts us at his table when we come in humble faith, with sorrow for our sins, and with a will to follow him as he commands.*

[And since it is necessary for us to come to the sacrament in good conscience, we urge any who lack this confidence to seek from the minister or any elder of this church such counsel as may quiet their consciences or lead to the conversion of their lives.]

All, then, who are truly sorry for their sins, who sincerely believe in the Lord Jesus as their Savior, and who earnestly desire to lead a godly life, ought to accept the invitation now given and come with gladness to the table of their Lord.

That we may rightly examine ourselves before God, let us seek his gracious help through prayer.

Almighty God, who has given us the gospel of Jesus Christ, and who has

---

Prepared in response to a mandate from the Synod of 1957, this form was finally adopted in 1964. While retaining the basic sections found in the Dutch form of 1566, this form is considerably shortened and simplified.

*If this preparatory exhortation and the communion formulary are combined for use in the communion service, omit the bracketed paragraph.

provided a most wonderful communion with him through the mystery of the sacrament, we ask you for grace to enable us to prepare our hearts to receive holy communion. To all who sincerely believe in your Son and truly repent of their sins, grant assurance of your gracious readiness to receive and bless them in the supper of their Lord. To all who have not repented and have not put their trust in the Lord Jesus, grant a restraining fear of this supper, lest their condemnation be greater. But have mercy upon these and grant them grace to repent of their sins and seek their salvation in your Son, our Lord Jesus Christ.

We confess, O Father, that we have all offended your majesty and deserved your judgment. We have transgressed in our thoughts, our words, and our deeds. We are truly weak. Be merciful, O God, and grant us your pardon. And let us come to the sacrament in the joy of your forgiving love.

Through Jesus Christ our Lord, who, with you and the Holy Spirit, one only God, lives and reigns forever. Amen.

Formulary

Beloved in the Lord, hear the words of the apostle Paul concerning the institution of the holy supper of our Lord Jesus Christ:

For I received from the Lord what I also passed on to you: the Lord Jesus, on the night he was betrayed, took bread, and when he had given thanks, he broke it and said, "This is my body, which is for you; do this in remembrance of me." In the same way, after supper he took the cup, saying, "This cup is the new covenant in my blood; do this, whenever you drink it, in remembrance of me." For whenever you eat this bread and drink this cup, you proclaim the Lord's death until he comes.

Therefore, whoever eats the bread or drinks the cup of the Lord in an unworthy manner will be guilty of sinning against the body and blood of the Lord. A man ought to examine himself before he eats of the bread and drinks of the cup. For anyone who eats and drinks without recognizing the body of the Lord eats and drinks judgment on himself (*1 Cor. 11:23–29*).

Let us hear also a brief instruction concerning the purpose for which the sacrament was ordained.

When our Lord said, "Do this in remembrance of me," he ordained this holy supper as a constant memorial and visible proclamation of his death. The apostle Paul also teaches us that as often as we eat the bread and drink the cup we proclaim the Lord's death. As we partake of this communion supper, therefore, we bear witness that our Lord Jesus was sent by the Father into the world, that he took upon himself our flesh and blood, and that he bore the wrath of God on the cross for us. We also confess that he came to earth to bring us to heaven, that he was condemned to die that we might be pardoned, that he endured the suffering and death of the cross that we might live through him, and that he was once forsaken by God that we might forever be accepted by him.

The sacrament thus confirms us in God's abiding love and covenant faithfulness. By his holy supper, our Lord seals to our hearts the promises of God's gracious covenant and so assures us that we belong to his covenant family. Let us then be persuaded as we eat and drink that God will always love us and accept us as his children for the sake of his Son.

Our Lord promises, moreover, that as we eat the bread and drink the cup, we are fed with his crucified body and shed blood. To this end he gives us his life-giving Spirit, through whom the body and blood of our Lord become the life-giving nourishment of our souls. Thus he unites us with himself and so imparts the precious benefits of his sacrifice to all who partake in faith.

The holy sacrament is also a means of grace that unites us with one another in the bond of the Spirit. For the apostle says that "we, who are many, are one body, for we all partake of the one loaf" (1 Cor. 10:17). Thus, even as he unites us with himself, he strengthens the bond of communion between us, his children.

Finally, the remembrance of our Lord's death revives in us the hope of his return. Since he commanded us to do this until he comes, the Lord assures us that he will come again to take us to himself. So, as we commune with him now under the veil of these earthly elements, we are assured that we shall sometime behold him face to face and rejoice in the glory of his appearing.

Our Lord Jesus will surely do what he has promised. Let us draw near to his table, then, believing that he will strengthen us in faith, unite us in love, and establish us more firmly in the hope of his coming.

Now "to him who loves us and has freed us from our sins by his blood, and has made us to be a kingdom and priests to serve his God and Father—to him be glory and power for ever and ever! Amen" (Rev. 1:5b–6).

Let us pray:

Almighty God, with one accord we give you thanks for all the blessings of your grace; but most of all we thank you for the unspeakable gift of your Son Jesus Christ. We most humbly thank you that your Son came to us in human form, that he lived a perfect life on earth, that he died for us on the cross, and that he arose victoriously from the dead. We bless you for the gift of your Holy Spirit, for the gospel of reconciliation, for the church universal, for the ministry and the sacraments of the church, and for the blessed hope of everlasting life.

We pray, gracious Father, that you will grant us your Holy Spirit, that through this sacrament our souls may truly be fed with the crucified body and shed blood of our Lord Jesus Christ. Grant us the full assurance of your grace as we draw near to your holy table, filling our hearts with humble gratitude for your mercies. Unite us more fully with our blessed Lord, and so also with one another. Enable us, in newness of life, to pledge ourselves in service to Christ and all your children. And lift our hearts to you, that in all the troubles and sorrows of this life we may persevere in the living hope of the coming of our Savior in glory.

Answer us, O God, through Jesus Christ our Lord, who taught us to pray, saying:

Our Father in heaven,
hallowed be your name,
your kingdom come,
your will be done
on earth as it is in heaven.
Give us today our daily bread.
Forgive us our debts,
as we also have forgiven our debtors.
And lead us not into temptation,
but deliver us from the evil one.
For yours is the kingdom
and the power
and the glory for ever.
Amen.

As we draw near to the table of our Lord, let us confess our Christian faith:

I believe in God the Father almighty,
maker of heaven and earth.
And in Jesus Christ, his only begotten
Son, our Lord;
who was conceived by the Holy Spirit,

born of the virgin Mary;
suffered under Pontius Pilate;
was crucified, dead, and buried;
he descended into hell;
the third day he rose again from the
dead;
he ascended into heaven,
and is seated at the right hand of God
the Father almighty;
from there he shall come
to judge the living and the dead.
I believe in the Holy Spirit;
I believe a holy catholic church, the
communion of saints;
the forgiveness of sins;
the resurrection of the body;
and the life everlasting. Amen.

[Having approached the table, the minister shall say]:

Beloved, hear these gracious words of promise spoken by our Lord:

"Come to me, all you who are weary and burdened, and I will give you rest. Take my yoke upon you and learn from me, for I am gentle and humble in heart, and you will find rest for your souls" *(Matt. 11:28–29).*

"I am the bread of life. He who comes to me will never go hungry, and he who believes in me will never be thirsty. . . . Whoever comes to me I will never drive away" *(John 6:35, 37b).*

"Blessed are those who hunger and thirst for righteousness, for they will be filled" *(Matt. 5:6).*

Beloved in the Lord Jesus Christ, let us lift up our hearts to the Lord; let us lift them up to the God of our salvation.

[As he breaks the bread, the minister shall say]:

The Lord Jesus, on the night he was betrayed, took bread, and when he had given thanks, he broke it and said, "This is my body, which is for you; do this in remembrance of me." *(1 Cor. 11:23b–24).*

[At the eating of the bread, the minister shall say]:

Take, eat, remember and believe that the body of our Lord Jesus Christ was given for the complete forgiveness of all our sins.

[As he takes the cup, the minister shall say]:

"Then he took the cup, gave thanks and offered it to them, saying, 'Drink from it, all of you. This is my blood of the covenant, which is poured out for many for the forgiveness of sins' "
(Matt. 26:27–28).

[At the drinking of the wine, the minister shall say]:

Take, drink, remember and believe that the precious blood of our Lord Jesus Christ was shed for the complete forgiveness of all our sins.

[When the communion is completed, the minister shall say]:

"Praise the Lord, O my soul; all my
inmost being,
praise his holy name.
Praise the Lord, O my soul,
and forget not all his benefits.
He forgives all my sins and heals all
my diseases;
he redeems my life from the pit
and crowns me with love and
compassion" *(Ps. 103:1–4).*

"You are worthy, our Lord and our God, to receive glory and honor and power, for you created all things, and by your will they were created and have their being" *(Rev. 4:11).*

"Worthy is the Lamb, who was slain, to receive power and wealth and wisdom and strength and honor and glory and praise" *(Rev. 5:12).*

My mouth will speak in praise of the LORD. Let every creature praise his holy name for ever and ever *(Ps. 145:21).*

Thanksgiving

Let us pray:

Almighty God, we give to you our humble and hearty thanks, that you in your great mercy have given us your Son to be our Savior from sin and to be our constant source of faith, hope, and love. We bless you for permitting us to show forth his death and to receive the communion of his body and blood through the holy sacrament. We praise you for uniting us more fully with the body of Christ, and for assuring us that we are heirs of your heavenly kingdom. Grant, we ask you, that our commemoration of his death may help to daily increase our faith, to establish our hope, and to strengthen our love. Enable us henceforth to live always for him who gave himself for us, even our Lord Jesus Christ. Amen.

Celebration of the Lord's Supper

Preparatory Exhortation

Beloved in the Lord Jesus Christ, listen to the words of the institution of the holy supper of our Lord as they have been handed down by the apostle Paul:

For I received from the Lord what I also passed on to you: the Lord Jesus, on the night he was betrayed, took bread, and when he had given thanks, he broke it and said, "This is my body, which is for you; do this in remembrance of me." In the same way, after supper he took the cup, saying, "This cup is the new covenant in my blood; do this, whenever you drink it, in remembrance of me." For whenever you eat this bread and drink this cup, you proclaim the Lord's death until he comes. Therefore, whoever eats the bread or drinks the cup of the Lord in an unworthy manner will be guilty of sinning against the body and blood of the Lord. A man ought to examine himself before he eats of the bread and drinks of the cup. For anyone who eats and drinks without recognizing the body of the Lord eats and drinks judgment on himself (*1 Cor. 11:23–29*).

In obedience to these words and in fellowship with the church universal we shall commemorate the death of our Savior in the sacrament of the Lord's Supper on the coming Lord's Day. (*Or:* we now commemorate the death of our Savior in the sacrament of the Lord's Supper.) However, to do so to our comfort, we must first examine ourselves, as the apostle has admonished.

Let all of us, therefore, consider our sin and guilt. God's anger against sin is so great that he has punished it in his beloved Son with the bitter and shameful death of the cross; and let us examine whether our hearts accordingly are filled with that "godly grief" which "produces a repentance that leads to salvation."

Let us also search our hearts to see whether we truly believe in Jesus Christ as our only Savior, and accept God's gracious promise that for the sake of the passion and death of Christ all our sins are now forgiven and we are clothed with the perfect righteousness of the Son of God.

Finally, let us examine our consciences to see whether we resolve sincerely and gratefully to serve Jesus Christ as Lord and to live by his commandment: "You shall love the Lord your God with all your heart, and with all your soul, and with all your mind . . . and . . . your neighbor as yourself."

As we thus examine ourselves, let us be assured that God will certainly receive in grace and welcome to the table of his Son all those who repent and walk in faith.

However, the Lord admonishes those who do not believe or have not repented to abstain from the holy supper so as not to eat and drink judgment on themselves. Therefore we also charge those who willfully continue in their sins to keep themselves from the table of the Lord *(such as all who trust in any form of superstition; all who honor images or pray to saints; all who despise God's Word

---

Prepared in response to a mandate from the Synod of 1957, this form was finally adopted in 1964. It is in part a translation of the 1566 Dutch form based in turn on earlier Reformed sources. There are both additions to and omissions from the original Dutch material. This form was the first in CRC liturgy to distinguish the preparatory exhortation from the communion formulary.

*The reading of the parenthetical list of gross sins is optional.

or the holy sacraments; all who take God's name in vain; all who violate the sanctity of the Lord's Day; all who are disobedient to those in authority over them; all drunkards, gamblers, murderers, thieves, adulterers, liars, and unchaste persons). To all such we say in the name of the Lord that as long as they remain unrepentant and unbelieving, they have no part in the kingdom of God.

However, this solemn warning is not intended, beloved in the Lord, to discourage the contrite believer, for we do not come to this supper claiming any merit in ourselves. On the contrary, we come testifying that we seek our salvation apart from ourselves in Jesus Christ. By this testimony we humbly confess that we are full of sin and worthy of death. By this testimony we also confess that we believe the sure promise of God: "If we confess our sins, he is faithful and just and will forgive us our sins and purify us from all unrighteousness" (1 John 1:9). This promise assures us that no sin or weakness which still remains in us against our will can hinder us from being received by God in grace at his table as worthy partakers of this holy food and drink.

*Thus assured, let us at the appointed hour come with quiet conscience and fullness of faith to keep this sacramental feast which our Lord appointed to be a continual memorial of his atoning death until he comes again.

Let us pray.

Almighty God, our Father, by whose law all are tried and by whose gospel we have hope, we your servants look to you for help in examining ourselves.

In your grace you invite us to the table of your Son. We confess that we have sinned. Have compassion on us in our weakness. Enable us in the light of your holy Word to read the secrets of our own hearts and to recognize the fruits of your work of grace within. Strengthen us by your Holy Spirit so that we may obediently respond to your call in sincere repentance and true faith.

Graciously remove whatever in us might keep us from your table. Let no love of sin or untruth, no pride or lust, no hatred or envy toward our neighbor, no remnant of unbelief remain within us to keep us from responding gladly. By your Spirit assemble us at the appointed hour to commemorate in an unbroken bond of Christian fellowship the atoning death of our Savior.

Hear us, we pray, in the name of our ever-living intercessor, to whom, with you and the Holy Spirit, belong all praise and glory. Amen.

Formulary

Beloved in the Lord Jesus Christ, in the night in which he was delivered up to be crucified, the Lord Jesus instituted the sacrament of holy communion, saying, "Do this in remembrance of me." In obedience to that command we now celebrate this memorial feast. We therefore invite all of you who have confessed your Lord, and who have truly examined yourselves as the apostle Paul commanded, to come in repentance and in assurance of faith to commune with Christ in this holy supper.*

As we now draw near, let us acknowledge that the Lord has instituted his supper so that by it we may remember him and he may nourish and refresh us for eternal life.

To observe this holy supper in remembrance of him is to proclaim our Lord's death until he comes again. In partaking of this supper, therefore, we remember that our Lord Jesus Christ is the Savior promised to the fathers in the

---

*Those who wish to use this form as a single formulary for the celebration of the Lord's supper may do so by omitting the paragraphs beginning and ending with *.

Old Testament; that he is the eternal and only begotten Son of God; that he assumed our human nature, in which he fulfilled for us all obedience and the righteousness of God's law; and that he bore for us the wrath of God under which we should have perished forever. We remember that he was bound that we might be loosed from our sins; that he was innocently condemned to death that we might be acquitted at the judgment seat of God; that he became a curse for us to fill us with his blessing; and that he humbled himself on the cross to hell's deep agony—which wrung from him the cry, "My God, my God, why have you forsaken me?"—that God might never forsake us. We remember also that he was buried to sanctify the grave for us, that he was raised for our justification, that he is exalted at God's right hand, and that he will come again to judge the living and the dead. And we remember that the shedding of his blood has confirmed for us the new and eternal testament, the covenant of grace.

Through this supper Jesus Christ assures us that he will truly nourish and refresh us with his crucified body and shed blood to everlasting life. He promises this in the institution to this supper, saying of the bread, "This is my body"; and of the wine, "This is my blood of the covenant, which is poured out for many for the forgiveness of sins" *(Matt. 26:26ff.)*. With these words our Lord directs our faith to his perfect sacrifice, once offered on the cross, as the only ground of our salvation. He also assures us that by his death he has taken away our sin, the cause of our eternal death, and has obtained for us the life-giving Spirit. By this Spirit, who dwells in Christ as in the head and in us as his members, he brings us into true communion with himself and makes us partakers of all his riches, of eternal life, righteousness, and glory. By this same

Spirit, he causes us, together with all true believers, to be united as members of one body. As the holy apostle says, "We, who are many, are one body for we all partake of the one loaf" *(1 Cor. 10:17)*

And as it is said to us, "For whenever you eat this bread and drink this cup, you proclaim the Lord's death until he comes" *(1 Cor. 11:26)*, we are assured by this holy supper that our Lord Jesus will come again to receive us to himself and that we shall sit down with him and drink with him the fruit of the vine in the newness of our Father's kingdom *(Matt. 26:29)*.

Let us pray.

Merciful God and Father, whose grace abounds beyond all our sins, we pray that in this supper, in which we commemorate the death of your dear Son, you will so work in our hearts, that we may yield ourselves ever more fully to Jesus Christ. May our contrite hearts, through the power of the Holy Spirit, be nourished and refreshed with his body and blood, with him, true God and man, the only heavenly bread, so that we may no longer live in our sins, but he in us, and we in him.

Confirm in us the covenant of grace, we pray, so that we may not doubt that you will forever be our gracious Father, no more imputing our sins to us and abundantly providing us with all things necessary for body and soul as your dear children and heirs.

Grant us your grace that we may cheerfully take up our cross, deny ourselves, confess our Savior, and in all temptations and trials expect our Lord Jesus Christ from heaven, who at his coming will make our mortal bodies like his glorified body and take us to himself in eternity.

Answer us, O God and merciful Father, through Jesus Christ our Lord, to whom, with you and the Holy Spirit, belong all praise and adoration now and evermore. Amen.

[While the table is being prepared an appropriate hymn may be sung.]

As we now come to the table of the Lord, let us with heart and mouth confess our catholic, undoubted Christian faith:
I believe in God the Father almighty,
    Maker of heaven and earth.
And in Jesus Christ, his only begotten
    Son, our Lord;
who was conceived by the Holy Spirit,
    born of the virgin Mary;
suffered under Pontius Pilate;
was crucified, dead, and buried;
he descended into hell;
the third day he rose again from the
    dead;
he ascended into heaven,
and is seated at the right hand of God
    the Father almighty;
from there he shall come
to judge the living and the dead.
I believe in the Holy Spirit.
I believe a holy catholic church, the
    communion of saints;
the forgiveness of sins;
the resurrection of the body;
and the life everlasting. Amen.

That we may be nourished with Christ, the true bread from heaven, let us lift up our hearts to Christ Jesus, our advocate, at the right hand of his heavenly Father. Let us firmly believe all his promises, not doubting that as surely as we receive the bread and wine in remembrance of him we shall be nourished and refreshed with his body and blood through the working of the Holy Spirit.

[In breaking and serving the bread, the minister shall say]:

The bread which we break is a communion of the body of Christ. Take, eat, remember, and believe that the body of our Lord Jesus Christ was given for the complete forgiveness of all our sins.

[In serving the cup the minister shall say]:

The cup of thanksgiving for which we give thanks is a communion of the blood of Christ. Take, drink, remember, and believe that the precious blood of our Lord Jesus Christ was shed for the complete forgiveness of all our sins.

[While the elements are being distributed, the minister may read fitting passages from Scripture, or a hymn may be sung].

[After the communion the minister shall say]:

Beloved in the Lord, since the Lord has now nourished our souls at his table, let us jointly praise his holy name with thanksgiving.

Sing together Psalm 103 or say in unison:
Praise the Lord, O my soul;
all my inmost being, praise his holy
    name.
Praise the Lord, O my soul,
and forget not all his benefits.
He forgives all my sins
and heals all my diseases;
he redeems my life from the pit
and crowns me with love and
    compassion.
The Lord is compassionate and
    gracious,
slow to anger, abounding in love.
He will not always accuse,
nor will he harbor his anger forever;
he does not treat us as our sins
    deserve
or repay us according to our
    iniquities.
For as high as the heavens are above
    the earth,
so great is his love for those who fear
    him;
as far as the east is from the west,
so far has he removed our
    transgressions from us.
As a father has compassion on his
    children,

so the Lord has compassion on
   those who fear him.
Praise the Lord, you his angels,
you mighty ones who do his bidding,
who obey his word.
Praise the Lord, all his heavenly
   hosts,
you his servants who do his will.
Praise the Lord, all his works
everywhere in his dominion.
Praise the Lord, O my soul.

(Ps. 103:1–4, 8–13, 20–22)

"To him who sits on the throne and to the
Lamb be praise and
   honor and glory and power, for ever
and ever!"

(Rev. 5:13)

Thanksgiving
   Let us pray:
   O merciful God and Father, we thank
you with all our hearts that in your
boundless grace you have given us your
only begotten Son as a mediator and a
sacrifice for our sins and as our food and
drink unto life eternal. We thank you too
for giving us the true faith through which
we can partake of your benefits. And since
your Son Jesus Christ ordained the holy
supper to strengthen our faith, we pray
that through your Holy Spirit, this supper
may increase our faith and enrich our
fellowship with Christ. May you also use
this proclamation of our Lord's death and
resurrection to bring others into this
blessed fellowship, so that all your
children may be gathered in to share with
us the joy of your salvation. Hear us,
Heavenly Father, in Jesus Christ our Lord.
Amen.

Excommunication

First Announcement

Beloved in the Lord, it is our painful duty as officebearers of this church to inform you that one of our fellow members, ___(name [optional])___, has committed the serious and offensive sin of _____ and persists unrepentant to this day, despite our prayers and admonitions. Through his/her persistence, our brother/sister is breaking the covenant bond with the Lord and his people. Because sacraments are signs and seals of this relationship with our Savior and with one another, we have already been compelled to bar our brother/sister from participation in the sacraments.

As members of this church of Jesus Christ, we should be deeply concerned when one of our fellow members obstinately turns his/her back on the Christian way and refuses to repent. We are and remain responsible for one another *(Gen. 4:9; Gal. 6:1–2; and 1 Cor. 12:12ff.)*. Therefore, let all of us pray that our brother/sister may respond positively to the admonitions of the church and return to the God and Father of our Lord Jesus Christ, who is seeking him/her in grace and faithfulness *(Matt. 18:10–14; Luke 19:10)*.

Second Announcement

Beloved in the Lord, we informed you previously that as officebearers of this church we barred a fellow member, ___(name)___, from the sacraments. We did so because he/she committed the serious and offensive sin of _____ and failed to show true repentance despite our frequent admonitions.

With a heavy heart we must tell you that his/her suspension from the sacraments, and all admonitions since that time, have not produced in our brother/sister any evidence of a desire to be restored to the covenantal relationship with the Lord and his people.

We have discussed this matter with Classis ___(name)___, and were advised that if our brother/sister does not repent, we may proceed to the extreme remedy of his/her excommunication from the church of Jesus Christ.

Therefore, all of us are urged to continue to pray for our brother/sister and to plead with him/her that he/she may mend his/her ways and return to the Lord and his people in genuine repentance and faith. Our Lord does not wish that the sinner should perish but desires that he/she should return from his/her ways and live *(Ezek. 18; Matt. 18)*.

Third Announcement

Beloved in the Lord, the officebearers of this church have twice informed you of the sin committed and the offense given by our fellow member, ___(name)___. We informed you that our brother/sister was barred from participation in the sacraments because he/she failed to show true repentance.

Our loving concern since that time, however, has not led him/her to demonstrate any sign of true repentance and faith. Because he/she persists in breaking the covenantal relationship with the Lord and his people, we are compelled to proceed with the final step of discipline, namely, the excommunication of our brother/sister from the church of the Lord. If our brother/sister does not show any evidence

---

This form, adopted for use by Synod of 1982, includes the three announcements that the Church Order requires before excommunication takes place.

of genuine repentance, he/she, to our deep sorrow, will be excommunicated in this church on ___(date)___. If any member of the church knows of any valid reason why we should not proceed, we urge that person to inform the consistory.

Let all of us continue to pray for ___(name)___ and to plead with him/her so that he/she may not harden his/her heart completely, but return to the God and Father of our Lord Jesus Christ, with true confession of sin.

Excommunication

Beloved in the Lord, our fellow member, ___(name)___, has brought discredit to the body of Christ by his/her sin, and in spite of the patient care of this church, remains unrepentant to this day.

Accordingly, we as officebearers of this church are compelled with great sorrow to proceed with the final step of discipline, namely, his/her excommunication from the church of the Lord. We do this in obedience to the command of God in his Word *(Matt. 18:15–18; 1 Cor. 5:1–5, 11–13; 1 Tim. 5:20).*

This excommunication is necessary so that we may maintain the honor of God, remove offense from the church of Christ, and lead the erring one to repentance. We pray that this action may cause our brother/sister to seek forgiveness of sin, union with Christ, and restoration into the covenant family of God and his people.

Prayer

Holy Father, we are humbled before you at this time. What we are about to do grieves us deeply. We do it, Lord, with fear and trembling, conscious of our imperfection, yet also of the responsibility you have given your church in using the keys of the kingdom. Grant that our action may build up your church and cause none to stumble. This we ask in the name and for the sake of Jesus Christ, our Lord. Amen.

Declaration

In the name and the authority of our Lord Jesus Christ, we hereby excommunicate ___(name)___ from the church of our Lord.

We believe that God himself excludes him/her from the fellowship of Christ, the holy sacraments, and all the blessings of faith as long as he/she persists in his/her impenitence.

Exhortation

Let all of us pray that the Holy Spirit grant ___(name)___ grace to recognize his/her sin, work in him/her genuine repentance, and restore him/her to fellowship with the Lord and his people *(Ezek. 18:23, 32; 33:11; Matt. 18:10–14).*

Let us be saddened by this event and warned to fear the Lord and live close to him and his Word. Today we clearly hear God's voice of judgment. Let us not harden our hearts *(Ps. 95:8)*, but place ourselves under the discipline of our Master, who lovingly and firmly renews our lives through the ministry of his Word and Spirit.

Since we are assured that the Lord forgives, let us together call on him, confessing our sin and pleading for mercy *(Ps. 130).*

[To be concluded with an appropriate prayer.]

Readmission

Announcement

Some time ago ____(name)____ was excommunicated from the church of the Lord because of his/her persistence in a serious and offensive sin without any token of genuine repentance. At that time we expressed the hope that God would use this excommunication as the extreme remedy unto conversion. We may now rejoice in the blessed results of Christian discipline and thankfully announce that our brother/sister has repented and expressed his/her desire to be restored into the covenantal relationship with the Lord and his people. If there are no lawful objections, this readmission will be celebrated on ____(date)____. Meanwhile, let us praise the Lord for this glorious manifestation of the power of his grace and ask him to keep our brother/sister in the grip of his hand during the days of preparation.

Form for Readmission

It is known to you that ____(name)____, who was excommunicated, has requested to be readmitted to the communion of Christ and his church. Since no one has presented any valid reason why this restoration should not take place, we now proceed with gladness to receive our brother/sister again into the church of Jesus Christ.

Our Lord declares in his Word that he takes no pleasure in the death of the sinner but rather that he/she should return from his/her ways and live *(Ezek. 18; Luke 15)*. Our Lord also declares that communion with him and his church is open to all who show sincere repentance. Again he declares, "If you forgive anyone his sins, they are forgiven," and "Whatever you loose on earth will be loosed in heaven" *(John 20:23; Matt. 16:19)*.

____(name)____, will you stand now, and in the presence of God and his people respond to the following questions:

1. Do you acknowledge before God and his people that you are truly sorry for your sin, and do you believe that the Lord has forgiven you?

2. Do you reaffirm your union with Christ and desire to be readmitted to the covenant family of God?

3. Do you promise to do all you can, with the help of the Holy Spirit, to strengthen your love and commitment to Christ by sharing faithfully in the life of the church, honoring and submitting to its authority; and do you join with the people of God in doing the work of the Lord everywhere?

Answer: I do, God helping me.

Declaration

By the authority of our Lord Jesus Christ this congregation, through its officebearers, restores you to full fellowship with Christ and his church. In the name of the Father and the Son and the Holy Spirit. Amen.

Reception

[The minister asks the congregation to rise.]

Minister: Brother/sister ____(name)____, we heartily and gladly welcome you back to all the privileges of full communion. We welcome you to full participation in the life of the church. We welcome you to its responsibilities, its joys, and its sufferings. May God by his Holy Spirit graciously enable you to continue steadfast in faith and godliness unto the end, through Jesus Christ, our Lord. Amen.

And you, beloved Christians, receive this brother/sister with all your love. Count him/her no longer as a stranger, but as a fellow member with the saints of the household of God. Let us together thank and praise the Lord!

Congregation: Thanks be to God! We promise you our love, encouragement, and prayers.

Minister: Let us say what we believe: I believe in God, the Father almighty . . .

[To be concluded with an appropriate prayer.]

Ordination/Installation of Ministers of the Word

The Announcement

Congregation of Jesus Christ:

Today we rejoice in Christ's special care and love for his church since we have the privilege of ordaining ___(name)___ [*or:* installing ___(name)___] to the ministry of the Word in this church [*or:* for a special ministry of this church]. Because he has accepted the call of the congregation, we shall now proceed with his ordination [installation].

The Introduction

From its beginning the entire New Testament church was called to proclaim the good news of salvation in Jesus Christ to the whole world: "Therefore go and make disciples of all nations, baptizing them in the name of the Father and of the Son and of the Holy Spirit, and teaching them to obey everything I have commanded you" *(Matt. 28:19–20).* It soon became apparent that the task committed to the church was extremely vast and complex. Therefore the church under the guidance of the apostles, instituted distinct ministries to ensure that the work would be done well *(Acts 6:1–6).* Those engaged in these ministries were to function with Christ's power and authority, a power and authority rooted in obedience to his Word and expressed in loving service.

These ministries are therefore to be distinguished from the more general ones given by Christ to all believers. The office of the minister of the Word is one of those distinct ministries.

The Instruction

The Scriptures portray the minister's duties in various ways. He is a servant both of Christ and of the church; he is a steward in the household of God; he is a teacher to explain the mystery of the gospel; he is a shepherd who cares for the flock; and he is an ambassador and a herald of his king, proclaiming the message of reconciliation.

The preaching of the Word is one of the minister's chief tasks. Such proclamation must faithfully reflect the Word of God and relate it to the needs of the listeners. Paul stressed this demand when he wrote, ". . . Preach the Word; be prepared in season and out of season; correct, rebuke and encourage . . ." *(2 Tim. 4:2).* And because the sacraments are closely related to the preaching of the Word, the minister has the privilege of administering holy baptism and the Lord's Supper. Since the minister has the responsibility to preach the Word and to administer the sacraments in public worship, it is his task to conduct the worship service in such a manner that God receives glory and the congregation is edified.

When Jesus said to Peter, "Feed my lambs," he entrusted the officebearers with special care for the young. The minister must instruct the baptized members of the congregation in the way of salvation, and he must also encourage and assist those who teach with him *(2 Tim. 2:2).*

As a pastor, the minister visits the members of the congregation. He calls on the sick and suffering, he comforts those who mourn, he admonishes those who stray, he counsels those in need of guidance, and he encourages the weak. He rejoices with those who rejoice and weeps with those who weep *(Rom. 12:15).*

Yet the minister is called not only to serve those who already are members of the church of Christ, but also to engage in and to promote the work of evangelism. As a true disciple of his Master, he should show that the church exists also for the world and that the missionary task of the church forms an essential part of its calling.

As a servant of Christ, the minister must help and encourage the people of God as they care for the hungry, the thirsty, the strangers, the naked, the sick, and those in prison *(Matt. 25:31–46).*

In all his work, the minister proclaims, explains, and applies Holy Scripture in order to gather in and build up the members of the church of Jesus Christ. For this work, the minister devotes himself to the ministry of prayer, joining all Christians in confession, intercession, thanksgiving, and praise.

The Questions

Brother ____(name)____, in order that all God's people assembled here may witness that you, in the strength of the Lord, accept the responsibilities of this office, you are requested to stand and answer the following questions:

Do you believe that in the call of this congregation God himself calls you to this holy ministry?

Do you believe that the Old and New Testaments are the Word of God, the only infallible rule of faith and life?

Do you subscribe to the doctrinal standards of this church, rejecting all teaching which contradicts them?

Do you promise to be a faithful minister, to conduct yourself in a manner worthy of your calling, and to submit to the government and discipline of the church?

____(name)____, what is your answer?

Answer: I do, God helping me.

[The officiating minister shall then say (with the laying on of hands in case of ordination)]:

God, our heavenly Father, who has called you to this great and glorious office, enlighten, strengthen, and govern you by his Word and Spirit that you may serve faithfully and fruitfully in your ministry, to the glory of his name and the coming of the kingdom of his Son, Jesus Christ. Amen.

[The members of the congregation are now requested to stand to make their vows. The officiating minister addresses them]:

Dear congregation of Christ:

Do you in the name of the Lord welcome this brother as your minister and pastor?

Do you promise to take to heart the Word of God as he proclaims it?

Do you promise to pray for him, to share with him in the work of his ministry, to encourage him in the exercise of his tasks, and to respond to his work with obedience, love, and respect?

Congregation, what is your answer?

Answer: We do, God helping us.

[The officiating minister (or whoever has been designated) shall then congratulate and encourage the minister and the congregation in the following manner]:

Dear brother and fellow servant of Christ:

We rejoice with you on this day that, after years of preparation, you have been ordained to the ministry of the Word. [*Or:* We all rejoice with you on this day as you begin your work in this congregation.]

May you experience much joy in fulfilling your calling. As you exercise the authority of the office entrusted to you, may you always remain a humble servant.

Look faithfully after the whole flock, the old and the young, the faithful and the unfaithful, the healthy and the sick, the strong and the weak. Rejoice with those who rejoice and suffer with those who suffer.

Use all your talents to the utmost of your ability, and do not neglect any of your gifts.

And one day our chief Shepherd will give you the crown of glory, saying, "Well done, good and faithful servant."

And to you, dear fellow Christians, congratulations also.

This is truly the day which the Lord has made. Let us rejoice and be glad in it.

Keep your vows. Receive your minister as a gift of God. Listen to him with all the respect due his office. Encourage him when he needs strength, and pray for him daily.

Anyone who receives a prophet because he is a prophet will receive a prophet's reward *(Matt. 10:41).*

May you as pastor and congregation live as the bride longing for the coming of our heavenly Bridegroom, praying, "Come, Lord Jesus" *(Rev. 22:20).*

Let us now give thanks and ask the Lord to help us do what we have promised.

Prayer:

Thank you, Lord, on this day for your many blessings. Thank you for your church, "elect from every nation, yet one o'er all the earth." Thank you for giving your church the task of calling others to your saving grace in Jesus Christ and to the fellowship of the covenant community.

Today we thank you in particular for giving the church the special office of the minister of the Word. We rejoice that we as a congregation have received a new pastor to work among us. We pray that you will bless him as a servant of Christ and the church. Help him to be an inspired ambassador for his King, bringing the message of salvation and reconciliation to all. Bless him as a preacher and a teacher, as a pastor and a counselor. May he prove himself a faithful steward in the household of God.

Enable us, as a congregation, to listen gladly and attentively to him, recognizing in his words the voice of the good Shepherd. Strengthen us all in the work of the ministry so that we may be the salt of the earth and the light of the world. Help us, congregation and pastor, to endure the heat of the day and the darkness of the night, sustained by your healing and guiding presence.

All this we ask with thankful hearts in the name of your dear Son, our Lord and Savior. Amen.

Ordination/Installation of Ministers of the Word

Congregation of Jesus Christ:

For some time you have known that ____(name)____ is to be ordained to the Ministry of the Word [or: installed in the ministry to which he has been called]. No one has alleged anything against his person or teaching. We shall therefore proceed, in the name of the Lord, to his ordination [installation].

The Holy Scriptures teach us that God, our heavenly Father, intends to gather his church out of the corrupt human race to life eternal, and to give to his church such teaching and care that it may grow in faith and love and service. Thus God, by a particular grace, appoints his people to preach the gospel and to build up the body of Christ. The apostle Paul solemnly charged Timothy to "preach the Word" *(2 Tim. 4:2)*, and our Lord Jesus charged his disciples to "make disciples of all nations, baptizing them in the name of the Father and of the Son and of the Holy Spirit, and teaching them to obey everything I have commanded you" *(Matt. 28:19–20)*. The apostle Paul declares that the Lord Jesus Christ intended "some to be apostles, some to be prophets, some to be evangelists, and some to be pastors and teachers, to prepare God's people for works of service, so that the body of Christ may be built up" *(Eph. 4:11–12)*.

Let us now hear what the Scriptures say concerning the office of minister of the Word: The minister of the Word is called by the command of God to preach the gospel of his kingdom. This preaching has the twofold object of calling sinners to reconciliation with God through Jesus Christ and nurturing believers in the faith and life of the kingdom of God. Ministers are called "Christ's ambassadors," as though God were pleading by them, "Be reconciled to God" *(2 Cor. 5:20)*. This preaching must be addressed to all people. The preaching of the gospel must also be addressed to the gathered congregation for the nurturing of Christian faith and life and for strengthening them against the ploys of the devil. Paul charged Timothy, "In the presence of God and of Christ Jesus . . . preach the Word; be prepared in season and out of season, correct, rebuke and encourage—with great patience and careful instruction" *(2 Tim. 4:1–2)*, and he charged Titus that a minister "must hold firmly to the trustworthy message as it has been taught, so that he can encourage others by sound doctrine and refute those who oppose it" *(Titus 1:9)*.

The minister of the Word is called to administer the sacraments which the Lord has instituted as signs and seals of his grace. Christ gave this charge to his apostles, and through them to all ministers of the Word, when he commanded them, "Therefore go and make disciples of all nations, baptizing them in the name of the Father and of the Son and of the Holy Spirit" *(Matt. 28:19)*; and when he said of the Lord's Supper: "Do this in remembrance of me" *(1 Cor. 11:24–25)*.

The minister of the Word is called to the service of prayer. In speaking of their calling, the apostles said: "We will give our attention to prayer and the ministry of the word" *(Acts 6:4)*. So, too, it is the calling of all God's ministers to lead the people of God in "requests, prayers, intercession and thanksgivings . . . for everyone—for kings and all those in authority" *(1 Tim. 2:1–2)*.

The minister of the Word is called, together with the elders, to shepherd the people of God in the Christian life, guiding and counseling, exhorting them to contend earnestly for the faith once for all delivered to the saints *(Jude 3)*, and keeping the church of God in good order and discipline. They are pastors, appointed to shepherd the church of Christ which he purchased with his own blood, in keeping with the Lord's command: "Feed my sheep!" "Feed my lambs!" They, together with the elders, watch over the house of God for the right and fruitful ordering of the faith, life, and worship of the people of God. In their exercise of the keys of the kingdom, what they bind on earth shall be bound in heaven, and what they loose on earth shall be loosed in heaven *(Matt. 18:18)*.

[The officiating minister shall now read section (1), (2), (3), or (4), depending on whether this is the ordination, or installation, of the pastor of an established congregation, a foreign missionary, or a home missionary, or the ordination of a teacher of theology.]

(1) For the Pastor in an Established Congregation

We will now ordain *[install]* a minister of the Word in this congregation. We rejoice that in his faithful love the Lord Jesus has provided a minister to serve as pastor and teacher to this people, and also as their leader in the missionary calling of this church. We receive this servant of our Lord from the hand and heart of the Shepherd and Bishop of our souls. We thank our Savior for committing preaching, teaching, and pastoral care to the office of the ministry, and we pray that he will continue to use sinful people for such high and holy purposes until the day of his return.

We are not equal to this holy ministry in our own strength. We put our hope in Jesus Christ, our Lord, who has said: "And surely I am with you always, to the very end of the age" *(Matt. 28:20)*.

Now, to show that you, ___(name)___, intend to accept this office, you are requested to stand and, in the presence of God and his church, answer the following questions:

Do you believe that in the call of this congregation, God himself calls you to this holy ministry?

Do you believe that the Old and New Testaments are the Word of God, the only infallible rule of faith and life; and do you subscribe to the doctrinal standards of this church, rejecting all teachings which contradict them?

Do you promise to do the work of your office faithfully, in a way worthy of your calling and in submission to the government and discipline of the church?

Answer: I do so believe and promise, God helping me.

[The officiating minister shall then say (in the case of ordination with the ceremony of the laying on of hands, other ministers present participating)]:

God, our heavenly Father, who has called you to this sacred office, guide you by his Word, equip you with his Spirit, and so prosper your ministry that his church may increase and his name be praised. Amen.

[The officiating minister shall address the congregation]:

Dear people of God and members of this church:
Since this solemn act obligates you also, I ask you before God:
Do you in the name of the Lord welcome this brother as your pastor? Do you promise to receive the Word of God proclaimed by him and to encourage him in the discharge of his duty?
Will you pray that he may, in the

power of the Spirit, equip you to build up the church, so that God's children may be saved and his kingdom advanced for the honor of Christ our Lord?
To these questions, what is your answer?
Answer: We do, God helping us.

[The officiating minister (and/or others designated) shall then exhort the ordained minister and the congregation in the following manner]:

Beloved brother and fellow-servant in Christ, keep watch over yourself and all the flock of which the Holy Spirit has made you an overseer. Shepherd the church of God which he bought with his own blood *(Acts 20:28).* Love Christ and feed his sheep, serving as an overseer not by constraint but willingly, not for shameful gain but eagerly. Set the believers an example in speech and conduct, in love, in faith, in purity. Attend to the public reading of Scripture, to preaching, to teaching. Do not neglect your gifts. Be patient in all trials. Be a good soldier of Jesus Christ, for by so doing you will save both yourself and your hearers. And when the chief Shepherd appears, you will be given the unfading crown of glory.

And you, brothers and sisters, joyfully receive your minister in the Lord and honor him. Remember that through him God himself speaks to you. Receive the Word which he, according to the Scripture, shall preach to you, not as the word of human beings but, as it is in truth, the Word of God. Let the feet of those who preach the gospel of peace and bring the good news be beautiful and pleasant to you. Submit to those whom God has placed over you, for they care for you as those who will give account. If you do these things, the God of peace will enter your homes. You who receive this person in the name of a prophet will receive a prophet's reward and, through faith in Jesus Christ, the inheritance of eternal life.

We cannot do these things on our own. Let us call upon the name of God: Merciful Father, we thank you that it pleases you by the ministry of your people to gather your church out of the lost human race to life eternal. We acknowledge the gift of your servant, sent to this people as a messenger of your peace.

Send now your Holy Spirit upon him. Enlighten his mind to know the truth of your Word. Give him speech to make known with boldness the mystery of the gospel. Endow him with wisdom to care for and guide the people over whom he is placed. Through his ministry preserve your church in peace and grant that it increase in number and in virtue. Give to your servant courage to fulfill his calling against every difficulty and power through your Spirit to be steadfast to the end.

Help these people receive him as your servant. May they receive his teaching and exhortation reverently, and believing in Christ through his Word, become partakers of eternal life.

Grant this, O heavenly Father, for the sake of your dear Son, in whose name we pray:
Our Father in heaven,
hallowed be your name,
your kingdom come,
your will be done
on earth as it is in heaven.
Give us today our daily bread.
Forgive us our debts,
as we also have forgiven our debtors.
And lead us not into temptation,
but deliver us from the evil one.
For yours is the kingdom
and the power
and the glory for ever.
Amen.

(2) For a Foreign Missionary

We will now ordain *[install]* ___(name)___ as a foreign missionary for service in ___(place)___. It is the task of the foreign missionary to bring the gospel to other lands, so that all people may learn of salvation and so that the church of Jesus Christ may be established in all the earth. Jesus Christ has said, "This gospel of the kingdom will be preached in the whole world as a testimony to all nations, and then the end will come" *(Matt. 24:14).* Through its missionaries the church reaches into the lives of those who are yet without God and without hope. It brings to all lands the witness that Jesus is the Son of God, that the glory of the nations belongs to him, and that his grace, love, and redemption are offered to them in the way of repentance and faith. In this work of missions the church may lift up its eyes to the Lord's coming and look with longing to the day when the earth shall be full of the knowledge of the Lord.

We are not equal to this holy ministry in our own strength. We set our hope on Jesus Christ our Lord, who has said, "And surely I am with you always, to the very end of the age" *(Matt. 28:20).*

Now, to show that you, ___(name)___, accept this office, you are requested to stand, and in the presence of God and his church to answer the following questions:

Do you believe that in the call of this congregation God himself calls you to this holy ministry?

Do you believe that the Old and New Testaments are the Word of God, the only infallible rule of faith and life; and do you subscribe to the doctrinal standards of this church, rejecting all teachings which contradict them?

Do you promise to do the work of your office faithfully, in a way worthy of your calling and in submission to the government and discipline of the church?

Answer: I do so believe and promise, God helping me.

[The officiating minister shall then say (in the case of ordination with the ceremony of the laying on of hands, other ministers present participating)]:

Go, then, brother, and bring the gospel to those to whom you are sent. Make disciples of them and baptize them in the name of the Father, and of the Son, and of the Holy Spirit. God, our heavenly Father, who has called you to this holy ministry, enlighten you with his Spirit, strengthen you with his hand, and so govern you in your ministry that you may be engaged in it faithfully and fruitfully, to the glory of his name and the coming of the kingdom of his Son Jesus Christ.

And you, brothers and sisters, be in continuing fellowship with this missionary whom you send forth in the name of Christ. Sustain him with your fervent prayers. Support him with your gifts. Strengthen his hand and heart in every need. As Christ received you, be ready to receive those who are brought into the body of Christ through his ministry, that there may be one flock, one Shepherd.

We cannot do these things on our own. Let us call upon the name of God: Merciful Father, we thank you that it pleases you by the ministry of your people to gather your church out of the lost human race to life eternal. We acknowledge the gift of your servant, now being sent by this people in your name, to be a messenger to others of the good news of your peace.

Send now your Holy Spirit upon him. Enlighten his mind to know the truth of your Word. Give him speech to make known with boldness the mystery of the gospel. Endow him with wisdom to care for and guide the people over whom he is placed. Through his ministry build up your holy church, and grant that it increase in number and in virtue. Give to your servant courage to fulfill his calling against every difficulty, and power through your Spirit to be steadfast to the end.

Let those to whom he comes see in him the ambassador of Christ, calling them to be reconciled to God. May they receive his teaching and exhortation reverently, and believing in Christ through his Word, become partakers of eternal life.

Grant this, O heavenly Father, for the sake of your dear Son, in whose name we pray:

Our Father in heaven,
hallowed be your name,
your kingdom come,
your will be done
on earth as it is in heaven.
Give us today our daily bread.
Forgive us our debts,
as we also have forgiven our debtors.
And lead us not into temptation,
but deliver us from the evil one.
For yours is the kingdom
and the power
and the glory for ever.
Amen.

(3) For a Home Missionary

We will now ordain *[install]* ___(name)___ as a home missionary for service in ___(place)___. The home missionary is called to preach the gospel and to care for the spiritual nurture and instruction of those in our homeland, who, though exposed to the witness of the church and the gospel have been alienated or are yet estranged from the Lord and his church. In the parable of the great banquet the Lord Jesus Christ spoke about the master who sent his servants out into the streets and lanes of the city, into the highways and hedges, to invite all people to his feast. Even so our Lord calls us to bring others into the house of the King through the ministry of his love in order that his house may be filled. The gospel of the kingdom shall be preached for a testimony to our own nation as well as to all nations of the world. In this way all people will be called to walk in the way of God's commands and promises. And together we look to the day of the coming of our Lord Jesus Christ, when the earth shall be full of the knowledge of the Lord.

We are not equal to this holy ministry in our own strength. We set our hope on Jesus Christ, our Lord, who has said: "And surely I am with you always, to the very end of the age" *(Matt. 28:20)*.

Now to show that you, ___(name)___, accept this office, you are requested to stand, and in the presence of God and his church to answer the following questions:

Do you believe that in the call of this congregation God himself calls you to this holy ministry? Do you believe that the Old and New Testaments are the Word of God, the only infallible rule of faith and life; and do you subscribe to the doctrinal standards of this church, rejecting all teachings which contradict them?

Do you promise to do the work of your office faithfully, in a way worthy of your calling and in submission to the government and discipline of the church?

Answer: I do so believe and promise, God helping me.

[The officiating minister shall then say (in the case of ordination with the ceremony of the laying on of hands, other ministers present participating)]:

Go then, brother, and bring the gospel to those to whom you are sent. Call the unbelieving to faith, the faithless to obedience, and invite people in the name of the Lord into the house of your King. God, our heavenly Father, enlighten you with his Spirit, strengthen you with his hand, and so govern you in your ministry that you may fulfill it faithfully and fruitfully, to the glory of his name and the coming of the kingdom of his Son Jesus Christ.

And you, brothers and sisters, be in continuing fellowship with this missionary whom you send forth in the name of Christ. Sustain him with your fervent prayers. Support him with your gifts. Strengthen his hand and heart in every need. As Christ received you, be ready to receive those who are brought into the body of Christ through his ministry, that there may be one flock, one Shepherd.

We cannot do these things on our own. Let us call upon the name of God: Merciful Father, we thank you that it pleases you by the ministry of your people to gather your church out of the lost human race to life eternal. We acknowledge the gift of your servant, now being sent by this people in your name, to be a messenger to others of the good news of your peace.

Send now your Holy Spirit upon him. Enlighten his mind to know the truth of your Word. Give him speech to make known with boldness the mystery of the gospel. Endow him with wisdom to care for and guide the people over whom he is placed. Through his ministry build up your holy church and grant that it increase in number and in virtue. Give to your servant courage to fulfill his calling against every difficulty and power through your Spirit to be steadfast to the end.

Let those to whom he comes see in him the ambassador of Christ, calling them to be reconciled to God. May they receive his teaching and exhortation reverently and, believing in Christ through his Word, become partakers of eternal life.

Grant this, O heavenly Father, for the sake of your dear Son, in whose name we pray:
Our Father in heaven,

hallowed be your name,
your kingdom come,
your will be done
on earth as it is in heaven.
Give us today our daily bread.
Forgive us our debts,
as we also have forgiven our debtors.
And lead us not into temptation,
but deliver us from the evil one.
For yours is the kingdom
and the power
and the glory for ever.
    Amen.

(4) For the Teacher of Theology
[This form is to be used only when the person assuming this position is to be ordained to the office of minister of the Word. For the appointment of those who are already ordained ministers, the form for the Teacher of Theology under "Forms for the Commissioning of Ministers to Extraordinary Tasks" is to be used.]

We will now ordain a minister of the Word and commission him to the particular task of teaching in the theological seminary of the Christian Reformed Church. We recognize the need for the training of those who, as ministers of the Word, shall preach the gospel of salvation to people both inside and outside the church of Christ.

The first messengers of peace in the days of the New Testament were personally taught and sent by our Lord Jesus Christ. After Pentecost the Holy Spirit gave the church a diversity of extraordinary gifts and knowledge of the mysteries, to continue this work of teaching for the salvation of sinners and the edifying of the saints. But these extraordinary methods lasted only as long as the Lord judged them to be necessary for the founding of his church among the nations. The church soon recognized the necessity of training pastors for the holy ministry under the ordinary dispensation of the Spirit by the regular methods of education. Thus Paul wrote to his fellow minister, Timothy: "And the things you have heard me say in the presence of many witnesses entrust to reliable men who will also be qualified to teach others" *(2 Tim. 2:2).*

To fulfill this task in our day, the church has established a theological school and appoints ministers of the Word who will serve the cause of the gospel by teaching and training those who are to become ministers of the Word in Christ's church. Our brother, ____(name)____, has been called to serve in this important task.

We are not equal to this holy ministry in our own strength. We set our hope on Jesus Christ our Lord, who has said: "And surely I am with you always, to the very end of the age" *(Matt. 28:20).*

Now, to show that you, ____(name)____, accept this office and fulfill this task, you are requested to stand and in the presence of God and his church answer the following questions:

Do you believe that in the call of this congregation God himself calls you to this holy ministry?

Do you believe that the Old and New Testaments are the Word of God, the only infallible rule of faith and life; and do you subscribe to the doctrinal standards of this church, rejecting all teachings which contradict them?

Do you promise to do the work of your office faithfully, in a way worthy of your calling and in submission to the government and discipline of the church?

Answer: I do so believe and promise, God helping me.

[The officiating minister shall then say (in the case of ordination with the ceremony of the laying on of hands, other ministers present participating)]:

God, our heavenly Father, enlighten you with his Spirit, strengthen you with his hand, and so govern you in your calling that you may discharge its duties faithfully and fruitfully, to the glory of his name, and the coming of the kingdom of his Son, Jesus Christ. Amen.

[The service is then concluded with appropriate prayer.]

Ordination of Evangelists

Congregation of Jesus Christ:

For some time you have known that ____(name)____ has accepted the call of God and of this church to serve as evangelist in ____(city)____. Today we ordain him to that office.

Jesus began his ministry by declaring, "The time has come. The kingdom of God is near. Repent and believe the good news!" He called disciples to follow him, saying, "Come, follow me," "and I will make you fishers of men" *(Mark 1:15, 17).* It was in this way that the gospel harvest began. Later the disciples received power at the Spirit's outpouring, and soon a large church was established in Jerusalem.

When the work of the church proved to be too much for the apostles, they appointed "seven men from among you who are known to be full of the Spirit and wisdom" to help them *(Acts 6:3).* At least one of these men, Philip, proved to be a gifted evangelist who "preached the good news of the kingdom of God and the name of Jesus Christ" and who baptized new believers *(Acts 8:12).* Later the apostle Paul declared that Christ "gave some to be apostles, some to be prophets, some to be evangelists, and some to be pastors and teachers, to prepare God's people for works of service, so that the body of Christ may be built up until we all reach unity in the faith and in the knowledge of the Son of God" *(Eph. 4:11–13).*

The work of an evangelist is to preach the good news. He calls people to heed the voice of the good Shepherd, who laid down his life for the sheep, and urges them in the name of Christ to be reconciled to God. He also gathers new believers into an emerging congregation, where he ministers the Word and sacraments. In our congregation ____(name)____ will be acknowledged as an

elder. Although every believer is called to bear witness to Christ, and every elder, deacon, and minister is called to engage in the work of evangelism, the evangelist is called to this work as his primary task under the supervision of the consistory.

____(name)____, we now ask you to answer the following questions here in the presence of God and his people:

Do you believe that in the call of this congregation, God himself calls you to the office of evangelist?

Do you believe that the Old and New Testaments are the Word of God, the only infallible rule of faith and life?

Do you subscribe to the doctrinal standards of this church, rejecting all teaching which contradicts them?

Do you promise to do the work of your office faithfully, in a way worthy of your calling, and in submission to the government and discipline of the church?

Answer: I do, God helping me.

Laying on of hands [optional]

God our heavenly Father, who has called you to your sacred office, guide you by his Word, equip you with his Spirit, and so prosper your ministry that his church may increase and his name be praised.

Charge to the Evangelist

____(name)____, hear the words of the apostle, "In the presence of God and of Christ Jesus, who will judge the living and the dead . . . : Preach the Word, be prepared in season and out of season, correct, rebuke and encourage—with great patience and careful instruction. But you, keep your head in all situations, endure hardship, do the work of an evangelist, discharge all the duties of your ministry" *(2 Tim. 4:1–2, 5).*

Charge to the Congregation

I charge you, people of God, to receive ___(name)___ as called by God to the office of evangelist. Recognize in him one way in which the church fulfills Christ's mandate to "therefore go and make disciples of all nations *(Matt. 28:19).* Hold him in honor as one called upon to seek and to save the lost. Support him with your gifts and assistance. Sustain him with your prayers. Accept him as one who brings the good news. Encourage him in times of difficulty and opposition.

Do you, congregation of the Lord, pledge to receive him as you have been charged?

Answer [by the congregation in unison]: We do, God helping us.

Prayer

Merciful and sovereign Father, we praise and thank you for the good news of salvation which has come to us and must come to many more. We thank you for equipping and ordaining ___(name)___ for the work of evangelism as your ambassador and our representative. Fill him with your Spirit of truth. Give him love for those who are as yet sheep without a shepherd. Encourage him with fruit on his labor, and renew your mercies to him from day to day.

We pray for this congregation and each of its members. You have entrusted to us the message of reconciliation. Give us courage to declare your wonderful deeds and show your love to the world. This we pray in the name of Jesus Christ and for the sake of his coming kingdom. Amen.

Ordination of Elders and Deacons

Congregation of Jesus Christ:

Today we celebrate God's gift of faithful leadership for his people. We joyfully thank him for elders and deacons who have served well and completed their terms of office. And we praise him for providing their successors.

In the officebearers of the church we see the love of Christ for his people. As the Lord of the church he appoints leaders and by his Spirit equips them, so that believers may grow in faith, develop disciplined Christian living, serve others in selfless love, and share with all the good news of salvation. He taught us the spirit of true leadership when he said, "Whoever wants to become great among you must be your servant, and whoever wants to be first among you must be your slave—just as the Son of Man did not come to be served, but to serve, and to give his life as a ransom for many" (Matt. 20:26–28).

Elders serve by governing the church in Christ's name. They received this task when Christ entrusted the apostles and their successors with the keys of the kingdom of heaven (Matt. 16:19). Elders are thus responsible for the spiritual well-being of God's people. They must provide true preaching and teaching, regular celebration of the sacraments, and faithful counsel and discipline. And they must promote fellowship and hospitality among believers, ensure good order in the church, and stimulate witness to all people.

Deacons serve by showing mercy to the church and to all people. They received this task in the early church when the apostles designated special persons for the work of mercy (Acts 6; 2 Cor. 8–9). In Christ's name the deacons relieve victims of injustice. By this they show that Christians live by the Spirit of the kingdom, fervently desiring to give life the shape of things to come. Deacons are therefore called to assess needs, promote stewardship and hospitality, collect and disburse resources for benevolence, and develop programs of assistance. They are also called to speak words of Christian encouragement. Thus in word as well as deed they demonstrate the care of the Lord himself.

These tasks of elders and deacons call for believers who are Christlike, who are mature in the faith, and who exercise their offices with prayer, patience, and humility.

Now we intend to ordain elders and deacons and to install them for terms of service in this congregation. Those appointed to the office of elder are ____(names)____. Those appointed to the office of deacon are ____(names)____.

To express your acceptance of these offices, you are asked to stand, and here in the presence of God and his church, to answer the following questions:

Do you believe that in the call of this congregation God himself is calling you to these holy offices?

Do you believe that the Old and New Testaments are the Word of God, the only infallible rule of faith and life?

Do you subscribe to the doctrinal standards of this church, rejecting all teaching which contradicts them?

Do you promise to do the work of your offices faithfully, in a way worthy of your calling and in submission to the government and discipline of the church?

Answer [by each officebearer]: I do, God helping me.

The officiating minister shall then say [the laying on of hands at this point is optional]:

God our heavenly Father, who has called you to these sacred offices, guide you by his Word, equip you with his Spirit, and so prosper your ministries that his church may increase and his name be praised. Amen.

Charge to the Elders

I charge you, elders, to "guard yourselves and all the flock of which the Holy Spirit has made you overseers. Be shepherds of the church of God, which he bought with his own blood" *(Acts 20:28)*. Be a friend and Christlike example to children. Give clear and cheerful guidance to young people. By word and example, bear up God's people in their pain and weakness, and celebrate their joys with them. Encourage the aged to persevere in God's promises. Be wise counselors who support and strengthen the pastor. Be compassionate, yet firm and consistent in rebuke and discipline. Know the Scriptures, which are "useful for teaching, rebuking, correcting and training in righteousness" *(2 Tim. 3:16)*. Pray continually for the church. Remember at all times that if you would truly give spiritual leadership in the household of faith, you must be completely mastered by your Lord *(1 Tim. 3:2–7)*.

Charge to the Deacons

I charge you, deacons, to inspire faithful stewardship in this congregation. Remind us that "from everyone who has been given much, much will be demanded" *(Luke 12:48b)*. Teach us to be merciful. Prompt us to seize new opportunities to worship God with offerings of wealth, time, and ability. Realize that benevolence is a quality of our life in Christ and not merely a matter of financial assistance. Therefore, minister to rich and poor alike, both within and outside the church. Weigh the needs of causes and use the church's resources discerningly. Be compassionate to the needy. Encourage them with words that create hope in their hearts and with deeds that bring joy into their lives. Be prophetic critics of the waste, injustice, and selfishness in our society, and be sensitive counselors to the victims of such evils. Let your lives be above reproach; live as examples of Christ Jesus; look to the interests of others.

Charge to the Congregation

I charge you, people of God, to receive these officebearers as Christ's gift to the church. Recognize in them the Lord's provision for healthy congregational life. Hold them in honor; take their counsel seriously; respond to them with obedience and respect; accept their help with thanks. Sustain them in prayer and encourage them with your support, especially when they feel the burden of their office. Acknowledge them as the Lord's servants among you.

Do you, congregation, pledge to receive them as you have been charged?

Answer [by the congregation in unison]: We do, God helping us.

Prayer

Our merciful Father in heaven, we thank you that you have provided faithful and gifted people to serve as elders and deacons. As these new officebearers assume their responsibilities, fill them with your Spirit, endow them with your wisdom, and grant them strength. Make them faithful workers in your vineyard. Under their guidance may your church grow in every spiritual grace, in faith which is open and unashamed, and in the committed service that promotes your reign in the world. Help them to perform their duties with enthusiasm and humility. In their work, grant them a sense of sustained awe which is rooted in daily adoration of you, their Lord. Through them may your name be honored and your church be served.

Help us, your people, to accept them gladly, encourage them always, and respect them for the sake of your precious Son, our Lord, in whose name we pray. Amen.

Marriage

[Where the wedding takes place before the congregation, the following announcement is to be made on the previous Sunday]:

___(name)___ and ___(name)___ have signified their desire to be united in marriage in this church on ___(date)___. If there are no lawful objections, the ceremony will take place on that date.

Beloved in the Lord, we are assembled here in the presence of God for the purpose of joining in marriage ___(name)___ and ___(name)___. Since we have received no lawful objections to their proposed union, let us reverently call to mind the institution, purpose, and obligations of the marriage state.

The holy bond of marriage was instituted by God himself at the very dawn of history. Making a man in his own likeness, he endowed him with many blessings and gave him dominion over all things. Moreover, God said, "It is not good for the man to be alone. I will make a helper suitable for him" *(Gen. 2:18)*. So God created woman of man's own substance and brought her to the man. "For this reason a man will leave his father and mother and be united to his wife, and they will become one flesh" *(Gen. 2:24)*.

Our Lord Jesus honored marriage by his blessed presence at the wedding in Cana and confirmed it as a divine ordinance, as an honorable estate, and as a lasting bond when he declared, "Therefore what God has joined together, let man not separate" *(Matt. 19:6)*. The apostle Paul shows its exalted nature when he calls marriage a symbol of the mystic union of the Savior and the church, his redeemed bride, commending it as a state honorable among all.

Marriage was established to extend the human race, to advance the kingdom of God, and to enrich the lives of those entering this state. To fulfill these purposes, a husband and wife must be lovingly devoted to each other, sharing responsibility for the nurture of the children the Lord may give them as his heritage and as parties to his covenant.

The Lord ordained that in marriage the husband should be the head of the wife, even as Christ is the head of the church, and that he should protect her and provide for her in love. This love, if exercised in the spirit and example of Christ, will be conducive to mutual happiness. God also ordained that the wife should be subject to the husband in all things that are according to his Word, showing him deference even as the church shows deference to Christ. Thus the liberty of both husband and wife is glorified by mutual loyalty to law, and the home begun in the name of the Lord and regulated by his commandments becomes the very foundation of a Christian society and provides a foretaste of the eternal home.

Marriage, then, is a divine ordinance intended to be a source of happiness to us, an institution of the highest significance to the human race, and a symbol of the union of Christ and his church. We may, therefore, as Christians look with confidence for grace in fulfilling our mutual responsibilities and for guidance and help in solving our common problems.

___(name)___ and ___(name)___, now that you have heard God's message concerning marriage, do you agree with it and do you desire to enter into this holy

This form first appeared in Dutch in 1566 as a translation from earlier Reformed sources. An English translation was adopted by the Synod of 1912 and substantially revised in 1934.

estate as ordained by God?

Each answers: I do.

[*Optional:* Who gives this woman to this man?

The father or guardian answers: I do.]

[*The minister shall cause the man to extend his right hand and to take the woman's right hand, and shall say*]:

May the Lord God confirm the desire and purpose of your hearts and may your beginning be in the name of the Lord, who made heaven and earth.

[*To the bridegroom*]:

____(name)____, do you solemnly declare that you take ____(name)____ as your wife, and do you promise that you will, with the gracious help of God, love, honor, and care for her, live with her in the holy bonds of marriage according to God's ordinance, and never forsake her, so long as you both shall live?

The bridegroom answers: I do.

[*To the bride*]:

____(name)____, do you solemnly declare that you take ____(name)____ as your husband, and do you promise that you will, with the gracious help of God, love, honor, and obey him in all things lawful, live with him in the holy bonds of marriage according to God's ordinance, and never forsake him so long as you both shall live?

The bride answers: I do.

[*Optional ring ceremony, either single or double.*]

____(name)____, do you give this ring as a symbol of your constant faithfulness and abiding love?

The bridegroom answers: I do. [*He shall then put the ring on the fourth finger of the bride's left hand.*]

[*To the bride*]:

____(name)____, do you receive [*or in case two rings are used:* Do you give] this ring as a symbol of your constant faithfulness and abiding love?

The bride answers: I do. [*In case two rings are used, she shall then put the ring on the fourth finger of the bridegroom's left hand.*]

[*Thereupon the minister says*]:

According to the laws of the state and the ordinances of the church of Christ, I now pronounce you, ____(name)____ and ____(name)____, husband and wife, in the name of the Father and of the Son and of the Holy Spirit. What therefore God has joined together let not anyone put asunder. Henceforth you go down life's pathway together, and may the Father of all mercies, who of his grace has called you to this holy state of marriage, bind you together in true love and faithfulness and grant you his blessing.

[*The bridegroom and the bride now kneel while the minister offers the following prayer*]:

Most merciful and gracious God, from whom the whole family of heaven and earth is named, we pray that you will confirm with your blessing the marriage into which our brother and sister have entered this day. Grant them your Holy Spirit to help them be true to the vow and covenant they have made. Guide them in the way of righteousness and peace so that, loving and serving you with one mind and heart all the days of their life, they may be abundantly enriched with the tokens of your everlasting favor in Christ Jesus our Lord. In all life's experiences lift up your countenance upon them, that they may be thankful in prosperity and patient in adversity. May their marriage be fruitful for this life and for the life to come. Grant them wisdom and strength to build a home which will glorify your name and promote the coming of your kingdom. May they live together many years, and in the hour of death may they part in the blessed hope of celebrating forever with all the saints of God the marriage of Christ and the church he loved. Hear our prayer in the name of our Lord Jesus Christ, who taught us to pray, saying:

Our Father in heaven,
hallowed be your name,
your kingdom come,
your will be done
on earth as it is in heaven.
Give us today our daily bread.
Forgive us our debts,
as we also have forgiven our
debtors.
And lead us not into temptation,
but deliver us from the evil one.
For yours is the kingdom
and the power
and the glory for ever.
Amen.

[The ceremony may be concluded with an appropriate song.]

Marriage

Declaration of Purpose

We have come together before the face of God to join ___(name)___ and ___(name)___ in marriage. We seek to honor the will of God for marriage, the concern of the Christian church for its well-being, and the interest of the state in the orderly development of society.

Invocation

God, our Father, we praise you for making and redeeming us to live together in love. We thank you for the love and trust which bring ___(name)___ and ___(name)___ to this their marriage day. Favor them with the honor of your presence at their wedding. Unite them by your Spirit so that together they may reflect the love of Christ for his church. Through Jesus Christ our Lord. Amen.

Parting from Parents [optional]

Today ___(name)___ and ___(name)___ leave their parents to establish a new home.

Do you, Mr. and Mrs. *[parents of the groom]*, give your blessing to them and promise them your continued love and support?

They answer: We give them our blessing, and so promise, God helping us.

Do you, Mr. and Mrs. *[parents of the bride]*, give your blessing to them and promise them your continued love and support?

They answer: We give them our blessing, and so promise, God helping us.

Institution and Meaning of Marriage

In marriage, as instituted by God, a man and a woman covenant to live together in a lifelong, exclusive partnership of love and fidelity *(Gen. 2:18;*

Matt. 19:5–6). The apostle Paul sees the union of husband and wife as a symbol of the union between Christ and his church *(Eph. 5:31–32).* If marriage is to be pleasing in the sight of God, those who enter into this covenant of life must share a common commitment to the Lord of life.

In putting his blessing on a marriage, God intended that it would provide:

a context within which husband and wife can help and comfort each other and find companionship;
a setting within which we may give loving and tender expression to the desires God gave us;
a secure environment within which children may be born and taught to know and serve the Lord; and
a structure that enriches society and contributes to its orderly function.

When these purposes are prayerfully pursued in union with Christ, the kingdom of God is advanced and the blessedness of husband and wife assured.

In Ephesians 5 the apostle Paul admonishes all Christians to develop a mutual respect and love when he says, "Submit to one another out of reverence for Christ." When he applies this to the marriage relationship, he instructs the wife to be subject to her husband as the church is subject to Christ, its head. He also instructs the husband to pattern his love for his wife after the example of Christ's love for his body, the church. Paul says, "Wives, submit to your husbands as to the Lord," and "Husbands, love your wives, just as Christ loved the church and gave himself up for her." In marriage this requires that the husband and wife serve

---

This form, adopted by the Synod of 1979, includes an (optional) concluding prayer adopted in 1981. The vows were revised by the Synod of 1986.

each other by providing the love, nurture, and faith which will enrich their lives together and build a Christ-centered home.

Our sinful and selfish tendency to break down what God has built threatens marriage with tensions, agony, and even with broken bonds. People who marry in the Lord, however, may trust that he will lead them and graciously provide for their needs when they follow the biblical pattern for love. "Love is patient, love is kind. It does not envy, it does not boast, it is not proud. It is not rude, it is not self-seeking, it is not easily angered, it keeps no record of wrongs. Love does not delight in evil but rejoices with the truth. It always protects, always trusts, always hopes, always perseveres. Love never fails." (1 Cor. 13:4–8a).

Declaration of Intent

_____(name)_____ and _____(name)_____, now that you have heard God's message concerning marriage, do you agree with it and do you commit yourselves to each other in accordance with it?

Each answers: I do.

Exchange of Vows

In the presence of God and before these people I now invite you to exchange your vows.

Groom: I take you, _____(name)_____, to be my wife and I promise before God and all who are present here to be your loving and faithful husband, as long as our lives shall last. I will love you and give myself up for you, as Christ loved the church and gave himself up for her. I will serve you with tenderness and respect, and encourage you to develop the gifts that God has given you.

Bride: I take you, _____(name)_____, to be my husband, and I promise before God and all who are present here to be your loving and faithful wife, as long as our lives shall last. I will love you and submit

to you, as the church loves and submits to Christ. I will serve you with tenderness and respect, and encourage you to develop the gifts that God has given you.

Exchange of Rings [optional]

Groom: _____(name)_____, I give you this ring as a symbol of our covenant in Christ.

Bride: _____(name)_____, I give you this ring as a symbol of our covenant in Christ.

Declaration of Marriage

As a minister of the church of Christ and by the authority which the state has vested in me, I now pronounce you, _____(name)_____ and _____(name)_____, husband and wife, in the name of the Father, Son, and Holy Spirit. Amen. "Therefore what God has joined together, let man not separate" (Matt. 19:6).

Promise of Support [optional]

Do you who are present here promise to pray for _____(name)_____ and _____(name)_____ and support them as times and circumstances may require?

People: We do, God helping us.

Pastor's Message

Prayer Following a Marriage Ceremony

Father in heaven,
give today your blessing
upon the marriage of _____(name)_____
and _____(name)_____.
We thank you for the vows
they have spoken
and the love in which
they are now united.
Keep them faithful and strong
in every trial.
Sustain their joy and affection
for many years.
We pray, Lord Jesus,
that you will be acknowledged
head of their home
and master of their lives.
Equip them, Holy Spirit,
with patient endurance,

sacrificial service, unfailing
courtesy,
endless trust, and lasting love.
Grant that their home
will often be a place of laughter;
and in times of difficulty or trouble,
a haven of healing and forgiveness.

May they and their children
give constant praise to you,
eternal Father, who with the Son
and the Spirit
is God, blessed and exalted forever.
Amen.

Responsive Readings of the Law

(1) Words of Jesus from the Gospels

Leader: You shall have no other gods before me.

People: It is written: "Worship the Lord your God, and serve him only."

Leader: You shall not make for yourself an idol.

People: God is spirit, and his worshipers must worship in spirit and in truth.

Leader: You shall not misuse the name of the Lord your God.

People: "Do not swear at all: either by heaven, for it is God's throne; or by the earth, for it is his footstool. . . .Let your 'Yes' be 'Yes', and your 'No,' 'No'; anything beyond this comes from the evil one."

Leader: Remember the Sabbath day by keeping it holy.

People: The Sabbath was made for man, not man for the Sabbath. So the Son of Man is Lord even of the Sabbath.

Leader: Honor your father and your mother.

People: For God said, "Anyone who curses his father or mother must be put to death."

Leader: You shall not murder.

People: Love your enemies and pray for those who persecute you, that you may be sons of your Father in heaven.

Leader: You shall not commit adultery.

People: Anyone who looks at a woman lustfully has already committed adultery with her in his heart.

Leader: You shall not steal.

People: For out of the heart come evil thoughts, murder, adultery . . . theft . . . . These are what make a man "unclean."

Leader: You shall not give false testimony.

People: For out of the overflow of the heart the mouth speaks. . . . For by your words you will be acquitted, and by your words you will be condemned.

Leader: You shall not covet.

People: Watch out! Be on your guard against all kinds of greed; a man's life does not consist in the abundance of his possessions.

(2) From the Epistles

Leader: You shall have no other gods before me.

People: For from him and through him and to him are all things. To him be the glory forever!

Leader: You shall not make for yourself an idol.

People: In Christ we have redemption, the forgiveness of sins. He is the image of the invisible God, the firstborn over all creation.

Leader: You shall not misuse the name of the Lord your God, for the Lord will not hold anyone guiltless who misuses his name.

People: Let us continually offer to God a sacrifice of praise—the fruit of lips that confess his name.

Leader: Remember the Sabbath day by keeping it holy. Six days you shall labor and do all your work, but the seventh day is a Sabbath to the Lord your God.

People: Let the word of Christ dwell in you richly as you teach and admonish one another with all wisdom, and as you sing psalms, hymns and spiritual songs with gratitude in your hearts to God.

Leader: Honor your father and your mother, so that you may live long in the land the Lord your God is giving you.

People: Children, obey your parents in everything, for this pleases the Lord.

Leader: You shall not murder.

People: Be kind and compassionate to one another, forgiving each other, just as in Christ God forgave you.

Leader: You shall not commit adultery.

People: You are not your own; you were bought at a price. Therefore honor God with your body.

Leader: You shall not steal.

People: He who has been stealing must steal no longer, but must work, doing something useful with his hands, so that he may have something to share with those in need.

Leader: You shall not give false testimony against your neighbor.

People: Instead, speaking the truth in love, we will in all things grow up into him who is the Head, that is, Christ.

Leader: You shall not covet your neighbor's house or anything that belongs to your neighbor.

People: I have learned to be content whatever the circumstances.

(3) From the Psalms

Leader: And God spoke all these words: I am the Lord your God. . . . You shall have no other gods before me.

People: Against you, you only, have I sinned and done what is evil in your sight.

Leader: You shall not make for yourself an idol . . . . You shall not bow down to them or worship them.

People: Come, let us bow down in worship, let us kneel before the Lord our Maker; for he is our God and we are the people of his pasture, the flock under his care.

Leader: You shall not misuse the name of the Lord your God.

People: O Lord, open my lips, and my mouth will declare your praise.

Leader: Remember the Sabbath day by keeping it holy.

People: How lovely is your dwelling place, O Lord Almighty! Better is one day in your courts than a thousand elsewhere.

Leader: Honor your father and your mother.

People: Remember not the sins of my youth and my rebellious ways; according to your love remember me, for you are good, O Lord.

Leader: You shall not murder.

People: Search me, O God, and know my heart; test me and know my anxious thoughts. See if there is any offensive way in me.

Leader: You shall not commit adultery.

People: You have set our iniquities before you, our secret sins in the light of your presence.

Leader: You shall not steal.

People: Have mercy on me, O God. . . blot out my transgressions.

Leader: You shall not give false testimony against your neighbor.

People: Keep me from deceitful ways; be gracious to me through your law.

Leader: You shall not covet your neighbor's house. You shall not covet your neighbor's wife, or his manservant or maidservant, his ox or donkey, or anything that belongs to your neighbor.

People: Turn my heart toward your statutes and not toward selfish gain. Save me from all my transgressions.

Leader: The Lord is near to all who call on him, to all who call on him in truth. He fulfills the desire of those who fear him; he hears their cry and saves them.

People: My mouth will speak in praise of the Lord. Let every creature praise his holy name for ever and ever.

(4) As a Teacher of Sin

Minster: Blessed are all who fear the
Lord, who walk in his ways.

People: Your word is a lamp to my feet
and a light for my path.

Leader: Blessed is the man who fears the
Lord, who finds great delight in his
commands!

People: Direct me in the path of your
commands, for there I find delight.

Leader: And God spoke all these words:

I am the Lord your God, who brought
you out of Egypt, out of the land of
slavery. You shall have no other gods
before me.

You shall not make for yourself an idol
in the form of anything in heaven
above or on the earth beneath or in
the waters below. You shall not bow
down to them or worship them; for I,
the Lord your God, am a jealous
God, punishing the children for the
sin of the fathers to the third and
fourth generation of those who hate
me, but showing love to a thousand
generations of those who love me and
keep my commandments.

You shall not misuse the name of the
Lord your God, for the Lord will not
hold anyone guiltless who misuses his
name.

Remember the Sabbath day by keeping
it holy. Six days you shall labor and
do all your work, but the seventh day
is a Sabbath to the Lord your God.
On it you shall not do any work,
neither you, nor your son or
daughter, nor your manservant or
maidservant, nor your animals, nor
the alien within your gates. For in six
days the Lord made the heavens and
the earth, the sea, and all that is in
them, but he rested on the seventh
day. Therefore the Lord blessed the
Sabbath day and made it holy.

People: Wash away all my iniquity and
cleanse me from sin. For I know my
transgressions, and my sin is always
before me.

Leader: Honor your father and your
mother, so that you may live long in
the land the Lord your God is giving
you.

You shall not murder.

You shall not commit adultery.

You shall not steal.

You shall not give false testimony against
your neighbor.

You shall not covet your neighbor's wife,
or his manservant or maidservant, his
ox or donkey, or anything that
belongs to your neighbor.

People: If you, O Lord, kept a record of
sins, O Lord, who could stand? But
with you there is forgiveness;
therefore you are feared.

(5) As a Rule of Gratitude

Leader: Hear, O people of God, the law which the Lord speaks in your hearing this day, that you may know his statutes and walk according to his ordinances.

People: Teach us, O Lord, the grace of your law, and give us life by your Word.

Leader: The God who saved us in Jesus Christ gave this law, saying: I am the Lord your God! You shall have no other gods before me.

People: We will worship the Lord our God and serve only him.

Leader: You shall not make yourself an image of anything to worship it.

People: Living no more in bondage to earthly gods, we will worship the Lord our God in spirit and in truth.

Leader: You shall not misuse the name of the Lord.

People: We will use the holy name of God with reverence, praising him in everything we do and say.

Leader: You shall observe the Sabbath by keeping it holy, for in six days you shall labor and do all your work.

People: This is the day the Lord has made; let us rejoice and be glad in it.

Leader: The first part of the law is this great commandment:

People: That we love the Lord our God with all our heart, with all our mind, and with all our strength.

Leader: The second part of the Law is similar to the first: you shall honor your father and mother, that you may live long in the land the Lord your God is giving to you.

People: As children we will be obedient to our parents in the Lord; as parents we will correct our children and guide them in the training and instruction of the Lord; we will respect the lawful authorities appointed by God.

Leader: You shall not murder.

People: We will be kind and compassionate to one another, forgiving each other, just as in Christ God forgave us.

Leader: You shall not commit adultery.

People: We will use our bodies in ways that are holy and honorable, and abstain from immorality and impurity.

Leader: You shall not steal.

People: We will do what we can for our neighbor's good, and work faithfully so that we may share with the poor.

Leader: You shall not give false testimony against your neighbor.

People: We will speak the truth with our neighbor in love, render judgments that are true and make for peace, and not devise in our hearts any evil against anyone.

Leader: You shall not covet anything that belongs to your neighbor.

People: We will be content whatever the circumstances through the strength of Christ within us.

Leader: Thus we must love our neighbor as ourselves.

People: For the Lord requires of us to do justice, to love kindness, and to walk humbly with our God. Amen!

(6) As Summarized in Matthew 22:37–40

Leader: What is the great and first commandment?

People: Love the Lord your God with all your heart and with all your soul and with all your mind.

Leader: What is the second commandment like it?

People: Love your neighbor as yourself.

Leader: What does this mean?

People: Love is the fulfilling of the law.

Leader: To what does this call us?

People: To a life of faith working through love.

Our World Belongs to God
A Contemporary Testimony

Preamble

1. As followers of Jesus Christ,[1]
   living in this world—
   which some seek to control,
   but which others view with despair—[2]
   we declare with joy and trust:
   Our world belongs to God![3]

   [1] Ps. 103:19–22
   [2] Ps. 4:6
   [3] Ps. 24:1

2. From the beginning,[1]
   through all the crises of our times,
   until his kingdom fully comes,[2]
   God keeps covenant forever.
   Our world belongs to him![3]
   God is King! Let the earth be glad!
   Christ is Victor; his rule has begun. Hallelujah!
   The Spirit is at work, renewing the creation. Praise the
      Lord!

   [1] Ps. 145
   [2] Rom. 11:33–36
   [3] Rev. 4–5

3. But rebel cries sound through the world:[1]
   some, crushed by failure
   or hardened by pain,
   give up on life and hope and God;
   others, shaken,
   but still hoping for human triumph,[2]
   work feverishly to realize their dreams.[3]
   As believers in God
   we join this struggle of the spirits,
   testing our times by the Spirit's sure Word.

   [1] Ps. 2
   [2] Eph. 6:10–18
   [3] 1 John 4

4. Our world has fallen into sin;
   but rebellion and sin can never dethrone God.[1]
   He does not abandon the work of his hand;
   the heavens still declare his glory.
   He preserves his world,
   sending seasons, sun, and rain,[2]
   upholding his creatures,
   renewing the earth,
   directing all things to their purpose.
   He promised a Savior;
   now the whole creation groans[3]
   in the birth pangs of a new creation.

   [1] Ps. 19
   [2] Acts 14:15–17
   [3] Rom. 8:18–25

5. God holds this world[1]
   in sovereign love.
   He kept his promise,
   sending Jesus into the world.
   He poured out his Spirit[2]
   and broadcast the news
   that sinners who repent and believe in Jesus[3]
   can live
   and breathe
   and move again
   as members of the family of God.

   [1] John 3:1–21
   [2] Acts 2
   [3] Acts 17:22–31

6. We rejoice in the goodness of God,
   renounce the works of darkness,
   and dedicate ourselves to holy living.
   As covenant partners,
   called to faithful obedience,[1]
   and set free for joyful praise,
   we offer our hearts and lives[2]
   to do God's work in his world.[3]
   With tempered impatience, eager to see injustice
   ended,
   we expect the Day of the Lord.
   And we are confident
   that the light which shines in the present darkness[4]
   will fill the earth when Christ appears.

   Come, Lord Jesus![5]
   Our world belongs to you.

   [1] Mic. 6:8
   [2] Rom. 12:1–2
   [3] 2 Pet. 3
   [4] 1 Cor. 15
   [5] Rev. 22:20

Creation

7. Our world belongs to God—
   not to us or earthly powers,[1]
   not to demons, fate, or chance.
   The earth is the Lord's!

   [1] Deut. 10:12–14

8. In the beginning, God—[1]
   Father, Word, and Spirit—[2]
   called this world into being[3]
   out of nothing,
   and gave it
   shape and order.

   [1] Gen. 1
   [2] Ps. 33:1–11
   [3] Isa. 40

9. God formed the land, the sky, and the seas,[1]
   making the earth a fitting home
   for the plants, animals,[2]
   and humans he created.
   The world was filled with color, beauty, and variety;
   it provided room for
   work and play,
   worship and service,
   love and laughter.
   God rested—[3]
   and gave us rest.
   In the beginning
   everything was very good.

   [1] Gen. 1–2
   [2] Ps. 104
   [3] Mark 2:27–28

10. As God's creatures we are made in his image[1]
    to represent him on earth,[2]
    and to live in loving communion with him.
    By sovereign appointment we are[3]
    earthkeepers and caretakers:
    loving our neighbor,
    tending the creation,
    and meeting our needs.
    God uses our skills
    in the unfolding and well-being of his world.

    [1] Gen. 1:26–30
    [2] Ps. 8
    [3] Matt. 22:35–40

11. Male and female,[1]
    all of us are to represent God[2]
    as we do our tasks.
    Whether single or married,
    we are called to live within God's order[3]
    in lives of loving service.

    [1] Gen. 1:26–28
    [2] Gal. 3:26–28
    [3] 1 Cor. 7

12. No matter what our age, or race, or color,[1]
    we are the human family together,
    for the Creator made us all.
    Since life is his gift,
    we foster the well-being of others,[2]
    protecting the unborn and helpless from harm.[3]

    [1] Acts 17:22–31
    [2] Ps. 139
    [3] Lev. 19; 25:35–38

13. God directs and bends to his will[1]
    all that happens in his world.
    As history unfolds in ways we only know in part,[2]
    all things—
    from crops to grades,
    from jobs to laws—
    are under his control.
    God is present in our world
    by his Word and Spirit.
    The faithfulness[3]
    of our great Provider
    gives sense to our days
    and hope to our years.
    The future is secure,
    for our world belongs to God.

    [1] Matt. 6:25–34
    [2] Ps. 147, 148
    [3] Ps. 111

The Fall

14. Early in human history
    our first parents listened to the intruder's voice.[1]
    Rather than living by the Creator's
    word of life,
    they fell for Satan's lie
    and sinned!
    They forgot their place;
    they tried to be like God.
    But as sinners they feared
    the nearness of God
    and hid from him.

    [1] Gen. 3

15. Apart from grace[1]
    we prove each day
    that we are guilty sinners.
    Fallen in that first sin,
    we fail to thank God,
    we break his laws,
    we ignore our tasks.
    Looking for life without God, we find only death;
    grasping for freedom outside his law,[2]
    we trap ourselves in Satan's snares;
    pursuing pleasure, we lose the gift of joy.

    [1] Rom. 1:18–3:23; 5:12
    [2] 1 John 1:8–10

16. When humans no longer show God's image,[1]
    all creation suffers.
    We abuse the creation or idolize it.[2]
    We are estranged from our Creator,
    from our neighbor, and from all that God has made.

    [1] Rom. 1
    [2] Eph. 4:17–19

17. All spheres of life—[1]
    marriage and family,
    work and worship,
    school and state,
    our play and art—
    bear the wounds of our rebellion.[2]
    Sin is present everywhere—[3]
    in pride of race,
    in arrogance of nations,
    in abuse of the weak and helpless,
    in disregard for water, air, and soil,
    in destruction of living creatures,
    in slavery, deceit, terror, and war,[4]
    in worship of false gods,
    and frantic escape from reality.[5]
    We have become victims of our own sin.

    [1] Rom. 1
    [2] Ps. 14
    [3] Amos 1–2
    [4] Jer. 17:9
    [5] Isa. 28:7–8

18. In all our strivings[1]
    to excuse
    or save ourselves,
    we stand condemned[2]
    before the God of Truth.
    But our world,
    broken and scarred,[3]
    still belongs to God.
    He holds it together[4]
    and gives us hope.

    [1] Ps. 89
    [2] Rom. 1:18
    [3] Jer. 14
    [4] Rom. 5:2–5; 15:13

Redemption

19. While justly angry[1]
    God did not turn his back
    on a world bent on destruction;
    he turned his face to it in love.[2]
    With patience and tender care he set out[3]
    on the long road of redemption
    to reclaim the lost as his people[4]
    and the world as his kingdom.

    [1] Gen. 3:9–15
    [2] John 3:16
    [3] Luke 1:68–75; 3:23–37
    [4] Rev. 11:15

20. Although Adam and Eve were expelled from the garden[1]
    and their work was burdened by sin's effects,
    God held on to them in love.
    He promised to crush
    the evil forces they unleashed.

    [1] Gen. 3:15–19

21. When evil filled the earth,[1]
    God judged it with a flood,
    but rescued Noah and his family[2]
    and animals of all kinds.
    He covenanted with every creature
    that seasons would continue
    and that such destruction would not come again
    until the final day.

    [1] Gen. 6–9
    [2] 1 Pet. 3:18–22

22. The Creator pledged to be God[1]
to Abraham and his children,
blessing all nations through them
as they lived obediently before him.
He chose Israel as his special people[2]
to show the glory of his name,[3]
the power of his love,[4]
and the wisdom of his ways.
He gave them his laws through Moses,[5]
he led them by rulers and teachers,
so that they would be a people
whose God was king.

[1] Gen. 12:1–3
[2] Deut. 7
[3] Rom. 9
[4] Mic. 6:8
[5] Ps. 103:7

23. When Israel spurned God's love[1]
by lusting after other gods,
by trusting in power and wealth,
and by hurting the weak,
God scattered his people among the nations.
Yet he kept a faithful few[2]
and promised them the Messiah:
a prophet to speak the clear word,
a king to crush the serpent's head,
a priestly servant willing to be broken for sinners.[3]
And he promised the gift of the Spirit[4]
to bend stubborn wills to new obedience.

[1] 2 Chron. 36
[2] Isa. 10
[3] Isa. 53
[4] Jer. 11; 31

Christ

24. God remembered his promise[1]
to reconcile the world to himself;
he has come among us[2]
in Jesus Christ,
the eternal Word made flesh.[3]
He is the long-awaited Savior,[4]
fully human and fully divine,
conceived by the Spirit of God
and born of the virgin Mary.

[1] 2 Cor. 5:18–21
[2] Gal. 4:4–7
[3] John 1:1–14
[4] Luke 1–2

25. In the events of his earthly life—[1]
his temptations and suffering,[2]
his teaching and miracles,
his battles with demons and talks with sinners—
Jesus made present in deed and in word
the coming rule of God.

[1] Luke 4
[2] Phil. 2:1–11

26. As the second Adam he chose[1]
the path we had rejected.
As our representative,
serving God perfectly,
and loving even those who scorned him,[2]
Christ showed us how
a righteous child of God lives.

[1] Rom. 5
[2] 1 Pet. 2:21–25

27. As our substitute[1]
he suffered all his years on earth,
especially in the horrible torture of the cross.
He carried God's judgment on our sin;[2]
his sacrifice removes our guilt.
He walked out of the grave, the Lord of life!
He conquered sin and death.[3]
We are set right with God,
we are given new life,
and called to walk with him[4]
in freedom from sin's dominion.

[1] Isa. 53
[2] Heb. 10
[3] Rom. 4:18–5:11
[4] Gal. 5

28. Being both God and man,[1]
Jesus is the only Mediator
between God and his people.
He alone paid the debt of our sin;[2]
there is no other Savior!
In him the Father chose those[3]
whom he would save.
His electing love sustains our hope:
God's grace is free
to save sinners who offer nothing
but their need for mercy.

[1] 1 Tim. 2:5–6
[2] Acts 4:10–12
[3] Eph. 1:1–14

29. Jesus ascended in triumph[1]
to his heavenly throne.[2]
There he hears our prayers,
pleads our cause before the Father,[3]
and rules the world.[4]
Blessed are all[5]
who take refuge in him.

[1] Acts 1:1–11
[2] Eph. 1:18–23
[3] 1 John 2:1–2
[4] Rev. 5
[5] Rom. 8:31–39

The Spirit

30. At Pentecost the Holy Spirit[1]
was given to the church.
In pouring his Spirit on many peoples
God overcomes the divisions of Babel;[2]
now people from every tongue, tribe, and nation
are gathered into the unity
of the body of Christ.

[1] Acts 2
[2] Rev. 7

31. Jesus stays with us in the Spirit,[1]
who renews our hearts,
moves us to faith,
leads us in the truth,[2]
stands by us in our need,
and makes our obedience fresh and vibrant.

[1] John 14
[2] 2 Cor. 3:7–18

32. The Spirit thrusts[1]
God's people into worldwide mission.
He impels young and old,[2]
men and women,
to go next door and far away[3]
into science and art,
media and marketplace
with the good news of God's grace.
The Spirit goes before them and with them,[4]
convincing the world of sin
and pleading the cause of Christ.

[1] Matt. 28:18–20
[2] Matt. 9:35–38
[3] Luke 14:15–24
[4] John 16:5–15

33. The Spirit's gifts are here to stay[1]
    in rich variety—
    fitting responses to timely needs.
    We thankfully see each other
    as gifted members of the fellowship[2]
    which delights in the creative Spirit's work.
    He gives more than enough
    to each believer
    for God's praise and our neighbor's welfare.[3]

    [1] 1 Cor. 12–14
    [2] Eph. 4
    [3] Rom. 12

Scripture

34. God has not left this world[1]
    without ways of knowing him.
    He shows his power and majesty
    in the creation;
    he has mercifully spoken
    through prophets, history writers, poets,[2]
    gospel writers, and apostles—
    and most clearly through the Son.
    The Spirit who moved humans[3]
    to write the Word of God[4]
    speaks to us in the Bible.

    [1] Rom. 1
    [2] Heb. 1
    [3] 2 Tim. 3:14–17
    [4] 2 Pet. 1:12–21

35. The Bible is the Word of God,
    record and tool of his redeeming work.
    It is the Word of Truth,[1]
    fully reliable in leading us[2]
    to know God
    and have life[3]
    in Jesus Christ.

    [1] James 1:18
    [2] Acts 8:26–39
    [3] John 20:30–31

36. The Bible tells God's mighty acts[1]
    in the unfolding of covenant history.[2]
    It is one revelation in two Testaments,
    which shows a single plan of salvation,
    and reveals God's will infallibly.
    As God's people hear the Word and do it,[3]
    they are equipped for discipleship,
    to witness to the good news:
    Our world belongs to God
    and he loves it deeply.

    [1] Acts 7
    [2] 1 Cor. 10:1–11
    [3] 2 Tim. 3:14–17

God's New People[1]

[1] Eph. 1–4

37. In our world, bent under the weight of sin,
    Christ gathers a new community.[1]
    Satan and his evil forces
    seek whom they may confuse and swallow;[2]
    but Jesus builds his church,[3]
    his Spirit guides,
    and grace abounds.

    [1] 1 Pet. 5:8–11
    [2] 1 Cor. 3:10–17
    [3] Matt. 16:13–19

38. The church is the fellowship of those[1]
    who confess Jesus as Lord.
    She is the Bride of Christ,
    his chosen partner,[2]
    loved by Jesus and loving him:[3]
    delighting in his presence,
    seeking him in prayer,[4]
    silent before the mystery of his love.

    [1] Rev. 21:9
    [2] 1 Pet. 2:4–10
    [3] Eph. 2
    [4] Col. 1:1–23; 3:1–17

39. Our new life in Christ[1]
    is celebrated and nourished
    in the fellowship of congregations[2]
    where God's name is praised,
    his Word proclaimed,[3]
    his way taught;
    where sins are confessed,[4]
    prayers and gifts are offered,[5]
    and sacraments are celebrated.

    [1] Acts 2:41–47
    [2] Eph. 4:1–5:20
    [3] Rom. 10
    [4] Eph. 3:1–13
    [5] Matt. 6:5–15

40. God meets us in the sacraments,[1]
    holy acts in which his deeds[2]
    elicit our response.
    God reminds and assures us in baptism,[3]
    whether of those newly born or newly converted,[4]
    that his covenant love saves us,
    that he washes away our guilt,[5]
    gives us the Spirit,
    and expects our love in return.
    In the supper our Lord offers[6]
    the bread and cup to believers
    to guarantee our share
    in his death and resurrection,
    and to unite us to him[7]
    and to each other.
    We take this food gladly,[8]
    announcing as we eat
    that Jesus is our life
    and that he shall come again[9]
    to call us to the Supper of the Lamb.

    [1] Gen. 17
    [2] Ex. 12
    [3] Matt. 28:18–20
    [4] Acts 2:37–41
    [5] Col. 2:9–14
    [6] Matt. 26:26–29
    [7] 1 Cor. 10:16–17
    [8] 1 Cor. 11:17–34
    [9] Rev. 19:6–9

41. The Spirit empowers each member[1]
    to take part in the ministry of all,
    so that hurts are healed
    and all may rejoice[2]
    in the life and growth of the fellowship.

    [1] 1 Cor. 12–13
    [2] 1 Cor. 1:1–9

42. The church is a gathering[1]
of forgiven sinners,
called to be holy,[2]
dedicated to service.
Saved by the patient grace of God,[3]
we deal patiently with others.
Knowing our own weakness and failures,
we bring good news to all sinners
with understanding of their condition,
and with hope in God.

[1] Eph. 2
[2] 1 Pet. 1
[3] Matt. 5:43–48

43. We grieve that the church[1]
which shares one Spirit, one faith, one hope,
and spans all time, place, race, and language[2]
has become a broken communion in a broken world.
When we struggle for the purity of the church
and for the righteousness God demands,
we pray for saintly courage.
When our pride or blindness blocks
the unity of God's household,
we seek forgiveness.
We marvel that the Lord gathers the broken pieces[3]
to do his work,
and that he blesses us still
with joy, new members,
and surprising evidences of unity.
We commit ourselves to seeking and expressing
the oneness of all who follow Jesus.

[1] Eph. 4
[2] Gal. 3:26–29
[3] John 17

The Mission of God's People

44. Following the apostles, the church is sent—[1]
    sent with the gospel of the kingdom[2]
    to make disciples of all nations,
    to feed the hungry,[3]
    and to proclaim the assurance that in the name of
    Christ[4]
    there is forgiveness of sin and new life
    for all who repent and believe—
    to tell the news that our world belongs to God.
    In a world estranged from God,
    where millions face confusing choices,
    this mission is central to our being,[5]
    for we announce the one name that saves.
    We repent of leaving this work to a few,
    we pray for brothers and sisters
    who suffer for the faith,
    and we rejoice that the Spirit[6]
    is waking us to see
    our mission in God's world.

    [1] Matt. 28:18–20
    [2] John 20:21–23
    [3] 1 John 3:11–24
    [4] 2 Cor. 5:11–6:2
    [5] Acts 1:8
    [6] 1 Thess. 1

45. The rule of Jesus Christ covers the whole world.[1]
    To follow this Lord is
    to serve him everywhere,[2]
    without fitting in,
    as light in the darkness,[3]
    as salt in a spoiling world.

    [1] Phil. 2:1–10; 4:8–9
    [2] Rom. 12
    [3] Matt. 5:13–16

46. We serve Christ by thankfully receiving our life[1]
    as a gift from his hand.
    We protest and resist
    all abuse and harm of this gift[2]
    by abortion, pollution, gluttony,
    addiction, and all foolish risks.

    [1] 1 Cor. 6:19–20
    [2] Ps. 139

47. Since God made us male and female in his image,[1]
    one sex may not look down on the other,
    nor should we flaunt or exploit our sexuality.
    Our roles as men and women must conform[2]
    to God's gifts and commands[3]
    as we shape our cultural patterns.
    Sexuality is disordered in our fallen world;[4]
    grief and loneliness are the result;[5]
    but Christ's renewing work gives hope
    for order and healing
    and surrounds suffering persons[6]
    with a compassionate community.

    [1] Gen. 1:26–2:25
    [2] Song of Songs
    [3] Gal. 3:28
    [4] Prov. 7
    [5] 1 Cor. 6:9–20
    [6] John 8:1–11

48. We serve Christ as singles,[1]
    whether for a time or a life,
    by undivided devotion to the work of God
    and so add our love and service
    to the building of his kingdom.

    [1] 1 Cor. 7:25–35

49. In marriage and family,[1]
    we serve God
    by reflecting his covenant love
    in life-long loyalty,
    and by teaching his ways,
    so that children may know Jesus as their Lord
    and learn to use their gifts in a life of joyful service.

    [1] Eph. 5:1–6:4

50. In education we seek to acknowledge the Lord[1]
    by promoting schools and teaching[2]
    in which the light of his Word shines in all learning,[3]
    where students, of whatever ability,
    are treated as persons who bear God's image[4]
    and have a place in his plan.

    [1] Prov. 4; 9:10
    [2] Ps. 119:105
    [3] Col. 1:17
    [4] Deut. 6:1–9

51. In our work, even in dull routine,[1]
    we hear the call to serve our Lord.
    We must work for more than wages,[2]
    and manage for more than profit,[3]
    so that mutual respect
    and the just use of goods and skills[4]
    may shape the work place,
    and so that, while we earn or profit,
    useful products and services may result.
    Rest and leisure are gifts of God[5]
    to relax us and to set us free
    to discover and to explore.
    Believing that he provides for us,
    we can rest more trustingly[6]
    and entertain ourselves more simply.

    [1] Eph. 4:17–32
    [2] 2 Thess. 3:6–13
    [3] Eph. 6:5–9
    [4] 1 Thess. 4:9–12
    [5] Phil. 4:8
    [6] Heb. 4:1–13

52. Grateful for the advances
    in science and technology,[1]
    we make careful use of their products,[2]
    on guard against idolatry
    and harmful research,
    and careful to use them in ways that answer[3]
    to God's demands
    to love our neighbor
    and to care for the earth and its creatures.[4]

    [1] Gen. 1:28–31; 9:1–7
    [2] 1 Chron. 29:1–19
    [3] 1 Tim. 4:1–5
    [4] Rom. 8:19–23

53. Since God establishes the powers that rule,[1]
we are called to respect them,[2]
unless they trample his Word.
We are to obey God in politics,[3]
pray for our rulers,
and help governments to know his will for public life.
Knowing that God's people
live under many forms of government,
we are thankful for the freedoms[4]
enjoyed by citizens of many lands;
we grieve with those who live under oppression,[5]
and we work for their liberty[6]
to live without fear.

[1] John 19:11
[2] Rom. 13:1–7
[3] Acts 4
[4] Isa. 61:1–2
[5] Gen. 18
[6] Rom. 6:16–19

54. We call on governments to do public justice[1]
and to protect the freedoms and rights[1]
of individuals, groups, and institutions,[3]
so that each may freely do[4]
the tasks God gives.
We urge governments to ensure the well-being of all citizens[5]
by protecting children from abuse and pornography,[6]
by guarding the elderly and poor,[7]
and by promoting the freedom to speak, to work,[8]
to worship, and to associate.

[1] Matt. 5:6
[2] Isa. 61:8
[3] Luke 4:17–21
[4] 1 Tim. 2:1–4
[5] Ps. 72
[6] Isa. 1:16–17
[7] Lev. 19:13–16
[8] Jer. 9:23–24; 22:15–17

55. Following the Prince of Peace,[1]
    we are called to be peacemakers,
    and to promote harmony and order.
    We call on our governments to work for peace;[2]
    we deplore the arms race[3]
    and the horrors that we risk.
    We call on all nations to limit their weapons
    to those needed in the defense of justice and freedom.
    We pledge to walk in ways of peace,[4]
    confessing that our world belongs to God;
    he is our sure defense.

[1] James 3:18
[2] Mic. 4:1–5
[3] Matt. 26:52
[4] Matt. 5:9

New Creation

56. Our hope for a new earth is not tied[1]
    to what humans can do,[2]
    for we believe that one day[3]
    every challenge to God's rule
    and every resistance to his will shall be crushed.
    Then his kingdom shall come fully,[4]
    and our Lord shall rule forever.

[1] 1 Pet. 1:3–12
[2] 2 Pet. 3:1–13
[3] 1 Thess. 4:13–5:11
[4] Rev. 11:15

57. We long for that day[1]
    when Jesus will return as triumphant king,
    when the dead will be raised[2]
    and all people will stand before his judgment.[3]
    We face that day without fear,
    for the Judge is our Savior.
    Our daily lives of service aim for the moment[4]
    when the Son will present his people to the Father.
    Then God will be shown to be true, holy, and gracious.
    All who have been on the Lord's side[5]
    will be honored,
    the fruit of even small acts of[6]
    obedience will be displayed;
    but tyrants and oppressors,
    heretics, and all who deny the Lord
    will be damned.

    [1] Rev. 20:11–21:8
    [2] 1 Cor. 15
    [3] John 5:28–29
    [4] 2 Thess. 1:5–10
    [5] 2 Cor. 5:10
    [6] Matt. 25:31–46

58. With the whole creation[1]
    we wait for the purifying fire of judgment.
    For then we will see the Lord face to face.[2]
    He will heal our hurts,
    end our wars,
    and make the crooked straight.
    Then we will join in the new song
    to the Lamb without blemish[3]
    who made us a kingdom and priests.[4]
    God will be all in all,
    righteousness and peace will flourish,[5]
    everything will be made new,
    and every eye will see at last
    that our world belongs to God!
    Hallelujah! Come, Lord Jesus.[6]

    [1] Rom. 8:18–39
    [2] Rev. 21–22
    [3] Rev. 5
    [4] 1 Cor. 15:28
    [5] Isa. 11:6–9; 60:11, 19–20; 65:17–25
    [6] Rev. 22:17, 20

INDEXES

Copyright Holders

We are grateful to all individuals and publishers who have granted us permission to print their copyrighted materials in this edition of the *Psalter Hymnal*. If you wish to reproduce (or reprint) any copyrighted words or music contained in this book, please contact the copyright holder for permission.

Abingdon Press
201 Eighth Avenue S.
P.O. Box 801
Nashville, TN 37202
(615) 749-6422

Anglican Church of Canada
600 Jarvis Street
Toronto, ON M4Y 2J6

Archdiocese of Philadelphia
Music Office
222 N. 17th Street
Philadelphia, PA 19103
(215) 587-3696

Augsburg Publishing Co.
426 S. Fifth St.
Box 1209
Minneapolis, MN 55440
(800) 328-4648

Barham-Gould, A. Cyril—Estate of
c/o D. R. Gould
34 Pollards Dr.
Horsham, West Sussex RH 13 5HH
England

Belwin Mills Publishing Corp.
c/o Columbia Pictures Publications
15800 N.W. 48th Ave.
P.O. Box 4340
Miami, FL 33014
(305) 620-1500

Bowers, The Reverend Canon J. E.
The Vicarage
Ashby-de-la-Zouch
Leicestershire LE6 5BX
England

Breitkopf & Hartel
Postfach 1707
D-6200 Wiesbaden 1
Germany

Broadman Press (SESAC)
127 Ninth Ave. N.
Nashville, TN 37234
(615) 251-2533

CRC Publications
2850 Kalamazoo SE
Grand Rapids, MI 49560
(616) 246-0797

Chinese Christian Literature Council
57 Peking Road, 2/F
Kowloon, Hong Kong

Christian Labour Association of
  Canada
81 Albion Rd.
Rexdale, ON M9V 1A3

Church Pension Fund
The Church Hymnal Corporation
800 Second Ave.
New York, NY 10017
(800) 223-6602

Church of the Brethren General
  Board
1451 Dundee Ave.
Elgin, IL 60120
(312) 742-5100

Concordia Publishing House
3558 S. Jefferson Ave.
St. Louis, MO 63118
(314) 664-7000

Covenant Press
5101 N. Francisco Ave.
Chicago, IL 60625
(312) 784-3000

Crawford, Mrs. Mary Babcock
2884 Galleon Rd.
Pebble Beach, CA 93953
(408) 372-6626

Davies, William
Oxford Cottage
Sackville Rd.
Cheam, Surrey
England

Daw, Carl P.
St. Mark's Chapel
42 N. Eagleville Rd.
Storrs, CT 06268
(203) 429-2647

de Lande Long, Mary N.
Estate of H. C. A. Gaunt
3 Bridle Path, Ewshot
Farnham, Surrey GU10 5BW
England

Edward B. Marks Music Corp.
Div. of Hal Leonard Pub. Corp.
8112 W. Bluemound Rd.
P.O. Box 13819
Milwaukee, WI 53213
(414) 774-3630

Erickson, John
Christ United Methodist Church
44 Highland Rd.
Bethel Park, PA 15102

Espinosa, Juan
c/o Alvin Schutmaat
Apartado 901
San Jose, Costa Rica

Faber Music Limited
3 Queen Square
London WC1N 3AU
England

Feed the Minds
Robertson House, Leas Road
Guildford, Surrey GU1 4QW
England

France, William M.—Estate of
355 Cooper St.
Ottawa 4, Ontario

Franciscan Communications Center
1229 S. Santee Street
Los Angeles, CA 90015

Fred Bock Music Company
P.O. Box 333
Tarzana, CA 91356
(818) 996-6181

G.I.A. Publications
7404 S. Mason Ave.
Chicago, IL 60638
(312) 496-3800

Geoffrey Chapman
1 Vincent Square
London SW1P 2PN
England

Geyer, John B.
5 Weoley Hill
Birmingham B29 4AA
England

Grant, John Webster
Victoria University
Birge Carnegie/22
75 Queens Park Cresc.
Toronto, ON M5S 1K7

Grotenhuis, Dale
Dordt College
Sioux Center, IA 51250

H. W. Gray Co., Inc.
(see Belwin Mills)

Harold Flammer, Inc.
Delaware Water Gap, PA 18327
(717) 476-0550

Harwood, Basil—Estate of
The Public Trustee
Mr. H. N. de v. Mather, Trust Officer
Stewart House
Kingsway, London WC2B 6JX
England

Hinshaw Music, Inc.
P. O. Box 470
Chapel Hill, N.C. 27514
(919) 929-0337

Hope Publishing Company
Carol Stream, IL 60188
(800) 323-1049

Hymn Society of America
c/o Hope Publishing Company

Hymns Ancient & Modern
St. Mary's Works, St. Mary's Plain
Norwich, Norfolk, NR3 3BH
England

International Commission on
English in the Liturgy
1275 K Street NW
Suite 1202
Washington, DC 20005
(202) 347-0800

InterVarsity Press
Box 1400
Downers Grove, IL 60515
(312) 964-5700

Ireland—The John Ireland Trust
Mr. P. B. A. Taylor
35 Saint Mary's Mansion
St. Mary's Terrace
London W2 1SQ, England

Isais, Juan M.
Mision Latinoamericana de Mexico
Apartado 21-983
04000 Mexico, D.F.
Mexico

Jabusch, Fr. Willard F.
St. Mary of the Lake Seminary
Mundelein, IL 60060
(312) 566-6401

Jackson, Frances
Nether Garth
Acklam, Malton
North Yorkshire YO17 9RG
England

Janson, Peter
St. Aidan's United Church
1891 Broadmead Avenue
Victoria, BC V8P 2V7
(604) 477-2089

JASRAC
Jasrac House
7-13 1-Chome Nishishimbashi
Minato-Ku, Tokyo 105
Japan

Kevin Mayhew Publishers
Rattlesden
Bury St. Edmunds
Suffolk IP30 0SZ
England

Koyzis, David
1512 Wadsworth Rd.
Wheaton, IL 60187

Lexicon/Spectra Distribution, Inc.
(ASCAP)
23 Music Sq. East, Suite 101
Nashville, TN 37203
(615) 244-1227

Liedboek voor de Kerken
Interkerkelijke Stichting voor Het
Kerklied
Prunuslaan 23
2641 AW Pijnacker
The Netherlands

Lillenas Publishing Company
P.O. Box 527
Kansas City, MO 64141
(816) 931-1900

Loh, I-to
Asian Institute of Liturgy and Music
P.O. Box 3167
Manila 2800
Philippines

Lutheran Church in America
Board of Publications
2900 Queen Lane
Philadelphia, PA 19129

Lutheran World Federation
Route De Ferney 150
1211 Geneva 20
Switzerland 333400

MacNutt, Walter
161 St. George St., Apt. 507
Toronto, ON M5R 2M3

Manna Music
22510 Avenue Stanford, Suite 101
Valencia, CA 91355
(805) 257-1191

Maranatha! Music
P.O. Box 1396
Costa Mesa, CA 92628
(714) 979-8536

Medema, Ken
627 Waller St., Apt. C
San Francisco, CA 94117
(415) 864-3725

Mills Music
Columbia Pictures Music Group
3500 W. Olive Ave., Room 428
Burbank, CA 91505
818-953-7756

Moody Press
2101 W. Howard St.
Chicago, IL 60645
(312) 973-7800

Novello & Co., Ltd.
Borough Green
Sevenoaks, Kent TN15 8DT
England

Order of St. Benedict, Inc.
The Liturgical Press
Collegeville, MN 56321
(612) 363-2213

OCP Publications
5536 NE Hassalo
Portland, OR 97213

Osborne, Stanley
705 Masson St.
Oshawa, ON L1G 5A6

Oxford University Press, NY
200 Madison Ave.
New York, NY 10016
(212) 679-7300

Oxford University Press
Miss Joyce Horn, Ely House
37 Dover St.
London W1X 4AH
England

Paideia Press
P.O. Box 1450
St. Catharines, ON L2R 7J8
(716) 284-7784

Paragon Music Corp. (ASCAP)
(see Zondervan Music Group)

Peacey, Mildred E.
10 Park Cottages
Manor Road, Hurstpierpoint
West Sussex BN6 9UW
England

Petter, Carol Vriend
c/o Mrs. Margaret Vriend
2151 Ridgecrest Rd. SE, Apt. 3
Grand Rapids, MI 49506

Pilgrim Press
132 W. 31st St.
New York, NY 10001
(212) 239-8700

Pitt-Watson, Ian
c/o Fuller Theological Seminary
135 N. Oakland
Pasadena, CA 91101-1790
(818) 449-1745

Praise Publications, Inc.
P.O. Box 246
65 Villiers Rd.
Padstow 2211
Australia

Rodborough Tabernacle United
    Reformed Church
The Limes, Kingscourt Lane
Stroud, Glos GL5 3QP
England

Rodeheaver Company
(see WORD, Inc.)

Rowthorn, Jeffery W.
Institute of Sacred Music
Yale Divinity School
New Haven, CT 06520

Royal School of Church Music
Addington Palace
Croydon CR9 5AO
England

Schalk, Carl F.
Concordia College
Music Department
River Forest, IL 60305

Smith, Leonard E., Jr.
New Jerusalem Music
Box 225
Clarksboro, NJ 08020
(609) 423-7028

Stassen-Benjamin, Linda
New Songs Ministries
P.O. Box 11662
Costa Mesa, CA 92627

E. C. Schirmer Music Co.
138 Ipswich St.
Boston, MA 02215
(617) 236-1935

Seerveld, Calvin
Institute for Christian Studies
229 College St.
Toronto, ON M5T 1R4

Smallwood, Richard
Essex Management
1111 Sixteenth Avenue South
Nashville, TN 37212
(615) 327-4935

Theodore Presser Company
Presser Place
Bryn Mawr, PA 19010
(215) 525-3636

Tyrrell, Mrs. J.
41 Minster Road
Godalming, Surrey
England

Unichappell Music, Inc.
Div. of Hal Leonard Pub. Corp.
8112 W. Bluemound Rd.
P.O. Box 13819
Milwaukee, WI 53213
(414) 774-3630

United Church Press
132 W. 31st St.
New York, NY 10001
(212) 239-8700

United Reformed Church
86 Tavistock Place
London WC1H 9RT
England

Voetberg, F. Wm.
374 Read Ave.
Tuckahoe, NY 10707

Ward, James
Music A.D.
Box 7465
Grand Rapids, MI 49510
(616) 241-3787

Waterloo Music, Ltd.
3 Regina St.
North Waterloo, ON N2J 4A5
(519) 886-4990

Watson, Sydney
Christchurch, Oxford
England

Wischmeier, Roger W.
Department of Music
Sterling College
Sterling, KS 67579

Witvoet, Bert
Calvinist Contact
99 Niaraga St.
St. Catharines, ON L2R 4L3
(416) 682-8311

WORD, Inc.
4800 West Waco Dr.
Waco, TX 76796
(817) 772-7650

Word of God
P.O. Box 8617
Ann Arbor, MI 48107
(313) 761-8505

World Library Publications
3815 N. Willow Rd.
Schiller Park, IL 60176
(312) 678-0621

Yale University Press
92A Yale Station
New Haven, CT 06520
(203) 432-0932

Yamaguchi, Tokuo
11-107 Seibujutaku
Muromachi, Toyohashi 440
Japan

Zondervan Music Group
365 Great Circle Rd.
Nashville, TN 37228
(615) 259-9111

Descants

Alternative Harmonizations

Rounds and Canons

Texts in Two Languages

Songs for Children

The following songs, in whole or part, are especially suited for singing by children. Some of these songs have a simple refrain; others contain a stanza that children would enjoy; still others are simple throughout.

Scripture References

Topical Index

**Lordship of Christ: see Ascension & Reign of Christ;
   King, God/Christ as**

Love
God's Love to Us

Our Love to God

Our Love for Others

Majesty of God

Marriage

Trial: see Temptation & Trial

Trinity

Trust in God

Victory

Vocation: see Ministry & Service

Authors, Composers, and Sources

Metrical Index of Tunes

Tune Names

Index of First Lines and Titles

*indicates first lines or titles by which some hymns in this book may also be known